THE PAPERS OF
WOODROW WILSON

VOLUME 37

MAY 9–AUGUST 7, 1916

SPONSORED BY THE WOODROW WILSON
FOUNDATION
AND PRINCETON UNIVERSITY

THE PAPERS OF

WOODROW WILSON

ARTHUR S. LINK, *EDITOR*

DAVID W. HIRST, *SENIOR ASSOCIATE EDITOR*

JOHN E. LITTLE, *ASSOCIATE EDITOR*

PHYLLIS MARCHAND AND MARGARET D. LINK,
EDITORIAL ASSISTANTS

Volume 37
May 9–August 7, 1916

PRINCETON, NEW JERSEY
PRINCETON UNIVERSITY PRESS
·1981·

Note to scholars: Princeton University Press
subscribes to the Resolution on Permissions of
the Association of American University Presses,
defining what we regard as "fair use" of copyrighted works. This Resolution, intended to encourage scholarly use of university press publications and to avoid unnecessary applications
for permission, is obtainable from the Press or
from the A.A.U.P. central office. Note, however,
that the scholarly apparatus, transcripts of
shorthand, and the texts of Wilson documents
as they appear in this volume are copyrighted,
and the usual rules about the use of copyrighted materials apply.

Publication of this book has been aided by a
grant from the National Historical Publications
and Records Commission.

Printed in the United States of America
by Princeton University Press
Princeton, New Jersey

INTRODUCTION

THE opening of this volume finds Wilson, indeed the entire country, basking in the afterglow of Germany's surrender on May 4, 1916, to Wilson's *Sussex* ultimatum of April 18. German-American relations grow increasingly friendly to the end of the period covered by this volume, so friendly, in fact, that it seems likely that the German government will soon appeal to Wilson to mediate the European war. At the same time, relations with the Allies, particularly with Great Britain, deteriorate dramatically on account of the ruthless suppression of the Irish Rebellion, the publication of the British blacklist, which carries the Allies' economic warfare to the territory of the United States, and Anglo-French seizure of American mail on the high seas. However, the most important factor in Wilson's own alienation from the Allied cause is the adamant refusal of the British Foreign Secretary, Sir Edward Grey, to permit the implementation of the House-Grey Memorandum which provided for Wilson's mediation in certain circumstances. Wilson considers Grey's refusal as virtually a slap in the face after he, Wilson, in an address to the League to Enforce Peace on May 27, commits the United States to membership in a postwar peacekeeping organization, which commitment Grey had hitherto said was a *sine qua non* of British acceptance of Wilson's mediation.

Meanwhile, a crisis in Mexican-American relations erupts in early May and threatens to cause war between the two countries. Generals Hugh L. Scott and Frederick Funston meet on the border near El Paso with the Mexican general, Alvaro Obregón, and conclude an agreement for Mexican-American cooperation for patrol of the border. Carranza not only repudiates the agreement but also, on May 22, sends a stern note which demands the immediate withdrawal of all American troops from Mexican soil. A few weeks later, the Mexican commander in northern Mexico warns General John J. Pershing, head of the Punitive Expedition, that Mexican troops will attack any American forces which move eastward, westward, or southward from the positions that they now occupy. Fighting occurs on June 21, when two American cavalry troops on patrol try to force their way through the town of Carrizal. The Americans suffer heavy losses in men killed, wounded, and taken prisoner by the Mexicans. First reports tell of a treacherous ambush by the Mexicans, and Wilson sends a peremptory demand to Mexico City for the immediate release and return of the captured Americans; he also drafts a message to Congress in which he asks for authority to occupy all of northern

Mexico. Reports soon make it clear that the American commander had acted recklessly and aggressively at Carrizal. Carranza releases the prisoners, and Wilson, in a speech to the National Press Club on June 30, asks whether war against helpless Mexico will enhance the glory of the United States. This speech prompts Carranza, on July 12, to suggest the appointment of a joint high commission to eliminate the causes of Mexican-American friction. Wilson agrees at once, and the commission is preparing to meet as this volume ends.

Against the backdrop of these tumultuous events, Wilson is hard at work on plans for the forthcoming presidential campaign. He reorganizes the Democratic National Committee and writes a platform that endorses woman suffrage and virtually all of the advanced social legislation demanded by the Progressive platform of 1912 and not yet enacted. Triumphantly renominated on June 15, Wilson plans to move soon to Shadow Lawn, his summer residence near the Jersey shore, after securing the passage of federal child-labor and workmen's-compensation bills. Then a domestic storm breaks out when negotiations between the railway managers and the heads of the railroad brotherhoods come to a complete impasse, and a nationwide railroad strike appears to be inevitable. Thus, as this volume ends, Wilson faces the direst crisis of leadership in his political career up to this point.

"VERBATIM ET LITERATIM"

In earlier volumes of this series, we have said something like the following: "All documents are reproduced *verbatim et literatim*, with typographical and spelling errors corrected in square brackets only when necessary for clarity and ease of reading." The following essay explains our textual methods and review procedures.

We have never printed and do not intend to print critical, or corrected, versions of documents. We print them exactly as they are, with a few exceptions which we always note. We never use the word *sic* except to denote the repetition of words in a document; in fact, we think that a succession of *sics* defaces a page.

We usually repair words in square brackets when letters are missing. As we have said, we also repair words in square brackets for clarity and ease of reading. Our general rule is to do this when we, ourselves, cannot read the word without stopping to determine its meaning. Jumbled words and names misspelled beyond recognition of course have to be repaired. We correct the misspelling of a name in the footnote identifying the person.

However, when an old man writes to Wilson saying that he is glad to hear that Wilson is "comming" to Newark, or a semiliterate farmer from Texas writes phonetically, we see no reason to correct spellings in square brackets when the words are perfectly understandable. We do not correct Wilson's misspellings unless they are unreadable, except to supply in square brackets letters missing in words. For example, for some reason he insisted upon spelling "belligerent" as "belligerant." Nothing would be gained by correcting "belligerant" in square brackets.

We think that it is very important for several reasons to follow the rule of *verbatim et literatim*. Most important, a document has its own integrity and power, particularly when it is not written in a perfect literary form. There is something very moving in seeing a Texas dirt farmer struggling to express his feelings in words, or a semiliterate former slave doing the same thing. Second, in Wilson's case it is crucially important to reproduce his errors in letters that he typed himself, since he always typed badly when he was in an agitated state. Third, since style is the essence of the person, we would never correct grammar or make tenses consistent, as one correspondent has urged us to do. Fourth, we think that it is obligatory to print typed documents *verbatim et literatim*. For example, we think that it is very important that we print exact transcripts of Charles L. Swem's copies of Wilson's letters. Swem made many mistakes (we correct them in footnotes from a reading of his shorthand books), and Wilson let them pass. We thus have to assume that Wilson did not read his letters before signing them, and this, we think, is a significant fact. Finally, printing typed letters and documents *verbatim et literatim* tells us a great deal about the educational level of the stenographic profession in the United States during Wilson's time.

We think that our series would be worthless if we produced unreliable texts, and we go to some effort to make certain that the texts are authentic.

Our typists are highly skilled and proofread their transcripts carefully as soon as they have been typed. The Editor sight proofreads documents once he has assembled a volume and is setting its annotation. The Editors who write the notes read through documents several times and are careful to check any anomalies. Then, once the manuscript volume has been completed and all notes checked, the Editor and Senior Associate Editor orally proofread the documents against the copy. They read every comma, dash, and character. They note every absence of punctuation. They study every nearly illegible word in written documents.

Once this process of "establishing the text" is completed, the manuscript volume goes to our editor at Princeton University

Press, who checks the volume carefully and sends it to the printing plant. The volume is set by linotype by two typographers who have been working on the Wilson volumes for years. The galley proofs go to the proofroom, where they are read orally against copy. And we must say that the proofreaders at the Press are extraordinarily skilled. Some years ago, before we found a way to ease their burden, they used to query every misspelled word, absence of punctuation, or other such anomalies. Now we write "O.K." above such words or spaces on the copy.

We read the galley proofs three times. Our copyeditor gives them a sight reading against copy to look for remaining typographical errors and to make sure that no line has been dropped. The Editor and Senior Associate Editor sight read them against documents and copy. We then get the page proofs, which have been corrected at the Press. We check all the changes three times. In addition, we get *revised* pages and check them twice.

This is not the end. Our indexer of course reads the pages word by word. Before we return the pages to the Press, she comes in with a list of queries, all of which are answered by reference to the documents.

Our rule in the Wilson Papers is that our tolerance of error is zero. No system and no person can be perfect. We are sure that there are errors in our volumes. However, we believe that we have done everything humanly possible to avoid error; the chance is remote that what looks at first glance like a typographical error is indeed an error.

We are grateful to Professors John Milton Cooper, Jr., William H. Harbaugh, and Richard W. Leopold for their careful reading of the manuscript of this volume and for their helpful criticisms and suggestions. We continue to profit from the help and suggestions of Judith May, our editor at Princeton University Press.

We want to express our warm gratitude to Dr. Frank G. Burke, Executive Director of the National Historical Publications and Records Commission, and his team of researchers in Washington: Dr. Mary Giunta, Research Supervisor, Anne H. Henry, Walter Hill, Dr. Sara Jackson, Teresa Matchette, and René Meachum. Over the years, they have searched out furtive archives and supplied us with hundreds of documents with cheerful dispatch. Our burden of research would have been much heavier without their generous help.

THE EDITORS

Princeton, New Jersey
April 27, 1981

CONTENTS

Introduction, vii
Illustrations, xxi
Abbreviations and Symbols, xxiii

The Papers, May 9–August 7, 1916

Wilson Materials

ILLUSTRATIONS

Following page 296

With his granddaughter, Ellen Wilson McAdoo
Library of Congress

Bust of Colonel House by Jo Davidson
National Portrait Galery

Bust of Wilson by Jo Davidson
Princeton University Library

The Wilsons leaving Memorial Continental Hall in Washington
Library of Congress

Signing the Federal Farm Loan Act, July 17, 1916
Princeton University Library

Leading the Flag Day parade, June 14, 1916
Princeton University Library

Louis Dembitz Brandeis
Library of Congress

James Watson Gerard
National Archives

ABBREVIATIONS

ALI	autograph letter initialed
ALS	autograph letter signed
CC	carbon copy
CCL	carbon copy of letter
CCLS	carbon copy of letter signed
CLS	Charles Lee Swem
CLSsh	Charles Lee Swem shorthand
CLST	Charles Lee Swem typed
EAW	Ellen Axson Wilson
EBW	Edith Bolling Wilson
EMH	Edward Mandell House
FR	*Paper Relating to the Foreign Relations of the United States*
FR-WWS 1915	*Papers Relating to the Foreign Relations of the United States, 1915, Supplement, The World War*
FR-WWS 1916	*Papers Relating to the Foreign Relations of the United States, 1916, Supplement, The World War*
Hw, hw	handwriting, handwritten
HwC	handwritten copy
HwCL	handwritten copy of letter
HwLS	handwritten letter signed
HwS	handwritten signed
JD	Josephus Daniels
JPT	Joseph Patrick Tumulty
JRT	Jack Romagna typed
MS	manuscript
MSS	manuscripts
NDB	Newton Diehl Baker
RG	record group
RL	Robert Lansing
T	typed
TC	typed copy
TCL	typed copy of letter
TCLS	typed copy of letter signed
TL	typed letter
TLI	typed letter initialed
TLS	typed leter signed
WGM	William Gibbs McAdoo
WHP	Walter Hines Page
WW	Woodrow Wilson
WWhw	Woodrow Wilson handwriting, handwritten
WWsh	Woodrow Wilson shorthand
WWT	Woodrow Wilson typed
WWTL	Woodrow Wilson typed letter
WWTLI	Woodrow Wilson typed letter initialed
WWTLS	Woodrow Wilson typed letter signed

ABBREVIATIONS FOR COLLECTIONS
AND REPOSITORIES

Following the National Union Catalog of the Library of Congress

AFL-CIO-Ar	American Federation of Labor-Congress of Industrial Organizations Archives
AGO	Adjutant General's Office
CPT	California Institute of Technology
CtY	Yale University
DLC	Library of Congress
DNA	National Archives
FFM-Ar	French Foreign Ministry Archives
FO	British Foreign Office
GFO-Ar	German Foreign Office Archives
InU	Indiana University
LDR	Labor Department Records
MH	Harvard University
MH-Ar	Harvard University Archives
NjP	Princeton University
NN	New York Public Library
NRU	University of Rochester
PRO	Public Record Office
PSC-P	Swarthmore College Peace Collection
RSB Coll., DLC	Ray Stannard Baker Collection of Wilsoniana, Library of Congress
ScCleU	Clemson University
SDR	State Department Records
ViU	University of Virginia
WC, NjP	Woodrow Wilson Collection, Princeton University
WDR	War Department Records
WP, DLC	Woodrow Wilson Papers, Library of Congress

SYMBOLS

[May 15, 1916]	publication date of a published writing; also date of document when date is not part of text
[*May 30, 1916*]	composition date when publication date differs
[[June 14, 1916]]	delivery date of speech if publication date differs
* * *	text deleted by author of document

THE PAPERS OF
WOODROW WILSON

VOLUME 37

MAY 9–AUGUST 7, 1916

THE PAPERS OF
WOODROW WILSON

To Edward Mandell House

Dearest Friend,   The White House. 9 May, 1916.

I am too tired to-night to write more than a line, but I want you to see and digest this editorial from the SPRINGFIELD REPUBLICAN[1] as soon as possible. The peace intimation contained in the German note seems now to be holding the attention of the country,[2] and it is my prediction that it is going to be increasingly difficult to keep off the insistent demand that I act. Perhaps you will think it best to send a somewhat full cable to Sir Edward. By the way, I will gladly arrange to pay for such messages.

We are all well, and all unite in affectionate messages.

Affectionately Yours,   W.W.

The portrait[3] is a great comfort.

WWTLI (E. M. House Papers, CtY).

[1] It is missing. However, it was "The Opportunity for Peace," *Springfield Republican*, May 9, 1916. The editorial referred to the military stalemate in the European war and the intimation about peace, quoted below, in the German note of May 4, and said that the question of an early peace deserved Wilson's "most careful and sympathetic consideration," for an "opportunity to initiate peace negotiations may be at hand." Wilson, the editorial continued, should act immediately without waiting for definite assurances by the belligerents that his offer would be welcome. It said that any prolongation of the war would almost necessarily draw the United States into the conflict and concluded: "This country, therefore, has an interest in the situation so vital that its right to seek the conclusion of peace can hardly be questioned in any quarter. And upon this ground of America's interest, as well as upon the high claims of civilization and humanity, the president might base his offer of mediation at the earliest day."

[2] J. W. Gerard to RL, May 4, 1916, enclosing G. von Jagow to J. W. Gerard, May 4, 1916, printed in *FR-WWS 1916*, pp. 257-60. It read, in part: "If the German Government, nevertheless, has resolved to go to the utmost limit of concessions, it has not alone been guided by the friendship connecting the two great nations for over a hundred years, but it also has thought of the great doom which threatens the entire civilized world should this cruel and sanguinary war be extended and prolonged.

"The German Government, conscious of Germany's strength, has twice within the last few months announced before the world its readiness to make peace on a basis safeguarding Germany's vital interests, thus indicating that it is not Germany's fault if peace is still withheld from the nations of Europe.

"The German Government feels all the more justified to declare that the responsibility could not be borne before the forum of mankind and history if, after 21 months' duration of the war, the submarine question under discussion between the German Government and the Government of the United States were to take a turn seriously threatening the maintenance of peace between the two nations."

[3] That is, the portrait of Mrs. Galt, about which see n. 1 to the extract from the House Diary printed at May 3, 1916, Vol. 36.

From Robert Lansing, with Enclosure

Dear Mr President, [Washington] May 9, 1916

I have just received the annexed letter from Mr Penfield.

Faithfully yours   Robert Lansing.

ALS (SDR, RG 59, 763.72/2664½, DNA).

E N C L O S U R E

Frederic Courtland Penfield to Robert Lansing

CONFIDENTIAL AND PERSONAL

My dear Mr. Secretary: Vienna April 15, 1916

Probably there is not one person in the Dual Monarchy who is not heartily sick of the war and wishes for an early peace.

On all sides one now hears expressions bearing out the above statement, as well as the inquiry "How much longer can Austria-Hungary continue in the war?" That is the eternal question asked thousands of times daily.

Persons influenced by skepticism profess to believe that the resources of the Monarchy can last but another six months.

On the other hand I have the opinion of a member of the Hungarian Cabinet, reaching me second-handed, that Austria-Hungary can stand two years more of war before reaching final exhaustion. This oracle's optimism is doubtless colored by official-ism and the fact that Hungary is always in a better material position than Austria.

Taking the mean of the many predictions reaching me it would be my prediction that Austria-Hungary can go through another twelvemonths on the resources of men, food and money at her command, but not longer.

Throughout the Monarchy every essential commodity is de-creasing in supply with an attendant increase in price of every-thing required by humanity. The practice of economy months since assumed an acute form. The country is supposed to have no cotton or copper, and we now hear of an alarming shortage of sugar, beer, butter and all fats. Having in mind that the Monarchy is essentially agricultural, I have maintained in all reports to the Department that the people cannot be starved. But it is a very different matter for the Empire-Kingdom to be in a condition to indefinitely carry on war with all its special require-ments and great waste.

The above brief statements sufficiently explain the popular wish for an early peace. But how it may be brought about no one has the temerity to announce. Baron Burian, the Minister for Foreign Affairs, started last night for Berlin for a conference with Bethmann-Hollweg. Although the object of the journey is not explained, the newspapers surmise that it may be in connection with the pacific attitude expressed in Mr. Asquith's recent speech.[1]

It is common knowledge that the coffers of the Dual Monarchy are practically empty. At the present moment the plans for the Fourth War Loan are being groomed by the press, preparatory to formal announcement in a few days.

American exchange is ruling at 7 crowns and 85 hellers, meaning that for a draft on New York one receives in local currency practically the equivalent of $1.50 for the dollar.

It is estimated that this season's crops will have an acreage of but 70 per cent. of normal. And it is admitted that fields tilled by women, children and Russian and Servian war prisoners do not yield as bountifully as when worked by native men whose occupation has never been other than farming. There are few cattle and horses in the country, and consequently little manure for the properties of small farmers. Farming utensils have long been uncared for, and factories usually producing agricultural machinery are occupied with war munitions.

There is no longer talk of Austria-Hungary receiving an indemnity from any of her foes. Hitherto it was the mode to predict that Austria-Hungary would recoup the cost of the war by the indemnities received.

It seems more than rumor that Austria-Hungary means to weld conquered Montenegro and the Belgrade section of Serbia into the Hungarian government of the Monarchy. This would be a political step of decided merit, as it would unify under a single control most of the co[so]-called "Sud-Slavs," a race believing it has political grievances and whose untiring agitation has been ever baneful. The assassination of the Archduke Franz Ferdinand at Sarajevo was claimed by many as directly traceable to the machinations of the "Sud-Slavs."

I am, my dear Mr. Secretary,

Yours very truly,   Frederic C. Penfield.

TLS (SDR, RG 59, 763.72/2664½, DNA).

[1] Asquith had replied to Bethmann Hollweg's speech in the Reichstag on April 5 (about which see n. 1 to Enclosure II in EMH to WW, April 8, 1916, Vol. 36, and n. 1 to Enclosure I in EMH to WW, May 14, 1916) at a reception for visiting French statesmen on April 10. Asquith referred to the Chancellor's peace intimations and he said that the Allies, too, were prepared for peace, but not for a peace on German terms. The result of the war, the Prime Minister con-

cluded, had to be the establishment of "the principle that international problems must be handled by free negotiation on equal terms between free peoples." *New York Times*, April 11, 1916.

From William Howard Taft

My dear Mr. President: New Haven, Conn May 9th, 1916.

I venture to take up again the question of your attending the banquet of the League to Enforce Peace, at the New Willard, on Saturday, May 27th at 7 o'clock. I do this with the hope that the stage of the issue with the German Government, which has at least a temporary settlement, may enable you to give a little more time to other questions, and to make some informal remarks at the dinner. Of course we realize that you cannot commit yourself in advance to any particular form of international agreement and that what we propose is a mere working hypothesis, to be amended as discussion and unforeseen conditions may require. It would, however, stimulate the movement much if we could have the countenance of your presence at the banquet.

Sincerely yours,   Wm H Taft

TLS (WP, DLC).

From Edward Mandell House, with Enclosure

Dear Governor: New York. May 9, 1916.

The League to Enforce Peace, with Mr. Taft presiding, is to hold its annual meeting in Washington on the 26th of May. There is to be a banquet on the evening of the 27th at which they wish you to speak. Is not this the occasion?

In my opinion, their proposals regarding the maintenance of peace are for the present impracticable. You cannot form "immediate judicial tribunals for hearing and judgment upon the merits of international issues."[1] Nor can you now get the great powers to submit differences among themselves to a council of conciliation.

Some such court and international force may in time be evolved out of the more practical plan which you will suggest and which will at once receive the support of England and perhaps every nation in Europe other than the Central Powers and Russia.

If your statement is to be made on May 27th it will be scant time to get a reply from Sir Edward if I send my letter by mail.

I believe it should be sent by cable and I am coding it today to send if you will telegraph me your approval.

Affectionately yours,   E. M. House

TLS (WP, DLC).
¹ House was quoting from *Program of the League*, a copy of which he enclosed.

E N C L O S U R E

New York, May 10, 1916.

There is an increasingly insistent demand here that the President take some action towards bringing the war to a close. The impression grows that the Allies are more determined upon the punishment of Germany than upon exacting terms that neutral opinion would consider just. This feeling will increase if Germany discontinues her illegal submarine activities.

I believe the President would now be willing to publicly commit the United States to joining with the other powers in a convention looking to the maintenance of peace after the war, provided he announced at the same time that if the war continued much longer, he purposed calling a conference to discuss peace. If the President is to serve humanity in a large way, steps should be taken now rather than wait until the opportunity becomes less fortunate. His statement would be along the lines you and I have so often discussed and which you express in your letter to me of September 22, 1915.

That is: The nations subscribing to this agreement should pledge themselves to side against any power breaking a treaty. The convention should formulate rules for the purpose of limiting armaments both on land and sea and for the purpose of making warfare more humane to those actually engaged and safe-guarding the lives and property of neutrals and non-combatants.

The convention should bind the signatory powers to side against any nation refusing in case of dispute to adopt some other method of settlement than that of war.

I am sure this is the psychological moment for this statement to be made and I would appreciate your cabling me your opinion as to the advisability of such a move. If it is not done now the opportunity may be forever lost.   Edward House.

TC telegram (WP, DLC).

From Edward Mandell House

Dear Governor: New York. May 9th, 1916.

I am told you are to be in Newark Saturday. If this is true will it not be possible for you to come to New York, go to the theater Saturday night and ride in the country on Sunday, or any other thing that would be pleasant to Mrs. Wilson and you?

There are some things we should talk over that have come up since I was in Washington.

I am delighted with the Note as, of course, you know. I hope there will be no more trouble and since everything is quiet there could be no possible criticism of a visit to New York.

Affectionately yours,   E. M. House

P.S. Dudley is just back from Washington and telephones me that the Fitzgerald matter has been attended to and he will not be there to disturb you next year.[1] He tells me, too, that anything of this sort you want in the future will be attended to with equal dispatch.

TLS (WP, DLC).
[1] John Joseph Fitzgerald was renominated and reelected in 1916.

From Pleasant Alexander Stovall

Personal and confidential.

Dear Mr. President: Berne, May 9, 1916.

Now, that the SUSSEX incident seems to be settled, I desire to communicate to you my thanks and congratulations for your address to Congress and your admirable notes to Germany relative to this incident.

I do not do this in a personal or perfunctory way, but situated as I am and bearing the relations to you as I do, I think it my duty to tell you that your threat to break off diplomatic realtions [relations] was timely and potent.

I did not obtrude this advice or this comment while the matter was under consideration. The situation was too delicate even for the slightest suggestion from outside sources. But I want to tell you that your message sent a thrill through the neutral countries. Even those which from their size and proximity dared not express themselves were immensely heartened by what you said and what you indicated. It was a bold and splendid stroke; you not only forced the hands of Congress but you called down a serious assailant; and although he has not submitted in good grace the lesson is boung [bound] to strike home. Holland, Spain and Brazil have felt the influence of your words and warnings. I mention these because they are maritime countries. Considerable concern was displayed in Switzerland whose neutrality has more than once been violated, and whose tranquillity is always threatened more or less.

Believing that you have scored another triumph in diplomacy and that the world and our country owe you a new debt for the statesmanship and self-control shown by you in this crisis, I must content myself with having said this much and with having detained you this long.

I fell [feel] so strongly upon this question and yet what I write seems so stiff and formal, that I am almost tempted to destroy what I have prepared.

I have the honor to be, Sir,

Your obedient servant: Pleasant A Stovall

TLS (WP, DLC).

From Newton Diehl Baker

My dear Mr. President: Washington. May 9, 1916.

I have just written Mr. Bernard M. Baruch, asking him to fix a time when I can see him here to discuss the "council of executive information."

I return the letter inclosed me by you, since it is addressed to Colonel House,[1] and you will perhaps want to have it in your files or destroy it, now that it has served its purpose.

Faithfully yours, Newton D. Baker

TLS (WP, DLC).
[1] That is, B. M. Baruch to EMH, April 24, 1916, Vol. 36.

From Elizabeth Gardiner Evans

My dear Mr. President: Boston. May 9, 1916.

May I express to you my pride in you for the letter you have just made public in regard to Mr. Brandeis,[1] and likewise my satisfaction that I have believed in you steadily since the first time I had the honor of an interview with you at Sea Girt when you were a candidate for the Presidency. There have been many occasions when I have been disappointed at things you have done and not done, but there has been no occasion when I have doubted the single-mindedness and the nobility of your aim. As regards Mr. Brandeis you have been discerning, and courageous, and generous, and just. Mr. Brandeis' many friends will love and honor you always.

God bless and guide you in the heavy duties of your office.

Respectfully,   Elizabeth Glendower Evans.

TLS (WP, DLC).
    ¹ That is, WW to C. A. Culberson, May 5, 1916, Vol. 36.

To Richard Heath Dabney

My dear Heath: The White House May 10, 1916

Alas, I am not to see you.¹ I find that this is my only chance to get away for an absolutely needed rest and I am going down the river Friday afternoon, to be gone until Monday morning. I am not very keen for any sort of public dinner, but I am genuinely disappointed that I am not to have the great pleasure of seeing you. Better luck next time!

Your guess as to the German note was certainly very close to the mark.²

In haste   Affectionately yours,   Woodrow Wilson

TLS (Wilson-Dabney Corr., ViU).
    ¹ Wilson was replying to R. H. Dabney to WW, May 8, 1916, ALS (WP, DLC).
    ² Dabney had written: "I wonder if I can guess the substance of your reply to the last irritating German note? It costs nothing to guess. So here goes! My guess is that you will express gratification at the orders issued by the German government to their submarine commanders, and will state that, so long as these orders are obeyed and no merchant ships (including those defensively armed) are illegally sunk, without reference to the conduct of any other belligerent, Germany has it in her power to maintain friendly relations with the United States."

To Henry Thomas Rainey

My dear Mr. Rainey: [The White House] May 10, 1916

I know I need not remind you of my very deep and intense interest in the proposed legislation for a Tariff Commission, and I am sure that in view of that interest you will pardon me if I ask what is the status of the bill now. I am exceedingly anxious that nothing should happen which would prejudice its passing even in the way of delay.

Cordially and sincerely yours,   Woodrow Wilson

TLS (Letterpress Books, WP, DLC).

Two Letters from Edward Mandell House

Dear Governor: New York. May 10, 1916.

I have read carefully the editorial in the Springfield Republican and I agree with it almost entirely.

I have had a feeling for sometime that it would be advisable and even necessary for you to act soon whether the Allies desire it or not.

I am revamping the letter in the form of a cable and will send it at once. We should get an answer by Saturday when I hope you will be here.   Affectionately yours,   E. M. House

I have a letter from Mr. Taft inclosing an invitation to you for the banquet on May 27.[1]

[1] Presumably W. H. Taft to WW, May 9, 1916, just printed.

Dear Governor: New York. May 10, 1916.

Last year when you sent me to Europe I could see signs of discontent in Page. This year there were many more and I was afraid there would be a disagreeable outbreak before I could accomplish your purposes and get away.

I will not go into details for the annoyance I was subjected to is of no importance. But what does count is that we have in Page a cog that refuses to work smoothly in the machinery you have set in motion to bring about peace and a reconstruction of international law.

I understand that I have offended Page's ambassadorial dignity not by transgressing any of the social or official niceties, but because there is "no place in one country for two Ambassadors."

His dissatisfaction is not confined to the single act of sending me to Europe, but your foreign policy and the administration of the State Department come under the ban of his displeasure. All of this together has led him to decide to protest to you in the event I am sent to England again, and to perhaps resign if the protest is ignored.

I am sorry to have to write this for I do not want to add to your troubles, but it has come to a point that it is necessary for you to know what is pending.

Sensing the trouble so far in advance I tried my best to avert it, but it seems I have failed.

Other Ambassadors and Ministers in Europe invited me most cordially to visit their capitals and seemed to think my failure to do so minimized their importance. I therefore believe this feeling is confined to London alone—where, indeed, I least expected it.

Affectionately yours,   E. M. House

TLS (WP, DLC).

From John Knight Shields

My dear Mr. President: Washington, May 10, 1916.

There has been a persistent rumor that you would veto Senate Bill 3331, providing for the improvement of navigation and development of water power in navigable rivers, which passed the Senate March 9th, last, in the event it should be concurred in by the House, and a statement in a letter you wrote Congressman Kent of California some time since upon the subject[1] is referred to as evidence tending to support such a rumor. This is, of course, having a hurtful influence against the bill in the House, as appears from the enclosed letter of Congressman Dill, of Washington, to one of his constituents.[2]

I have given this rumor little credence, because I knew you would not be influenced by the false and slanderous propaganda of Mr. Pinchot, in which he attacks the bill in general terms, as against the deliberate opinion and approval of more than two-thirds of the Senators who were present upon its final consideration and passage, and that you would not dispose of so important a measure upon an ex parte hearing of any kind.

If I am correct in my assumption that you have not so expressed yourself adversely to the bill, I think the rumor ought to be corrected, as it is evidently doing the measure injustice, and, I may add, is being used as the basis for personal assaults upon me.

I will also ask that, before acting adversely to the bill, you give those who believe it has merits and ought to be the law an opportunity to be heard upon it.

I gave this bill very earnest and careful consideration, and feel confident that it is free from any constitutional or economic objection, and that the jurisdiction of the Federal Government over navigable rivers, the sovereignty and interests of states in such rivers, the rights of riparian proprietors, are recognized and provided for, and that the interests of the general public—investors and consumers—are all fully safeguarded in every respect.

While there has been some criticism of this bill, most of it inspired by Mr. Pinchot and his satellites, I believe the great majority of the press of the country has approved it. This is especially true in Tennessee, where all the leading papers, save one, as I am informed, have endorsed it in strong terms.

I would regret that the work the majority of the Senate, including myself, has done in the matter should be prejudged and made abortive without our views being fully presented and considered.   Very truly yours,   Jno K. Shields

TLS (WP, DLC).
    [1] WW to W. Kent, March 9, 1916, Vol. 36.
    [2] C. C. Dill to Milton Dam, April 24, 1916, TLS (WP, DLC). Clarence Cleveland Dill, Democrat.

From Robert Lansing

PERSONAL AND PRIVATE:

My dear Mr. President: [Washington] May 10, 1916.

In the submarine controversy we will unavoidably be forced to meet a situation which will arise, if it has not already arisen, and to determine on a course of action.

The problem is this: A German submarine torpedoes, without conforming in any way to the rules of international law, a merchant vessel of the enemy, which has no Americans on board. No American life is directly endangered by this lawless act, but how did the German submarine commander know that? Is it to be supposed that he considered the matter at all? Did he not simply take a chance?

Now, if the attack is made without definite knowledge as to the nationality of the persons on board, then the action of the submarine commander as a part of a general policy, becomes a serious menace to Americans traveling on merchant ships within the sphere of submarine activity. Though in the particular case cited our rights are not directly affected, they are affected indirectly by making their exercise hazardous.

In our "SUSSEX note" we took a position based on humanity and insisted on respect for neutral rights in general. The rights of all non-combatants are impaired by the conduct referred to. Are we or are we not to consider a sudden attack by a submarine a violation of the assumed pledge of the German Government to comply with the rules of naval warfare even though no American life is immediately endangered?

My own impression is that we will have great difficulty in explaining our position, if we do not resent every lawless attack on a merchant ship whether Americans are or are not among the passengers or crews. On the other hand, I realize that public opinion in this country would not support drastic action unless

Americans were killed or imperiled by the submarine warfare. It is to me a very difficult problem to solve, and I would be gratified if you would advise the policy to be followed.

Faithfully yours,   Robert Lansing

TLS (Lansing Letterpress Book, SDR, RG 59, DNA).

From Jessie Woodrow Wilson Sayre

Dearest Father,   [Williamstown, Mass.] May 10, 1916.

I realize with dismay how long I have been home with no word of my love and gratitude to you. I had to let Frank do the writing for me, for these first two weeks have been very tiring ones, and very busy. Our new routine is, however, happily established. We have an excellent nurse who gets things done so quickly and efficiently and yet is so sweet with the children that she bids fair to prove a treasure.

Eleanor has not done well since we came home, has not gained at all since the Monday after our arrival, but we feel that she is over the upset now and that all will be well. She looks well, still, and is a joy to have in the house.

I am gaining strength steadily. Spring is at last here and we are all out of doors a great deal. It is so heavenly that I wish you and dear Edith could be here to share the entrancing beauty of spring on these hills with us. Dearest Father, we love you so, you can't know how wonderful it was to see you in Philadelphia and to see my darling in your arms. I shall always remember it. Dear Father, I am wordless when I try to express all our love for you and our appreciation of your generosity towards us. It makes me cry when I try to write.

I can only say again how much I love you both,

Devotedly your own daughter   Jessie.

ALS (WC, NjP).

To Louis Wiley

My dear Mr. Wiley: The White House May 11, 1916

That was a very generous letter you wrote me on the ninth[1] and I thank you for it most sincerely. I find that one has to detach oneself in large measure from the talk going on around one in order to see things steadily and see them whole, and sometimes that is very difficult indeed to do. Besides, one does not always know just how safe it is to do it and to trust one's own judgment;

but I always try to think what the verdict would be after the event rather than in the midst of it.

Cordially and sincerely yours,   Woodrow Wilson

TLS (L. Wiley Papers, NRU).
1 It is missing.

To James Paul Clarke

My dear Senator: [The White House] May 11, 1916

I do not know what stage the Rivers and Harbors Bill has reached, because amidst a multitude of other things I find it very difficult to keep posted, but there is one matter I thought I would take the liberty of dropping you a line about because of its general importance. That is the appropriation for the East River in New York and the approaches to the Navy Yard there. This is so important an item in the preparedness business that I thought I would commend it to your special consideration if it should be an item of discussion in the final determination of the contents of the pending measure.

Cordially and sincerely yours,   Woodrow Wilson

TLS (Letterpress Books, WP, DLC).

From David Lawrence

Dear Mr. President: [Washington] May 11, 1916

I am venturing to present herewith some thoughts on the Mexican situation that may prove, I hope, of constructive value.

The recognition of Carranza seemed six months ago the logical and proper development of our policy since his faction had obtained military control of the country. Aside from the fact that it gave an important stimulus to the Carranza party, bringing about the surrender of many of the Villista bands, it afforded us a government with which to deal, an authority that could be held responsible for violations in *any* part of Mexican territory of the rights of foreigners. Gen. Carranza may or may not have realized at the time the responsibilities imposed upon him. I recollect (and I have confirmed my recollection by reference to memoranda and messages of those dates) that in conversation with the First Chief at Vera Cruz in August, just prior to recognition, I pointed out the dangerous consequences which recognition would entail since in preferring one faction to the other vindictiveness might bring about border raids and efforts to produce intervention. Gen Carranza waved aside the suggested possibility, contending that such things wouldn't happen. But that identical situation has arisen. I sought at the time to impress Carranza with the fact that not intervention but war might follow continued hostile acts or incursions, that there might be no legal basis for intervention but that attacks on American territory might prove a just cause for war.

The situation has veered around to the point where the de facto government realizes that failure to cooperate with us means war. For Carranza personally this would be disastrous. His will be the blame for failing to avert it. His will be the responsibility if an ignominious occupation by American troops results and a military government under foreign supervision such as we maintained in Cuba grows out of it all.

To Carranza, therefore, every consideration of selfishness and even far-sightedness would seem to dictate the necessity of an agreement with us for the joint patrol of the border and for the continuation of our troops on Mexican territory until banditry is extirpated.

No matter how Obregon or Carranza may wriggle and squirm, they cannot [can] reject our decision only with disastrous consequences to themselves.

The Mexican is an odd character. He applauds altruism, he courts generosity but he most often abuses it. That is why offhand so many of our Americans in Mexico dismiss all idea of gentle dealing and urge "the strong hand." There is a happy combination, a compromise between these two extremes of policy that could prove effective. We need not threaten to overrun Mexico but we can insist on staying there until our objects are accomplished. As soon as the Mexican understands we are adamant in our decision, he will accept that situation as inevitable. He will swallow it because he feels he must.

But every moment that affairs continue on the precarious basis that they seem to be, I am hoping that vital precautions with respect to coast towns will not be omitted. If there were some mobilizing—perhaps sending one vessel at a time—in Atlantic and Pacific waters the dangers to our citizens which may result from a sudden flare-up can be promptly minimized. I am familiar, for example, with conditions at Vera Cruz and Tampico. We should have cruising about in those waters several gunboats and one or two battleships, and a few hundred marines. Tampico is the most dangerous spot of all. Americans are way up the river as you know. Two light draft boats—the Machias and the Marietta —are there now but one must not forget that the Mexican gunboats, three in all, when concentrated in Tampico as they frequently are could seriously embar[r]ass our two little boats. Mexico is like a tinder-box and while so many of our troops are on Mexican soil, events may happen so rapidly as never to give our citizens a chance to escape. Certainly it would be nothing short of terrible to have a riot or something of that sort and no ships available for protection. Since the Mexican question has gotten in to politics, it would produce a bad impression if such a flare-up came in the midst of the campaign. I am not one of those who believe the presence of ships inflames the people. The Mexicans don't like them but they take them philosophically. My idea in general however is to suggest naval precautions which could be instantaneously effective in case of developments in other parts of Mexico, developments that we might not be able to foresee or even control.

Assuming the temporary or tentative settlement of questions relating to the presence of our troops in Mexico, there is another branch of policy even more urgent. It relates to the economic situation. I am not only convinced that we must exercise a quasi-coercive influence to insure protection of our border but that we must initiate steps practically compelling the reconstruction process to get started. We have waited patiently for the de facto government to devise an economic policy, a system of taxation or revenue that would stabilize exchange but inexcusable delay and the unprecedented drop in exchange rates has been the lamentable result. This is not, as might seem at first plausible, due to inherent incapacity on the part of the de facto government officials. It is primarily due to an unwillingness on their part to recognize, if they yet realize it, that the basis of financial reconstruction in Mexico is purely political, that domestic business will not flourish, that plants will not reopen, that taxes will not be forthcoming, that imports will drop, unless there is some guarantee, some assurance of protection for property and certainly the lives of foreigners.

Protection for foreign property comes only when there is political order. The Mexican is not inherently a robber. He confiscates because of necessity, to assure him sustenance. Whichever way one turns, there is the economic situation—the absence of money with which to pay disaffected troops, to buy supplies and keep the government machinery in motion—as the most vital factor.

To permit the economic situation to drift on will hasten that which we all do or should desire to avoid—general war with Mexico. If intervention is inevitable because the economic situation will compel it, we should be fully justified in breaking any precedent or brushing aside any previous policy in order to avert that contingency. I refer now to government cooperation in the financing of Mexico.

Money is to be obtained nowhere except in the United States on account of the European war. New York bankers have told me from time to time that while Mexico was not a profitable investment, they would as a matter of patriotism assist in rehabilitating Mexico but they must have good security, virtually a guarantee by our government of the obligations. The bankers want an American financial adviser, they want American supervision of the customs. But these suggestions are of course extreme and Carranza off-hand would be inclined to reject them but the time is coming when he must grasp at even that straw to save the government and his country from ruin.

I would suggest these concrete things:

1. That Ambassador Fletcher start at once for Mexico and present his credentials. This would be hailed in Mexico as an evidence of good faith on our part, as an indication that we wish to continue good relations and that the presence of our troops has not altered our original purpose. It would give valuable moral support to the de facto government. It might be done the moment a satisfactory agreement is reached between Obregon and Scott on military matters.[1] That would be the psychological moment for the step.

2. That Ambassador Fletcher make a careful study of the economic situation and make recommendations within the next month or so—as rapidly as possible.

3. Acting on the Ambassador's facts or such information as the Department of State may have as to the state of Mexican finances, the Secretary of the Treasury might approach banking groups in New York and get the most reasonable terms possible. These could be submitted to the de facto government.

4. As for security, the New York bankers probably realize that if the United States becomes morally interested in a big loan, the government will be morally obligated to safeguard that interest. If the de facto government succeeds as a result of the loan, well and good. If it fails, intervention must result and in that event, the interests of Americans become almost prior claims, the satisfaction of which would, as I understand it, devolve upon the United States government as the receiver of Mexican finances.

Whether the de facto government accepts any plan for American cooperation in financing Mexico or not, the position of the

[1] About the conferences between Generals Scott, Funston, and Obregón, see H. P. McCain, to H. L. Scott, April 26, 1916, Vol. 36, and subsequent documents in Vol. 36 and this volume.

United States in the future will be materially strengthened. If we are able to show Latin America that we sought even to give financial help and Mexico refused, preferring bankruptcy and anarchy to self-rehabilitation, the record is bound to be one that will elicit sympathy abroad and approval at home. We have extended recognition. We must be ready to do more than that but responsibility for the failure of the de facto government must always be placed squarely on them.

I have outlined in a much more general and vague way the above ideas to Arredondo who told me he was quite sure Carranza would look with favor on some plan for financial help provided it was of an "unofficial" character and did not compromise him with his people.

In conclusion, something in the financial line should be started soon. If Mexico seems unwilling to take our help, it ought almost be forced upon them because the alternative seems certain war and in the face of that pride and precedent should vanish.

In opposition to this policy, it might be urged at home that we withdrew from the six power loan because our government refused to go into partnership with banking interests. This is quite a different case because in China other powers were *jointly* interested, governments over which we could exercise no control. Under the peculiar circumstances in this hemisphere, liberty of action is not circumscribed. It is entirely ours. We have assisted other Latin countries in a financial way. There should be some equitable way of doing the same for Mexico—and at an early date. Hoping that the above may be of some benefit to you in your general survey of the situation, I am,

Very sincerely yours,   David Lawrence

TLS (WP, DLC).

From Joseph Edward Willard

Madrid, May 11th, 1916

240. CONFIDENTIAL FOR THE PRESIDENT. Following is in Colonel House Cipher: His Majesty[1] sent for me this afternoon and asked that I telegraph immediately to the President as follows:

From information just received from the Spanish Ambassador, Berlin,[2] His Majesty feels that the German forces are now willing to consider peace and that His Majesty is ready to cooperate with the President toward securing arbitration protocol.

In the course of an hour's further conversation His Majesty stated that he had the assurance of the Pope's full cooperation. His Majesty feels that while his own influence on Austria and

Germany may be stronger than the President's and that he could take the initiative with these Governments yet (cipher badly garbled but inference is apparently made that the President's influence is greater with France and England), that France was nearing the end of her resources and would really welcome peace, that Italy and Turkey were desperately tired, that Russ[i]a though possessed of more available military forces for the ranks was almost without officers and was encountering great difficulty in organizing her fresh forces, that by inference Austria would follow Germany's lead, (that), though England might be perhaps opposed to any movement looking to peace as proposed by (Germany), yet she could not resist the influence of the United States, sovereignty (? Spain) and the Vatican supported by the sentiment of the civilized countries, and that from a military point of view the belligerents were quite harmless (? hopelessly deadlocked). The King expressed himself interested solely on the ground of humanity and on account of the irreparable loss that his and other neutral powers were sustaining in the continuance of the war. (He concluded ?) by asking that I secure as soon as possible an expression of the President's wishes.

Willard

T telegram (SDR, RG 59, 763.72119/10494, DNA).
  1 That is, Alfonso XIII.
  2 Luis Polo de Bernabé.

From Edwin Stockton Johnson

Dear Mr. President: [Washington] May 11, 1916.

Since coming from the White House,[1] I have been to see Mr. Hollis to get his list of those who were opposed to the appointment of Mr. George Rublee as a member of the Federal Trade Commission.

I have agreed to see, personally, six of our Democrats who, I understand, are opposed to his confirmation. I will go over the ground very thoroughly with them and hope that I may be of some assistance in getting them to favorably consider the matter. I will certainly do my best in that direction.

Sincerely yours,   E. S. Johnson

TLS (WP, DLC).
  1 He had seen Wilson there at 11 A.M. on May 1.

Edward Mandell House to Sir Edward Grey

Dear Sir Edward: New York. May 11, 1916.

I enclose you a copy of a cable which I sent you yesterday.

We have been on the eve of a break with Germany so long that I have not written as it seemed it would come each day. For the moment, matters are quiet again and unless Germany transgresses further, there will probably be no break.

If we should get into the war, I feel sure, it would not be a good thing for England. It would probably lead to the complete crushing of Germany; and Russia, Italy and France would then be more concerned as to the division of the spoils than they would for any far-reaching agreement that might be brought about looking to the maintenance of peace in the future and the amelioration of the horrors of war.

The wearing down process, as far as Germany is concerned, has gone far enough to make her sensible of the power we can wield. This is an enormous gain and will help in the final settlement. A year ago we could not have made her come to the terms to which she has just agreed, and it seems certain that at a peace conference she would yield again and again rather than appeal to the sword.

From my cable you will see how far the President has gone within the year. Public opinion, we feel sure, will uphold him in his purpose to insist that the United States should do her part in the maintenance of peace.

I am sure, too, that this is the psychological moment to strike for those things which the President and you have so near at heart. Delay is dangerous and may defeat our ends.

While the program we have outlined means as much to the other nations, yet they will not see it clearly now as England and the United States see it. Therefore, England should be immediately responsive to our call. Her statesmen will take a great responsibility upon themselves if they hesitate or delay, and in the event of failure because they refuse to act quickly, history will bring a grave indictment against them.

All the things that you and I have wished to bring about seem ready now of accomplishment and I earnestly hope you may bring your Government to a realization of the opportunity that is seeking fulfillment.   Sincerely yours,

Dear Governor: I have supplemented my cable of yesterday by this letter, which I trust you will approve and which will be mailed Saturday morning. Affectionately, E.M.H.[1]

CCL (WP, DLC).
[1] EMHhw.

Hugh Lenox Scott and Frederick Funston
to Newton Diehl Baker

El Paso, Texas, May 11, 1916.

NUMBER 23. General Obregon and Juan Amador[1] arrived 10:00 a.m., and conferred until 1:30 p.m., when although invited to luncheon, they left to keep a previous engagement with Francisco Elias[2] and their families stating they would return at 4:00 p.m. today.

The result of the Mexican statements is in substance as follows: General Obregon spent all yesterday conferring by wire with all the commanders and Governors of provinces adjoining our border from Brownsville to lower California, with a view to ascertaining conditions and forces available to protect our border and orders were issued yesterday to General Trevino[3] to take ten thousand of best disciplined troops occupy the Parral district as well as the Rio Grande district east of Chihuahua and make a vigorous and effective campaign against all bandits and to show results as soon as practicable with a view of convincing the United States that the presence of American troops in Mexico can safely be dispensed with; that United States forces are now in Mexico and will not be molested while this bandit campaign is going on. He finds it impracticable to sign a written agreement but earnestly disclaims any thought other than that the United States will do as it has said it would, viz; leave Mexico when convinced of the safety of United States border likewise the earnest belief that all our affairs can be adjusted in a way satisfactory to both Governments as soon as the results of the bandit campaign becomes evident.

Amador asks us not to press an honorable and high minded general like Gen. Obregon to write down a permission for a foreign force to remain on the soil of his country. Obregon offers to intercept from south the bandits now fleeing from Boquillas towards where they are thought to have come from viz: San Pedro de Lagunas near Torreon, capture or kill them and release Deemer and fellow captive.[4] Other than this he says he has no power to act and refers us to his Government through ours.

---

[1] Dr. Juan Neftali Amador, Sub-secretary of Foreign Relations.

[2] Probably a resident of Juárez who served as Minister of Agriculture and Development in the 1930s.

[3] That is, Jacinto B. Treviño, military commander in Chihuahua.

[4] In a raid on Glen Springs on May 5, bandits kidnapped Jesse Deemer, proprietor of a country store, and Monroe Paine, a rancher. Major George Tayloe Langhorne tried to exchange three Mexican prisoners for the Americans. That plan failed, and, on May 12, Langhorne led troops A and B of the 8th Cavalry across the Rio Grande in an effort to surprise the bandits and retrieve the hostages. The troops caught up with the bandits on May 14 at Santa Fe Del Pino, ninety miles south of the border, rescued Deemer and Paine, and killed five of their captors.

Mexican conferees were informed that it is not known what effect it will have on our Government to learn that they are willing to tell us things they will not sign, that in the meanwhile our Government proposes to remain in Mexico until it feels that results mentioned by the De facto Government have been accomplished sufficiently for it to withdraw its troops with safety to its own soil. After reading the above twice to Obregon he made no objections to it as a statement of facts when interpreted to him by Amador. We believe that Obregon is sincere in his wish to avoid a clash with us, and will make an earnest effort to carry out his promises, but feels it necessary for his own protection to be able to say to his own people that he has signed no agreement to permit a foreign force to remain in Mexico which would be used with fatal effect to his prestige. Upon reassembling at 4:00 p.m. there was a discussion covering two and a half hours. Obregon produced two papers asking for agreement for stationing troops along both sides of the border. The same answer was given as before that this could better be arranged after our withdrawal from Mexico. One paper had the statement in it that orders had been given to withdraw our troops from Mexico immediately. It was pointed out that such order was never contemplated. The papers were not left with us.

The following conversation was held:

General Obregon: That the American troops are now in Mexican territory without the existence of a previous agreement and with my knowledge, and consequently there is no necessity to have an agreement for their withdrawal. General Scott, I state furthermore that in these papers General Obregon makes the declaration that he has received instructions from his Government and to patrol the border line and to garrison the section of Parral in order to get rid of these troubles as soon as possible, and as soon as these troubles are overcome, it is natural that our troops will get out of Mexican territory.

General Obregon: I make correction of that statement that withdrawal depends on the fact that you do not want to retire immediately. I cannot justify the presence of these troops by declaring of my own accord that the presence of the troops will be necessary for longer time in Mexico when I believe it is not necessary because I have troops in sufficient number to not permit of the forming of any bands of outlaws; and besides the troops I have in that section, I have mobilized a greater number of them.

General Scott: I will embody this in the telegram. End of Conversation.

The following statement was agreed upon for the press:

"That after several conferences marked throughout with conspicuous courtesy and good will in which conference mutual impressions were exchanged and information was collected upon the military situation on the frontier, it was agreed upon by the conferees to suspend the conference and report back to their Governments in order that these may be able, through their respective foreign departments to conclude this matter.

The ending of these conferences does not mean, in any way, a rupture of the good relations of friendship between the conferees nor between the respective Governments.

Signed: A. Obregon, H. L. Scott, and Frederick Funston."

The subject of use of railroads was discussed, Amador thought there would be no change.

Obregon said that the matter would be finally decided by his Government. By this time it was fully evident that the conferees would be unable to agree upon the main point at issue which was about the remaining of American troops on Mexican soil, and feeling that an agreement on this subject could not be reached, Obregon suggested adjournment, which was determined upon.

Although the subject of immediate withdrawal of American troops from Mexico was often discussed, it never came up as a demand or an ultimatum from Obregon.

Scott, Funston.

T telegram (SDR, RG 59, 812.00/18998, DNA).

To Edward Mandell House

The White House DC [May] 12 [1916]

Supplementary letter admirable   Glad you are sending it Thanks for the letter about Yucca [Walter Page]   Wilson

T telegram (E. M. House Papers, CtY).

To Robert Lansing

My dear Mr. Secretary,   The White House. 12 May, 1916.

Thank you for letting me see this.[1] It is very interesting and informing. I return it for your files.

Faithfully Yours,   W.W.

WWTLI (SDR, RG 59, 763.72/2665½, DNA).
   [1] F. C. Penfield to RL, April 15, 1916, printed as an Enclosure with RL to WW, May 9, 1916.

To Atlee Pomerene

My dear Senator:　　　　　[The White House] May 12, 1916

You have always been so generous and friendly that I know you will let me speak to you confidentially, and with the greatest freedom, about a matter which is troubling me a great deal. I mean the efforts that Senator Gallinger is making to defeat the appointment of Mr. Rublee to the Federal Trade Commission. It is a very serious matter to have a nomination of such importance defeated on the personal objection of a single Senator who cannot allege anything with regard to the record or qualifications of Mr. Rublee which show unfitness for the position, and it would be a still more serious business to let the independent and progressive voters of the country get the impression that we on our side would let those who are distinctly reactionary defeat appointments of this sort. Our whole fortune in the coming election depends upon whether we gain or do not gain the confidence of the independent voters, and I could not imagine anything that would be more likely to defeat us than the rejection of such nominations as this and that of Mr. Brandeis.

It has given me so much anxiety that I have taken the great liberty,—I hope, my dear Senator, you will not consider it too great,—of laying the matter before you personally and expressing my very great solicitude about it, and, at the same time, asking if it will not be possible for me to receive your active aid. As leader of the party, I feel that there is nothing which it is more clearly my duty to urge than favorable action in such matters as this.

　With warmest regard,

　　　Cordially and sincerely yours,　Woodrow Wilson

TLS (Letterpress Books, WP, DLC).

To Edward Nash Hurley[1]

My dear Mr. Hurley:　　　The White House May 12, 1916

Your Boston speech is before me, in which you outline some of the work which the Federal Trade Commission is doing for the business men of the country. I wish to commend your efforts generally, and in particular your endeavor to assist the small manufacturer and merchant to better his condition by helping him to improve his cost accounting and bookkeeping methods.

This is a step in the right direction and one of the main fundamentals of any successful business. It is most important to the future success of a business man that he should know what his goods actually cost to manufacture and to sell. If he has these facts, they will enable him to present a modern balance sheet to his bank, and as a result he will be better able to obtain credit with which to expand and develop his business.

Your suggestion that trade associations, associations of retail and wholesale merchants, commercial clubs, boards of trade, manufacturers' associations, credit associations, and other similar organizations should be encouraged in every feasible way by the Government seems to me a very wise one. To furnish them with data and comprehensive information in order that they may more easily accomplish the result that they are organized for is a proper and useful government function. These associations, when organized for the purpose of improving conditions in their particular industry, such as unifying cost accounting and bookkeeping methods, standardizing products and processes of manufacture, should meet with the approval of every man interested in the business progress of the country.

Too much emphasis cannot be placed on your suggestion that materials, methods, and products in industry should be standardized upon the basis of specifications drawn up in friendly cooperation with engineering societies, industrial experts, and trade associations. Further standardization in our industries will not only reduce the cost of production, but assure the producer better materials and more efficient workmanship, and to the consuming public the manifest benefit resulting from not having to pay for a wide and increasing variety of products and materials. Judicious standardization also means a greater return on a given investment. Capital now tied up because of inefficient methods will be released and can be used effectively elsewhere.

If we are to be an important factor in a world's markets, we must be more thorough and efficient in production. The encouragement of trade associations and standardization, and the installing of better cost accounting methods in our business concerns will go a long way toward accomplishing this end.

It is my hope that, in addition to the other work which the Federal Trade Commission is doing, it will ascertain the facts regarding conditions in our various industries. If it finds that an industry is not healthy, it should, after carefully considering the facts, in cooperation with the parties interested, suggest a practical and helpful remedy. In this way many of our difficult business problems might be solved.

I am very anxious to see you continue to cooperate with the

business men of the country along the lines upon which you are working.

Cordially and sincerely yours,   Woodrow Wilson

TLS (Berg Coll., NN).
¹ The following letter was drafted by Hurley and edited slightly by Wilson. Hurley's draft with Wilson's emendations is in WP, DLC.

From Joseph Patrick Tumulty

Dear Governor: The White House May 12, 1916.

I spoke to you a few days ago about the apparent dissatisfaction of the country with regard to the attitude of Congress toward preparedness. You seemed to feel that it was not nation-wide. I send you herewith an editorial from the Milwaukee Journal (Nieman's paper) which has supported you on everything. It denounces the action of the House as "criminal folly."¹ Also an editorial from the Kansas City Star which speaks of the lack of leadership; and editorials from the Brooklyn Eagle, the St. Louis Post Dispatch, the Baltimore Sun, the New York Times and our old friend, the Philadelphia Record.²

Respectfully,   J P Tumulty

TLS (WP, DLC).
¹ *Milwaukee Journal*, May 9, 1916, clipping in WP, DLC. This editorial described the country's defense capability as "incredibly inadequate" and derided both Democratic and Republican congressmen for "criminal folly" and for "lacking in patriotic vision" when they voted down the Senate's army reorganization bill.
² *Kansas City Times* (not the *Kansas City Star*), May 9, 1916, *Brooklyn Eagle*, May 11, 1916, *St. Louis Post-Dispatch*, May 9, 1916, Baltimore *Sun*, May 11, 1916, *New York Times*, May 9, 1916, *Philadelphia Record*, May 9, 1916, all clippings in WP, DLC.

From James Paul Clarke

Dear Mr. President: [Washington] May 12, 1916.

Your letter of yesterday did not reach me until 10 o'clock to-day.

The Committee on Commerce in considering the Rivers and Harbors Bill recommended the East River item for rejection. This was done not because any single member of the Committee was opposed to its being ultimately included in the bill, but for certain tactical reasons of peculiar importance in the consideration of the whole bill in conference. The Senate took the liberty of adding several items which it supposed severally to be quite important. It was thought by putting the East River item on the same footing as these when all come to be finally considered by the conference would not be unfair nor otherwise improper. No concealed nor factional motive prompted the Committee in taking the action indicated. It is altogether likely that you will be satisfied with the result that will finally be evolved. It may be that when the matter is considered in the Senate, that that body will not agree with the Committee that the item should be left out of the bill even temporarily.

Very sincerely yours,   James P. Clarke.

TLS (WP, DLC).

From Walter Hines Page

Dear Mr. President: 12, May 1916—London

The message that you were kind enough to telegraph about Shakespeare[1] was enthusiastically received at the Mansion House meeting, whereat men representing most countries (other than the German, of course) paid their countries' tribute to the poet; and I have had many persons speak to me since about it. It added just the right American touch to a notable meeting. . . .[2]

The English ought to be drawn and quartered for their sluggish stupidity in forever abusing one another and for forever grumbling. They seem to have (with their Allies, all of whom they maintain by money and supplies,) the military situation well in hand. The Germans have had a hard blow and a serious set-back at Verdun. In spite of that the prevalent English mood is a mood of depression. They fear they can never win a real victory but only a draw—and this just when they have voted for conscription and can thus continue to put men into the field—a larger reserve than Germany has. Waves of feeling sweep over them as billows break on a rocky shore. But the rock remains after the billows are all gone—luckily for them. My own belief is that the only invincible thing in Europe are these same English. If all Europe were against them instead of the Germans, still they'd win in the long run. Yet they wrangle and become "grouchy" and decline even to permit their friends to know what they are doing. I cd. with truth tell the whole race what I've often told groups of them—that they are good for nothing except to become ancestors of Americans and Colonials. In America and their large Colonies, the English become free and hopeful. The despair—the depression—the melancholy—the slow ichor[3] in the blood—of all Europeans, with the possible exception of the French—is what damns them all. It turns their eyes inward and backward. And yet these are the only invincible people in this world—this race. Perhaps I've told you that I talk with many women who come to ask me to have inquiries made about their sons and husbands who are "missing." "Missing" generally means dead, and that is what they all fear. But they hope that it may mean imprisonment. They tell their stories with the same fortitude, the same self-restraint, the same sorrowful pride—noble women and working women alike. Of the hundreds that I have heard recite the same sad story, only one whimpered. I found out afterwards that she was a Belgian married to an Englishman. She was not of the breed. The Spartan women were weaklings beside the English. I daily grow stronger in my Americanism—real Americanism, not the hyphenated counterfeit. For the British race (*i.e.* Scotch and English, for your Irishman is a sort of yellow dog and your Welshman has a tendency to lying) is the best race yet mixed & developed on this globe, and this race comes to its best under freer and more mobile conditions than this rainy isle of dukes and earls permits. People here now discuss everything with reference to "after the war." "What are we going to do after the war? What do we do best?" I have an easy answer: "Send your children to the United States. Your daughters will become handsomer and your sons more adaptable —they'll be English set free: that's what an American is. The best thing you've ever done is to breed men for freer lands." And they believe it—some of 'em do at least. These English are the most interesting study in the world. Just when you'd like to hang them for their stupidity, you become aware of such noble stuff in them that you thank God that they were your ancestors. And Europe wd. be a bloody slave-pen today but for them. It's a shambles as it is.

They are not going to get tired. Peace? Yes, on their terms. And, while they are fighting for their lives, they are the only nation that is not fighting also for booty. And among many things that this war is teaching them is the stupidity of their arrogance when they twice provoked us to war. They pathetically yearn for our utmost good-will—even while they (some of them at least) curse us. My admiration for their racial qualities deepens while my impatience with their ways is heightened. I cd. write a book in worship of them and another book damning them—both true, both concrete, both definitely proving its thesis.

And now Stabler,[4] the senior Second Secretary here, is called home to (I fear) the death-bed of his father in Baltimore[5]—a faithful, patriotic man of good judgment and prudent. If you wish a true report about any particular thing here—about our activities & methods—ask the Department to send him to see you. You will get a true report.

The more I have thought of your last Note to Germany, the more admirable its content and especially its strategy appear. They are bagged. I find nobody here who believes that they will cease their submarine recklessness—unless they are preparing for an early surrender, wh. nobody here believes. But everybody believes that the beginning of the end has begun, however far off the end may be. I know that this is the feeling of the Government here—both the civil and the military ends of it; and, in spite of their grumbling, they will not slacken their resolution or their work till they get what they want—security, on a more trustworthy basis than German promises or pledges.

And thus the weary, wearing, endless but interesting days go on. A sort of new Old World will emerge at last, wherein the English will still be dominant and—let us hope—chastened and humbler and, therefore, greater than ever.

Sincerely Yours,   Walter H. Page

ALS (WP, DLC).

[1] WW to the Shakespeare Tercentenary Committee, April 30, 1916, Vol. 36.

[2] Here Page reported on the first annual meeting of the British National Committee for Relief in Belgium, and then followed with a long paragraph on the valuable services of Lieutenant Colonel George Owen Squier, the American military attaché in London.

[3] Watery discharge from certain wounds and sores.

[4] Jordan Herbert Stabler.

[5] Jordan Stabler, prominent businessman of Baltimore; founder and owner of the Jordan Stabler Co., the largest wholesale and retail grocery house in the South. He died on June 20, 1916.

From James Cardinal Gibbons

My dear Mr. President: Baltimore. May the 12th, 1916.

I have received a cipher cable message from the Pope in which His Holiness expresses the hope that you have favorably considered his communication of the fifth instant,[1] presented to you through your Secretary, Mr. Tumulty, by His Excellency the Apostolic Delegate.[2]

Should you be pleased to make any acknowledgment of the message, I am authorized by His Holiness to receive it.

With sentiments of the highest esteem and respect, I am

Most faithfully Yours,   J. Card. Gibbons,
Archbishop of Baltimore.

Handed to me by Mons. Russell[3] to be delivered to Pres't in case he intends to answer Pope's message. 5/15/16   RL[4]

TLS (WP, DLC).

[1] It is printed as an Enclosure with WW to RL, May 15, 1916.

[2] The Most Rev. Giovanni Bonzano, Archbishop of Melitene.

From William Calhoun McDonald

Mr. President: Santa Fe May 12, 1916.

The suggestion in yours of May 8th, relative to the cases of the seven men sentenced to be hanged May 19th for participating in the raid on Columbus, New Mexico in March and now held in the penitentiary for safe keeping,[1] is in accord with what I have had in mind with reference to these cases. The delicacy of the situation at the present time undoubtedly requires careful handling. I scarcely think that their execution would result in any serious reprisal on the part of the Mexicans, though of course no one can tell just what might happen.

I have been waiting for the court record of the trial of these men, which I have not yet received. It seems to me now that it will probably be necessary to reprieve these men in order to have such investigation as I desire, so that I may be thoroughly informed in regard to everything relating thereto before reaching a final determination.

You will readily understand that there is considerable feeling in New Mexico, and I believe these cases should be handled carefully in order to prevent, so far as possible, any objectionable developments here as well as in Mexico. I think, however, I shall be able to handle the cases in such a way as to prevent any serious complications here or in Mexico, and at the same time act in accordance with your suggestion.

I have the honor to be,
                    Your obedient servant,   W. C. McDonald

TLS (WP, DLC).
1 See WW to W. C. McDonald, May 8, 1916, Vol. 36.

A Memorandum by Ray Stannard Baker of a Conversation at the White House[1]

[May 12, 1916]

I had a wonderful talk with Mr. Wilson, two hours long, from 8 to 10, in the evening in his library upstairs in the White House. I want to set it down fully, just as it was & before the impression begins to be distorted by reflection or perspective: or influenced

1 The conversation took place on May 11, 1916.

by discussion with other people. I'll put it all down, just as it was, though much of it could not possibly now be used in public. Just as we were parting Mr. Wilson said: "I've tried to open my mind completely to you: to show you just what I am thinking upon these questions." He used the expression, he would "put me in possession of his mind" on this or that subject. And I think he did. I talked with both Roosevelt & Taft when they were in the White House, especially the former, & often, but neither could deliver himself so completely, reasons & all, as Wilson. Wilson applies the scientific method to his own mental processes.

Well, I was shown into the study a few minutes before he arrived & had a moment to look about. Two very large paintings: one a fine copy of Watts' Love & Life with a written poem on the book case at one side entitled "Love & Life." The other painting represented the moment of the signing of the treaty with Spain in the McKinley admr. McK is standing at the end of the table: a fine figure & Hay & the Spanish Amb. are rep. as sitting & signing the treaty. Genthe's photograph of the new Mrs. Wilson has a prominent place on a near book case. A book by Earl Grey[2] on "Fly-Fishing"[3] (never heard of it) on the table. Mr. Wilson's desk a great litter of books & papers: filing cabinet behind it: a stenographer's desk in the corner. It is the quiet place where, he said, he does all his serious work. He came in stepping quickly & lightly. "How are you Baker?" He always looks—well "natty"—well buttoned up & he has a peculiary *live* face: *live* eyes. He looks very well, though he told me that he grows very tired. His complexion is that seen on so many public men: rather bronzed & full of fine veins & lines.

I never have talked with any public man who has such a complete control of his whole intellectual equipment as he. Men talk or write clearly & easily who think clearly & easily: & good expression is one of the soundest evidences of good thought. Contrary to popular belief, I think, he has a very vivid & expressive face. The rise & fall of his intellectual interest & enthusiasm express themselves wonderfully in his eyes & face. Two or three times when I told him some new fact or something that interested him a look as of keen *appetite* came into his eyes. He *pounces* upon things half said & consumes them before they are well out of one's mind. And his pounce is sure, accurate, complete. He instantly adds what you give him, whether fact or opinion, to his own view of the situation: so that to an extraordinary degree you go along with him & arrive at that meeting of minds which is so

---

2 Sir Edward Grey, ennobled as Viscount Grey of Fallodon on July 27, 1916.
3 *Fly Fishing* (London, 1899).

rare a thing in discussion. So many men are little habituated to quick thought, so little equipped to weigh & take in instantly a new fact or idea that you may pass a whole evening with them & find them lumbering along on their track & you on yours, & though much talk has passed, you have really never met! Not so, Mr. Wilson!

One of the first things he said was this: "I am delighted with your namesake in the Cabinet (Baker, the new War Secretary). It is a comfort to have him with me." He said that Baker had a trained mind: an administrative mind & that his experience as Mayor of Cleveland, with the responsibility of decisions in large matters, made him especially useful.

"He is a very different type from Mr. Garrison?" I asked.

"Entirely different. Garrison was an intensely argumentative man. He wore me out with argument. When he met a fact, instead of accepting it, as facts must be accepted, as inevitable, he wanted to argue about it indefinitely. Baker accepts it, makes room for it & goes ahead."

This led to a consideration of Mr. Bryan. He said that, different as they were in character & temperament, Bryan & Garrison were somewhat alike in mental processes. Bryan also an argumentative man, to whom facts, when they conflicted with his logical processes were not acceptable. He told me how he had labored to show Bryan what were the *conditions* they had to meet: & that Bryan, after listening, would immediately slip back into the smooth channel of his theories & begin to argue along the old lines. Bryan had not the scientific mind. But he gave Bryan great credit for the one-year delay treaties. This was his own idea, Wilson said, & some such delay-method must be one of the corner stones of future international relationships, if peace was to come in the world.

I asked him if he was less a party man than when he came into the W. H. recalling that he had told me in a former talk that he believed strongly in party government. His recent experiences with Congress—dull tools—might have changed him I thought. But he is still a strong party man. Told me the story of a barber who once shaved him—in N. Y.—during the Seth Low-Van Wyck contest.[4] He talked with him about the elec. The barber said he was going to vote for Van Wyck. Why, isn't he a less able man than Low? That may be, said the barber, but if we elect Low & he doesn't make good there will be no one left to punish. Low had

---

[4] Seth Low ran as an independent candidate in the first election for Mayor of Greater New York in 1897. Robert Anderson Van Wyck, a Democrat, defeated Low and General Benjamin Franklin Tracy, the Republican candidate.

no party behind him but only a dissolving committee, while Van Wyck had a powerful party org. which could be held responsible. This, he thought illus. the use of parties fully.

Said he regretted personally the fact that the president was said to be stronger than the party. It placed heavier resp. & obl. upon him. The best work was done when party & president were of equal regard.

He reiterated again his belief in "responsible government," & a closer working together of party and president. Said the president had an undue advantage now: that what he said had universal publicity while what congressmen said in reply or modification did not reach the people in any such degree. He thought some modification of the English system would bring about better team work in public affairs.

He made many references to this nation as being intensely conservative—conserv-minded—& explained it, as he explains so many things, historically. A written Constitution, diverse population elements—an instinctive fear of interfering with the cement of our national charter & institutions. But the only way for a party to live was to be going somewhere—moving—in short, being *progressive*. One could only think *ahead*. He said he had labored with a group of senators that day on this point referring to the confirmation of Brandeis & Rublee—both progressives.

"But, most of them never think ahead," I remarked.

"Most of them never think at all," he said.

We then fell to talking about his program. He quoted Oliver's book on Hamilton, that passage which comments upon the power of the leader or party with a program against the leader or party having none.[5]

His success in the first 16 mos of his admr. was due to having a definite program—approved by the people & in the party platform, which he carried out. His only important variation from this was in the Panama Canal tolls matter—which concerned

[5] Wilson probably recalled the following passage from Frederick Scott Oliver's *Alexander Hamilton: An Essay on American Union* (New York and London, 1916), p. 486: "Men are prepared for sacrifices, if only the leaders would understand, and will hardly be satisfied that their object has been attained unless they are called upon for sacrifices. Confidence in the old policy of disintegration is utterly destroyed. Nor will people believe that the new policy of union is to be achieved without an effort. They are suspicious of advice which assures them that true safety is to be found by drifting with the easiest currents. Their minds are fully possessed by the greatness of the endeavour, and they have judged rightly that the difficulties which attend it must be in proportion. A problem of this magnitude, in their opinion, cannot be solved without guidance of the forces. The industrious cupidity of distracted individuals, the energies, ambitions and rivalries of particular states can never carry them to their goal." There is a copy of Oliver's book in the Wilson Library, DLC.

foreign affairs & was properly within the initiative of the president.

Very interesting his talk about his new program which came in with the war. He referred to the passage in his book on the Constitution[6] (see!) in which he shows that in times of peace when domestic problems are uppermost Congress comes to the front, but when foreign affairs intrude the people look to the president. His foreign affairs policy must then be his own. Humanity in former expressions. He went West on the preparedness campaign to test out public opinion. He does not, he says, read newspapers, though he glances over headlines & reads certain editorials. Spoke with warmth of editorials in Springfield *Republican*. Said Tumulty reads everything & reports what he finds. Has certain close friends who are ears for him. Spoke warmly of Col. House & of his disinterested service. House goes about meeting & seeing people & reports to him. Sent him abroad twice to Europe (Said Bryan didn't like it. Bryan himself wanted to go—actually!)

We talked of the qualifications of leadership. Wilson's mind wholly different from T.R's. I remember some such conv. with T.R. in which it could be seen that when T.R. defined a leader he described himself: but Wilson's mind is scientific & he divides & classifies leaders & one could *feel him* placing himself here or there: I am this, I am that, I have that qualification, not this & so on. Such a satisfying mind! The first need of a leader that he mentioned was *enthusiasm*. He must believe something strongly. Therefore he must have a program & be going somewhere. He must understand his people & stir them to response, either an emotional response or an intellectual approval. (Wilson himself inspires people with confidence. He is *safe*. We trust him. He is not magnetic, he does not awaken emotion as T.R. does.) He told humorously how it was possible for the president to winnow out the truth of a matter by talking with a sufficient number of liars as in the Mexican matter. Said that the lying about Mexico was prodigious. But this was the situation regarding liars: what they all agreed upon was probably true. What they all differed upon was probably lies.

Told story of Scotch friend who read Bishop Burnett's book.[7] "It's lies Jamie, & again "It's all lies Jamie" & when he came to end said, "It's lies, Jamie & ye *ken* it's lies."

[6] That is, *Constitutional Government in the United States* (1908).
[7] Wilson was probably referring to Bishop Gilbert Burnet's famous book, *Bishop Burnet's History of His Own Time* (1723).

People don't know Wilson as a story teller. He is full of them: not Lincolnesque but anecdotal.

He said his Mexican policy was based upon two of the most deeply seated convictions of his life: first his shame as an American over the first Mexican war & his resolution that while he was president there should be no such predatory war. Second, upon his belief in the Virginia bill of rights: that a people had the right "to do what they damned pleased with their own affairs" (He used the word "damned"). He wanted to give the Mexicans a chance to try. Said he had asked a man named Holder,[8] formerly with the British embassy at Mexico, who had come to see him, to name a single instance in history in which the blessing of free government had been bestowed upon a people from above: & had not come with struggle & trials from below. He wants to give the Mexicans a chance, but is not dogmatic about it. Here, as always, he respects the facts, the events, & it may prove, as he said, that we shall have to go in finally & make peace. He is ashamed of our attitude toward Mexico, spoke of our Ambassador down there at the time of the Madero revolution (Wilson)[9] as "unspeakable" & believes—so he said—that Wilson played an evil part in the overthrow of Madero. Said that the greatest trouble was not with Mexicans but with people here in America who wanted the oil & metals of Mexico & were seeking intervention to get them.

Referred to the Mexican boundary as one of the longest in the world & declared with shut jaw that he would not be forced into war with Mexico if it could possibly be avoided. Did not want one hand tied behind him at the very moment the nation might need all its forces to meet the German situation. In no way does he show his fundamental progressiveness & democracy [more] than in his attitude toward Mexico. He also emphasized the enormous undertaking it would be to pacify Mexico—500 000 men at least, he said (a point I did not quite like: for if here lies our duty, it must be done).

He is thinking more than almost anything else, he said, just now, about what he, or this nation might be called upon to do toward helping to bring about peace. Not a word of this is now to be breathed abroad of course. When is the time to offer our good offices? Shall he outline tentatively some plans or ideas at the dinner of the League to Enforce Peace which is to meet the latter part of the month? He asked my advice & I told him I thought the time had not arrived to enter the serious stage of offering

8 Thomas Beaumont Hohler.
9 That is, Henry Lane Wilson.

good offices or calling a peace conference but that I thought he could help prepare opinion by guarded statements in his coming speech.

I asked him also of the proposal to call a conference of neutral nations, which I have long thought to be a good one, but he said he thought it would hamper rather than help us to be associated with a group of little nations. He said that in any event we should have to bear the brunt of the conflict & that responsibility was better not divided.

He talked at length & with great enthus. of the new Pan-American treaties which are to make us partners with S. & Central America, rather than guardians. He thought it a great step in advance: This is not public yet & will make a great stir when announced. He thinks some such idea as this must be applied to the world situation. His views are near to those of the League to Enforce Peace.

Spoke of tariff commission: did not believe in it when he came to the White House but here the facts were plain. Must be prepared for stormy conditions & quick action at close of war. Need an expert commission. Tariff could never be taken wholly from politics, because tariff a form of taxation.

He is a man humble before facts & events.

He has stolen most of the thunder of the Progressives & Republicans.

I asked him squarely which he would rather meet in the coming elections, Roosevelt or Hughes.

"It matters very little," he said. "We have definite things constructive things to do, & we shall go ahead and do them. Roosevelt deals in personalities & not argument upon facts & conditions. One does not need to meet him at all. Hughes is of a different type. If he is nominated, he will have to be met."

He commended many Congressmen highly, said Congress was under-rated. Spoke of the ability of Mr. Glass of Virginia—"a man we shall hear more from."

Said he was convinced that the people of the country—the mass —wanted peace, not war, but also that if war came now after every effort had been made to avoid it that we would go into it sadly but strongly.

Wilson's favorite poem, he says is Wordsworth's "Happy Warrior."

A great democrat here & a great man. Fearless because sure of himself. A great president.

We talked two hours in the quiet of his library & were not once disturbed. He sees very few people compared with former presidents & never gives interviews. His talk with me was not an interview but a conversation the purpose of which was to enable me to found soundly & truly whatever I may write about him & his policies. A thoughtful leader like him needs interpretation. T.R. interprets himself. His look is forward & his thinking is forward.[10]

Hw memorandum, Notebook No. 10, pp. 42-64 (RSB Papers, DLC).
[10] Baker published an article based upon this interview—"Wilson," *Collier's*, LVIII (Oct. 7, 1916), 5-6. However, it was a personal and character sketch with few quotations from the conversation itself.

From Newton Diehl Baker, with Enclosures

My dear Mr. President: Washington. May 13, 1916.

I send you herewith copies of two telegrams from General Funston and General Scott, which are interesting as giving their view of the effect of the conferences they have held with General Obregon and the present status of the case.

Cordially yours,   Newton D. Baker

TLS (WP, DLC).

E N C L O S U R E   I

El Paso, Texas.
Received at the War Department May 12, 1916, 7:55 P.M.

Number 1357-A. Following just received from Pershing: "Lakeitascate, Mexico, May 11th. Number 179. No evidence so far that de facto troops intend no [to] attack columns. Believed contact with our troops have been severe experience. Their idea of American prowess have been changed since this expedition started. Do not anticipate molestation unless they have overwhelming numbers coupled with every other possible advantage. No considerable bodies reported anywhere near us. Coalition believe factions south of San Antonio against Americans confirmed. Again proving universal opposition experienced from the start. Carrancistas have been recently distributing arms to natives vicinity Andres. Presumably to drive out Americans. Any assemblage of Mexicans for that purpose of whatever size would be without intelligent leadership or organization, and their easy defeat by this command would be certain. Any army they can muster would be nothing but a mob without training or discipline and with little courage, and not to be feared in the slightest. District organizations were in good working order when instructions changed plans. Result would undoubtedly soon have been general clean up all Villista bands unless Carrancistas interfered. Withdrawal progressing smoothly. One regiment Cavalry and one battery present rear guard Wilder's[1] Brigade will encamp tonight at Dolores fifteen miles south."   Funston

[1] Colonel Wilber Elliott Wilder, commander of the 5th United States Cavalry.

E N C L O S U R E   I I

El Paso, Texas, May 12, 1916.

Number twenty five period. Both General Funston and I greatly appreciate the kind expressions contained in your telegram of this date and thank you therefor period. We believe that the acute situation is over for the present, that the Mexicans will do their best to carry out their part and Obregon will have greater strength with his people to carry it out than if an agreement had been actually ratified period. Amador made following statement to stenographer in car this morning, quote. That [in] all of these talks General Obregon, in my opinion, has had the conviction of the good faith in which General Scott, on the part of the American government, has been acting; but the simple promise to control the situation not being sufficient, he is now going to show evidently to the government of the United States that he is able to handle the situation in Mexico, with full control of his troops, which he is going to distribute in the zone of Parral and on the Mexican side of the Rio Grande frontier in sufficient numbers as to guarantee safety for that region and try to avoid future trouble period. That by that way, it being the intention of the U. S. to withdraw, as it has been repeatedly stated by General Scott, the withdrawal of the troops will have to occur because of the demonstration of the fact of the Government of Mexico being powerful enough to control the situation unquote.   Scott

TC telegrams (WP, DLC).

From Josephus Daniels

My dear Mr. President: Washington, May 13, 1916.

House of Representatives Bill 406, now before the Senate and familiarly known as the General Leasing Bill,[1] a conservation measure, contains, in Sections 9 and 10, provisions, not a fundamental part of the Bill, which, if the Bill becomes a law, will so seriously jeopardize the future supply of fuel oil for the Navy that I feel it my duty to bring this matter to your attention.

In 1909, the President, influenced by "the further reason that it seemed desirable to reserve certain fuel-oil deposits for the use of the American Navy," withdrew from entry or disposal certain public lands in California and Wyoming, some of which were subsequently, by Executive Order, specifically set aside and reserved "for the exclusive use or benefit of the United States Navy."

Question having been raised regarding the validity of this withdrawal, Congress in 1910 specifically authorized the President to withdraw public lands, and upon the representations of the claimants of withdrawn oil lands incorporated in the same Act (the Pickett Act) a provision designed to protect those prospectors who were at the time of the 1909 withdrawal in diligent prosecution of work looking to the discovery of oil.

The Pickett Act gives full protection to everyone who had a just claim to the withdrawn lands, but as it has been acknowledged by the oil men themselves before the Public Lands Committee of the House, that about 90% of the claimants have no valid claim whatever to the land, they can not obtain a patent, and in many instances dare not apply for one. They have, therefore, sought to obtain by Congressional action title to these lands, and if H.R. 406 becomes a law, these trespassers on the public domain will be given either a patent to the land to which they admit they have no legal claim, or a lease of it as long as oil can be extracted from it. They will, therefore, be rewarded merely because of their disregard of the Presidential order of withdrawal (since declared by the Supreme Court to be valid) and of their financial ability and willingness to complete or initiate the drilling of an oil well; and the citizens who respected the order of withdrawal will get absolutely nothing.

An argument that the oil men have used in urging this legislation is that they have equities based on the expenditure of large sums of money which should not be ignored. The attorney for the Department of Justice who has been prosecuting these cases in California has stated that the number who have claims of such a character as to deserve consideration is very small, but even if every man who claims it had such an equity, it would be far better for the Government to make the most reasonable determination of the value of their equities and pay it to them than that the oil in the lands should pass out of the hands of the Government.

Another statement made by these claimants and others is that in order that the so-called equities of these claimants may be protected the Navy might well surrender its rights in these Reserves and seek other lands for Naval Petroleum Reserves, but the answer to this proposition is found in the letter of the Director of the Geological Survey, under date of August 8, 1912, prior to the creation of these Reserves:

"There does not exist in the United States a tract of land better fulfilling the requirements of a naval reserve in respect to (a) probable existence of a large supply of oil; (b) favorable conditions for preservation of that supply; (c) ready accessibility of lines of transportation to the seaboard; and (d) a position protected from the danger of foreign invasion."

This matter is of such vital interest to the Navy Department because—

1. The Navy relied upon this reserve of oil when the policy of building oil-burning battleships was adopted.

2. A naval vessel built to burn oil can not be converted to a coal burner without practically rebuilding her and even then at a great sacrifice of military efficiency.

3. The Secretary of the Interior has estimated that there exists in the oil fields of the United States only enough oil to supply this nation for about 28 years at the present rate of consumption.

4. With the completion of the naval program the annual requirements of the Navy for fuel oil will be 4,800,000 barrels, and the estimated total fuel oil content of the existing Naval Petroleum Reserves Numbers 1 and 3 would supply the Fleet for 15 years in peace and 5 years in war; but this Bill will dispose of the only proven part of Number 1, and all of Number 2 Reserve.

The enactment of this Bill as it now stands will dispose of all the proven public oil lands and render it necessary for the Navy Department to consider the abandonment of oil and the return to coal as fuel for the Fleet. If this should be done, it will put the stamp of inferiority on our ships in comparison with the ships of a nation which can secure a supply of oil for fuel.

This matter is one of such national importance, and so vitally affects the efficiency of the Navy, that I earnestly request that the elimination of these so-called relief provisions be urged.

Sincerely yours,   Josephus Daniels

TLS (J. Daniels Papers, DLC).
1 See WW to J. W. Kern, April 12, 1916, n. 1, Vol. 36.

From Edward Mandell House, with Enclosures

Dear Governor: New York, May 14, 1916.

Here is a cable which came from Sir Edward yesterday. It is disappointing in a way and yet there is nothing final about it. He does not give his own opinion firmly, much less that of any of his colleagues.

That is the difficulty we have in dealing with the British Government. Sir Edward has been talking to me for two years concerning the necessity of the United States doing just what you now propose, and yet when you are ready to do it, he hesitates.

What do you think of the enclosed cable to him? I shall also write him a letter by the next mail enclosing some clippings culled from the papers today bearing such headings as these: "Urges the President to offer his services for peace" "Bryan demands move for peace" etc. etc.

Sir Edward wants to know whether he shall take the matter up with Asquith. What would you advise about this? Shall we go ahead upon his negative approval rather than risk a more positive statement from Asquith?

Do you think it would serve any purpose for me to talk to Jusserand and have him get in touch with Briand and Cambon?

I see evidences of the Allies regaining their self-assurance and not being as yielding to our desires as they were when they were in so much trouble. We have given them everything and they ever demand more.

One thing that works against you is the alienated Americans living in both Paris and London. By their wealth and position they have the ears of the members of the governments. Whitney Warren in Paris[1] is a type and I have been told is very close to Briand. Bacon[2] is another. The members of the firm of Morgan & Company are close to both governments and you may be sure there is nothing your Administration does but what is condemned.

They try to create the feeling, and never more so than now, that if the republicans were in it would be a triumph for the Allies and that if the war continues until after November things will be different.

It should be borne in mind that Page may resign in any event for the reason that their children are married and Mrs. Page is very lonely and desires to come home. I believe Cleve Dodge would be an excellent substitute for Page. He is loyal and has good sense and that is all you want in an ambassador.

Affectionately yours,   E. M. House

TLS (WP, DLC).

[1] Distinguished New York architect and member of the firm of Warren and Wetmore; he had studied at École des Beaux Arts and was a member of L'Académie des Beaux Arts of the Institut de France and of numerous other French architectural and artistic societies.

[2] That is, Robert Bacon.

ENCLOSURE I

May 12, 1916.

I have received your telegram. My opinion without consulting colleagues and Allies is of little value and for me to consult them now as to a peace conference would I think at best lead to a reply that mediation or a conference was premature, especially after the German Chancellor's last speech of which both the terms and tone were resented by the Allies.[1]

The President's suggestion of[2] summoning a peace conference without any indication of a basis on which peace might be made would be construed as instigated by Germany to secure peace on terms unfavourable to the Allies while her existing military position is still satisfactory to her.

The difficulty of avoiding this impression without offense to Germany, is one which you can estimate perhaps better than I, but the danger of making the undesirable impression on the Allies is very real, for there is a belief, wide-spread through perhaps over confidence, that Germany is in grave difficulties which may lead her to collapse especially if failure to take Verdun becomes final.

For the rest, my letter of September 22[3] contemplated diminution of arms as the result of a league of nations binding themselves to side against any power which broke a treaty or certain rules of war on sea or land.

I hesitated to advocate rules for directly limiting armaments not on the ground of principle but because of the practical difficulty in drawing up such rules.

Otherwise my personal view is in favour of agreement between nations such as you suggest; though I cannot guarantee how others would receive it. I believe it would secure a reduction of armaments. I sympathize with the President's aspirations and feel that his proposal as regards a league of nations may be of the greatest service to humanity, but as to the desirability of it now and with a summoning of a peace conference I cannot express an opinion beyond what I have stated above.

A month ago I gave an interview to Bell of the Chicago Daily News;[4] which I have hitherto asked him to refrain from publishing as I doubted the opportuneness of publication, but in view of what you imply as to the impression that the Allies are vindictive I hope the interview will be now published. If it appears please remember it was completed a month before your telegram was received, but I do not think the contents will be inconvenient to the President.

I hope you will realize this telegram is a purely personal opinion sent in reply to your request without consulting my colleagues, not even the Prime Minister who is now in Ireland, but if you desire it I will consult him upon his return.

E. Grey.

TC telegram (WP, DLC).

[1] In his speech in the Reichstag on April 5, 1916, Bethmann Hollweg had again insisted on Germany's right to use all its available weapons against the English policy of starvation. As far as peace negotiations were concerned, the Chancellor stated that Germany would never agree to a peace that was based on the destruction of German military power, but would answer any such suggestion by the sword. He then maintained that Germany would give up neither Belgium nor Poland without providing for future securities. "History," he declared, "does not know the *status quo ante* after these monumental events. Belgium after the war will no longer be the old Belgium before the war. The Poland that the Russian Cossack left burning and looting does not exist any more. . . . We will provide for real guarantees that Belgium will not become an Anglo-French vassal state, that it will not be turned into a bastion against Germany militarily and economically." Friedrich Thimme, ed., *Bethmann Hollwegs Kriegsreden* (Stuttgart and Berlin, 1919), pp. 90-102. See also the *New York Times*, April 6, 1916.

[2] Corrections from the TC of this telegram in the E. M. House Papers, CtY.

[3] E. Grey to EMH, Sept. 22, 1915, quoted in full in n. 3 to the extract from the House Diary printed at Oct. 15, 1915, Vol. 35.

[4] That is, Edward Price Bell. Bell's interview with Grey appeared in the *Chicago Daily News* on May 13. It was reprinted in the *New York Times*, May 14, 1916.

E N C L O S U R E   I I

Proposed cable to E.G.

It is not intended that the President's statement regarding the calling of a peace conference should be definite. It would be scarcely more than an intimation in order to satisfy the growing insistence that he take some action.

His proposal for a league of nations would be definite. The cause of the Allies is at high tide here, but if there comes a recession it would not be possible to do the things that would now be approved.

CC MS (WP, DLC).

Two Letters from Edward Mandell House

Dear Governor: New York, May 14, 1916.

Bernstorff came this morning. He has a message from his government saying that Gerard was rather premature in his announcement that they, the German Government, would welcome you as a mediator.[1]

They believe this state of mind will come about shortly, particularly if we can have a period of quiet between the two governments. In order that this may come to pass, he suggests again that the Lusitania matter be closed and that the von Igel case be disposed of by an intimation from Lansing that von Igel be sent home and by the return to him, Bernstorff, of the papers.

These papers, he says, relate to a case nearly two years old. He expressed the belief that those connected with the attempted destruction of the Welland Canal, would be punished by our courts.

He advised very strongly that both governments stop nagging each other. As an instance of our doing so he mentioned Lansing's insistence that the German Government inform this Government how the commander of the submarine that sank the Sussex was punished. And again his statement that no demand would be made upon England for the present simply because Germany had insisted upon it in her note.

He calls these pin-pricks, but said it was impossible to allay irritation and to bring about good feeling while they continued.

Affectionately yours,   E. M. House

[1] After House, on May 4, had informed Bernstorff of Gerard's message (J. W. Gerard to RL, May 2, 1916, enclosed in RL to WW, May 3, 1916, Vol. 36), the German Ambassador immediately got in touch with Berlin. See J. H. von Bernstorff to the Foreign Office, May 4, 1916, T telegram (Der Weltkrieg, No. 2, geheim, Vermittlungsaktionen, Vol. 17, p. 144, GFO-Ar). In his reply, Bethmann Hollweg said that Wilson would first have to take measures against England before the German people would accept him as an impartial mediator. Therefore, the Chancellor added, Gerard's report had been premature. See T. von Bethmann Hollweg to J. H. von Bernstorff, May 6, 1916, printed in Alfred von Tirpitz, *Politische Dokumente* (2 vols., Hamburg and Berlin, 1926), Vol. II: *Deutsche Ohnmachtspolitik im Weltkriege*, p. 542. Bernstorff's telegram to the Foreign Office is printed in *ibid*. See also Karl E. Birnbaum, *Peace Moves and U-Boat Warfare: A Study of Imperial Germany's Policy towards the United States, April 18, 1916-January 9, 1917* (Stockholm, 1958), pp. 96-98.

Dear Governor: New York, May 14, 1916.

Since we talked over campaign matters I have had discussions with many of our friends and have tentatively mentioned what would seem to be a good Executive Committee.

If Polk is Chairman how would this do: Homer Cummings

for New England. Morganthau for New York. Hudspeth for New Jersey. Carter Glass for the South. Senator Kern, Chas. R. Crane, Fred. Lynch, Senator Stone and Phelan or someone from the Pacific Coast?

The officials might be Polk for Chairman, Morganthau, Chairman of the Finance Committee, Woolley, Chairman of the Publicity Committee with headquarters, perhaps, in the West and in charge of the Western Division. Goltra for Treasurer.

The Eastern campaign could be run by Polk, Cummings, Morganthau, Hudspeth and Glass and the Western campaign run by Kern, Crane, Woolley, Stone, Lynch and Phelan. I mention Kern and Goltra because of their Bryan proclivities. If Kern is objectionable to the Taggart element in Indiana he might be dropped.

Will you not think of this and talk with Morganthau when he comes over on Tuesday.

Lynch and others think that by buying the paper[1] for the campaign now it can be gotten much cheaper than later, and Morganthau has authorized Woolley to contract for $80,000. worhth [worth], he agreeing to stand good for it. They believe they can save some $15,000. or $20,000. by contracting for it now.

I wish someone could be found other than Polk for it seems a pity to disorganize the State Department, as I am afraid it will even if he leaves only temporarily.

McAdoo might have some suggestions other than these that would be of value.   Affectionately yours,   E. M. House

TLS (WP, DLC).
[1] That is, paper for campaign materials.

Remarks to the National Press Club[1]

[May 15, 1916]

Mr. President and gentlemen of the Press Club: I am both glad and sorry to be here; glad because I am always happy to be with you and know and like so many of you, and sorry because I have to make a speech. One of the leading faults of you gentlemen of the press is your inordinate desire to hear other men talk, to draw them out upon all occasions, whether they wish to be drawn out or not. I remember being in the Press Club once before, making many unpremeditated disclosures of myself,[2] and

[1] At a dinner given in Wilson's honor. Theodore Hance Tiller, Washington correspondent for the Munsey newspapers and president of the National Press Club, introduced Wilson.
[2] On March 20, 1914. Wilson's speech is printed at that date in Vol. 29.

then having you, with your singular instinct for publicity, insist that I should give it away to everybody else.

I was thinking, as I was looking forward to coming here this evening, of that other occasion when I stood very nearly at the threshold of the duties that I have since been called upon to perform, and I was going over in my mind the impressions that I then had by way of forecast of the duties of President and comparing them with the experiences that I have had. I must say that the forecast was very largely verified, and that the impressions I had then have been deepened rather than weakened.

You may recall that I said then that I felt constantly a personal detachment from the presidency; that one thing that I resented, when I was not performing the duties of the office, was being reminded that I was President of the United States. Because I felt toward it as a man feels toward a great function which, in working hours, he is obliged to perform, but which, out of working hours, he is glad to get away from and almost forget and resume the quiet course of his own thoughts. I am constantly reminded, as I go about, as I do sometimes at the weekend, of the personal inconvenience of being President of the United States. If I want to know how many people live in a small town, all I have to do is to go there and they at once line up to be counted. I might, upon a census-taking year, save the census takers a great deal of trouble by asking them to accompany me and count the people on the spot. Sometimes, when I am most beset, I seriously think of renting a pair of whiskers or doing something that will furnish me with an adequate disguise, because I am sorry to find that the cut of my jib is unmistakable and that I must sail under false colors if I am going to sail incognito.

Yet, as I have matched my experience with my anticipations, I, of course, have been aware that I was taken by surprise because of the prominence of the things to which I had not looked forward. When we are dealing with domestic affairs, gentlemen, we are dealing with things that to us, as Americans, are more or less calculable. There is a singular variety among our citizenship, a greater deal of variety even than I had anticipated. But, after all, we are all steeped in the same atmosphere, we are all surrounded by the same environment, we are all more or less affected by the same traditions, and, moreover, we are finding out anything that has to be worked out among ourselves, and the elements are there to be dealt with at first hand. But when the fortunes of your own country are, so to say, subject to the incalculable winds of passion that are blowing through other parts of the world, why, then the strain is of a singular and unprece-

dented kind, because you do not know by what turn of the wheel
of fortune the control of things is going to be taken out of your
hand. It doesn't make any difference how deep the passion of
the nation lies. That passion may be so overborne by the wheel
of fortune in circumstances like those which now exist that you
feel the sort of—I had almost said resentment—that a man feels
when his own affairs are not within his own hands. You can
imagine the strain upon the feeling of any man who is trying to
interpret the spirit of his country when he feels that that spirit
could not have its own way beyond a certain point. And one of the
greatest points of strain upon me, if I may be permitted to point
it out, was this:

There are two reasons why the chief wish of Americans is
for peace. One is that they love peace and have nothing to do with
the present quarrel. And the other is that they believe the present
quarrel has carried those engaged in it so far that they cannot be
held to the ordinary standards of responsibility, and that, therefore, as some men have expressed it to me, when the rest of the
world is mad, why not simply refuse to have anything to do with
the rest of the world in the ordinary methods of transaction? Why
not let the storm pass, and then, when it is all over, have the
reckonings? So that, knowing that, from these two points of view,
the passion of America was for peace, I was, nevertheless, aware
that America is one of the nations of the world, not only, but one
of the chief nations of the world—a nation that grows more and
more powerful almost in spite of herself; that grows, morally,
more and more influential even when she is not aware of it; and
that, if she is to play the part which she most covets, it is necessary that she should act more or less, at any rate, from the point
of view of the rest of the world. If I cannot retain my moral influence over a man except by occasionally knocking him down,
because that is the only basis upon which he will respect me,
then for the sake of his soul I have got occasionally to knock him
down. You know how we have read—isn't it the Reverend Connor's[3] stories of western life in Canada?—and how all his sky
pilots are ready for a fracas at any time, and how the ultimate
salvation of the souls of their parishioners depends upon their
using their fists occasionally? If a man won't listen to you quietly
in a seat, sit on his neck and make him listen, just as I have
always maintained, particularly in view of certain experiences of
mine, that the shortest road to a boy's moral sense is through his
cuticle. I am not pointing to the proper spot, but there is a direct

---

[3] Ralph Connor, the pseudonym of Charles William Gordon, Canadian clergy-
man and novelist.

and, if I may be permitted the pun, a fundamental connection between the surface of his skin and his moral consciousness. And you arrest his attention first in that guise and then get the moral lesson conveyed to him in milder ways that, if he were grown up, would be the only ways you would use.

So I say, in order to do the very thing that we are proudest of the ability to do, I have been aware that there might come a time when we would have to do it in a way that we would prefer not to do it. And the great burden on my spirits, gentlemen—since we are speaking in the family, I know I have got you where I want you, and you could count on me—the burden on my spirits has been that it has been up to me to choose when that time came. Can you imagine a thing more calculated to keep a man awake at nights than that? Because, just because I did not feel that I was the whole thing, and was aware that my duty was a duty of interpretation, how could I be sure that I had the right elements of information by which to interpret truly?

I believe that I have told you how I found out what little I know about Mexico. I found out that little by hearing a multitude of liars telling me all about it on a very interesting principle, which I believe I have explained to some of you before, that the liar has to invent, and very few men have enough invention to fill half an hour, and in the course of half an hour they must tell you a number of things that are true because they can't think fast enough to make up things that aren't so. Now, if you hear a large number of men, half an hour apiece, do that thing you will find certain broad consistencies in their narratives. That's the truth. And the variances can be then eliminated because all that they are making up and inventing. And if you hear liars enough, you will know all about a subject, because the limitations upon human invention are very great, and the likelihood is that more than half of what a man tells you will be so.

But I found that advantage in a man of this sort that we are speaking of, because it is largely spiritual. You say, "All the people out my way think so and so." Now, I know perfectly well that you have not talked with all the people out your way. And I also find out this very interesting thing, which I mention here in confidence, that the newspapers seldom contain what the majority of people in their neighborhood are thinking, and that what an editorial says and what the people think is not, let me say, necessarily the same. I found that out. Again and again, you will find cases. Take the City of New York. There have been cases where a man was elected mayor who was opposed by every paper in the town—some of the greatest papers in the world—except one paper that nobody out of the town had ever heard of. And so you are taken by surprise. The people of the United States are not asking anybody's leave to do their own thinking, and are not asking anybody to tip them off what they ought to think. They are thinking for themselves, every man for himself. And you do not know, and, the worst of it is, since the responsibility is mine, I do not know what they are thinking. I have the most imperfect means of finding out, and yet I have got to act as if I knew. That is the burden of it, and I tell you, gentlemen, it is a pretty serious burden, particularly if you look upon the office as I do—that I am not put here to do what I damn please. If I were, it would be very much more interesting than it has been. But I am put here to interpret, to register, to suggest, and, more than that, and much greater than that, to be suggested to.

Now, that is where the experience that I forecast has differed from the experience that I have had. In domestic matters, I think I can, in most cases, come pretty near a guess where the thought of America is going. But in foreign affairs, the chief element is where action is going on in other quarters of the world, and not where thought is going on in the United States. Therefore, I have several times taken the liberty of urging upon you gentlemen not yourselves to know more than the State Department knew about foreign affairs. Some of you gentlemen have shown a singular range of omniscience, and certain things have been reported as understood in administration circles which I never heard of until I read the newspapers. I am constantly taken by surprise in regard to decisions which are said to be my own, and this gives me an uncomfortable feeling that some Providence is at work with which I haven't had any communication at all. Now, that is pretty dangerous, gentlemen, because it happens that remarks start fires. There is tinder lying everywhere, not only on the other side of the water, but on this side of the water, and a man that spreads sparks may be responsible for something a great deal worse than burning a town on the Mexican border. Thoughts may be bandits. Thoughts may be raiders. Thoughts may be invaders. Thoughts may be disturbers of international peace. And, when you reflect upon the importance of this country keeping out of the present war, you will know what elements we are all dealing with because we are all in the same boat. That importance is this: If somebody does not keep the processes of peace going, if somebody does not keep their passions disengaged, by what impartial judgment and suggestion is the world to be aided to a solution when the whole thing is over? If you are in a conference in which you know nobody is disinterested, how are you going to make a plan? I tell you this, gentlemen—the only thing that saves the world is the little handful of disinterested men that are in it.

Now, I have found a few disinterested men. I wish I had found more. I can name two or three men with whom I have conferred again and again and again, and I have never caught them by an inadvertence thinking about themselves for their own interests. And I tie to those men as you would tie to an anchor. I tie to them as you would tie to the voices of conscience if you could be sure that you always heard them. Men who have no axes to grind! Men who love America so that they would give their lives for it and never care whether anybody heard that they had given their lives for it, willing to die in obscurity if only they might serve! Now, those are the men, and nations like those men are the nations that are going to serve the world and save it. There never was a time in the history of the world when character, just sheer character all by itself, told more than it does now. A friend of mine says that every man who took office in Washington either grew or swelled, and when I give a man an office, I watch him carefully to see whether he is swelling or growing. The mischief of it is that, when they swell, they do not swell enough to burst. If they would only swell to the point where you might insert a pin and let the gases out, it would be a great delight. I do not know any pastime that would be more delightful except that the gases are probably poisonous, so that we would have to stand from under. But the men who grow, the men who think better a year after they are put in office than they thought when they were put in office, are the balance wheel of the whole thing. They are the ballast that enables the craft to carry sail and to make port in the long run, no matter what the weather is.

So I have come willing to make this narrative of experience to you, that I have come through the fire since I talked to you last. Whether the metal is any purer than it was or not, God only knows. But the fire has been there, and the fire has penetrated every part of it, and, if I may believe my own thoughts, I have less partisan feeling, more impatience of party maneuver, more enthusiasm for the right thing, no matter whom it hurts, than I ever had before in my life. And I have something that is dangerous to have, what I can't help having. I have a profound intellectual contempt for men who cannot see the signs of the times. I have to deal with some men who don't know anything more of the modern processes of politics than if they were living in the eighteenth century, and for them I have a profound and comprehensive intellectual contempt. They are blind. They are hopelessly blind. And the worst of it is I have to spend hours of my time talking to them when I know before I start, as much as after I have finished, that it is absolutely useless to talk to them. I am talking *in vacuo*.

So that I often think of a poem that a colleague of mine at Princeton wrote about three colleagues of ours who were decided back numbers. And he wrote an apostrophe, which I wish I could quote altogether—to get a rag and rag the cobwebs off their brains and wake them up. And the refrain was "In vain, still snooze the snoozers lie, dreaming of things as they used to be."

But that is the prayer I should like to make to some of these gentlemen—to get a rag. Nothing less than a rag would be strong enough to penetrate the depths of the cobwebs that have accumulated on their unused brains—brains that are real antiques, because they have not been molested with thought or disturbed by information.

The business of every one of us, gentlemen, is to realize that if we are correspondents of papers which have not yet heard of modern times we ought to send them as many intimations of modern movements as they are willing to print. You can insert a great deal more than they will know you are inserting, because they don't know it when they see it, and you can be indirect in informing them and soon go all the way up from them to the best informed and most modern newspaper. I wouldn't go beyond that to the newspapers which know things that haven't happened yet and which are constantly anticipating what they hope will be events, whether they turn out to be so or not. So there is a happy mean to follow of enlightenment, which is neither retrogressive nor too progressive. There is a simile that was used by a very interesting English writer that has been much in my mind. Like myself, he had often been urged not to try to change so many things. I remember, when I was president of a university, a man said to me, "My God, man, why don't you leave something alone and let it stay the way it is?" And I said, "If you will guarantee to me that it will stay the way it is, I will let it alone. But if you knew anything, you would know that, if you leave a live thing alone, it will not stay where it is. It will develop and will either go in the wrong direction or decay." I reminded him of this thing that the English writer said, if you want to keep a white post white you cannot let it alone. It will get black. You have to keep doing something to it. In that instance, you have got to keep painting it white, and you have got to paint it white very frequently in order to keep it white, because there are forces at work that will get the better of you. Not only will it turn black, but the forces of moisture and the other forces of nature will penetrate the white and get at the fiber of the wood, and decay will set in. And the next time you try to paint it, you will find there is nothing but punk to paint. Then you will remember the Red Queen in *Alice in Wonderland*, or *Alice through the Looking-Glass*—it has been so long since I was a boy—who takes Alice by the hand and they rush along at a great pace, and then, when they stop, Alice looks around and says, "But we are just where we were when we started." "Yes," says the Red Queen, "you have to run twice as fast as that to get anywhere else."

Now, that is true, gentlemen, of the world and of affairs. You have got to run fast merely to stay where you are, and, in order to run anywhere, you have got to run twice as fast as that. That is what people do not realize. That is, all these hopeless dams against the stream known as reactionaries and standpatters and other words of obloquy. That is what is the matter with them: they are not even staying where they were. They are sinking further and further back in what will some time comfortably close over their heads as the black waters of oblivion. I sometimes imagine that I see their heads going down, and I am not inclined even to throw them a life preserver. The sooner they disappear, the better. We need their places for people who are awake. And we particularly need now, gentlemen, men who will divest themselves of party passion and of personal preference and will try to think in the terms of America. If a man describes himself to me now in any other terms but those terms, I am not sure of him. And I love the fellows that come into my office sometimes and say, "Mr. President, I am an American." Now, I don't care if he really means that. I am with him, because his heart is right, and his instinct is right, and he is going in the right direction, and he will take the right leadership if he believes that the leader is also a man who thinks first of America.

You will see, gentlemen, that I did not premeditate these remarks, or they would have had some connection with each other. They would have had some plan. I have merely given myself the pleasure of telling you what has really been in my heart, and not only has been in my heart, but is in my heart every day of the week. If I did not go off at weekends occasionally and throw off, as much as it is possible to throw off, this burden, I could not stand it. This week I went down the Potomac and up the James and substituted history for politics, and there was an infinite, sweet calm in some of those old places that reminded me of the records that were made in the days that are past. And I comforted myself with the recollection that there were just as many

crooks then as there are now, in proportion, and that the men
we remember are the men who overcame the crooks and gave
us the deeds that have covered the name of America all over with
the luster of imperishable glory.[4]

JRT transcript (WC, NjP) of CLSsh (C. L. Swem Coll., NjP).
　[4] Wilson edited this speech and permitted its publication as *The President, at National Press Club, May 15, 1916* (n.p., n.d.).

To Robert Lansing, with Enclosure

My dear Mr. Secretary,　　　　　The White House. 15 May, 1916.

This is the communication from the Pope to which I referred
the other day. I would value your suggestion as to the manner
and substance of my reply.　　Faithfully Yours,　W.W.

It was brought to the Office by the Apostolic Delegate

WWTLI (SDR, RG 59, 763.72/2691½, DNA).

E N C L O S U R E

Translation dictated to Mr. Tumulty by Monsignor Bonzano.

To his Excellency President Wilson

We pray Your Excellency to be kind enough to suspend your
decision on the question of Submarine Warfare with Germany,
since we see the possibility of peaceful settlement, & we hope that
as far as you are concerned no incident will embarrass our effort.
We are sending the same telegram to His Majesty, the Emperor.
　　　　　　　　　　　　　　　　　　　Benedict[1]

HwC telegram (SDR, RG 59, 763.72/2690½, DNA).
　[1] The original telegram, written in French, is in the State Department archives and bears the same file number as the above.

To James Paul Clarke

Personal.

My dear Senator:　　　　　　[The White House] May 15, 1916

Thank you very warmly for your frank letter of May twelfth. I
did not doubt that I could count on the Committee to give the
most public-spirited attention to the needs of New York Harbor,
and I shall feel that the outcome will be satisfactory all around.

My only object was to express my great interest in a particular item which has latterly become of special importance.

Cordially and sincerely yours,   Woodrow Wilson

TLS (Letterpress Books, WP, DLC).

From Robert Lansing, with Enclosures

PERSONAL AND CONFIDENTIAL:

My dear Mr. President: Washington May 15, 1916.

I received your letter of today enclosing a copy of the communication which you received from the Pope. I enclose a letter which I suggest as a reply.

This morning Monseignor Russell called upon me with a letter addressed to you from Cardinal Gibbons,[1] which he asked me to read and if I thought you intended to answer the Pope's communication to deliver it to you.

I have also drafted a reply to Cardinal Gibbons which provides for the transmission of your answer to the Pope's communication through him.

Monseignor Russell indicated to me that there was some feeling on the part of the Cardinal that no reply had been made to the Pope before this. I believe, although your letter does not indicate it, that you received the Pope's communication on May sixth. Monseignor Russell said that you had agreed to make answer on Monday, the 8th, and for that reason they were disappointed it had not been received before.

Faithfully yours,   Robert Lansing

TLS (WP, DLC).
[1] That is, Cardinal Gibbons to WW, May 12, 1916.

E N C L O S U R E   I

His Holiness, Benedict XV,   May 15, 1916

I greatly appreciate the friendly sentiment of broad humanity that prompted your personal communication to me concerning the questions that have arisen between this country and Germany.

I am gratified to say that before the receipt of your message, the discussion had already entered upon a state of satisfactory understanding.

With great respect I have the honor to be, Your Holiness,

Very sincerely,[1]

¹ Tumulty handed this letter, presumably written by hand by Wilson, to Msgr. Bonzano.

E N C L O S U R E   I I

Your Eminence: May 15, 1916.

In reply to your note of the 12th instant, it gives me pleasure to enclose my reply to the message which the Pope was good enough to have presented to me a few days ago through His Excellency the Apostolic Delegate.

I hope you will find it possible to transmit my reply to His Holiness.

I am, Your Eminence,   Very respectfully yours,[1]

CC MSS (WP, DLC).
[1] These letters were sent as WW to J. Cardinal Gibbons, May 15, 1916, TLS (Baltimore Cathedral Archives).

From William Joel Stone

PERSONAL.

Dear Mr. President: [Washington] May 15 1916.

Information has just come to me that there is some proposal pending—how originating I know not—that Mr. Brandeis should appear before the Judiciary Committee and make a statement. I wish merely to say that in my opinion that ought not to be done. The idea of a man nominated by the President for a place on the Supreme Bench appearing, at least voluntarily or on his own motion, before a Committee to make an argument or statement in support of what might be termed his candidacy, would be exceedingly obnoxious to right thinking members of the Senate and right thinking people everywhere. I think it would be the height of folly.

I just wanted to say this much to you. No answer desired.
                              Yours, etc.   Wm. J. Stone

TLS (WP, DLC).

From Edward Mandell House

Dear Governor: New York, May 15, 1916.

Governor Glynn is actively at work upon his speech for the St. Louis Convention and I am in constant touch with him.

We now have all the data from the Departments, but he very much desires copies of your speeches, both before and after your election, if that is possible,

Will you not ask Mr. Tumulty to send them to me at the earliest possible moment, or those of them that are available.

Affectionately yours,   E. M. House

What do you think of Vance McCormick as a substitute for Polk as National Chairman? I do not know him, but I am to see him on Wednesday.

TLS (WP, DLC).

To Edward Mandell House

My dearest Friend,   The White House. 16 May, 1916.

I have been giving some very careful thought to your question, how we should deal with Sir Edward and his Government at this turning point,—for it really is that.

It seems to me that we should get down to hard pan.

The situation has altered altogether since you had your conferences in London and Paris. The at least temporary removal of the acute German question has concentrated attention here on the altogether indefensible course Great Britain is pursuing with regard to trade to and from neutral ports and her quite intolerable interception of mails on the high seas carried by neutral ships. Recently there has been added the great shock opinion in this country has received from the course of the British Government towards some of the Irish rebels.

We are plainly face to face with this alternative, therefore. The United States must either make a decided move for peace (upon some basis that promises to be permanent) or, if she postpones that, must insist to the limit upon her rights of trade and upon such freedom of the seas as international law already justifies her in insisting on as against Great Britain, with the same plain speaking and firmness that she has used against Germany. And the choice must be made immediately. Which does Great Britain prefer? She cannot escape both. To do nothing is now, for us, impossible.

If we move for peace, it will be along these lines 1) Such a settlement with regard to their own immediate interests as the belligerents may be able to agree upon. We have nothing material of any kind to ask for ourselves and are quite aware that we are in no sense or degree parties to the quarrel. Our interest is only in peace and its guarantees; 2) a universal alliance to maintain freedom of the seas and to prevent any war begun either a) contrary to treaty covenants or b) without warning and full inquiry, —a virtual guarantee of territorial integrity and political independence.

It seems to me to be of imperative and pressing importance that Sir Edward should understand all this and that the crisis cannot be postponed; and it can be done with the most evident spirit of friendliness through you. Will you not prepare a full cable putting the whole thing plainly to him? We must act, and act at once, in the one direction or the other.

With affectionate messages from us all,

Faithfully Yours,   Woodrow Wilson

16 May, 1916.

I have noted what you send me from Bernstorff and also your suggestions about the Campaign committee. I shall profit by the former and write you soon about the latter, with any suggestions I may pick up here.   W.W.

WWTLS (E. M. House Papers, CtY).

To William Joel Stone

My dear Senator: [The White House] May 16, 1916

I had heard of the suggestion referred to in your letter of May fifteenth. I entirely agree with you about it and shall look into it.

In haste   Faithfully yours,   Woodrow Wilson

TLS (Letterpress Books, WP, DLC).

From Joseph Patrick Tumulty

My dear Governor: The White House May 16, 1916.

As I have discussed with you on frequent occasions, it seems to me that the time is now at hand for you to act in the matter of *Peace*. The mere process of peace negotiations may extend over a period of months. Why should we wait until the moment of exhaustion before ever beginning a discussion? Everybody admits that the resources of the nations involved cannot last through another year without suffering of an untold character. It is now May. Let us assume that everybody accepts your offer. It would be physically impossible to get Commissioners from various parts of the world, including Japan, in less than two months. Then the discussion would perhaps last until the Fall, no matter what conclusion might be reached. Therefore, allowing for the time that must be consumed in persuading all the parties that the time is now ripe, the whole business will require almost a year in itself, during which time the hostilities would still be continuing, and certainly the chance of getting a truce would be better after the discussion had been in progress for sometime. Similarly, as the time for the Winter campaign approached, the inducement to agree on a truce on any terms would become more powerful each day.

Let us look at it from the point of view of postponement. If we waited until the Fall and the negotiations stretched out through the Winter, the temptation for making new drives in the Spring, with the preparations made throughout the Winter, would incline the militaristic element in the different countries involved to block peace negotiations. *It seems, therefore, that the time to act is now when these drives are spending their force.*

AS TO THE PROCEDURE:

It seems that no belligerent should be put in the position by your note of weakening or suing for peace, for we must keep in mind the pride and sensibilities of all. The initiative must be ours—to all nations, on equal terms. We must so word our note that a belligerent will not be in a position of seeming to weaken if it wishes to accept our suggestion. One way to do this would be to send a note, saying that from the German note and from statesmen representing the entente powers the Government of the United States assumes that the belligerent nations are willing at least to discuss suggestions for peace, each only reserving to itself liberty of action. The United States can, therefore, announce that it is willing to meet at The Hague a Commission sent by the respective governments to discuss means for making peace, *and for establishing a world court or international tribunal to safeguard the peace of the world after the close of the war*.

In the latter, namely, *world peace*, the United States has a direct interest. The United States can in the note assume that Commissioners will meet with it and hopes to be advised if there is any feeling to the contrary.

My idea is to go ahead with the plan on the theory that all the belligerents are in accord with the idea, so that in answering our note they will not have accepted anything but our proposals to discuss, *first*, the suggestion of peace, and, *secondly*, the idea of a world court.

The President should say, in order to elicit the sympathy of the world and mankind in general, that the note of the United States suggesting a meeting between the powers will be made public within a few days after its receipt by the respective powers. This will give each government not only its own public opinion to reckon with, but the public opinion of the civilized world. The nation that objects to a discussion of peace will by no means be in an enviable position.

I hope you will read the article I am sending you by Mr. Strunsky—"POST IMPRESSIONS,"[1] especially that part which I have indicated in the margin. It is from this article that I got the idea of suggesting the alternative proposition of a world court. Your note setting forth your position in this matter should be an appeal to the heart and to the conscience of the world.

Yours Sincerely,   Tumulty

TLS (WP, DLC).

[1] Simeon Strunsky, "Post: Impressions," New York *Evening Post*, May 13, 1916. In this piece, Strunsky advocated bringing the belligerents together to establish a world court. This would provide them with an opportunity to meet, put aside their differences, and return to the *status quo ante bellum* without tarnishing their national honor. When the representatives returned home and were asked to justify the tremendous cost of the war, they could say: "Dear friends, we have brought you back a new world order, we have brought you back a federation of nations, we have brought you a guarantee for as long a future as human foresight can provide for, against another such calamity as our wretched little system plunged you into two years ago. Territories? Indemnities? We had no time to think of such matters. We were too busy building up the brotherhood of the nations."

From Harry Augustus Garfield

Williamstown, Massachusetts

Dear Mr. President: May 16, 1916

I am in receipt of a letter from Mr. Droppers,[1] in which he refers to the fact that he has written to you concerning his return to America. As I understand it, he has told you that he leaves the case in your hands, and will remain as long as you need him. I wish merely to say that we are holding Mr. Droppers's place open for him and have arranged with his substitute to remain for another year.

I am planning to attend the meetings of the League to Enforce Peace on the 26th and 27th inst., and shall give myself the pleasure of calling at some convenient hour.

As always, with warm regard,

Faithfully yours,   H. A. Garfield.

TLS (WP, DLC).

[1] G. Droppers to WW, March 23, 1916, Vol. 36.

Two Letters to Edward Mandell House

Dearest Friend,   The White House. 17 May, 1916.

I find I have not acknowledged youh [your] letter about Walter Page.

Thank you for it very much. Of course it was painful reading, but it was clearly right and necessary for you to tell me about it. It lowers my opinion of the man immensely. I thought he was bigger and more capable of gratitude (I mean gratitude to you, of which he must know he owes a great deal) than that. But we must take facts as they come and make the best of them. I am always grateful for the guiding light of the truth.

What would you advise? Lansing is so dissatisfied with Page's whole conduch [conduct] of our dealings with the Foreign Office in London that he wants to bring him back for a vacation, to get some American atmosphere into him again. What do you think? And is there any one there who would be sufficient as *chargé*?

Affectionately Yours,   Woodrow Wilson

Dearest Friend,   The White House. 17 May, 1916.

Your request about sending my speeches to Governor Glynn is being attended to. I do not know how many of them are available but those that are will be sent as promptly as possible.

Affectionately,   Woodrow Wilson

WWTLS (E. M. House Papers, CtY).

To Robert Lansing

My dear Mr. Secretary,   The White House. 17 May, 1916.

I have thought a great deal about the questions you here put, —both before and since you sent me this letter.[1]

Undoubtedly there is an awkward quandary here, but I think we would not be justified in as[s]uming the general representation of neutral rights in this matter, whether our own citizens are affected or not.

If Germany should show a purpose to return to the practices we have objected to by attacking ships again without warning, I think we would be justified in making pointed inquiries of her as to the facts in any given case, even if no Americans were on board; but we would not be justified in acting, unless her reply to those inquiries indicated a departure form [from] the policy she has now agreed to follow.

At any rate, this is my present judgment.

Faithfully Yours,   W.W.

WWTLI (SDR, RG 59, 763.72/2755, DNA).
  [1] RL to WW, May 10, 1916.

Two Letters to Joseph Patrick Tumulty

Dear Tumulty,   The White House. 17 May, 1916.

The memorandum about existing political conditions is most interesting and useful and I thank you for it very warmly.[1]

Faithfully,   W.W.

  [1] JPT to WW, May 12, 1916.

Dear Tumulty,   The White House. 17 May, 1916.

Thank you for the memorandum about peace suggestions. I have read it very carefully and find my own thoughts travelling very much the same route. You may be sure I am doing a great deal of serious thinking about it all.   Faithfully,   W.W.

WWTLI (J. P. Tumulty Papers, DLC).

To William Calhoun McDonald

[The White House]

My dear Governor McDonald: May 17, 1916

I warmly and sincerely appreciate your kind letter of May twelfth and beg to be permitted to express my admiration for the admirable prudence and patriotic feeling with which you are handling the cases about which I ventured to speak in my letter to you of May eighth. I know just how delicate you must find the whole thing, but I have every confidence that you will work it out in the wisest way.

Cordially and sincerely yours,   Woodrow Wilson

TLS (Letterpress Books, WP, DLC).

From Edward Mandell House, with Enclosure

Dear Governor: New York, May 17, 1916.

Your letter of yesterday came last night too late to answer.

I am enclosing you a suggestion for a cable to Sir Edward

Grey. Please make the necessary changes and I will code and send it immediately.

It has been apparent that when our difficulties with Germany were settled, our difficulties with the Allies would begin and the solution has disturbed me greatly.

The more I see of the dealings of governments among themselves, the more I am impressed with the utter selfishness of their outlook. Gratitude is a thing unknown and all we have done for the Allies will be forgotten overnight if we antagonize them now. Nevertheless, I am convinced that it is your duty to press for a peace conference with all the power at your command, for whether they like it or whether they do not, I believe you can bring it about.

That was an inspiring speech you delivered before the Press Club. You have never done anything of the kind I think so well. It is one that will live and will be to future generations an index of you.   Affectionately yours,   E. M. House

TLS (WP, DLC).

ENCLOSURE

My cables and letters of the past few days have not been sent with any desire to force the hands of the Allies or to urge upon them something for which they are not ready. But rather to put before them a situation that arose immediately Germany agreed to discontinue her illegal submarine warfare.

America has reached the crossroads and if we cannot soon inaugurate some sort of peace discussion there will come a demand from our people in which all neutrals will probably join, that we assert our undeniable rights against the Allies with the same insistence we have used towards the Central Powers.

There is a feeling here, which is said to exist in other neutral countries, that the war should end, and any nation or nations that reject peace discussions will bring upon themselves a heavy responsibility.

If we begin to push the Allies as hard as we needs must, friction is certain to arise and our people will not sustain the President in doing those things that they would now welcome.

I am speaking in all frankness, as I have always done with you, without reservation or any motive other than that the relations between our countries may become what we have so earnestly desired. The time is critical and delay is dangerous.

If England is indeed fighting for the emancipation of Europe,

we are ready to join her in order that the nations of the earth, be
they large or small, may live their lives as they may order them
and be free from the shadow of autocracy and the spectre of war.
If we are to link shields in this mighty cause, then England must
recognize the conditions under which this alone can become possible and which we are unable to ignore.

Germany has made no overtures to us looking to a peace conference, but on the contrary, the German Ambassador gave me a
message from his Government yesterday that German public
opinion would not at present tolerate the President as a mediator.

It is not the President's thought that a peace conference could
be immediately called and the Allies would have ample time to
demonstrate whether or not Germany is indeed in a sinking condition and the deadlock can be broken.

I would suggest that you talk with the three of your colleagues
with whom we discussed these matters for it is something that
will not bear delay.

CC MS (E. M. House Papers, CtY).

From Edward Mandell House

Dear Governor: New York, May 17, 1916.

In making your announcement on May 27th, do you not think
it would be a good idea to come out again for a strong Navy?

If we are to join with other great powers in a world movement
to maintain peace, we ought to immediately inaugurate a big
naval programme. We have the money and if we have the will,
the world will realize that we are to be reckoned with. Its effect
will be far-reaching and it will give us the influence desired in the
settlement of European affairs, make easy your South American
policy, and eliminate the Japanese question.

Your desire to stop the war and your willingness to help maintain the peace of the world afterwards would not be inconsistent
with a demand for a navy commensurate with these purposes.

Our Naval Attache at Berlin, who is one of the most valuable
men we have in Europe winds up a letter with these two sentences.

"Finally, the American note has exerted a very evident depres-
sive effect on the German people. Never before have they recognized the isolation of their position and the power of the forces
working against Germany.

I am of the opinion that the delivery of this note, whether accepted or not, marks the turning point of the war. Its moral

effect on belligerents and neutrals will play a large factor in coming events, political and military."[1]

Affectionately yours,   E. M. House

TLS (WP, DLC).
[1] House was quoting from W. R. Gherardi to EMH, April 25, 1916, TLS (E. M. House Papers, CtY).

From Alexander Jeffrey McKelway

Dear Mr. President: [Washington] May 17, 1916.

I take the liberty of enclosing to you some suggestions for the Democratic platform,[1] which I hope this time will be satisfactory to you before it is presented to the Convention for adoption. I have taken this matter up with Colonel House[2] and with Secretary Baker.[3]

I am very clear that with your economic programme so nearly completed we shall need some additions to our domestic policy on which to appeal to the country, especially if, through the coming of peace, there should be more time for attention to domestic affairs before the November election.

Cordially yours,   [A. J. McKelway]

CCL (A. J. McKelway Papers, DLC).
[1] The Enclosure is missing. However, it was "Suggestions for Democratic Platform," n.d., CC MS (A. J. McKelway Papers, DLC). McKelway's proposals for a social-justice program included: (1) To make the federal government a "model employer" by providing for such measures as old-age pensions, a decent living wage, and adequate workmen's compensation for its employees; by adhering to the standards of the "Uniform Child Labor Law"; and by guaranteeing healthy and comfortable working conditions. (2) The development of the "Human Welfare Agencies of the Government," such as the Public Health Service, the Children's Bureau, the Bureau of Mines, and the Bureau of Education, and the extension of federal aid to education to include primary schools. (3) The reform of the federal penal system by the training of prisoners in "remunerative occupations"; the liberal extension of the federal parole law; the adoption of the probation system; and the establishment of a Federal Board of Pardon and Parole. (4) The federal regulation of interstate commerce "in the interests of the public health, the public morals, the public safety and the public welfare" through a federal child labor law and a measure to control the shipment of prison-made goods. (5) Making the District of Columbia a model in its laws and institutions relating to human welfare.
In addition, McKelway sent to Wilson a "Memorandum in Exposition of the Suggestions for the Platform," n.d., CC MS (A. J. McKelway Papers, DLC), in which he elaborated on his individual proposals.
[2] A. J. McKelway to EMH, May 15, 1916, CCL (A. J. McKelway Papers, DLC).
[3] Baker's reply is N. D. Baker to A. J. McKelway, May 19, 1916, TLS (A. J. McKelway Papers, DLC).

From Josephus Daniels

Dear Mr. President: Washington. May 17th, 1916.

The matter of the oil reservation in California is so important that I am sending you a carefully prepared statement of history, hearings and propositions.[1] If you could snatch the time to read it I believe you would feel repaid. I am also enclosing the Phelan bill.[2] You will find certain paragraphs marked and also my letter to the Chairman of the Committee pointing out the errors in the Phelan report.[3]

This question will come before the Senate as soon as the River and Harbor bill is disposed of and that is why I am sending you this data to-day.   Sincerely,   Josephus Daniels

ALS (WP, DLC).

[1] What Daniels actually sent was a rather jumbled mass of typed and printed extracts of congressional hearings and copies of correspondence among the Navy, Interior, and Justice departments, all relating to the problem of the oil reservations in California. This material, seventy-two pages in all, is filed with Daniels' letter of May 17 in WP, DLC.

[2] Actually, this was 64th Cong., 1st sess., Senate Report No. 319, *Exploration for and Disposition of Oil, Gas, Etc.*, the report of the Committee on Public Lands, presented by Senator Phelan, to accompany H.R. 406. The committee had in fact substituted a completely new bill for the original H.R. 406, but the report merely described and justified the new measure briefly; it did not include a text of it.

[3] J. Daniels to H. L. Myers, May 8, 1916, TCL (WP, DLC). Daniels charged that portions of Senate Report No. 319 were not in accord with the official record of the Senate hearings on H.R. 406.

From Benjamin Ryan Tillman

"I am put here to interpret, to register, to suggest; and more than that, much greater than that, to be suggested to."
          President Wilson; Press Club Speech.

Dear Mr. President: [Washington] May 17, 1916.

Emboldened by the sentence quoted above I want to make two suggestions to you.

First: You ought to reconcile Lane and Daniels, and you three decide promptly the policy in regard to the navy's oil reserve fields. Then you use your wonderful influence with Congress to have such legislation enacted as will preserve this oil *in the ground* for the navy's future use. Otherwise, our "active" western Senators, always on the look-out for their "constituents," will smuggle through legislation which will enable outsiders to tap these fields and draw the navy's oil off for private benefit or uses.

Every day more and more I come face to face with that element in the man which I can best describe as hoggishness. I have yet to come across a human being who has not got a reasonable quantity of it. Enlightened selfishness is patriotism, but hoggishness is bestial.

Second: The Army Bill, which the conferees have just reported to the Senate, and which will be agreed on and become a law soon, gives you full power in regard to the manufacture of nitrates for the Army, *and nitrates for the farmers too.* Some fossils in the Senate—Democrats, I am sorry to say—have been debating all the morning the constitutional power of Congress to manufacture nitrates for the farmer's use. They make me sick.

I beg to suggest this idea to you: There is a water-power on the Savannah River—two or three of them, perhaps, at least one—that can develop 30,000 horse-power or more. Developed by the U. S. Government for the purpose of making nitrates for explosives, it is in the very heart of the cotton belt, which needs fertilizers most. High grade phosphate rock is found in Florida and Tennessee, and a lower grade in South Carolina.

A perfect fertilizer for corn, cotton and tobacco requires phosphate, potash and nitrogen. Nitrogen is the most costly and at the same time is the most valuable for crops. Nitrogen makes stalk and leaf; phosphate and potash are necessary for the seed. Potash in commercial quantities has not yet been found in the United States. With cheaper nitrogen, the states from Virginia to Alabama will blossom like a rose.

I beg you to look very carefully to the development of one government nitrogen plant on the Savannah River, and believe that 30,000 horse-power would be ample for an experiment like this is bound to be.

You will doubtless suspect me of having some of the hog in me too. I believe I have enough to claim to be a patriot; and if South Carolina doesn't possess the very best power for this purpose, then let it go to that locality possessing the very best power, all things being considered.

I merely "make the suggestions" because of your invitation.

Very respectfully,   B. R. Tillman

TLS (WP, DLC).

From Joseph Patrick Tumulty

Dear Governor: [The White House, c. May 17, 1916]

You will probably have to make some short platform speeches on the way to North Carolina.[1] Might it not be a good idea to discuss the evil of Senatorial courtesy? Rublee is a prominent progressive. The whole country is interested in this matter and, if handled properly, it might easily develop into an issue as big in its proporitions [proportions] as the Cannon issue. Gallinger typifies everything that constitutes "standpatism"; Rublee, everything that appeals to the progressive heart of the country. The vote is on Tuesday. Why wouldn't it be a good idea to discuss this matter?   Faithfully,   Tumulty

TCLS (J. P. Tumulty Papers, DLC).
  1 Wilson was to speak in Charlotte on May 20.

Two Letters to Edward Mandell House

Dearest Friend,   The White House. 18 May, 1916.

This cable message is admirable. There is nothing I could add or wish to take away. I hope that you will send it entire.[1]

It is deeply discouraging to think what the effect will be upon the minds of the men who will confer about it. They have been blindly stupid in the policy they have pursued on the seas, and must now take the consequences. They would not in any case have been able, even if willing, to be even handed with us in the trade rivalries which must inevitably follow the war.

With affectionate messages from us all,
                    Affectionately Yours,   Woodrow Wilson

  1 House dispatched the cable on May 19.

Dearest Friend,   The White House. 18 May, 1916.

I am thinking a great deal about the speech I am to make on the twenty-seventh, because I realize that it may be the most important I shall ever be called upon to make, and I greatly value your suggestion about the navy programme.

Would you do me the favour to formulate what you would say, in my place, if you were seeking to make the proposal as nearly what you deem Grey and his colleagues to have agreed upon in principle as it is possible to make it when concretely formulated as a proposal? Your recollection of your conferences is so much more accurate than mine that I would not trust myself to state the proposition without advice from you, though it may be wise to strengthen and heighten the terms a little.

Why do you say so confidently that it is idle to hope that the European nations will at this time consider the establishment of some such tribunal as the programme of the League to Enforce Peace proposes? It is a body only to inquire and report and is given no right of decision. How else can we secure the deliberate consideration of all situations that may threaten war and lay a foundation for the concerted action of nations against unjustifiable breaches of the peace of the world? The only inducement we can hold out to the Allies is one which will actually remove the menace of Militarism.

Affectionately Yours,   Woodrow Wilson

WWTLS (E. M. House Papers, CtY).

To William Howard Taft

My dear Mr. Taft: The White House May 18, 1916

I have left your kind letter of May ninth, about the banquet of the League to Enforce Peace, so far unanswered because I was sincerely desirous of accepting the invitation which it conveyed and did not wish to write until I could be measurably sure that it would be possible.

I need not explain to you how unavoidable it is to make the acceptance of such invitations provisional upon the demands of public business at the time that the fulfillment of the promise falls due, but I am hoping with a good deal of confidence that it will be possible for me to be present, and I am very much obliged to you and the other officers of the League for the courtesy and compliment of the invitation.

Cordially and sincerely yours,   Woodrow Wilson

TLS (W. H. Taft Papers, DLC).

To Alexander Jeffrey McKelway

My dear Mr. McKelway: The White House May 18, 1916

Let me acknowledge the receipt of your letter of May 17th, and thank you for [your] kindness in sending me the enclosures, which I shall carefully examine.

Sincerely yours,   Woodrow Wilson

TLS (A. J. McKelway Papers, DLC).

To John Knight Shields

My dear Senator: [The White House] May 18, 1916

Pardon me for not having replied sooner to your letter of May tenth. I have been carried along in a rush of business which I could not stem.

You may be sure, my dear Senator, that any report that I have announced my intention of vetoing this, that, or the other bill is false, for I have never felt that it was right to take that attitude or to make up my mind about a bill until I had seen it in its final form, as passed by the Houses, and really made myself acquainted with the detail of it.

The so-called Shields Bill as first reported to the Senate did contain a number of provisions which were, in my judgment, unwise, but I understand that a number of changes were made in it in the course of its passage through the Senate, and since its passage I have not had an opportunity to acquaint myself with its provisions. You may be sure that I shall welcome any elucidation of it that you may be kind enough to put me in the way of getting.

Cordially and sincerely yours,   Woodrow Wilson

TLS (Letterpress Books, WP, DLC).

To Edwin Stockton Johnson

My dear Senator: [The White House] May 18, 1916

Thank you warmly for your little note of May eleventh. I warmly appreciate your cooperation in the effort to confirm the nomination of Mr. George Rublee as a member of the Federal Trade Commission, and I earnestly hope the adverse vote may be reconsidered and reversed.

Cordially and sincerely yours,   Woodrow Wilson

TLS (Letterpress Books, WP, DLC).

To Ralph Pulitzer

My dear Mr. Pulitzer: [The White House] May 18, 1916

You may be sure that I did not at all regard it as an imposition to have you introduce Mr. Davidson to me, and I have waited to reply to your letter[1] because I wanted to see if it was not possible to give Mr. Davidson a sitting. Unhappily, it has turned out not to be possible, for reasons which you will readily imagine, and I can only hope that at some future time I may have the distinction of being sculptured by so accomplished an artist.

Cordially and sincerely yours,   Woodrow Wilson

TLS (Letterpress Books, WP, DLC).
[1] R. Pulitzer to WW, April 27, 1916, enclosed in R. Pulitzer to JPT, April 27, 1916, Vol. 36.

To Josephus Daniels

My dear Daniels: The White House May 18, 1916

May I not wish you many, many happy returns? I hope you have felt with how sincere and warm a sympathy and approval

I have stood by you during the trials you have had to go through to get the right established, and I hope you feel, as I do, that the outcome is now becoming more and more certain. We must put none but the tried on guard and when we get through, the Navy will, I hope, have a new spirit.

            Cordially and faithfully yours,   Woodrow Wilson

TLS (J. Daniels Papers, DLC).

From Josephus Daniels

My Dear Friend: Washington. May 18th, 1916.

    You made my birth-day very happy by your words of friendship and your note of confidence and approval. The years here for me have been crowded with work and with trial. When I came to Washington I had but one ambition and that was to help in the spirit of the great service to which you had consecrated yourself. More than once, when severely criticized, it has troubled me chiefly because I feared it might embar[r]ass the complete success of your administration. Your belief in me and your counsel and cheer have given me strength and happiness.

    Faithfully and with affection

                      your friend Josephus Daniels

ALS (WP, DLC).

From Edward Mandell House

Dear Governor: New York, May 18, 1916.

    I do not think we need worry about Page. If he comes home at once I believe we can straighten him out. You will remember I have urged his coming for more than a year.

    I do not believe he is of any service there at present and the staff are able to carry on the work. They have just added Hugh Gibson[1] from Brussels who is a good man—better, indeed, than any they had.

    No one who has not lived in the atmosphere that has surrounded Page for three years can have an idea of its subtle influence, therefore he is not to be blamed as much as one would think. He seems to have gone about his job wrong in some way. While he is popular among the English people generally, he has but little influence in governmental circles other than with Grey who likes him much.

    He would have done admirably in times of peace, but his mind has become warped by the war.

He may wish to remain after he comes home, for private reasons, and if he does, I would not dissuade him. On the other hand, if he remains here for the ordinary sixty days leave he will probably recover his equilibrium and there will be no further trouble with him. I cannot believe he has any personal feeling in regard to me.

If it becomes necessary to send me to Europe again in order to get in personal contact with the belligerent governments about the matter you are now negotiating, this Page incident should be out of the way as quickly as possible. We will find it difficult to push the matter in hand to a conclusion by cables and letters.

My coming on such a mission would doubtless not be welcome to the Allies, but that is beside the mark if you think it best for me to go in order to bring those governments to a realization of the situation.   Affectionately yours,   E. M. House

TLS (WP, DLC).
  1 Hugh Simons Gibson, former secretary of the American legation at Brussels, had been appointed secretary of the American embassy at London on May 16, 1916.

From Henry Morgenthau

My dear Mr President!   Washington May 18/16

I was with Senator Hoke Smith for 2½ hours yesterday discussing the *Brandeis* matter & listening to his & his colleagues grievances.

Smith stated that Senators Shield, Reed of Mo. and O'Gorman would vote as he does and that [although] he is disposed to vote *for* Brandeis's confirmation, he still wants to dispel some slight doubts he has as to the Lenox case.[1]

I feel that I made an impression upon him and that he will vote for Brandeis

Smith feels keenly that you did not consult any of the democratic members of the Judiciary Comtee. about the nomination & as it was a National position & both Mass. Senators are Republicans, he thinks you should have done so

He also stated that since January he has not been at the White House for conference

I think it would help greatly if you would send for him *after* Brandeis has been confirmed and discuss with him the English question and thereby give him back his "self-respect" about which he is much concerned.

He & some of the other Senators have been nursing their discontent so long that it may become chronic, while now, a few soothing words from you will produce a prompt cure.

With kindest regards,

Yours Devotedly   H. Morgenthau

ALS (WP, DLC).
  [1] About this case, see Alpheus T. Mason, *Brandeis: A Free Man's Life* (New York, 1946), pp. 232-37, 474-75.

Sir Cecil Arthur Spring Rice to the Foreign Office

Washington 18 May 1916.

My tel. No. 1500. President has allowed publication of extracts from his speech.[1] He received Sir J Chancellor[2] yesterday and used same language to him regarding his desire to do anything possible for establishment of satisfactory and permanent peace.

His utterances as to duty of U S to keep out of the war are very clear and show that his present desire is to act as mediator on good terms with both parties in the war. It is thought that if he succeeds in being accepted as mediator before elections take place his reelection would be secured. The papal delegate denies absolutely that he made any peace proposal but press continues to hint at a correspondence on the subject of peace between President and Pope.

The peace rumours here are probably of German origin and German pressure is no doubt being brought to bear to induce President to offer mediation. His present bent seems to be in that direction and rumours are current that USG is about to address a "severe" note to the allies about restrictions of trade, although Secretary of State had stated that German threats would make it difficult for USG to take action against the blockade. It looks as if USG might be prepared to use pressure in order to induce us to accept mediation

Hw telegram (FO 115/2090, p. 27, PRO).
  [1] That is, Wilson's speech to the National Press Club, printed at May 15, 1916.
  [2] Major Sir John Robert Chancellor, the new Governor of Trinidad, who made a courtesy call on Wilson en route to his new post.

To Henry Morgenthau

My dear Morgenthau: The White House May 19, 1916

Thank you warmly for your note of May eighteenth about your talk with Senator Hoke Smith. I think the matter goes deep with him and is incurable, having been born with him, but, of course,

I am willing to do anything that I reasonably can to accomplish the great results we have all set our hearts upon.

I was heartily sorry I was tied up so as not to be able to hear about your interview in person.

In haste

Cordially and sincerely yours,   Woodrow Wilson

TLS (WP, DLC).

To Wilbur Fisk Sadler, Jr.

My dear General: [The White House] May 19, 1916

I am warmly obliged to you for your letter of May fifteenth, giving me a full account of the way the Secretary of War spent his day at Newark and the impression he made.[1] I felt confident that he would make just that impression. He is one of the most genuine and gifted men I know, and I am sure that the better he is known the more he will be trusted, not only, but loved and admired. It was generous of you to give me the pleasure of hearing all about it.

Cordially and sincerely yours,   Woodrow Wilson

TLS (Letterpress Books, WP, DLC).
   [1] W. F. Sadler, Jr., to WW, May 15, 1916, TLS (WP, DLC).

To Joseph Swagar Sherley

My dear Mr. Sherley: [The White House] May 19, 1916

I hope that you will not think that I am making too many suggestions when I urge upon you the strategic importance of having the naval bill go through before the conventions meet. I make this suggestion to you because I know how interested you are in the fortifications bill (and I am sure I need not assure you of my own deep interest in it) and because I thought, therefore, that there might be some question of order of precedence as between these two bills. My own judgment is on strategic grounds, and because public attention is focused upon it, that the naval bill should be put through at the earliest possible date.

Cordially and sincerely yours,   Woodrow Wilson

TLS (Letterpress Books, WP, DLC).

From Joseph Patrick Tumulty, with Enclosure

For the President—   [The White House] May 19th [1916].
  How should this matter be taken care of?

The Secretary.

TLS (WP, DLC).

ENCLOSURE

From Hamilton Holt

To the President   New York May 11, 1916

I have received last night a cablegram from H. G. Dresselhuijs and B. De Jong Van Beek en Donk,[1] and this morning the Associated Press called me on the 'phone, saying that the announcement had been made in Holland, that such a cable had been sent me, and giving its context in substance. As the matter was public, I therefore gave out the cablegram, which appears in this afternoon's papers. I herewith enclose a copy for you.[2]

I was greatly impressed by the interview you gave to the Committee of the American Union against Preparedness, which appeared before you on May eighth,[3] especially since in that interview you practically endorsed the underlying principles of the League to Enforce Peace, of which Mr. Taft is president, and of which I was one of the founders. As all the nations in the present war are professing to fight for the purpose of establishing the basis of a durable peace which will guarantee their legitimate aspirations, I am wondering if you have considered the possibility of whether it would be practicable to offer mediation now on the basis of a League to Enforce Peace? Perhaps if the future peace of the world can be guaranteed, the immediate problems will become relatively insignificant and can be easily arranged.

Yours respectfully   Hamilton Holt

TLS (WP, DLC).

[1] Hendrik Coenraad Dresselhuys and Benjamin de Jong van Beek en Donk, both of the Netherlands Anti-War Council.

[2] H. C. Dresselhuys and B. de Jong van Beek en Donk to H. Holt, May 10, 1916, TC telegram (WP, DLC). It stated that the Netherlands Anti-War Council believed that recent German-American diplomatic exchanges, along with speeches by Bethmann Hollweg and Asquith, provided new opportunities for mediation by the neutral powers. Sweden and Switzerland had already expressed interest in cooperation toward this end. The Dutch council hoped that American peace organizations would cooperate and also urge President Wilson to "promote" a conference of neutral nations to offer mediation for a "durable peace and [an] international system which will secure [the] principle of equal rights for all civilized states."

[3] See the colloquy printed at May 8, 1916, Vol. 36.

To Joseph Patrick Tumulty

Dear Tumulty: [The White House, c. May 19, 1916]

I wish you would be kind enough to acknowledge for me this letter of Mr. Hamilton Holt's. Say that I appreciate very warmly his friendly suggestions and want to assure him that I am watching the opportunities in this great matter with the keenest and most profound interest.   The President.

TL (WP, DLC).

Two Letters from Edward Mandell House

Dear Governor: [New York] May 19, 1916.

Your letter of yesterday came last night in time to permit the cable to Sir Edward being coded and it has been sent just as written.

My day is very full and I may not be able to make the suggestions in regard to your speech until tomorrow. I will certainly have the letter before you Monday morning.

Vance McCormick is to be here today. I am having him to both lunch and dinner in order to get a thorough view of him. I will let you know about it later.

Frank Polk, Dudley, Woolley, Newton Baker, Daniels, Morganthau and others think he is the man you want for Chairman. The fact that he comes from Pennsylvania is not altogether against him for the reason that he will not be involved in any of the factional quarrels that seem to prevail in the doubtful states. Every faction would feel with such a man that they would have a hearing without prejudice.

Did you see what Bryan had to say at Mohonk yesterday? I am sending it and also what Bryce said in London.[1] It is strange they should have spoken upon the same subject at the same time. Knowing the two men, however, it does not seem strange that their views should be so wide apart.

Professor Ford has given us some valuable suggestions for the Glynn speech.

Since dictating the above I have spent some time with Vance McCormick. Unless something develops that is not apparent I believe he is the man you want. He reminds me very much of Frank Polk. He seems to be of the same high type. He appears to have poise and good judgment. I cannot judge on so short an acquaintance of his political sagacity, but I am favorably impressed with him.

If you take Polk you will have Lansing a sick man on your hands.[2] Of this I am convinced and so is Polk.

If possible I hope you can make a decision within the next few days as I would like to talk freely with whomsoever you select and discuss the plan of organization. I can do it so much better now than later when the real hot weather sets in.

If you think favorably of McCormick I will arrange to see him frequently between now and the time I leave for Sunnapee. If anything unfavorable develops before the St. Louis Convention[3] I would likely find it out by frequent intercourse with him and you could shelve him for someone else.

I believe he would meet the favour of your friends generally better than Polk for he has had a wider national acquaintanceship than Polk.   Affectionately yours,   E. M. House

[1] These enclosures are missing. However, at the Lake Mohonk Conference on International Arbitration on May 18, Bryan stated that he opposed preparedness because it would provoke rather than prevent war. He said, also, that, if the United States joined European nations to enforce peace, the United States would be forced to abandon the Monroe Doctrine. Lord Bryce believed that the United States, as a great power, had to participate in world affairs, and he looked forward to the use of her "authority and strength" in a "League to restrain aggression." *New York Times*, May 19, 1916; James Viscount Bryce, "America's Traditional Isolation," *The New Republic*, VII (May 20, 1916), 58-59.

[2] Lansing suffered from chronic diabetes.

[3] The Democratic national convention, scheduled to open on June 14.

Dear Governor: New York, May 19, 1916.

I am sending you some data to look over which may be of service to you in formulating your speech.[1]

Norman Angell gave me the quotations from the speeches of Asquith, Grey, Balfour and others and Bryce's article in the New Republic has a direct bearing upon the same subject.

My reason for thinking the programme of the League to Enforce Peace impracticable at this time is that I believe the first thing to do is to get the governments to agree to stand together for the things which you have so admirably outlined in your letter to me and which I in substance cabled to Grey.

When there is a committal upon these points then the question of putting them into practical use will arise and some such tribunal as they suggest may be worked out. I think the initial step, however, should not include any definite plan to put the agreement into operation.

As soon as you begin to discuss details you will find differences arising that might obscure the real issue.

I shall write you further Sunday.

                    Affectionately yours,   E. M. House

TLS (WP, DLC).
¹ The material included excerpts from speeches by Asquith, Grey, Balfour, Frederick Edwin Smith, and Lloyd George, extracts from the London *Times*, and James Bryce, "America's Traditional Isolation." They all emphasized the need for a postwar international peacekeeping system in which the United States would participate.

From Jessie Woodrow Wilson Sayre

Dearest Father,   [Williamstown, Mass.] May 19, 1916.

The beautiful silver plate for Francis came today. We made him open it—with our help—and he loved it, as did we. It is such a particularly pretty one and, as Helen suggested, his wife can use it *forever* and *ever*. We are enchanted with it!

He is like a young lord, now, with an entire silver outfit of cup, porringer, and plate.

Do you suppose it would be possible in the next six or eight months, in our happiest dream moments, to plan to have you here at another Christening Party?

We don't want Eleanor to be less fortunate than Ellen¹ and Francis were but we feel very bold indeed to even suggest such a thing. We wouldn't want you to consider it unless it would mean something of a rest or change for you, dear Father, too. So I know you will tell us truthfully what you think of such a project.

Little Eleanor is slowly gaining again now and we are all very much relieved.

With deepest love and thanks to you both from us all.

Your ever loving daughter   Jessie.

ALS (WC, NjP).
¹ Ellen Wilson McAdoo, born on May 21, 1915.

Remarks from a Rear Platform
at Salisbury, North Carolina

May 20, 1916.

My friends, I told the Senator¹ that I was loaded with only one cartridge this morning, which was to be exploded at Charlotte, but I am very glad, indeed, to give you my very cordial greetings and to say how very glad I am to find myself here in Senator Overman's old home. You have reason to be proud of your Senator, ladies and gentlemen, and I am very glad to give him the tribute of my praise and, if he will permit me to add it, of my friendship.

There are very serious things to be done nowadays, ladies and gentlemen, and it is a satisfaction to be associated with men who know how serious they are, and with what spirit they must be approached. Because, whether we will or not, we are at the beginning of a new age for the world, and America will have to play a very great part in that new age. And we will have to be very sure not to encourage or to give countenance to the men who are trying to hold us back. There are some men—I do not believe they represent the great rank and file of the Republican party—but the men who now control the Republican party have their heads over their shoulders. They are looking backward, not forward. They do not know the problems of the new day. And whenever I, for example, try to show my sympathies for the forward looking men of their own party by nominating men of that sort, they at once try to block the process. They have no sympathy with the forward looking men of their own party. Now, I am for forward looking men, not for backward looking men. We have come down here to celebrate an historical episode, but we have not done it because we are looking backward. We have done it merely in order to give ourselves the excuse to get together and feel the thrill of being Americans and living in an age when it is worthwhile being Americans. (Train pulls out)

T MS (WP, DLC).
    1 That is, Lee Slater Overman, Democrat, from Salisbury, whom Wilson had invited to accompany him on his trip to North Carolina. Wilson had reluctantly agreed to Overman's request for a brief speech in the Senator's home town in order not to antagonize him any further in the fight over the Brandeis confirmation. See Josephus Daniels, *The Wilson Era: Years of Peace, 1910-1917* (Chapel Hill, N. C., 1944), pp. 545-47.

An Address in Charlotte, North Carolina[1]

May 20, 1916

Your Excellency, ladies and gentlemen: It is with unaffected pleasure that I find myself in the presence of this interesting company today, for I have come back for a visit all too brief to a region very familiar to my heart, and the greeting of whose people is peculiarly welcome to me.

I do not know, my fellow citizens, whether I can interpret for you today the spirit of this occasion, but it is necessary, when we get together in celebrations like this, to take counsel together with regard to just what it is that we wish to celebrate. You will say we wish to celebrate the memories of that time to which we look back with such pride—when our fathers, with singular wisdom of counsel and stoutness of heart, undertook to set up an

    1 At the ceremony commemorating the one hundred and forty-first anniversary of the so-called Mecklenburg Declaration of Independence. Governor Locke Craig introduced Wilson.

independent nation on this side of the water. But it is very much
more important that we should remind ourselves of the elements
with which our forefathers dealt. There were only three million
citizens in that original republic of the United States of America.
Now there are one hundred millions. It is a long cry back to those
modest beginnings. A great period of time, not only, but a great
period of profound change, separates us from that time, and yet
I would remind you that the same elements were present then
that are present now.

What interests my thought more than anything else about the
United States is that it has always been in process of being made
ever since that little beginning, and that there have always been
the same elements in the process. At the outset, there was at the
heart of the men who led the movement for independence a very
high and handsome passion for human liberty and free institutions. And, yet, there lay before them a great continent which it
was necessary to subdue to the uses of civilization if they were
going to build upon it a great state among the family of nations.
I heard a preacher once point out the very interesting circumstance that our Lord's prayer begins with the petition for "our
daily bread," from which he drew the inference that it is very difficult to worship God on an empty stomach, and that the material
foundations of our life are the first foundations. What I want to
call your attention to is that this country, ever since that time, has
devoted much of its attention, perhaps too much of its attention,
to the material foundations of its life—to subduing this continent
to the uses of the nation and to the building up of a great body of
wealth and material power. I find some men who, when they
think of America, do not think of anything else but that. But, my
friends, there have been other nations just as rich and just as
powerful, in comparison with the other nations of the world, as
the United States is, and it is a great deal more important that we
should determine what we are going to do with our power than
that we should possess it.

You must remember, therefore, the elements with which we
are dealing. Sometimes those of us who were born in this part of
the country persuade ourselves that this is the characteristic part
of America. Here, more than anywhere else, has been preserved
a great part of the original stock which settled this country,
particularly that portion of the stock which came from the British
Isles. (I am not meaning to exclude Ireland.) And then I find a
great many of my friends who live in New England imagining
that the history of this country is merely the history of the expansion of New England, and that Plymouth Rock lies at the

foundation of our institutions. As a matter of fact, my fellow citizens, however mortifying it may be to them or to us, America did not come out of the South, and it did not come out of New England. The characteristic part of America originated in the middle states of New York and Pennsylvania and New Jersey, because there, from the first, was that mixture of populations, that mixture of racial stocks, that mixture of antecedents, which is the most singular and distinguishing mark of the United States. The most important single fact about this great nation, which we represent, is that it is made up out of all the nations of the world. I dare say that the men who came to America then, and the men who have come to America since, came with a single purpose, sharing some part of the passion for human liberty which characterized the men who founded the republic. But they came with all sorts of blood in their veins, all sorts of antecedents behind them, all sorts of traditions in their family and national life, and America has had to serve as a melting pot for all these diversified and contrasted elements. What kind of fire of pure passion are you going to keep burning under the pot in order that the mixture that comes out may be purged of its dross and may be the fine gold of untainted Americanism? That is the problem.

I want to call your attention to another picture. America has always been making and to be made, and, while we were in the midst of this process, apparently at the acme and crisis of this process, while this travail of soul and fermentation of elements was at its height, came this great cataclysm of European war, and almost every other nation in the world became involved in a tremendous struggle which was what, my fellow citizens? What are the elements in the struggle? Don't you see that, in this European war, is involved the very thing that has been going on in America? It is a competition of national standards, of national traditions, and of national polities—political systems. Europe has grappled in war, as we have grappled in peace, to see what is going to be done with these things when they come into hot contact with one another. For, do you not remember that, while these processes were going on in America, some very interesting things were happening? It was a very big world into which this nation came when it was born, but it is a very little world now. It used to take as many days to go from Washington to Charlotte in those days as it now takes hours. I heard an Irishman say that, if the power of steam continued to increase in the next fifty years as it had increased in the last, we would get to Charlotte two hours before we left Washington. And, as these processes of intercommunication have been developed and quickened, men of the same nation, not only, have grown closer neighbors, but men of different nations have grown closer neighbors with each other. And, now that we have these invisible tongues that speak by the wireless through the trackless air to the ends of the world, every man can make every other man in the world his neighbor and speak to him upon the moment. While these processes of fermentation and travail were going on, men were learning about each other, nations were becoming more and more acquainted with each other, nations were more and more becoming interrelated, and intercommunication was being quickened in every possible way, so that now the melting pot is bigger than America. It is as big as the world. And what you see taking place on the other side of the water is the tremendous—I had about said final—process by which a contest of elements may, in God's Providence, be turned into a coordination and cooperation of elements. For it is an interesting circumstance that the processes of the war stand still. These hot things that are in contact with each other do not make very much progress against each other. When you cannot overcome, you must take counsel.

See, then, ladies and gentlemen, what a new age we have come into. I should think that it would quicken the imagination of every man, and quicken the patriotism of every man who cared for America. Here, in America, we have tried to set the example of bringing all the world together upon terms of liberty and cooperation and peace. And in that great experience that we have been going through, America has been a sort of prophetic sample of mankind. Now, the world outside of America has felt the forces of America—felt the forces of freedom, the forces of common aspiration, the forces that bring every man and every nation face to face with this question: "What are you going to do with your power? Are you going to translate it into force, or are you going to translate it into peace and the salvation of society?" Does it not interest you that America has run before the rest of the world in making trial of this great human experiment? And is it not the sign and dawn of a new age that the one thing upon which the world is now about to fall back is the moral judgment of mankind?

There is no finer sentence in the history of great nations than that sentence which occurs in the Declaration of Independence (I am now referring to the minor declaration at Philadelphia, not to the Mecklenburg Declaration) in which Mr. Jefferson said, "A decent respect for the opinion of mankind makes it necessary"—I am not now quoting the words exactly—"that we should state the grounds upon which we have taken the important step of assert-

ing our independence." "A decent respect for the opinion of mankind"—it is as if Jefferson knew that this was the way in which
mankind itself was to struggle to realize its aspirations and that,
standing in the presence of mankind, this little group of three million people should say: "Friends and fellow citizens of the great
moral world, our reason for doing this thing we now intend to
state to you in candid and complete terms, so that you will never
think that we were merely throwing off a yoke out of impatience,
but know that we were throwing off this thing in order that a
great world of liberty should be open to man through our instrumentality."

I would like, therefore, to think that the spirit of this occasion
could be expressed if we imagined ourselves lifting some sacred
emblem of counsel and of peace, of accommodation and right-
eous judgment, before the nations of the world and reminding
them of that passage in Scripture, "After the wind, after the
earthquake, after the fire, the still small voice of humanity."[2]

T MS (WP, DLC).
   [2] There are two WWT outlines of this address, each with the composition
date of May 19, 1916, in WP, DLC.

From Robert Lansing

PERSONAL AND PRIVATE:

My dear Mr. President: Washington May 20, 1916.
   I enclose a draft of a note to the British Ambassador on the
subject of interference with the mails. I have been delayed in
preparing this because it required considerable research and in
addition I have not been to the Department for the past three
days and may not be for two or three days to come.
   I consider it very important that this note should be delivered
as soon as possible because the mail detentions are becoming
more and more irritating to our people. I believe a way can be
found for Great Britain to modify her present practice, but such a
consideration will come after the note is delivered.
   I would be obliged for any suggestions or changes you may see
fit to make in the draft, which you will oblige me by sending to
my house after you have examined it.
                        Faithfully yours,   Robert Lansing.

TLS (SDR, RG 59, 841.711/349, DNA).

From Newton Diehl Baker

(PERSONAL AND CONFIDENTIAL.)

My dear Mr. President: Washington. May 20, 1916.

I have just had a note from Governor Cox to the effect that William Durbin, who is Chairman of the Democratic State Committee of Ohio, is personally opposed to Senator Pomerene and is endeavoring to stir up an opposition candidacy in the Ohio State primary.

I know Durbin very well. He is one of your enthusiastic admirers. If I send for him, would you be willing to see him for five minutes and ask him quite frankly to do all that he can for Senator Pomerene? If you would rather not see him, I will send for him on my own account and see if I can do anything with him, although, of course, a word from you would be conclusive, while from me it would be merely argumentative.

Cordially yours,   Newton D. Baker

TLS (WP, DLC).

From Herman Bernstein

Personal.

Dear Mr. President: New York   May 20th, 1916.

Permit me to acknowledge Secretary Tumulty's letter of recent date with regard to the document by the Pope to the rulers of the nations, which I had the honor to give you, at the request of Pope Benedict, whom I saw last summer.[1] Mr. Tumulty writes as follows:

"I have brought your letter of May 8th to the attention of the President,[2] who asks me to say that he is sorry if any courtesy was omitted. He did not suppose that a printed document needed an acknowledgment beyond what he roally [orally] gave you; but if you will indicate what you think was expected, he would be very glad to receive your suggestion."[3]

[1] Benedict XV, on July 28, 1915, had addressed a letter to the heads of state of the belligerent nations in which he appealed for an end to the war. *New York Times*, July 31 and Aug. 1, 1915.

[2] H. Bernstein to JPT, May 8, 1916, Vol. 36.

[3] Tumulty was paraphrasing WW to JPT, *c.* May 15, 1916, TL (WP, DLC):
"I don't know which message he is referring to. The one he himself delivered to me did not seem to be really from the Pope but from Cardinal Gasparri. If you would be kind enough to look it up, I would be obliged. I did not know that it required a personal acknowledgment." And another note of same date:
"Will you not write to Mr. Bernstein that we are sorry if any courtesy was omitted, but that I did not suppose that a printed document needed an acknowledgment beyond what I orally gave to him; that if he will indicate what he thinks was expected, I should be very glad to receive his suggestion."

The reason why I inquired whether the receipt of the letter was acknowledged to the Vatican is this:

Last year when I visited a number of European countries and talked with many statesmen and leaders of thought in the belligerent lands about the prospects for peace and the readjustment after the war, I also had a private audience with Pope Benedict and several interviews with his Secretary of State Cardinal Gasparri. As an American writer and student of European affairs, believing that the present interruption of European civilization by violence is the greatest misfortune that has befallen mankind in centuries, I felt that every effort, be it ever so humble, in the direction of peace, should be made, or, at least, every effort should be made to ascertain to what extent the wave of war-madness is taking hold of the people abroad, and of the leaders of thought as well as of religion. When I heard of the efforts made by [the] Vatican in the direction of peace, I sought the Pope's views on this subject. I found that Pope Benedict was dealing with the problem not only from a moral but also from a practical viewpoint. When I learned that certain Governments actually authorized him to start peace negotiations, outlining the terms upon which they would be willing to conclude peace, when I learned that he was working in the matter not as a sympathizer with only one group of the nations involved in the war, but that he was concerned in bringing about a just and reasonable peace because he was moved by the awful calamity that has befallen mankind, and that he was in position to offer terms that might make it possible for the nations to end the conflict without loss of dignity on either side, I became deeply interested in his efforts. In the course of the conversations at the Vatican, the Pope and Cardinal Gasparri expressed the view that you, as the President of the greatest neutral power, could act most effectively as the mediator between the nations, and they also expressed their admiration for you personally, for your policy of neutrality and peace, as well as for your offer of the good offices of America in the beginning of the war. Then I mentioned that I had the honor of knowing you personally and I expressed my admiration for your statesmanship and your readiness to help in the service of mankind, as evidenced on numerous occasions. It was then that Cardinal Gasparri and later the Pope himself asked me to bring to you the letter on Peace addressed to the rulers of the world, as a token of their appreciation of your efforts in behalf of peace, with the request that you continue your endeavors in that direction and with the assurances that they would be glad to be of any assi[s]tance to you in your efforts to bring about peace. At the time the Vatican had definite proposals, authorized by the Central powers, for the beginning of peace negotiations. I was given to understand that there were influential elements also among the official spheres in England who knew of these efforts and approved of them, and that even the Italian Government was not opposed to these endeavors on the part of the Pope.

I tried to ascertain what the motives of the Vatican were in these activities, and I gathered from my conversations with Cardinal Gasparri that the Pope desired to be represented at the coming peace conference as a religious head, that he believed the heads of other religious denominations should also be represented there, so that many questions not of a political nature that have irritated Europe and have served as causes of wars in the past, might be settled this time. I understood that, if represented at the peace conference, the Pope would not raise the question of temporal power under any circumstances, that he was concerned only with the moral influence and advice he could bring to the councils of the conference; but that, on the other hand, if he should not be represented at the peace conference, there might be the danger of the German Government and particualrly [particularly] the Austrian Government raising the question of temporal power ende[a]voring to secure more rights and privileges for the Vatican, in order thus to weaken the Italian Government.

When I came to Germany and interviewed Professor Hans Delbrueck, the former tutor of the Kaiser, the editor of the Preussische Jahrbuecher, and one of the most influential German statesmen, and he stated to me that you and the Pope could bring about peace within two months; when Maximilian Harden,[4] whom I have known for many years, discussed with me your statesmanship and leadership, and then declared that you alone could be the peace mediator; and when Dr. Ludwig Stein,[5] immediately after a conference with Prince Von Buelow, made to me the statement that you could end the war within a short time, if you took the initiative as a peace mediator,—when I heard the same thing in neutral countries as well as in England, Italy and even France, I was eager to meet you immediately after my return from Europe and I considered it my duty to tell you all that I have learned abroad. Upon my return to America, you were occupied with grave and pressing problems, and you informed me twice that you could not receive me at the time. About two

4 Maximilian Felix Ernst Harden, editor of *Die Zukunft* of Berlin, outspoken antimilitarist, liberal, and peace advocate.
5 Formerly Professor of Philosophy at the University of Bern; now a journalist in Berlin and an advocate of peace and of international organization.

months thereafter I went to Europe again, on the Ford ship, and as you may perhaps know, I was the only one to sever my connection with that expedition as soon as a resolution was submitted in which the members were asked to criticise you and to oppose the plans outlined in your message to Congress.

On March 29 I had the keen pleasure of meeting you, but during the few minutes I had not the opportunity of telling you under what circumstances the letter was sent to you by the Pope.[6]

It seems to me that several months ago there was a psychological moment when peace negotiations would have been welcomed by almost all the nations at war, but that moment passed. For a time the nations were in a temper to resent any attempts at mediation. But it appears to me that the psychological moment for peace negotiations is at hand again. And it is my belief that if no energetic endeavors will now be made to ascertain the terms upon which peace could be secured, the opportunity may be lost once more, and the war may be prolonged for years.

From my personal observations I feel justified in believing that practically all the nations are looking upon you as the only mediator, for you have succeeded, by reason of your brilliant and sane statesmanship, in keeping America out of this war, and it is my feeling that your greatest achievement will be your success in bringing the bleeding nations to their senses, in ending the violence and the bloodshed abroad.

I have not mentioned anything about my interviews with the Pope to anyone and have not published a line about this matter. It was my intention to inform you of all this immediately upon my return from Europe in October, but unfortunately circumstances shaped themselves so that you could find no time to see me then.

I am writing this to you just now because I have seen from the press that the Pope has communicated with you and has perhaps suggested some of the things which I was asked to transmit to you personally. When I was in Europe recently I was asked whether I had delivered to you the letter and the message. I was not in a position to say that I had. That is the reason why I inquired whether the receipt of the letter was acknowledged.

I do not know whether I have made myself clear in this letter. Should you you [sic] desire any additional information on this subject, I shall be happy to give it to you at any time. I expect to

---

[6] "Please ask Mr. B. to express my appreciation and say that I am sorry if I seemed unappreciative." WW to JPT, ALI, c. May 31, 1916 (WP, DLC).

be in Washington on Friday and Saturday, at the convention of the League to Enforce Peace, and I hope to have the pleasure of hearing you speak and of meeting you on that occasion.[7]

With highest esteem and the best of wishes, I am,

Sincerely and faithfully yours,   Herman Bernstein.

TLS (WP, DLC).
[7] The Executive Office and head usher's diaries do not indicate that Bernstein visited the White House on May 26 or 27.

From Edward Mandell House, with Enclosure

Dear Governor: New York, May 21, 1916.

I am sending you my thoughts on the speech you have in hand. It is roughly and quickly done and is no more than a suggestion.

I do not believe I would make the calling of the conference any more definite. Something should perhaps be said about Belgium for you might be criticized for not taking action before and then taking it now. The difference is easily expla[i]nable.

I hope you will show Lansing the speech before it is delivered. He might be useful and he would surely be offended if he did not know of this important step.

I am writing hastily but with deep affection.

Your devoted,   E. M. House

TLS (WP, DLC).

E N C L O S U R E

May 21, 1916.

One Reason this war has come, one reason why other wars will come is because nations are secretive as to their intentions towards one another and do not in advance outline their thoughts and purposes   If England had said before the war, if France is attacked by the Central Powers we will join her, Germany would in all human probability have consented to a conference as proposed by Grey.

In the interest of international comity we should give voice to the convictions that lie near the heart of a vast majority of Americans. If we had said before this war, what I shall say tonight, the war in all human probability would not have occurred. It would have been notice to each of the belligerents that we are fundamentally opposed to certain policies and that we would use all our moral and economic strength, and under certain circumstances, even our physical strength against the nation or nations violating these principles.

It is clear the world must come to this new and more whole-some diplomacy. If an agreement can be reached by the great powers as to what fundamentals they hold to be to their common interest and agree to act in concert when any nation or nations violates these fundamentals, then we can feel that our civiliza-tion has begun to justify its being. Nations in the future must be governed by the same high code of honor as we demand of indi-viduals. It must be said in some humiliation that the United States has not always maintained so high a level, but the lapses have been few and have constituted the exception and not the rule.

If we may take the utterances of the spokesmen in other na-tions—belligerent as well as neutral—we must believe that this feeling lies as deep and strong with them as it does with us. It is confined to no one land but circles the earth. If its voice is clearer and more definite in the Americas it is perhaps because we are under less restraint than the other continents and can ex-press ourselves without the fear of being misunderstood.

We have Mr. Asquith at Dublin September 25, 1914 repeating what Mr. Gladstone had said nearly a half century ago:

"The greatest triumph of our time will be the enthronement of the idea of public right as the governing idea of European poli-tics" and he added that "it seems to me to be now at this moment as good a definition as we can have of our European policy." ["]The idea of public right: what does it mean when translated into concrete terms? It means, first and foremost, the clearing of the ground by the definite repudiation of militarism as the gov-erning factor in the relations of States, and of the future mold-ing of the European world. It means next, that room must be found and kept and for the independent existence and the free development of the smaller nationalities—each with a corporate consciousness of its own. Belgium, Holland, Switzerland and the Scandinavian countries, Greece and the Balkan states, they must be recognized as having exactly as good a title as their more powerful neighbors—more powerful in strength as in wealth—ex-actly as giid [good] a title to a place in the sun. And it means finally, or it ought to mean, perhaps by a slow and gradual process, the substitution for force, for the clash of competing ambition, for grouping and alliances and a precarious equipoise, the substitution for al[l] these things if [of] a real European partnership based on the recognition of equal right and estab-lished and enforced by a common will."

We have Sir Edward Grey saying in one of his historic papers "My own endeavor will be to promote some arrangement, to which Germany could be a party, by which she could be assured that no aggressive or hostile policy would be pursued against her or her allies by France, Russia and ourselves, jointly or separately"

Speaking at the City Temple on November 11, 1915, Mr. Lloyd George said:

"We are all looking forward to a time when swords shall be beaten into plowshares and spears into pruninghooks and nation cannot rise up against nation, and there will be no more war. The surest way of establishing a reign of peace upon earth, is by making the way of the transgresser of the peace of the nations, too hard for the rulers of men to bear it."

Speaking at Bristol on December 14th, 1914, Mr. Balfour said:

"It seemed that the international future of our race lay in as far as possible, spreading wide the grip and power of international law, in the raising more and more of the dignity of treaties between states, and that controversies which arose between governments (as in every community they arose between different individuals) should be decided not by the sword but by arbitration"

Mr. Bonar Law said on December 4th:

"We know we can gain nothing from the war except two things: Peace when it is over, and security for peace in the future."

In the Reichstag debate December 9th Herr Scheidemann[1] said:

"If a chance is offered to the Government to conclude a peace assuring to the German people its political independence, its security and freedom of development, we demand that peace should be concluded. If it has the chance to enter into peace negotiations on the basis of these conditions, it ought to do it in the interest of human civilization."

In Russia we hear Prof. Milyukov[2] (Leader of the Constitutional Democrats in Russia) saying:

"The limitation of armaments the conclusion of a general and obligatory arbitration treaty, the final assertion of the liberty of life and private property, and, before all, a strong and efficacious

[1] Philipp Scheidemann, secretary of the Social Democratic party, and a member of the Reichstag.

[2] Pavel Nikolaevich Miliukov, historian, former lecturer at Moscow University; founder and leader of the Constitutional Union (Kadet) Party and its principal spokesman in the third and fourth Dumas (1907-1917); and an expert on foreign affairs.

sanction to be applied in future by a legally organized Europe to the attempted violations of international law."

Expressions of like tenor from the statesmen and the press of all countries could be given. It seems therefore that this war has been caused by a hideous misunderstanding and what is necessary is for some friend to bring about a reconciliation—a reconciliation that will be lasting. Nations are not unlike individuals. It would be well if we could better understand that. We have the international mischief makers just as we have the social scandal mongers and mischiefmakers. The result is that nations do not understand one another.

It is a much more common fault among nations than among individuals to place too low an estimate upon the courage, the integrity and the purposes of their neighbors, for we have all become neighbors now. It is not wise to underestimate an antagonist. It creates friction and friction creates war and war creates surprises. If then, every belligerent desires peace upon an honorable and lasting basis, it should not be difficult to bring it about, provided some plan may be suggested by which the peace may be permanent and by which the belligerents in the future may be friends and not enemimies [enemies] that have merely ceased to fight.

This it would seem might be accomplished by putting into concrete expression what they all declare they desire—a desire in which we share.

There should be a universal alliance to maintain freedom of the seas and to prevent any war begun either contrary to treaty covenants or without warning and full inquiry. This alliance should formulate rules for the purpose of limiting armaments both on land and sea and for the purpose of making warfare more humane to those actually engaged, and in safe-guarding the lives and property of neutrals and non-combatants. This should be the initial step. Later details could be worked out so that the agreement could be put into practical operation.

This, then, is the message that America is sending to stricken Europe—this is our promise of help. The call of the Centuries has come and is seeking fullfilment. Must we not answer it and justify our place among the nations of the world.

T MS (WP, DLC).

From William Charles Adamson

Dear Mr. President: Washington, D. C. May 21, 1916.

I think I emphasized to you the one great obstacle to our General Dam Legislation is the insistence of some people on authorizing the imposition of a federal tax, and I think I suggested to you that at your convenience you try to mollify some of the leading democrats of the House who have been insisting on that proposition. I think I mentioned to you Mr. Sherley and Mr. Ferris, possibly Mr. Rainey and Dr. Foster. I know Judge Cullop has been uncontrollable on the subject, and our friend Kent of California has been the same way.

No man can insist more strenuously than I on guarding and protecting all the rights and interests of the Government and the people, but private capital will not invest unless we have some liberality in the terms offered, and the one thing above all others that deters capital from investing under the General Dam Act is the uncertainty of what will be required of them. A federal tax changeable at the pleasure of the Secretary of War would absolutely prevent any investment.

If you should have occasion to talk to any of these democrats on that subject you can help us considerably.

With high regards and best wishes, I remain,

Yours truly,   W C Adamson

TLS (WP, DLC).

To Edward Mandell House, with Enclosure

Dearest Friend,   The White House. 22 May, 1916.

Signs multiply that The Allies are becoming alarmed at the possibility of our making a move for peace. I send you the enclosed from Polk as one of the bits of evidence. Lansing has been laid up in bed for a few days.

Mrs. Wilson and I are to be in New York on Wednesday for the Grayson-Gordon wedding.[1] I shall take Mrs. Wilson directly to Miss Gordon's. Will you not join me there at two o'clock that day? We can ride about or go somewhere for an hour and a half or so and confer about things,—particularly about the speech Saturday night.

Thank you warmly for taking so much trouble and sending me so much material and such full suggestions for the speech. It will all help me immensely.

I shall be deeply interested to learn what you think about

Vance McCormick now that you have seen and personally sampled him. The suggestion about making him chairman of the National Committee interests me very much. I want reassurance on this doubt: whether he is aggressive enough and whether he is not too "high-brow" and intolerant of the rougher elements that have to be handled and dealt with.

Will you be kind enough to let me have a copy of the letter I wrote you which formed the basis of your cable to Sir Edward in regard to a basis for peace? Perhaps I can get it on Wednesday?

In haste and amidst many interruptions,

Affectionately Yours,   Woodrow Wilson

WWTLS (E. M. House Papers, CtY).
    1 Grayson married Alice Gertrude Gordon at St. George's Church on May 24.
Mrs. Wilson served as the bride's witness.

E N C L O S U R E

From Frank Lyon Polk

My dear Mr. President: Washington May 22, 1916.

The French Ambassador called at the Department this afternoon and, in the absence of the Secretary, saw me. After taking up one or two routine matters, he spoke of the rumors in the press of your taking some steps toward bringing about peace. He referred to the construction put on one of your recent speeches and said he sincerely hoped that nothing would be said at present which would indicate an intention on the part of this Government to offer mediation or an intention to take any other steps toward bringing about peace. As he put it, his country wanted peace before the war, but now, after making all the sacrifices that had been made, France could not consider peace until it could be assured that it was a real peace and not a breathing spell for Germany; in other words, the people of France feel that they must continue the war so as to make the result decisive, not a draw, in order to make it a lasting peace.

The Ambassador spoke with great earnestness and some emotion. His attitude during his talk was most friendly and complimentary toward this Government, but he said, in closing, that anyone suggesting peace now would be considered by his people a friend of Germany.

He did not ask to see you, but I gathered that he would welcome the opportunity of discussing the subject with you in person. As he is very anxious that I should get the substance of our conversation before you, I take the liberty of writing you as soon after the interview as possible. I will send a copy of this letter to Mr. Lansing.   Yours faithfully,   Frank L. Polk

TLS (E. M. House Papers, CtY).

To Robert Lansing

My dear Mr. Secretary,   The White House. 22 May, 1916.

I have just been able to complete my careful reading of this note, and hasten to return it to you for transmission. I have made a few alterations in the verbiage which seem to me to make it clearer.[1]

I hope that you are feeling a great deal better. We missed you at the Cabinet Friday very much.

Faithfully Yours,   W.W.

WWTLI (SDR, RG 59, 841.711/488½, DNA).
[1] Wilson's emendations were indeed mainly literary and few in number. This draft of the note is RL to "Excellency," n.d., TL (SDR, RG 59, 841.711/349, DNA). The note as sent to Ambassadors Jusserand and Spring Rice and dated May 24, 1916, is printed in FR-WWS 1916, pp. 604-608.

To Benjamin Ryan Tillman

My dear Senator: [The White House] May 22, 1916

You may be sure that the words which you quote at the head of your letter of May seventeenth were most sincerely uttered, and that such letters as yours of that date are most welcome.

I am very much concerned about the Navy oil situation and am going to try my best to carry out your suggestion about reconciling the views and policies of the Departments of the Interior and the Navy.

The nitrate business interests me deeply, too, and I am going to take very seriously the power conferred upon me by the Army Bill, prefacing whatever I do with some very thorough inquiry as to the best methods and the best places.

Thank you again.

Cordially and faithfully yours,   Woodrow Wilson

TLS (Letterpress Books, WP, DLC).

A Telegram and a Letter from Edward Mandell House

[New York, May 22, 1916]

I have a cable from Sir E. G. saying, "No letter has arrived recently but situation as presented in your telegram of May nineteenth will be considered with Asquith at once and I hope to send a reply in a few days." unquote

EBWhw decode (WP, DLC) of T telegram (WP, DLC).

Dear Governor: New York, May 22, 1916.
We hope you and Mrs. Wilson will take both lunch and dinner with us Wednesday and go to the play at night.
Will you not telegraph me tomorrow so we may know that you will give us that pleasure.
I have some things to tell you but will defer them until you come.   Affectionately yours,   E. M. House

TLS (WP, DLC).

From the Most Reverend Giovanni Bonzano

Your Excellency: Washington, May 22, 1916.
Having forwarded to Rome by cablegram your esteemed reply of May 15 to His Holiness, Benedict XV, I am directed to make known to Your Excellency that His Holiness was gratified by the sentiments expressed in it and to assure you that he is very thankful for the same.
With great respect I have the honor to be Your Excellency's Humble Servant Archbishop John Bonzano,
                    Apostolic Delegate.

ALS (WP, DLC).

From Joseph R. Wilson, Jr.

My dear Brother: Baltimore, Md. 5-22-16.
The papers say you will occupy a theater box here May 30. I suppose you will be the guest of honor, so we cannot join your party, but we *do* hope *so* much that you and Sister Edith will come over in time to dine with us on the date named.
If you will dine with us it will at least show the Baltimore people that we are on good terms with our own family, a fact which many kind (?) critics seem to doubt because we prefer to live a quiet, home life. We have tried to ignore the criticisms to which we are constantly subjected because we do not seek the lime-light of official Washington and such other social prominence as we might have by reason of our family connections, but the comments often hurt by reason of their personal nature, and

they are even detrimental to me in a business way. We feel, therefore, that we must take advantage of every opportunity to set ourselves right in the public eye, on your account as well as on our own. Then too, we *want* you both with us whenever you can come.

With deep love from us three to you all,

Your affectionate Brother,   Joseph R. Wilson.

TLS (WP, DLC).

To Newton Diehl Baker

Personal and Confidential.

My dear Mr. Secretary: [The White House] May 23, 1916

Thank you for your note of the twentieth about Mr. Durbin's attitude towards Senator Pomerene. I sincerely regret that he should be opposing the Senator.

I shall be very glad indeed to see him and have a talk with him about the matter if you would be kind enough to arrange it.[1]

Cordially and faithfully yours,   Woodrow Wilson

TLS (Letterpress Books, WP, DLC).

[1] Durbin had an appointment with Wilson on May 25, which was apparently canceled. Former Representative John Jacob Lentz opposed Pomerene unsuccessfully in the Democratic primary on August 8, 1916.

To William Charles Adamson

My dear Judge: [The White House] May 23, 1916

I have your letter of May twenty-first about the obstacles in the way of general dam legislation and you may be sure I shall help upon every opportunity that offers. I shall keep in mind the names of the men you have mentioned.

In haste   Faithfully yours,   Woodrow Wilson

TLS (Letterpress Books, WP, DLC).

To Henry Morgenthau

My dear Mr. Morgenthau: The White House May 23, 1916

I need not tell you with what regret I accept your resignation as Ambassador to Turkey.[1] Your services there have been of a most unusual sort and entitle you to the genuine gratitude of all Americans, not only, but of the many people of many nationalities whom you were able generously to serve while at your post in Constantinople. But I know I am yielding to your desire in accepting the resignation, and that it is the thought that you can be more serviceable for the present in America than in Constantinople that has prompted you to offer your resignation.

May I not add an expression of my warm personal appreciation, regard and best wishes?

Cordially and sincerely yours,   Woodrow Wilson

TLS (WP, DLC).
¹ See H. Morgenthau to WW, March 23, 1916, Vol. 36.

To Harry Augustus Garfield

My dear Garfield: The White House May 23, 1916

I am sincerely obliged to you for your letter of May sixteenth about Droppers. It would be unwise, I think, for him to leave Greece at this time, and since you are able to make provision for holding his place open and are willing to do so, I very gratefully accept the arrangement.

I shall look forward with a great deal of pleasure to seeing you at the end of the week.

In haste

Cordially and sincerely yours,   Woodrow Wilson

TLS (H. A. Garfield Papers, DLC).

From Newton Diehl Baker, with Enclosure

My dear Mr. President: Washington. May 23, 1916.

The enclosed report, made by Colonel Squier who has just returned from London, seems an interesting view of the situation from the English standpoint. This copy being made for you can be destroyed when you are through with it; the original is, of course, in the confidential files of the War College.

Respectfully yours,   Newton D. Baker

TLS (WP, DLC).

ENCLOSURE

A Memorandum by George Owen Squier

CONFIDENTIAL   London, April 27th, 1916.

MEMORANDUM for the Ambassador:

Subject: Interview with Field Marshal Earl Kitchener, K.G., etc.,
        Secretary of State for War.

1. Field Marshal Earl Kitchener sent for me yesterday, and I went to his office by appointment at 3 p.m. in full dress uniform to say "good-bye" on leaving England.

2. His Lordship was in dress uniform, and received me alone as usual, the visit lasting about three-quarters of an hour. He was most cordial, frank, and even intimate. As on previous visits, on [an] air of perfect peace and quiet prevailed about his office, and there were no visitors waiting to see him.

3. His Lordship spoke with great pride of the creation of the New Armies of Great Britain, and said that the six Divisions that first went to France had now been increased to the point where there were 1,200,000 men in France, 1,600,000 abroad in other theatres, and 1,300,000 in the United Kingdom. He said at the start, the Expeditionary Force had 486 guns in the field, they now had 5,613 guns, and were still increasing at a rapid rate.

4. He told me of an instance in the early months of the war when the Staff recommended to him to order 200 extra guns, and after hearing them he said "make it 2,000," which was done.

5. He spoke in great confidence of the present position of France, and said that France had very few reserves left, in fact, without aid in men, she could not maintain resistance longer than the end of the present year. He said France had lost large numbers in prisoners in the early part of the war, during the retreat from Mons, which had crippled her very much. He also said that the Russians, recently landed at Marseilles, were only 6,000 in number.

6. He then began to talk of the present attitude of the United States, and spoke with great feeling and appreciation of the last Note which the President had sent to Germany,[1] and of his address before the joint meeting of Congress in Washington.[2] He said the Note would be a historical document.

7. I then asked him if, in his opinion, the United States should break off diplomatic relations with Germany, war would necessarily follow, or whether it would be possible to maintain such a break, without actual declaration of war. He was very positive and definite in his answer. He said "Either Germany will declare war on your country, or you will be forced to declare war on her within three weeks after the break in relations." He said that Germany would be sure to sink some American ship, which would force the United States to make a declaration of war.

8. I asked him if the entrance of the United States into this war would hasten its conclusion. He replied that in his judgment, it would make a very great difference, and would be the beginning of the end of the war. I asked him if he would name a date when it would end if we came in, and after some hesitation, he said "at least by the end of the present year." I then asked him in case we did not come in, how long he thought the war would last,

and he replied that he saw no reason to change his original estimation of 3 years, and that the war in that case would continue into next year.

9. He then spoke very earnestly of the difficulties in keeping the aims and objects of the present Allies in harmony. He said these difficulties were very great, and then said "England is in this war solely on principle, and wants absolutely nothing, while all the other Allies have vital interests at stake." Great Britain, he felt, would have difficulty, single-handed, in adjusting these conflicting interests of the other Allied Nations.

10. He felt that if the United States came into this war, she would also come in solely on principle, and like Great Britain, would desire no material advantage, and in that case, he felt confident, that Great Britain and the United States would be strong enough on principle to prevent at the end, conflicting claims causing dissensions among the Allies themselves.

11. Futhermore, he thought that with the two English-speaking peoples working together on broad principles, it might be possible to ensure a lasting peace.

12. He charged me with a message to our Secretary of War, to the effect that if we break off diplomatic relations, which in his opinion meant war, he would give all possible help to our War Department. He said "tell your Secretary of War, if he will merely send me a wire for any assistance that I can give, it will be given immediately without the necessity of regular diplomatic channels." He said the War Offices of the two countries should work together directly, exactly as he was now working with Russia. He said the Military Attache in London would be assigned an office in the War Office here.

13. He also said that if it came to sending American troops to France, the best possible school for instruction was over here, in training camps directly behind the lines, where the officers could be sent into the trenches for days at a time, just as was done in the case of the Canadian troops. In other words, after a minimum amount of volunteer training in the United States, they should be sent here to finish that training in the shortest possible time in the theatre of war.

14. I thanked His Lordship for his unusual courtesies to us during the war, and bespoke a continuance of the same for the future.   George O. Squier

Lieut.-Col., Signal Corps, Military Attache.

TCL (WP, DLC).
  1 That is, Wilson's *Sussex* note, printed at April 17, 1916, Vol. 36.
  2 Printed at April 19, 1916, *ibid.*

Edward Mandell House to Sir Edward Grey[1]

Dear Sir Edward: New York. May 23, 1916

Enclosed is a copy of the cable sent you May 19th.

We believe that the war may be ended upon terms that will make its recurrence nearly impossible, if not entirely so. Militarism is I think, already broken, and any further prosecution of the war will not add to a desirable settlement but rather prevent it.

We are much more able to influence a just settlement now than we would be if the war continued very much longer, or if we should be drawn into it. The favorable position which the Allies have made for themselves in this country can be used to their advantage, but it is evident that as the war goes on this advantage may lessen day by day.

I am sorry that England does not realize this. England and France seem to think that the cooperation America is willing to give them in a just settlement of the vexatious questions that are sure to follow peace do not outweigh the doubtful advantage they would gain if Germany were completely crushed. It seems certain if this happens a new set of problems will arise to vex us all.

Your seeming lack of desire to cooperate with us will chill the enthusiasm here—never, I am afraid, to come again, at least in our day. There is a fortunate conjunction of circumstances which makes it possible to bring about the advancement and maintenance of world-wide peace and security, and it is to be hoped that the advantage may not be lost. If it is, the fault will not lie with us.

I am, my dear Sir Edward, with all good wishes,

Sincerely yours,   [E. M. House]

CCL (E. M. House Papers, CtY).

[1] House undoubtedly showed this letter to Wilson when they conferred in New York on May 24.

From Ralph Pulitzer

My dear Mr. President: New York May 23, 1916.

I wish to thank you most sincerely for the sympathy you showed my suggestion concerning Mr. Davidson, and for the entirely unexpected trouble which you took to answer my letter.

I certainly do hope that you will see your way clear in the not distant future to let Davidson make the bust of you. I really believe that it is, in a way, a public duty which should over-ride any but the gravest objections in the way of sacrifice of time, especially as his methods of work are such that the sitter is at full liberty to continue talking or working and does not at all have to pose in the ordinary sense of the word.[1]

Thanking you again, I am, with kindest regards,

Faithfully yours,   Ralph Pulitzer

TLS (WP, DLC).
    [1] See J. Davidson to WW, June 13, 1916.

To Edward Mandell House

The White House May 24 1916

Edith and I warmly appreciate invitation and regret with all our hearts we must start back at six   We lunch on the train

WW

T telegram (E. M. House Papers, CtY).

From Henry French Hollis

Dear Mr. President: [Washington] May 24, 1916

I am naturally disappointed that Mr. Rublee failed of confirmation.[1] Everything possible was done to get that extra vote, but it could not be effected. If Senator Jones of Washington had stayed with us, we should have had a margin of two votes. He was the one man that I could not cover personally so as to be sure where he stood. Senator La Follette and Senator Clapp thought that he would stand firm. They said as much to him on the subject as they dared to.

The Senate of the United States has not voted against George Rublee. They are evenly divided in spite of the anti-administration forces and the Senatorial courtesy rule. I very much hope that you will not appoint a successor to Mr. Rublee during this session of Congress and that you will give him another recess appointment. In no other way could you show so plainly your sympathy with the Progressive element in the Republican party. I shall hope to see you before long to talk this over. At least, I hope you will not appoint Mr. Rublee's successor until I have seen you.

Senator Clapp of Minnesota has stood with us firmly on the Rublee and Brandeis nominations. If a successor is to be appointed to Mr. Rublee, he wishes to present for your consideration Congressman Davis[2] of Minnesota, a Progressive Republican. I think it would be an excellent idea to talk this matter over with Senator Clapp before you make another appointment. I think he would appreciate the attention and I feel you would be glad to recognize him in any reasonable way.

I just have news of the favorable report on Mr. Brandeis by a strict party vote.[3] Politically, I think this could not be better. I think there will be no difficulty in confirming him before June first.   Sincerely,   Henry F. Hollis

TLS (WP, DLC).

[1] The Senate, on May 15, had rejected Rublee's nomination by a vote of forty-two to thirty-six. On May 23, a motion to reconsider the nomination was lost by a tie vote of thirty-eight to thirty-eight. Vice-President Marshall was absent and hence unable to break the tie. *New York Times*, May 16 and 24, 1916.

[2] That is, Charles Russell Davis.

[3] The Judiciary Committee had recommended Brandeis' confirmation by a vote of ten to eight on May 24.

To Sir Edward Grey

[New York, May 24, 1916]

I can assure you, on the authority of the President, that no thought of putting separate responsibility on Great Britain has ever been entertained here and that no influences to that end are at work in the State Department. The cases complained of with regard to the mails have all arisen out of the action of British authorities but a duplicate note will be sent to the French government.

WWhw draft telegram (E. M. House Papers, CtY).

A Memorandum

[May 24, 1916]

1) The right of every people to choose the sovereignty under which they shall live.

2) The right of small states to the same respect for their integrity and sovereignty that big states expect to enjoy.

3) The right of the world to be free from every disturbance of the peace that proceeds from aggression.

4) The willingness of the United States to go into a partnership for these objects. There is nothing that the United States wants for herself, and she is seeking to limit herself along with the others.

T transcript (WC, NjP) of WWsh MS (WP, DLC).

From the Diary of Colonel House

May 24, 1916.

Since the President is to come over for the Grayson-Gordon wedding, the usual accompaniments have followed and I have scarcely had time to breathe.

I went with Dudley Malone to meet the President at one o'clock. The first thing he told me was that the Senate Committee by a strict party vote had reported Brandeis' nomination favorably.

We drove to Miss Gordon's where we left Mrs. Wilson, and the President and I came to our apartment. He first suggested a drive, to which I assented. Afterward I thought it would not be possible for us to work in that way so we remained for an hour and a half working assiduously. It was one of the most important sittings we have had for a long while.

I showed him Sir Edward Grey's note to the British Ambassador,[1] and was surprised to hear him say that our note had already gone to the British Government. I asked him to send at once a duplicate to France, which he agreed to do. He thought it would be wise for me to cable Grey that this was being done. I handed him a pad and asked him to write what he thought should be sent. His memorandum is attached.

Miss Denton coded it at once. I have the advantage of the President in having a secretary to whom I can intrust every delicate and secret matter. The President seems entirely satisfied to accept my judgment of her discretion, and he knows that no one excepting himself, myself and Miss Denton have knowledge of these confidential negotiations.

We discussed the European situation and the futility of trying to please the different belligerents. I told him of my conversation with Gaunt.[2] I also read extracts from letters I had received from

[1] E. Grey to C. A. Spring Rice, May 23, 1916, TC telegram (E. M. House Papers, CtY). Grey said that the American note protesting against seizure of mails from neutral ships (about which see RL to WW, May 20, 1916, and WW to RL, May 22, 1916) should be sent to France as well as to Great Britain, since the mail seizures had been undertaken by both governments following the suggestion of the French government. In these circumstances, a protest sent to Great Britain alone would be regarded by that nation as "unfair and unfriendly."

[2] House invited Captain [Reginald Archer] Guy Gaunt, the naval attaché of the British embassy in Washington, to dine with him in his New York apartment on May 22. Gaunt told House that Australia (Gaunt had been born in Victoria, Australia), which had always regarded the United States as her ideal, bitterly resented the failure of the United States to enter the war on the side of the Allies, as did France also. "He believes," House wrote in his diary for May 22, "all the Allies are resolved that we shall have no part in the peace conference." "At this point," House recorded, "I began to talk and tell him how little we cared what they thought or did, if we were conscious we were right. The part we had taken, and the part we intended to take was entirely unselfish. We were the only nation that desired nothing, and I did not believe the democracies engaged in this fight would be stupid enough to refuse help from the greatest democracy of them all."

Paris, and a letter which had come from Sir Horace Plunkett.[3]
It is evident that unless the United States is willing to sacrifice
hundreds of thousands of lives and billions of treasure we are not
to be on good terms with the Allies.

One of the difficulties, I explained to the President, was that
neither Great Britain or the United States was represented in the
right way at Washington or London. We agreed it would be wise
in the circumstances to greatly modify the speech he is to make
next Saturday before the League to Enforce Peace. He is to treat
the subject as we have outlined it with the exception that he is not
to do more than hint at peace. He asked for a pad and made a
memorandum. We divided the subject into four parts, and indicated just how far he should go. I shall not give this in detail
for his speech itself will indicate our conclusions.

I asked if he thought it wise for him to see the French Ambassador and have a talk with him to inform him just what advantage France would have under the plan we have in mind. He
thought it would be better for me to see him. I cannot go to Washington, but will ask Jusserand to come over, although I understand he has not left Washington for a year or more.

I explained France's real feeling, that is, she had best stick to
this war until Germany is crushed, for she could never again hope
to have Great Britain, Russia, Italy and Belgium fighting by her
side.

I spoke about the New York political situation and outlined
it as I saw it. He agreed that Dudley Malone would be a satisfactory man for Senator and authorized me to arrange it if it could
be done without involving him. He authorized me to offer Governor Glynn a place on the shipping Board when it is created. I told
him Glynn could fill any position and could be put in the Cabinet
with safety. He thought the country would not approve of his putting a Catholic in the Cabinet. I disagreed with him and contended that the country would not object in the slightest. What
they do object to is having the President's Secretary a Catholic.
Many Protestants do not believe that communications reach the
President. While this is probably not true, nevertheless, the feeling cannot be overcome. Much to my surprise, the President
asked me to suggest some[one] for Secretary in Tumulty's place.
I asked him when he would make the change, and he again surprised me by saying, "immediately, if I can find the right man. I
will offer Tumulty something else."

I took this occasion of telling him if Tumulty is a mistake,
McAdoo and I are responsible for it. I remember quite well the

3 H. Plunkett to EMH, April 20, 1916, TLS (E. M. House Papers, CtY).

type of man the President desired for that important and responsible place, and I persuaded him to take Tumulty. I knew Tumulty but slightly, and took him at McAdoo's estimate. I remember, too, that he thought it would not be a place in which to have a Catholic. Again, I overcame his objections. The truth is my experience had been limited to gubernatorial secretaries and I did not realize the difference.

Knowing that Governor Hamlin's term on the Federal Reserve Board expires during the summer we discussed his reappointment. We also talked of McAdoo's probable resignation. He suggested Houston for his place and I warmly endorsed it. I suggested to the President that he show Lansing his speech before he makes it Saturday night. He promised to do this because he said the speech was of such importance that he dared not deliver it extemporaneously. He is to write it between now and Saturday for he has the matter of it well in hand.

I urged him to accelerate the Navy program and to mention it in his speech Saturday. We decided upon what he should say. It will not please the British, but it will please Americans and I shall be content with that. The balance of the speech will not please the Germans and the Allies should take comfort there.

We talked of Mexico and of the hopelessness of that situation. I thought it was an economic problem and we should reach it in that way through governmental aid. He thought I was right, but declared Congress would never take such a step. I believed it would if he would get back of it properly, which I doubt being able to get him to do. Poor man, I hate to crowd more work upon his shoulders, and yet it is important for him to settle the Mexico question with something more of vigor than he has yet shown.

We talked of the Vice Presidentcy and whether we should sidetrack Marshall and give the nomination to Baker. He felt that Baker was too good a man to be sacrificed. I disagreed with him. I did not think any man was too good to be considered for Vice President of the United States. I thought if the right man took it, a man who had his confidence as Baker has, a new office could be created out of it. He might become Vice President in fact as well as in name, and be a co-worker and co-helper of the President. He was interested in this argument but was unconvinced that Baker should, as he termed it, be sacrificed. He was afraid he could not educate the people in four years up to the possibilities of the office. He reminded me that no Vice President had ever succeeded a President by election.[4]

---

[4] Wilson had obviously forgotten John Adams, Jefferson, Van Buren, and Theodore Roosevelt.

The President showed some signs of fatigue and it was time for him to call for Mrs. Wilson to take her to the wedding. We went to the door together. There was a large crowd assembled to see him come out and I was gratified to hear the cheers that greeted him.

Loulie and I went to the wedding and afterward to the reception at Miss Gordon's apartment at No. 12 West 10th Street. It was a notable wedding and a notable gathering.

I had a few minutes conversation with Mrs. Wilson and with the President. Afterward, McAdoo and I motored for an hour in order to have some talk. The President evidently does not tell McAdoo much of what is in his mind. I was surprised to find that he knew so little excepting of matters current in his own department.

T MS (E. M. House Papers, CtY).

Two Letters from Robert Lansing

PERSONAL AND PRIVATE:

My dear Mr. President: Washington May 24, 1916.

Here is a characteristic CONFIDENTIAL communication from Ambassador Gerard.[1] I think you will find it of interest and of possible information on certain subjects.

You will oblige me if you will return it for my files after reading.   Faithfully yours,   Robert Lansing.

TLS (SDR, RG 59, 763.72/2757½, DNA).
  [1] J. W. Gerard to RL, May 10, 1916, TLS and T memorandum (SDR, RG 59, 763.72/2757½, DNA). Scattered among his usual gossip were a few points of interest: that he had become "great friends" with Bethmann at Charleville; that the Germans would "gladly" accept Wilson's mediation; and that half the products in German army stores came from Holland. The typed memorandum concerned a report in the Berlin *Continental Times* to the effect that Gerard had heard of Sir Roger Casement's plan to land in Ireland, that Gerard had sent this news to Wilson in cipher, and that Wilson, or two members of his cabinet, had betrayed Casement to Spring Rice.

PERSONAL AND PRIVATE:

My dear Mr. President: Washington May 25, 1916.

I had hoped to see you tomorrow at Cabinet meeting but today the Doctor refused to allow me to leave the house this week. I intended when I saw you to say something about the purposes of the League to Enforce Peace, which is to meet here, and at the banquet of which I understand you are to speak on Saturday night. I would have preferred to talk the matter over with you but as that is impossible I have taken the liberty to write you this letter, although in doing so I am violating the directions of the Doctor.

While I have not had time or opportunity to study carefully the objects of the proposed League to Enforce Peace, I understand the fundamental ideas are these, which are to be embodied in a general treaty of the nations: *First*, an agreement to submit all differences which fail of diplomatic adjustment to arbitration or a board of conciliation; and, *second*, in case a government fails to comply with this provision, an agreement that the other parties will unite in compelling it to do so by an exercise of force.

With the first agreement I am in accord to an extent, but I cannot see how it is practicable to apply it in case of a continuing invasion of fundamental national or individual rights unless some authoritative international body has the power to impose and enforce an order in the nature of an injunction, which will prevent the ag[g]ressor from further action until arbitration has settled the rights of the parties. How this can be done in a practical way I have not attempted to work out, but the problem is not easy, especially the part which relates to the enforcement of the order.

It is, however, the second agreement in regard to the imposition of international arbitration by force, which seems to me the most difficult, especially when viewed from the standpoint of its effects on our national sovereignty and national interests. It is needless to go into the manifest questions arising when the *modus operandi* of the agreement is considered. Such questions as: Who may demand international intervention? What body will decide whether the demand should be complied with? How will the international forces be constituted? Who will take charge of the military and naval operations? Who will pay the expenses of the war (for war it will be)?

Perplexing as these questions appear to me, I am more concerned with the direct effect on this country. I do not believe that it is wise to limit our independence of action, a sovereign right, to the will of other powers beyond this hemisphere. In any representative international body clothed with authority to require of the nations to employ their armies and navies to coerce one of their number, we would be in the minority. I do not believe that we should put ourselves in the position of being compelled to send our armed forces to Europe or Asia or, in the alternative, of repudiating our treaty obligation. Neither our sovereignty nor our interests would accord with such a proposition, and I am convinced that popular opinion as well as the Senate would reject a treaty framed along such lines.

It is possible that the difficulty might be obviated by the establishment of geographical zones, and leaving to the groups of nations thus formed the enforcement of the peaceful settlement
of disputes. But if that is done why should all the world participate? We have adopted a much modified form of this idea in
the proposed Pan-American Treaty by the "guaranty" article. But
I would not like to see its stipulations extended to the European
powers so that they, with our full agreement, would have the right
to cross the ocean and stop quarrels between two American
Republics. Such authority would be a serious menace to the
Monroe Doctrine and a greater menace to the Pan-American
Doctrine.

It appears to me that, if the first ideas of the League can be
worked out in a practical way and an international body constituted to determine when steps should be taken to enforce
compliance, that the use of force might be avoided by outlawing
the offending nation. No nation today can live unto itself. The
industrial and commercial activities of the world are too closely
interwoven for a nation isolated from the other nations to thrive
and prosper. A tremendous economic pressure could be imposed
on the outlawed nation by all other nations denying it intercourse
of every nature, even communication, in a word make that nation
a pariah, and so to remain until it was willing to perform its
obligations.

I am not at all sure that this means is entirely feasible. I see
many difficulties which would have to be met under certain conditions. But I do think that it is more practical in operation and
less objectionable from the standpoint of national rights and interests than the one proposed by the League. It does not appear
to me that the use of physical force is in any way practical or
advisable.

I presume that you are far more familiar than I am with the
details of the plans of the League and that it may be presumptious
on my part to write you as I have. I nevertheless felt it my duty
to frankly give you my views on the subject and I have done so.

Faithfully yours,   Robert Lansing

TLS (WP, DLC).

To Robert Lansing

My dear Mr. Recretary,   The White House. 25 May, 1916.

I am deeply distressed that you should still of necessity be confined to the house. I am glad that you are obeying the orders of

the doctor and taking the necessary precautions to ensure your recovery. We shall all be exceedingly glad when you are well and free again.

Thank you for letting me see the enclosed papers. I have read them with the greatest interest.

Faithfully Yours,   W.W.

WWTLI (SDR, RG 59, 763.72/2758½, DNA).

From Simon Wolf

To the President: Washington, D. C. May 25, 1916.
I had the honor on February 9, 1915, of addressing you as follows:

"As Chairman of the Board of Delegates of the Union of American Hebrew Congregations, and as resident member of the Executive Committee of the International Order of B'nai B'rith, I beg to present to you the wishes of your fellow citizens of Jewish faith, who are, in every sense of the word, patriotic and loyal American citizens, and therefore are deeply concerned in the outcome of the present war when terms of peace shall be determined on. You are well aware of the conditions of our co-religionists in certain parts of Europe; that for centuries in those countries they have been denied equal rights, either political or religious, in consequence of which a large number have sought refuge in this land of opportunity, and that unless our Government can be instrumental in securing those rights, to the enjoyment of which they have so far been denied, the influx of such refugees from the land of oppression will not only continue, but be largely increased.

"John Hay, when Secretary of State, made this proposition very clear in his famous Roumanian note.[1] He regarded the persecution of the Jews as an act of hostility to the United States, as it brought to our shores immigrants that would have remained in the land of their birth, were they treated in a spirit of fairness and justice.

"We do not believe that at any time in the world's history has the time been so opportune to secure equal rights for the Jews in Europe as at the time when terms of peace shall be agreed upon by the belligerent powers. The United States Government has a vantage ground equaled by none; one that can, I am sure, through your wise and sane statesmanship, become a dominating factor in the solution of this great and important question. It will not only be conducive to the welfare and prosperity of the people in question, but aid very materially the citizens of the United States, and we, therefore, must respectfully but earnestly suggest that you give this great international problem due consideration to the end of securing justice.

"With sincere regards, I have the honor, Mr. President, to subscribe myself,

"Your very obedient servant and fellow citizen."
to which on April 7, 1915, you were kind enough to answer as follows:

"I read with the greatest interest the letter you were kind enough to leave with me a short time ago bearing the signatures of representatives of the Order of B'nai B'rith and the Hebrew Congregations of the United States. I beg that you will assure those who were kind enough to send me this interesting letter that I follow from time to time with the greatest interest the fine work of the organizations which they represent, work which undoubtedly contributes to the uplift and betterment of the nation, and I have been particularly interested in the work of education and philanthropy and the effort to destroy so far as they can the provincialism of prejudice as between races.

"Will you not be kind enough to convey to them my warm appreciation of their letter and my assurance that whenever and in whatever way it may be possible for me to serve the interests which they represent, I shall conceive it a privilege to do so?

"Cordially and sincerely yours,"
Since that date various groups of American citizens of Jewish faith have concluded to call a congress for the purpose of formulating plans to secure equal rights for their co-religionists in every part of the world, especially in Russia and Roumania. In the present European conditions, it is hard to prognosticate or conclude as to what may or may not be done when the belligerents shall have concluded on terms of peace, but when that hour comes, we wish to be assured on the part of our great Government, so far as the Executive can promise, that every means consistent with diplomacy and with the demands of humanity, shall be exercised to secure those rights which are inherent in every human-being, and which when conceded by all Nations, will strengthen the kinship, no matter what the nationality or creed may be, and materially contribute to solve a great problem, coincident with the prosperity and development of the United States.

Is it asking too much, my dear Mr. President, for you to express yourself as far as is consistent and proper at this juncture, that your determination to do the right thing at the right time has not changed; on the contrary, has been accentuated by the present conditions and by the ultimate prospects of universal peace.   Very sincerely yours,   Simon Wolf

TLS (WP, DLC).
1 J. Hay to C. L. Wilson, July 17, 1902, printed in *FR* 1902, pp. 910-14.

To Franklin Knight Lane

My dear Lane: [The White House] May 26, 1916

I know that I showed the other day in our discussion at the Cabinet how deeply interested I am and how much perplexed I am about the oil question and the naval reserve in California. No doubt it is unnecessary to ask you if you will do me the favor to hold up any patents that might otherwise be issued until I can have looked into the matter a little further, but for fear my desire in that matter was not made sufficiently clear in the debate, I am writing to ask this of you now. I want to have a full talk with you about the matter just as soon as I have studied it a little further.

                 Cordially and faithfully yours,   Woodrow Wilson

TLS (Letterpress Books, WP, DLC).

To William Gibbs McAdoo

My dear Mac: [The White House] May 26, 1916

I am distressed that anything should have occurred in New York which was mortifying or uncomfortable for you and Nell.[1] I took it for granted that the Secret Service men knew how our little group ought to be handled, though I suppose they can hardly be held responsible since that is not part of their job.

I have no master of ceremonies to whom such things in connection with journeys away from home can be referred, and so feel personally responsible. I can only send my apologies for not having attended to the matter.

         Always   Affectionately yours,   Woodrow Wilson

TLS (Letterpress Books, WP, DLC).
1 The McAdoos attended the wedding of Dr. Grayson and Miss Gordon but arrived separately from the Wilson party. The police, who had cordoned off the square in front of the church, and who had instructions to screen all guests, probably asked the McAdoos for identification.

To Joseph R. Wilson, Jr.

Dear Joe: [The White House] May 26, 1916

Our plans have been so conjectural that I have not sooner been able to write you about Tuesday night.

It is evident, my dear fellow, that we can't get off in time to dine with you, but we shall count on you to go to the show with us. It will be delightful to have Kate and Alice and you there. I have no idea what the show is to be or how good, but we can, at any rate, have a jolly time together. It is to be at the Academy of Music.

I am going to send over an extra car and have it call for you and bring you to the theatre under the escort of somebody who will know how to get you into the box if we don't happen to arrive at the same time.

In haste, with love from us all,
          Your affectionate brother,   Woodrow Wilson

TLS (Letterpress Books, WP, DLC).

From Edward Mandell House, with Enclosure

Dear Governor: New York, May 26, 1916.

The enclosed cable from Sir Edward Grey came last night. I did not think it important enough to repeat to you by wire.

Captain Gaunt, British Naval Attache, who has just returned from Washington tells me that Spring-Rice and Jusserand had a conference concerning the mail seizure note and they had decided there was no conflict of principle that could not be met. They thought, however, some sentences in the note were unnecessarily harsh and made for bad feeling instead of good. They thought the same thing might have been said in a softer tone.

Gaunt told me this in great confidence and it is not supposed to be repeated to you.

He said the British Government were much disturbed over the trouble brewing in Nicaragua and British Honduras and also Mexico. That there were indications of renewed German activities in those countries.

Whether you succeed in starting a peace movement at this time or not you are making I think, a good record to go before the world with. If the dead-lock continues and peace is finally made when the armies are practically where they are today, it will be a great indictment against the British and French Governments. The only thing that could justify their stubbornness would be a complete military success which does not see[m] possible.   Affectionately yours,   E. M. House

TLS (WP, DLC).

E N C L O S U R E

May 25, 1916.

Your two last telegrams and letter are being carefully considered by my colleagues and I hope to send a reply very soon.

E. Grey.

TC telegram (WP, DLC).

An Address in Washington to the League to Enforce Peace

[May 27, 1916]

When the invitation to be here tonight came to me, I was glad to accept it—not because it offered me an opportunity to discuss the program of the League—that you will, I am sure, not expect of me—but because the desire of the whole world now turns eagerly, more and more eagerly, towards the hope of peace,[1] and there is just reason why we should take our part in counsel upon this great theme. It is right that I, as spokesman of our government, should attempt to give expression to what I believe to be the thought and purpose of the people of the United States in this vital matter.

This great war that broke so suddenly upon the world two years ago, and which has swept within its flame so great a part of the civilized world, has affected us very profoundly, and we are not only at liberty, it is perhaps our duty, to speak very frankly of it and of the great interests of civilization which it affects.

With its causes and its objects we are not concerned. The obscure fountains from which its stupendous flood has burst forth we are not interested to search for or explore. But so great a flood, spread far and wide to every quarter of the globe, has of necessity engulfed many a fair province of right that lies very near to us. Our own rights as a nation, the liberties, the privileges, and the property of our people have been profoundly affected. We are not mere disconnected lookers-on. The longer the war lasts, the more deeply do we become concerned that it should be brought to an end and the world be permitted to resume its

[1] In his shorthand draft of this address (WP, DLC), Wilson struck out the following at this point: "and while we have the attention of the whole world it is."

normal life and course again. And when it does come to an end, we shall be as much concerned as the nations at war to see peace assume an aspect of permanence, give promise of days from which the anxiety of uncertainty shall be lifted, bring some assurance that peace and war shall always hereafter be reckoned part of the common interest of mankind. We are participants, whether we would or not, in the life of the world. The interests of all nations are our own also. We are partners with the rest. What affects mankind is inevitably our affair as well as the affair of the nations of Europe and of Asia.

One observation on the causes of the present war we are at liberty to make, and to make it may throw some light forward upon the future, as well as backward upon the past.[2] It is plain that this war could have come only as it did, suddenly and out of secret counsels, without warning to the world, without discussion, without any of the deliberate movements of counsel with which it would seem natural to approach so stupendous a contest. It is probable that, if it had been foreseen just what would happen, just what alliances would be formed, just what forces arrayed against one another, those who brought the great contest on would have been glad to substitute conference for force. If we ourselves had been afforded some opportunity to apprise the belligerents of the attitude which it would be our duty to take, of the policies and practices against which we would feel bound to use all our moral and economic strength, and in certain circumstances even our physical strength also, our own contribution to the counsel which might have averted the struggle would have been considered worth weighing and regarding.

And the lesson which the shock of being taken by surprise in a matter so deeply vital to all the nations of the world has made poignantly clear is that the peace of the world must henceforth depend upon a new and more wholesome diplomacy. Only when the great nations of the world have reached some sort of agreement as to what they hold to be fundamental to their common interest, and as to some feasible method of acting in concert when any nation or group of nations seeks to disturb those fundamental things, can we feel that civilization is at last in a way of justifying its existence and claiming to be finally established. It is clear that nations must in the future be governed by the same high code of honor that we demand of individuals.

We must, indeed, in the very same breath with which we avow this conviction admit that we have ourselves upon occasion in the past been offenders against the law of diplomacy which we

2 Here Wilson's shorthand draft reads: "House's first two paragraphs."

thus forecast; but our conviction is not the less clear, but rather
the more clear, on that account. If this war has accomplished
nothing else for the benefit of the world, it has at least disclosed
a great moral necessity and set forward the thinking of the statesmen of the world by a whole age. Repeated utterances of the leading statesmen of most of the great nations now engaged in war
have made it plain that their thought has come to this[3]—that
the principle of public right must henceforth take precedence
over the individual interests of particular nations, and that the
nations of the world must in some way band themselves together
to see that that right prevails as against any sort of selfish aggression; that henceforth alliance must not be set up against alliance,
understanding against understanding, but that there must be a
common agreement for a common object, and that at the heart
of that common object must lie the inviolable rights of peoples
and of mankind. The nations of the world have become each
other's neighbors. It is to their interest that they should understand each other. In order that they may understand each other,
it is imperative that they should agree to cooperate in a common cause, and that they should so act that the guiding principle
of that common cause shall be evenhanded and impartial justice.

This is undoubtedly the thought of America. This is what we
ourselves will say when there comes proper occasion to say it. In
the dealings of nations with one another, arbitrary force must be
rejected and we must move forward to the thought of the modern
world, the thought of which peace is the very atmosphere. That
thought constitutes a chief part of the passionate conviction of
America.

We believe these fundamental things: First, that every people
has a right to choose the sovereignty under which they shall live.
Like other nations, we have ourselves no doubt once and again
offended against that principle when for a little while controlled
by selfish passion, as our franker historians have been honorable
enough to admit; but it has become more and more our rule of
life and action. Second, that the small states of the world have a
right to enjoy the same respect for their sovereignty and for their
territorial integrity that great and powerful nations expect and
insist upon. And, third, that the world has a right to be free from
every disturbance of its peace that has its origin in aggression and
disregard of the rights of peoples and nations.[4]

So sincerely do we believe in these things that I am sure that I
speak the mind and wish of the people of America when I say

[3] Here Wilson's shorthand draft reads: "See addresses quoted by House."
[4] There is a WWsh outline of this paragraph in WP, DLC.

that the United States is willing to become a partner in any feasible association of nations formed in order to realize these objects and make them secure against violation.

There is nothing that the United States wants for itself that any other nation has. We are willing, on the contrary, to limit ourselves along with them to a prescribed course of duty and respect for the rights of others which will check any selfish passion of our own, as it will check any aggressive impulse of theirs.

If it should ever be our privilege to suggest or initiate a movement for peace among the nations now at war, I am sure that the people of the United States would wish their government to move along these lines:[5] First, such a settlement with regard to their own immediate interests as the belligerents may agree upon. We have nothing material of any kind to ask for ourselves, and are quite aware that we are in no sense or degree parties to the present quarrel. Our interest is only in peace and its future guarantees. Second, an universal association of the nations to maintain the inviolate security of the highway of the seas for the common and unhindered use of all the nations of the world, and to prevent any war begun either contrary to treaty covenants or without warning and full submission of the causes to the opinion of the world—a virtual guarantee of territorial integrity and political independence.

But I did not come here, let me repeat, to discuss a program. I came only to avow a creed and give expression to the confidence I feel that the world is even now upon the eve of a great consummation,[6] when some common force will be brought into existence which shall safeguard right as the first and most fundamental interest of all peoples and all governments, when coercion shall be summoned not to the service of political ambition or selfish hostility, but to the service of a common order, a common justice, and a common peace. God grant that the dawn of that day of frank dealing and of settled peace, concord, and cooperation may be near at hand![7]

Printed reading copy (WP, DLC).
    [5] Here Wilson's shorthand draft reads: "See copy of letter to House."
    [6] Here Wilson's shorthand draft reads: "Return to 2nd paragraph House's suggestions."
    [7] There is also an elaborate WWsh outline of this address in WP, DLC.

From Edward Mandell House

[New York, May 27, 1916]

Following cable received from Sir E.G. "Much relieved note about mails is to be addressed to both France and ourselves. This will greatly facilitate discussion of the question. My colleagues will have what I hope will be final answer discussion of your telegram on Monday and I hope to telegraph you then. You will realize how difficult and delicate is the consideration any public statement about a conference to end a war in which we are united to Allies. Convention to maintain peace after war   Have no doubts about present same difficulties["]

EBWhw decode (WP, DLC) of T telegram (WP, DLC).

Norman Hapgood to Joseph Patrick Tumulty

The White House Saturday
Dear Mr. Tumulty: May 27 9:15 a.m. [1916]
Harris, Rublee, and several others think I am the person to tell the President the truth about recent events.[1] It is not a pleasant job, but I can't very well dodge it. It ought to be done, for the future good of the Commission, as well as for other reasons. I have to leave Washington Thursday morning, to be gone some time. Will you fix up a few minutes with the President before then? I shall be greatly obliged.[2]
Yours sincerely   Norman Hapgood

Harris, Stevens, and Hurley want to take up other aspects, but they do not care to deal with the more personal side of it.

ALS (WP, DLC).
[1] A bitter personal struggle had been going on in the Federal Trade Commission for many months between Joseph E. Davies, chairman, and Edward N. Hurley, vice-chairman. Davies charged that Hurley, a former president of the Illinois Manufacturers' Association was a reactionary and wanted to turn the F.T.C. into an agency friendly to big business and one that failed to protect small competitors. J. E. Davies to E. M. House, June 9, 1916, TLS (E. M. House Papers, CtY). Hurley, as documents in this and other volumes reveal, had been striving hard to make the F.T.C. a friend and counselor to businessmen, particularly small businessmen, and was a strong supporter of business cooperation through trade associations.
[2] Hapgood met with Wilson at the White House at 12:15 P.M. on Wednesday, May 31. See J. E. Davies to WW, June 10, 1916.

From Edward Mandell House

Dear Governor: New York, May 28, 1916.
I cannot tell you how pleased I am with your speech last night. It will be a land mark in history. Mezes agrees with me in this estimate and I am sure this will be the general verdict.
Vance McCormick was with me for a long sitting today. Much to my surprise he tells me he does not believe he can accept the Chairmanship of the National Committee. He gi[v]es personal

reasons. He thinks, too, that his record on the liquor question would make him undesirable for the place. As a matter of fact, he stands just where you do, that is he is for local option, but the fight was so bitter against him that the liquor interests were practically all arrayed on the other side when he made his campaign for Governor.

He thinks he is "a spotted man" and would be considered unfriendly to the anti-prohibitionists. What do you think of this?

Jusserand comes Wednesday and I will give him the talk we agreed upon. I believe it will do good.

The weather is growing so warm and I am so beset on all sides that I am afraid I shall have to leave in a few days for cooler surroundings where I can work to better advantage. I would soon be incapacited here.

Affectionately yours,   E. M. House

TLS (WP, DLC).

To Edward Mandell House

Dearest Friend,   The White House. 29 May, 1916.

I am immensely pleased that you approved and liked the speech. I was handling critical matter and was trying to put it in a way that it would be very hard for the Allies to reject, as well as for Germany.

There is a good deal in what McCormick urges about the questions associated with his name in Pennsylvania. I should like to have your own candid judgment.

And, if not Vance McCormick, who? What can we do without him. I confess to being myself at a loss, unless we are to turn again to Polk.

The Speaker declines to be permanent chairman,[1] and for very good reasons connected with the work of Congress.

What would you say to Ollie James, who could physically dominate the Convention, who was originally a Clark man, and a Bryan man too, for that matter, and who would make a stunning speech. The speech he made at the Kentucky convention was very remarkable and very telling? He has been one of the most generous and consistent supporters of the Administration in the Senate throughout the whole of the time since it came in.

Be sure not to linger too long in this heat. Much as I hate to see you go further away, you must take no risks.

Affectionately Yours,   Woodrow Wilson

WWTLS (E. M. House Papers, CtY).
[1] Of the St. Louis convention.

To Simon Wolf

Personal.

My dear Mr. Wolf: [The White House] May 29, 1916

I have your letter of May twenty-fifth. I hope that it is not necessary for me to state again my determination to do the right and possible thing at the right and feasible time with regard to the great interests you so eloquently allude to in your letter.

I hope that I may be fully apprised of the results of the congress to which you are looking forward and of the plans which they may think it best to suggest.

Cordially and sincerely yours,   Woodrow Wilson

TLS (Letterpress Books, WP, DLC).

To William Gibbs McAdoo

My dear Mac.,   The White House. 29 May, 1916.

I fear we shall have to accept the Speaker's decision: the reasons he gives are very cogent; but I hope that you will express to him my very great and sincere regret. I wish there were some right way of getting him free for the service, which would be a very great one. I had heard it suggested that the House would adjourn for the period of the convention, though I wondered how it would do that in the case of one of the conventions and not in that of the other.

Have you any suggestion as to Permanent Chairman now that the Speaker has declined?   Affectionately Yours,   W.W.

WWTLI (W. G. McAdoo Papers, DLC).

From Charles Richard Crane

Dear Mr President   Woods Hole Massachusetts May 29 1916

I am very happy about the speech on Saturday evening. It is a fine use you have put this hemisphere to during the last two years. You have made a kind of laboratory of it to try out ideas that will certainly be of service to the world later on. I am especially happy about your declaration regarding the smaller nations. Very often their ideals are more precious to them and more necessary to their comfort and welfare than almost any economic condition. And I have been much among the small nations and feel very close to them. I am also glad to see you facing the fourth year of your administration with so much serenity. I feel that it will be the most convincing one of them all and I would not allow any possible condition to in any way qualify the high standard you have set and which I am sure will be appealed to for many years to come. It certainly is most inspiring to be shown that it is possible to govern a strong commercial and industrial democracy without the slightest disloyalty to the highest ideals, *and make it go*. Four years of it were very necessary to establish the principle. We shall pray for eight years of it but that is not so vital. So please "go to it" strong for the fourth year!

With affectionate greetings to you, the pretty lady and the children,   Always faithfully   Charles R. Crane

ALS (WP, DLC).

From Hamilton Holt

To the President   New York May 29, 1916

I have had no severer disappointment in my life than not to have been present to hear your epochal address before the League to Enforce Peace on Saturday night. After giving my address Friday before the League I was summoned home to the bedside of my brother[1] who is desperately ill with pneumonia. But I cannot help writing to tell you how much the American people, and the world, are in your debt for this utterance which cannot fail to rank in political importance with the Declaration of Independence and the Monroe Doctrine.

I am sending you under separate cover a copy of The Independent out tomorrow, in which the first three editorials feebly express some of my views on the subject.[2]

The League to Enforce Peace, of which I am one of the founders, I am sure will do everything in its power to acquaint the public of the United States with the principles which you have laid down, and I hope and trust that when the Great War is over, and the nations assemble around the common board to establish the basis of a durable peace at that supreme hour, thanks to your leadership, the United States will stand united for your great practical proposal which is destined to enthrone reason instead of force as the arbiter of the destinies of nations.

                              Yours respectfully   Hamilton Holt

TLS (WP, DLC).
    [1] Henry Chandler Holt, Hamilton's only surviving brother. He died on February 20, 1955.
    [2] "The President on the Enforcement of Peace," "A Declaration of Interdependence," and "The League to Enforce Peace," *The Independent*, LXXXVI (June 5, 1916), 357-58. The editorials summarized Wilson's address before the League to Enforce Peace and emphasized his statements on self-determination

and equality among nations. Holt viewed Wilson's statements as an "almost official endorsement" of the principles of the League to Enforce Peace. Holt expressed the hope that Wilson might develop the basis for a lasting peace. Then, after giving a brief history of the idea for a league of peace, Holt said that Wilson was now, as spokesman for the United States, "at the head of this movement to enthrone reason instead of force as the final arbiter of the destinies of nations."

From Edward Mandell House

Dear Governor: New York. May 29, 1916.

Do you not think that your speech before the League to Enforce Peace should be endorsed by the St Louis Convention?

Many people with whom I have talked today regard it as the real democratic platform. Some of them say it leaves the republicans without a single issue either foreign or domestic. That Taft, Root, Choate and most of the republican leaders are compelled to endorse it because of their previous positions.

I am delighted the way it has been accepted. I expected some criticism and you have gotten it, but the chorus of approval makes the criticism seem very vain and partisan.

Affectionately yours,   E. M. House

TLS (WP, DLC).

From Newton Diehl Baker

My dear Mr. President: Washington. May 29, 1916.

I am leaving to-night for Ohio, and will return on Friday morning with my family. The Ohio Convention is on Thursday, so that unless I should be suddenly needed I will not return until after that day.

I have asked General Scott to take up with you directly any developments on the Mexican border. There is apparently a substantial accumulation of troops by the De Facto Government in the neighborhood of Chihuahua. Newspaper reports attribute aggressive intentions to these troops, but General Funston has sent a personal messenger to Chihuahua to get accurate information, and until his messenger has returned and reported to him we can have no sure judgment of the situation.

Should the note from General Carranza which is reputed to be on its way[1] to you turn out to be a peremptory demand for immediate withdrawal or otherwise show hostile intentions on the part of the Mexican Government, it would seem desirable to increase the forces on the border at once, both as a safeguard against surprise and as a moral deterrent to aggression.

General Scott and I have talked over the situation and are agreed upon the Militia forces next to be summoned in the event any are needed, our general thought being that it would be better to take troops from southern States who are to some extent acclimated to the hot weather which will be experienced in Texas, and also not to rob the States of Militia in which there are large cities.

I shall keep in touch with the Department by telegraph, and will of course return should there be any sudden change in the situation.   Cordially yours,   Newton D. Baker

TLS (WP, DLC).
  ¹ See F. L. Polk to WW, June 1, 1916, n. 1.

Frank Lyon Polk to the American Embassy, Santiago

Washington, May 29, 1916. 3 pm

About a month ago the Brazilian Ambassador here presented on behalf of Brazil and Chile, a counter proposal for the Pan American treaty.¹ This counter proposal was amended in a few particulars by the President and unofficially returned to the Braziliam Ambassador and has been communicated through his Government to the Chilean Government.

The Department learns that Brazil has accepted our amendments and is endeavoring to persuade Chile to do so also. Discreetly ascertain unofficially the attitude of the Chilean Government in regard to our amendments and urge favorable reply. Period. For your confidential information, Lauro Muller expects to sail from Rio June seventh to visit the United States.

Polk

T telegram (SDR, RG 59, 710.11/284, DNA).
  ¹ It is printed at May 3, 1916, Vol. 36.

A Proclamation

[*May 30, 1916*]

My Fellow-Countrymen: Many circumstances have recently conspired to turn our thoughts to a critical examination of the conditions of our national life, of the influences which have seemed to threaten to divide us in interest and sympathy, of forces within and forces without that seemed likely to draw us away from the happy traditions of united purpose and action of which we have been so proud.

It has, therefore, seemed to me fitting that I should call your attention to the approach of the anniversary of the day upon which the flag of the United States was adopted by the Congress as the emblem of the Union, and to suggest to you that it should, this year and in the years to come, be given special significance as a day of renewal and reminder, a day upon which we should direct our minds with a special desire of renewal to thoughts of the ideals and principles of which we have sought to make our great Government the embodiment.

I, therefore, suggest and request that throughout the nation, and if possible in every community, the 14th day of June be observed as Flag Day with special patriotic exercises, at which means shall be taken to give significant expression to our thoughtful love of America, our comprehension of the great mission of liberty and justice to which we have devoted ourselves as a people, our pride in the history and our enthusiasm for the political program of the nation, our determination to make it greater and purer with each generation, and our resolution to demonstrate to all the world its vital union in sentiment and purpose, accepting only those as true compatriots who feel as we do the compulsion of this supreme allegiance.

Let us on that day rededicate ourselves to the nation, "one and inseparable," from which every thought that is not worthy of our fathers' first views of independence, liberty, and right shall be excluded, and in which we shall stand with united hearts for an America which no man can corrupt, no influence draw away from its ideals, no force divide against itself, a nation signally distinguished among all the nations of mankind for its clear, individual conception alike of its duties and its privileges, its obligations and its rights.

Printed in the *New York Times*, May 31, 1916.

A Memorial Day Address[1]

[[May 30, 1916]]

Mr. Chairman, ladies, and gentlemen: Whenever I seek to interpret the spirit of an occasion like this, I am led to reflect upon the uses of memory. We are here today to recall a period of our history which, in one sense, is so remote that we no longer seem to keep the vital threads of it in our consciousness, and yet is so near that men who played heroic parts in it are still living, are still about us, are still here to receive the homage of our respect and our honor. They belong to an age which is past, to

1 Delivered in the amphitheater at Arlington National Cemetery. The Grand Army of the Republic sponsored the affair. The Rt. Rev. Alfred Harding, Bishop of Washington, the Rev. Henry Noble Couden, chaplain of the House of Representatives, and Osborn Hamiline Oldroyd, a past president of the Potomac Division of the G.A.R., were among the speakers.

a period the vital questions of which no longer vex the nation, to a period of which it may be said that certain things which had been questionable in the affairs of the United States were once for all settled, disposed of, put behind us, and, in the course of time, have almost been forgotten.

It was a singularly complete work that was performed by the processes of blood and iron at the time of the Civil War, and it is singular how the settlement has ruled our spirits since it was made. I see in this very audience men who fought in the Confederate ranks. I see them taking part in these exercises in the same spirit of sincere patriotism that moves those who fought on the side of the Union. And I reflect how singular and how handsome a thing it is that wounds such as then were opened should be so completely healed, and that the spirit of America should so prevail over the spirit of division. It is the all-prevailing and triumphant spirit of America, where, by our common action and consent, governments are set up and pulled down, where affairs are ruled by common counsel; and where, by the healing processes of peace, all men are united in a common enterprise of liberty and of peace.

And yet, ladies and gentlemen, the very object for which we are met together is to renew in our hearts the spirit that made these things possible. The Union was saved by the processes of the Civil War. That was a crisis which could be handled, it seems, in no other way. But I need not tell you that the peculiarity of this singular and beloved country is that its task, its human task, is apparently never finished, that it is always making and to be made. And there is at present upon us a crisis which at one time seemed to threaten to be a new crisis of division. We know that the war which is to ensue will be a war of spirits and not of arms. We know that the spirit of America is invincible, and that no man can abate its power. But we know that that spirit must, upon occasion, be asserted, and that this is one of the occasions. America is made up out of all the nations of the world. Look at the rosters of the Civil War. You will see names there drawn from almost every European stock. Not recently, but from the first, America has drawn her blood and her impulse from all the sources of energy that spring from the fountains of every race. And, because she is thus compounded out of the peoples of the world, her problem is largely a problem of union all the time—a problem of compounding out of many elements a single triumphant force.

The war in Europe has done a very natural thing in America. It has stirred the memories of men drawn from many of the

belligerent stocks. It has renewed in them a national feeling
which had grown faint under the soothing influences of peace,
but which now flares up when it looks as if nation had chal-
lenged nation to a final reckoning, and they remember the nations from which they spring and know that they are in this
life and death struggle. It is not singular, my fellow citizens, that
this should have occurred, and up to a certain point it is not just
that we should criticize it. We have no criticism for men who love
the places of their birth and the sources of their origin. We do
not wish men to forget their mothers and their fathers, their fore-
bears running back through long, laborious generations, who
have taken part in the building up of the strength and spirit of
other nations. No man quarrels with that. From such springs
of sentiment we all draw some of the handsomest inspirations of
our lives. But all that we do criticize is that, in some instances—
they are not, my fellow countrymen, very numerous—but, in some
instances, men have allowed this old ardor of another nationality to overcrow their ardor for the nationality to which they have
given their new and voluntary allegiance. So the United States
has again to work out by spiritual process a new union, when men
shall not think of what divides them, but shall recall what unites
them, when men shall not allow old loves to take the place of
present allegiances; where men must, on the contrary, translate
that very ardor of love of country of their birth into the ardor
of love for the country of their adoption and the principles which
it represents. I have no harshness in my heart even for the
extremists in this thing, which I have been trying in moderate
words to describe. But I summon them, and I summon them very
solemnly, not to set their purpose against the purpose of America.
America must come first in every purpose we entertain, and
every man must count upon being cast out of our confidence, cast
out even of our tolerance, who does not submit to that great ruling principle.

But what are the purposes of America? Do you not see that
there is another significance in the fact that we are made up
out of all the peoples of the world? The significance of that fact
is that we are not going to devote our nationality to the same mistaken, aggressive purposes that some other nationalities have
been devoted to; that, because we are made up, and consciously
made up, out of all the great family of mankind, we are cham-
pions of the rights of mankind. We are not only ready to cooperate, but we are ready to fight against any aggression, whether
from without or from within. But we must guard ourselves
against the sort of aggression which would be unworthy of

America. We are ready to fight for our rights when those rights are coincident with the rights of man and of humanity. It was to set these rights up, to vindicate them, to offer a home to every man who believed in them, that America was created and her government set up. We have kept our doors open because we did not think we, in conscience, could close them against men who wanted to join their force with ours in vindicating the claim of mankind to liberty and justice.

America does not want any additional territory. She does not want any selfish advantage over any other nation in the world. But she does wish every nation in the world to understand what she stands for, and to respect what she stands for. And I cannot conceive of any man of any blood or origin failing to feel an enthusiasm for the things that America stands for, or failing to see that they are infinitely elevated above any purpose of aggression or selfish advantage.

I said the other evening, in another place, that one of the principles which America held dear was that small and weak states had as much right to their sovereignty and independence as large and strong states. She believes that because strength and weakness have nothing to do with her principles. Her principles are for the rights and liberties of mankind, and this is the haven which we have offered to those who believe that sublime and sacred creed of humanity.

And I also said that I believed that the people of the United States were ready to become partners in any alliance of the nations that would guarantee public right above selfish aggression. Some of the public prints have reminded me—as if I needed to be reminded—of what General Washington warned us against. He warned us against entangling alliances. I shall never, myself, consent to an entangling alliance. But I would gladly assent to a disentangling alliance—an alliance which would disentangle the peoples of the world from those combinations in which they seek their own separate and private interests and unite the people of the world to preserve the peace of the world upon a basis of common right and justice. There is liberty there, not limitation. There is freedom, not entanglement. There is the achievement of the highest things for which the United States has declared its principles.

We have been engaged recently, my fellow citizens, in discussing the processes of preparedness. I have been trying to explain to you what we are getting prepared for, and I want to point out to you the only process of preparation which is possible for the United States. It is possible for the United States to get ready only if the men of suitable age and strength will volunteer to get ready. I heard the president of the United States Chamber of Commerce speak the other evening of a referendum to 750 of the chambers of commerce of the United States upon the question of preparedness, and he reported that 99 per cent of them had voted in favor of preparedness.[2] Very well now, we are going to apply the acid test to those gentlemen, and the acid test is this: Will they give the young men in their employment freedom to volunteer for this thing? I wish the referendum had included that, because that is of the essence of the matter. It is all very well to say that somebody else must prepare, but are the businessmen of this country ready, themselves, to lend a hand and sacrifice an interest in order that we may get ready? We shall have an answer to that question in the next few months. A bill is lying upon my table now ready to be signed, which bristles all over with that interrogation point, and I want all the businessmen of the country to see that interrogation point staring them in the face. I have heard a great many people talk about universal training. Universal voluntary training, with all my heart, if you wish it. But America does not wish anything but the compulsion of the spirit of America.

I, for my part, do not entertain any serious doubt of the answer to these questions, because I suppose there is no place in the world where the compulsion of public opinion is more imperative than it is in the United States. You know, yourself, how you behave when you think nobody is watching! And now all the people of the United States are watching each other. There never was such a blazing spotlight upon the conduct and principles of every American as each one of us now walks and blinks in it. And, as this spotlight sweeps its relentless rays across every square mile of the territory of the United States, I know a great many men, even when they do not want to, are going to stand up and say, "Here." Because America is roused, roused to a self-con-

2 Robert Goodwyn Rhett, president of the United States Chamber of Commerce, had announced the results of his organization's referendum on national defense at the dinner meeting of the League to Enforce Peace. The recommendations submitted to the chambers of commerce were, among others: that the army and navy should be increased and the nation's industrial resources be made fully available to the military branch; that a council of national defense be created by law to aid in the development of an adequate policy for national defense; that a "Staff of Industrial Mobilization" be created by law and maintained in peacetime to insure the effective use of the country's economic resources in the event of war; that the United States begin a program of naval construction to build and maintain the second largest force in the Atlantic and a force sufficient to protect the Panama Canal and trade routes in the Pacific; that the regular army be increased until it was sufficient to serve as the first line of land defense; and that universal military service be instituted. Chamber of Commerce of the United States, *Referendum Number Fifteen, on the Report of the Special Committee on National Defense* (Washington, 1916).

sciousness and a national self-consciousness such as she has not had in a generation. And this spirit is going out conquering and to conquer until, it may be, in the Providence of God, a new light is lifted up in America which shall throw the rays of liberty and justice far abroad upon every sea, and even upon the lands which now wallow in darkness and refuse to see the light.[3]

Printed in *Address of President Wilson at Arlington National Cemetery May 30, 1916* (Washington, 1916); with corrections from a reading of the CLSsh notes (C. L. Swem Coll., NjP).
[3] There is a WWT outline of this address, dated May 30, 1916, in WP, DLC.

To Henry French Hollis

My dear Senator: [The White House] May 30, 1916
I am deeply sorry about Rublee, and you may be sure will ponder your suggestions.
In haste
Cordially and sincerely yours,   Woodrow Wilson

TLS (Letterpress Books, WP, DLC).

Two Letters from Edward Mandell House

Dear Governor: New York, May 30, 1916.
Glynn has just sent me his speech and I am forwarding it to you at once. He very much desires to get it back almost immediately so he may give it to the press. Unless they have it by June 4th they cannot guarantee its publication except in an abbreviated form.

I have read it hastily and have made but one correction which you will notice in brackets on page 45 in reference to you. I think he has done it marvellously well and I hope you will agree with this conclusion.

Will you not give some care to what he says about keeping our Government free from entangling alliances. This part of it might be modified. Unless I mistake it he has written a speech that will appeal to our public and will be a campaign document of great value.

I am glad Clark will not be Permanent Chairman. I never liked that suggestion. In my opinion Ollie James is far better in every way.

For two days I have done but little else than look for a suitable Chairman of the National Committee to suggest to you, but it is next to impossible to find one that is satisfactory.

In seeking I have endeavored to eliminate the three r's. Rum, Romanism and Rebellion and in doing so our best material is not available. If you get a Roman Catholic, the religious question might become an issue. If you get a Southerner, there is a possibility of that being raised, and of course the liquor question in any form should be shunned.

I have not only sifted the country by states and by districts, but have gotten the help of almost everyone whose opinion is of value, even including such men as Cobb of the World and McAneny of the Times.[1]

John W. Davis, Solicitor General, has occur[r]ed to me as being the most available one, provided you think West Virginia is not too far south. As a matter of fact, their affiliations are more western than southern.

I would appreciate it if you will let me know tomorrow what you think of Davis.

Polk, I believe, must be considered unavailable. Lansing is a much sicker man than even his close friends know and to take Polk from him would be to put the finishing touch upon him. I suggested Polk to Cobb and he thought it would not do to take a man from the State Department to use for personal or party reasons. This view is held by many others.

It will not do to get an old time politician. He should be of the new school, able and forward looking and willing to play the game with all that seek to help. I have never known a national campaign to be properly organized, and organization is almost the most essential element in success. If we can get the right man I think we can get the organization, for it is a simple matter to an intelligent man when he is told how.

Affectionately yours,   E. M. House

[1] George McAneny, executive manager of *The New York Times*. He had been Borough President of Manhattan and was extensively involved in New York reform politics.

Dear Governor: New York, May 30, 1916.

Since writing you this morning Dudley suggests that the man for National Chairman is Billings, Collector of the Port at Boston.

In some ways I agree with him. He is said to be a fine organ-[i]zer, he is a business man, forward-looking and American to the core.

I remember looking him over for you for Collector and found him practically flawless from a political viewpoint.

I have asked him to come over and spend the evening with me

(I mean evening and not afternoon). I will let you know further about him tomorrow.

Affectionately yours,   E. M. House

B. voted for Bryan three times—stands well with labor and is said to be a good mixer.

TLS (WP, DLC).

From Harry Augustus Garfield

Dear Mr. President: Williamstown, Mass. May 30/16

I was rejoiced. The address was all that anyone not a rabid partisan could desire. It directs us & the world in a new path. My most heartfelt congratulations. Now I am eager to hear the verdict of the belligerents. But I remember to have read that the Gettysburg address had to sink in. Then people awoke to it.

Thank you also for the qualified promise you gave Mr. Bok & me for next November.[1]

With high & affectionate regards, as always,

Faithfully Yours,   H. A. Garfield.

ALS (WP, DLC).

[1] Garfield had lunch with Wilson (Bok was not present) at the White House on May 26. Wilson told Garfield that he would consider giving the first in a series of lectures at Williams College sponsored by Bok. See WW to F. B. Sayre, Oct. 9, 1916.

From Frank Lyon Polk

My dear Mr. President: Washington May 31, 1916.

This morning Mr. Arredondo, the Mexican Agent, delivered a long note in Spanish, addressed to the Secretary of State.[1] I enclose a translation, which has just been hurriedly completed and, therefore, is not as accurate as it might be. However, I think it desirable that it be placed in your hands as soon as possible.

The tone, as you will notice, is decidedly unsatisfactory and, in some places, impertinent. I assume it is for home consumption, but it seems to be a little overdone. Mr. Arredondo, when he called, told me that it was not an ultimatum, but merely a continuation of the diplomatic discussion. I quoted him to the press to that effect, as I assume this should not be given out until you have had an opportunity to give it some consideration.

I have sent a copy to Mr. Lansing and given a digest to General Scott for his information and guidance. General Scott suggests that it might be desirable to make a further concentration of troops now in Mexico and to consider the advisability of calling out more militia, if this note should impress you as being un-friendly.

I hope the Secretary will be at the office tomorrow for a short time, and he will probably communicate with you on this subject.

Yours faithfully,   Frank L Polk

TLS (WP, DLC).
1 See F. L. Polk to WW, June 1, 1916, n. 1.

From Edward Mandell House, with Enclosure

Dear Governor—   [New York] May 31, 1916.

Here is a cable from Sir Edward. Like most of his countrymen he travels by freight. This cable should have been here days ago. It is after ten o'clock and I am trying to get this to you on the mid-night.

Billings has come. I believe he is just what you want for a Chairman. I wish you would look him over. Polk tells me he is pretty sure Davis would not want to be Chairman. He has in view a judicial career.

Affectionately yours,   E. M. House

I shall talk freely with Jusserand tomorrow as Sir Edward suggests.

ALS (WP, DLC).

E N C L O S U R E

May 29, 1916.

Your direct question to me is whether in my opinion it is advisable for the President to make a public announcement committing the United States to joining after the war with other powers in a convention looking to the maintenance of peace after the war, provided he announce at the same time that if the struggle continued much longer he proposed calling a conference to discuss peace.

First, such an announcement would be welcomed and meet with public response from me giving cordial support in terms of my letter of September 22nd.

As regards second part, the calling a conference to discuss peace if the struggle continued much longer, I should have to say that I could give no opinion until after consultation and in agreement with Allies. No other reply would be honorably consistent with our alliance with them.

If the President desires the Allies to be consulted he should, if he does not wish to approach them all simultaneously, take the French Government at any rate into his confidence as directly as he has taken us.

The French Government in this way may be sufficiently impressed with his real intentions and goodwill. I should like them to know directly and not only through me the situation as presented in your telegrams to me of the tenth and nineteenth of May, but the following observations are suggested by careful consideration with my colleagues of your two telegrams.

These telegrams raise two questions, different though closely connected. The first relates to territorial arrangements to be made at the conclusion of the war. The second to methods by which a lasting peace may thereafter be secured.

As regards the first of these, we are evidently bound to our allies. Separate negotiations are impossible and even separate interchange of ideas with a friendly neutral is not easy.

But this much may perhaps be said. While no British statesman desires to wage a bloody and costly war in order to either "destroy" Germany or to be "revenged" on her, there is real danger that if Germany succeeds in obtaining terms of peace satisfactory to her and preventing terms giving essential satisfaction to the Allies, militarism in Germany will remain the dominant force, and will render ineffective and insecure any convention for maintaining future peace.

The terms must be sufficiently favourable to the Allies to make the German people feel that aggressive militarism is a failure.

The best chance for the great scheme is the President's willingness that it should be proposed by the United States in convention a peace favourable to the Allies obtainable with American aid. The worst chance would be that it should be proposed in connection with an inconclusive or disastrous peace accompanied, perhaps promoted, by diplomatic friction by [between] the Allies and the United States over maritime affairs.

Between these two extremes there are endless interminable possibilities. But evidently a premature announcement of intervention by the President might be dangerous to the cause he and we have at heart because it would be interpreted as meaning that he desired peace on a basis favourable to Germany and for the reasons above stated. No such peace could secure a reliable and enduring international organization of the kind he contemplates.   E. Grey.

TC telegram (WP, DLC).

From Edward Mandell House

Dear Governor: New York, May 31, 1916.

I had a long talk with Billings last night and I believe he is the kind of man you want.

The only objection from a party viewpoint that can be brought against him is that he has not been regular in municipal politics. If he had been he would not be the man you desire. No one living in the large cities can with any self respect always trail along with either of the regular parties.

He has always voted the democratic ticket for Governor and for President. He is a good organizer and has had enough experience in politics to be able to maintain himself.

I am getting him to go to Washington tomorrow with Dudley so you may look him over again, and if you think well of him, he can meet some of the party leaders and get acquainted with them. It is a great thing to have him start off right and to have those who are to be active in the campaign feel they have had something to do with the selection.

I am leaving tomorrow for Manchester, Massachusetts where I shall be until Monday. After that, my address will be, New London, Lake Sunnapee, New Hampshire.

Affectionately yours,   E. M. House

If you decide upon Billings and will wire me at Manchester, Mass. before Monday, I will get in touch with him at once, and go over with him the organization of the campaign.

TLS (WP, DLC).

To Martin Henry Glynn

My dear Governor: [The White House] June 1, 1916

Mr. House sent me the speech and I have read it with real approval and gratification. I congratulate you. I asked Mr. Tumulty to read it also and between us we have made several minor suggestions. I have asked him to send you the speech today,[1] so that you may get it back at the earliest possible moment.

It gratifies me very deeply that you have undertaken this important thing, and I congratulate you upon the way in which you have done the work.

Cordially and sincerely yours,   Woodrow Wilson

TLS (Letterpress Books, WP, DLC).
[1] Wilson did not keep a copy.

To Charles Richard Crane

My dear Friend: [The White House] June 1, 1916

Thank you warmly for your note of May twenty-ninth about the speech before the League to Enforce Peace. I think you do not know how much your approval means to me, or how much encouraged I am by such a message.

With warmest regards from us all,

Faithfully yours,   Woodrow Wilson

TLS (Letterpress Books, WP, DLC).

From Edward Mandell House, with Enclosure

Dear Governor: New York. June 1, 1916.

Jusserand came as planned and we talked for two hours or more.

He believes that the salvation of France depends upon her courage and he believes that any peace talk at this time will have a tendancy to encourage her enemies and break the spirit of her people. He thinks the thing for us to do now is to encourage her to fight on for the present. That Germany would would [sic] come out of the war now triumphant and would be ready within a few years to do more thoroughly what she planned to do at the beginning.

He said Russia and Japan had formed an alliance, the details of which were drawn up and signed in Washington recently.[1] He seemed to think that Germany might later drift into that alliance and if so, the balance of us would have a strong combination to reckon with. He thinks they would first direct their attention to us because he believes both Germany and Japan have an unforgivable grievance against us. He hinted we would have no sympathizers in our [hour] of trouble unless we more actively took the part of the Allies.

In reply to this, I said, we could take care of ourselves for within a few years we would probably have a navy large enough to withstand both Germany and Japan.

And this leads me to say that I do think it is of vital importance that we accelerate the building of a navy commensurate with our position in the world. If we do not, some such trouble may come.

It is none too sure that when this war is over, it will be settled to our liking, and while I believe that a long peace will follow and a reduction of armament come about, yet we should not gamble upon that. If after all the warning we have had, trouble should follow this war, the people would feel that their interests had not been properly protected.

Jusserand thought that there were several unfortunate expressions in your recent speeches, particularly in regard to our having no interest in this quarrel, seeming, he said, to place the Allies upon a level with Germany. He expressed a profound admiration for you and believed that you had done nothing intentionally unfriendly to the interests of France. Only he wanted to call attention to the interpretation the French people had placed upon some things you had said.[2]

Bernstorff followed Jusserand. He had nothing in particular to say. He was calm, fairminded and optimistic as usual. He hoped all differences between our two countries had subsided for good. The difference between Bernstorff and the representatives of the Allies is that the one never complains and is always ready to see our side.

I am enclosing you the first half of Governor Glynn's speech which he has rewritten. Will you not return this to him direct with such corrections as you care to make.[3] I do not know why he has rewritten it as I have not had time to look it over.

Affectionately yours,   E. M. House

TLS (WP, DLC).

[1] If we may believe Jusserand's account of this conversation, printed below, House began to fabricate at this point. Moreover, he was confused or ill-informed. The Russo-Japanese agreement was not negotiated and signed in Washington. It was signed in Petrograd on July 3. About this convention, see F. L. Polk to WW, July 13, 1916.

[2] Jusserand's report of this conversation (J. J. Jusserand to A. Briand, June 1, 1916, CCL [J. J. Jusserand Papers, Vol. 16, FFM-Ar]) follows (our translation):

"No. 421 *Very confidential.* To continue my telegram 339, which I have sent in code to New York so that it might be given directly to our own cable company, I believe I should add some information to what has been thus transmitted to Your Excellency regarding my conversation with Mr. House, which seems to be quite timely. Neither the President, in fact, nor his most heeded adviser, seems to have foreseen or believed (although I had pointed it out to Mr. Wilson) that the advances in favor of peace contained in the address of May 27 could not have produced anything but misunderstandings and would ruin the very plans of the speaker had those plans been feasible in the first place, which is not the case.

"As my telegram indicates, the status of Mr. House remains truly extraordinary. Especially with regard to Europe, the President does nothing without consulting him. The State Department is constantly in communication with him by a telephone service specially controlled to avoid indiscretions. A secretary of the American embassy in Berlin, Mr. Grew, whose trip provoked a great deal of comment and who is allegedly the bearer of documents relating to German desires to obtain peace, received orders to see Mr. House in New York as soon as he docked, and before seeing anyone else.

"Mr. House, in poor health and fearing travels during the hot season, avoids going to Washington as much as possible, and does not even always go when the President would wish, and must leave this very day for New Hampshire in order to rest. Communications with him will continue as before by secure telephone line.

"I saw him yesterday in New York. The extreme difficulty I am having in keeping abreast of the burdens of this post hardly permits me to make these trips frequently. But in this case, the occasion was of particular importance.

"I allowed him to speak first. Begging my pardon for the liberty with which he expressed himself, he voiced the opinion that the war could last a great while longer, with increased sufferings and eventual exhaustion on both sides, without any decisive results. This is the opinion of Lord Kitchener, he assures me, who foresees still two or three more years of war (and who furthermore declares that the Germans are the only type of enemy with whom he cannot imagine shaking hands after the war) without any great change in the military positions, and with only the more or less firm hope of exhausting the enemy. According to Mr. House, the Allies have lost the principal occasion they had to end the war by force when, without any agreement among themselves, the Russian army crossed the Carpathians. An action on their part, joined by one by the Serbs, striking Austria from the rear, would have knocked that tottering empire out of the war and would have swept along all the Balkan countries behind our lead. But, on the contrary, Austria, seasoned to war, reorganized, aided, rebuilt, was able to prevail in the Balkans and now makes the Italians beg for help. Who knows whether, filled with anxiety, the Italians might not wish for peace for themselves and, without breaking their treaty with the Allies, make entreaties to them, difficult to ignore, in favor of an end to the hostilities which threaten the Italians with serious misfortunes as much on the home front as from outside, if not more? Under these conditions, would it not be better to seek an end of the war at a less distant date than that envisioned by Lord Kitchener and to see whether a conference would be possible? Whether or not it was included in such a conference, acting from within or from without, the United States would exercise its influence in favor of those countries which have suffered the most, and the most unjustly, and whose heroism has won them the sympathies of the world, in particular, France and Belgium. The latter must be recompensed for its losses, the former to recover Alsace-Lorraine, a point to which Mr. House came back several times. The exercise of this 'influence' could go to the point of war.

"I did not conceal from Mr. House that nearly everything about these projects seemed chimerical to me. If, by every means possible, by every sound, by every route, the Germans call for peace, it is because it would be to their advantage to make it and ours, consequently, to continue the war. It is they who made the war, but it is we who will make the peace. We could not help but be distressed that an appeal so clearly inspired by German interest should have found an echo from the lips of the President of the greatest friendly republic. The mistrust on the part of the Allies and the unfavorable commentaries were certain and easy to predict. I had endeavored, though in vain, to make certain that they foresaw that this would happen (in particular by turning to Mr. Polk, who manages the State Department, who transmitted to the President, whom he, or anyone else, seldom sees, a note summarizing my statements).

"We are determined, I continued, to carry things through to their conclusion, as should be manifest from the declarations of the President of the Republic and the President of the Council, who are not in the habit of talking for nothing or saying anything other than what they think. While less serious than our enemies' losses, our own losses are increasing; we watch the blood of our children being shed. So much blood, and so many tears! But we stand firm. We will pursue the struggle on behalf of nations that are the friends of liberty, both those who have been satisfied to be spectators (and who will later lack power for having been only spectators) and on behalf of our comrades in arms. It is to the greatest advantage of the United States that we persevere in this attitude; an inconclusive peace, which would allow renewed attempts, would be a disaster for the United States and liberalism throughout the world. These German appeals advocate an inconclusive peace, even worse than inconclusive if one could take seriously the monstrous peace terms which they make public by their propagandists as bargaining terms. Anything that can enervate Allied resistance or further German propaganda is being done to harm the Allies and no less the United States, whose interests are being defended without risk or loss to themselves on the battlefields of France.

"Thereupon, I elaborated on the idea indicated in my telegram of the distress naturally caused in France and England by the President's proclaimed indifference to the causes and the objects of the war and by his imprecise declarations about the security of the oceans, formulated in such a way that one cannot tell precisely whether it is a question of German submarine crimes or of this freedom of the seas, which our enemies demand in order to annul, by negotiation, the Allied naval predominance, which they have not even tried to challenge by force.

"The hypothesis of an American recourse to force had already come up, I said further, in the Paris and London conversations, but nothing ever came of it (my telegram No. 95 of 15 February had already pointed out to Your Excellency my doubts on this subject). Can a country kept in a state of atony by a regime of procrastination following each grave incident, can it take such action? Would it even countenance such action? Procrastination about the *Lusitania*, and now about the affair of the Von Igel papers. When these papers come to light, the effect will be no more than when the servant explains that the precious broken plate has been broken last year.

"Mr. House objected that these impressions were ill-founded, but his arguments did not seem very convincing to me. Nevertheless, the accuracy of his remark about the last American note to Germany on the *Sussex* must be acknowledged: 'Who would have believed that Germany would accept it, and that it would not result in war? We were clearly taking the risk at that moment.'

"I said, and I willingly acknowledged, that the result could have been war in case of rejection. Its acceptance was the greatest sign of weakening that we have been able to perceive beyond the Rhine: it is proof that the Germans do not believe themselves capable of many years of resistance as they have suggested, and we must therefore be encouraged by that fact to hold fast, as we would be prepared to do anyway, even if the chances were worse. I then furnished numerous proofs that our confidence about the outcome was built on facts and realities.

"Mr. House, who foresees after the war an *entente* of Japan with Russia and Germany, said to me in conclusion that he understood perfectly well the point of view I had explained to him and that he would not neglect any opportunity to see that the President understood it as well.

"In addition, I will apply myself, come what may, to corroborating his action by other means. As my telegram indicates, if my language was of a force and a clarity which left no doubt about our way of thinking, the *tone* was constantly friendly; for no good could have come if House doubted it was as a friend (albeit a distressed friend, a friend nonetheless) who spoke to him as I did. Without that precaution, the most probable effect would have been to reinforce the tempting attraction of the 'German vote' in the forthcoming elections, and this vote, which usually goes to the Republicans and which Mr. Roosevelt just rejected with éclat, cannot be a free gift.

"It would, in my opinion, conform to our interests that this friendly tone, strained without any doubt, remain friendly nevertheless to the American republic and also be the one adopted by the Allied press. The temptation to resort to irony and sarcasm can be very strong, but we would gain nothing by yielding to it."

3 It is still in the Wilson Papers, with no changes by Wilson.

E N C L O S U R E

May 29, 1916.

The passages that refer to rights of small nations and particularly America's willingness to pledge an assurance, is very gratifying.

The announcement of unconcern with the causes and with the objects of this war has shocked those who only entered the war to defend Belgium. Freedom of the seas given such prominence has disappointed those that expect America to uphold sea power, it being the most effective curb on military aggression.

In your opinion has the Irish rebellion seriously increased anti-British feeling? Would you think that full official publication of facts and reason for executions would be opportune and desirable?   Sir Horace Plunkett.

This cable has just come.

TC telegram (WP, DLC).

From Frank Lyon Polk

My dear Mr. President: Washington June 1, 1916.

The translation I sent you last night was hurriedly made and I am sending you a correct copy.[1] I spoke to Mr. Lansing today and he sees no reason for any haste in answering it.

Mr. Fletcher and one or two men in the Department who read Spanish are very much impressed with the language used. They say it is not only unusual, but unnecessarily strong and aggressive. It would seem as if this Note was not written by a Mexican and, in Mr. Fletcher's opinion, indications are that it was written either by a European or a Chilean.

It has been suggested that it might be well to consider the advisability of returning the Note on account of its offensive tone.   Yours faithfully,   Frank L Polk

TLS (WP, DLC).
    [1] C. Aguilar to RL, May 22, 1916, TCL (WP, DLC); printed in FR 1916, pp. 552-63. The lengthy note reviewed the earlier negotiations over an agreement for hot pursuit and the futile Obregón-Scott-Funston talks. The Punitive Expedition's entry, it charged, had constituted an invasion of Mexico. The Mexican government, it said, had appealed for its withdrawal. Now it had to insist upon that withdrawal. Although it would exhaust all pacific means to solve the conflict, the Mexican government would defend Mexican territory by force if the United States Government refused to evacuate its troops. The Mexican government called upon the President, Secretary of State, the Senate, and the American people for a frank statement of their intentions toward Mexico. Wilson had promised to recall the Punitive Expedition once its work had been accomplished, and the American government had agreed that the *Villistas* had been dispersed. Yet Wilson had failed to withdraw Pershing's forces—a failure which accentuated "the discrepancy between the assurances of respect for Mexico's sovereignty and the actual fact that for purely political reasons in the United States this state of affairs, so unjust towards the Mexican Republic, is allowed to continue." The Mexican government had been eager to cooperate with American military forces in defense of the border. However, the United States Government had tried to prevent the Mexican government from establishing its control in northern Mexico in order to protect American interests in that region. The Washington government had supported Villa and prolonged the civil war in Mexico, permitted Mexican rebels to organize conspiracies against Mexico on American soil, and impeded the export of arms and ammunition to the Mexican government, all for the same reason. "The Mexican Government does not wish war with the United States, and if this should occur it will be as a consequence of the deliberate cause by the United States. Today these measures of precaution by the American Government show that there is a desire to be prepared for such an emergency, or, what amounts to the same thing, they manifest an attitude of hostility on the part of the United States toward Mexico." The Mexican people and government were certain that the American people did not want a war with Mexico; however, the Mexican people and government were uncertain of the

attitudes of the governmental and military authorities of the United States. These latter could best prove their friendly intentions by withdrawing all United States troops from Mexican territory.

From Franklin Knight Lane

Dear Mr. President: Washington June 1, 1916.

I have your note of May 26th regarding the oil matter and regret that it is bothering you. Perhaps I can help you in a few words. There are three matters that are of immediate concern:

(1) The Honolulu case. This is a decision given by Mr. Tallman[1] and approved by me, awarding to the Honolulu Company certain lands in one of the Naval petroleum reserves upon the ground that the lands were located and developed prior to their withdrawal for any purposes; that as a matter of law and of fact the claimants are entitled to the patents. At the request of the Attorney General and the Secretary of the Navy I have withheld the issuance of patents to these lands, although I regarded it as my duty to issue such patents, and furnished a copy of Mr. Tallman's decision to the Attorney General and gave him two months time in which to review it. His answer was that he could not say that we were wrong either in law or in fact, but he would advise that the patents be not granted. If you will send for Mr. John W. Davis, the Solicitor General, to whom the matter was referred by the Attorney General, he will tell you that Mr. Tallman's opinion is sound; so will Mr. Lenroot, of the Public Lands Committee, one of the strongest conservationists in the country, who has taken a great interest in these oil reserves.

However, I told Mr. Tallman as soon as Mr. Gregory's first letter came to me some three months ago, that I was going to see that the safe course was followed regarding this matter and would direct that patents be withheld if the Attorney General's opinion was adverse to us, so that the matter could be determined by the courts. The Attorney General's opinion was not adverse, although critical and dubious, and I determined upon an effort to convince him that we were right by having a memorandum prepared extensively reviewing the case again for presentation to him. I spoke of this matter, you will remember, at the Cabinet meeting. Of course, in advance of the presentation of this memorandum I would not think of issuing patents nor would I have thought at all of doing so unless upon mature reflection and consideration the Attorney General could be brought to see that we were right. Of course you will understand that in tak-

[1] Clay Tallman, Commissioner of the General Land Office.

ing this position I am yielding my own judgment to that of the Attorney General, and this the law does not contemplate, for the Secretary of the Interior and the Commissioner of the General Land Office are quasi-judicial officers whose decisions are not subject to review by the Attorney General or any other administrative officer.

It has been my effort for three years to minimize your troubles so far as this Department could effect that end and to allow no opportunity for those charges and scandals which have been too frequent in this Department under other administrations. So that I have sought to follow the safe path, and for that reason I suggest that if after the presentation to the Attorney General of the review now in course of preparation as to the Honolulu case Mr. Gregory is not satisfied that Commissioner Tallman is right, that he (the Attorney General) be requested to institute a proceeding in the courts in which the matter will be determined.

(2) The general leasing bill. This measure was drafted by me after consultation with Senator Walsh, Senator Myers, Congressmen Ferris, Lenroot, Kent, and others, and I have supported it through two sessions of Congress. If there were any objections to this measure they should have been stated two years and more ago, for they were advocated by me in my reports, speeches and testimony before committees of both Houses. There was no possibility of passing this bill without the passage of some relief measure for those who were affected by the Mid-West decision,[2] which was the decision holding that the withdrawals under President Taft of 1909 were good.

(3) The relief provisions of the general leasing bill. The House Committee added to the general leasing bill certain relief provisions which I endorsed. These provisions allowed the leasing of lands under certain conditions but expressly provided that lands withdrawn for military or naval purposes should not be leased. The amendments that have been added to the bill in the Senate were added without my knowledge or approval. My opinion has never been asked as to the so-called Phelan Amendments. Early in the winter a delegation headed by the Lieutenant-Governor of California,[3] a man of very high rank who received the Democratic nomination as well as the Progressive nomination for Lieutenant-Governor in the last election, called on me and presented an outline of the so-called relief which he and his committee thought

desirable, needed and just. I said that I would not undertake to speak for anything other than the House provisions and that I knew the House Committee would not stand for the proposed amendments. Lieutenant-Governor Eshleman later said that he called upon you to urge these amendments and saw Mr. Tumulty, who said that "If Lane had any guts he would get this relief for you." This was reported to me frequently on my last visit to California, so that the State believes that I stand in the way of securing what Lieutenant-Governor Eshleman and his committee endorsed, and this is the fact. The Secretary of the Navy, however, has apparently assumed that this was my amendment, for I understand that the Phelan amendments and the Eshleman proposals are very similar. I have not read the Phelan amendments nor the Phelan report, although I have been told their purport.

Now the upshot of this whole business is this: That the Secretary of the Navy has attempted to create a scandal involving one of his colleagues where no scandal exists and none could possibly exist, because the record is so clear and simple. Had Mr. Daniels not spoken of this matter some sort of bill would have passed the Senate. The House conferees would then have brought the bill down to reasonable shape and while not acceptable to the oil men they would have taken it as the best they could get. There would have been no scandal or talk of depriving the Navy of oil and the Navy reserves would not have been touched but allowed to remain just as they are. I assume that Mr. Daniels was responsible for the articles that appeared in the New York Herald and which were written, I understand, by Mr. Howe, the secretary to Assistant Secretary Roosevelt, formerly of the New York Herald, Mr. Donald Craig, of the New York Herald, and Mr. Brown, of the New York Herald.[4] The latter gentleman is responsible for the statement that he got his information from the Navy Department and one of the correspondents tells me that both Mr. Craig and Mr. Brown say that they talked with the Secretary of the Navy as to the matter.

[4] Louis McHenry Howe, journalist, long-time friend and political mentor of Franklin D. Roosevelt, at this time Roosevelt's private secretary in the Navy Department; Donald Alexander Craig, manager of the Washington bureau of the *New York Herald*; and Sevellon Ledyard Brown, at this time the Washington representative of the *Paris Herald*. The articles, which were attributed only to the "Herald bureau" in Washington, were as follows: "Scheme to Grab Navy's Oil Lands Revealed in Conservation Bill," *New York Herald*, May 27, 1916; "2,077 Acres of Navy Oil Land Saved by Attorney General" and "Navy Names a Board to Deal with Oil Supply," both in *ibid.*, May 28, 1916; "Navy Needs Support to Combat Oil Land Grab; Fight Becoming Bitter," *ibid.*, May 29, 1916; "Oil Land Grab Would Be a Serious Blow to Navy, Mr. Daniels Declares," *ibid.*, May 30, 1916; "Western Oil Interests Urged Attorney General Not to Hamper Reserve Field Grabs," *ibid.*, May 31, 1916; and "Two Senators Enter Fight to Save Navy's Oil Tracts from Grasp of Speculators," *ibid.*, June 1, 1916.

There is nothing so far as I see now that you can do unless you wish to ask the members of the Senate to bring these Senate amendments down so as to accord with the House amendments. A wiser course, it seems to me, is to allow the bill to pass practically in the best shape that it can be put in by the Senate, and then that it should be fought out in conference, for Ferris, Lenroot and Taylor will not allow any bill to go out that is not reasonable.

Tell me if you can, why the Secretary of the Navy and the Attorney General have twice brought this matter up in Cabinet without giving me any notice or telling me that the matter was to be raised? I should also like to know why the Secretary of the Navy did not avail himself of my suggestion made three years ago that an effort be made to develop special oil fields for the Navy. I should also like to know why the Secretary of the Navy has never interested himself in the proposition which I made to him that out of the two and a half million acres of public lands classified as oil lands by the Geological Survey, that new reserves should be created for the Navy. There is abundant oil land left in the public domain for fuel supply for the Navy, and I should have thought that one who desired to protect the interests of the Navy would have spent his time in securing an opportunity to prove some of these fields rather than in an effort to prevent the passage of legislation which no one has ever opposed excepting the strong anti-conservationists. The Secretary of the Navy by his policy has played directly into the hands of the great oil magnates and those who have been opposing for years the opening of the two and a half million acres of oil lands that are under withdrawal. The upshot of his policy will be to force the Navy to buy oil from those who now hold the land—the railroads, the Standard Oil, the Prairie Oil and Gas Company, and others,—because the leasing bill will not be passed and in the meantime these companies, which have alternate sections in the withdrawn reserves, will be draining the field so that the Government at the end will get a sucked lemon.

I think that this is the first letter that I have had occasion to write you in explanation of anything that has been done by me during my term of office, and I would not trouble you now but for your letter which called for a rather frank and full reply.

Faithfully yours,   [F. K. Lane]

TL (WP, DLC).

From Dudley Field Malone

Dear Mr. President, Washington Thursday, June 1, 16.

I am here. Collector Billings is with me. Col. House thinks it best for you to see me *alone first*, as he wishes me to tell you some things for him. I can come over to the White House *at once* or whenever it is convenient for you. Hoover can reach me.[1]

You ought to know that Billings never heard of this matter until Col. House sent for him

Yours affectionately   Dudley Field Malone.

ALS (WP, DLC).
[1] Wilson saw Malone and Billings at three o'clock that afternoon.

From Josephus Daniels

Dear Mr. President: Washington. June 1, 1916.

It seems a sin to add a single thing to your burdens, but the importance of the oil legislation is my justification for sending you the report of the Committee on Public Lands, written by Senator Phelan, and the minority report by Senator Husting. The minority report seems to me to be unanswerable and I hope you will have time to read it.[1]

Sincerely,   Josephus Daniels

ALS (WP, DLC).
[1] 64th Cong., 1st sess., Senate Report No. 319, Parts 1 and 2. For a summary of both the majority and minority reports, see WW to J. W. Kern, April 12, 1916, n. 1, Vol. 36.

From Walter Hines Page

Dear Mr. President: London, June 1, '16

I have periods of great irritation by the English—almost of impatience with them. I suppose that any people wd. be put on edge by such a strain as this war. But not even such a strain can excuse the foolish flurry that public opinion here is having over one word in your speech to the League for Insuring Peace. You are reported to have said that we are not concerned with the causes or the *objects* of this war. Forgetting all the rest of your speech, the press and the people have singled out the word "objects" and read it to mean that you see no purpose in the conflict etc. etc. etc—I am sending House a lot of newspaper clippings: I spare *you* such things—except the enclosed letter that Lord Cromer wrote to *The Times*.[1]

[1] Evelyn Baring, 1st Earl of Cromer, "Mr. Wilson's Part: Good Intentions

My analysis of this whole unhappy incident—for it has its serious as well as its silly side—is this: The German people are getting tired of the war—as who is not? They have been fed on "victories" that were fictitious and especially on the promise of victories that have not been won. Now their loyalty and submission must be fed on some other diet. The German leaders, therefore, have set going a great peace hubbub: *We* want peace; *we'll* make peace. It's the stupid English, who are whipped, that will not make peace. The continuance of the war, therefore, is wholly the fault of the English and their allies. Thus, they seek to shift the responsibility for whatever fighting must yet be done off their own shoulders—to save their face to their own people and incidentally to affect neutral opinion. The English, who have received no peace-proposal from the Germans and who, Sir Edward Grey recently informed me, have not even discussed peace with their allies, of course understand this piece of German strategy, are annoyed by it—so annoyed that they have, for a time at least, banishd. the word "peace" from their vocabulary. A lady said to me to-day: "I no longer use the word: it smells German—as German as *kultur*."

It is on this mood that your word "objects" fell; and the anti-American-Government feeling is again all ablaze. Even our best friends of the London press—papers that have hitherto refrained from unfriendly comment—have broken over the censorship and berated us; and all London is talking about the American desire and design to force—or to try to force—peace. Many sections of

---

and Hard Facts. To the Editor of The Times," London *Times*, May 31, 1916, clipping in WP, DLC.C romer referred to Wilson's recent statements on the European war and observed that the official British attitude of acquiescence in America's policy was not indicative of the true feelings of a great number of Englishmen. Wilson, he argued, had to be made to understand that the British people, although willing to listen to any plans for the diminution of the risk of future wars, would not accept any peace terms that were not entirely satisfactory to the Allies. Furthermore, Wilson had to realize that the "meaningless and misleading phrase invented in Berlin about the 'freedom of the seas'" was a mere euphemism for the destruction of Britain's naval supremacy. Any responsible British government could only reject such a proposal, all the more since the crucial role of the Royal Navy had again become evident in the blockade of Germany and the suppression of the Irish Rebellion. Cromer acknowledged Wilson's "good intentions and his lofty aims," but he nevertheless doubted whether the British people would welcome him as an impartial mediator. "As Note has succeeded Note and speech speech," Cromer concluded, "the conviction has been steadily gaining ground that President Wilson has wholly failed to grasp the view entertained by the vast majority of Englishmen on the cause for which we and our Allies are fighting. . . . Confidence in President Wilson's statesmanship has been rudely shaken, neither for the moment does it appear likely to be restored to the extent of acquiescence in the proposal that he should be in any way vested with the power of exercising any decisive influence on the terms of peace upon which the future destinies of this country and of the civilized world will greatly depend."

society and of opinion have worked themselves into an ugly temper.

I am trying, without seeming to pay too much attention to it, to set some corrective influences at work. I am glad to say that the best of the American correspondents here, who are very loyal fellows, are giving their help. I can hardly say, as I wish I cd., that this is merely a passing mood. Of course the subject will presently be changed, but something of this unfortunate mood, I am afraid, will persist.

The serious aspect of it—apart from the gross misreading of your speech—is that our Government is suspect of preferring a premature peace—a peace that wd. be really a German victory. The English no longer expect a stalemate: they expect a definite result in their favor. They have no foolish idea of driving the German armies to Berlin nor of imposing humiliating terms; but they do feel sure of a victory over the German army and of the complete restoration of Belgium etc. etc. Just when this expectation has become fixed, he who talks peace talks treason.

Gossip (none of wh., so far as I know, has yet got into print) even busies itself with House's visits: "What did he come here for? What message did he bring? He *said* nothing, but he was feeling for peace—in the interests of the peace-cranks & perhaps even of the Germans. We want no peace emis[s]aries. We know ourselves when we shall want peace. The American Government is playing the German game. They don't wish us harm—we know that—but they don't yet even know what the war is about." This is the kind of talk that buzzes everywhere. With House in mind, a questioner askd. Sir Edward Grey in the House of Commons yesterday whether the Government meant to send a special diplomatic envoy to Washington. The answer was: "No. His Majesty's Government have complete confidence in its Ambassador to the United States." Thus this English mood smites everybody, on every side.

From this point of observation, the less said about peace, at least till some new and decisive event happen, the better.

This mood has even revived talk about the submarine truce. We are reminded that the submarine warfare has ceased not out of respect for American protests or fear of American threats, but because so many submarines have been destroyed by the British. I heard one story to-day that a single British torpedo-boat-destroyer has destroyed ten submarines. What truth there is in this narrative or in the whole flood of such talk, I have not been able to find out.

All these things and suchlike, though, I take it, you wish to know them, unfortunate as they are, have nothing in them seriously to disturb the philosophic mind. They are, rather measures of the abnormal effects of the strain of the war. Still, you may be sure that the English mood has reachd. a fixed determination to spend their last shilling and to send their last man rather than stop before their enemy gives up; and this German peace-talk all about the world makes that determination all the stronger. The League to Insure Peace will have its day, but it's day will not come till peace come

I resolutely refuse to be made the least unhappy by any such outburst of excitement—or the least uncomfortable. The fluctuations of feelings, like the fluctuations of battle, wd. confuse you if you watch them too minutely: the inevitable result after a while begins to be visible. The inevitable result, as regards our relations with the English, will be that they and we will, in time, become the League for Insuring Peace; and they will thank you, as I now thank you, for showing that when Washington spoke of entangling alliances, he didn't mean to discourage disentangling alliances.

You wouldn't believe that a three-year's absence and the study all the while of no domestic problem but always of the U. S. *vs.* the rest of the world, could bring such a mass of ignorance to a man of fair intelligence, as my mind now holds about the domestic political condition at home. All my cues are lost. I can't guess what will happen at Chicago next week;[2] but I can't imagine that anything will happen wh. will put the election in any doubt. All the Americans that I see—tho' these days they are fewer than at any preceding time for 50 years—hold this opinion. This reminds me, by the way, to say that the resident Americans in London are a right-minded, well-behaved, patriotic group, although of no great importance, (a black sheep here & there) who stand up for their country. They are now, for example, quietly and continuously trying to make their English friends understand the indecency of criticizing a speech they haven't read; for only two short paragraphs of what you said have been telegraphed here.

Yours Sincerely & faithfully   Walter H. Page

P.S. As I read this letter over, it seems to me unspeakably dull and depressing and most uninterestingly true. I am always, these recent days, swinging from pity and indignation to admiration: the English compel all these emotions and more. I swear at them

---

2 When the Republican and Progressive national conventions were to meet.

and I bow low to them. This is not my bowing week. Great Heavens! it's a crazy world—a slaughter-house where madness dwells. I keep calm—as calm as one can; and one must keep calm, well-balanced, philosophical. That's half the battle.

W.H.P.

ALS (WP, DLS).

Remarks to the Graduating Class of the Naval Academy

[[June 2, 1916]]

Mr. Superintendent,[1] young gentlemen, ladies and gentlemen: It had not been my purpose when I came here to say anything today, but, as I sit here and look at you youngsters, I find that my feeling is a very personal feeling indeed. I know some of the things that you have been through, and I admire the way in which you have responded to the new call of duty. I would feel that I had not done either you or myself justice if I did not tell you so.

I have thought that there was one interesting bond that united us. You were at Washington three years ago and saw me get into trouble, and now I am here to see the beginning of your trouble. Your trouble will last longer than mine, but I doubt if it will be any more interesting. I have had a liberal education in the last three years, with which nothing that I underwent before bears the slightest comparison. But what I want to say to you young gentlemen is this. I can illustrate it in this way. Once and again, when youngsters, here or at West Point, have forgotten themselves and done something that they ought not to do and were about to be disciplined, perhaps severely, for it, I have been appealed to by their friends to excuse them from the penalty. Knowing that I have spent most of my life at a college they commonly say to me: "You know college boys. You know what they are. They are heedless youngsters very often, and they ought not to be held up to the same standards of responsibility that older men must submit to." And I have always replied: "Yes, I know college boys. But, while these youngsters are college boys, they are something more. They are officers of the United States. They are not merely college boys. If they were, I would look at derelictions of duty on their part in another spirit; but any dereliction of duty on the part of a naval officer of the United States may involve the fortunes of a nation and cannot be overlooked." Don't you see the difference? You cannot indulge yourselves in weaknesses, gentlemen. You cannot forget your duty for a moment, because there might come a time when that weak spot in you should affect you in the midst of a great engagement, and then the whole history of the world might be changed by what you did not do or did wrong.

So that the personal feeling I have for you is this: We are all bound together, I, for the time being, and you, permanently, under a special obligation—the most solemn that the mind can conceive. The fortunes of a nation are confided to us. Now, that ought not to depress a man. Sometimes I think that nothing is worthwhile that is not hard. You do not improve your muscle by doing the easy thing; you improve it by doing the hard thing, and you get your zest by doing a thing that is difficult, not a thing that is easy. I would a great deal rather, so far as my sense of enjoyment is concerned, have something strenuous to do than have something that can be done leisurely and without a stimulation of the faculties.

Therefore, I congratulate you that you are going to live your lives under the most stimulating compulsion that any man can feel—the sense, not of private duty, merely, but of public duty, also. And, then, if you perform that duty, there is a reward awaiting you which is superior to any other reward in the world. That is the affectionate remembrance of your fellow men—their honor, their affection. No man could wish for more than that or find anything higher than that to strive for. And, therefore, I want you to know, gentlemen, if it is any satisfaction to you, that I shall personally follow your careers in the days that are ahead of you with real personal interest. I wish you Godspeed and remind you that yours is the honor of the United States.

Printed in *Responding to the New Call of Duty. . .* (Washington, 1916).
  [1] Captain Edward Walter Eberle, Superintendent of the United States Naval Academy from 1915 through 1919.

After-Dinner Remarks in Washington[1]

June 2, 1916.

Mr. Toastmaster, Bishop Cranston, ladies and gentlemen: Your toastmaster has been kind enough to say that it was a very gracious act on my part to come tonight, but I want to say, for myself, that I came under the compulsion of my own heart. I have known Bishop Cranston well enough and long enough to love him as you do, and, therefore, it seemed to me that I should be missing a privilege if I did not arrange to be here tonight to render my tribute to him.

I have been asking the Bishop, as I sat here beside him, how it felt, and he has said something to me that has been corroborated by my observation on many occasions when that observation has been of genuine and really big men. I remember that, a good many years ago, I attended the celebration of the fiftieth anniversary of the appointment of the great Lord Kelvin to his professorship at the University of Glasgow.[2] I never knew a simpler man than Lord Kelvin. He had that delightful quality, which belongs to so few of us, of an entire absence of self-consciousness. He never seemed for a moment to think about himself, but, at the banquet which concluded the exercises of the celebration, he was obliged to say something about himself, for the toast was to him. I suppose that no great physicist ever filled a life with more tangible achievements than did Lord Kelvin. I had just been to one of the rooms of the university where I saw a table as long almost as this at which I am standing filled from one end to the other with the inventions of Lord Kelvin—inventions most of which had been contributions to the safety of the navigation of the seas. It was Lord Kelvin who made it possible to telegraph around the globe, and I was standing near him when he received a telegram of congratulations from the other side of the globe by means of an invention of his own. When he was called upon to speak about himself, he said with that delightful simplicity which characterized him: "If I were asked to choose a single word in which to express my own impression of my career, it would have to be the word 'failure' "; and when everyone cried, "No, No, No," I was near enough to see the tears come into his eyes. And he said, "What I mean is that, when I compare what I have accomplished with what I dreamed of accomplishing, there is no other word for it." And I imagine, from what the Bishop has told me tonight, that that is his impression. When you look back upon a career, it seems so short, and the things that seem to stick in your memory are the things that did not happen rather than the things that did.

I have been wondering how you have managed to differentiate Bishop Cranston from other bishops in describing his career and rendering the meed of praise which he has so richly earned. I suppose that the life of one bishop is very much like the life of another, and to describe the career of one, as discriminated from that of another, is very much like describing one human face as distinguished from other human faces, which is as difficult an exercise in the use of the language as I know of. And, as I have thought of that, I realize that what you really must attempt to describe is not a career but a spirit. In any given career, if it be the career in a well-organized profession, one man goes through the same functions as another, but you do not retain the same impressions of him. There is a distinctive note of individuality which he contributes and which, if there be genuine force in him, nobody else could have contributed. And so you remember something that makes it very proper to speak, particularly in his profession, of the ghostly influences which have characterized him.

It is not, I take it, by accident that we speak of our ghostly advisers, not meaning that they are ghosts, but that, in their advice, spirit speaks to spirit. And the things that are invisible are the things that are vital. So what we have assembled to celebrate tonight, it seems to me, is the spiritual influence of an individual coming like the fragrance of a flower out of the way in which he has done ordinary things, out of the way in which he has performed accustomed functions. It is the particular tone and flavor of the man that we like, just as we can make friends with some people and we cannot make friends with others. Some men give me a creepy feeling the minute I am in the room with them, and with other men I feel like opening to them every thought that I have. When a man like Bishop Cranston comes into the room, I feel like opening to him every handsome thought that I have and concealing all the rest, because I have an instinctive feeling that that is the thing that would be acceptable to him. That is the test of the man—the kind of confidence you think he would relish, the kind of story you think he would laugh at, the kind of principle that you believe he would approve. Those are the tests of a man, and Bishop Cranston's contribution to the great church which he serves is the contribution which he has made in building up other spirits and making them, in some sort and degree, kin to his own spirit. It is this fine spiritual propagation which is the true lineage of the Christian Church.

I am glad, therefore, to come and express my meed of gratitude to Bishop Cranston for what his example and suggestion have put into my life and the privilege I have had of touching here and there a spirit which stimulates and elevates and guides.

T MS (WP, DLC).
    1 Wilson addressed some two hundred clergy and laypersons gathered at a dinner at Rauscher's Restaurant to honor Methodist Bishop Earl Cranston upon his retirement as resident Bishop of Washington, D. C. The toastmaster, the Rev. Whitford L. McDowell, delivered the opening remarks. In addition to Wilson, Josephus Daniels and Bishops John William Hamilton of Boston, Joseph Flintoft Berry of Washington, D. C., Franklin Elmer Ellsworth Hamilton of Pittsburgh, John L. Neulsen of Zurich, Switzerland, and William Alfred Quayle of St. Paul, Minnesota, praised Bishop Cranston, a Civil War veteran and one of the founders of the University of Denver, for his pastoral work and his efforts to unite the several branches of the Methodist Episcopal Church in the United States.
    2 See WW to EAW, June 17, 1896, Vol. 9.

From Edward Mandell House

Dear Governor—   [New York] June 2nd, 1916.

Vance McCormick has just telephoned me that he is available if you desire him. Dudley also telephones about Billings and the doubts you have there. I knew that question would be raised and why, but I have a feeling it would not be serious. I could find out in Boston if it really exists and if so how far it would go. There is no need to do this unless you favor him otherwise. I am wondering whether you have tried out Davis? I think one of these three is the best solution.

Affectionately yours,   E. M. House

Dudley hopes you will make no New York appointments until after the St Louis Convention. In this I concur.

Please pardon the pencil.

ALS (WP, DLC).

From Robert Latham Owen

Sir: [Washington] June 2, 1916.

I wish to emphasize on your attention the importance of having the Democratic Platform in St. Louis contain the progressive principles which were set forth in the Progressive Platform of 1912, in which ninety-nine Democrats out of a hundred believe, and which would make special appeal to the progressive Republicans of the Nation. I wish you would very carefully consider this matter and not overlook its importance as a means of promoting social and industrial reforms, as well as political reforms, and as a means of attaching to our party progressive Republicans who are in sympathy with us in so large a degree.

Yours respectfully,   Robt L. Owen

TLS (WP, DLC).

From Henry Morgenthau

My dear Mr. President: New York June 2nd, 1916.

My best congratulations to [on] Brandeis' confirmation.[1] I know you had set your heart on it and rejoice with you that it has been accomplished.

I hope that in the midst of your many other duties you will *not forget* to ask Hoke Smith to call on you for a conference.

During my western trip I met and talked with and at a great many people, and found that they are not as "heroic" as T.R. wants them to be. They want to keep us out of the war at almost any price. The majority of the Republicans want Hughes and principally because they think he would conduct the government on the Wilsonic method,—the deliberate watchful-waiting style and not the flamboyant 'T.R.' style.

I think and purpose saying it publicly, that the nomination or desire to nominate Hughes, the "bewhiskered Wilson" is the strongest vote of confidence and approval that the Republican party can give you.

With kind regards,
                 Sincerely and Cordially Yours,   H Morgenthau

TLS (WP, DLC).
    ¹ The Senate had confirmed Brandeis' nomination on June 1 by a vote of forty-seven to twenty-two.

From George Weston Anderson

Dear Mr. President: Boston June 2nd, 1916.

It is fitting that one who has played his small part in the fight for genuine democracy in this old New England community should pay his tribute of respect and admiration to the President who had the courage, insight and persistency to make Louis D. Brandeis a member of the Supreme Court. You, the Attorney General and others who have never lived in New England, do not, I think, even now appreciate what this appointment, fought to a successful finish in the confirmation of yesterday, means to us of New England.

This victory is a new victory for freedom: freedom from the trammels of race prejudice; freedom from subservience to the money power; freedom to think and to act and to speak as men ought to think and act and speak in a real democracy.

Accept my personal thanks and congratulations for the appointment and for the confirmation.
                 Respectfully yours,   G W Anderson
TLS (WP, DLC).

From David Lawrence

PERSONAL AND CONFIDENTIAL

Dear Mr. President: [Washington] June 2, 1916

I had a long talk with Arrendondo today the details of which I am giving you for your general information. He was very

curious as to what our attitude would be on the latest note from
Carranza. I told him that since Mr Lansing was ill, no one
knew that except yourself and so far as I knew no one had discussed it with you. He asked me what my personal opinion was
and I told him very frankly that I believed the troops would not
be withdrawn and could not be until the American people were
convinced Carranza could control the situation in northern Mexico and prevent a recurrence of raids. I told him I believed the last
note had hurt the chances of an early withdrawal and that whatever opinion Carranza or his officials might have as to motives
or considerations involved in prolonging the stay of American
troops, to make the charge of internal politics was not only highly indiscreet from a diplomatic point of view but very offensive.
He countered with the statement that if all the notes sent by our
government to Carranza were made public, there would be
revealed some very insulting documents. He complained that the
United States had promised time and again to withdraw the
troops and had not even answered the note of April 12th.[1] He
said if there had only been some oral understanding as to the
length of time the troops were to stay, the note would not have
been necessary.

I told Arredondo that regardless of what had happened, no
matter what interpretations had been or would be placed on what
conversations or notes were sent, the thing he must realize is that
the troops will not be withdrawn, for the present anyway. He
said he feared very much that war would come. He said Carranza was being called "traitor" on every side since he was con-
senting to the occupation of Mexican territory by foreign troops.
He added that the desire for a war with the United States was
growing, that Carranza was not writing his notes for "home
consumption" since he had suppressed the first series of exchanges and had only begun to make the documents public because his own position was growing untenable.

I pointed out the futility of war from the Mexican point of
view, the certain loss to Mexico and the incalculable results that
might flow from such a situation. He said that many officials
in the Mexican government were beginning to feel that it would
be better for Mexico to die, better for it to be strangled while
fighting than to submit in humiliation to what would in the end
be the same thing. I suggested to him that there were many people in the United States who thought the use of force was the
only way out of the dilemma and that if therefore Carranza took
the offensive it might be a relief. The United States would not

[1] See RL to WW, April 13, 1916, n. 1, Vol. 36.

be the aggressor but would appear in a defensive position, justifying its original expedition on the ground, too, of retaliating against an attack originating in Mexican territory and constituting an invasion of Columbus N. M. He argued that Latin America would understand. (Incidentally I have strong reason to suspect that the Mexican government already is at work among the Latin-American governments and their diplomats here to arrange some sort of diplomatic back-fire.)

After I had repeated that it did not seem likely that our troops would be withdrawn and urged that he look at the situation from that point of view, he suggested that perhaps there might be a solution through the proposal of a new convention, somewhat after the form of the proposed protocol, the principles of which we accepted some time ago. His idea was that if we were specifically granted the right of re-entering Mexico at any time should a raid occur or bandits threaten our boundary, this might compensate us for a withdrawal. He suggested that as long as our troops were "in contact" or pursued a hot trail they could by agreement remain and even for eight or ten days after they had "lost contact." He suggested that a force of 2000 men could be allowed to enter at any point. I thought 5,000 might be more adequate and he said that all this could be arranged. His chief idea was that some kind of protocol could be discussed if it were now proposed by the United States. I asked him if this would be agreeable to Carranza. He said he thought so. I told him I thought it would be a good idea for him to sound out Carranza and find out whether that would solve the difficulty. He said he didn't want to do that of his own initiative but that if a suggestion to sound out Carranza on that idea were to come from the State Department in oral conversation he would transmit it and push it. I told him I wouldn't make any suggestion myself to the government authorities here because I didn't want to be in the position of making suggestions which later might not prove to be Carranza's real attitude. He is going to see Mr Lansing or Mr Polk on Monday to inquire informally when an answer is expected. That is only a pretext to get talking on the subject generally. I have a theory that Arredondo has private instructions to get a discussion going on the subject of a new protocol if he discovers that we are firm in our refusal to withdraw. He certainly has some alternative proposals back in his mind sent secretly by Carranza, these to be used only in the event that he sees war or general intervention is inevitable.

May I add this suggestion: in all our correspondence with Carranza since the Columbus raid we have never, it seems to me, made clear our lawful equity. We have never shown the basis under international law for our presence in Mexico. It seems to me that we could still by reviewing the circumstances of the Columbus raid make it very clear that under international law a recognized government must be held responsible for all acts committed on its territory, for all acts flowing from its territory. The incursions of Villa Bandits proceeded from territory under the sovereign jurisdiction of the de facto government. These attacks were hostile acts against a friendly government and people. They were acts of invasion. No active steps had been taken by the de facto government from the days of the Santa Ysabel raid[2] to crush out banditry. Failure to proceed actively leaves a presumption of assent. Our troops therefore have merely moved in defense of our international line. In moving south of the line, we have begun a pursuit which the de facto government was either unable or unwilling to accomplish. But we have not occupied Mexican towns or set up any government. We have merely placed our troops in such defensive positions as would guard the approaches to our boundary. Defense of a boundary under conditions of lawlessness could justifiably include defense of such strategic positions in a neighboring country as command the approaches to our line.

Briefly, I think we should place on record our intention to hold the de facto government responsible for the protection of foreigners and property *throughout all* of Mexican territory and to hold it responsible for raids begun on Mexican territory against the United States. Something very unequivocal on this subject of protection to foreigners would have a wholesome effect throughout Mexico. Should we accomplish by our next note a better feeling between the [de] facto government and our own, I think it imperative that something constructive be attempted at once in connection with Mexico's financial and economic situation.

Very sincerely yours,   David Lawrence

TLS (WP, DLC).
2 About this incident, see C. H. Dodge to WW, Jan. 14, 1916, n. 1, Vol. 35.

From Dudley Field Malone

Personal and Confidential.

Dear Mr. President: New York, N. Y. June 2, 1916.

Though it is very difficult to handle this New York political situation alone, I have already been in touch with Harris and we will try to get the situation straightened out. However, please do not send in any nominations for postmaster here or for the judgeship here until after the St. Louis Convention; and when I get back from the Convention I will see you again about these matters. I am trying hard to get Harris and the Party gladly to accept your wishes in the premises. It is most important that nothing be done now.   Yours affectionately,   Dudley Field Malone

TLS (WP, DLC).

To William Frank McCombs

The White House, June 3, 1916.

I have heard with gratification of the selection of Martin Glynn as temporary chairman. A strong body of opinion with which I concur centers on Ollie James for permanent chairman. I would be gratified by his selection.   Woodrow Wilson.

T telegram (WP, DLC).

Two Letters from Newton Diehl Baker

CONFIDENTIAL AND URGENT.

My dear Mr. President: Washington. June 3, 1916.

On my return to the office I had another conference with the Judge Advocate General, and am satisfied that your Constitutional power to call out the State Militia for the purposes named in the Constitution is not in any way attempted to be interfered with by the new Army Bill, but that the correct interpretation of the bill is that should you desire to *draft* the Militia for any other than the purposes named in the Constitution, previous authority of Congress would be necessary, just as it would if you were to call the volunteers under the old law. It is very much better, in my judgment, under these circumstances, not to raise the question by asking the Congress to pass any resolution of the kind I indicated to you. I am sure you will be relieved to know that the Act does not do what I had been told it did.

I send this hurriedly so that you will not make public any comment that would be based on this information as to the effect of the Act.   Sincerely yours,   Newton D. Baker

Dear Mr. President: Washington. June 3, 1916.

One of the grave concerns of America, after the close of the European war, is going to be to close up the breaches between our people growing out of their sympathies with the contestants.

My own notion is that the wholesome part of our German population is eager for some note of recognition and reconciliation and that we can afford to forget the unwholesome part for a while. Would it not be worth while for you, in some speech, to recast the following suggestion and analogy:

One obvious result of the War in Europe has been to introduce a new division among us, based upon sympathies with the respective contestants there. This is not strange for where [while] we were not ourselves a party the sentiments of many of our people were naturally enlisted in behalf of those who spoke the same language and cherished the same traditions as their ancestors. Friendships, kinships and national literatures inspired sentiments and emotions both tender and partisan, it is natural and would be unfortunate only if it were allowed to become a division among us in our sentiment about America or to introduce distrusts among us about one another. But we have high comfort and assurance from our own history on that subject. We were torn by a conflict which divided us on vital issues for four years and left homes everywhere desolated by war. The idea of America which triumphed over the bitter memories of that struggle will cure the lesser divisions of this and leave us now as it left us then strong and united for all that makes up the great purpose of our national being.

I know Germans who would welcome such a message, and it would be a wholesome restraint upon some others who are "indicting a whole nation" of Germans among us because of the bad behavior or [of] a few Germans.

Sincerely yours,   Newton D. Baker

TLS (WP, DLC).

From Frank Lyon Polk, with Enclosure

My dear Mr. President: Washington June 3, 1916.

A question of policy has arisen as to what should be done in Santo Domingo and the Secretary of the Navy felt that your views should be obtained before any further messages are sent.

You probably recall that the President of that country resigned during the revolution.[1] The Cabinet is now the constitutional authority. It has been the opinion of Admiral Caperton and our Minister[2] that an election of a President should be prevented until peace is restored. We are informed the last two or three days, by a series of messages, that an election by Congress is imminent. The suggestion made by the Admiral and our Minister was that if nothing else would stop it, it would be well to arrest some of the Senators.

This impresses us as too high-handed and not necessary. After a conference today with the Secretary of the Navy, Admiral Benson, and Mr. Harrison, of this Department, two messages were prepared, one to be sent by the Secretary of the Navy[3] and one by this Department. I attach copies of the two messages for your approval.

If the present state of affairs cannot be maintained until peace is restored, and something has to be done, a solution of the present difficulties is indicated in these messages for the guidance of our representatives. Unless this is done, a great deal of ground already gained will be lost and it will be more difficult than ever to accomplish the reforms that you have had in mind.

As some action may be taken on Monday, these messages should be sent tonight or tomorrow. If they meet with your approval, I will have them sent on receiving word from the White House. If you desire to see me, I can be reached at my house any time this evening.

I am, my dear Mr. President,

Faithfully yours,   Frank L Polk

TLS (WP, DLC).

[1] President Juan Isidro Jiménez resigned on May 5 during an attempted *coup d'état* by the Minister of War, Desiderio Arias. In the course of this event, some one hundred and fifty United States marines had landed in support of the Jiménez regime. Lansing seized the attempted *coup* as an opportunity for full-scale intervention, and, under his direction, some six hundred marines and sailors took control of Santo Domingo on May 15. Within the next two months, the entire country was under the military occupation of some two thousand American sailors and marines. For these and other recent events in the Dominican Republic, see Arthur S. Link, *Wilson: The Struggle for Neutrality, 1914-1915* (Princeton, N. J., 1960), pp. 538-45.

[2] That is, William Worthington Russell.

[3] J. Daniels to *U.S.S. Dolphin*, June 3, 1916, T radiogram (WP, DLC). It repeated in compacted form the telegram that follows and also asked Caperton whether he needed an additional marine regiment.

E N C L O S U R E

AMLEGATION SANTO DOMINGO   Washington, June 3, 1916.

Your June 2, 4 p.m.

Senators should not be arrested.

Inasmuch as the United States will not tolerate revolution and will, if necessary, enforce peace in Santo Domingo, this Government cannot countenance the election of Arias or any of his friends or even Henriquez[1] in view of his present attitude, since the election of any of the foregoing would result in further revolution and bloodshed.

The Department believes that the present status quo should be maintained until peace is restored. But if the Senate insists upon the election, no candidate should be chosen who is not acceptable to the country and who will not be in sympathy with the policy of the United States, as set forth in the Department's instruction No. 139 of September 17 last.[2]

If therefore the Senate breaks its agreement not to proceed with election of President you will endeavor to induce Congress to agree on a desirable candidate and inform him of our intention to keep our forces in Santo Domingo until the reforms proposed by us are initiated and obtain his promise to support our policy, which Congress must likewise agree to make effective. Period. If this should prove impracticable, would it not be possible to assure the Council of Ministers now exercising the executive power, that they would have our support should they undertake to carry out our policy even if it were necessary for them to dissolve Congress, which apparently no longer has the support of nine of the twelve provinces, and proceed to the election of a new Congress which would properly represent the country and elect a President who would be acceptable to the country and carry out the reforms desired by the United States.

Regarding your recommendation to appoint financial controller, whom have you in mind? Would it not be well for receivership to act for the time being, as proposed in your May 29, 8 a.m.?

CC telegram (WP, DLC).
    [1] Federico Henríquez y Carvajal, president of the Dominican Supreme Court.
    [2] F. L. Polk to W. W. Russell, Sept. 17, 1915, printed in *FR 1915*, pp. 321-25.

From William Calhoun McDonald

Santa Fe, New Mexico, June 3, 1916.

Investigation in cases of Mexicans convicted of murder at Columbus March 9, 1916, shows that they had fair trial. Perhaps it was mistake to try cases in border county, but everything appears to have been fair. Six of men were probably taken in Mexico, but were legally in jurisdiction of court that tried them. Defense was that Villa impressed them into his service and that they did not know where they were. One of them was shown to have been in United States prior to March 9th; one admitted having been close to Miller[1] when he was killed.

W. C. McDonald

T telegram (WP, DLC).
    [1] Most primary and secondary accounts of the Columbus raid agree that two persons named Miller were killed in the attack: Charles DeWitt Miller of Albuquerque (occupation unknown) and C. C. Miller, usually identified as a druggist of Columbus. See the *El Paso Morning Times*, March 10 and 12, 1916.

From William Cox Redfield with Enclosure

PERSONAL.

My dear Mr. President: Washington June 3rd, 1916.

The suggestion has been made to me in which I concur heartily that the Democratic platform at the National Convention should contain a "Foreign Trade Plank." This should emphasize the importance of foreign trade and what the Democratic Party has done to promote it and embody the modern policy of our Party respecting same. The suggestion comes to me as per enclosed. I submit it as merely embodying an idea and as probably subject to amendment. My present thought is merely to urge that something of this kind be done.

Yours very truly,   William C. Redfield

TLS (WP, DLC).

E N C L O S U R E

Foreign trade is a vital element in our domestic prosperity. Under the Democratic Administration more has been done to promote and develop this trade than ever before. New forces in the foreign field have been created which with enlarged appropriations for their support have greatly enhanced our foreign business. The Democratic Administration has discovered and brought to the attention of the public new and valuable opportunities for the oversea sale of the products of American labor and enterprise.

Under the Federal Reserve Act American national banks have for the first time established foreign branches, and Democratic legislation has recently extended the opportunity so afforded. To enable our smaller producers and industries to compete effectively in foreign markets where they are confronted by combinations of foreign rivals equipped to resist American competition and leagues of foreign buyers organized to depress the prices of American products, particularly those derived from our natural resources, it is desirable that legislation be enacted which shall establish the unquestioned legality of cooperative effort among exporters while fully safeguarding the public interest against restraint of domestic trade.

T MS (WP, DLC).

Two Letters from Robert Latham Owen

PERSONAL.

My dear Mr. President: Washington. June 3, 1916.

The declaration of the Democratic National Platform on Pure Foods and Public Health, I quote as follows:

"We reaffirm our previous declaration advocating the union and strengthening of the various governmental agencies relating to pure food, quarantine, vital statistics, and human health. Thus united and administered without partiality to or discriminating against any school of medicine or system of healing, they would constitute a single health service, not subordinated to any commericial [commercial] or financial interest, but devoted exclusively to the conservation of human life and efficiency. Moreover, this health service should cooperate with the health agencies of our various states and cities, without interference with their prerogatives or with the freedom of individuals to employ such medical or hyg[i]enic aid as they may see fit."

I venture to remind you that since March 1913, I have before the beginning of each session of Congress urged this plank upon your attention, but other matters more urgent demanded and obtained the right of way, so that there is a very large group of people throughout the United States who are deeply disappointed at the failure of the Democratic Administration to establish a Department of Health, or an independent Bureau of Health, as we promised.

I am desirous of conciliating this element, but I am extremely anxious that the Democracy should pledge itself definitely and [un]equivocably to an independent Department of Health, with a Secretary of dignity in charge of it.

I therefore earnestly urge that you shall, as the leader of the Democratic Party, recommend such a plank, which I venture to suggest as follows:

"We favor a Department of Health under a Secretary, with a seat in the Cabinet, in which shall be united and administered the governmental agencies relating to human health, purefood and water, quarantine, vital statistics, which shall be conducted without any discrimination, for or against any school of medicine or system of healing, but devoted exclusively to the conservation and advancement of human health and physical efficiency."   Yours very respectfully,   Robt L. Owen

PERSONAL

My dear Mr. President: Washington. June 3, 1916.

I wish particularly to call your attention to the progressive doctrines which were set forth in relation to social and industrial justice in the platform of the Progressive Party in 1912. It expressed the aspirations of four million men who followed the progressive flag, and I am extremely anxious that since these doctrines represent fundamental Democracy we shall cause declarations to be put in the Democratic Platform which will emphasize the importance of these doctrines on the minds of the people of the country.

First, because it will educate the country along the right lines, and second because it will attach to the Democratic Party a very large number of Progressives who will be confused in mind at a coalition between Roosevelt and Barnes,[1] and whose confidence will be impaired by a fusion of standpatters and Progressives.

Yours faithfully,   Robt L. Owen

TLS (WP, DLC).
[1] William Barnes, conservative Republican boss of New York State.

To Frank Lyon Polk

My dear Polk: The White House June 5, 1916

Here is an interesting paper from David Lawrence, the correspondent of the New York Evening Post, which I think you would like to read.

In haste   Cordially yours,   Woodrow Wilson

TLS (F. L. Polk Papers, CtY).

To Robert Latham Owen

My dear Senator: [The White House] June 5, 1916

I have your letter of June second and realize the importance of the suggestion you make. Many of the Progressive principles set forth in the Progressive platform of 1912, however, were merely in thesis, because they affected matters controlled by the state and not by the national government. I would be very glad if you would let me have a memorandum as to those which you think we could all agree upon.

Cordially and sincerely yours,   Woodrow Wilson

TLS (Letterpress Books, WP, DLC).

To Henry Morgenthau

My dear Friend: The White House June 5, 1916

Thank you for your note of June second. I am indeed relieved and delighted at the confirmation of Brandeis. I never signed any commission with such satisfaction as I signed his. I understand that he is to be sworn in today.

Next time I see you I want to say a word to you about consulting with the senior Senator from Georgia.

What you tell me of your trip West and the temper of the people you met interests me very much indeed. I wish I myself had time to get out quietly among the people who are doing their own thinking.

In haste

Cordially and sincerely yours,   Woodrow Wilson

TLS (WP, DLC).

From Edward Parker Davis

My dear Woodrow,   [Philadelphia] June 5 1916

There are so many things to felicitate you about! but I know you are pleased about Brandeis; I am very, very glad. You won a signal victory for Justice.

Affectionately your   E P Davis.

ALS (WP, DLC).

To Edward Mandell House

Dearest Friend,   The White House. 6 June, 1916.

There are a score of things I want to speak to you about and take counsel with you about, but here is the chief one, and the only one I have time for to-day:

I am very much perplexed about the choice of a Chairman for the National Committee. I believe that if we are to get the best work out of the men in the trenches we ought, if possible, to select some man who knows them and whom they know not to be an alien or a highbrow. Homer Cummings is such a man, and is, I have reason to believe, in every way loyal to me and to what I try to represent. He is undoubtedly and sincerely progressive, is a gentleman and man of principle, and would know better than a stranger how to govern those whom we would wish to have guided and restrained, at the same time that his choice would greatly gratify the members of the National Committee. What do you think. I have not been able to bring my own judgment to either McCormick or Billings.

In haste,   Affectionately Yours,   Woodrow Wilson

WWTLS (E. M. House Papers, CtY).

Two Letters from Frank Lyon Polk

My dear Mr. President: Washington June 6, 1916.

Many thanks for Lawrence's interesting letter, which I return. I gave a copy to Mr. Lansing. As you know, Lawrence is a great friend of the Mexicans and we have heard that he receives a salary. I give this information to you for what it is worth.

Believe me, my dear Mr. President,
                              Yours faithfully,   Frank L Polk

My dear Mr. President: Washington June 6, 1916.

On Saturday, June 3, the French Ambassador called, apparently on a routine matter, but he at once plunged into the subject of peace rumors and the attitude of this Government towards a peace conference. He was with me some time and expressed the opinion over and over again that his country was not ready to treat with Germany. He begged me, if ever I heard of any intention on the part of this Government of offering mediation, to let him know so that he could request an interview with you, in order personally to explain the attitude of the French people.

I think that the French are particularly nervous over these peace rumors, as they rather fear that some of their allies may be tempted to listen to such suggestions and leave them in their hour of need.

Believe me, my dear Mr. President,
                              Yours faithfully,   Frank L Polk

TLS (WP, DLC).

From Melvin A. Rice

My dear Friend: New York City June 6, 1916

You will be interested in reading this long delayed letter received this morning,[1] relative to Fraulein Clara Bohm.[2] I hope that you will consider me justified in taking to myself the name of having been of more assistance to this lady than the actual facts warrant. Miss Bohm knows full well the source of this bounty,[3] and if at all necessary, my connection with the matter can be straightened out after the war.

If I can be of further assistance, will you kindly command me.

Respectfully,   Melvin A. Rice

TLS (WP, DLC).
[1] The letter is missing.
[2] Governess for the Wilson girls, 1897-98. She lived with the Wilson family in Princeton until at least 1900. See the numerous index references to her in Vols. 10 and 11 of this series.
[3] Wilson had arranged to send money through Rice to Fräulein Böhm, who was destitute.

To Albert Sidney Burleson

Dear Burleson,   The White House 7 June, 1916.

Many, many happy returns! May you live long to continue your admirable service to the country and may I have the good fortune to be associated with you.   Woodrow Wilson

ALS (A. S. Burleson Papers, DLC).

To Edward Parker Davis

My dear E. P.:   [The White House] June 7, 1916

I am indeed deeply glad about the Brandeis appointment, and thank you for thinking of me in connection with it. I am going to see the new Justice today and tell him how happy it makes me to see him on the great court.

Affectionately yours,   Woodrow Wilson

TLS (Letterpress Books, WP, DLC).

To Harry Augustus Garfield

My dear Garfield: The White House June 7, 1916

Thank you warmly for your little note about my address before the League to Enforce Peace. That is the kind of thing that warms my heart when it comes from people whom I know and trust.

Cordially and sincerely yours,   Woodrow Wilson

TLS (H. A. Garfield Papers, DLC).

To William Cox Redfield

My dear Mr. Secretary: [The White House] June 7, 1916

Your reminder about the importance of saying something about foreign trade in the platform was most welcome. You may be sure that I have that matter very much at heart.

In haste   Faithfully yours,   Woodrow Wilson

TLS (Letterpress Books, WP, DLC).

To Henry French Hollis, with Enclosure

My dear Senator: [The White House] June 7, 1916

Thank you warmly for having let me see the enclosed from Lippmann. I value his high opinion very much indeed.

Cordially and sincerely,   Woodrow Wilson

TLS (Letterpress Books, WP, DLC).

E N C L O S U R E

Walter Lippmann to Henry French Hollis

Dear Senator: [New York] May 29, 1916.

Thank you so much for your letter. It is all very kind of you.

Could you let me know where to find you in St. Louis?

I think the President's speech on Saturday night one of the greatest utterances since the Monroe Doctrine was proclaimed. In historic significance it is easily the most important diplomatic event that our generation has known.

Sincerely yours,   [Walter Lippmann]

CCL (W. Lippmann Papers, CtY).

To Hamilton Holt

My dear Mr. Holt: [The White House] June 7, 1916

I greatly value your kind letter of May twenty-ninth about my declaration before the League to Enforce Peace. I thank you for it and for the editorials with all my heart.

I am sincerely sorry to hear of the serious illness of your brother and hope that ere this he has taken a decided turn for the better.

Only an extraordinary pressure of business has prevented my acknowledging sooner your kind letter.

Sincerely yours, Woodrow Wilson

TLS (Letterpress Books, WP, DLC).

To Li Yüan-Hung[1]

Washington, June 7, 1916.

On this sad occasion of the death of President Yuan Shi Kai[2] I extend to the Government and people of China the deep sympathy of the Government and people of the United States and my own sincere condolences. Pray extend to Madam Yuan the personal sympathy of Mrs. Wilson and myself.

I also convey to you my best wishes for the continued prosperity of the Chinese people under your administration.

Woodrow Wilson

T telegram (SDR, RG 59, 893.001 Y9/16a, DNA).
[1] Formerly Vice-President of the Republic of China, now President.
[2] He had died on June 6, 1916.

From Dudley Field Malone

Chicago, Ill., June 7, 1916.

Consensus opinion here now is Harding's speech[1] a frost and Republicans as cheerful as the weather, which is awful. Have talked fifty six men yesterday and today, leading men of their party, and not one is sure anyone they name can beat you.

Man direct from Oyster Bay who saw Roosevelt yesterday says he is resigned to fact that Republicans will not name him and that in that event he does not care whom the Republicans name, or whether he runs on third ticket himself, as failure to name him—Roosevelt—will mean your reelection anyway. Roosevelt's great embarrassment is he does not see how he can refuse accept Progressive nomination without being called a traitor, and then deserted by both parties here. Spoke at women party convention last night against Pinchot,[2] Murdock, John Hays Hammond, Osborne, of Mich.,[3] had a battle royal and gave the whole convention a real dressing down for Mrs. Belmont's disrespectful and bad mannered speech of Monday.[4] They wanted equality and I gave it them, and yet the great national reason for your reelection received the only prolonged demonstration of the night. Am most anxious see you Saturday or Sunday before I go St. Louis. Will you wire me here Lasalle Hotel, what day and time will be convenient.

Dudley Field Malone.

T telegram (WP, DLC).

¹ Senator Warren G. Harding's keynote speech to the Republican national convention.

² That is, Gifford Pinchot.

³ Chase Salmon Osborn, Governor of Michigan, 1911-12.

⁴ The Congressional Union for Woman Suffrage held a convention in Chicago on June 5-7 to launch a Woman's Party, whose sole purpose was to secure passage of a woman suffrage amendment to the Constitution. Not even *The Suffragist*, the weekly newspaper published by the Congressional Union, reported on the speeches at the convention in any detail. The New York *World*, June 6, 1916, printed brief extracts from the speech of Alva Erskine Smith Vanderbilt (Mrs. Oliver Hazard Perry) Belmont on June 5. She was quoted as saying in part: "You are here to create a new woman's world. You are breaking down all the old platitudes that have kept women under. . . . There are in this country many men pleading, praying and paying for the Presidential nomination. Some of them are big, some little, all knowing about politics. They will be taught something more this year by the women. Our business is with these men who want to be President. . . . We of the Congressional Union ask the three million women who have the vote to here officially notify the candidates of all parties and all varying degrees of selfishness and indifference, that unless they pledge themselves to free all women of the United States and work for that freedom, they will not get one woman's vote."

The newspapers had even less to say about the speeches made by representatives of the Progressive, Republican, and Democratic parties on June 6, although they do indicate that all received a rough reception from the women delegates. The Democratic spokesman, Malone, according to the *New York Herald*, June 7, 1916, "roundly scolded the women for what he termed 'hypocritical criticism of big men in public life.' 'President Wilson is not impelled by a spirit of meanness,' he said. Mr. Malone attempted to tell why he favored the enactment of federal suffrage legislation. 'Tell it to the President,' said a voice in the audience. 'I shall be happy to tell it to the President,' replied Mr. Malone. 'But I shall tell it in a tone of respect.' "

From Edward Mandell House

New London, Lake Sunnapee,
New Hampshire. June 7, 1916.

Dear Governor:

I am wondering if you saw this from the Independent.¹ I think you have won Hamilton Holt permanently and that the Independent will support you as strongly as Howland² will permit.

In answer to Sir Horace Plunkett's queries in the cable a copy of which I sent you, I told him that I thought the execution of the Irish rebels had accentuated opinion against Great Britain.

In answer to his second as to whether the British Government should give out a statement concerning all their reasons I advised against it. Things are soon forgotten these tragic days and the quicker that is forgotten the better.

Enclosed is a copy of a letter which I have just written Sir Edward in answer to his long cable. I hope you will approve

I had an advance copy of Senator Harding's keynote speech and thought to send it to you, but it was so tame that I decided it was not worth while.

I either over-estimated Glynn's speech as it was first written or he did not rewrite it nearly so well. I did not have the first copy to compare with it.

Affectionately yours,   E. M. House

I will send a copy of my letter to Sir Edward tomorrow.

TLS (WP, DLC).
  [1] The enclosure is missing. It was undoubtedly one of the editorials cited in H. Holt to WW, May 29, 1916, n. 1.
  [2] William Bailey Howland, publisher of *The Independent*; incorrectly identified as Harold Jacobs Bailey on p. 307, n. 3, Vol. 34.

From Albert Sidney Burleson

My dear Mr. President: Washington June 7, 1916.

The enclosures have just been handed to me.[1]

Late yesterday afternoon Senator Walsh informed me that he was gathering together memoranda prepared by various Senators in the nature of suggestions to be considered by you in drafting the platform. Senator Walsh also said to me that he was going to leave for Saint Louis on Saturday.

I beg again to suggest that you avail yourself of an opportunity to confer with a few of the Senators and Representatives before they leave for the convention; I know that they would appreciate a word or two from you by way of suggestion; they desire to do what you want done.   Sincerely yours,   A. S. Burleson

TLS (WP, DLC).
  [1] Five undated T MSS (WP, DLC), written by Senators William J. Stone, Henry F. Hollis, Furnifold M. Simmons, Oscar W. Underwood, and Thomas J. Walsh. All were suggestions for the Democratic platform of 1916. Senator Stone stressed the administration's accomplishments in foreign affairs: keeping the United States at peace, defending American rights, and standing ready to offer mediation to the European belligerents. He recommended that the platform specifically endorse the dispatch of the Punitive Expedition to Mexico and keeping it there "as long as necessary." He also suggested a resolution commending the administration's Pan-American policy. Senator Hollis provided a list of the administration's achievements in domestic affairs and called for further social and economic legislation. Someone had penciled out Hollis's more radical proposals: compulsory arbitration of labor disputes, full suffrage rights for women, and universal military training. Senator Simmons also devoted himself to Democratic achievements at home, including "prosperity." Simmons discussed in some detail the tariff and banking laws enacted since 1913 and suggested that the Democrats stress the virtues of the income tax. Senator Underwood's half-page memorandum was devoted entirely to singing the praises of the Underwood-Simmons Tariff Act. Senator Walsh provided a fairly full draft of a complete platform, which discussed both foreign and domestic policy in some detail. He recommended that the Monroe Doctrine be "reasserted as a principle of democratic faith" and stressed that, in addition to guaranteeing the republics of the hemisphere against "aggression from another continent," the doctrine implied as well "the more scrupulous regard upon our part for the sovereignty of each of them." He applied this principle specifically to Mexico and drew a careful distinction between the pursuit of bandits over the border and "intervention." Walsh also urged support of the administration's policy of adequate military and naval preparedness. He, too, provided a long list of legislative and administrative accomplishments in the domestic sphere, particularly social-justice legislation.

He urged that the federal deficits made unavoidable by necessary expenditures for defense be met by a tax on munitions for the duration of the war, by an increase in the income tax, and by a graduated inheritance tax. Finally, Walsh called for a government-owned merchant fleet and for legislation to regulate the development of water power and mineral resources.

To Samuel Gompers

My dear Mr. Gompers: The White House June 8, 1916

I have been a long time answering your letter of April twenty-ninth about the conditions in Porto Rico[1] because I wanted to be more certain than I was at the time I received it that I knew what I was talking about.

Of course, it is not, literally speaking, possible to know entirely at a distance the conditions existing in the island, but I feel that I can assure you of this, of the sound character and patriotic attention[2] of the Governor. I have known him for a great many years and know how sincere and genuine he is. Of course, it is possible that he has made mistakes and has been unconsciously misled, but I feel certain of his inclination to justice and fairness.

Cordially and sincerely yours,   Woodrow Wilson

TLS (S. Gompers Corr., AFL-CIO-Ar).
[1] S. Gompers to WW, April 29, 1916, Vol. 36.
[2] Wilson dictated "intention."

To Lemuel Phillips Padgett

My dear Mr. Padgett: [The White House] June 8, 1916

Even before the bill passes the Senate in its final form, I want to express to you my warm admiration of the way in which you have handled a difficult matter in framing and putting through the naval bill. The attitude of the House shows in a most gratifying way the determination to make thoughtful preparation for national defense, and I could not deny myself the pleasure of telling you how sincerely I have admired the spirit and patriotism with which you have worked.

Cordially and sincerely yours,   Woodrow Wilson

TLS (Letterpress Books, WP, DLC).

To William Calhoun McDonald, with Enclosure

[The White House]
My dear Governor McDonald: June 8, 1916

It was very gracious of you to send me the message you did about the Mexicans convicted of murder at Columbus, and to give me the privilege of consulting with you about them.

I have been talking the matter over with the Secretary of War and he has written me the letter of which I take the liberty of enclosing you a copy. I am sure that you will regard it as as [*sic*] frank and fair as it seems to me, and I submit it for your generous consideration.

Cordially and sincerely yours,   Woodrow Wilson

TLS (Letterpress Books, WP, DLC).

ENCLOSURE

Newton Diehl Baker to Joseph Patrick Tumulty

(PERSONAL.)

My dear Mr. Tumulty: Washington. June 6, 1916.

Under date of June 3rd Governor W. C. McDonald of New Mexico telegraphed the President with regard to the cases of the Mexicans convicted of murder at Columbus. To-day you sent me a copy of that telegram with request that I advise the President what embarrassments attach to the trial referred to.

The case is that of the six Mexicans convicted in the New Mexico State courts of complicity in the raid on Columbus. These men were tried, found guilty and sentenced to death. I suggested to the President that he ask the Governor of New Mexico to postpone their execution in order to avoid creating a hostile sentiment in Mexico by reason of our inflicting the death penalty upon these raiders while their chief, Villa, was still unapprehended. I still have a feeling that Villa is the responsible criminal and that these men were his ignorant dupes, and that therefore the extreme penalty is too severe. I have no doubt, however, that the trial accorded them was fair and that they are legally convicted under the laws of New Mexico, so that there cannot be any just criticism if the laws of that State are carried into effect. I beg leave to suggest, however, that in view of the fact that Villa has not yet been apprehended, and in view of the additional fact that these men were captured on Mexican soil, brought to the United States without the consent of the Mexican Government or of the men themselves, and therefore without a resort to the ordinary processes of extradition, which would be the usual way for the United States to secure custody of Mexican citizens who had offended against her laws, it would seem to me better if Governor McDonald would simply commute their sentences to life imprisonment, so that if in the round-up the Republic of Mexico undertakes to object to our abducting her citizens without going through the formalities of extradition as provided by treaty between that Republic and ours, she will at least not be able to say that we carried off her citizens and executed them.

It may well be that my feeling on this subject is in part affected by my complete aversion to capital punishment, but I do not think it is.   Cordially yours,   Newton D. Baker

TLS (WP, DLC).

To James Duval Phelan

My dear Senator: [The White House] June 8, 1916

Your letter of May thirty-first[1] gave me a great deal of concern and I have delayed replying to it in order that I might thoroughly inform myself. Since receiving it, I have fully conferred with the Attorney General and the Secretary of the Navy and feel that I can assure you that your impression is altogether wrong that there has been anything done by either the Attorney General or the Secretary which was intended, or even in their opinion calculated, to reflect upon the motives of anybody connected with the present pending legislation with regard to the oil lands of California, particularly the oil lands in Reserve No. 2. I am taking the liberty of sending you a copy of a statement I have just received from the Secretary of the Navy.[2] I send it for your information merely, because I have not obtained the consent of the Secretary to treat it otherwise than as a letter to myself. The Attorney General went over the matter very fully with me orally and assured me that, so far as his department was concerned, nothing had been accessible to the gentlemen of the Press except the official documents and public testimony accessible to everybody, and so far as he could ascertain even these had not been supplied the Press from anyone in his department.

I am very happy indeed to remove from your mind the impression under which you were laboring with regard to the publicity in this matter.

Cordially and sincerely yours,   Woodrow Wilson

TLS (Letterpress Books, WP, DLC).
   1 It is missing in both the Wilson and Phelan papers.
   2 "MEMORANDUM FOR THE PRESIDENT. Re pending legislation affecting the naval petroleum reserves. Prepared jointly by the Department of Justice and the Navy Department." T MS (WP, DLC). It discussed the probable productivity of the naval oil reserves in California and Wyoming and, in particular, how much of the total oil content of the reserves might be siphoned off to private companies if their claims to patents within the naval reserves were validated by the Phelan amendment to the general leasing bill.

To Hoke Smith

My dear Senator: [The White House] June 8, 1916

I appreciate very much your seeking my opinion about the bill on vocational education,[1] and I am dropping you a line just now to confess that I have not had time yet to give it the study it deserves and to say that I hope in a few days to write you. I am going to take the liberty of bringing it up at the next Cabinet meeting in order to get the opinions of some of my colleagues.[2]

Sincerely yours,   Woodrow Wilson

TLS (Letterpress Books, WP, DLC).

[1] H. Smith to WW, June 1, 1916, TLS (WP, DLC), enclosing printed bill S. 703, *To provide for the promotion of vocational education*. . . . Smith asked Wilson to submit any changes he might desire in the bill and especially requested Wilson's opinion of the proviso that the members of the Federal Board of Vocational Education had to be members of the cabinet.

[2] After the cabinet meeting on June 9, Wilson wrote to Smith on June 10 (TLS [Letterpress Books, WP, DLC]) and said that he did think that the members of the board should be cabinet members.

To William Joel Stone

My dear Senator: [The White House] June 8, 1916

I am ashamed to find that your memorandum of June first about the dinner at the Mercantile Club in St. Louis[1] has not been replied to. The fact is, my dear Senator, that when it was suggested to me that I speak to the Club over the telephone, I recalled the single effort I made to do that on a former occasion a couple of years ago and how utterly flat and unsuccessful it was, because of the impossibility of my taking any kind of fire when speaking merely into the transmitter of a telephone. I made up my mind then that that was the particular thing I could not and must not try again.

I wanted to give you this explanation at the same time I made my sincere and humble apologies for not having replied to your memorandum before the banquet came off.

Cordially and sincerely yours,   Woodrow Wilson

TLS (Letterpress Books, WP, DLC).

[1] It is missing.

To Melvin A. Rice

My dear Friend: [The White House] June 8, 1916

Thank you for the letter about Fraulein Bohm which you were kind enough to send me. You need not bother about relative services. The initiative was yours and you are not getting any credit which does not belong to you.

In haste

Cordially and sincerely yours,   Woodrow Wilson

TLS (Letterpress Books, WP, DLC).

From Robert Latham Owen, with Enclosure

My dear Mr. President: [Washington] June 8, 1916.

I enclose what I think would be of special value as a plank to attract the progressive elements in the country who ought to be with us, and not dividing their forces as an independent party, much less in the impossible relation of supporting Barnes, Penrose, Cannon and Root, who are absolutely hostile to the progressive program.   Yours, respectfully,   Robt L. Owen

TLS (WP, DLC).

E N C L O S U R E

The Democratic Party has persistently, for many years, strenuously contended for the fullest recognition of the rights of the people to govern themselves, free from machine rule.

In the platform of 1900, under this policy, we demanded the direct election of Senators, and declared in favor of direct legislation wherever practicable.

In 1908 we raised this issue in favor of giving the greatest possible power to the people in controlling their own government, and declared the overwhelming issue to be the right of the people to rule.

We now repeat and emphasize again the declaration of the platform of 1912 and we direct attention to the fact that the Democratic Party's demand for a return to the rule of the people, expressed in the National Platform of 1908, has now become the accepted doctrine of a large majority of the electors.

We again remind the country that only by the larger exercise of the reserve power of the people, can they protect themselves from the misuse of delegated power and the usurpation of governmental instrumentalities by special interests.

The Democratic Party offers itself to the country as the agency through which the complete overthrow and extirpation of corruption from machine rule in American politics can be effected.

With the triumph of these principles, the people both in the Nation and in the States, can carry out the spirit of Progressive Democracy in the conservation of human resources through enlightened measures of social and industrial justice; for the prevention of industrial accidents, occupational diseases and overwork; involuntary unemployment and other injurious effects incident to modern industry; the fixing of minimum safety and health standards for the various occupations, and the harmonious exercise of the public authority of State and Nation in maintaining such standards; the prohibition of child labor; the establishment of minimum wage standards for working men, women and children, and a living wage scale in industrial occupations; the establishment of an eight hour day for women and young persons, and one day's rest in seven for all wage workers; improved methods of dealing with delinquent citizens in prison and out of it; the preservation of the rights of human beings to the opportunity of labor, self support and development, and the establishment of such social and industrial reforms as will increase to the highest point the efficiency, the self respect, and the happiness of the American people.

T MS (WP, DLC).

From Albert Sidney Burleson

Personal

My dear Mr. President,   Washington June 8, 1916.

When I reached home yesterday afternoon I found the beautiful flowers and your highly appreciated note. I feel that it was well worth while to live fifty three years in order to receive such commendation.   Faithfully yours,   A. S. Burleson

ALS (WP, DLC).

To Newton Diehl Baker

My dear Baker: The White House June 9, 1916

I have failed to thank you for the suggestion contained in your letter of June third about a message to our fellow-citizens of German extraction along the lines of the results of the Civil War. I am sincerely obliged to you for it and shall certainly act upon it on the first favorable occasion.

Cordially and sincerely yours,   Woodrow Wilson

TLS (WDR, RG 94, AGO Document File, No. 2638801, DNA).

To Robert Lansing, with Enclosure

My dear Lansing: The White House June 9, 1916

I hope sincerely that no official impropriety prevents our acceding to the request of the enclosed letter. Henry Lane Wilson was one of the worst men we ever had to deal with and it would be a shame if for lack of the necessary evidence he were permitted to injure an honorable and public-spirited man.

Cordially and faithfully yours,   Woodrow Wilson

TLS (SDR, RG 59, 812.00/24727, DNA).

E N C L O S U R E

From Jesse Corcoran Adkins[1]

Dear Mr. President: Washington, D. C. June 6, 1916.

I am one of the counsel for Mr. Norman Hapgood in the suit filed in this District against him by Mr. Henry Lane Wilson for libel.

The articles complained of were written by Mr. Murray,[2] who is now in Mexico City and it is quite uncertain when we will be able to see him. The articles were based very largely upon dispatches from Mr. Wilson while Ambassador to Mexico.

It is essential that we prepare our pleas as soon as possible, and to do this safely and intelligently we should see the dispatches of Mr. Wilson.

Mr. Hapgood tells me that he spoke to you about the matter a few days ago, and that you were good enough to say that we might see the dispatches.

May I ask therefore that you request the Secretary of State to permit me to examine these dispatches at an early day?

Respectfully,   Jesse C Adkins

TLS (SDR, RG 59, 812.00/24727, DNA).
  [1] Lawyer of Washington, Assistant Attorney General of the United States 1912-14.
  [2] Robert Henry Murray, "Huerta and the Two Wilsons," *Harper's Weekly*, LXII (March 25-April 29, 1916), 301-303, 341-42, 364-65, 402-404, 434-36, and 466-69.

To Dudley Field Malone

[The White House] June 9, 1916

Have not wired before because of uncertainty as to my engagements. Will you see me here at the house at twelve thirty on Sunday. Thank you for the telegram as to the interesting meeting you attended.   Woodrow Wilson.

T telegram (Letterpress Books, WP, DLC).

To Byron Rufus Newton

My dear Newton: The White House June 9, 1916

Alas, I have to observe the very utmost ceremonial cleanliness in all matters touching the awful struggle on the other side of the water, and I do not think there would be at present propriety in Mrs. Wilson's receiving a cutting from a rose bush sent from the battlefield of Verdun.[1] It is true that both sides are engaged there, but Verdun is a French fortress, and you know the old maxim, "In case of doubt do nothing."

        Cordially and sincerely yours,   Woodrow Wilson

TLS (B. R. Newton Papers, CtY).
  [1] B. R. Newton to JPT, June 7, 1916, TLS (WP, DLC).

To Sir Cecil Arthur Spring Rice

My dear Mr. Ambassador: [The White House] June 9, 1916

Only the other day did I hear of the distressing loss you have suffered in the death of your brother.[1] May I not convey to you my warmest sympathy? The tragical circumstances of the time are a burden upon all our spirits, and I can imagine what the added burden must be of those who suffer irreparable losses like yours.

        Cordially and sincerely yours,   Woodrow Wilson

TLS (Letterpress Books, WP, DLC).
  [1] Lt. Gerald Spring Rice of the British army, a younger brother of Sir Cecil, was killed in action in France on May 27, 1916, at the age of fifty-two.

From Edward Mandell House, with Enclosure

                                        New London,
Dear Governor: Lake Sunapee, N. H. June 9, 1916.

I have your letter of the 6th concerning Homer Cummings.

The objections to Cummings are several unless my information is incorrect. You will be able to determine this. I have just talked with Gordon over the telephone and have asked him to find out certain things and let me know. He will get in touch with

Morganthau and others and I should hear from him tonight or tomorrow.

I am told he represented the New Haven Railroad and also some of the directors that were indicted and are still awaiting a new trial.

Second. That there was a very disagreeable scandal connected with him some years ago the details of which I have completely forgotten, but the truth of which can be easily verified.

The fact that he is a member of the National Committee and is in touch with the old line politicians is an advantage. I understand, too, that he is capable. I have never met him therefore I speak without any personal knowledge whatever. I did not meet him because I accepted without investigation the objections mentioned.

I am not nearly so afraid of losing the rank and file as I am of not getting the necessary votes from the outside to win. The regulars have nowhere to go and if we got them all we are still in the minority and I think we should be more concerned in bringing into the fold those that are on the outside.

I am almost content to be here for awhile for I believe I can be of more service to you at present than if I were in New York where I hardly have a moment to think.

The enclosed is a copy of a letter to Sir Edward Grey.

Affectionately yours,   E. M. House

I shall probably be able to wire you about Cummings tomorrow.

TLS (WP, DLC).

ENCLOSURE

Edward Mandell House to Sir Edward Grey

Dear Sir Edward: New York, June 8th, 1916.

There is nothing much to add to the short cable I sent you on June 1st acknowledging receipt of yours of May 29. I had a long conference with the French Ambassador who came to New York for that purpose. I did not show him the cables sent you nor your replies, but told him in substance what was said to you without mentioning your Government.

He thinks France will not consider peace proposals of any sort at this time no matter how far we might be willing to go towards preventing aggressive wars in the future. The feeling of France is that never again can they ever have as strong a combination fighting with them as now and they desire to defeat Germany decisively.

I am afraid another year will go by leaving the lines much as they are today. I am told, on high authority, that Lord Kitchener thought just this.

What France could probably get out of it now is peace largely upon the basis of the status quo ante with perhaps Alsace and Lorraine added and Germany given compensation elsewhere perhaps in Asia Minor. Russia could get a warm seaport and Italy what she is entitled to. The world at large could have peace and, as far as human foresight could arrange, might have something akin to permanent peace.

The President has gone a long way towards placing upon this country its share of the responsibility for the future. I sometimes feel discouraged when the Allied Governments and press overlook the weight the President has thrown on their side at almost every turn of the war and pick out some expression he makes giving it a meaning and importance he never meant. If we are to take part in maintaining the peace of the world we could hardly be indifferent to the war and its causes and the President never intended to leave such an impression.

Unless you have better means of knowing the situation than we have, there does not seem to be much reason for the optimism of the Allies. It is true that the blockade is gnawing Germany and giving her much concern, but our reports are that she can hold out indefinitely as far as the food supply.

Your belief that the President's proposal for permanent peace cannot be successful with a victorious Germany does not seem to us to enter into the matter for what is proposed would surely be anything but that. Looking at the situation from this distance, it seems that England might easily be in a worse position later, even though the fortunes of Germany recede. I think it must be looked at not only from the present viewpoint, but from what is likely to come later. In getting rid of the German peril, another might easily be created. The matter requires a dispassionate outlook free from all present prejudices.

I wonder, too, whether the Allies fully realize that their position here may materially change after November.

As far as I can see there is nothing to add or to do for the moment and if the Allies are willing to take the gamble which the future may hold, we must rest content.

Lord Kitchener's death has deeply distressed me.[1] While I know his work had largely been accomplished, yet I doubt whether England realizes how potential his name was throughout the world and what a pillar of strength it seemed.

With warm regards and good wishes, I am, my dear Sir Edward, Sincerely yours, [E. M. House]

CCL (WP, DLC).
¹ Horatio Herbert Kitchener, 1st Earl Kitchener of Khartoum, perished on June 5, 1916, when *H.M.S. Hampshire*, on which he was sailing to Russia, sank off the Orkneys. *H.M.S. Hampshire* apparently struck a mine.

From Frederic Clemson Howe, with Enclosure

My dear Mr. Wilson: Ellis Island, N. Y. June 9, 1916.

I take the liberty to enclose copy of a suggested plank for insertion in the Democratic platform. It is self-explanatory, and looks to the raising of the direct issue between democracy and imperialism. There is every evidence that the privileged interests in this country, especially the banking and concession seeking interests, are urging what they term "a strong foreign policy" as an aid to the same kind of financial imperialism that has brought over 100,000,000 people under the dominion of the greater powers of Europe during the last thirty years, and led to countless irritations, conflicts and diplomatic contests, which formed a prelude to the present war. We are the only country with surplus capital to invest. The European countries will be kept from the field of overseas exploitation for a generation to come; and this, with the monopoly of the resources of America, creates a condition in which surplus wealth will inevitably seek foreign fields, which requires dollar diplomacy, the use of the State Department and the Navy to make their concessions secure.

It seems obvious to me that the Republican party stands for this policy. I am satisfied that these influences stand behind Colonal [Colonel] Roosevelt, and see in his election an agency for the promotion of just such a programme. I am satisfied, too, that the American people would rise to a repudiation of this doctrine if presented to them, and I believe it is eminently good politics to place this issue in the forefront and frankly develop it before the people.

I have the honor to remain,

Very sincerely yours, Frederic C. Howe

TLS (WP, DLC).

ENCLOSURE

SUGGESTED PLATFORM DECLARATION OF THE DEMOCRATIC PARTY
REGARDING DEMOCRACY OR IMPERIALISM.

We adhere to the democratic doctrine that all peoples have a right to establish their own form of government and control their internal affairs.

We commend as one of his most distinguished achievements the action of President Wilson in refusing to lend the sovereign power of the United States to private interests in Mexico, Central America and China, and take pride in his solicitous respect for the political integrity of these countries.

We condemn as undemocratic and dangerous to the peace of the nation the doctrine that the State Department and the flag should follow the investor; and hold that such a doctrine is inimical to friendly relations with weaker peoples.

We believe that imperialism is one of the gravest dangers to democracy, and declare the Democratic Party to be irretrievably opposed to dollar diplomacy, the acquisition of new territory, or to any act which threatens the sovereignty or political integrity of any people.

T MS (WP, DLC).

From Edward William Pou

Dear Mr. President: Smithfield, N. C. June 9th, 1916.

I was elected a delegate to the National Convention because I have consistently supported the policies of your administration. It has not been difficult to do this, for the reforms demanded by your administration are reforms for which I have fought the most of my life.

I have read in the newspapers that the Progressive party demands in its platform a navy second in power and efficiency. Why should a great rich nation like America have a navy second to any other? In one of your speeches you said, if I remember correctly, that the navy of the United States should be "unconquerable." Why not put that in our platform? It is a fine word. I suggest for your consideration to go in our platform the words unconquerable navy. I believe the words unconquerable navy represent the wishes, the aspirations of the great majority of Americans. They certainly represent my own views. If we are to have a navy, why should it be second? I believe there are very few Americans who will not say let it be first.

With every good wish, Mr. President, I beg to remain,

Sincerely your friend,   Edwd W. Pou.

TLS (WP, DLC).

From Li Yüan-Hung

Peking, June 9, 1916.

On behalf of the government and people of China, I thank the Government and people of the United States and yourself for your message of sympathy on the occasion of the death of President Yuan Shih Kai. Madame Yuan desires me to express to Mrs. Wilson and yourself her heartfelt thanks for your kind expression of sympathy guided by the great ideas that have made the United States an enduring Republic and a prosperous country. I hope to see realized your wishes for the prosperity of the Chinese people.

Li Yuen Hung

T telegram (WP, DLC).

From Walter Hines Page

Dear Mr. President: London, June 9. '16

The atmosphere here is far from clear. The British are annoyed by the German peace-propaganda all over the world and especially in the United States. The German purpose, as the British see it, is not a sincere wish for peace, unless, indeed, peace cd. be got with an acknowledgment that Germany is victorious; but they regard it as an effort to convince the German people and neutrals that the blame for continuing the war must fall on England. The more that peace-talk is indulged in now the further the English are driven from peace. Peace? The word and the idea have never before been in such bad repute here. Of course the English want peace just as they want culture. But, as culture must not be *Kultur*, so peace must be security from a repetition of this war. I cannot officially verify what I am about to write, but I have heard it from credible sources. A Swedish gentleman of good standing came here recently directly after a visit to Berlin and (it is said) after an audience with the Kaiser. He talked peace. I have not heard that he was authorized to make a definite proposal, but he did have authority to discuss some sort of general proposition. He saw the Prime Minister and he saw Sir Edward

Grey. The mere fact that they gave him an audience has been kept very secret. I am told that a mere handful of people know even that such a man has been here. From Mr. Asquith and Sir Edward he got very cold comfort.

Not only does this peace-talk muddy the waters, but also a fear of an angry time coming with us over the blockade. They are not going to relax the blockade: if there had ever been any chance of its being relaxed, such a chance was shot to pieces in the big sea-fight.[1] The British navy, with the full force of British opinion behind it, will make its strangle-hold the tighter, be the consequences what they may. Item in proof of that—An officer of this Government whom I know is now in Holland on the secret errand of outbidding the Germans for all the foodstuffs that Holland will export, including the oncoming harvest. All food in Germany is, of course, taken by the Government, and the British Government will increase its efforts to prevent any food from getting in. If, therefore, we return to the contest about the blockade in general, we'll make no progress in inducing the English to relax it, but we will strain relations. They will do almost anything else for us. They are what might truly be called morbidly anxious to retain our good will. But our good relations will not endure the strain of any stiffer or renewed contention by us, looking towards relaxing the blockade. We have forcibly set down our position: that's our contention for international law. We have made a practical basis for claims for such damages as we suffer. We cannot do more that can have practical value.

Much uneasiness is produced here on this general subject by our diplomatic methods. I will illustrate. The cases of Americans who wishd. to get permits to bring goods out of Germany were at first presented both in Washington and in London. The State Department was—quite properly—displeased that this business was transacted through two channels. I was instructed to ask Sir Edward Grey if he wd. consent to have *all* these cases presented at Washington. He consented and the British Gov't, to please us, refused further to see the American lawyers here who seemed to think that they got some advantage by coming here instead of going to our trade advisers in Washington. The Department instructed me to thank Sir Edward Grey. The British Gov't thereupon adjusted itself to this change, at our request. Now comes a request from the Department that the British Gov't shall receive one of our trade advisers (or a man to be sent by them) and go over a lot of these cases here with him. We ask them to make a change and concentrate all this business in Washington. They

[1] The Battle of Jutland, which occurred on May 31.

assent. We thank them. They adjust themselves to the change. Now we ask them to change back.

In a private conversation between an important under-officer in the Foreign Office and one of the Secretaries of the Embassy, the Englishman said: "How can we ever tell what you want? God knows we try to please you. But you ask one thing today and the very opposite tomorrow; and, when we've finished a piece of business with you—or think we have finished it—we discover that the negotiation has just begun." I mention such a subject not because of its intrinsic importance, but to illustrate, by a concrete case, what I mean when I say that our zigzag presentation of an endless number of private commercial cases with the full machinery of our diplomatic establishment produces an atmosphere unfavorable to success in larger matters. Other countries do not do it. The result is, we seem to nag the British Gov't rather than to conduct important controversies with them.

I am, therefore, somewhat apprehensive. We present hundreds of nagging protests and objections that enforce no large principle but that at last produce a cumulative effect of sheer quarrelsomeness—a policy of "hit-'em-ag'in," "give his tail another twist." I can't tell you what a joy it is when a case comes along that involves some clear principle, such as the case of the Germans who were taken off the American ship "China"[2]—a *Trent* case reversed. That was worth while and we got what we contended for. And Sir Edward Grey is becoming apprehensive—the friendliest and most patient and most courteous Forn. Secretary imaginable. He told an English friend of his the other day that the blockade is necessary to win the war, the blockade as tight as it can be made; that if the U. S. makes embarrassing demands, those demands will have to be disregarded—a very painful thing for him to do— or the war will be lost; and that, if the U. S. does not make em-

---

[2] The British armed merchant cruiser, *Laurentic*, on February 18 removed twenty-eight Germans, eight Austrians, and two Turks from the American mail steamer *China*, bound from Shanghai to Nagasaki, on the high seas about ten miles off the entrance to the Yangtze River. Lansing and Page pursued this case vigorously. They contended that the details were very similar to the *Trent* affair during the American Civil War and that, under international law, civilian subjects of belligerent nations could not be removed from neutral vessels proceeding from one neutral port to another. Finally, they demanded the immediate release from detention of the thirty-eight men involved. By May 3, Sir Edward Grey had agreed informally to the release of the prisoners; moreover, in an official memorandum dated May 8, he substantially agreed with the principle argued by Lansing and Page, although he maintained that the case should not be a precedent for the future. However, the Foreign Office was quite dilatory about ordering the release of the detained men and, consequently, on June 28, Lansing sent a sharp note demanding their immediate freedom. On July 31, Grey informed Page that orders had been sent to release the men from their detention in Australia. The American consul general in Shanghai reported on November 15 that they had been returned to that port. See the correspondence on the *China* affair in *FR-WWS 1916*, pp. 632-67 *passim*.

barrassing demands, the war will be won and won within a reasonable time and American good-will retained. He has, in effect, expressed the same idea to me more than once. But to this Englishman he expressed a degree of fear that he has never expressed to me. I get the impression from my neutral and Allied colleagues here that they all together have less business—fewer items of diplomatic business—with the Forn. Officer—than we alone have.

So much for present peace-talk and so much for our relations to these over-wrought folk of this Kingdom, which, praise God, in spite of many jars, are not yet bad. They need our good-will and value it and will do everything to retain it short of changing their war-programme or of surrendering what they conceive to be a necessary policy for their ultimate victory. They have thought it all out. They have made up their minds—the Government and the whole Nation. They will not relax their sea pressure for any consideration whatsoever.

And when the war will end nobody knows. I have lately heard such opinions as these advanced by men whose judgment I respect—(1) that the sea-war is over, for the German fleet will not venture out again, and (2) that a British drive will be made in France when the situation at Verdun and on the Russian frontier seem to have brought the favorable moment—a drive wh. the English expect to be successful. If this hope be realized the war may end then or soon thereafter. If not, it will go on into next year. These opinions are, perhaps, as good as any others. There is a sort of general expectation here that the German submarine activity will at some time be renewed.

The sea-fight did more than all preceding events to rouse the English interest and to strengthen the English resolve. Sea-fights appeal to their imagination as nothing else does. You hear in every gathering of men or women the spirited story of the fleet's return after the battle. It steamed into the Frith of Forth majestically in regular order, every ship, whether sound or battered, in its proper place in the line, with an appropriate gap for every one that had been lost. When the battle began, the *Invincible*, wh. had been assigned to the head of the battle-cruiser line, was out of place—by some misunderstanding was behind. But, as soon as the first shot was fired and it was evident that a battle had begun, the *Invincible* put on all her steam and came past the other ships at a rate that no cruiser ever ran before—passing them all; and every ship cheered her as she ran to her place in the front of the line. Then in half-an-hour she went down. On one ship all the officers were killed but an 18-year-old lieutenant. The charts were destroyed and, I think, the compass. The machinery was disabled

& a large part of the crew were dead or wounded. That boy brought her into port a day late.

Such events as these will take their place in the immortal annals of the British navy; and so far as the English are concerned, the war is just begun. The day after the battle, Admiral Jellicoe telegraphed: "My fleet is ready for action."

Yours Sincerely,   Walter H. Page

ALS (WP, DLC).

From Charles Evans Hughes

To the President: Washington, D.C. June 10, 1916.

I hereby resign the office of Associate Justice of the Supreme Court of the United States.[1]

I am, Sir,   Respectfully yours,   Charles E. Hughes.

TLS (WP, DLC).
[1] Hughes had been nominated for the presidency by the Republican national convention on June 10.

To Charles Evans Hughes

Dear Mr. Justice Hughes: [The White House] June 10, 1916.

I am in receipt of your letter of resignation and feel constrained to yield to your desire. I, therefore, accept your resignation as Justice of the Supreme Court of the United States to take effect at once.

Sincerely yours,   Woodrow Wilson

TLS (Letterpress Books, WP, DLC).

From William Gibbs McAdoo

Dear Mr. President: Washington June 10, 1916.

1. On page 2 of your draft,[1] which I return herewith, I would suggest the substitution of the following for lines 8 to 18, inclusive, beginning with the words "the archaic system":

"The archaic system of banking and currency under which the country was living, a system which has[2] proved

[1] McAdoo was commenting upon Wilson's first full draft of the platform. This draft is a CC MS in WP, DLC, and has many WGMhw emendations, which McAdoo explains in his letter. Wilson's penultimate draft was in turn based upon WWsh outlines, a shorthand draft, and a WWT draft, all in WP, DLC.

For the degree to which Wilson accepted McAdoo's suggestions, see the draft of the platform printed as the next document.

[2] Wilson changed this to "had."

the prolific cause of panic and financial disaster and the impregnable stronghold *of selfish control*[3] in the field of credit and enterprise, has been utterly done away with and, by the enactment of the Federal Reserve Act, the Democratic Party has substituted a system under governmental control, which has resulted in the establishment of a true democracy of credit and a bulwark of financial resources which have successfully withstood the shock of a great world war and has produced an ease and prosperity of business enterprise such as the country has never known before."

Reason: It is important, I think, to bring out clearly the fact that the Federal Reserve Act, for which the Democratic Party is responsible, has produced these results. Nowhere in your draft is allusion made to the Federal Reserve Act, which is generally conceded to be one of the strongest claims we have upon the support of the business interests of the country.

2. At the end of line 11, after the words "any quarter," paragraph VI, page 6, I suggest the insertion of the following:

"And be able to assert and protect their just rights upon the high seas and in every quarter of the globe."

Reason: It seems to me that we should not limit the uses of the Navy and the Army to the extent that you have done in the sentence embraced within lines 7 and 11, paragraph VI, page 6.

For the same reasons I think there should be inserted in line 13, paragraph VI, page 6, after the words "and safety," the following:

"and the protection of the national rights,"
or something to this effect.

It may be necessary, in view of these suggestions, to broaden the whole of paragraph VI so as to convey fully the meaning that we want an adequate army and navy, not only for domestic order and tranquility, but also for the assertion and maintenance of our just rights throughout the world and to enable us to perform our proper part in the great "international tasks" which, as you very happily state, we hope and expect to "take a part in performing."

3. In line 7, page 9, paragraph VIII, instead of saying

"and her neighbors to the South of us,"
I would substitute

"and her Latin American neighbors."

By adding to the end of this paragraph the suggestion I submitted to you yesterday,[4] endorsing specifically the Pan American

3 WWhw.
4 "We commend the action of the Administration in holding the Pan American

Financial Conference of 1915 and the work of the International High Commission as the most practical measures or steps in this direction yet taken, I think this ground would be properly covered.

4. It seems to me that you have not brought out strongly enough the "social and industrial justice" phase in section XI, pages 11 and 12, and I would suggest that you broaden this, if possible. A few general words might cover this. Perhaps you would be interested in reading what the Progressive platform as adopted in Chicago has to say on this subject:

"A nation to survive must stand for the principles of social and industrial justice. We have no right to expect continued loyalty from an oppressed class. A country must be worth living in to be worth fighting for."

These are, of course, mere generalizations, but it seems to me that if we could make a specific declaration that the party pledges itself to do every possible thing for the betterment of social and industrial conditions in the country, it would be wise. To ignore it altogether would be misunderstood.

5. You have omitted what I think is a most important declaration, all references to the paragraph in the Democratic Platform of 1912 in relation to the Russian Treaty and the determination of the Democratic Party to stand for the "equality of all our citizens, irrespective of race or creed * * * and the fundamental right of expatriation." A failure to reiterate the position we took in 1912 would be a serious mistake, and would, I fear, alienate the support of large numbers of our foreign born citizens.

Louis Marshall, a prominent lawyer and Jew of New York, has suggested the following:

"We again declare that the sacred rights of American citizens must be preserved at home and abroad, and that no treaty with any other government shall receive the sanction

---

Financial Conference at Washington in May 1915 and organizing the International High Commission which represented the United States in the recent meeting of representatives of the Latin American Republics at Buenos Aires, April 1916, as the most effective and practical steps yet taken for the strengthening of our relations with Latin-America." WGMhw MS (WP, DLC).

About the financial conference, see n. 1 to Wilson's welcome to the Pan American Financial Conference, printed at May 24, 1915, Vol. 33. One important result of the conference was the establishment of an International High Commission, composed of five to seven members, along with the finance ministers of every American nation. Its purposes were to solve international legal problems, to facilitate commercial treaties and foreign exchange, unify trade laws, and deal with other issues affecting the commercial relations of the nations of the western hemisphere. The first meeting of the commission was held in Buenos Aires, April 3-13, 1916. The United States delegation was headed by McAdoo. See W. G. McAdoo, *Crowded Years* (Boston and New York, 1931), pp. 353-54, 358-59; and John J. Broesamle, *William Gibbs McAdoo: A Passion for Change, 1863-1917* (Port Washington, N. Y., 1973), pp. 207-11.

of our government which does not express or recognize the absolute equality of all our citizens, irrespective of race, *Too long*[5] creed or previous nationality, and which does not guarantee the right of expatriation. The constitutional rights of American citizens should protect them on our borders and go with them throughout the world, and those of them who may reside or have property in any foreign country are entitled to and must be given the full protection of our Government. At the earliest practicable opportunity our country should strive earnestly for peace among the warring nations of Europe and seek to bring about the fundamental principle of justice and humanity that all men should enjoy equality of right and freedom from discrimination in the lands wherein they dwell."

I enclose a letter from Mr. Marshall,[6] which I thought I had sent to you, and which I think it would be well if you would read. You can contrast his proposal with what was contained in the 1912 Democratic Platform, which is set out in his letter. I also enclose a letter of June 9th from Mr. Marshall, in which he recites the declarations of the Republican and Progressive platforms adopted the other day in Chicago.[7] Mr. Marshall, you will observe, has added an expression of hope for peace in Europe. Both the Republican and Progressive platforms, just adopted, contain an expression of this sort. For the sentimental effect I think it would be well if the Democratic platform contained, as a separate paragraph, some such provision. No one can phrase it in such admirable language as you can and, therefore, I do not offer a concrete suggestion.

6. The Democratic Platform of 1912 expressly condemned the "money trust" and the "present methods of depositing government funds in a few favored banks," and declared in favor of interest on government deposits. In view of this fact, it seems to me that it would be wise to put in a provision to the following effect:

"We commend the action of the administration in using the public money in the Treasury to move the crops, thereby destroying the long standing practice of the money trust to create tight money every year at crop moving time, to the injury of the farming industry of the country, and we endorse the policy adopted by the administration of charging interest on all government deposits instead of permitting favored banks to have the free use of government funds

5 WWhw.
6 McAdoo had just quoted the proposed plank in L. Marshall to WGM, June 7, 1916, TLS (WP, DLC).
7 L. Marshall to WGM, June 9, 1916, TLS (WP, DLC).

under the long established practice of Republican administrations."

7. The platform of 1912 also declared in favor of

"the establishment of a parcel post or postal express, and
also the extension of the rural delivery system as rapidly
as possible."

In view of the fact that the Republicans in their platform, just
adopted, say

"We favor the extension of the rural delivery system and
condemn the democratic administration for curtailing and
crippling it,"

I think it would be wise to insert the following:

"We commend the Democratic administration for redeem-
ing the pledge in the 1912 platform for the establishment of
a parcels post and the extension of the rural delivery system. The parcels post service has been highly developed,
the postal savings system has been enlarged, and the rural
delivery service has been increased and extended by the
addition of 2,500 rout[e]s and 8,000 extensions or rural
routes since March 4, 1913."

Faithfully yours,   W G McAdoo

TLS (WP, DLC); one page CC MS (W. G. McAdoo Papers, DLC).

A Draft of the National Democratic Platform of 1916[1]

[c. June 10, 1916]

The Democratic party in National Convention adopts the following declaration to the end that the people of the United States
may both ⟨see⟩ *realize* the achievements wrought by four years
of Democratic administration and be apprised of the policies to
which the party is committed for the further conduct of national
affairs.

In looking back over the eventful years which have elapsed
since the Presidential campaign of 1912, during which the Democratic party has been in control of both the legislative and executive branches of the government, we feel that we can safely
challenge comparison of the record of achievement, of redeemed
promises and constructive legislation with that of any dominant
party during any previous generation. Brief as the time has been,

[1] This final draft represented a revision of the penultimate typed draft (WP,
DLC), which Newton Baker had slightly emended. Words in angle brackets
were deleted by Wilson; words in italics were added by him in making his final
literary changes. Baker took the ribbon copy of the revised final draft to St.
Louis on June 12.

it has yet sufficed to produce great legislative enactments in the interest of justice and of better and freer business enterprise. The unprecedented has happened. A great political party has within the term of a single administration redeemed the pledges of a platform full of specific promises with regard to every great subject of national concern.

When the Democratic party came into the control of the government in March 1913, the life of the country was hampered on every hand by the existence of special privilege. The tariff laws in operation were admitted to be the fertile soil of selfish advantage, credit was restricted, and the currency fatally inelastic. The foreign affairs of the nation were dominated by the commercial interests of those who ⟨governed⟩ *controlled* the field of credit and the course of enterprise rather than by considerations of impartial justice and the general interests of the nation as a body politic. The Republican party had proved impotent to correct the most flagrant abuses, though expressly pledged to attempt their correction. It had conspicuously failed as an instrument of progressive government and had as a consequence split asunder into hopelessly divergent factions. Special privilege had grown more rank and insolent than ever under the very administrations that had professed to be about to destroy it. Since the inauguration of the present administration at Washington, the whole aspect of affairs in all of these essential matters has been altered. Under a Democratic leadership which never hesitated or halted and which no obstacles retarded, the legislative axe has been laid to the root of the tree of special privilege and the refreshing spectacle has been witnessed of a complete release of the energies of a free people within all the great fields of business enterprise. The archaic system of banking and currency under which the country was living—a system which had proved the prolific cause of panic and financial disaster and the impregnable stronghold of selfish control in the field of credit and enterprise —has been utterly done away with by the enactment of the Federal Reserve Act, and a system has been substituted, under government control, which has resulted in the establishment of a true democracy of credit, and which has proved a true bulwark of *financial* strength in time of stress. The financial resources of the country have been mobilized and placed at the disposal of business and industry by a system which has not only proved sufficient for our ordinary demands but has successfully withstood the severe and sudden strain of a great world war and given ease and prosperity to business enterprise such as the country has never known before.

By the establishment of the Federal Trade Commission, many difficult questions concerning the accommodation of business method to the anti-trust laws of the country have been taken out of the field of debate and conjecture and put in the way of adjustment.

By a thorough and yet conservative reform of the customs duties, the business of the country has been taken out of the hands of special groups of favored manufacturers and restored to the wholesome and stimulating air of regulated competition. In *connection with* these customs laws there ⟨has been⟩ *was* given to the country provision for an income tax, which not only instituted a scientific and equitable method of taxation but *which has* maintained the revenues necessary to carry on the government during a period when the interruption of our foreign trade inevitably cut down the receipts from duties on imports.

For monopoly in the field of production fair business methods have been substituted and a tribunal created for their certain definition and determination.

Federal taxation, which, under Republican legislation, was altogether a burden on consumption, upon the expenses of the poor as well as the rich, has been put in a way to be equalized by the adoption of an equitable income tax, which affords the government an elastic means of adjusting taxation to the fair taxpaying capacity of the individual citizen.

By a much needed revision of the anti-trust laws human labor has been lifted out of the false position of being treated as a commodity in the view of the law and has been placed once for all in its right light as a human right.

The present Democratic administration has intelligently developed and made useful the parcels post service, enlarged the postal savings system, increased and extended the rural delivery service by adding 10,500 additional routes and extensions, thus reaching two million five hundred thousand people who theretofore had been denied any delivery service; it has increased the effiency of the postal service in all its branches, and at the same time so successfully administered its finances that it has for the first time in the history of the government placed the postal establishment upon a self-supporting basis, having produced actual surpluses for the years 1913, 1914 and 1916.

II

We have thus sought to clear and set at rest the most pressing and difficult questions of reform that had for many years demanded solution. What the business of the country now needs is stability, in order that it may have a definite, confident, and continuous development. We hold it to be the immediate duty of those who guide the counsels and shape the legislation of the nation to remove so far as possible every remaining element of unrest, uncertainty, apprehension or uneasy conjecture from the path of the business men of America, and to secure for them a period of quiet, assured and confident achievement. The reforms which were most obviously needed to clear away privilege, prevent unfair discrimination and release the energies of men of all ranks and advantages have been effected by recent legislation. We must now make sure of a period of constructive progress during which laws will promote, not alter or deflect, the course of enterprise and industry.

III

The future, however, bids fair to force upon the consideration of those responsible for the guidance of the nation's affairs many new matters of deep consequence and some old matters which will wear a new face. The events of the last two years have brought about many momentous changes. These changes have been operative chiefly outside of the United States and in the field of the large world of international relationship. In some respects their effects are yet conjectural and wait to be disclosed. They are likely to affect the United States chiefly in regard to its foreign trade and with regard to its relations with the other nations of the world. Two years of a war which has directly involved six of the chief industrial nations of the world, and which has indirectly affected the life and industry of all nations, are bringing about economic changes more varied and far-reaching than the world has before experienced. In order to ascertain just what those changes may disclose themselves to be, the Sixty-fourth Congress, controlled in both branches by Democratic majorities, is providing for a non-partisan tariff commission to make dispassionate and thorough study of every economic fact that might throw light either upon our past or upon our future fiscal policy with regard to the imposition of taxes on foreign trade or with regard to the general conditions under which our trade is carried on. We cordially endorse this timely and provident act of legislation and declare ourselves heartily in sympathy with the principle and purpose of shaping future legislation within that field in accordance with clearly established facts rather than by preconceived theory or the arbitrary demands of selfish interest.

IV

It is equally important that immediate provision should be made for the development of the carrying trade of the United States. Our foreign commerce has in the past had many unnecessary and vexatious obstacles placed in its way by the legislation of Republican Congresses. Until the recent tariff legislation, it was hampered by unreasonable burdens of taxation. Until the recent banking legislation, it had at its disposal few of the necessary instrumentalities of international credit and exchange. Until the formulation of the pending act to promote the construction of a merchant marine, it lacked even the prospect of adequate carriage by sea. We heartily endorse the pending shipping bill and favor all such additional measures of constructive or remedial legislation as may be necessary to restore our flag to the seas and to provide further facilitation for our foreign commerce, particularly such laws as may be made to remove unfair conditions of competition in the dealings of American merchants and producers with competitors in foreign markets.

We further urge the passage of such additional laws as may be necessary or proper to promote and foster the orderly and efficient development of the industry and commerce of the nation, both at home and abroad.

V

The part that the United States will play in the new day of international relationships which is now upon us will depend upon our preparation and our character. The Democratic party recognizes the assertion and triumphant demonstration of the indivisibility and coherent strength of the nation, therefore, as the supreme issue of this day in which the whole world faces the crisis of manifold change. It summons all men, of whatever origin or creed, who would count themselves Americans to join in making clear to all the world the unity and consentaneous[2] power of America. This is an issue of patriotism. To taint it with partisanship would be to defile it. In this day of test America must show itself, not a nation of partisans, but a nation of patriots.

VI

Along with the proof of our character as a nation must go the proof of our power to play the part that legitimately belongs to us. The people of the United States love peace. They respect the

---

2 Done with one consent; unanimous.

rights and covet the friendship of all other nations. They desire neither any additional territory which cannot be acquired by honorable purchase, nor any advantage which cannot be peacefully gained by their skill, their industry, or their enterprise. But they love and insist upon having absolute freedom of national life and policy, and feel that they owe it to themselves and to the role of spirited independence which it is their sole ambition to play that they should render themselves secure against the hazard of interference from any quarter, and should be able to protect their just rights upon the seas or in any part of the world. We, therefore, favor the maintenance of an Army fully adequate to the requirements of order, of safety and of the protection of the nation's rights which are constantly liable to disclose themselves even in times of settled peace; of an adequate reserve of citizens trained to arms and prepared to safeguard the people and territory of the United States against any danger of hostile action which may unexpectedly arise; and a fixed policy for the continuous development of a Navy worthy to support the great naval traditions of the United States and fully equal to the international tasks which the United States hopes and expects to take a part in performing. The plans and enactments of the present Congress afford substantial proof of our purpose in this exigent matter.

VII

The Democratic administration has throughout the present war scrupulously and successfully held to the old paths of neutrality and of the peaceful pursuit of the legitimate objects of our national life which statesmen of all parties and creeds have prescribed for themselves in America since the beginning of our history. But the circumstances of the last two years have ⟨disclosed⟩ *revealed* necessities of international action which no former generation can have foreseen. We hold that it is the duty of the United States to use its power, not only to make itself safe at home, but also to make secure its just interests throughout the world, and, both for this end and in the interest of humanity, to assist the world in securing settled peace and justice. We believe that every people has the right to choose the sovereignty under which it shall live; that the small states of the world have a right to enjoy the same respect for their sovereignty and for their territorial integrity that great and powerful nations expect and insist upon; and that the world has a right to be free from every disturbance of its peace that has its origin in aggression or disregard of the rights of peoples and nations; and we believe that the time has come when it is the duty of the United States to join with the other nations of the world in any feasible association that will effectively serve these principles, to maintain inviolate the complete security of the highway of the seas for the common and unhindered use of all nations, and to prevent any war begun either contrary to treaty covenants or without warning and frank submission of the provocation and causes to the opinion of mankind.

The present administration has consistently sought to act upon and realize in its conduct of the foreign affairs of the nation the principles that should be the object of any association of the nations formed to secure the peace of the world and the maintenance of national and individual rights. It has followed the highest American traditions. It has preferred respect for the fundamental rights of smaller states, even to property interests, and has secured the friendship of the people of those states for the United States by refusing to make a mere material interest an excuse for the assertion of our superior power against the dignity of their sovereign independence. It has regarded the lives of its citizens and the claims of humanity as of greater moment than material rights, and peace as the best basis for the just settlement of commercial claims. It has made the honor *and ideals* of the United States its standard alike in negotiation and action.

VIII

The Democratic party reaffirms its adherence to the principles of the Monroe Doctrine. Moreover, we recognize now, as we have always recognized, a definite partnership of the United States with the other peoples and republics of the Western Hemisphere in all matters of national independence and free political development. We favor the establishment and maintenance of the closest relations of amity and mutual helpfulness between the United States and the other republics of the American continents for the support of peace and the promotion of a common prosperity. To that end we favor all measures which may be necessary to facilitate intimate intercourse and promote commerce between the United States and her neighbors to the south of us, and such international understandings as may be practicable and suitable to bind the countries of the two Americas together in the assertion of their common rights and interests.

We commend the action of the Democratic administration in holding the Pan American Financial Conference at Washington in May 1915, and organizing the International High Commission which represented the United States in the recent meeting of representatives of the Latin-American republics at Buenos Aires, April 1916.

IX

For the safeguarding and quickening of the life of our own people, we favor the conservation and development of the natural resources of the country by means of a legal policy which shall be positive rather than negative, a policy which shall not withhold those resources from development but which, while permitting and encouraging their use, shall prevent both waste and monopoly in their exploitation. This policy has already been exemplified in legislation proposed in the present Congress regarding the use and development of water power within the public domain and forests and on the navigable streams of the country, and regarding the leasing of coal and oil producing lands, and we earnestly favor the passage of acts which will accomplish these objects.

X

We favor the vigourous prosecution of investigations and plans to render agriculture more profitable and country life more healthful, comfortable and attractive, and we believe that this should be the dominant aim of the nation as well as of the states. With all its recent improvement, farming still lags behind other occupations in development as a business, and the advantages of an advancing civilization have not accrued to rural communities in a fair proportion. A great deal has been accomplished in this field under the present administration—far more than under any previous administration. In the Federal Reserve Act of the last Congress and the Rural Credits Act of the present Congress, the machinery has been created which will make credit available to the farmer constantly and readily, and the farmer has at last been put upon a footing of equality with the merchant and the manufacturer in securing the capital *necessary* to carry on his enterprises. Grades and standards necessary to the intelligent and successful conduct of the business of agriculture have also been established, or are in the course of being established by law. The long-needed Cotton Futures Act, passed by the Sixty-third Congress, has now been in successful operation for nearly two years. A Grain Grades Bill, long equally needed, and a Permissive Warehouse Bill, intended to provide a means of supplying the farmer with the facilities he has needed to obtain the storage certificates upon which he may secure advances of money, have passed the House of Representatives, have been favorably reported to the

Senate, and will probably become law during the present session of the Congress. Both Houses have passed a good roads measure which will be of far-reaching benefit to all agricultural communities. Above all, the most extraordinary and significant progress has been made, under the direction of the Department of Agriculture, in extending and perfecting the practical farm demonstration work which is so rapidly substituting scientific for empirical farming. But it is also necessary that rural activities should be better directed through cooperation and organization, that unfair methods of competition should be eliminated and the conditions requisite for the just, orderly, and economical marketing of farm products created. We warmly applaud the Democratic administration for having emphatically directed attention for the first time to the essential interests of agriculture involved in farm marketing and finance, for creating the Office of Markets and Rural Organization in connection with the Department of Agriculture, and for extending the cooperative machinery necessary for conveying information to farmers by means of demonstrations. We favor continued liberal provision, not only for the benefit of production, but also for the study and solution of agricultural marketing and finance and for the extension of existing agencies for improving country life.

XI

We hold that the life, health and strength of the individual men, women and children of the nation are its greatest asset, and that in the conservation of these the Federal Government, wherever it acts as the employer of labor, should *both* on its own account and as an example put into effect the following principles of just employment:

1. A living wage for all employees.

2. A working day not to exceed eight hours, with one day of rest in seven.

3. The adoption of safety appliances and the establishment of thoroughly sanitary conditions of labor.

4. Adequate compensation for industrial accidents.

5. The standards of the "Uniform Child Labor Law" wherever minors are employed.

6. Such provisions for decency, comfort, and health in the employment of women as should be accorded the mothers of the race.

7. Adequate provision for aged employees entitled to retirement by long and faithful service.

We believe also that the adoption of similar principles *should be urged and applied* in the legislation of the states with regard to labor within their borders ⟨should be urged,⟩; that through every possible agency the life and health of the people of the nation should be conserved; that the Federal Government should develop upon a systematic scale the means already begun under the present administration to assist laborers throughout the Union to seek and obtain employment; and that the same assistance and encouragement should be extended by the Federal Government to systematic vocational training as is now extended to agricultural training. It is our judgment that there should *also* be a thorough legislative reconsideration of the means and methods by which the national government handles questions of public health.

[XII]

We favor such an alteration of the rules of procedure of the Senate of the United States as will permit the prompt transaction of the nation's legislative business.

XIII

We demand careful economy in all expenditures for the support of the government, and to that end favor a return by the House of Representatives to its former practice of initiating and preparing all appropriation bills through a single committee chosen from its membership, in order that responsibility may be centered, expenditures standardized and made uniform, and waste and duplication in the public service as much as possible avoided. We favor this as the only practicable first step towards a budget system.

XIV

We heartily endorse the provisions of the bill, recently passed by the House of Representatives, further promoting self-government in the Philippine Islands as being in fulfillment of the policy declared by the Democratic party in its last national platform, and we reiterate our endorsement of the purpose of ultimate independence for the Philippine Islands, expressed in the preamble of that measure.

XV

We recommend the extension of the franchise to the women of the country by the states upon the same terms as to men.

XVI

We again declare that the rights of American citizens must be preserved at home and abroad, and that no treaty with any other government ⟨shall⟩ *should* receive the sanction of our government which does not express or recognize the absolute equality of all our citizens, irrespective of race, creed or previous nationality, and which does not guarantee the right of expatriation. The constitutional rights of American citizens should protect them ⟨on our borders and⟩ *not only at home but* go with them *also* throughout the world.

This is a critical hour in the history of America, a critical hour in the history of the world. Upon the record above set forth, which shows great constructive achievement in the following out of a consistent policy for our domestic and internal development; upon the record of the Democratic administration, which has maintained the honor, the dignity, and the interests of the United States and, at the same time, retained the respect and friendship of all the nations of the world; and upon the great policies for the future strengthening of the life of our country, the enlargement of our national vision and the ennobling of our international relations, as set forth above, we appeal with confidence to the voters of the country for a retention of our party in power.[3]

CC MS (WP, DLC).

[3] As has been noted, Newton D. Baker took this draft to St. Louis on June 12. He was afterward in consultation with the resolutions committee and in frequent telephonic communication with Wilson while the resolutions committee prepared the final draft of the platform.

The platform as adopted, generally speaking, incorporated most of Wilson's text *verbatim*, although some sections were compacted. However, it emphatically endorsed by name the Underwood-Simmons Tariff Act and the principle of a tariff for revenue only. Moreover, Wilson helped to frame a new plank on Americanism that condemned "as subversive of this Nation's unity and integrity, and as destructive of its welfare, the activities and designs of every group or organization, political or otherwise, that has for its object the advancement of the interest of a foreign power."

Wilson yielded to the resolutions committee, which insisted upon the inclusion of a special plank on Mexico. It reaffirmed the Monroe Doctrine and the independence of all American states. However, the absence of a stable and responsible government in Mexico capable of suppressing bandit gangs who had invaded American soil and murdered American citizens had made it necessary for the United States Army temporarily to occupy "a portion of the territory of that friendly state." It would be necessary to continue that occupation until the causes for it had been eliminated. On the other hand, "intervention" and "military subjugation" were "revolting" to the people of the United States "and should be resorted to, if at all, only as a last recourse." The plank on labor was revised so as to endorse, specifically, the adoption of a federal child labor law. To Wilson's plank XVI was added the following: "At the earliest practical opportunity our country should strive earnestly for peace among the warring nations of Europe and seek to bring about the adoption of the fundamental principle of justice and humanity, that all men shall enjoy equality of right and freedom from discrimination in the lands wherein they dwell." The resolutions committee added new planks on waterways and flood control, Alaska, and territorial status for Alaska, Hawaii, and Porto Rico. It added a penultimate plank endorsing Wilson and Marshall and ended: "In particular, we commend to the

American people the splendid diplomatic victories of our great President, who has preserved the vital interests of our Government and its citizens, and kept us out of war. Woodrow Wilson stands today the greatest American of his generation." "Certified copy of the platform adopted by the Democratic National Convention held at Saint Louis, Missouri, June 16, 1916," T MS (WP, DLC).

Two Letters from Edward Mandell House

New London,

Dear Governor: Lake Sunapee, N. H. June 10, 1916.

A great deal of foreign mail has come yesterday and today.

One of the most interesting correspondents I have over there is Arthur Bullard,[1] an American who writes on international affairs. He has just been in England for two months and he sees danger of the conservatives regaining their hold. He believes it is not impossible that Germany may be more liberal than England within the next decade.

Bullard thinks all our energies should be spent upon reaching a maritime accord with Great Britain. He thinks the way to accomplish this is to smash through obstacles of diplomacy and get the matter to the people.

The difficulty is to make the English people realize that we have a real grievance against the policy pursued by their government, a grievance that is based upon principle and idealism and respect for law. He says the most intelligent English have not the slightest comprehension of the charges being brought against them by the neutrals. It is generally believed that the United States is trying to overthrow the principle of blockade and contraband. He believes if the British people understood the nature of the controversy an accord could be speedily reached.

He suggests that when you have occasion to send another note you send a short note designed for the edification of the general public, and that you say the United States approves in theory and practice the use of naval power to produce economic pressure of blockade and the seizure of contraband.

He thinks this statement would startle everyone into attention. He then suggests it might be well to quote Sir Edward Grey's instructions to Lord Dessart (Blue Book, Miscellaneous, No. 4, 1909, p. 25) "His Majesty's Government are now desirous of limiting as much as possible the right to seize for contraband, if not eliminating it altogether" and say that all you wish is to pursue that right.

Then follow our main contention that we hold these weapons, (naval pressure), like all other weapons in accordance with international law which have received the sanction of general useage.

That we do not admit the right of any one nation to change, according to their convenience, the law of nations.

He suggests also that you state that the judicial committee of the Privy Council, as in the case of the S.S. Zamora[2] has borne out our contention that the means taken by the British Fleet and Prize Courts to exercise this pressure (in itself legitimate) has been illigitmate.

I have two long letters from Page. He seemed to be in good humor, but tells nothing of particular value.

He declares that any suggestion of peace angers the British; that, outside of a féw cranks, the Empire is solid for a continuation of the war, even if it takes any number of years. He says, too, that Sir Edward has become the most popular man in the Kingdom because of the position he has taken against peace overtures.

As a matter of fact, both the British and French Governments are afraid of peace discussions for the reason that there is such a sentiment in both countries in favor of it that it might break loose at any time and force them to act. Jusserand admitted as much as this.

Gerard thinks that the Germans will pull through and cannot be starved into submission. On the contrary, his Secretary writes that the food situation is very serious, that there is much suffering and there will be more. He adds, "the bottom of the barrel is in sight."

My letters from France indicate that they are deeply hurt because of such expressions from you as "We have nothing to do with the present quarrel," "This quarrel has carried those engaged in it so far that they cannot be held to the ordinary standard of responsibility," "If the rest of the world is mad why should be [we] not simply refuse to have anything to do with the rest of the world."

One sentence in an article from the Temps says: "Our deep attachment to the Americans renders us particularly sensitive to that which they say of us."

I believe it would be wise to leave Europe alone, for the moment, and not refer to them in any way. All the belligerents as of course you know are extremely sensitive and if you are to hold a commanding position with them, this will have to be reckoned with. It is irritating to feel that they overlook your high and splendid purposes and lay such stress upon minor phrases of your speeches.   Affectionately yours,   E. M. House

[1] At this time a war correspondent for magazines such as *The Outlook, The Century,* and the *Atlantic Monthly.*

[2] *S.S. Zamora,* a Swedish vessel, sailed from New York for Stockholm on

March 20, 1915, with a cargo which included four hundred tons of copper. She was captured by a British naval vessel on April 8. In June 1915, the British Prize Court decided that the copper should become the property of the Crown on the ground that the Prize Court was bound to observe the Order in Council under which the seizure had been made. The judicial committee of the Privy Council reversed the Prize Court decision on April 7, 1916. It declared that, while the Prize Court had to take cognizance of Orders in Council, just as it would of any other relevant law or regulation, it could not enforce such orders if they were in conflict with the accepted dictates of international law.

Bullard in his comment probably had in mind the following passage from the decision of the judicial committee:

"Further, the Prize Court will take judicial notice of every Order in Council material to the consideration of matters with which it has to deal, and will give the utmost weight and importance to every such Order, short of treating it as an authoritative and binding declaration of law. Thus an Order declaring a blockade will *prima facie* justify the capture and condemnation of vessels attempting to enter the blockaded ports, but will not preclude evidence to shew that the blockade is ineffective and therefore unlawful. An Order authorising reprisals will be conclusive as to the facts which are recited as shewing that a case for reprisals exists, and will have due weight as shewing what, in the opinion of His Majesty's advisers, are the best or only means of meeting the emergency; but this will not preclude the right of any party aggrieved to contend, or the right of the Court to hold, that these means are unlawful, as entailing on neutrals a degree of inconvenience unreasonable, considering all the circumstances of the case." *FR-WWS 1916*, pp. 492-93. See also *ibid.*, pp. 364-68 and, for the original decision of the Prize Court, *FR-WWS 1915*, pp. 469-72.

New London,
Lake Sunapee, N. H. June 10, 1916.

Dear Governor:

I now have a complete record of Homer Cummings. I do not believe the divorce and suit for breach of promise can be used against him.

Cobb and Seitz[1] of the World do not think his connection with the New Haven Railroad is serious. They do not regard him as a heavy weight but think he would answer in lieu of someone better.

He represented, as you probably know, Mellon in 1914[2] and Billard[3] last year and now.

The news of the nominations at Chicago has just reached me. I hope T.R. will accept as readily as Hughes has.[4] Now that Hughes is the candidate it is all the more necessary for us to gather in the progressive vote. I think we can show Hughes up as a thorough conservative who obtained the name of progressive because of his refusal to let the bosses dictate to him. His veto of the income tax[5] and the support which the Germans have and will give him, will, I think, insure his defeat.

Affectionately yours,   E. M. House

P.S. Gregory saw something of Cummings during the New Haven trial and thinks very well of him.

TLS (WP, DLC).
[1] Don Carlos Seitz, business manager of the New York *World*.
[2] Charles Sanger Mellen, living in retirement since his resignation from the

presidency of the New Haven Railroad in 1913. He was the target of numerous civil and criminal actions arising out of his real and/or alleged misdeeds as president of the New Haven.

3 John Leander Billard, a coal dealer of Meriden, Conn., who became notorious when he led a syndicate which "bought" 110,000 shares of Boston & Maine Railroad stock from the New Haven Railroad in 1908 in order to comply on paper with a law of the Massachusetts legislature which required the New Haven to sell its B. & M. stock. The passage of other legislation soon allowed the New Haven to repurchase the stock. Billard was later reported to have made $2,700,-000 on the deal without having invested any of his own money. A suit for the recovery of that sum brought against Billard, Mellen, and others by the new management of the New Haven was settled out of court on March 1, 1916, by the agreement of the defendants to pay $1,250,000 to the company. Homer S. Cummings negotiated the settlement. *New York Times*, March 2, 1916.

4 The national convention of the Progressive party, acting in defiance of Theodore Roosevelt himself, voted to nominate him for the presidency at 12:37 P.M. on June 10, about three minutes after Hughes had won the Republican nomination. Later that afternoon, Roosevelt telegraphed to the convention a conditional refusal of the nomination. He made his official withdrawal on June 22. For the full story of Roosevelt's complicated maneuvering to win both the Republican and Progressive nominations in 1916, see George E. Mowry, *Theodore Roosevelt and the Progressive Movement* (Madison, Wisc., 1946), pp. 320-66, and John A. Garraty, *Right-Hand Man: The Life of George W. Perkins* (New York, 1960), pp. 327-53.

5 House's use of the word "veto" was somewhat imprecise. On January 5, 1910, Hughes, then Governor of New York, submitted the proposed Sixteenth, or income tax, Amendment to the legislature. In a special message, he said that, while he favored a federal income tax, he felt obliged to recommend that the amendment as then proposed should not be ratified. He objected to the phrase that permitted the taxation of incomes "from whatever source derived." Hughes said that this would permit the federal government to tax income derived from state or municipal securities, and that such taxation would in effect make the operations of local government "a matter of Federal grace." The legislature rejected the amendment. Hughes's special message is printed in State of New York, *Public Papers of Charles E. Hughes, Governor, 1910* (Albany, 1910), pp. 71-76, and in *Cong. Record*, 64th Cong., 1st sess., Appendix, pp. 1171-72. See also Merlo J. Pusey, *Charles Evans Hughes* (2 vols., New York, 1951), I, 253-54.

From Joseph Edward Davies

My Dear Mr. President: Washington [c. June 10, 1916]

Wont you please pardon this intrusion. There are two matters I omitted & want you to know.[1]

Excuses were assigned for this action.[2] But the allegations of my omissions & deficiencies which I learned for the first time from Joe Tumulty are self serving ex parte declarations. They are excuses and not reasons. Of course, it could not be done without some justification. What I want to impress is, that *all* that I have said is subject to verification from disinterested sources, & from men who are honorable & who do not lie.

And again. I would appreciate it for myself & for my country & those things which you stand for, if you could add the weight of your personal appeal to Harris. He has a phone No 6587. I feel sure that he could not withstand your request.[3]

With all your burdens, I regret this more than I can say:— but it is of vital importance I know to the successful issue of one of your greatest achievements in legislation: and I know you would not believe in me, unless I did just this.

    With Devotion, & Faithfully Yours   Joseph E. Davies

ALS (WP, DLC).

¹ Davies had talked with Wilson at the White House at 6:30 P.M. on June 8.

² William J. Harris, at a meeting of the Federal Trade Commission on May 31, had moved that the chairmanship of the commission rotate, and that the vice-chairman, Hurley, be elected chairman. The motion carried three (Hurley, Harris, and Rublee) to two (Davies and Will H. Parry). Davies then said that his wife was pregnant and begged the members to defer announcement of Hurley's election until after the birth of the baby, which was imminent. According to Davies, the commissioners agreed to postpone the announcement two weeks and to permit Davies to make the announcement himself. The baby was born on June 2. Davies wanted to postpone the announcement for another six days. However, at Hurley's insistence, the announcement was given to the Associated Press on June 7. J. E. Davies to E. M. House, June 9, 1916, TLS (E. M. House Papers, CtY). In this letter, Davies also wrote: "It may become so bad that [it may become] my duty to the President and to the country to make public what the differences are in the Commission. It will feed the opposition with satisfaction, and ammunition to attack one of the agencies of this administration. It is inevitable that this will result if the situation is permitted to obtain."

³ That is, that Wilson ask Harris to reverse his vote and form a new majority to reinstate Davies. Norman Hapgood wrote to Colonel House on June 18, 1916, as follows: "Probably there is nothing for you to do about it, but Davies has been to the President and caused him to send such a message to Hurley that Hurley and Harris will probably both resign this week. I promised over the long distance to try and get their side of the case to the President if they would hold back their resignations a few days. I reached 1712 H Street, Washington, Tuesday morning   Davies simply told the President a mass of lies. The President asked to have a recent vote of the Commission rescinded (which it will not do), and said he did not care to see Hurley on the other side, fearing publicity. I hope it can be straightened out, but fear Davies is bent on revenge." ALS, *ibid.*

Hapgood conferred with Wilson about this matter on June 21. There is no record of their conversation, but Wilson must have agreed to withdraw his request to Hurley, whatever it may have been. Moreover, House mollified Davies, who agreed to remain on the commission and not to issue his public statement "exposing" Hurley (J. E. Davies to EMH, July 1, 1916, TLS, *ibid.*) and his "underhanded manipulations to undermine my position as Chairman of which I knew nothing and tales were carried, I believe, to Secretary Tumulty finding fault with my administration, charging that I had become a prosecutor and any other number of alleged facts." J. E. Davies to EMH, June 7, 1916, TLS *ibid.*

From Sir Cecil Arthur Spring Rice

My dear Mr President   Washington. June 10 1916

    I am deeply touched by your kind words of sympathy for which my wife and I are deeply grateful. I shall tell my brother's wife¹ of your kindness and I know she will feel it very much. My brother and I worked on a farm together in Canada just 30 years ago and I have been with him continually since so that the loss is a very great one.

    With deep gratitude and respect,
        Believe me dear Mr President
                    Yours sincerely   Cecil Spring Rice

ALS (WP, DLC).

¹ Mary Isabella Bush (Mrs. Gerald) Spring Rice.

From Charles Richard Crane

Chicago, Ills., June 11, 1916.

The Progressives are in a resentful mood and probably will drift in large numbers towards us without propaganda. Any sympathetic moves at St. Louis would be most effective. Cordial greetings.   Charles R. Crane.

T telegram (WP, DLC).

To Edward Mandell House

[The White House, June 11, 1916]

For various reasons fear neither Boston nor Harrisburg man would be wise choice. Besides Your judgment on present vice chairman of committee would like to know what you would think of Hugh Wallace. Could you possibly act yourself?

WWT telegram (WP, DLC).

From Norman Hapgood

New London New Hampshire
Sunapee Lake
Dear Mr. President: Sunday June 11 [1916]

I have just had a full and interesting talk with Col. House about the chairmanship of the national committee. Since you asked me, 10 days ago, what I thought of various names, the situation has been considerably developed by the nomination of Mr. Hughes and by his repeated references to partisanship in his first statement. That shows that he means to try for the independent vote as definitely as he did when he was Governor. Therefore I feel that Mr. Cummin[g]s is at least questionable. Personally I feel the same about Mr. Wallace.

Col. House brought up Mr. Hurley, who would be splendid, except that, as Col. House points out, he would be charged with working the corporations through knowledge acquired on the Trade Commission,—"frying the fat."

Certainly nothing can be said against John Davis, except that he comes from the South (if West Virginia is the South) and much, very much, for him.

My own choice is Robert Woolley, and Col. House says that if Virginia is not too serious an objection he inclines to think Woolley combines most. I do not believe the slip in tact you noticed at all characteristic. He has drive, devotion, knowledge of the country, judgement, and full comprehension of party men and independents.

With Hughes running we need broad inspiration.

Very sincerely Yours   Norman Hapgood

ALS (WP, DLC).

To Edward William Pou

My dear Mr. Pou: [The White House] June 12, 1916

I have your letter of June ninth. My own feeling about the plank on the Navy is that we should not declare for either the first, second, or third, but go entirely on our own hook and declare for a Navy adequate for the defense of the nation and for the performance of the international tasks we may expect to be obliged to perform. I am heartily with you in the whole feeling expressed in your letter.

In haste

Cordially and sincerely yours,   Woodrow Wilson

TLS (Letterpress Books, WP, DLC).

To Robert Latham Owen

My dear Senator: [The White House] June 12, 1916

Your letter of June eighth with its enclosure reached me, and I think you will find in the suggestions I have made to the Resolutions Committee by their kind invitation the substance of a greater part of what you so opportunely suggest.

In haste

Cordially and sincerely yours,   Woodrow Wilson

TLS (Letterpress Books, WP, DLC).

To Dudley Field Malone

[The White House] June 12, 1916

Do not go up from here by boat but from New York where we take boat tonight about ten o'clock. I suppose it would not be possible for friend to join us at that time. If not suggest West Point tomorrow morning nine thirty or train returning from West Point to New York three eighteen tomorrow afternoon.

Woodrow Wilson.

T telegram (Letterpress Books, WP, DLC).

To Joseph Leland Kennedy[1]

My dear Joe: [The White House] June 12, 1916

I have your letter of recent date (it wasn't dated).[2]

In reply, I will say that it would really be impossible for me to give an appointment of any kind to anyone so nearly related to me in blood, as you are. I think it would be regarded on every hand as a misuse of my power, no matter what your qualifications might be.

I am sure that when you think the matter over, you will see that I am right about this.

Moreover, I am sure that the appointment of directors would not lie with me but with the Central Board which is to be established here in Washington.

I was glad to hear from you, and hope that you are getting along well. You are certainly to be congratulated on the confidence in you expressed in Mr. Murtaugh's letter.[3]

Faithfully yours,   Woodrow Wilson

TLS (Letterpress Books, WP, DLC).

[1] Wilson's nephew, of Sheldon, Ia., since 1913 a National Bank examiner, under the Comptroller of the Currency, for the district including northern Iowa and southern Minnesota. Wilson had agreed to his accepting this position because it required no action on the part of the President.

[2] J. L. Kennedy to WW, c. June 8, 1916, TLS (WP, DLC), requesting a position in one of the Federal Land Banks to be created under the Federal Farm Loan Act of 1916 (about which see R. L. Owen to WW, Jan. 26, 1916, n. 1, Vol. 35).

[3] Wilson returned Murtaugh's letter.

From Sara Bard Field[1]

St. Louis, Missouri, June 12, 1916.

Dear Mr. President: I beg to inform you of the feeling of certain Western democratic women with regard to the national suffrage situation. I have been informed that the democratic party considers the attitude of the congressional union for woman suffrage toward the party one of hostility and that our activities in behalf of the Susan B. Anthony amendment are directed by republican zeal. I know that you as statesman could not so misinterpret our policy of holding the party in power responsible for the failure or success of legislative measures. I need therefore spend no time assuring you that our course has been wholly free from personal or party antagonisms. What I do want to tell you very earnestly as a democratic woman and what I fear you do not realize is that many members of the congressional union and the new national womans party are loyal democrats eager that their party should have the honor of freeing the women of this country politically as the republicans had the honor of freeing politically the negroes. Therefore the pressure which democratic women in the congressional union have brought to bear upon the democratic party in regard to the passage of this amendment has been one of desire for party service as well as service to women. I have had the privilege of assisting in three state campaigns for woman suffrage, California, Oregon and Nevada. In Oregon which was formerly my home I know the people of every little and big town.

So great is my belief in what you stand for as our party leader that I am willing to offer my services to the democratic party in the coming presidential campaign without remuneration if our party will put through the amendment before that time. Moreover I know of at least five other prominent democratic women, women whose influence was powerful enough to win suffrage in their own states, who would also gladly give their services in the same way. If I had so great a reason as the accomplishment of womans political freedom by the democratic party to lay before voting women when asking support of you it would be an easy matter for me and many other women to give gladly of our time and our influence telling women up and down the Pacific Coast what the democratic party with you as its leader has done for womans emancipation and the progress of the race. This is not written to you in a spirit of bargaining, to that you would turn a deaf ear. It is asking you to make it possible as far as you are able to give democratic women a chance to tell our women voters that you have done the thing of paramount importance to women and of significant advantage to the democratic party. May I take this opportunity to add that through my friend Mr. Lincoln Steffens I have learned much of your belief and that I share your hopes for social and industrial justice. It would give me great joy to tender you my services in the coming campaign. I ask that you make such services possible by effective action which would furnish me and other democratic leaders with the most persuasive arguments.

Very sincerely,   Sara Bard Field, San Francisco.

T telegram (WP, DLC).
1 Of San Francisco; poet, suffrage leader, active in the peace movement.

From Edward William Pou

Dear Mr. President: Smithfield, N. C. June 12th, 1916.

Your administration has been such a tremendous success that some of our political enemies have forgotten how to behave. At one time I thought Mr. Roosevelt a sincere square man, but his attitude towards your administration is not worthy of a man who has been President of this nation. His attacks upon your administration are so cheap that they hardly arouse comment in the newspapers. When the record is completed and submitted to the voters of the nation our pol[i]tical adversaries probably will be still more desperate.

The purpose of this letter is not to discuss the attitude of Roosevelt or of Hughes who might have been a little more polite; but to offer a suggestion in the interest of the people of the nation, and secondarily in behalf of your administration.

I believe it will be a fine thing if you will offer Mr. Taft the place made vacant by Judge Hughes. I will say candidly that personally I do not admire Mr. Taft, but he is really a great lawyer. If you should decide to appoint him I believe a majority of the American people would clap their hands.

I am with you, Mr. President, in whatever action you take; and I will say in this connection, that the House is now working like a well oiled machine. We shall put through your program sooner than some suppose.

I venture to make this suggestion for what it is worth. Be assured it is made by one who has stood steadfastly with you and who has your interest at heart.

Sincerely your friend,   Edwd W. Pou.

TLS (WP, DLC).

From Norman Hapgood

Windsor, Vermont.

Dear Mr. President: Monday morning June 12 [1916]

Col. House called up last night, after I wrote you, about Secretary Baker as Chairman. I have been hoping he might be the nominee for vice-President, as in my opinion no man could so strengthen the ticket, especially as against Hughes. The several hundred thousand,—perhaps a million,—Progressives who are displeased with the failure of the Colonel to run, and who think Hughes too conservative, all like Baker, and his campaigning in the doubtful states would be very effective. His resignation (even if it were necessary) to run for vice-President would not be criticised, while his resignation for the chairmanship would be. However, on the other side it can at least be said that the satisfaction of having him as chairman would in itself be very great. I think with Hughes running the issue will be sound, tested, and successful liberalism versus able Toryism; and Baker (in either position) will be a power in that fight. I am much worried over Marshall, and think the Indiana situation much exaggerated.

Wishing you peaceful nights and days, and confident in your inspiration   Very sincerely Yours   Norman Hapgood

My address will be the University Club, New York, for about a week, and then Washington.

ALS (WP, DLC).

From Edward Mandell House

New London,
Dear Governor: Lake Sunapee, N. H. June 12, 1916.

I am sorry I cannot get to New York to meet you tomorrow. I am sure you understand that I would go if it were at all possible.

I am absolutely convinced that no greater mistake could be made than to make me Chairman or to have me an official part of the campaign. Even in Texas I always had someone else as chairman who could relieve me, not only of the details, but of the constant pressure of seeing unimportant people that demand interviews of a chairman.

I am not writing at length about the matter because I have talked it out so fully over the telephone with Dudley who has in turn talked with you and it seems unnecessary.

I can only add that, in my opinion, neither Baker nor Vance McCormick would be a mistake and perhaps Cummings would also answer, though of him, I have no personal knowledge.
                    Affectionately yours,   E. M. House

TLS (WP, DLC).

From William Cox Redfield

My dear Mr. President   [Washington] June 12. 1916

I hand you the enclosed telegram from a well-known New York merchant for such action as you deem wise[1] The suggestion has also been made to me and has force that a strong anti-dumping clause would be very helpful in our platform. I hope you will find time amid your cares to give both matters some thought   Sincerely   William C. Redfield

ALS (WP, DLC).
    [1] F. R. Chambers to W. C. Redfield, June 12, 1916, T telegram (WP, DLC), suggesting that the Democratic platform include a plank favoring "a budget system of national finances."

Walter Lippmann to Henry French Hollis

Dear Senator: [New York] June 12, 1916.

I was very much pleased to get your letter and the President's.[1]

Having just come back from Chicago I am convinced that you people have all the cards in your hands, in the sense that all the positive program will be yours. Chicago was a terrible and disgusting spectacle.

I find that I cannot come to St. Louis, and since nothing but harmony is to prevail I do not suppose I shall miss any excitement.

But all good luck to you.

Sincerely yours, [Walter Lippmann]

CCL (W. Lippmann Papers, CtY).
[1] That is, WW to H. F. Hollis, June 7, 1916.

A Commencement Address at the United States Military Academy

[June 13, 1916]

Colonel Townsley,[1] young gentlemen, ladies and gentlemen: I look upon this body of men who are graduating today with a peculiar interest. I feel like congratulating them that they are living in a day not only so interesting because fraught with change, but also because so responsible. Days of responsibility are the only days that count in time, because they are the only days that give test of quality. They are the only days when manhood and purpose are tried out as if by fire.

I need not tell you, young gentlemen, that you are not like an ordinary graduating class of one of our universities. The men in those classes look forward to the life which they are to lead after graduation with a great many questions in their minds. Most of them do not know exactly what their lives are going to develop into. Some of them do not know what occupations they are going to follow. All of them are conjecturing what will be the line of duty and advancement and the ultimate goal of success for them. There is no conjecture for you. You have enlisted in something that does not stop when you leave the Academy, for you then only begin to realize it—which then only begins to be filled with the full richness of its meaning. You can look forward with absolute certainty to the sort of thing that you will be obliged to do.

[1] Col. Clarence Page Townsley, U.S.A., Superintendent of the United States Military Academy, 1912-1916.

This has always been true of graduating classes at West Point, but the certainty that some of the older classes used to look forward to was a very dull certainty. Some of the old days in the army, I fancy, were not very interesting days. Sometimes men, like the present Chief of Staff,[2] for example, could fill their lives with the interest of really knowing and understanding the Indians of the western Plains, knowing what was going on inside of their minds and being able to be intermediary between them and those who dealt with them by speaking their sign language, and so could enrich their lives. But the ordinary life of the average officer at a western post cannot have been very exciting, and I think, with admiration, of those dull years through which officers, who had not a great deal to do, insisted, nevertheless, upon being efficient and worthwhile and keeping their men fit, at any rate, for the duty to which they were assigned. But in your case, there are many extraordinary possibilities, because, gentlemen, no man can certainly tell you what the immediate future is going to be, either in the history of this country or in the history of the world. It is not by accident that the present great war came in Europe. Every element was there, and the contest had to come sooner or later. And it is not going to be by accident that the results are worked out, but by purpose—by the purpose of the men who are strong enough to have guiding minds and indomitable wills when the time for decision and settlement come. And the part that the United States is to play has this distinction in it, that it is to be, in any event, a disinterested part. There isn't anything that the United States wants that it has to get by war, but there are a great many things that the United States has to do. It has to see that its life is not interfered with by anybody else who wants something.

These are days when we are making preparation, when the thing most commonly discussed around every sort of table, in every sort of circle, in the shops and in the streets, is preparedness. And, undoubtedly, gentlemen, that is the present imperative duty of America—to be prepared. But we ought to know what we are preparing for. I remember hearing a wise man say once that the old maxim that "everything comes to the man who waits" is all very well provided he knows what he is waiting for. And preparedness might be a very hazardous thing if we did not know what we wanted to do with the force that we mean to accumulate and to get into fighting shape.

America, fortunately, does know what she wants to do with her force. America came into existence for a particular reason. When

2 That is, Hugh Lenox Scott.

you look about upon these beautiful hills, and up this stately stream, and then let your imagination run over the whole body of this great country from which you youngsters are drawn, far and wide, you remember that, while it had aboriginal inhabitants, while there were people living here, there was no civilization which we displaced. It was as if, in the Providence of God, a continent had been kept unused and waiting for a peaceful people who loved liberty and the rights of men more than they loved anything else, to come and set up an unselfish commonwealth. It is a very extraordinary thing. You are so familiar with American history, at any rate in its general character—I don't accuse you of knowing the details of it, for I never found the youngster who did—but you are so familiar with the general character of American history that it does not seem strange to you, but it is a very strange history. There is none other like it in the whole annals of mankind—of men gathering out of every civilized nation of the world on an unused continent and building up a polity exactly to suit themselves, not under the domination of any ruling dynasty or of the ambitions of any royal family; doing what they pleased with their own life on a free space of land which God had made rich with every resource which was necessary for the civilization they meant to build up. There is nothing like it.

Now, what we are preparing to do is to see that nobody mars that, and that, being safe itself against interference from the outside, all of its force is going to be behind its moral ideas, and mankind is going to know that, when America speaks, she means what she says. I heard a man say to another, "If you wish me to consider you witty, I must really trouble you to make a joke." We have a right to say to the rest of mankind, "If you don't want to interfere with us, if you are disinterested, we must really trouble you to give the evidence of that fact." We are not in for anything selfish, and we want the whole mighty power of America thrown into that scale, and not into any other.

Now, you know that the chief thing that is holding many people back from enthusiasm for what is called preparedness is the fear of militarism. I want to say a word to you young gentlemen about militarism. You are not a militarist because you are military. Militarism doesn't consist in the existence of an army, not even in the existence of a very great army. Militarism is a spirit. It is a point of view. It is a system. It is a purpose. The purpose of militarism is to use armies for aggression. The spirit of militarism is the opposite of the civilian spirit, the citizen spirit. In a country where militarism prevails, the military man looks down upon the civilian, regards him as inferior, thinks of him as intended for

his, the military man's, support and use. And just so long as
America is America, that spirit and point of view is impossible
with us. There is as yet in this country, as far as I can discover,
no taint of the spirit of militarism. You young gentlemen are not
preferred in promotion because of the families you belong to.
You are not drawn into the Academy because you belong to certain influential circles. You do not come here with a long tradition
of military pride back of you. You are picked out from the citizens
of the United States to be that part of the force of the United
States which makes its polity safe against interference. You are
the part of American citizens which says to those who would
interfere, "You must not and you shall not." But you are American
citizens, and the idea I want to leave with you boys today is this:
No matter what comes, always remember that, first of all, you are
citizens of the United States before you are officers, and that
you are officers because you represent in your particular profession what the citizenship of the United States stands for. There
is no danger of militarism if you are genuine Americans, and I,
for one, do not doubt that you are. When you begin to have the
militaristic spirit—not the military spirit, that is all right, but
the militaristic spirit—then begin to doubt whether you are Americans or not.

You know that one thing in which our forefathers took pride
was this, that the civil power is superior to the military power in
the United States. Once and again the people of the United States
have so admired some great military man as to make him President of the United States, when he became commander in chief
of all the forces of the United States. But he was commander in
chief because he was President, not because he had been trained
to arms, and his authority was civil, not military. I can teach you
nothing of military power, but I am instructed by the Constitution to use you for constitutional and patriotic purposes. And that
is the only use you care to be put to. That is the only use you
ought to care to be put to, because, after all, what is the use in
being an American if you do not know what it is.

You have read a great deal in the books about the pride of the
old Roman citizen, who always felt like drawing himself to his
full height when he said, "I am a Roman." But, as compared with
the pride that must have risen to his heart, our pride has a new
distinction—not the distinction of the mere imperial power of a
great empire, not the distinction of being masters of the world,
but the distinction of carrying certain lights for the world that
the world has never so distinctly seen before, certain guiding
lights of liberty and principle and justice. We have drawn our

people, as you know from all parts of the world, and we have been somewhat disturbed recently, gentlemen, because some of those—though I believe a very small number—whom we have drawn into our citizenship have not taken into their hearts the spirit of America and have loved other countries more than they loved the country of their adoption. And we have talked a great deal about Americanism. It ought to be a matter of pride with us to know what Americanism really consists in. Americanism consists in utterly believing in the principles of America and putting them first, as above anything that might by chance come into competition with it. And I, for my part, believe that the American test is a spiritual test. If a man has to make excuses for what he has done as an American, I doubt his Americanism. He ought to know at every step of his action that the motive that lies behind what he does is a motive which no American need be ashamed of for a moment. Now, we ought to put this test to every man we know. We ought to let it be known that nobody who doesn't put America first can consort with us. But we ought to set them the example. We ought to set them the example by thinking American thoughts, by entertaining American purposes. And those thoughts and purposes will stand the test of example anywhere in the world, for they are intended for the betterment of mankind.

So I have come to say these few words to you today, gentlemen, for a double purpose: first of all, to express my personal good wishes to you in your graduation and my personal interest in you, and, second of all, to remind you how we must all stand together in one spirit as lovers and servants of America. And that means something more than lovers and servants merely of the United States. You have heard of the Monroe Doctrine, gentlemen. You know that we are already spiritual partners with both continents of this hemisphere and that America means something which is bigger even than the United States, and that we stand here, with the glorious power of this country, ready to swing it out into the field of action whenever liberty and independence and political integrity are threatened anywhere in the western hemisphere. And we are ready—nobody has authorized me to say this, but I am sure of it—we are ready to join with the other nations of the world in seeing that the kind of justice prevails anywhere that we believe in.

So that you are graduating today, gentlemen, into a new distinction. Glory attaches to all those men whose names we love to recount, who have made the annals of the American army distinguished. They played the part they were called upon to play with honor and with extraordinary character and success. I am congratulating you, not because you will be better than they, but because you will have a wider world of thought and conception to play your part in. I am an American, but I do not believe that any of us loves a blustering nationality—a nationality with a chip on its shoulder, a nationality with its elbows out and its swagger on. We love that quiet, self-respecting, unconquerable spirit which doesn't strike until it is necessary to strike, and then strikes to conquer. Never since I was a youngster have I been afraid of the noisy man. I have always been afraid of the still man. I have always been afraid of the quiet man. I had a classmate at college who was most dangerous when he was most affable. When he was maddest, he seemed to have the sweetest temper in the world. He would approach you with a most ingratiating smile, and then you knew that every red corpuscle in his blood was up and shouting. If you work things off in your elbows, you do not work them off in your mind; you do not work them off in your purposes. So my conception of America is a conception of infinite dignity, along with quiet, unquestionable power. I ask you young gentlemen to join with me in that conception, and let us all in our several spheres be soldiers together to realize it.

Printed copy with corrections from a reading of the CLSsh notes (C. L. Swem Coll., NjP).

From Joseph Patrick Tumulty

Dear Governor: The White House June 13, 1916.

It is clear as the editorial appearing in this morning's New York World says that the "hyphenate vote is a definite factor that cannot be discredited"; and that from the activities of the German American Alliance every effort, as their own supporters declare, should be made to elect Justice Hughes. That there is abundant proof of this is clear, so that he who runs may read. This is evident from the attitude of the German American press, and from the statements of professional German agitators, and from the campaign that has been carried on against you from the very beginning.

Annexed to this is a copy of a letter addressed to ex-Congressman FitzHenry[1] which is proof that some protest against your nomination, emanating from the National German American Alliance will presently make its appearance at St. Louis.

[1] Louis FitzHenry, Democratic congressman from Illinois, 1913-1915. The copy of his letter is missing.

I have not read the platform to be proposed by you. The only part that I have any knowledge of is that which you read to me over the telephone some nights ago; that had to do with the question of Americanism.

Frankly, your mention of Americanism is on all fours with the declarations found in the Bull Moose and regular Republican platforms. The characteristic of all these references to Americanism is vagueness and uncertainty as to what is really meant. I believe that the time has come when the Democratic party should set forth its position on this vital matter in no uncertain tones for efforts will soon be made, from stories appearing in the newspapers, by professional German Americans, to dominate our convention, either in an effort to discredit you or to have embodied in the platform some reference to the embargo question, or a prohibition against the sale of munitions of war. We ought to meet these things in a manly, aggressive and militant fashion. It is for that reason that I suggest an open letter to the Chairman of the Committee on Resolutions, setting forth your position in this matter so that the convention may know before it nominates you the things for which you stand. Mr. Baker at the convention will doubtless know when the representatives of the German American Alliance make their appearance, asking for consideration at the hands of the Committee of their resolutions. As soon as they do, it appears to me to be the time for you to strike. Mr. Roosevelt set forth completely the whole situation in his letter to Mr. Jackson when he said *"The professional German-Americans acting through various agencies, including so-called German-American alliances, are at this moment serving notice on the members of your Convention that your action must be taken with a view to the interests, not of the United States but of Germany and of that section of the German-American vote which is anti-American to the core. I believe with all my heart that the action of these sinister professional German-Americans will be repudiated with angry contempt by the great mass of our fellow citizens who are in whole or in part of German blood and who, as I well know, are unsurpassed in rugged and whole-souled Americanism by any other citizens of our land. But the professional German-Americans are seek[ing] to terrorize your convention for they wish to elect next November a man who shall not be in good faith an American President, but the viceroy of a foreign government. It is for your Convention in emphatic fashion to repudiate them. This can be done in effective manner only if such action is taken as to enable the Republicans, Progressives, Democrats who are true to the principles of Andrew Jackson and inde-*

pendents—in short, all loyal Americans—to join in the effort to reach the goal we all have in view."[2]

I wish to call your attention to what you said in your last annual message bearing upon the efforts of those "welcomed under our generous naturalization laws to the full freedom and opportunity of America." You discussed the problem of divided citizenship in all of its phases. At the time you addressed the Congress these included attempts to destroy munitions plants, plots to destroy munition carrying ships, fomenting of strikes, conspiracies to violate the neutrality of the United States, and as you said, "to debase our politics to the uses of foreign intrigue." This last has now become the paramount issue before you in connection with divided loyalty. It is the immediate problem to be dealt with as regards Americanism. An effort is under way to debase our politics through the creation of the German voters in the United States as a power. The instrumentality through which this power is to be exerted is the present candidacy of Justice Hughes. It does not need to be established that Justice Hughes is seeking the support of German-Americans by un-American commitments, in order to prove that what I have said is true. It is a fact not susceptible of being controverted that there is an organized movement among the Teutonic-Americans to deliver their three million or more votes to Mr. Justice Hughes in November.

I annex to this letter two statements from prominent officials of the German American Alliance (A and B); also an editorial from the New York World (C); a letter to Mr. FitzHenry (D); excerpt from your last Message (E); copy of Mr. Roosevelt's letter to Mr. Jackson (F); editorial from the New York Tribune (G); and article from the New York World (H).[3]

---

[2] T. Roosevelt to William Purnell Jackson, June 8, 1916, printed in Elting E. Morison *et al.*, eds., *The Letters of Theodore Roosevelt* (8 vols., Cambridge, Mass., 1951-54), VIII, 1060. Actually, Roosevelt wrote "and independent—in short, all loyal Americans."

[3] All these enclosures are missing. Those that can be identified are (following Tumulty's letter enumeration):

A. and B. One of the statements was probably that of Louis E. Brandt, secretary of the German-American Alliance of Illinois, who was quoted as saying on June 10 that the national alliance had not only worked for the nomination of Hughes but would also urge its 3,000,000 members to vote for Hughes. *New York Times*, June 11, 1916. The other statement was probably that of Alphonse G. Koelble, president of the United German Societies of New York, who remarked on June 11 that Wilson's chances of being reelected were slim, that the Republican and Progressive platforms were a virtual repudiation of Wilson's stand on the "so-called hyphen issue," and that he (Koelble) opposed any "concerted effort" on the part of German Americans to support any candidate. *New York World*, June 12, 1916.

C. "Can the Kaiser Defeat the President?", New York *World*, June 13, 1916.

D. Presumably the missing letter mentioned in n. 1 above.

I discussed this matter over the telephone yesterday with Mr. Henry C. Campbell,[4] one of our devoted friends, and editor of the Milwaukee Journal. Mr. Frank Polk, Counsellor of the State Department, who was at the Convention, tells me that he was discussing this matter with Mr. Nieman of the Milwaukee Journal, and that Mr. Nieman made the statement that both parties were "pussy-footing" and that he would not support the Democratic party unless its attitude in this matter was unequivocal. When Mr. Campbell discussed this matter with me over the telephone, I told him to send me a telegram setting forth what he thought ought to find lodgment in the platform, by way of expressing our attitude in this matter. This morning I received the attached telegram from Senator Husting, expressing Mr. Campbell's and Mr. Nieman's views. (I).[5] The part I have underlined I think should be expressed in less emphatic language.

The purpose of this letter therefore is to urge you as strongly as I can to address at once an open letter to the Chairman of the Committee on Resolutions embodying the following ideas:

First—You might start in this way, "It has been brought to my attention through the public press and by means of circulars that have reached me at the White House offices that attempts will be made by certain gentlemen claiming to represent certain organizations of our foreignborn citizens, to prevail upon your Committee to embody in the platform some reference to our foreign relations.

"Before your Committee acts on these matters it is only fair, inasmuch as there is little doubt of my nomination at your hands, that I should state my position with reference to these matters in the frankest possible fashion so that our attitude on the questions brought forward by these gentlemen shall be stated in an unequivocal way in the platform adopted by the party."

Second—Call attention again to what you said in your last annual message. (The purpose of introducing this is to show that your position has not changed and that since that time there has

E. Tumulty discusses it in the paragraph above. It was from Wilson's Annual Message printed at Dec. 7, 1915, Vol. 35.

F. Cited in n. 2 above.

G. "The First Step," *New York Tribune*, June 13, 1916, which called on Hughes to make "a prompt, frank and specific statement upon the Hyphen question."

H. This could have been either "Germans Generally Pleased with Naming of Hughes; Alliance and Its Allied Societies Will Conduct Campaign for Him from Chicago," New York *World*, June 11, 1916, or "Calls on Germans to Vote for Hughes; New Yorker Herold Says Wilson or T. R. Supporters Merit Kicking," *ibid.*, June 13, 1916.

4 Henry Colin Campbell.

5 This enclosure is also missing.

been evidence on all sides of this purpose). Then you should state, as a request coming from you in terms of deepest solemnity, just what to embody with reference to these things. You can find no better expressing of these ideas than is found in Mr. Husting's telegram, which was dictated by Mr. Nieman. (I).[6]

Tumulty

TLS (WP, DLC).
[6] For Wilson's response, see his Flag Day address printed at June 14, 1916.

From Jo Davidson

Dear Mr President   Washington Tuesday [June 13, 1916]

I want to express my thanks and appreciation for your kindness in having given me so much of your valuable time in sitting to me for your portrait bust particularly in these times when I realize how busy you are,[1] and only hope that the Bust I have made is both worthy of my art and also of one [of] *The* Great Statesmen that this Country has produced

I sincerely hope that I will have the great pleasure of seeing you again

Believe me Mr. President

Most Sincerely Yours   Jo Davidson

ALS (WP, DLC).
[1] Wilson sat for Davidson on June 5, 7-10, and 12. The bust, generally regarded as the finest of Wilson, was completed soon afterward. The two copies known to exist are in the Woodrow Wilson School of Princeton University and the Woodrow Wilson Birthplace in Staunton, Va. See Jo Davidson, *Between Sittings: An Informal Autobiography* (New York, 1951), pp. 120-23.

A Flag Day Address[1]

[[June 14, 1916]]

Mr. Secretary, ladies, and gentlemen: I have not come here this afternoon with the purpose of delivering to you an elaborate address. It seems to me that the day is sufficiently eloquent already with the meaning which it should convey to us. The spectacle of the morning has been a very moving spectacle indeed—an almost unpremeditated outpouring of thousands of

[1] Wilson spoke from a temporary platform erected near the Washington Monument. He was introduced by Secretary of State Lansing. Wilson's speech followed a parade for preparedness in which some 66,000 marchers participated. Wilson, himself, led the parade, which started at 9:30 A.M., from a point near the Capitol down Pennsylvania Avenue to the White House. There Wilson left the parade to join his wife in a reviewing stand, where he spent another three and a half hours. Following luncheon at the White House, Wilson went to the Washington Monument to deliver his speech at 3 P.M. *Washington Post*, June 15, 1916.

sober citizens to manifest their interest in the safety of the country and the sacredness of the flag which is its emblem.

I need not remind you how much sentiment has been poured out in honor of the flag of the United States. Sometimes we have been charged with being a very sentimental people, fond of expressing in general rhetorical phrases principles not sufficiently defined in action. And I dare say there have been times of happy and careless ease in this country, when all that it has been necessary to do for the honor of the flag was to put our sentiments into poetic expressions, into the words that, for the time being, satisfied our hearts.

But this is not a day of sentiment. Sentiment is a propulsive power, but it does not propel in the way that is serviceable to the nation, unless it have a definite purpose before it. This is not merely a day of sentiment. It is a day of purpose.

It is an eloquent symbol of the unity of our history that, upon this monument which commemorates the man who did most to establish the American Union, we should have hoisted those stars that have so multiplied since his time, associated with those lines of red and white, which mean all that is pure in our purpose and all that is red in our blood in the service of a nation whose history has been full of inspiration because of his example.

But Washington was one of the least sentimental men that America has ever produced. The thing that thrills me about Washington is that he is impatient of any sentiment that has not got definite purpose in it. His letters run along the lines of action, not merely along the mere lines of sentiment. And the most inspiring times that this nation has ever seen have been the times when sentiment had to be translated into action.

Apparently this nation is again and again and again to be tested, and always tested in the same way. The last supreme test that this nation went through was the test of the Civil War.

You know how deep that cut. You know what exigent issues of life were at issue in that struggle. You know how two great sections of this Union seemed to be moving in opposite directions, and, for a long time, it was questionable whether that flag represented any one united purpose in America. And you know how deep that struggle cut into the sentiments of this people and how there came a whole generation following that great struggle, when men's hearts were bitter and sore and memories hurt as well as exalted, and how it seemed as if a rift had come in the hearts of the people of America.

And you know how that ended. While it seemed a time of terror, it has turned out a proof of the validity of our hope. Where are now the divisions of sentiment which cut us asunder at the time of the Civil War? Did you not see the blue and the gray mingled this morning in the procession? Did not you see the sons of a subsequent generation walking together in happy comradeship? Was there any contradiction of feeling or division of sentiment evident there for a moment?

Nothing cuts so deep as a civil war, and yet all the wounds of that war have been healed, not only, but the very passion of that war seems to have contributed to the strength of national feeling which now moves us as a single body politic.

And, yet again, the test is applied, my fellow countrymen. A new sort of division of feeling has sprung up amongst us. You know that we are derived in our citizenship from every nation in the world. It is not singular that sentiment should be disturbed by what is going on on the other side of the water, but, while sentiment may be disturbed, loyalty ought not to be.

I want to be scrupulously just, my fellow citizens, in assessing the circumstances of this day, and I am sure that you wish with me to deal out with an even hand the praise and the blame of this day of test.

I believe that the vast majority of those men whose lineage is directly derived from the nations now at war are just as loyal to the flag of the United States as any native citizen of this beloved land. But there are some men of that extraction who are not; and they, not only in past months, but at the present time, are doing their best to undermine the influence of the Government of the United States in the interest of matters which are foreign to us and which are not derived from the questions of our own politics.

There is disloyalty active in the United States, and it must be absolutely crushed. It proceeds from a minority, a very small minority, but a very active and subtle minority. It works underground, but it also shows its ugly head where we can see it; and there are those at this moment who are trying to levy a species of political blackmail, saying, "Do what we wish in the interest of foreign sentiment or we will wreak our vengeance at the polls."

That is the sort of thing against which the American nation will turn with a might and triumph of sentiment which will teach these gentlemen, once for all, that loyalty to this flag is the first test of tolerance in the United States.

That is the lesson that I have come to remind you of on this day—no mere sentiment. It runs into your daily life and conversation. Are you going, yourselves, individually and collectively, to see to it that no man is tolerated who does not do honor to that flag?

It is not a matter of force. It is not a matter, that is to say, of physical force. It is a matter of a greater force than that which is physical. It is a matter of spiritual force. It is to be achieved as we think, as we purpose, as we believe. And, when the world finally learns that America is indivisible, then the world will learn how truly and profoundly great and powerful America is.

I realize personally, my fellow citizens, the peculiar significance of the flag of the United States at this time, because there was a day, not many years ago, when, although I knew what that flag stood for, it had not penetrated my whole consciousness as it has now.

If you could have gone with me through the space of the last two years, and could have felt the subtle impact of intrigue and sedition and have realized with me that those to whom you have entrusted authority are trustees, not only of the power, but of the very spirit and purpose of the United States, you would realize with me the solemnity with which I look upon that sublime symbol of our unity and power.

I want you to share that consciousness with me. I want you to realize that, in what I am saying, I am merely your spokesman, merely trying to interpret your thoughts, merely trying to put into inadequate words the purpose that is in your hearts. I regard this day as a day of rededication to all the ideals of the United States.

I took the liberty a few weeks ago to ask our fellow citizens, all over the United States, to gather together in celebration of this day—the anniversary of the adoption of our present flag as the emblem of the nation. I had no legal right to declare it a holiday. I had no legal right to ask for the cessation of business. But when you read in the papers tomorrow morning, I think you will see that authority was not necessary; that the people of the country were waiting for an opportunity to cease their ordinary business and gather together in united demonstrations of their feeling as a nation.

It was a very happy thought that led the committee of gentlemen who had charge of the demonstrations of the forenoon to choose the fourteenth of June for the parade which most of us have witnessed. It is a tiresome thing, my fellow citizens, to stand for hours and see a parade go by, but I want to take you into this secret: It was not half as tiresome as the inauguration parade.

The inauguration parade is a very interesting thing, but it is painfully interesting to the man who is being inaugurated, because there then lie ahead of him the four years of responsibility whose horoscope cannot be guessed by any man.

But today was interesting, because the inauguration parade of the day of my inauguration is more than three years gone by. I have gone through deep waters with you in the meantime.

This parade was not a demonstration in honor of any man. It was an outpouring of people to demonstrate a great national sentiment. I was not the object of it. I was one citizen among millions whose heart beat in unison with it.

I felt caught up and buoyed along by the great stream of human purpose which seemed to flow there in front of me by the stand by the White House, and I shall go away from this meeting, as I came away from that parade, with all the deepest purposes of my heart renewed. And, as I see the winds lovingly unfold the beautiful lines of our great flag, I shall seem to see a hand pointing the way of duty, no matter how hard, no matter how long, which we shall tread while we vindicate the glory and honor of the United States.[2]

Printed in *Address of President Wilson . . . Flag Day June 14, 1916* (Washington, 1919), with corrections from a reading of the CLSsh notes (C. L. Swem Coll., NjP).

[2] There is a brief WWsh outline of this address in WP, DLC.

From Edward Mandell House, with Enclosures

New London,

Dear Governor: New Hampshire. June 14, 1916.

Your speech at West Point was fine, particularly the part concerning international affairs. I think you were on firm ground.

Our representatives abroad should bring these speeches not only to the attention of the government to which they are accredited, but to the public through the press.

I am enclosing you a copy of another letter which has just come from Page, and also some editorial clippings which you might look over.[1]

I have another letter from Arthur Bullard in which he complains that the press of both England and France publish garbled reports of your utterances and do not give your true meaning.

If you approve, I will get Frank Polk to have letters sent to our representatives in Europe asking them to see that your views are brought properly before the governments and the public. Those parts of your speeches relating to international affairs should be cabled to them and they, in turn, should be instructed to make them public.

I take it, this would be perfectly proper. However, the Department would know this.

Affectionately yours,   E. M. House

TLS (WP, DLC).
1 The clippings are missing.

ENCLOSURE   I

Two Letters from Walter Hines Page to Edward Mandell House

Dear House: London. May 30, 1916.

All this peace-talk from Germany causes amusement here and is construed as a confession that Germans know they have lost the war. All the peace-talk that comes from the United States causes surprise and is taken to confirm the old opinion that the people in the United States do not yet know anything about the war.

The President's peace speech before the League for the Enforcement of Peace has created confusion. Some things in it were so admirably said that the British see that he does understand; and some things in it seem to them to imply that he does not in the least understand the war and show (as they think) that he was speaking only to the gallery filled with peace cranks Bryans and Fords and Jane Addamses. They are, therefore, skittish about the President.

You know how very friendly the Northcliffe papers have all been to us from the beginning. Well, they now shy off. The President's apparent idea—as they suspect—of the possibility of promoting peace has made them—very critical, to say the least.

There isn't any early peace in sight here, and the discussion of the subject at all puts the British and the French on edge. They are just beginning to see results of their fighting and of their blockade. They know they are going to win and they haven't the slightest idea of listening to any peace-talk on the basis of a German victory nor even on the basis of a draw. They don't any longer consider a draw a possibility. They can't quite see what the President is driving at. Hence they say, as you will observe from the enclosed clippings, that he is merely playing politics.

To that extent, therefore, the waters are somewhat muddied again. The peace racket doesn't assuage anybody: it raises doubts and fears—fears that we don't understand the war at all.

I can't resist the fear that the more peace-talk there is now the longer peace will be in coming.

But you can read these few clippings (I do not send you a lot of scurrilous ones, as I might) as well as I can.

Heartily yours,   W.H.P.

ENCLOSURE II

London. June 2, 1916.

The confounded flurry gets worse. There is just now more talk in London about the American (and the President's) "inability to understand the war" and about our falling into the German peace-talk trap than there is about the war itself. The President's sentence about our not being concerned with *the objects* of the war is another too-proud-to-fight, as the English view it.

I have moods in which I lose my patience with them and I have to put on two muzzles and a tight corset to hold myself in.

But peace talk doesn't go over here now, and the less we indulge in it, the better. The German peace-talk game has made the very word offensive to Englishmen. Then, too, they get more and more on edge as the strain becomes severer. There will soon be very few sane people left in the world.   W.H.P.

TCL (WP, DLC).

From Alexander Mitchell Palmer

Saint Louis, Mo., June 14, 1916

Chairmanship of National Committee ought to be settled immediately. Members of Committee are organizing for Cummings, whose election would be a mistake. Chairman ought to be man who can make strong appeal to Progressives. Best man in my judgment is Vance C. McCormick. He is trained in executive management of large affairs, clean aggressive and progressive. When Democrats in Pennsylvania nominated him for Governor in 1914 the Progressives pulled down Lewis[1] one of their National leaders to make him Progressive nominee. He will attract more Progressive support than any other chairman. New committee should organize Saturday. If you will indicate preference for McCormick now campaign will immediately start right.

A. Mitchell Palmer.

T telegram (WP, DLC).

[1] William Draper Lewis, professor and former Dean of the Law School of the University of Pennsylvania.

From Charles Richard Crane

St. Louis, Mo., June 14, 1916.

I am sure you would be happy to see your flock in assembly. It is a fine looking body, working its program without direction of any plutocratic committee in its enthusiasm and unity of purpose in proclaiming its allegiance to you and the party's achievements under your leadership. It is in every way in marked contrast with Chicago convention. If you were to appear here the town would not be safe. The confidence in the coming campaign is unqualified in any way, affectionate greetings.

Charles R. Crane.

T telegram (WP, DLC).

Remarks to Virginia Democratic Leaders

June 15, 1916.

Mr. Woods[1] and gentlemen: I had had the pleasure of seeing these resolutions when they were printed after the adjournment of the convention,[2] and I had already felt the encouragement which they brought me in generous measure. But it is an especially gracious act on the part of the convention to have appointed a committee to come in person to present these resolutions to me. I want you to know, in the first place, that, when you do me honors of this sort, you make me feel very proud. But you make me feel also very humble, because, in the midst of a great many unexpected difficulties, a man can never be sure that he is taking the wisest course. He can only be sure of the motives that prompt him in that course and of the thoughts that lie back of the course.

I have been saturated all my life in the traditions of American history, to which Virginia has made such abundant contributions, and I feel that the spirit that animates a nation is the spirit which its executive ought at least to try to interpret and put into action. That has been my endeavor, and that I have won, in acting upon those principles, the affectionate admiration and support of my native state gives me deep and proud gratification. You have greatly overstated my claims to credit, but I accept what you have said very gladly as a tribute of the heart rather than a tribute of the judgment, though I know you intended it as both. And, as a tribute of the heart, it gives me peculiar pleasure. It is not often, gentlemen, that there is personal contact of this sort in this rather strenuous and lonely business of conducting a government, and, therefore, it was with an instinct of real friendship that you came

in such interesting numbers[3] to bring me this encouragement and
to tell me that you do believe in the motives and in the purposes
that have characterized this administration. I can only thank you
very humbly and very heartily for the great compliment and the
great pleasure that this visit has given me.

T MS (WP, DLC).
  [1] James Pleasant Woods, lawyer of Roanoke, Va.
  [2] The resolutions adopted by the Virginia state Democratic convention on June
2 included the following statement: "The Democratic party of Virginia, in convention assembled, heartily indorses the policies of the national administration
and gives its unqualified approval of the masterly conduct of the public affairs
of the nation under Woodrow Wilson, a great Democratic President, and it but
expresses the unanimous demand of our people in asking for his renomination
at St. Louis and instructing the delegates from this State to vote as a unit to
make him again our standard bearer." The document went on to praise Wilson
for his conduct of policies toward the European war and the Mexican Revolution.
The resolutions are printed in the *Richmond Times-Dispatch*, June 3, 1916.
  [3] There were twenty persons in the delegation.

To Homer Stillé Cummings

The White House June 15 1916

In pursuance of our conversation and your kind suggestion I
suggest for chairman Vance McCormick of Pennasylvania for
vice chairman Homer S Cummings for secretary Carter Glass of
Virginia for treasurer W W Marsh of Iowa[1] and that committee
authorize chairman to appoint the campaign and other necessary committees   For your information let me say that I shall
suggest Lynch as chai[r]man executive committee

Woodrow Wilson

T telegram (H. S. Cummings Papers, ViU).
  [1] Wilbur W. Marsh, cattle farmer and manufacturer of cream separators of
Waterloo, Ia.

To Carter Glass

The White House June 15 1916

Am suggesting your selection as secretary national committee   I earnestly beg that you will not decline   We will see that
you are relieved of all detail of work   I greatly need your moral
influence and your guidance which I perfectly trust

Woodrow Wilson

T telegram (C. Glass Papers, ViU).

To Norman Hapgood

Personal.

My dear Hapgood: The White House June 15, 1916

Thank you for your interesting suggestion. I wish that it were possible to explain to you, as it is not, in a letter the various phases through which my thought has been going in the matter of the chairmanship. I hope and believe that you will in the end be satisfied with the result. It did not seem to me possible to take Baker from the War Department at this particular time without seeming to prefer my interests in the campaign to the interests of the country itself.

In haste

Cordially and sincerely yours,   Woodrow Wilson

TLS (WC, NjP).

To Edward William Pou

My dear Mr. Pou: [The White House] June 15, 1916

Your suggestion about Mr. Taft is one to which I have given really a great deal of consideration, but I think that when I see you next I can convince you that it would not be wise to act upon it. I shall be very much interested to talk it over with you when we can get together again.

In haste

Cordially and sincerely yours,   Woodrow Wilson

TLS (Letterpress Books, WP, DLC).

To Frederic Clemson Howe

My dear Howe: [The White House] June 15, 1916

Thank you for your letter of June ninth. I do not believe that it would be best to put into the platform the plank you suggest in the form in which you have suggested it, but I think that when the platform is finally completed you will find that it breathes throughout just the spirit of what you have embodied in what you have sent me.

I am warmly obliged to you for the suggestion, and hope with all my heart that everything goes well with you.

In haste   Faithfully yours,   Wodrow Wilson

TLS (Letterpress Books, WP, DLC).

To Robert Price[1]

My dear Doctor Price: [The White House] June 15, 1916

May I not stop in the midst of busy days to send you a word of affectionate greeting? I know that my father would have done this, and I have inherited his warm feeling about you. Not only that, but I have also the great pleasure of having known you personally.

I congratulate you and all your friends upon the remarkable preservation of your health and faculties, and wish that I could bring these greetings in person.

Cordially and sincerely yours,   Woodrow Wilson

TLS (Letterpress Books, WP, DLC).
[1] The Rev. Dr. Robert Price, colleague of Wilson's father at the Southwestern Presbyterian University in Clarksville, Tenn. Wilson thought that he was writing a birthday greeting. Dr. Price was born on January 16, 1830.

From Carter Glass

St Louis, Mo., June 15, 1916.

I gravely doubt the wisdom of your suggestion but I will not withhold any service which it is thought I may render you or the party.   Carter Glass.

T telegram (WP, DLC).

From Robert Lansing

PERSONAL AND CONFIDENTIAL:

My dear Mr. President: Washington June 15, 1916.

Here is a draft[1] of the reply to the Mexican note of May 22d. I believe that it embodies the suggestions which you made to me this morning and sets forth clearly the case between us and the *de facto* Government.

I have not shown this draft to General Scott for the purpose of correcting any minor errors of fact in regard to the conferences at El Paso, because I thought it would be unwise to do so until it had received your approval as to substance. It was my idea after you had made such changes as you desire to submit it to him for the purpose of any corrections which might be necessary.

The note does not include reference to the two raids into American territory made during the past few days,[2] but they can be inserted if so desired.

Faithfully yours,   Robert Lansing.

TLS (SDR, RG 59, 812.00/18450, DNA).
    1 It is printed as Enclosure I with WW to RL, June 18, 1916.
    2 Small bands of Mexicans carried out these minor raids near Laredo, Texas, on June 10 and 11. See A. B. Garrett to RL, June 11 and 12, 1916, *FR 1916*, pp. 573-74, and the *New York Times*, June 12 and 13, 1916.

From Robert Lansing, with Enclosures

Personal and Confidential.

Dear Mr. President: Washington June 15, 1916.

The telegrams from Minister Reinsch which accompany this show that there is a critical financial situation in China and raise an important question as to the policy which our Government should adopt.

The action of Japan to which reference is made in the telegram of June 15, 1 a.m., was withholding from the Chinese Government the surplus receipts from the Chinese Salt Gabelle deposited in the Yokohama Specie Bank at Shanghai.

The Reorganization Loan Contract of 1913 provided that the revenue from the salt tax, which formed the security for the loan, should be deposited in certain foreign banks, among them the Yokohama Specie Bank. The revenue from the Gabelle is far greater than the sums needed for the interest on the loan. Amortization does not begin until 1924. The Gabelle itself is managed by Europeans and Japanese so that there was no need for the action taken by Japan. The European banks were quite willing to hand over the monies deposited with them, but the action of Japan damaged the credit of China and very nearly produced a panic. The European and American banks, however, came to the relief of native banks and enabled them to meet the runs on their deposits. Japan is pressing her advantage and availing herself of China's distress to force Japanese control.

Confidential reports from a representative of our own Legation at Peking, who was sent quietly into Shantung to investigate the situation there, show a systematic attempt on the part of Japanese officers to create such disorders there as would justify Japanese intervention.

The results of Japanese aggression in Manchuria show what we may expect elsewhere.

No one can complain of fair competition but that we cannot expect from Japan and the increase of her power in China, as proposed by this latest move to control China's finances, will undoubtedly work great injury to American interests.

American bankers seem disposed to make a loan to China in association with European financiers. The proposed plan is that

American banks shall carry the European shares until the war is over.

There is danger, however, of a conflict between the banks represented by Messrs. Lee, Higginson and Company of Boston and those associated with the American Group in New York. The former state that they have already begun negotiations for a large loan to be secured upon the land taxes of China. The latter, apparently ignorant of any such negotiations, are considering the advisability of joining with other members of the Sextuple Group of 1913 in a second reorganization loan, secured, as was the first, upon the Salt Gabelle. Article XVII of the loan contract gives the lenders an option upon such additional loans. The American Group claim that, although they refused to participate in the loan of 1913, they still hold a right under the original articles of agreement to participate in any further loans by that Group. It seems probable that the British, French and Russian members of that Group are willing, not to say eager, to have the American Group make this proposed loan and carry them along.

That there would be considerable advantage in this arrangement is evident. The negotiations could be closed very quickly, for the security is already created and is being handled skillfully by European experts. The corruption and waste, which occurred under the old Chinese management are disappearing and the revenue is large enough now to cover another loan. The arrangement would be advantageous, too, in that it would give Japan participation but keep her controlled by her European associates, and in this way probably check her enroachments upon China.

On the other hand Messrs. Lee, Higginson and Company accepted the post of fiscal agents of China in the United States some months ago and provided a small loan of $5,000,000 when others would do nothing. They have paid already one million on this loan and are arranging to pay the balance. They, therefore, deserve the privilege, if they so desire, of sharing in the profits to accrue from further loans.

If these two groups are allowed to struggle with one another the Japanese may secure the prize.

Three courses are open to us:

(1) Refrain from any action, and allow China to decide whether to deal with either group or with Japanese,

(2) Support one group against the other, or

(3) Advise the bankers of both groups to combine. The last mentioned seems a reasonable course.

Very sincerely yours,   Robert Lansing.

TLS (SDR, RG 59, 893.51/3009, DNA).

ENCLOSURE I

Peking, China, May 27, 1916, 9 p.m.

STRICTLY CONFIDENTIAL. The situation has developed in a manner to place great responsibility on the United States as the chief neutral power interested in China and as the only power able to give effective financial assistance. Responsible Chinese as well as Europeans look upon American assistance as the last resort of Chinese independence and of international rights in China.

Japanese utilize the alliance for the purpose of independent action of the European Allies and to force them to follow Japan's lead. Political power of Yuan shaken by the joint advice in November was undermined by Japan refusing to turn over salt revenue and to join in assistance to Chinese banks. Meanwhile revolutionists were furnished every assistance by Japanese and the Bank of Shantung *fostered.*

The consequences of disorganization can be relieved only by assistance from without. Foreign banks should organize a clearing house which could take in hand rehabilitation and sound control of the national banks but joint action is impossible because of war. Only if the United States will take the initiative with a banking loan of fifteen million dollars can the reorganization be secured without loss of sovereignty.

The same applies to general finance. A loan of thirteen million secured on the land reorganization which would then be reformed under an American inspector similar to successful salt Gabelle would restore the Government. Rates and securities of these loans may be made such as to satisfy bankers.

Though American activity in China is not welcomed by Japan a last opportunity is afforded. A just, straightforward policy of the United States, strongly supported, would compel respect and prevent developments extraterritorially perilous to our future. Menacing ambitions of Japan though given much scope by the complications in Europe still rest on slender basis and could be held in check by display of active interest in China. Once realized, however, they could not be controlled except by great force. In China there would be enough to do for all. The Chinese Government would pursue policy of friendly cooperation with Japan in many ways and would raise no obstacles in Manchuria.

In its results the moderate investment suggested would equal military expenditure of hundred millions because it would prevent realization of exclusive control in the Far East inevitably hostile to America. The issues involved exceed those in Europe in ultimate importance.

Therefore it is very advisable financial assistance should come from United States without delay unless the abandonment of our position in China and of Chinese independence is required by other weighty considerations. By preserving evidences of non-political character of American action through confining assistance to the necessary auditing control required by interest of all and by showing a frank desire for co-operation with others, such a policy while highly effective could avoid seriously antagonizing other interests.   Reinsch.

ENCLOSURE   II

Peking, June 14, 1916, 6 p.m.

STRICTLY CONFIDENTIAL. The considerations adduced by my telegram of May 27, 9 p.m. apply with equal force under existing conditions. The President has received telegrams from the Governors of all seceded provinces pledging their allegiance. The convocation of the National Assembly, dissolved 1913, is likely and there is every reason to believe there will be cooperation in substances among the various parties but funds are required for reorganization and therefore serious difficulties would follow were the Government to be made dependent on any one power.
                                                  Reinsch.

ENCLOSURE   III

Peking, June 15, 1916, 1 a.m.

STRICTLY CONFIDENTIAL. The financial condition has taken a turn which makes necessary immediate and favorable decision on the part of American financiers, if complete domination of Chinese finance by Japan is to be prevented. The Chinese Government is very anxious to have American interests established so as to avoid sole reliance on Japan. The action of Japan has succeeded in obstructing sources from which funds should come and now it is offering China a large loan on condition of destruction of financial independence, including the demand to act as exclusive fiscal agent for China throughout the world. The Chinese Government can hold out only a few days longer, then it will be forced to capitulate and accept fiscal protectorate damaging to all. American financiers here have a last opportunity for acquiring interests in China in their interest, and that on an exceptionally favorable basis.

Unless a decision is made now American opportunity will be irrevocably lost. It is not necessary for Americans to assert primacy or to antagonize anyone, but simply to make use of the right which still exists to participate in Chinese affairs on an equal and independent basis. An immediate decision of policy, whether of inaction or of independent or joint financial assistance to China imperatively required. Reinsch.

E N C L O S U R E   I V

Peking, June 15, 1916, 8 p.m.

My telegram of June 15, 1 a.m.

Words *here lost an opportunity for* should read *have a last opportunity for*. Between *inaction* and *or joint* insert the clause *or of independent*.

In case financial cooperation with a neutral power would be looked upon as advantageous, I beg to say I have authoritative indications that the Dutch Minister,[1] financiers, and the Netherlands Government would be willing to consider proposals to that end. Reinsch.

T Telegrams (SDR, RG 59, 893.51/30009, DNA).
[1] Jonkheer F. Beelaerts van Blokland, Netherlands Minister to China, 1908-1918; Foreign Minister of the Netherlands, 1927-1933.

From Edward Mandell House

New London,
New Hampshire. June 15, 1916.

Dear Governor:

I am delighted at your choice for campaign manager and his associates. You have done the best, I think, that could be done in all the circumstances. I am receiving telegrams from St. Louis indicating satisfaction. I have just talked with McCormick from Harrisburg and we have arranged to get together soon.

If the campaign is properly organized—and it must be—we will win. It is only necessary to do the thing right for we are in the position of advantage. This must not be a slip-shod campaign and we must definitely know by the first of October how you stand with the voters.

I was never so eager to get at it im [in] my life for it seems to me to be the only thing in the world now that is worth while.

Your Flag Day Speech struck the keynote. No matter what

Hughes may say or do, before November it will be firmly fixed in the minds of the voters that a vote for Hughes will be a vote for the Kaiser. Say what he will, do what he will, he cannot get from under that. Affectionately yours, E. M. House

TLS (WP, DLC).

To Sara Bard Field

My dear Mrs. Field:[1]   [The White House] June 16, 1916
Your frank and friendly telegram of June twelfth sent from St. Louis was warmly appreciated. I have been in frequent conference with my party associates about the platform declaration with regard to woman suffrage and sincerely hope that the outcome has been acceptable to you.
In haste, with sincere appreciation,
Cordially yours, Woodrow Wilson

TLS (Letterpress Books, WP, DLC).
[1] Her marital status at this time is unknown; she had earlier been married to a man named Ehrgott.

From Carrie Clinton Lane Chapman Catt

St. Louis, Missouri, June 16, 1916.
Inasmuch as Governor Ferguson of Texas and Senator Walsh of Montana made diametrically opposite statements in the democratic Convention today with regard to your attitude towards the suffrage plank adopted by the convention[1] we apply to you directly to state your position on the plank and give your precise interpretation of its meaning. Carrie Chapman Catt

T telegram (WP, DLC).
[1] The exchange between James E. Ferguson and Thomas J. Walsh took place during a debate over Ferguson's proposed substitute for the plank presented by the platform committee recommending that the states extend the franchise to women. Ferguson's substitute, presented as a minority report on the platform, would have simply reaffirmed the traditional Democratic doctrine that control of elections and the suffrage were the sovereign prerogatives of the states. Senator Walsh declared, in the course of his remarks, that Wilson was well aware of exactly what was included in the platform and that the suffrage plank had his approval: "He deems it vital to his success that it shall stay there." Ferguson replied that he had heard something quite different during the discussions of the platform committee: "I put the question to them yesterday and I said: 'If you tell me that President Wilson is requesting this, I shall give up the fight and march like a soldier to support his judgment in this proposition.' And they said, 'No.' And they ran away from it, and they said President Wilson was leaving the Democratic Convention free to act according to the dictates of their consciences." The substitute plank was resoundingly defeated. *Official Report of the Proceedings of the Democratic National Convention, Held in Saint Louis, Missouri, June 14, 15 and 16th, 1916. . . .* (n.p., n.d), pp. 144-45.

From Edward Mandell House, with Enclosures

Dear Governor: New London,
        New Hampshire. June 16, 1916.

It is pleasing to receive this letter from Fletcher. It looks as if in a short time that matter would be closed.

If you can find it convienient, will you not see Fletcher as he requests and tell him directly, as I know you will, that you desire the smaller republics to sign simultaneously with the A.B.C. governments.

Bryce's letter you may also find interesting.

Your selections for the campaign seem to me in every way admirable. I am glad Carter Glass is to be a potential part of the Committee.

Gordon[1] tells me you intend to see Baruch. In many ways he is the most valuable man we have among the "Plunderbund" of which he is indeed not one, for he is progressive as far as one of his type can be.   Affectionately yours,   E. M. House

TLS (WP, DLC).
[1] That is, Gordon Auchincloss, his son-in-law.

E N C L O S U R E   I

Henry Prather Fletcher to Edward Mandell House

My dear Colonel House: New York City, June 15, 1916.

May I break in upon your intrenched repose "somewhere in Vermont" long enough to continue my report on the progress of the P.A.T. negotiations?

Brazil has accepted the amended draft. The new Chilean Consul General,[1] who has been Assistant Secretary for Foreign Affairs until appointed here, tells me he believes Chile will come along. Mr. Liano [Lauro] Muller will arrive here in the course of the next month and has signified his desire to sign the Treaty during his stay in this country.

After hearing from Brazil I journeyed up to Manchester to go over the matter with Naon. I have just returned from seeing him. He is ready also to sign, so that I think we may safely say we have arrived.

Naon believes it is of the utmost importance, and I agree with him, that some of the other American republics should sign at the same time, in order to make it a real Pan American document and not merely an agreement amongst the four largest. A number have signified their desire to join and if the President approves, I shall submit the final draft (when in treaty shape) to Uraguay and the others which have accepted and get as many more to sign on the same day as possible.

We believe if the United States and the A.B.C. countries are the only ones to sign that it will have a bad effect and unnecessarily so. They are to come in later so we might as well have as many of them as possible in from the very beginning and on the ground floor.

Naon has prepared a draft[2] which differs slightly in arrangement and phraseology from the one which Brazil has accepted but is substantially the same. I like it better than the draft we now have but will not risk losing the bird in hand.

However, on my return to Washington I shall submit the matter to the Secretary of State and we may be able to arrange it. Naon's draft leaves the first article almost word for word as originally drafted by the President and takes care of the territorial disputes in the second, leaving the guarantee of all such territory in suspense until disputes with regard to it shall have been settled.

I shall send you a copy of this from Washington. I do not like to risk a public stenographer making a copy here. After going over it with Mr. Lansing next week I think I shall ask the President to see me and give me ten or fifteen minutes. If you happen to have occasion to write to him will you please second this motion.

I shall return to 1718 H. Street, Washington early next week. I am staying here in the hope of getting Chile in line through Castro, the new Consul General, who is familiar with the matter from its inception.

Hoping you are enjoying your stay in the Hills, I am with very kind regards,   Sincerely yours,   Henry P. Fletcher.

TCL (WP, DLC).

1 Carlos Castro Ruiz, Consul General since June 1, 1916.
2 It is printed as an Enclosure with RL to WW, June 17, 1916.

E N C L O S U R E   I I

James Viscount Bryce to Edward Mandell House

Private.

My dear Colonel House: London. May 31, 1916.

As you asked me to tell you from time to time how opinion seemed to be moving here, I send this line to say that the indications of a wish on the part of the German Government to negotiate vague and unofficial indications, but not without some significance, find no more response here than in France or in Russia.

Our people are convinced that the German Government would not make peace on any terms the Allies could accept. That is perfectly clear from the language they hold. We are therefore resolved to prosecute the war till it is plain that Germany, recognizing her failure, is prepared to accept the terms the Allies think necessary for their own security.

I fear this moment is still some way off. But great as are the sufferings the war is causing, the feeling here is that a peace on the basis which the Germans indicate would leave us in a position of insecurity, with the dread of another war hanging over us, and with the need of continuing to maintain huge armaments.

There is no wish to break up Germany or humiliate or injure her. But her conduct has made us feel that no promise she might make would be worth the paper it is written on, and the securities for future peace must therefore be of a tangible nature.

From what I know of the French, they also think that the chance for any mediation has not yet come. We are pretty hopeful of the issue, and the perfect unanimity of the nation is quite remarkable; witness the ease with which at last compulsory service was accepted.

Is there any chance of our having the pleasure and benefit of seeing you here before Autumn? I am,

Sincerely yours,   James Bryce.

TCL (WP, DLC).

From Robert Lansing, with Enclosure

PERSONAL AND PRIVATE:

My dear Mr. President: Washington June 17, 1916.

I enclose you a confidential memorandum dated June 16th which I asked Mr. Fletcher to prepare, showing the progress and present *status* of the negotiations concerning the Pan-American Treaty. I believe Mr. Fletcher's suggestions are very well worth considering.

May I add a suggestion? It is that you see Mr. Fletcher before returning the memorandum to me with your views as to the course which we should adopt as to the language and signature of the treaty. I make this suggestion for two reasons—first, he could explain any doubtful point in the memorandum, and, second, I think that it would inspire him to additional efforts to carry out your policy in the matter. I am not complaining of the loyalty and energy Mr. Fletcher has shown in the task assigned to him. He has, in my opinion, done extremely well due in large measure to his knowledge of the Chilean attitude. It would, however, be wise to accord him an interview, outside of the real benefit to be obtained, as a mark of appreciation of what he has already accomplished, and also a courtesy to an American Ambassador. It always puts enthusiasm in a man to come in contact with the fountainhead.

If this latter suggestion meets with your approval, will you please indicate the day and time when you would be willing to receive Mr. Fletcher?

Faithfully yours,   Robert Lansing.

TLS (R. Lansing Papers, DLC).

E N C L O S U R E

Henry Prather Fletcher to Robert Lansing

CONFIDENTIAL

Dear Mr. Secretary: [Washington] June 16, 1916.

On the 27th of April last the Brazilian Ambassador submitted on behalf of the Brazilian and Chilean governments the text of a counter-project for the Pan-American treaty. This counter-project was accepted by the President and the Secretary of State with slight modifications and additions and as so modified and amended reads as follows, the words underlined being those added by the President, to wit:

ARTICLE I.

The High Contracting Parties will guarantee to one another their *present undisputed* territorial possessions in America and political independence under republican forms of government.

ARTICLE II.

The High Contracting Parties undertake to settle by arbitration or other amicable process the territorial questions that may arise in the future between two or more of them and declare, in this instrument, their purpose to settle those that are now pending or those that may flow therefrom by friendly means and without resort to violence.

ARTICLE III.

The High Contracting Parties undertake not to permit the organization and departure of military or naval expeditions hostile to *American* governments already established. They therefore undertake to prohibit the exportation of arms and munitions of war intended for insurgents against established American Governments, *unless such insurgents have been recognized as belligerents.*

On the 3rd of May a copy of the draft with our amendments was handed by me to the Brazilian Ambassador for transmission to his government, and copies of the same were handed also within a short time thereafter to the Argentine Ambassador and to the Chilean Charge d'Affaires. The Department was advised on the 3rd. day of June of the acceptance by the Brazilian Government of the draft of the treaty as amended and as above quoted. We were informed at the same time that it was the intention of Mr. Lauro Müller, Minister of Foreign Affairs of Brazil, to visit the United States for the purpose of taking the cure at French Lick Springs, and it has been arranged that during his visit to the United States he will sign the treaty. Mr. Müller is expected to arrive on the 12th of July. The Department was informed also that Brazil was using its good offices with Chile to persuade that Government to accept and sign also.

Pursuant to your instructions, I visited Ambassador Naon on the 14th of June at his summer residence in Manchester, Mass., and acquainted him with the fact of the acceptance by Brazil and of the desire of our Government to conclude the negotiations and sign the treaty during the visit of Mr. Lauro Müller, and asked him if he also had authority and would sign at the time indicated. He replied that he was so authorized and would be ready to sign. He stated, however, that he would prefer that the treaty should contain the first article as originally drafted by the President and that the matter relating to pending territorial disputes be covered in the second article. He handed to me a draft, copies of which in English and Spanish are attached hereto, of the treaty as he would prefer to have it signed. He stated that he felt sure that Mr. Lauro Müller would sign the treaty as he (Naon) had drafted it. I promised him to submit this draft to you but pointed out the difficulty and danger of delay in changing a formula at which we arrived with so much difficulty. I returned to New York on the 15th instant and submitted the two drafts to Mr. Castro, the new Chilean Consul-General in New York, who has been until his appointment there one month ago, the Sub-Secretary of Foreign Affaires of Chile, and perfectly acquainted with the negotiation from its inception. Mr. Castro, after studying Mr. Naon's draft in comparison with the draft of the treaty as amended by the President, stated that he did not believe the Chilean Government would accept Mr. Naon's draft but that he felt confident that the Chilean Government would accept and would sign the treaty as above set forth. I explained to him that it was necessary for us to have a reply from the Chilean Government within the shortest possible time; that the amendments in the original draft had been introduced solely to meet the views of the Chilean Government and that if in spite of all our efforts to meet their ideas with regard to the treaty they did not intend to accept it, there was no reason that I could see why we should not proceed to sign along the broader lines of the President's draft as modified by Mr. Naon. He promised to take up the matter informally with the Chilean Embassy here and to urge prompt acceptance by Chile of the draft above quoted.

SIGNATURE OF THE TREATY:

Mr. Naon informed me that he was strongly averse that the treaty should be signed by the ABC powers and the United States on one day and with the other American Republics signing at a subsequent date,—his idea being that this being a Pan-American document it should be signed by all the republics of America who were willing to sign it, on the same day, and he felt that if it were signed only by the United States and the ABC powers it would create a bad impression among the smaller republics and would lose much of its force. I might observe, in parenthesis, that Mr. Naon is decidedly opposed to the ABC pact and believes that it is not sound American policy that there should be a grouping of powers. The Chilean point of view is quite the opposite, as I imagine is also that of Brazil, and Mr. Castro feels that if the other and smaller republics are asked to sign at the same time that it will be an indication on our part of hostility to, and an attempt to break up the ABC. Mr. Castro believes also that its effect in Europe would be greater if signed by the United States and the ABC allowing the smaller republics to adhere subsequently. I personally am inclined to agree with Mr. Naon that it would be better to[o] if the treaty should be signed simultaneously by as many of the American powers as care to join in it. I would respectfully suggest therefore that advantage be taken of the formal call of the new Chilean Charge d'Affaires upon the Secretary of State, to impress upon him the necessity for a prompt and categorical reply from his government so that the draft as above quoted may be embodied in a formal treaty which can be submitted to all the American governments who have accepted the idea of this treaty in principle, and arrangements be made for signature during the visit of Mr. Lauro Müller, say sometime during the first fortnight in August.

Should Chile definitely decline the modified draft above quoted, I see no objection if Brazil will agree to going ahead along the broader lines of Mr. Naon's draft hereto annexed. Mr. Naon is confident that Mr. Lauro Muller, in the event of Chile's refusal to accompany us, would be willing to sign the Naon draft.

H.P.F.

TCL (R. Lansing Papers, DLC).

ENGLISH TEXT. (Naon Draft)

I.

The High Contracting Parties agree upon a common and mutual guarantee of their territorial integrity and of their full political independence under a Republican form of government.

II.

The High Contracting Parties agree to settle by arbitration or by any other amicable procedure, any question which may arise between them in the future and they express their purpose of settling those now pending or those which may be derived therefrom, by amicable means, without having recourse to violence. Until the final settlement among themselves of the questions of territorial limits now pending between two or more of the High Contracting Parties, the mutual guarantee of territorial integrity referred to in Article I, shall apply only to the territories not in dispute.

III.

The High Contracting Parties agree not to permit the organization and departure of naval or military expeditions hostile to the Governments constituted in any of the countries of the continent. To this end they likewise agree to prohibit the exportation of arms and munitions of war intended for insurgents against said Governments, unless such insurgents have been recognized as belligerents.

TC MS (R. Lansing Papers, DLC).

From Frank Lyon Polk

My dear Mr. President: Washington June 17, 1916.

Last night I was quite at a loss as to how to express my very sincere appreciation of your willingness to consider me for Chairman of the National Committee. The thought is most gratifying and I am more than grateful for this evidence of your confidence.

As I said when I was appointed to my present position, I consider it an honor indeed, to be connected with your Administration in any capacity, but I feel that I can be more useful where I am, than in the place McCormick will fill with so much ability.

Yours faithfully,   Frank L Polk

TLS (WP, DLC).

From William Bauchop Wilson

My dear Mr. President: Washington June 17, 1916.

Referring to the Mexican situation you may recall that under date of May 23, 1916, President Gompers of the American Federation of Labor, sent a communication to the Casa Obrero Mundial and other labor organizations of Mexico, suggesting a conference of representatives of the labor unions of Mexico with representatives of labor unions of the United States "to propose a practical method of mutual cooperation between organized labor in Mexico and in the United States." Mr. Gompers suggested that "matters for the mutual welfare of the sister republics could then be discussed and a future cooperative policy outlined."

He advises me that he has had a response from the Casa Obrero Mundial and seven or eight other labor organizations of Mexico, but suggesting Eagle Pass instead of El Paso as the place of meeting. As the result of the correspondence, two representatives of the labor unions of Yucatan, Carlos Loveira, chief of the Department of Labor of Yucatan, and Baltasar Pages, editor of The Voice of the Revolution, published in Merida, have been sent to the United States to confer with Mr. Gompers and others concerning the proposed conference. Upon arriving in the United States and finding Mr. Gompers on a tour of the Middle West, they issued an appeal to the United States workers, a copy of which I am enclosing you herewith.[1] It is quite lengthy, but if you can find time to read it, it will give you a very clear concept of the ideals these people are struggling for. Mr. Gompers feels very confident that great good will result from the proposed conference, the date for which has not yet been set, and expresses the hope that no feeling of exasperation growing out of recent correspondence or actions will change the sentiment of friendly forbearance which has characterized the Administration's treatment of the Mexican situation in the past. He feels that if a crisis can be averted until the conference he is arranging for can be held, the mutual understandings growing out of such a conference will assist in clarifying the situation to the mutual benefit of both countries. He also calls attention to a report that there is under consideration the appointment of a commission to be composed of representatives of the United States and representatives of Mexico to attempt to adjust matters between these two countries, and suggests that as the labor movement of Mexico has been a very considerable factor in the recent changes in that country, and, since the time of Madero, the workers of Mexico have been organizing and have been successfully pressing their demands for their rights as citizens and as workers, if such a commission is to be appointed, organized labor should be represented on it.

I am bringing these matters to your attention because Mr. Gompers is absent from the city and is consequently unable to present them to you in person. He has communicated his viewpoint to me by letter and by messenger and I feel that both suggestions are of such importance that they should be brought to your attention at once.   Faithfully yours,   W B Wilson

TLS (WP, DLC).
¹ "Yucatan Unions Send Peace Plea in Proclamation to U. S. Workers," *New York Call*, June 13, 1916, newspaper clipping (WP, DLC). The proclamation gave a brief statement of the objectives of the revolution in Mexico. The statement characterized it as a class struggle between the Mexican workers and peasants, on the one hand, and domestic and foreign capitalists and imperialists, on the other hand. The reactionary forces in the United States and Mexico now hoped to destroy the revolution by pitting the workers of both nations in a war against each other. The Mexican workers urged their American "comrades" to help to bring about the withdrawal of United States military forces in Mexico in order to avoid a disastrous clash. If a war did occur, they concluded, the "magnates" and all other persons seeking intervention in Mexico should be put at the head of the American army.

From Margaret Woodrow Wilson

Darling Father,   [New York, c. June 17, 1916]

So now you are in for being president again! I am sorry for you but happy for our beloved country.

I stayed over another night in New York as Mrs David was not quite ready for me and telegraphed Mr David, who is in New York, to bring me down today.

I saw Mr Adams[1] and he was so lovely. He is going to do this work for us with a great deal of deep and true feeling. Often while talking about it with me his eyes would fill with tears.

As a result of our conversation he asked me to get a consensus of opinion from the family as to just what qualities we would most like the figure in the bas-relief to express and then write him before he goes south so that he may go with something definite in his mind that might take form while he is there. Now, Father dear, I know that what we three most want is to have your wishes and ideas carried out in this monument. As we cannot possibly all get together will you write to Mr Adams telling him what qualities of Mother's you would most like to see expressed or symbolized in her monument? I take it that you like the general design of the stone that Mr Adams has made and the idea of having a bas-relief of Greek character on it. I do very much. Mr Adams said that he could draw the figure on a larger scale if it were a kneeling figure than if it were a standing one, and that because the space for the bas-relief cannot be large a standing figure might not be as striking as a kneeling figure. It was I that suggested a standing figure, but I am perfectly willing to bow to his and Nell's opinion in the matter. Nell said the same thing as he about it. He says that he can make the kneeling figure stronger than it is in his sketch. He will try to express too symbolically, in the treatment of the details of the carving, other sides of Mother's character than those expressed in the action of the figure and also I suppose some of her gifts. He was going to work out some symbolism for instance in the things that are in the left hand of the figure in his sketch. They are only suggested in it now of course. He has I think hit upon a significant thing in having the right hand reaching out to the flower, suggesting the way she always reached out to people, but I think that he can make a much stronger thing than he has. I always think of all the strong qualities in connection with Mother as well as the sweet and gentle ones, and always of the light that radiated from her.

Will you have time to write to Mr Adams next week? He wants to go to Rome as soon after the twenty first of June as possible. I did not speak to him about letters to Rome people; I forgot to do so. I should think that he would want to be at the grave alone, but perhaps Helen could write to Miss Berry asking her to meet him and take him there.

I love you so much, dear Father and it was such a wrench leaving you the other day. The last few weeks have been happy ones for me, because I have seen more of you and dear Edith than I have for a long time. They have been a real blessing to me. (I still put the punctuation in the wrong place sometimes, but aren't you glad that I am using a typewriter?)

Don't bother to answer this letter, dear Father unless there is something you want me to do for you.

Give my dear love to Edith.

With love and devotion for you,

Your loving daughter,   Margaret.

TLS (WC, NjP).
[1] That is, Herbert Adams, sculptor of the monument over Ellen Axson Wilson's grave.

To Robert Lansing, with Enclosures

My dear Mr. Secretary,   The White House. 18 June, 1916.

I have gone very carefully through this note and think it adequate and excellent. I have here and there altered the wording, but nowhere the meaning of it.

I showed it to Baker last evening, and he makes, after taking it away for careful perusal, the enclosed suggestion, which I think an excellent one. They might as well know at once *all* that they will be up against if they continue their present attitude.

How will you send this,—by post or wire?

Faithfully yours,   W.W.

WWTLI (SDR, RG 59, 812.00/18516½, DNA).

E N C L O S U R E   I[1]

Sir:

I have read your communication, which was delivered to me on May 22, 1916 under instructions of the Chief Executive of the *de facto* Government of Mexico, on the subject of the presence of American troops in Mexican territory, and I would be wanting in candor if I did not, before making answer to the allegations of fact and the conclusions reached by your Government, express the surprise and regret which have been caused this Government by the *discourteous* tone and temper of this last communication of the *de facto* Government of Mexico.

The Government of the United States has viewed with deep

[1] Words in the following document in angle brackets deleted by Wilson; words in italics (except *de facto* and *ad referendum* and words noted below) added by him.

concern and increasing disappointment the progress of the revolution in Mexico. Continuous bloodshed and disorders have marked its progress. For three years the Mexican Republic has been torn with civil strife; the lives of Americans and other aliens have been sacrificed; vast properties developed by American capital and enterprise have been destroyed or rendered non-productive; bandits have been permitted to roam at will through the territory contiguous to the United States and to seize, without punishment or without effective attempt at punishment, the property of Americans, while the lives of citizens of the United States who ventured to remain in Mexican territory or to return there to protect their interests, have been taken, and in some cases barbarously taken, and the murderers have neither been apprehended nor brought to justice. It would be difficult to find in the annals of the history of Mexico conditions more deplorable than those which have existed there during these recent years of civil war.

It would be tedious to recount instance after instance, outrage after outrage, atrocity after atrocity, to illustrate the true nature and extent of the ⟨almost incredible⟩ *widespread* conditions of lawlessness and violence which ⟨has⟩ *have* prevailed. During the past nine months in particular, the frontier of the United States along the lower Rio Grande has been thrown into a state of constant ⟨terror⟩ *apprehension* and turmoil because of frequent and sudden incursions into American territory and depredations and ⟨massacres⟩ *murders* on American soil by Mexican bandits, ⟨destroying lives and⟩ *who have taken the lives and destroyed the* property of American citizens, ⟨and carrying across the international boundary⟩ *sometimes carrying* American citizens *across the international boundary* with the booty seized. ⟨during these raids.⟩ American garrisons have been attacked at night, American soldiers killed and their equipment and horses stolen; American ranches have been raided, property stolen and destroyed, and American trains wrecked and plundered. The attacks on Brownsville, Red House Ferry, Progresso Post Office, and Las Peladas, all occurring during September last, are typical. In these attacks on American territory, Carrancista adherents and even Carrancista soldiers took part in the looting, burning, and killing. Not only were these murders characterized by ruthless brutality, but uncivilized acts of mutilation were perpetrated. Representations were made to General Carranza and he was emphatically requested to stop these reprehensible acts in a section which he has long claimed to be under the complete domination of his authority. Notwithstanding these representations and the promise of

General Nafarrete[2] to prevent attacks along the international boundary, in the following month of October a passenger train was wrecked by bandits and several persons killed seven miles north of Brownsville, and an attack was made upon United States troops at the same place several days later. Since these attacks leaders of the bandits well known both to Mexican civil and military authorities as well as to American officers have been enjoying with impunity the liberty of the towns of Northern Mexico. So far has the indifference of the *de facto* Government to these atrocities gone that some of these leaders, as I am advised, have received not only the protection of that Government, but encouragement and ⟨financial⟩ aid as well. ⟨have been furnished by its authorities without rebuke or interference.⟩

Depredations upon American persons and property within Mexican jurisdiction have been still more numerous. This Government has repeatedly requested in the strongest terms that the *de facto* Government safeguard the lives and homes of American citizens and furnish the protection, which international obligation imposes, to American interests in the Northern States of Tamaulipas. Nuevo Leon, Coahuila, Chihuahua, and Sonora, and also in the States to the South. For example, on January 3d troops were requested to punish the bands of outlaws which looted the Cusi mining property, eighty miles west of Chihuahua, but no effective results came from this request. During the following week the bandit Villa with his band of about 200 men was operating without opposition between Rubio and Santa Ysabel, a fact well known to Carrancista authorities. Meanwhile a party of unfortunate Americans started by train from Chihuahua to visit the Cusi mines, after having received assurances from the Carrancista authorities in the State of Chihuahua that the country was safe, and that a guard on the train was not necessary. The Americans held passports or safe conducts issued by authorities of the *de facto* Government. On January 10th the train was stopped by Villa bandits and eighteen of the American party were stripped of their clothing and shot in cold blood, in what is now known as "the Santa Ysabel massacre." General Carranza stated to the Agent of the Department of State that he had issued orders for the immediate pursuit, capture, and punishment of those responsible for this atrocious crime, and appealed to this Government and to the American people to consider the difficulties of according protection along the railroad where the massacre occurred. Assurances were also given by Mr. Arredondo, presumably under instructions from the *de facto* Government, that the murderers

[2] Emiliano P. Nafarrate, *Carrancista* commander in Matamoros.

would be brought to justice, and that steps would also be taken to remedy the lawless conditions existing in the state of Durango. It is true that Villa, Castro, and Lopez[3] were publicly declared to be outlaws and subject to apprehension and execution, but so far as known, only a single man personally connected with this massacre has been brought to justice by Mexican authorities. Within a month after this barbarous slaughter of inoffensive Americans it was notorious that Villa was operating within twenty miles of Cusihuiriachic, and publicly stated that his purpose was to destroy American lives and property. Despite repeated and insistent demands that military protection should be furnished to Americans, Villa openly carried on his operations, constantly approaching closer and closer to the border. He was not intercepted, nor were his movements impeded by troops of the *de facto* Government, and no effectual attempt was made to frustrate his hostile designs against Americans. In fact, as I am informed, while Villa and his band were slowly moving toward the American frontier in the neighborhood of Columbus, New Mexico, not a single Mexican soldier was seen in his vicinity. Yet the Mexican authorities were fully cognizant of his movements, for on March 6th as General Gavira[4] pub[l]icly announced he advised the American military authorities of the outlaw's approach to the border, so that *they*[5] might be prepared to prevent him from crossing the boundary. Villa's unhindered activities culminated in the unprovoked and cold-blooded attack upon American soldiers and citizens in the town of Columbus on the night of March 9th, the details of which do not need repetition here in order to refresh your memory with the heinousness of the crime. After murdering, burning, and plundering, Villa and his bandits fleeing south passed within sight of the Carrancista military post at Casas Grandes, and no effort was made to stop him by the officers and garrison of the *de facto* Government stationed there.

In the face of these depredations not only on American lives and property on Mexican soil, but on American soldiers, citizens and homes on American territory, the perpetrators of which General Carranza was unable or possibly considered *it* inadvisable to apprehend and punish, the United States had no recourse other than to employ force to disperse the bands of Mexican outlaws⟨,⟩ who were with increasing boldness systematically raiding across

---

[3] Rafael Castro and Pablo López. López, a chief lieutenant of Villa, commanded the force responsible for the Santa Ysabel massacre.

[4] Gabriel Gavira, the *Carrancista* commander in Juárez.

[5] Emphasis in the text; also as in the case of "gradually" and "immediate," *infra*.

the international boundary. The marauders engaged in the attack on Columbus were driven back across the border by American cavalry, and subsequently, as soon as a sufficient force to cope with the band could be collected, were pursued into Mexico in an effort to capture or destroy them. Without co-operation or assistance in the field on the part of the *de facto* Government, despite repeated requests by the United States, and without apparent recognition *on its part* of the desirability of putting an end to these systematic raids, or of punishing the chief perpetrators of the crimes committed, because they menaced the good relations of the two countries, American forces pursued the lawless bands as far as Parral, where the pursuit was halted by the ⟨instigated⟩ hostility of Mexicans, presumed to be loyal to the *de facto* Government, who arrayed themselves on the side of outlawry and became in effect the protectors of Villa and his band.

In this manner and for these reasons have the American forces entered Mexican territory. Knowing fully the circumstances set forth, the *de facto* Government cannot be blind to the necessity which compelled this Government to act and yet it has seen fit to ⟨conjure up⟩ *recite* groundless sentiments of hostility toward the expedition and to impute to this Government ulterior motives for the continued presence of American troops on Mexican soil. It is charged that these troops crossed the frontier without first obtaining the consent or permission of the *de facto* Government. Obviously, as immediate action alone could avail, there was no opportunity to reach an agreement (other than that of March 10th-13th now repudiated by General Carranza) prior to the entrance of such an expedition into Mexico if the expedition was to be effective. Subsequent events and correspondence have demonstrated to the satisfaction of this Government that General Carranza would not have entered into any agreement providing for an effective plan for the capture and destruction of the Villa bands. While the American troops were moving rapidly southward in pursuit of the raiders, it was the form and nature of the agreement that occupied the attention of General Carranza rather than the practical object which it was to attain— the number of limitations that could be imposed upon the American forces to impede their progress rather than the obstacles that could be raised to prevent the escape of the outlaws. It was General Carranza who suspended through your note of April 12th all discussions and negotiations for an agreement along the lines of the Protocols between the United States and Mexico concluded during the period 1882-1896, under which the two countries had so successfully restored peaceful conditions on their common boundary. It may be mentioned here that, notwithstanding the statement in your note that "the American Government gave no answer to the note of the 12th of April," this note was replied to on April 14th, when the Department instructed Mr. Rodgers by telegraph to deliver this Government's answer to General Carranza. Shortly after this reply, the conferences between Generals Scott, Funston and Obregon began at El Paso, during which they signed on May 2d a project of a memorandum *ad referendum* regarding the withdrawal of American troops. As an indication of the alleged bad faith of the American Government, you state that though General Scott declared in this memorandum that the destruction and dispersion of the Villa band "had been accomplished," yet American forces are not withdrawn from Mexico. It is only necessary to read the memorandum, which is in the English language, to ascertain that this is clearly a misstatement, for the memorandum states that "the American punitive expeditionary forces have destroyed or dispersed many of the lawless elements and bandits, * * * or have driven them far into the interior of the Republic of Mexico," and further, that the United States forces were than [then] "carrying on a vigorous pursuit of such small numbers of bandits or lawless elements as may have escaped." The context of your note gives the impression that⟨,⟩ the object of the expedition being admittedly accomplished, the United States had agreed in the memorandum to begin the withdrawal of its troops. The memorandum shows, however, that it was not alone on account of partial dispersion of the bandits that it was decided to begin the withdrawal of American forces, but equally on account of the assurances of the Mexican Government that their forces were "at the present time being augmented and strengthened to such an extent that they will be able to prevent any disorders occurring in Mexico that would in any way endanger American territory," and that they would "continue to diligently pursue, capture or destroy any lawless bands of bandits that may still exist or hereafter exist in the northern part of Mexico," and that it would "make a proper distribution of such of its forces as may be necessary to prevent the possibility of invasion of American territory from Mexico." It was because of these assurances and because of General Scott's confidence that they would be carried out that he stated in the memorandum that the American forces would be "*gradually* withdrawn." It is to be noted that, while the American Government

was willing to ratify this agreement, General Carranza refused
to do so, as General Obregon stated, because, among other things,
it imposed improper conditions upon the Mexican Government.

Notwithstanding the assurances in the memorandum, it is well
known that the forces of the *de facto* Government have not
carried on a vigogous [vigorous] pursuit of the remaining bandits
and that no proper distribution of forces to prevent the invasion
of American territory has been made, as will be shown by the
further facts hereinafter set forth. ⟨On the whole,⟩ I am reluctant-
⟨ly⟩ *to be* forced to the conclusion *which might be drawn from
these circumstances* that the *de facto* Government, in spite of
the crimes committed and the sinister designs of Villa and his
followers, did not and does not now intend or desire that these
outlaws should be captured, destroyed, or dispersed by American
troops or, at the request of this Government, by Mexican troops.

While the conferences at El Paso were in progress, and after
the American conferees had been assured on May 2d that the
Mexican forces in the northern part of the Republic were then
being augmented so as to be able to prevent any disorders that
would endanger American territory, a band of Mexicans, on
the night of May 5th, made an attack at Glenn Springs, Texas,
about twenty miles north of the border, killing American soldiers
and civilians, burning and sacking property and carrying off two
Americans as prisoners. Subsequent to this event, the Mexican
Government, as you state, "gave instructions to General Obregon
to notify that of the United States that it would not permit the
further passage of American troops into Mexico on this account,
and that orders had been given to all military commanders along
the frontier not to consent to same." This Government is of course
not in a position to dispute the statement that these instructions
had been given to General Obregon, but it can decisively assert
that General Obregon never gave any such notification to General Scott or General Funston or, so far as known, to any other
American official. General Obregon did, however, inquire as to
whether American troops had entered Mex in pursuit of the Glenn
Springs raiders, and General Funston stated that no orders had
been issued to American troops to cross the frontier on account
of the raid, but this statement was made before any such orders
had been issued, and not afterwards, as the erroneous account
of the interview given in your note would appear to indicate.
Moreover, no statement was made by the American Generals
that "no more American troops would cross into our territory."
On the contrary, it was pointed out to General Obregon and to
Mr. Juan Amador, who was present at the conference, and

pointed out with emphasis, that the bandits de la Rosa and Pedro Vino,[6] who had been instrumental in causing the invasion of Texas above Brownsville, were even then *reported to be* arranging, in the neighborhood of Victoria ⟨, according to reports,⟩ for another raid across the border, and it was made clear to General Obregon that if the Mexican Government did not take immediate steps to prevent another invasion of the United States by these marauders, who were frequently seen in the company of General Nafarrete, the Constitutionalist commander, Mexico would find in Tamaulipas another punitive expedition similar to that then in Chihuahua. American troops crossed into Mexico on May 10th, upon notification to the local military authorities, under the repudiated agreement of March 10-13th, or in any event in accordance with the practice adopted over forty years ago, when there was no agreement regarding pursuit of marauders across the international boundary. These troops penetrated 168 miles into Mexican territory in pursuit of the Glenn Springs marauders without encountering a detachment of Mexican troops or a single Mexican soldier. Further discussion of this raid, however, is not necessary, because the American forces sent in pursuit of the bandits recrossed into Texas on the morning of May 22d, the date of your note under consideration—a further proof of the singleness of purpose of this Government in endeavoring to quell disorder and stamp out lawlessness along the border.

During the continuance of the El Paso conferences, General Scott, you assert, did not take into consideration the plan proposed by the Mexican Government for the protection of the frontier by the reciprocal distrubition [distribution] of troops along the boundary. This proposition was made by General Obregon a number of times, ⟨every⟩ *but each* time conditioned upon the immediate withdrawal of American troops, and the Mexican conferees were invariably informed that *immediate* withdrawal could not take place, and that therefore it was impossible to discuss the project on that basis.

I have noted the fact that your communication is not limited to a discussion of the deplorable conditions existing along the border and their important bearing on the peaceful relations of our Governments, but that an ⟨obvious⟩ effort is made to connect it with other circumstances in order to support, if possible, a ⟨fallacious definition⟩ *mistaken interpretation* of the attitude of the Government of the United States toward Mexico. You state

6 Luis de la Rosa, former deputy sheriff of Cameron County, Texas; now allegedly involved in a plot to invade the southwestern United States and create an independent republic therein. See R. Robertson to RL, June 9, 1916, *FR 1916*, pp. 570-72. Pedro Viño cannot be further identified.

in effect that the American Government has placed every obstacle in the way of attaining the pacification of Mexico, and that this is shown by the volume of diplomatic representations in behalf of American interests which constantly impede efforts to reorganize the political, economical, and social conditions of the country; by the decided aid lent at one time to Villa by American officers and by the Department of State; by the aid extended by the American Catholic clergy to that of Mexico; by the constant activity of the American press in favor of intervention and the interests of American business men; by the shelter and supply of rebels and conspirators on American territory; by the detention of shipments of arms and munitions purchased by the Mexican Government; and by the detention of machinery *intended* for their manufacture.

In reply to this sweeping charge, I can truthfully affirm that the American Government has given every possible encouragement to the *de facto* Government in the pacification and rehabilitation of Mexico. From the moment of its recognition, it has had the undivided support of this Government. An embargo was placed upon arms and ammunition going into Chihuahua, Sonora, and Lower California, in order to prevent their falling into the hands of the armed opponents of the *de facto* Government. Permission has been granted from time to time, as requested, for Mexican troops and equipment to traverse American territory from one point to another in Mexico in order that the operations of Mexican troops against Villa and his forces might be facilitated. In view of these friendly acts, I am surprised that the *de facto* Government has construed diplomatic representations in regard to the unjust treatment accorded American interests, private assistance to opponents to the *de facto* Government by sympathizers in a foreign country, and the activity of a foreign press as interference by the United States Government in the domestic politics of Mexico. If a denial is needed that this Government has had ulterior and improper motives in its diplomatic representations, or has countenanced the activities of American sympathizers and the American press opposed to the *de facto* Government, I *am glad most emphatically to* deny it. It is, however, a matter of common knowledge that the Mexican press has been more active than the press in the United States in endeavoring to inflame the two peoples against each other and to force the two countries into hostilities. With the power of censorship of the Mexican press, so rigorously exercised by the *de facto* Government, the responsibility for this activity cannot, *it would seem*, be avoided by that Government, and the issue of the appeal of General Carranza himself in the press of March 12th, calling upon the Mexican people to be prepared for any emergency which might arise, and intimating that war with the United States was imminent, evidences the attitude of the *de facto* Government toward these publications. It should not be a matter of surprise that, after such manifestations of hostile feeling, the United States was doubtful of the purpose for which the large amount of ammunition was to be used which the *de facto* Government appeared eager to import from this country. Moreover, the policy of the *de facto* Government in refusing to co-operate and in failing to act independently in destroying the Villa bandits and in otherwise suppressing outlawry in the vicinity of the border so as to remove the danger of war materials, while passing southward through this zone, falling into the hands of the enemies of law and order is, in the opinion of this Government, a sufficient ground, even if there were no other, for the refusal to allow such materials to cross the boundary into the bandit-infested region. To have permitted these shipments without careful scrutiny would, in the circumstances, have been to manifest a *sense of* security which would have been unjustified.

Candor compels me to add that the unconcealed hostility of the subordinate military commanders of the *de facto* Government toward the American troops engaged in pursuing the Villa bands and the efforts of the *de facto* Government to compel their withdrawal from Mexican territory by threats and show of military force instead of by aiding in the capture of the outlaws constitute a menace to the safety of the American troops and to the peace of the border. As long as this menace continues and there is any evidence of an intention on the part of the *de facto* Government or its military commanders to use force against the American troops instead of co-operating with them, the Government of the United States will not permit munitions of war or machinery for their manufacture to be exported from this country to Mexico.

As to the shelter and supply of rebels and conspirators on American territory, I can state that vigorous efforts have been and are being made by the agents of the United States to apprehend and bring to justice all persons found to be conspiring to violate the laws of the United States by organizing to oppose with arms the *de facto* Government *of Mexico*. Political refugees have undoubtedly sought asylum in the United States, but this Government has vigilantly kept them under surveillance and has not hesitated to apprehend them upon proof of their criminal intentions, as the arrest of General Huerta and others fully attests.

Having corrected the erroneous statements of fact⟨,⟩ to which

I have adverted, the real situation stands forth in its true light. It is admitted that American troops have crossed the international boundary in hot pursuit of the Columbus raiders and without notice to or the consent of your Government, but the several protestations on the part of this Government by the President, by this Department, and by other American authorities, that the object of the expedition was to capture, destroy, or completely disperse the Villa bands of outlaws or to turn this duty over to the Mexican authorities when assured that it would be effectively fulfilled, have been carried out in perfect good faith by the United States. Its efforts, however, have been obstructed at every point; first, by insistence on a palpably useless agreement which you admit was either not to apply to the present expedition or was to contain impracticable restrictions on its organization and operation; then by actual opposition, encouraged and fostered by the *de facto* Government, to the further advance of the expedition into Villa territory, which was followed by the sudden suspension of all negotiations for an arrangement for the pursuit of Villa and his followers and the protection of the frontier; and finally by a demand for the immediate withdrawal of the American troops. Meantime, conditions of anarchy in the border States of Mexico were continually growing worse. Incursions into American territory were plotted and perpetrated; the Glenn Springs raid was successfully executed, while no effective efforts were being made by General Carranza to improve the conditions and to protect American territory from constant threat of invasion. In view of this increasing menace, of the inactivity of the Carranza forces, of the lack of co-operation in the apprehension of the Villa bands, and of the known encouragement and aid given to bandit leaders, it is unreasonable to expect the United States to withdraw its forces from Mexican territory or to prevent their entry again when their presence is the only check upon further bandit outrages and the only efficient means of protecting American lives and homes—safeguards which General Carranza, though internationally obligated to supply, is manifestly unable or unwilling to give.

In view of the actual state of affairs as I have outlined it above, I am now in a position to consider the conclusions which you have drawn in your note under acknowledgment from the erroneous statements of fact which you have set forth.

Your Government (insinuates) *intimates*, if it does not openly charge, that the attitude of the United States is one of insincerity, distrust, and suspicion toward the *de facto* Government of Mexico, and that the intention of the United States in sending its troops into Mexico is to extend its sovereignty over Mexican territory, and ⟨is⟩ not *merely* for the purpose of pursuing marauders and preventing future raids across the border. The *de facto* Government charges by implication⟨,⟩ which admits of but one interpretation, that this Government has as its object territorial aggrandizement even at the expense of a war of aggression against a neighbor weakened by years of civil strife. The Government of the United States, if it had had designs upon the territory of Mexico, would have had no difficulty in finding during this period of revolution and disorder many plausible arguments for intervention in Mexican affairs. ⟨Believing,⟩ *Hoping*, however, that the people of Mexico would through their own efforts restore peace and establish an orderly government, the United States has awaited with patience the consummation of the revolution.

When the superiority of the revolutionary faction led by General Carranza became undoubted, the United States, after conferring with six others of the American Republics, recognized unconditionally the present *de facto* Government. It hoped and expected that the Government would speedily restore order and provide the Mexican people and others, who had given their energy and substance to the development of the great resources of the Republic, opportunity to rebuild in peace and security their shattered fortunes.

This Government has waited month after month for the consummation of its hope and expectation. ⟨Yet,⟩ *In* spite of increasing discouragements, in spite of repeated provocations to exercise force in the restoration of order in the northern regions of Mexico, where ⟨the⟩ American interests have suffered most seriously from lawlessness, the Government of the United States has refrained from aggressive action and sought by appeals and moderate though explicit demands to impress upon the *de facto* Government the seriousness of the situation and to arouse it to its duty to perform its international obligations toward citizens of the United States who had entered the territory of Mexico or had vested interests within its boundaries.

In the face of ⟨the⟩ *constantly* renewed evidences of the patience and restraint of this Government in circumstances which only a government imbued with unselfishness and a sincere desire to respect to the full the sovereign rights and national dignity of the Mexican people⟨,⟩ would have endured, ⟨the⟩ doubts and suspicions as to the motives of the Government of the United States ⟨, which⟩ are expressed in ⟨the⟩ *your* communication of May 22d, ⟨can only be made with the sole purpose of⟩ *for which I can imagine no purpose but to* impugn⟨ing⟩ the good faith of this Government; ⟨although⟩ *for I find it hard to believe that such imputations are not universally* known to be without the least shadow of justification in fact.

Can the *de facto* Government doubt that, if the United States had turned covetous eyes on Mexican territory, it could have found many pretexts in the past for the gratification of its desire? Can that Government doubt that months ago, when the war between the revolutionary factions was in progress, a *much* better opportunity *than the present* was afforded for American intervention, if such has been the purpose of the United States as the *de facto* Government now insinuates? What motive could this Government have had in refraining from taking advantage of such opportunities other than unselfish friendship for the Mexican Republic?

I have *of course* given consideration to your argument that the responsibility for the present situation rests largely upon this Government. In the first place, you state that even the American forces along the border whose attention is undivided by other military operations, "find themselves physically unable to protect effectively the frontier on the American side." Obviously, if there is no means of reaching bands roving on Mexican territory and making sudden dashes at night into American territory it is impossible to prevent such invasions unless the frontier is protected by a cordon of troops. No government could be expected to maintain a force of this strength along the boundary of a nation with which it is at peace for the purpose of resisting the onslaughts of a few bands of lawless men, ⟨and⟩ especially ⟨so⟩ when the neighboring state makes no effort to prevent these attacks. The most effective method of preventing raids of this nature, as past experience has fully demonstrated, is to visit punishment or destruction on the raiders. It is precisely this plan which the United States desires to follow ⟨out⟩ along the border without any intention of infringing upon the sovereign rights of her neighbor, but which, although obviously advantageous to the *de facto* Government, it refuses to allow or even countenance. It is in fact protection to American lives and property about which the United States is solicitous and not the methods or ways in which that protection shall be accomplished. If the Mexican Government is unwilling or unable to give this protection by preventing its territory from being the rendezvous and refuge of murderers and plunderers, that does not relieve this Government from its duty to take all the steps necessary to safeguard American citizens on American soil. The United States Government cannot and will not allow bands of lawless men to establish themselves upon its borders with liberty to invade and plunder American territory with impunity and, when pursued, to seek safety across the Rio Grande, relying upon the plea of their Government that the integrity of the soil of the Mexican Republic must not be violated.

The Mexican Government further protests that it has "made every effort on its part to protect the frontier" and that it is doing "all possible to avoid a recurrence of such acts." Attention is again invited to the well-known and unrestricted activity of de la Rosa, Aniceto Piscano[,][7] Pedro Vino and others in connection with border raids and to the fact that, as I am advised, up to June 4th de la Rosa was still collecting troops at Monterey for the openly avowed purpose of making attacks on Texan border towns and that Pedro Vino was recruiting at other places for the same avowed purpose. I have already pointed out the uninterrupted progress of Villa to and from Columbus, and the fact that the American forces in pursuit of the Glenn Springs marauders penetrated 168 miles into Mexican territory without encountering a single Carranzista soldier. This does not indicate that the Mexican Government is doing "all possible" to avoid further raids; ⟨but on the other hand,⟩ *and* if it is doing "all possible," this is not sufficient to prevent border raids, and there is every reason, therefore, why this Government must take such preventive measures as it deems sufficient.

It is suggested that injuries suffered on account of bandit raids ⟨is⟩ *are* a matter of "pecuniary reparation" but "never the cause for American forces to invade Mexican soil." The precedents which have been established and maintained by the Government of the Mexican Republic for the last half century do not bear out this statement. It has grown to be almost a custom not to settle depredations of bandits by payments of money alone but to quell such disorders and to prevent such crimes by swift and sure punishment.

The *de facto* Government finally argues that "if the frontier were duly protected from incursions from Mexico there would be no reason for the existing difficulty"; thus the *de facto* Government attempts to absolve itself from the first duty of any Government, namely, the protection of life and property. This is the paramount obligation for which governments are instituted, and governments neglecting or failing to perform it are not worthy of the name. This is the duty for which General Carranza,

---

[7] The surname also appears as Pisano or Pizano. He was another former resident of Cameron County, Texas, and closely associated with De la Rosa in the plot to revolutionize the American Southwest. See the diplomatic report cited in n. 5 above.

it must be assumed, initiated his revolution in Mexico and organized the present Government and for which the United States Government recognized ⟨it⟩ *his government* as the *de facto* government of Mexico. Protection of American lives and property, then, in the United States is first the obligation of this Government, and in Mexico is, first, the obligation of Mexico and, second, the obligation of the United States. In securing this protection along the common boundary the United States has a right to expect the cooperation of its neighboring Republic; *and yet,* instead of taking steps to check or punish the raiders, the *de facto* government demurs and objects to measures taken by the United States. The Government of the United States does not wish to believe that the *de facto* government approves these marauding attacks, yet as they continue to be made, they show that the Mexican Government is unable to repress them. This inability, as this Government has had occasion in the past to say, may excuse the failure to check the outrages complained of, but it only makes stronger the duty of the United States to prevent them, for if the Government of Mexico can not protect the lives and property of Americans *exposed to attack from Mexicans*, the Government of the United States is in duty bound, so far as it can, to do so.

In conclusion, the Mexican Government invites the United States to support its "assurances of friendship with real and effective acts" which "can be no other than the immediate withdrawal of the American troops." ⟨This⟩ *For the reasons I have herein fully set forth, this* request of the *de facto* Government can not now be entertained. The United States has not sought the duty⟨,⟩ which has been forced upon it⟨,⟩ of pursuing bandits who, under fundamental principles of municipal and international law, ought to be pursued and arrested and punished by Mexican authorities. Whenever Mexico will assume and effectively exercise that responsibility the United States, as it has many times before publicly declared, will be glad to have this obligation fulfilled by the *de facto* Government of Mexico. If, on the contrary, the *de facto* Government is pleased to ignore this obligation and to believe that "in case of a refusal to retire these troops there is no further recourse than to defend its territory by an appeal to arms," the Government of the United States would surely be lacking in sincerity and friendship if it did not frankly impress upon the *de facto* Government that the execution of this threat will lead to the gravest consequences. While this Government would deeply regret such a result, it cannot recede from its settled determination to maintain its national rights and to perform its full duty in preventing further invasions of the territory of the United States and in removing the peril which Americans along the international boundary have borne so long with patience and forebearance.[8]

T MS (SDR, RG 59, 812.00/18450, DNA).
   [8] The note was sent in this revised form as RL to E. Arredondo, June 20, 1916, and is printed in *FR 1916*, pp. 580-92.

E N C L O S U R E   I I

From Newton Diehl Baker

My dear Mr President: Washington June 18, 1916

   I have read the note with great care. It seems to me fine in substance and manner and makes a strong case.

   On the subject of the embargo upon shippments of arms and munitions would it not be better to say that while a part of its purpose was and is to prevent such supplies falling into the hands of enemies of the *de facto* government yet so long as our commanders are menaced by subordinate commanders of the Mexican Government and the Mexican Government itself spends its efforts in threats upon us instead of action against the disturbers of our common peace, we do not propose to allow them to have any munitions from the U. S.[1]

   Might they not as well understand at once the fact?

   Instances could be cited of the approval of the Chihuahua mob by General Carranza;[2] the approval of Trevinos orders to Pershing;[3] the Carranza uniform and papers of the Brownsville raiders &c.   Respectfully   Newton D. Baker

ALS (SDR, RG 59, 812.00/18516½, DNA).
   [1] Baker's suggestion was incorporated in the note in the paragraph beginning: "Candor compels me to add. . . ."
   [2] Extensive anti-American rioting, including attacks on the United States consulate, took place in Chihuahua City on the nights of June 6 and 7. The trouble followed immediately after General Jacinto B. Treviño, commander of the *Carrancista* military forces in Chihuahua, had issued an inflammatory proclamation which called on citizens to assemble to discuss defense against an American invasion and after the ensuing, equally inflammatory, public meeting presided over by Treviño himself. *New York Times*, June 9, 1916.
   [3] General Treviño, on June 16, sent to General Pershing the following telegram: "I have orders from my Government to prevent, by the use of arms, new invasions of my country by American forces and also to prevent the American forces that are in this State from moving to the south, east or west of the places they now occupy. I communicate this to you for your knowledge for the reason that your forces will be attacked by the Mexican forces if these instructions are not heeded." Pershing replied in a telegram of the same date that he intended to maintain his freedom of action and that the responsibility for the consequences of any attack by Mexican forces would lie with the Mexican government. *FR 1916*, p. 577.

From Norman Hapgood

Dear Mr. President: [New York] June 18/16

Many thanks for your letter of the 15th. I certainly think the choice an admirable one. It will fit in pleasantly with our campaign among the independents.

My conferences with Bull Moose leaders this last week have been very encouraging. We shall have many of them, and all whom I have seen, whether with us or not, think the chances favor our winning.

Raymond Robins[1] (who I think is going to support you) said: "It would be wonderful if the President's choice for the Supreme Court should happen to fall on Lehmann.[2] Next to Brandeis I consider him the finest lawyer in the United States, (among the liberals at any rate), and he is respected equally by big business, law, and labor."

Others speak in the same way of him. One said he had Jewish blood, but Robins is sure he hasn't. He was born in Prussia.

In New York the bar situation is difficult. James Byrne[3] is spoken of most. He is rather enlightened, for a Wall Street lawyer, but how hard it is for them to see straight! Byrne said to his partner H. B. Brown:[4] "I have read the Brandeis record. One might vote for him, but no one can say he did right." The best man on the bench in New York is Cardoza,[5] but he is a Jew. I like Seabury,[6] for his progressive tendencies, but while a good judge he is hardly a great one, and his interest in politics somewhat obscures in the public mind his judicial standing.

One of the cleverest of the Progressives (who also probably will support you, tho he is going to watch Hughes for a while) said: "If the President should put Secretary Lane on the court it would not only strike the country as a distinguished appointment but it might give a chance to shift Mr. Daniels and thus make a much needed repair in the fences."

I feel extremely cheerful about the outlook. There are a few things I do not wish to write as I hope for the privilege of a few moments of your time this week.

                    Very sincerely Yours   Norman Hapgood

Oh, by the way, Mr. Hughes has indicated to certain Progressive leaders that he will put practically the whole Armageddon programme—the Bull Moose platform of 1912—into his formal acceptance, making a really striking Social Justice play.

I reach Washington early Tuesday morning.[7]

ALS (WP, DLC).

1 Lawyer, reformer, leader of religious lay movements, including the Y.M.C.A and the Y.W.C.A., and a prominent figure in the Progressive party.

2 That is, Frederick William Lehmann of St. Louis.

3 Of the firm of Byrne & Cutcheon, 24 Broad Street, New York.

4 Benjamin Henry Inness Brown.

5 Benjamin Nathan Cardozo, associate judge of the New York Court of Appeals.

6 Samuel Seabury, also an associate judge of the New York Court of Appeals. He was soon to become the Democratic candidate for Governor of New York.

7 Wilson saw Hapgood at 11:30 A.M. on June 21.

From Edward Mandell House

New London,

Dear Governor: New Hampshire. June 18, 1916.

I remember your having called attention to the fact that if we left the wording in Article One of the Pan American Peace Pact as it now is, (guaranteeing territorial and political integrity under republican forms of government) British America could not come in.

In talking it over with Gregory today he suggests having it read "existing forms of government." This would cover our desires and would leave Great Britain free to come in if she wished. If you think this a good suggestion, will you not communicate it to Secretary Lansing so he may instruct Mr. Fletcher.

It need not be necessary for Fletcher or the South American governments to know just why the change was made.

But few people realize the tremendous import of this pact but I believe you will find as soon as it is closed, it will create worldwide interest. It is epoch making and the outside nations will soon begin to give it a proper place.

This campaign is certain to center around international questions and those that are inter-related with it like Preparedness and Americanism. I shall endeavor during the summer to keep in closer touch with European affairs than ever.

I am enclosing a cabled synopsis of another article by Gardiner.[1] He evidently wrote this in response to a letter in which I enclosed him a verbatim copy of your address before the League to Enforce Peace. I sent Bryce, Loreburn and others copies for I felt sure they would only get garbled reports of it from the English papers and, perhaps, miss its main purposes.

You already know how thoroughly I agree with Gardiner in regard to a large naval program, for if we are to play the part that destiny seems to indicate, we must impress foreign governments with our ability to carry out our purposes. They know our latent strength, but unless we put it in concrete form, or indicate an intention to do so, we cannot make them give serious consideration to our aims.

Affectionately yours,   E. M. House

TLS (WP, DLC).

¹ "Says U. S. Election Is Vital to Europe," New York *Sun*, June 17, 1916, newspaper clipping (WP, DLC). This dispatch summarized Gardiner's, "What Does America Stand For?", *London Daily News*, June 17, 1916. Gardiner declared that the coming American election was of momentous importance: "It is to decide what America stands for with regard to the future of the world, and with that decision not the interests of America alone but the interests of Europe and the whole earth are bound up." The old world would emerge from the present war, not only terribly battered, but also totally unable to prevent itself from falling into new conflicts in the future. Only the United States, which would soon emerge as "the greatest power on the face of the globe," could lead the world in new directions. Therefore, the political struggle now going on in the United States, symbolized by the tumult over "preparedness" and "Americanism," was of vital importance to all mankind since it would determine America's course in the postwar era. Gardiner believed that the idea underlying the preparedness agitation was a hopeful one: "It is the idea that the power of America should be used to deliver humanity from the toils in which it is enmeshed by the past; that it is to be the weapon of a new dispensation; that the affairs of men shall henceforth be subject to arbitrament, not force, but justice." Gardiner recognized that this idea was not confined to any one American party, but he asserted that Wilson had given it the most explicit utterance, especially in his speech before the League to Enforce Peace, which he described as "opening a new chapter in the history of civilization."

To Carrie Clinton Lane Chapman Catt

My dear Mrs. Catt: The White House June 19, 1916

I was away from the city and did not get your telegram of June sixteenth promptly.

I am very glad to make my position about the suffrage plank adopted by the convention clear to you, though I had not thought that it was necessary to state again a position I have repeatedly stated with entire frankness. The plank received my entire approval before its adoption and I shall support its principle with sincere pleasure. I wish to join with my fellow-Democrats in recommending to the several states that they extend the suffrage to women upon the same terms as to men.

Cordially and sincerely yours,   Woodrow Wilson

TLS (National American Woman Suffrage Association Papers, DLC).

To William Bauchop Wilson

My dear Mr. Secretary: The White House June 19, 1916

I am very much gratified by what you tell me of the prospects of a conference between the representatives of labor in Mexico and this country, and thank you sincerely for your letter of June seventeenth. You may be sure the crisis with Mexico will be avoided by us if there is any way at all of avoiding it. If it comes, it will come upon their action and initiative, not ours.

I do not know what conference it is between representatives of the United States and Mexico to which Mr. Gompers refers in suggesting that organized labor be represented at it. No such conference, so far as I know, is at present in contemplation, though, of course, events may develop in a way to make it very desirable.

In haste

Cordially and sincerely yours,   Woodrow Wilson

TLS (received from Mary A. Strohecker).

To George Weston Anderson

My dear Mr. Anderson: [The White House] June 19, 1916

I have read your letter of June twelfth[1] with the greatest interest. You may be sure that I subscribe to your estimate of Mr. Gregory. My association with him has taught me not only to trust him, but to love him. The only thing is I do not know how I could do without him as Attorney General.

In haste

Cordially and sincerely yours,   Woodrow Wilson

TLS (Letterpress Books, WP, DLC).
[1] G. W. Anderson to WW, June 12, 1916, TLS (WP, DLC), a carefully reasoned argument for nominating Gregory to the Supreme Court.

From Josephus Daniels

Dear Mr. President: Washington. June 19th, 1916.

The Senate Naval Affairs Committee will meet to-morrow to take up the Naval bill. I am to see them this afternoon at 4:30 o'clock. They are anxious that all three of us talk with you about several important matters and hope you can arrange it before the Senate Committee meets to-morrow. Could you see us at 6 o'clock this afternoon or to-night? If not, at 9:30 Tuesday morning? It would be better to-day if your engagements will permit.[1] Please let me know as I am to see them at 4:30.

Sincerely,   Josephus Daniels

ALS (WP, DLC).
[1] Wilson saw Daniels and Senators Tillman and Swanson at 9 A.M. on Tuesday, June 20.

From Edward Mandell House

New London,
Dear Governor: New Hampshire. June 19, 1916.

When Gregory was here yesterday we discussed the Supreme Court vacancy and he will probably make a recommendation to you tomorrow.

There are one or two things that seem to me clear and that is the appointment should be made from the North, unless you believe it would be of greater advantage to appoint Gregory in order to get an Attorney General from the North.

From what I can learn Judge George W. Wheeler of Connecticut[1] would be an excellent appointment. James Byrne of New York or Judge Jenks[2] of New York seem available material.

If you do not decide upon either ot [of] these, do you not think it would be well to go to the Middle West?

I think some care should be used not to appoint a man of too advanced ideas. It will frighten the business element, for they will realize that if you are re-elected you will have perhaps four more judges to appoint and, in this way, change the character of the Court entirely.

I am sorry to hear of the trouble in the Trades Commission. I sympathize with Davies and yet from what Gregory, Hapgood and others tell me, there is another side to it. I hope you will be able to reconcile their differences in a way that will prevent public exposure. I understand that Hurley and Harris are about to resign and may do it before this reaches you.

I have been praying that we could get out of the Mexican difficulty without war, but it looks now as if it were inevitable. If it comes to that, I hope you will prosecute it with all the vigor and power we possess, for to do less, will entail unnecessary loss of life and an infinite amount of criticism.

Affectionately yours,   E. M. House

TLS (WP, DLC).
  [1] George Wakeman Wheeler, associate justice of the Supreme Court of Errors of Connecticut.
  [2] Almet Francis Jenks, presiding justice of the appellate division of the Supreme Court of New York.

From Joseph Patrick Tumulty

The White House.
Memorandum for the President: June 20, 1916.

Senator Stone, of Missouri, called this morning to say that he was very anxious to see the President. He wished to talk with the

President about some things he learned in St. Louis, but principally as to the advisability, in view of the present Mexican situation, of pressing at this time the Colombian Treaty.

The Senator asked that he be notified as soon as the pressure upon the President would permit him to see the Senator.[1]

T MS (WP, DLC).
[1] Wilson saw Stone at 2 P.M. on June 21.

From Edward Mandell House

New London,
Dear Governor: New Hampshire. June 20, 1916.

There has been some doubt concerning Charles W. Eliot. I have been in touch with him recently and received the following from him today.

"I am indeed much interested in the international situation, but also in the success of the Democratic Party next November. I should be very glad of an opportunity to talk with you on either subject."

I am planning to go to Northeast Harbor where he will be during the summer in order to talk over with him both matters.

I have in mind one or two letters which I hope we can get him to write for our campaign literature. Have you any suggestions regarding what you think would be the best subjects for his pen?

I am enclosing a memorandum[1] which I will give Vance McCormick tomorrow. I will enlarge upon it, but this is the meat of it.

If you approve and have occasion to talk with him, I would suggest that you do not let him know that I have sent you a copy but tell him we have talked along those lines.

Affectionately yours,   E. M. House

TLS (WP, DLC).
[1] T MS dated June 20, 1916 (WP, DLC), of suggestions for the conduct of the presidential campaign.

From Thomas James Walsh

My dear Mr. President: Washington. June 20, 1916.

You will recall that when a number of Senators called on you some three or four weeks ago to confer with you about the so-called leasing bill, we all urged upon you, and you recognized, the wisdom of getting Secretary Lane and Secretary Daniels together at once that one department should not be at war with another concerning any feature of the bill. Since that time the differences have, unfortunately, become so acute as not only to threaten the measure, whose passage would be an additional achievement for the administration, but have stimulated efforts to discredit the Interior Department and its eminently successful head before the country.

Perhaps your attention may not have been called to a series of articles appearing in some of the papers, the purpose of which is to impress the country with the belief that the present administration of the public land laws is no improvement upon the method and spirit which prevailed under Ballinger.

I am far from charging that these attacks have been inspired by any one connected with the Navy Department, but the controversy which has arisen has afforded the occasion for the making of them. It is to my mind singularly unfortunate that after Secretary Lane has so richly earned the confidence of the country, heretofore so unstintedly extended to him, suspicion should be aroused at this exceedingly critical juncture.

I hope you may find it possible in the midst of the multitude of cares that oppress you to find time to adjust whatever differences may exist with reference to the bill. I feel certain that if it is put through with the understanding that there is no division in the Cabinet with respect to it, and that it has the unqualified indorsement of the administration, criticism that may develop into something serious will be stilled and the troublesome issue avoided. You may command me at any time in connection with any effort you may make.   Cordially yours,   T. J. Walsh

TLS (WP, DLC).

From Sylvester Woodbridge Beach

Dear Wilson: Princeton, N. J. June 20, 1916.

I have had so many letters from prominent men in different branches of the Church of similar purport to the one I enclose.[1] To all of them I have sent an absolute and indignant denial of the many devilish lies that your enemies have been coining.

I would so much like to talk with you a few minutes as to the best way to deal with these infamous rumors which may or may not have come to your knowledge.

Dr. Watson[2] is a very influential man, and it seems to me that it might be well to allow him to come to see me that I might more fully than is possible in a letter refute the horrible slanders that many people are industriously circulating.

I will wait to hear from you before answering Dr. Watson's letter.

Lovingly and always faithfully,   Sylvester W. Beach

TLS (WP, DLC).
¹ Wilson returned the enclosure to Beach.
² Undoubtedly the Rev. Dr. Robert Watson, pastor of the Scotch Presbyterian Church of New York.

Two Letters to Robert Lansing

My dear Mr. Secretary,   The White House. 21 June, 1916.

Now that the negotiations with regard to this important matter have reached the stage indicated in Mr. Fletcher's report, I should like to have a talk with Fletcher, to acquaint myself with the details.[1]

My present judgment is with Mr. Naon and Mr. Fletcher, for a simultaneous signing by the big and little states alike which have indicated their assent; and I hope that this can be arranged to take place not later than the time when Dr. Muller will be here to sign for Brazil.

Fletcher seems to have pressed this matter very wisely and successfully.   Faithfully Yours,   W.W.

WWTLI (R. Lansing Papers, DLC).
¹ Wilson saw Fletcher on June 24.

My dear Mr. Secretary,   The White House. 21 June, 1916.

I have already conferred with you orally about this matter,[1] but return your letter now for the completeness of your record, with the comment that it seems to me wise to bring the two sets of American bankers together in this matter.

I was glad to learn from you the other day that there was good reason to hope that this could be done.

Faithfully Yours,   W.W.

WWTLI (SDR, RG 59, 893.51/3009, DNA).
¹ RL to WW, June 15, 1916, with Enclosures.

From Robert Lansing, with Enclosure

PERSONAL AND PRIVATE:

My dear Mr. President: Washington June 21, 1916.

I send you a letter which I have just received from Mr. Gerard, at Berlin. Will you please return this letter after reading it as it has not been answered.

Faithfully yours,   Robert Lansing

TLS (SDR, RG 59, 763.72/2796½, DNA).

ENCLOSURE

James Watson Gerard to Robert Lansing

Personal.

My dear Mr. Secretary.   Berlin, June 7th. 1916.

I am sorry to lose Ruddock[1] who is sent to Belgium, but it is a good appointment for him. His knowledge of German and relations here will help matters. Harvey[2] will be better in the Argentine. He is too nervous for a job like this in a hostile population where even the Americans or most of them are against the Administration. But please on no account send Kirk away. He works until late each night on our finances and accounts which are complicated and extensive and no one can take his place. Also if Osborne[3] passes into the service please send him here.

The debates in the Reichstag have been quite interesting yesterday and the day before. The Chancellor irritated by the anonymous attacks on him in pamphlets etc. made a fine defense. In the course of the debate allusions were made to President Wilson and the U boat question. Summaries enclosed. The U boat question may break loose again any day.

I do not think that either Austria or Germany wishes President Wilson to lay down any peace conditions, there may possibly be a Congress after the Peace Congress but meanwhile all parties here feel that America has nothing to do with peace conditions. America can bring the parties together but that is all. The speech about the rights of small peoples has, I hear, made the Austrians furious as Austria is made up of many Nationalities and the Germans say that if the rights of small peoples and peoples choosing their own Sovereignty is to be discussed that the Irish question, the Indian question and the Boer question, the Egyptian question and many others involving the Allies must be discussed. I think that generally there is a big change in public opinion and the Germans are begin[n]ing to realize that the President is for peace with Germany.

The Germans expect that by September preparations will be finished and that the Suez Canal will be cannonaded, bombed and mined so that it will dry up, and then the Indian-Afghan troubles will begin. The crops are fine and the food question will soon be solved.   Yours ever   J.W.G.

TLS (SDR, RG 59, 763.72/2796½, DNA).
   1 Albert Billings Ruddock, Second Secretary of the embassy in Berlin, who was being transferred to the same position in Brussels.
   2 Roland Bridendall Harvey, another Second Secretary at Berlin. He was listed in the *Register of the Department of State, December 15, 1916* (Washington, 1917), p. 98, as "unassigned from September 4, 1916."

3 Lithgow Osborne, an attaché in the Berlin embassy since January 1915; he became Third Secretary in August 1916.

To Robert Lansing

My dear Mr. Secretary,   The White House. 21 June, 1916.

Thank you for sending me this letter. I have read it with the mixture of interest and mental query with which I read all of the Ambassadors communications.

Faithfully Yours,   W.W.

WWTLI (SDR, RG 59, 763.72/2797½, DNA).

From Robert Lansing, with Enclosure

PERSONAL AND PRIVATE:

My dear Mr. President: Washington June 21, 1916.

I send you a letter I have just received from Mr. Penfield at Vienna. Will you please return it after reading it as it has not been answered.   Faithfully yours,   Robert Lansing

E N C L O S U R E

Frederic Courtland Penfield to Robert Lansing

CONFIDENTIAL & PERSONAL

My dear Mr. Secretary: Vienna June 3, 1916

I feel I should write you of the Austrian opinion on the subject of bringing the war to a close, a theme that a fortnight ago dominated the speech of almost every human being in the Habsburg capital. All seemingly wanted peace, while many believed it was certain to come in a few months and through the efforts of President Wilson.

Newspapers rang with these opinions, and the man in the café was as certain of early peace as the man in the street. That was immediately following the President's North Carolina speech.

Day by day I have seen the idea contract until the Austrian official now is far from certain that the Monarchy of Francis Joseph wants the war to end before some of the issues of the vast struggle have been settled in a way making a recurrence of strife impossible for generations.

There seem to be four reasons for this reaction of judgment, and are:

Firstly, the Fourth War Loan of Austria-Hungary recently closed succeeded beyond expectation, giving encouragement for fresh borrowing.

Secondly, the forces of the Monarchy are having such success on the Italian front and on Italian soil that many Austrians want to go on until the Archduke Eugen's armies are in Verona and on the plain of Venice and hated Italy is humbled.

Thirdly, the triumph this week of Germany over the British fleet in the North Sea[1] gives color to the belief that the Central Powers in the not distant future may practically dictate terms of peace without submitting to mediation.

Fourthly, in certain circles there is growing fear that our President may not be the best mediator to bring benefit to a Monarchy peopled by a congeries of nationalities as is Austria-Hungary with its nine or ten different races. Many persons have been circulating the report that more than once President Wilson has stated his belief that it was the inherent right of every race to govern itself, and that this belief might conflict with the interests of a Monarch ruling Austrians, Hungarians, Bohemians, Slavs, Croats, and various other races. Some debaters of the peace proposal pretend that the King of Spain, half Habsburg and a Roman Catholic, and for the most part reared in Vienna, might give the Dual Monarchy a larger measure of advantage than the well-intentioned American President.

I know that some members of the Imperial Family, near relations of the King of Spain, are doing their utmost to eventually have the Archduchess Christina's[2] son[3] officiate as sole mediator; and failing this, then as joint mediator with America's Chief Executive. There seems to be but little real sentiment in favor of the Pope as a co-arbitrator. Austrians revere the Holy Father but prefer as peace-maker a potentate whose influence is more than spiritual.

It is widely published here that the President recently told the Peace League that each people should have the right to choose the form of its Constitution; and that small States, like the Great Powers, should be entitled to have their sovereignity and integrity respected. This may not be pleasing reading to a people conquering Montenegro, Albania, and a portion of Serbia in the present war.

A newspaper before me states that the number of orphans in Hungary caused by the war now exceeds 400,000, that misery is everywhere growing there, while the cry for peace is becoming louder. These statements only show that the masses of poor—the man with the hoe and the widow with numberless children to feed—want peace, and want it quickly. They care not through whose instrumentality it comes so long as it arrives in time to keep them from perishing.

I am informed from good sources that Germany is far more desirous of early peace than is class-ruled Austria-Hungary.

These rambling observations I am aware can have but little value, and are only sent in the performance of what I deem a duty—to advise you frankly of the current state of opinion in Vienna.

I am, my dear Mr. Secretary,

Yours most sincerely,   Frederic C. Penfield.

TLS (SDR, RG 59, 763.72/2803½, DNA).
¹ Early reports had told of a great German victory in the Battle of Jutland.
² Maria Cristina of Hapsburg, second wife of Alfonso XII of Spain.
³ Alfonso XIII of Spain.

To Robert Lansing

My dear Mr. Secretary,   The White House. 21 June, 1916.

Thank you very much for having let me see the enclosed very interesting letter. I dare say that it is now very much out of date because of the Russian successes and of the altered aspect of the fight in the North Sea.   Faithfully Yours,   W.W.

WWTLI (SDR, RG 59, 763.72/2804½, DNA).

From Robert Lansing, with Enclosure

PERSONAL AND CONFIDENTIAL:

My dear Mr. President: Washington June 21, 1916.

As there appears to be an increasing probability that the Mexican situation may develop into a state of war I desire to make a suggestion for your consideration.

It seems to me that we should avoid the use of the word "Intervention" and deny that any invasion of Mexico is for the sake of intervention.

There are several reasons why this appears to me expedient:

First. We have all along denied any purpose to interfere in the internal affairs of Mexico and the St. Louis platform declares against it. Intervention conveys the idea of such interference.

Second. Intervention would be humiliating to many Mexicans whose pride and sense of national honor would not resent severe terms of peace in case of being defeated in a war.

Third. American intervention in Mexico is extremely distasteful to all Latin America and might have a very bad effect upon our Pan-American program.

Fourth. Intervention, which suggests a definite purpose to "clean up" the country, would bind us to certain accomplishments which circumstances might make extremely difficult or inadvisable, and, on the other hand, it would impose conditions which might be found to be serious restraints upon us as the situation develops.

Fifth. Intervention also implies that the war would be made primarily in the interest of the Mexican people, while the fact is it would be a war forced on us by the Mexican Government, and, if we term it intervention, we will have considerable difficulty in explaining why we had not intervened before but waited until attacked.

It seems to me that the real attitude is that the *de facto* Government having attacked our forces engaged in a rightful enterprise or invaded our borders (as the case may be) we had no recourse but to defend ourselves and to do so it has become necessary to prevent future attacks by forcing the Mexican Government to perform its obligations. That is, it is simply a state of international war without purpose on our part other than to end the conditions which menace our national peace and the safety of our citizens, and that it is *not* intervention with all that that word implies.

I offer the foregoing suggestion, because I feel that we should have constantly in view the attitude we intend to take if worse comes to worse, so that we may regulate our present policy and future correspondence with Mexico and other American Republics with that attitude.

In case this suggestion meets with your approval I further suggest that we send to each deplomatic representative of a Latin American Republic in Washington a communication stating briefly our attitude and denying any intention to intervene. I enclose a draft of such a note. If this is to be done at all, it seems to me that it should be done at once, otherwise we will lose the chief benefit, namely, a right understanding by Latin America at the very outset.　　Faithfully yours,　　Robert Lansing

TLS (SDR, RG 59, 812.00/18533A, DNA).

E N C L O S U R E

Sir:　　　　　　　　　　　　　　　　　　　　June 21, 1916.

I enclose for your information a copy of this Government's note of June 20th to the Secretary of Foreign Relations of the *de facto*

Government of Mexico on the subject of the presence of American troops in Mexican territory. This communication states clearly the critical relations existing between this Government and the *de facto* Government of Mexico and the causes which have led up to the present situation.

Should this situation eventuate into hostilities, which this Government would deeply regret and will use every honorable effort to avoid, I take this opportunity to inform you that this Government would have for its object not intervention in Mexican affairs, with all the regrettable consequences which might result from such a policy, but the defense of American territory from further invasion by bands of armed Mexicans, protection of American citizens and property along the boundary from outrages committed by such bandits, and the prevention of future depredations, by force of arms against the marauders infesting this region and against a Government which is encouraging and aiding them in their activities. Hostilities, in short, would be simply a state of international war without purpose on the part of the United States other than to end the conditions which menace our national peace and the safety of our citizens.

T MS (SDR, RG 59, 812.00/18533A, DNA).

To Robert Lansing

My dear Mr. Secretary,   The White House. 21 June, 1916.

I agree to all of this. I was myself about to say something to you to the same effect, though I had not thought of making an occasion of the sending of copies of our note to Mexico to the Latin American representatives but had thought to wait until hostilities were actually forced upon us. As I write this "extras" of the evening paper are being cried on the Avenue which, if true, mean that hostilities *have* begun.[1] At any rate, my doubt upon that point (the time for the notification you suggest) is so slight that I beg that you will carry out the plan you suggest at once.

Faithfully Yours,   W.W.

WWTLI (SDR, RG 59, 812.00/18533½, DNA).

[1] On June 17, General Pershing dispatched two scouting parties of cavalry, commanded by Captains Charles T. Boyd and Lewis S. Morey, to investigate reports of a concentration of *Carrancista* troops at Villa Ahumada. Both commanders were specifically ordered to avoid a fight and not to enter any place garrisoned by *Carrancistas*. The two forces, comprising together eighty-two soldiers and two guides, converged at Santo Domingo ranch, twelve miles west of the pueblo of Carrizal, in the evening of June 20. Boyd, the senior officer, assumed command, and the combined force set out for Villa Ahumada the next morning. The most direct road ran through Carrizal. Captain Morey suggested an alternate route around the village. Boyd, however, decided to go through the town and requested permission of the local authorities to pass through. The

local Mexican commander, General Félix Uresti Gomez, warned Boyd that he would resist with force if the Americans attempted to enter the town, and between 120 and 200 Mexican soldiers took up a defensive position near the village. Boyd ordered an advance, and firing began. In the ensuing, hour-long battle, Boyd and Gomez were killed and Morey was wounded. The Mexicans lost thirty dead and forty-three wounded. Nine Americans were killed; twenty-five, including a Mormon guide, were captured and sent as prisoners to Chihuahua City; and twelve Americans were wounded. The first reports of the encounter indicated that the Mexicans had ambushed the Americans. However, careful investigation later brought out the fact that Boyd had unquestionably been the aggressor. For a definitive account of the Carrizal incident, see the Enclosure printed with W. M. Ingraham to WW, Oct. 9, 1916. See also Link, *Confusions and Crises*, pp. 303-308.

From Newton Diehl Baker

CONFIDENTIAL.

My dear Mr. President: Washington. June 21, 1916.

I am sure you will pardon this note.

During the past day or two I have been conferring with the Attorney General, at his instance, about several people whose qualifications he is canvassing for your information. The upshot of it all is that I have been so deeply impressed by his fine spirit and his devotion to every ideal I cherish that while he obviously does not want for himself the great place under consideration, yet the need of the place for him seems almost imperative. Of course there are plenty of lawyers who know as much, but I cannot think of the name of one who knows as much *rightly*, and while the sacrifice of doing without him as an aide would be great I can think of no place for which so much sacrifice on your part would be so well justified.

Your fuller knowledge of all the circumstances will of course weight the relative values, and because I know that I venture to suggets [suggest] that you ask him to yield to your judgment as to his duty. He is really very rare!

Respectfully yours,   Newton D. Baker

TLS (WP, DLC).

From Pleasant Alexander Stovall

Dear Mr. President: Berne, June 21, 1916.

I take advantage of the departure of Mr. Charles Spach, Special Treasury Agent of the United States at St. Gall, to forward you my letter of congratulation upon your re-nomination for the office of President.

You must know how much I am delighted by this news and you

will probably remember how the "Old Guard" sat up for seven days and nights in Baltimore in 1912 and worked and prayed for your nomination which this year comes easily and unanimously.

I believe that every neutral state in Europe endorses this action, and it is only for the neutral states that I am in a present position to speak.

Your splendid diplomatic triumphs have been the wonder and the admiration of all Europe. On the 29th of November last, I had the honor to write you as follows: "I note by the papers that the German-American element has lined up in the United States to defeat your re-election, if possible. I want to congratulate you that the line has at last been drawn thoroughly between the Americans and the hyphenated Americans, and to say that in my judgment there can be no doubt about the outcome of such an issue. This line is not of our drawing, but if it is forced upon us, I do not doubt that the real Americans will respond in no uncertain way. This is the legitimate outcome of the propoganda in the United States in favour of a foreign power and also of the numerous attempts to burn factories, blow up ships, and to assassinate American people. For some time I have seen that this issue must be made, and the recent announcement by an element of German-American citizens have finally brought it to pass. I thought it my duty to write to you this much and to say that if the foreign-born Americans and their connections insist upon precipitating this issue in Amerca, the verdict of the Presidential election will have no uncertain sound."[1]

I have the honor to be, Sir,

Your obedient servant: Pleasant A Stovall

TLS (WP, DLC).
[1] P. A. Stovall to WW, Nov. 29, 1915, TLS (WP, DLC).

From Robert Price

My Dear Mr Wilson,   Clarksville [Tenn.] June 21, 1916

The growing infirmities of age (I am now in the 87th year of my age) render it difficult for me to write, but I cannot deny myself the privilege & pleasure of answering your kind letter received a few few [sic] days ago. Your father was one of my most highly valued and beloved friends, and I have followed your distinguished career with great pleasure for his sake especially. I thank you for your kindly interest & rejoice in your distinguished career.   Yours truly   Robert Price

ALS (WP, DLC).

Frederick Funston to Henry Pinckney McCain

Fort Sam Houston, Tex., June 21, 1916. 9:00 P.M.

NUMBER SEVENTEEN NAUGHT EIGHT PERIOD. Following received from General Bell[1] quote: Mexican consul Garria[2] telephoned me six P.M. as follows quote: There was a clash this A.M. at Carrizal near Villa Ahumada between Carranzista and American troops in which General Gomez and other Mexicans were killed number unknown period. Number of Americans killed or wounded unknown period. That General Gomez sent a Captain with an order to American Commander to go back but American said he was going to Villa Ahumada and opened fire on Mexican Captain wounding him and killing a private who was with him. period. That Americans attacked General Gomez but were driven back and that several were taken prisoners period. Prisoners were sent to Chihuahua period. Garria says this is telephoned at request General Gonzales[3] period. Unquote: An American who was on the train to-day passing Villa Ahumada about two thirty P.M. states that he saw several dead Mexicans put on his train and among them was a dead Mexican General period. There were also several Mexican wounded period. He gathered from talk of Mexicans that fight was with American cavalry about nine miles west and that the Americans were decoyed into a trap by using a flag of truce period. That they were then fired on by Machine guns and then had to retire period. Copy furnished Pershing period. Report states our troops engaged were tenth cavalry period. More particulars later unquote.   Funston.

T telegram (WP, DLC).
   [1] George Bell, Jr., brigadier general, U.S.A., commander of the El Paso district.
   [2] Andres G. Garcia, Mexican consul in El Paso.
   [3] Francisco Gonzáles, *Carrancista* commander of the military zone of the border, based in Ciudad Juárez.

To Edward Mandell House

Dearest Friend,   The White House. 22 June, 1916.

I have treated you shamefully in the matter of letters of late, but, thank God, you understand and are generous enough to forgive!

Meanwhile you have sent me no end of useful matter and have filled my thoughts with many suggestions that are of the highest value to me, and promptly become part of my thinking after I have read your letters. I thank you with all my heart!

The letters and the glimpses of opinion (official opinion) from the other side of the water are not encouraging, to say the least, and indicate a constantly narrowing, instead of a broad and comprehending, view of the situation. They are in danger of forgetting the rest of the world, and of waking up some surprising morning to discover that it has a positive right to be heard about the peace of the world. I conclude that it will be up to us to judge for ourselves when the time has arrived for us to make an imperative suggestion. I mean a suggestion which they will have no choice but to heed, because the opinion of the non-official world and the desire of all peoples will be behind it.

Your letter to-day brings your sketch of a plan of campaign. I remember that these have long been your ideas as to organization and action, and they seem to me thoroughly practical and altogether admirable. I will speak to McCormick about them when I see him, as you desire. I am expecting to see him on Saturday.

I am not clear as to the states that should be put under your several Classes, but that is a matter of detailed common counsel.

The break seems to have come in Mexico; and all my patience seems to have gone for nothing. I am infinitely sad about it. I fear I should have drawn Pershing and his command northward just after it became evident that Villa had slipped through his fingers; but except for that error of judgment (if it was an error) I cannot, in looking back, see where I could have done differently, holding sacred the convictions I hold in this matter.

Right or wrong, however, the extremest consequences seem upon us. But INTERVENTION (that is the rearrangement and control of Mexico's domestic affairs by the U. S.) there shall not be either now or at any other time if I can prevent it!

We as yet know nothing from our own officers about the affair at Carrizal. We shall no doubt have heard from them before this reaches you.

I hope with all my heart you are taking real care of yourself, that you find Sunnapee what you hoped, and that you are ever so much better than you were when Dudley last talked with you about the Chairmanship.

You were of course right about that. I was so desperate to get the man I can absolutely trust to judge and act rightly that I for a moment yielded to temptation and asked you!

Good night. God Bless you!

Affectionately Yours,   Woodrow Wilson

WWTLS (E. M. House Papers, CtY).

To Martin Henry Glynn

My dear Governor: [The White House] June 22, 1916

The extraordinary and deserved success of your remarkable speech at the convention has already received the most unusual acknowledgment from the convention itself and from the Press of the country, but I want to add my word of appreciation and gratitude. It was and I am sure will remain one of the notable things of a campaign which, before we get through with it, should stir to the very bottom the conscience and thought of the United States.

Cordially and sincerely yours,   Woodrow Wilson

TLS (Letterpress Books, WP, DLC).

To Ollie Murray James

My dear Senator: [The White House] June 22, 1916

I have already congratulated you orally over the telephone on the wonderful success of that remarkable speech of yours, but I want to send you this line of congratulations and of affectionate and grateful admiration. The speech evidently got the reception it richly deserved and I rejoice with all your friends in a triumph which had many unique features and which must have made you feel that you had with unusual vision interpreted the real feeling and purpose of the party and of the country.

Cordially and sincerely yours,   Woodrow Wilson

TLS (Letterpress Books, WP, DLC).

To Louis Wiley

My dear Mr. Wiley: The White House June 22, 1916

Your letter of June seventeenth[1] is the sort that makes me glad that I have been able to serve the country and in some degree the ideals which true Democrats revere and wish to see maintained against all obstacles. I thank you for it with all my heart. We are apparently getting into deep waters to the south of us, but we must be the more careful in entering them to do nothing which will put any doubt upon our purpose and our ability to keep faith with Latin-America in all matters that touch independence and territorial integrity.

Cordially and sincerely yours,   Woodrow Wilson

TLS (L. Wiley Papers, NRU).
    [1] L. Wiley to WW, June 17, 1916, TLS (WP, DLC), which expressed his satis-
faction with both the tone and the actions of the Democratic national convention.

To Dudley Field Malone

My dear Dudley: [The White House] June 22, 1916

It was fine to get your telegram.[1] Everything that you do increases my affection for you, and your trust in me touches me
more deeply than I can say. I hope with all my heart that I shall
always deserve it.

This is just a line of affectionate acknowledgment.

In great haste,   Faithfully yours,   Woodrow Wilson

TLS (Letterpress Books, WP, DLC).
    [1] D. F. Malone to WW, June 17, 1916, T telegram (WP, DLC).

A Memorandum by Newton Diehl Baker

MEMORANDUM FOR THE ADJUTANT GENERAL.

Washington. June 22, 1916.

The Secretary of War directs the following telegram, sufficiently coded to make it obscure, be sent to the Commanding General,
Southern Department for his confidential information and not to
be allowed to become public:

"It is believed that should open hostilities begin before rein-
forcements can reach you the most you can do is to guard the
border, seize the international bridges and occupy Mexican
towns directly on the border period. There will be temptation
to send expeditions to protect interests at certain places period.
The danger in doing so, before additional troops reach you, is
that such expeditions may become tied up, requiring troops
to assist them which you cannot spare and others to keep open
lines of supply period. But in the event of hostilities it is necessary to force Mexican organized troops to evacuate as much of
north Mexico south from the boundary as possible period. It
is most desirable to accomplish this, if possible, without actual
collision period. In anticipation of possible hostilities the following project is tentatively accepted as one that will permit
modifications subsequently found necessary and meanwhile
will facilitate the most orderly concentration of troops on the
border period. It is assumed that whatever is done must be
done with the regular troops now on the border and the militia

at the strength it will have on assembling at its mobilization camps period. It is assumed that this will give approximately one hundred and fifty thousand troops comma approximately thirty thousand regulars and one hundred and twenty thousand militia period. It is proposed to send the militia to the border by organizations as rapidly as they are assembled and reasonably equipped for field service period. As rapidly as they arrive you can relieve regular troops on the border and send them to reinforce General Pershing until his command amounts to approximately twenty thousand combatants properly organized period. As additional militia arrive you can distribute them so as to relieve the remainder of the regular troops for concentration at Brownsville comma El Paso and Nogales period. At these places they will form the nucleus of columns of thirty thousand men at Brownsville comma thirty thousand at El Paso and ten thousand at Nogales period. Without depleting your present border guard you can assign additional arriving militia organizations until the above numbers of these three columns are completed period. These assignments will of course be made by you so as to have these columns properly organized for any advance movement that may become necessary period. At the same time you will continue assigning additional militia organizations for border guard duty between Brownsville and El Paso and between El Paso and Nogales and from Nogales to Yuma period. This movement being completed you will have troops as follows colon twenty thousand with General Pershing comma thirty thousand at Brownsville comma thirty thousand at El Paso comma ten thousand at Nogales and thirty thousand no border patrol duty between the places above indicated period. Your border patrol will in numbers be much stronger than now, while of course Brownsville, El Paso and Nogales will be more than amply garrisoned period. The foregoing leaves thirty thousand troops yet to be disposed of period. Of these it is proposed if practicable to send five thousand with the Navy to Tampico and five thousand with the Navy to Guaymas period. These latter two forces would occupy thoroughly defensible positions near their base to be used as circumstances may dictate period. This still leaves twenty thousand troops in reserve comma to be used to strengthen if desired either of the foregoing columns or to strengthen garrison at Laredo or Eagle Pass or Douglas and advance from these places if desired period. It is believed that with twenty thousand men under Pershing in his present position and thirty thousand

ready to advance from El Paso all organized Mexican troops
in Chihuahua will withdraw to a point south of the city of
Chihuahua period. It is believed that with thirty thousand men
ready to advance from Brownsville and with the entire river
well guarded and with five thousand men making a demonstration at Tampico the Mexican troops in Coahuila and Nuevo
Leon and Tamaulipas will withdraw as far as Monterey and
it is believed that for the same general reason the Mexican
troops in Sonora will similarly withdraw period. If this can be
accomplished all hope on part of Mexicans of a successful
attack on any part of the border will be gone. It is hoped that
during the foregoing process recruiting will be stimulated and
the militia will soon be largely in excess of its above estimated
strength of one hundred and twenty thousand men period. The
same cause would increase to an unknown extent the recruiting of regular troops period. If popular feeling enabled us to
recruit to war strength we would have approximately seventy
five thousand regular troops and two hundred and fifty thousand militia period. We cannot count on this in advance of
the fact comma but if it should so result we would have a force
sufficient comma in case the Mexicans refuse to make any
terms comma to force them entirely out of the northern states
of Mexico and ourselves to occupy positions which would
prevent their return until we permitted it period. The essential
object now is to get the force first available promptly on the
border and in the most orderly way period. Department commanders have been instructed to notify you the moment an
organization is ready to move from a mobilization camp period.
You will designate the destination and the department commander will immediately order the movement period. As far
as practicable you should assign incoming militia regiments
to points where you desire the complete brigade to ultimately
be period. In the same way as far as practicable the brigades
should be in the sections where you desire the complete division to be period. This will bring about the concentration of
the militia in their larger tactical units and will avoid confusion period. To whatever extent this is not practicable at the
outset these organizations may be completed by subsequent
shifting of troops period. Department commanders have been
directed to wire you any shortage in field transportation of
each organization so that you may take steps to complete it
after arrival as far as possible period. The Quartermaster's
Department has been directed to provide one hundred additional motor truck companies period. Acknowledge receipt and

wire your suggestions comma bearing in mind that it is better to get the troops promptly in some such way as indicated rather than have an indefinite delay period.["]

Foregoing general plan has been approved by the President with suspension of movement to Tampico and Guaymas.

T MS (WP, DLC).

To John Wesley Wescott

My dear Judge: The White House June 23, 1916

I have been so busy making the preliminary arrangements for the campaign that it has not seemed possible to turn away from the day's work to express my real gratitude to you for your generous speech of nomination, but you may be sure that in the midst of all my duties my debt of friendship and gratitude to you has not been forgotten.

I am sincerely indebted to you. You have been generous beyond my deserts, and I can only say with simplicity but entire earnestness that I am proud to be so trusted and believed in.

    Cordially and faithfully yours,   Woodrow Wilson

TLS (J. W. Wescott Coll., NjP).

To Ray Stannard Baker

My dear Mr. Baker: [The White House] June 23, 1916

That is a most generous statement you prepared of your reasons for supporting me for the Presidency.[1] It has heartened me more than I think you can realize that a man who thinks as you do, as clearly and as genuinely, should repose such unqualified confidence in me. It gives me an additional pride in succeeding along the lines I have laid out for myself. I thank you with all my heart.

    Cordially and sincerely yours,   Woodrow Wilson

TLS (Letterpress Books, WP, DLC).

[1] This was a statement which Baker prepared for the use of the Woodrow Wilson Independent League. Baker asserted that the Republicans were being forced into a selfish and nationalistic position. Wilson's internationalism and his emphasis upon America's duties, Baker believed, would constitute the most successful appeal to the independent voter. In his judgment, the public would respond "only to a real call to duty & a larger vision of the service to the world, for which we feel, gropingly, that the nation has so long been in undisturbed preparation." John E. Semonche, *Ray Stannard Baker: A Quest for Democracy in Modern America, 1870-1918* (Chapel Hill, N. C., 1969), p. 302.

From Robert Lansing

PERSONAL AND PRIVATE:

My dear Mr. President: Washington June 23, 1916.

If you have not had time to read carefully the enclosed telegram of the 20th from Paris reciting the resolutions adopted by the Economic Conference of the Allied Powers,[1] I think that it would be well worth reading as the results of these measures may be very far reaching on the commerce and trade of the whole world after the war is over.

The proposed measures must be viewed from two standpoints, that of their effect on the present and future trade of the enemies of the Allies, and that of their effect on the present and future trade of neutral countries.

The drastic measures against the enemies of the Allies are not only intended to strangle their industries and commerce during the war, which is of course a legitimate war measure, but they go much further and purpose to prevent as far as possible the rebuilding of their industries and commerce after the war. It seems to me that the persistence of the Allied Governments in this policy will make the negotiations of a satisfactory peace most difficult, and that the knowledge of this intention to continue the war industrially after actual warfare ceases will cause the central Powers to hesitate in taking steps toward a restoration of peace. I believe that this Conference will have the effect of prolonging the war.

In regard to the trade of neutrals, both now and after the war, the intentions of the Allied Powers are disquieting and I think should receive very careful consideration. We neutrals, as well as the Central Powers, will have to face a commercial combination which has as its avowed purpose preferential treatment for its members. It will be a strong combination of nations, which on account of their colonies and great merchant marine will be able, I fear, to carry through their preferential program. The consequent restriction upon profitable trade with these commercial allies will cause a serious, if not critical, situation for the nations outside the union by creating unusual and artificial economic conditions.

In view of these possibilities as to the future and the present restraints upon free commerce between neutrals as a consequence of blacklisting firms, agreements as to non-exportation, influence upon steamship companies and insurance, with the accompanying censorship of mail, would it not be well to consider the advisability of holding a Congress of Neutrals to take up these various questions and determine upon ways and means to relieve the present situation and to provide for the future?

If some step of this sort is not taken, the neutral countries acting independently will be impotent against this commercial combination. United and with some definite plan to meet the proposed measures of the Allies, I believe that the neutrals could better protect their interests by preventing radical action both during and after the war.

I have up to the present consistently opposed any action other than independent, but this economic and commercial conference of the Allied Powers with the purpose of union when peace is restored has materially changed conditions. The policy, which they propose to adopt, requires different treatment as it will materially affect our industrial and commercial life. It must be met in some practical way, and the best way to fight combination is by combination.

At least it seems to me a subject which we should consider, and the consideration of which ought not to be long delayed.

Faithfully yours,   Robert Lansing

TLS (WP, DLC).
    ¹ W. G. Sharp to RL, June 20, 1916, T telegram (WP, DLC), summarizing the resolutions adopted by the Economic Conference of the Allied governments held at Paris, June 14-17, 1916. For the full text of these resolutions, see *FR-WWS 1916*, pp. 975-77.

From Benjamin Ryan Tillman

Dear Mr. President: [Washington] June 23, 1916.

The more I think about it, the more I am convinced that a trump card which ought to be played by the Democratic Party at this time is to raise the graduated income tax to the limit. Preparedness is demanded by wealth for its protection, as much as from patriotic motives, and the poor people throughout the country who have votes are watching us to see if the Party is going to call on these millionares to pay for this preparation for the defense of the country, or even their just share of it.

Therefore, I take the liberty of urging you to press this view. I have talked with many men from all parts of the country, and they all entertain the same ideas that I do. Let us see to it that the millionares and multi-millionares contribute very very liberally to this condition in which we find ourselves.

Very respectfully,   B. R. Tillman

TLS (WP, DLC).

From Edward Mandell House, with Enclosure

New London,
Dear Governor: New Hampshire. June 23. 1916.

I am enclosing you a copy of a letter which has just come from Lord Bryce. It bears out what I told you concerning the French and English press misrepresenting you by publishing only parts of your speeches.

If Page would think more about presenting your views favorably to the English people and less about our mistreatment of them, it would go a long way towards helping to accomplish the purposes you have in mind.

Jusserand is constantly after his Government not to permit the French press to be discourteous.

I have a letter from Penfield in which he says:

"On may 15th a low-class journal printed the enclosed cartoon against the President. I demanded an immediate interview with Baron Burrian and protested vigorously against the publication of such attacks against a sovereign ruler of a land with which Austria was not at war. Within twenty-four hours I had a written apology and the assurance of the Government that the unfriendly attitude of the papers would cease at once."

If Penfield can do it in Austria, Page and Sharp can do it in England and France. We cannot hope to make much headway with the Allies if their press and music halls are permitted to show disrespect to you and our Government. In times of peace it is impossible to do what can easily be done in times of war when there is a censorship.

Affectionately yours,   E. M. House

TLS (WP, DLC).

E N C L O S U R E

James Viscount Bryce to Edward Mandell House

Dear Colonel House: London. June 8th, 1916.

Those of us who have been working in this country at and for a scheme for the prevention of war, after this war has ended, by a League of Nations against aggressive and wanton breaches of the peace of the world are greatly cheered and encouraged by the President's recent deliverances on the subject.

It seems to have been misunderstood by a section of the English press, which by mistaking in one single sentence what I am sure was the President's meaning, mistook the general purport and bearing of the speeches as a whole.

But I think that the general feeling of thoughtful men, and especially of those who know what have hitherto been the trends of United States policy, was that his pronouncement was not only a significant new departure, but one of great value for the prospects of peace in the future.

I ventured, in an article published in the "New Republic"[1] just about the time when the President was speaking, to suggest that the cooperation of the United States in any international scheme for the avoidance of war would be of supreme importance, and rejoice to believe that he deems this possible.

Believe me,   Sincerely yours,   Bryce.

P.S. I now always put my name on the outside of envelope to avoid censorship of letters.

TCL (WP, DLC).

[1] See EMH to WW, May 19, 1916 (first letter of that date), n. 1.

Two Letters from Edward Mandell House

New London,
Dear Governor: New Hampshire. June 23, 1916.

Judge Shearn[1] has talked to Gordon in confidence asking him what would be thought of Hearst making the race for Governor of New York on a platform endorsing the National Administration.

Gordon dodged the question and has put it up to me and I am passing it along to you. Judge Shearn will probably be here in a day or two to talk it out.

I have a feeling that our candidate for Governor should be Seabury or Shearn himself, provided Tammany will nominate them. Either of them would bring a large independent vote and the labor vote. Shearn would also bring the Hearst people in line.

I have an idea that the republicans are going to work the sectional issue in this campaign. They may not do it openly, but it will be done quietly and vigorously, therefore I am hoping you will choose Northern men for almost every office that is to be filled between now and November.

Affectionately yours,   E. M. House

[1] Clarence John Shearn, justice of the Supreme Court of New York for the 1st district and a long-time associate of William Randolph Hearst.

New London,

Dear Governor: New Hampshire. June 23, 1916.

I have a letter from Warburg with which I hate to disturb you, but the matter is serious.

Before I left New York both Miller and Warburg talked to me about Hamlin and they both thought he was unfit for Governor and that his reappointment would cause the gradual resignation of every other member of the Board.

Warburg thought the remedy lay in rotation, Miller, however, said there was not a man on the Board that was fit, in his opinion, to be Governor. He thought some man should be appointed that was big enough to command not only the respect of the Board, but of the country.

In my opinion, you will never have peace in these different commissions until you permit them to select their own chairmen. The Interstate Commerce Commission started the pace, the Trades Commission has followed and the Federal Reserve Board will have no peace under any other plan and it might be well to recognize it before their differences become public.

Affectionately yours,   E. M. House

TLS (WP, DLC).

From Newton Diehl Baker

Mr President: [Washington, June 24, 1916]

This, from the New York World of this morning,[1] probably accounts for Mr Bryan's telegram[2]   Newton D. Baker

ALS (WP, DLC).
  [1] "Anti-Militarism Union Works for Peace in Mexico," New York *World*, June 24, 1916. It reported that officials of the American Union Against Militarism had requested William J. Bryan, David Starr Jordan, and Frank P. Walsh to meet in El Paso, Texas, with three prominent Mexicans "as an unofficial Mexican peace commission . . . in an effort to get at the difficulties which have arisen between the two governments."
  [2] Bryan's telegram is missing but it undoubtedly requested Wilson's opinion and approval of the proposed mediation effort. Bryan stated on June 25 that such a movement, to be successful, had to have Wilson's approval, and that he did not wish to participate in any project which might embarrass the administration. *New York Times*, June 26, 1916. Bryan did not participate in the talks sponsored by the American Union Against Militarism which took place in New York in July 1916. C. Roland Marchand, *The American Peace Movement and Social Reform, 1898-1918* (Princeton, N. J., 1972), p. 243.

From Joseph Patrick Tumulty

Dear Govenor: [The White House] June 24, 1916.

The Mexican authorities admit that they have taken American soldiers and incarcerated them. The people feel that a demand should be made for their immediate release, and that it should not take the form of an elaborate note. Only firmness and an unflinching insistence upon our part will bring the gentlemen in Mexico City to their senses.

If I were President at this moment, or acting as Secretary of State, my message to Carranza would be the following:

Release those American soldiers or take the consequences.

This would ring around the world.

Respectfully,   [Tumulty]

CCL (WP, DLC).

Eliseo Arredondo to Robert Lansing

My dear Mr. Lansing: Washington, D. C. June 24, 1916.

I am directed by my Government to inform Your Excellency, with reference to the Carrizal incident, that the Chief Executive, through the Mexican War Department, gave orders to General Jacinto B. Treviño not to permit American forces from General Pershing's column to advance further south, nor to move either east or west from the points where they are located, and to oppose new incursions of American soldiers into Mexican territory. These orders were brought by General Treviño to the attention of General Pershing, who acknowledged the receipt of the communication relative thereto. On the 22nd instant, as Your Excellency knows, an American force moved eastward quite far from its base, notwithstanding the above orders, and was engaged by Mexican troops at Carrizal, State of Chihuahua. As a result of the encounter, several men on both sides were killed and wounded and seventeen American soldiers were made prisoners.

With the assurance of my highest consideration, I have the honor to be,

Your Excellency's most obedient servant,

E. Arredondo

TLS (SDR, RG 59, 812.00/18574, DNA).

Henry Prather Fletcher to Edward Mandell House

Dear Colonel House,   [Washington] June 24, 1916

I have just had an interview with the President He thinks it safer to proceed with the draft already accepted by Brazil. So I have written to Naon to that effect asking him to inform me definitely whether he will sign. I also enclosed him a copy of the draft and asked him to write the Spanish text. I told him as soon as I heard from him that—acting on the President's orders—I would then present it to the other diplomatic representatives of American countries here and endeavor to have everything agreed upon and arranged ready for signature during Müllers visit.

He told me in N. Y. day before yesterday that he feared the Mexican complications might incline his and the other governments to hold back, but I think this can easily be arranged. I mentioned this to the President and he said it was an additional reason for signing rather than otherwise.

I shall keep you advised. Meantime I hope you are enjoying your rest.   Faithfully yours,   Henry P. Fletcher

ALS (E. M. House Papers, CtY).

A Plan of Action

[c. June 25, 1916]
Course of Action.

1) Send demand to Mexico for release of prisoners.

2) Immediately thereupon send for the ranking members of the two houses and apprise them of any information with regard to Chihuahua.

3) If the prisoners are not returned go at once to Congress and lay the whole matter before them as follows:

   a) If we were dealing with a regular government, I should have no choice but to advise a declaration of war; but

   β) We are dealing, as a matter of fact, with a distressed and stricken people whose government represents no authority that can be counted upon even to maintain internal order; therefore

   γ) I request authority to take the necessary steps to safeguard the United States and our own people against a government whose attitude is one composed of aggression and incompetence.

State once again our purpose in Mexico.

(N.B. Draw up the necessary resolution.)

T transcript (WC, NjP) of WWsh MS (WP, DLC).

To James Linn Rodgers

Washington, June 25, 1916.

Mr. Arredondo yesterday delivered to this Government the following communication: Quote. . . .[1]

You are hereby instructed to hand to the Minister of Foreign Relations of the *de facto* Government the following: Quote. The

Government of the United States can put no other construction upon the communication handed to the Secretary of State of the United States on the twenty fourth of June, by Mr. Arredondo, under instruction of your Government, than that it is intended as a formal avowal of deliberately hostile action against the forces of the United States now in Mexico, and of the purpose to attack them without provocation whenever they move from their present position in pursuance of the objects for which they were sent there, notwithstanding the fact that those objects not only involve no unfriendly intention towards the Government and people of Mexico, but are on the contrary, intended only to assist that Government in protecting itself and the territory and people of the United States against irresponsible and insurgent bands of rebel marauders.

I am instructed, therefore, by my Government to demand the immediate release of the prisoners taken in the encounter at Carrizal, together with any property of the United States taken with them, and to inform you that the Government of the United States expects an early statement from your Government as to the course of action it wishes the Government of the United States to understand it has determined upon, and that it also expects that this statement be made through the usual diplomatic channels, and not through subordinate military commanders. Unquote.[2]

CONFIDENTIAL. If you are asked, or opportunity offers, you may state that the expectation of an early statement means that the Government of the United States will not wait many hours for a reply.   Lansing.

T telegram (SDR, RG 59, 812.00/18574, DNA).
   [1] Here follows the text of E. Arredondo to RL, June 24, 1916, just printed.
   [2] There is a WWsh draft of the above two paragraphs in WP, DLC.

From Edward Mandell House, with Enclosure

                                                      New London,
Dear Governor: New Hampshire. June 25, 1916.

I am enclosing you part of a letter from Sir Horace Plunkett. I am also sending some articles from the London Nation, The Manc[h]ester Guardian, The Dailey News and The Statesman which you may find interesting since they concern your speech before the League to Enforce Peace.[1]

Noel Buxton,[2] Member of Parliament, who is identified with the Peace Party in England, has been with me here for two days. He believes you have given those who think like himself an opportunity to do some effective work in England towards creating a peace sentiment.

The sentiment is there and the Government fear it, therefore your conclusion that when in your judgment the time has arrived for us to make an imperative suggestion, you will make it, interests me greatly. This is why I think thorough preparedness is so necessary, because it will strengthen your position when you make the demand.

I believe, too, that the way the Mexican affair is handled will have great influence upon the European situation. Heaven knows, you have done all that a man could to help the people there, and the fact that they are not able to follow your kindly lead, is no fault of yours.

I am sure I need not tell you how deeply I appreciate your letter of June 22nd. Please do not ever get me on your mind. I understand perfectly when I do not hear from you and your silence does not disturb me in the least.

Affectionately yours,   E. M. House

TLS (WP, DLC).

¹ These editorials and articles were: "If America Backs the Bill!" and "A Disentangling Alliance," London *Nation*, XIX (June 3, 1916), 276-78; "The League of Peace," Manchester *Guardian*, May 31, 1916; "The Peacemaker," London *Daily News and Leader*, May 29, 1916; "The Enforcement of Peace," *New Statesman*, VII (June 3, 1916), 196-97; and Norman Angell, "Mr. Wilson's Contribution," *War and Peace*, III (June, 1916), 136-38. These articles and editorials all stressed the significance of Wilson's departure from the traditional American foreign policy of isolation from the affairs of the rest of the world in his suggestion that the United States might participate in an international organization to preserve peace in the postwar world. Several of the writers called attention to the similarities of view on the ultimate objectives of the war among Wilson and British leaders such as Grey, Asquith, and Balfour and argued that close cooperation between England and the United States was vital to secure a viable peace settlement. The second editorial in the London *Nation*, "A Disentangling Alliance," was the only one to raise the question of whether or not Wilson could in fact persuade the American people and many conservative politicians to abandon isolationism in favor of participation in an international organization. It pointed out in particular that such participation would require the United States Senate to give up much of its control over foreign policy.

² Noel Edward Noel-Buxton, Liberal M.P. since 1910; hereinafter referred to as Noel Buxton.

E N C L O S U R E

Extract from letter of Sir Horace Plunkett.   June 7th, 1916.

Unquestionably, the misunderstanding of the President's Peace League speech has done immense harm to the popular feeling in England. I took the words "With its causes and objects we are not concerned" to mean that the United States had absolutely no part or responsibility in the outbreak of the war, that the immediate issues were restricted to the international relations in Europe and that, whatever objects were sought by the belligerents, whether in Europe, in Asia or in Africa, were equally of no concern to your country. On the other hand, principles which vitally concerned the whole of western civilization were at stake and the neutral rights which had been prejudiced were largely American.

All this, of course, is perfectly true, but you cannot prevent people in these stirring times seizing upon some sentence—the shorter the better, because the easier remembered—and putting their own interpretation upon it.

A careful reading of the speech as a whole not only makes its meaning and purport perfectly clear but, in my judgment, raises it to a high place among the prophetic visions of international statesmanship. It recognizes that Washington's warning against European entanglements no longer holds good, and that the United States must join with other nations in thinking out and working out the means of saving our common civilization from the appalling menace of militarism.

Knowing how mere reiteration will set up a lie in formidable competition with the truth, I feel that you ought to get the President to re-state his fine case as often as possible. His literary sense may revolt at this; but it would be well for him to approach the question from many angles and so appeal to many different kinds of intelligence. I should like to see frequent utterances upon this greatest of world problems from him, the first of them clearing up in the minds of simple folk those parts of his argument which, as I have explained above, have not been rightly understood.

T MS (WP, DLC).

From Newton Diehl Baker, with Enclosure

Dear Mr President: Washington. June 26, 1916

I have marked with pencil the particular sentence in the enclosed which tries to state your idea[1]—the rest was written just to get a start and I have not delayed to revise it.

Perhaps a word of argument might be added by showing the transitory allegiance of the armed forces in Mexico, as a reason for the plan to require a complete suspension of all military operations by Mexicans in the Northern States

Respectfully,   Newton D. Baker

With his granddaughter, Ellen Wilson McAdoo

Bust of Colonel House by Jo Davidson

Bust of Wilson by Jo Davidson

The Wilsons leaving Memorial Continental Hall in Washington

Signing the Federal Farm Loan Act, July 17, 1916

Leading the Flag Day parade, June 14, 1916

Louis Dembitz Brandeis

James Watson Gerard

ALS (WP, DLC).
1 It is the first sentence of the third paragraph. He drew a line alongside it in the margin.

ENCLOSURE

I do not ask you to declare war upon Mexico. With the people of that Republic we have no quarrel, and with their sufferings we are moved by all the sympathies of neighborhood and humanity. We have no purpose of aggrandizement or aggression, but we have a duty which we must perform toward the people of the United States who live along the frontier and to whom we must secure freedom from raids which menace their lives and from fears which paralyze all the ordinary processes of their industrial and commercial life. Were we to go to war, our object would necessarily be in part political and our success would result in the enforced acceptance by Mexico of some part of our theory and practice of political organization; but the very nature of our theory in these matters is that they are voluntary and unforced, and it is likewise an essential part of our own freedom that we accord freedom in equal fulness to others. Our right in this matter rests upon our duty to save and safeguard the lives and rights of our own people, and the action we take should be only such as is adapted to and limited by the object to be attained.

Our border is approximately eighteen hundred miles long. Immunity from marauding bands and local attacks cannot be secured by the stationing of troops on our own side of the international line, in the absence of either the ability or the willingness of Mexico adequately to cooperate on the other side. We have already been obliged to send upon Mexican soil an expedition to scatter a formidable band of outlaws which with growing head menaced both our peace and that of Mexico herself, and with even the remnants of which the Mexican forces continue to show themselves unable to deal. This expedition we have not been able to withdraw, as the mere suggestion of our intention so to do summons into new hope and fresh outrage the lawless and desperate people among whom aggressions upon our soil are planned. We must therefore maintain this force and by adding to the forces on the border make our power at every point such that an end of the disturbances will be reached. It may be, too, that additional expeditionary forces will be necessary to be sent into the northern States of Mexico, especially if the de facto Government concerts its action with the common enemy and refuses its assent to measures which we must take because that Government cannot or will not. I do not conceal from myself that these measures, were they taken against a responsible and able but unwilling government, would be acts of international war. But in the present case, for the purposes which we should declare most solemnly to the world and the limits which we should steadfastly observe, I am persuaded that we shall not be held by the candid judgment of the world to be doing otherwise than at once securing our own rightful peace and aiding a distracted people to secure for themselves an ordered government of their own making and choice, which will give them peace and opportunity and at the same time assume its just relations and burdens in the family of nations.

I ask you, therefore, Gentlemen of the Congress, not to declare war, but to authorize me so to use the military powers of the Government as effectively to guard our frontier, if necessary to enter upon Mexican soil and to require the entire suspension, in those Mexican states which border upon the United States, of all military activities of every kind on the part of the Mexican people, until by the establishment of a responsible and responsive authority among themselves they are prepared to resume the performance of their full obligation to us as a neighboring and friendly state. By such uses of our power and by such alone can we hope to satisfy the just expectation which our own citizens entertain as to the safety of their lives and property, and in no other manner can we hope successfully to answer the call of humanity towards our neighbors, destitute, torn by faction and wasted by want, disease and unceasing war.

T MS (WP, DLC).

A Draft of an Address to a Joint Session of Congress[1]

TO THE CONGRESS.   June [26], 1916.

Gentlemen of the Congress: The relations between the Government of the United States and the *de facto* government of the Republic of Mexico have come to a turning point so critical and so set about with the gravest questions of public policy that it has become my duty to lay the facts before you for such action as you may deem it wise and right to take: for action of some sort is necessary.

1 Words in angle brackets in the following document deleted by Wilson; those in italics (except for Latin words and personnel), added by him. Wilson made many of these changes in response to Lansing's suggestions, presumably in conference. Lansing also made some handwritten emendations which have not been printed. He also made the marginal comments. There is a WWsh draft of this address in WP, DLC.

Allow me to recall briefly some of the events of the last three months. During the night of March eighth to ninth last a band of armed men out of Mexico attacked the town of Columbus, New Mexico, partially burned and sacked it, and sought to kill every one they encountered there, whether offering resistance or not, guards and citizens alike. One of the most disturbing circumstances connected with the raid was that the plan to make it was known beforehand to at least one of the commanders of the military forces of the *de facto* government near at hand and that no measures were taken by the Mexican authorities to prevent it. ⟨No steps have since been taken by them either to punish or to apprehend the bandits who took part in it.⟩ Repeated raids into the territory of the United States have since been made from the Mexican side of the border, upon a smaller scale, often at points upon the frontier which are very near stations where troops of the *de facto* government are known to be on guard. The bandits who attacked Columbus were pursued across the border by our troops, as ⟨the⟩ subsequent bands of marauders have also been. The territory of the United States joins that of Mexico for a distance of eighteen hundred miles. For a large part of that distance no natural barrier or even visible line marks the boundary of the one country and the other. Towns are infrequent. No direct line of road or railway runs along the length of the border to afford quick and ready means of transportation. It is impossible to defend such a frontier against raiders by any arrangement of mere patrol on this side the line that it is fea[s]ible to effect. If the lives of our people there are to be adequately defended, the daily peaceful course of their industry protected from intolerable interruption, and fear as intolerable, it is necessary that the Mexican authorities should be as active as we in such times as the present in assuring their safety. But they are not; and they have not been. Because they have not been it has been necessary for us ourselves to cross the border and drive marauders away from its vicinity.

The force under General Pershing which was sent into Mexico to pursue the men who attacked Columbus found it necessary, if they were in fact to break the forces of the bandits ⟨up⟩ and inflict effective punishment which would be heeded and remembered, to penetrate far into the interior and establish posts there from which they could strike at the outlaws as they disclosed their whereabouts; but they have been scrupulously careful to meddle in no way with the life of the peaceful people there and never at any time to interfere with the operations or the control of ⟨the officers or forces⟩ *either the civil authorities or the military forces* of the Mexican government. We have sought to act with the utmost consideration and with constant respect for the sov-

? ereignty of the Republic. General Carranza was ⟨promptly⟩ informed of the entrance of our troops into Mexican territory, and
was explicitly assured that they would not be permitted to do anything that would in fact interfere in any way with the independent authority of his government. Our purpose was fully and
frankly stated, and the active cooperation of his own forces was
asked in the ⟨performance⟩ *suppression* of disorders which manifestly threatened his own authority and control as much as they
menaced the peace of our people near the border. We expressed
our willingness not only but our desire to arrive at a practicable
modus vivendi by which the forces of the two governments might
effectively coöperate; and offered to withdraw our own forces so
soon as we should be convinced that the forces of the *de facto*
government were in fact so disposed and so employed as to make
our people and territory safe. But General Carranza opposed
arguments of pride to arguments of necessity, points of form to
points of fact, and offered promises in the stead of effectual
action.

Without something more than that we could not withdraw.
The mere suggestion of our intention to do so would certainly
excite to new hope and fresh outrages the desperate men of
whom northern Mexico is full among whom the attacks upon
our soil and people are hatched, and with whom the Mexican
authorities have not attempted to deal.

Again and again General Carranza has demanded that we
withdraw. When he found that we would not do so until he himself actually disbanded and crushed the outlaws of the northern
States of the Republic which he professed to control, he issued
orders to his commanders to attack any portion of the forces of
the United States in Mexico ⟨that⟩ *which* sought to move east or
west or south; and on the twenty-first of the present month those
orders were obeyed by General ⟨Garza,⟩ *Gomez*, who at Carizel
on that day attacked two troops of the tenth *United States* cavalry
⟨of the United States⟩ who were moving northeastward from General Pershing's headquarters ⟨in pursuit of bandits known to be in
that neighbourhood,⟩ *on ordinary scouting duty*, notwithstanding

Capt. ? the fact that Colonel Boyd, in command, had in the most friendly spirit informed him of his errand and courteously sought his

Omit permission to pass through the town. All the circumstances of the
attack are not yet known; but the details do not for the moment
concern us. It has become evident that the *de facto* government
will neither use its own forces in any effectual way to protect
the people of Texas, New Mexico, and Arizona nor permit us to

take the steps absolutely necessary to protect them. There seems to be no alternative but to clear the northern States of Mexico, for the time being, of armed forces of every kind. We had hoped that an arrangement manifestly in the interest of both Mexico and the United States might be effected by the concurrent action of the two governments; but Mexico has disappointed us and withheld cooperation. An end must be put to an intolerable situation, and we are left to put an end to it alone.

If we were dealing with a government which in fact exercised undisputed authority in Mexico, which really governed and was in a position to assume the responsibility ⟨of⟩ *that should go with* a regularly constituted and freely employed control, it would obviously be my duty to advise the Congress to exercise its constitutional power to declare war. But we are not dealing with such a government. There has been no such government in Mexico since February, 1913. At no time since the tragic assas[s]ination of President Madero have we had any certain evidence that those who were assuming to exercise authority in that distracted country represented anybody but themselves. Amidst the endless confusions of inconstant revolution it has apparently been impossible to consult the wishes or ascertain the sentiments of the Mexican people, for whom all government in that country should exist. The Government of the United States recognized the present self-constituted government of Mexico as the *de facto* government of the Republic only because it seemed at the time of the recognition to be about to succeed in establishing order over a sufficiently large part of the country to permit the early resumption of constitutional government there, and because it did not bear upon it the infamous stain of blood guiltiness and ⟨upon⟩ *of* having laid violent hands upon the constitution itself that the ⟨unspeakable⟩ *lawless* Huerta bore. We do not know whether it represents the people of Mexico or not. We shall not know until it has been judged by the people at the polls.

I cannot bring myself to recommend that the United States make war upon Mexico for what the *de facto* government has ⟨?⟩ done or has failed to do, in its mistaken pride and unfriendliness. I cannot dismiss from my mind the pitiable distress of the People of Mexico, and particularly of the people of the northern states. Their lives and their property alike have been stripped of all security by the events of more than four years of incalculable change. Their homes have been devastated, their fields swept bare, their very money,—such pittance as they were able to scrape together,—made valueless. In many parts of the country they are starving. Their crops ⟨are⟩ *have been* stolen or consumed and they are without seed to renew them. Their draft cattle have been taken away. They face desolation and death. Violence has been substituted for authority, force for right. The law⟨s, the very thing that⟩ *and every essential thing that should* sustain the life of the country ⟨itself,⟩ are in suspense. They are beyond measure harried and distracted. Their men crowd into the ranks of the armed levies, under any captain who offers, officer of the *de facto* government or sullen rebel or reckless outlaw, oftentimes only because in no other way can they get food or keep body and soul together. No man who has a heart under his jacket can wish or consent to make war on a people in such a case. No American who has really grasped and comprehended the principles of humanity and of right upon which the life of free and just America is founded could ⟨with the⟩ *without an* utter renunciation of every ideal he holds dear advocate any such heartless and un-righteous thing. What we do must be adapted to the extraordinary circumstances of the case and must be justified by the highest standards of political justice and necessity. So far as the people of Mexico may be affected by what we do, we must help them, not harm them, restore their op[p]ortunity to live and to work, not destroy or interfere with it, feed them rather than take anything away from them.

With such feelings, with such principles held with passionate conviction,[2] and standing here in the full light of what ⟨is⟩ *has* actually happened and is happening in Mexico, I make this earnest recommendation and request: that the Congress author-ize me to use the military and naval forces of the Government in any way that may be necessary to guard our frontier effectively, if necessary to enter on Mexican soil and there require the entire suspension, in the states which touch our own *of* all military activities of every kind on the part of the Mexican people until by the establishment of a responsible and adequate authority among themselves they are prepared to resume their full obliga-tions to us as a neighbouring and friendly state. By such uses of our power, and only by such uses, can we hope to satisfy the just expectations of our own citizens with regard to the protec-

---

[2] This paragraph in Wilson's shorthand draft reads as follows: "With such feeling, with such principles held with unfaltering conviction, and standing here in the full light of what has actually happened and is happening in Mexico, I make this earnest request: that the Congress authorize me, if it should prove necessary to use the armed forces of the United States to secure beyond question the peace and safety of our own people and territory against attacks of any kind from Mexico, to employ those forces within Mexico itself, not only for the purpose of policing bands of marauders who have crossed our borders, but also for the purpose of checking the movements and preventing the military con-trol of all armed Mexican forces responsible for the disorders of northern Mexico and for the consequent constant disturbance of our peace and security."

tion of their lives and property. In no other manner can we hope successfully to answer the call of humanity towards our neighbours, destitute, torn by faction, wasted and exhausted by want, disease, and violence.

The root of the trouble we face in Mexico is that the military commanders now nominally under the direction of the *de facto* government in the northern states of that Republic are unable or unwilling to protect our territory against violence from their own side of the border, and that armed men in that part of Mexico of all ranks, officers and enlisted men, seem to change their allegiance at will. Those who to-day profess allegiance to the *de facto* government may to-morrow adhere to some insurgent chief, and ⟨next⟩ *the* day *after* resume their former standing as regular soldiers of the Republic. There is no control and no certain or fixed military power. Men in the uniform of the *de facto* forces do not hesitate to play bandit at pleasure, and there is no effectual restraint or punishment. The ⟨immediate⟩ presence of troops of the *de facto* government does not make even their immediate neighbourhood on our side of the border safe against organized lawless attack.

I am careful to set the whole situation before you and to ask your authorization in the terms I have used because I feel bound in conscience, as the official representative of the American people, *to act* in these critical circumstances as a friend of the people of Mexico even when proposing to use force against those who profess to be their government, but do not govern. I am not willing to be a party to intervention in the internal affairs of Mexico. By intervention I mean an attempt to determine for the Mexican people what the form, the circumstances, and the *personnel* of their government shall be, or upon what terms and in what manner a settlement of their disturbed affairs shall be effected. To such intervention I am, and shall remain, unalterably opposed.

I know too well why it is desired, and by whom. I know the infinite perils it involves to the liberties and rights of the Mexican people, now face to face, constantly face to face, with those who would exploit and make selfish use of them. Very few of those who desire a settlement of Mexican affairs by the force and power of the United States desire it for the sake of Mexico. It does not lie with the American people to dictate to another people what their government shall be or what use shall be made of their resources, what laws or rulers they shall have or what persons they shall encourage and favour. I have been bred in an old school of American principle and practice: I know what American history means and what spirit in affairs the American

?

Haiti
S. Domingo
Nicaragua
Panama

peo[ple] have have [*sic*] most passionately and habitually preferred. I know that they desire no one who professes to speak for them to interfere with the liberties of any people and that I am speaking their deepest principle of action when I say that we wish not a single foot of Mexican territory, not a single hour of political control in Mexico. The present situation, if fortunate in no other respect, is at least fortunate in this, that it affords us an opportunity to prove ourselves as great as our professions. We shall seek in the very act of protecting our southern frontier to succour the people whose territory we enter, and to set them free to look to their own affairs, bring order out of their con-
? fusion. They shall be as free to act in all matters of their own self-government where our forces are as if no American soldier were to be found anywhere in Mexico, and they shall know, when these anxious and troubled days have passed, that we are in deed and in truth their friends.

WWT MS (WP, DLC).

A Draft of a Resolution

[June 26, 1916]

RESOLUTION.

BE IT RESOLVED, etc., etc., that the President be and is hereby authorized and empowered to use the military and naval forces of the United States in any way that may be necessary to guard the southern frontier of the United States most effectively, if necessary to enter on Mexican soil and there require the entire suspension, in the Mexican states which touch and border upon our own, of all military activities of every kind on the part of the Mexican authorities and people until by the establishment of a responsible and effective political authority among themselves they are prepared to resume and meet their full obligations towards us as a neighbouring and friendly state.

WWT MS (WP, DLC).

To Thomas James Walsh

My dear Senator: [The White House] June 26, 1916

I appreciate the importance of the matter you call my attention to in your kind letter of June twentieth and I have not been inactive in the matter.

I made the most careful inquiry as to the origin of the articles in the newspapers you refer to about the oil leasing question and can assure you that nothing emanated from either the Navy Department or the Department of Justice by way of suggestion or stimulation of the attacks which put the Secretary of the Interior in so unjust a light.

I took the matter up very frankly with Secretary Lane and he has prepared me a memorandum[1] which I think will form a basis for our working out a satisfactory accommodation of the views of the several departments.

With warm regard and appreciation,

Sincerely yours,   Woodrow Wilson

TLS (Letterpress Books, WP, DLC).

[1] The Editors have been unable to find this document.

To Sylvester Woodbridge Beach

My dear Mr. Beach: [The White House] June 26, 1916

I warmly appreciate the kindness of your letter of June twentieth. I do not know how to deal with the fiendish lies that are being invented and circulated about my personal character other than to invite those who repeat them to consult anybody who has known me for any length of time.

It would be a very good idea, I think, if you were to let Doctor Watson come to see you and talk with anybody he cares to talk with in Princeton, and I am certainly your debtor for bestirring yourself in this matter, even though there may be nothing effective to do. Poison of this sort is hard to find an antidote for.

Cordially and sincerely yours,   Woodrow Wilson

TLS (Letterpress Books, WP, DLC).

From Newton Diehl Baker

Dear Mr. President: Washington. June 26, 1916.

May I suggest the wisdom of the Secretary of State undertaking to discover, if he can, what action the British Government would be likely to take in the event of trouble in Mexico of such character as to lend probability to General Nafarette's threat to destroy the Tampico oil fields.

As I understand the situation, the British interests there are very large, and are in some way of especial importance to their naval operations, perhaps, because of oil-burning ships in the British Navy.

The thought in my mind is that, if there is likelihood of British intervention at Tampico, we ought to forestall it, if trouble comes, by intervening there ourselves, so as to make outside interference unnecessary, and having a force at Tampico would fit in well with the military plan which you have already discussed with me.

Respectfully yours,   Newton D. Baker[1]

TLS (SDR, RG 59, 812.00/1879½, DNA).
[1] Wilson sent this letter to Lansing in WW to RL, July 20, 1916, TLS, same file number as above.

A Memorandum by Robert Lansing[1]

MEMORANDUM.   June 26, 1916.

ATTITUDE ON MEDIATION IN MEXICAN CONTROVERSY.

1. This Government is always averse to the use of force when other means can be found to protect the rights of the United States and its citizens.

2. This Government has always, whenever it could consistently with its dignity and the practical security of its just rights, listened sympathetically to friendly powers seeking to find an amicable way of settling differences.

3. The relative attitude of this Government and the Carranzista Government was shown in the acceptance of mediation of the A.B.C. Powers by the United States in 1914, and the flat refusal of Carranza to do so.

4. It is not the part of the Government, which has done an indefensible and hostile act, to seek mediation as a cloak to protect itself from the consequences of such act. Its only course is to admit the wrong and to offer restitution as far as possible. If the aggrieved Government does not consider the admission of wrong or the offer of restitution sufficient, and there is an honest difference of opinion as to the sufficiency, mediation might then be invoked as a means of composing this difference.

5. In the present case the Carrizal incident does not at present offer a fit subject for mediation in view of the fact that the Mexican forces attacked our troops under direct orders from the *de facto* Government, and, therefore, that Government is wholly responsible for the lives lost and for the capture and imprisonment of American soldiers.

6. Until the demand, which has been made by this Government on the *de facto* Government, has been fully complied with, it is impractical to consider mediation. A demand, of which the

justness is beyond controversy, is not a proper subject for mediation.

7. Even after compliance with the demand, the previous attitude of the Carranza Government toward mediation makes the subject one of doubtful expediency, as the motive of that Government if it accepts mediation in principle may be doubted.

T MS (SDR, RG 59, 812.00/18607½, DNA).
   1 Lansing read this memorandum over the telephone to Wilson. Ignacio Calderon, Bolivian Minister to the United States, had unofficially suggested mediation of the Carrizal affair on June 24, and Arredondo had accepted the suggestion "in principle" on the following day. *New York Times*, June 25 and 26, 1916. See also Link, *Confusions and Crises*, p. 311.

Frederick Funston to Henry Pinckney McCain

Fort Sam Houston, Tex. Received at the War
Department June 26, 1916, 12:44 P.M.

Number 1787. Following just received from General Pershing: "Dublan, Mexico, June 25th, 1916 Commanding General Southern Department Fort Sam Houston, Tex. Number 293. Message from Major Jenkins,[1] Saint Louis Ranch dated this morning reports Captain *Hower* [Howze] and four colored troopers as having arrived there. Jenkins scouted country vicinity San Domingo ranch with four troops in line deployed as skirmishers with wide intervals and positive none of our men left in that vicinity. Total of two troops so far returned to lines one officer and forty three enlisted men, and one reported gone north from Sabinal, may turn up later. Counting seventeen prisoners now seems probable twenty-two killed although possibly others may turn up. Major Howze sends report of American foremen San Domingo, stating horseholders reached ranch in bunches saying were going for reenforcements, refused return assist commanders or attempt make stand at ranch. Boyds note book taken from his body by Sergeant contains carbon copy his note to Jefe Politico Carrizal, advising latter he was passing Carrizal on peaceful mission, and requesting usual authority and that military authority be notified of his movements, also message to me written before fight anticipating his arrival and departure from Ahumada. Papers taken from Boyd's body include note sent by General Gomez, inviting Boyd and his command to come to Carrizal for conference. Strong indication that treachery was planned by Mexicans. Also that conference between Mexican officials and Boyd held for purpose of delay in order to draw him into trap. Where Capt. Boyd in error in thinking Mexicans would not fight, de facto government no less responsible for firing upon our troops. Morey's report will be

forwarded tomorrow. Morey just reached camp, wounded in right
shoulder, not serious."   Funston.

T telegram (WP, DLC).
 [1] John Murray Jenkins.

To Benjamin Ryan Tillman

My dear Senator: The White House June 27, 1916
   Thank you for your letter of the twenty-third. It certainly expresses a view which can be pressed home with very strong
arguments. I have been rather leaving the matter to the Committee on Ways and Means of the House. I would appreciate it very
much if you would tell the Secretary of the Treasury what you
have told me in this letter, for I know the Committee is constantly
seeking his advice.
             Cordially and faithfully yours,   Woodrow Wilson

TLS (B. R. Tillman Papers, ScCleU).

From Jane Addams and Others

                              Chicago, Ills., June 27, 1916.
   The Executive Board of the Woman's Peace Party urges the
administration by means of direct conference or by mediation
through other American nations to avoid hostile conflict with the
people of Mexico within their own borders, so that there may not
be sown seeds of distrust and enmity which will prevent us—
strong enlightened and free—from aiding in the near future, our
weak neighbor, uneducated and poor, to secure education economic independence and political stability.
             Miss Jane Addams, Mrs. Anna Garlin Spencer,
             Mrs. William Kent, Mrs. Louis F. Post,
             Mrs. Frederick J. Taussig, Mrs. Lu[c]ia
             Ames Mead, Miss Sophonisba P. Breckinridge.

T telegram (WP, DLC).

From Harry Allen Overstreet and Others[1]

The President: New York, N. Y. June 27, 1916.
   We, citizens of the United States, in mass meeting assembled,[2]
profoundly appreciative of the patience and understanding shown
by the present Administration in its handling of foreign issues,
and deeply regretting the strained relations now existing between

the United States and Mexico, ask that the differences between the two nations be submitted to mediation or to arbitration in accordance with the spirit of the treaty of 1848 with Mexico, so that it may not be said that any treaty of the United States is a "mere scrap of paper."   Very respectfully,   H. A. Overstreet

Gertrude M Pinchot.

Irving Fisher

For Joint Committee On Arbitration

in Mexico.

TLS (WP, DLC).

1 Overstreet was Professor of Philosophy at the College of the City of New York. The other signers of the letter were Irving Fisher, Professor of Political Economy at Yale, and Gertrude Minturn (Mrs. Amos Richards Eno) Pinchot, former president of the Women's Peace Society.

2 The mass meeting was held on the evening of June 27 at the Hotel Le Marquis in New York under the auspices of the Civic Club. Representatives of many peace and social reform organizations were present at the meeting, and the speakers included Lincoln Steffens, Sidney L. Gulick, and Amos Pinchot. *New York Times*, June 28, 1916.

From Robert Underwood Johnson

Dear Mr. President: [New York] June 27, 1916.

I am greatly impressed with the editorial in today's "Evening Post" "The Two Paths."[1] I know you want peace, as the country does, but if war is to come we want a clear basis of right—a cause to be proud of. Capt. Morey's statement[2] beclouds the issue as to the Carrizal affair.

In this crisis, may Heaven guide you to the right decision!

Respectfully and faithfully yours,   R. U. Johnson.

And always *noblesse oblige!*

ALS (WP, DLC).

1 "The Two Paths," New York *Evening Post*, June 27, 1916. This editorial declared that Wilson stood "at the parting of the ways" in his Mexican policy and went on to point out that, despite Wilson's repeated statements that the United States would never coerce Mexico, he now seemed prepared to do just that. If he did invade Mexico, Wilson would lose his reputation as a peacemaker. Moreover, the administration seemed to have left the decision for war in Carranza's hands, and over a relatively trivial issue at that. "Is Mr. Wilson's and Mr. Lansing's statesmanship so bankrupt," asked the editorial, "that war must come unless Carranza immediately releases the seventeen Carrizal prisoners with ample apology?" Even at the present late hour, the editorial concluded, war was not the only recourse. The other Latin American republics could still be persuaded either to mediate the dispute or to bring pressure on Carranza to make a satisfactory settlement.

2 Captain Morey, the senior surviving officer involved in the Carrizal fight, made a brief written report immediately after the battle which indicated clearly that Captain Boyd had ordered an attack after being refused permission to pass through the town. Morey's message did not reach Pershing until June 25. It was transmitted to Washington that day and published in the morning newspapers on June 26. See F. Funston to NDB, June 25, 1916, *FR 1916*, p. 596, and *New York Times*, June 26, 1916.

From Arthur Hoag Howland[1]

Dear Mr. President: New York, N. Y. June 27, 1916.

Your kind acknowledgement of my telegram sent the other day from Flushing, N. Y.,[2] gives me courage to follow that brief message with a letter. I am particularly anxious to do this because my second telegram,[3] to which you were so kind as to reply, did not state definitely my position, which is to urge you with all the vehemence I am capable of to prevent hostilities between the United States and Mexico.

I have to confess that on a number of occasions I have felt it necessary in my editorial work to condemn certain positions you have taken, but in the last few months my faith in you as one of the supreme leaders in these times of world anguish has been greatly strengthened. I recall the first time I was made to realize how different you are from the ordinary line of influential men. It was the reading of one of your baccalaureate addresses at Princeton that made me open my eyes. "What manner of college president is this?" I thought, "who cares so much for the working man and the poor!"

Since then I have been getting into closer touch with the labor movement, and while I have heard on all sides criticism of your work and doubt of your motives, I have found my faith in you growing stronger. You settled the Colorado strike and, I believe, made the workers out there feel that you were their friend and champion, and would later do something positive and constructive for them; you put and kept Walsh at the head of your Industrial Relations Commission in the face of terrific opposition. You put Brandeis into the Supreme Court. You have seemed to understand Carranza, and what he is trying to do for the oppressed populace of Mexico. I have hailed and repeated again and again your noble utterances: "A flag too great to be stained by selfishness."—A nation whose highest honor and purpose is not to contend with but to *serve* the other nations of the world. You are a real democrat, a real pacifist, a real internationalist. So I cannot bear the thought that now, when Mexico, after so many years of bitter sorrow, is just about to find life and liberty, you should allow our great nation to destroy her hope.

No man in the world ever had so great an opportunity as you have at this moment to lift the race of men toward the plane of peace and brotherhood toward which it has been struggling, to point not only our own nation but the world the way to life, liberty and the best happiness. You have the opportunity of showing the practicability of the principles for which Jesus laid down his life.

Please let me venture to repeat my plea of the telegram. I know you will seek your guidance in the very presence of God, that God whom we love to think of and commune with as the "God of peace." Most respectfully yours, Arthur H. Howland

TLS (WP, DLC).
  ¹ Editor of the New York *Christian Herald*.
  ² A. H. Howland to WW, June 23, 1916, T telegram (WP, DLC).
  ³ Howland sent a second telegram on June 23. Both telegrams are stamped "acknowledged," but no copies of either of Wilson's replies are in WP, DLC.

From Edward Mandell House, with Enclosures

New London,
Dear Governor: New Hampshire. June 27, 1916.

I am enclosing you copies of letters from Lord Bryce and A. G. Gardiner which came this morning.

My information now is that the Liberal press of England are actively taking up your proposals to enforce peace. Mr. Buxton told me that when he returned to England (within the next three weeks) his party would begin an active propaganda for peace based upon your suggestion that America would be willing to help maintain it in the future.

He thought that put an entirely different phase upon the situation and they no longer required the crushing defeat of Germany in order to rid the world of militarism. He also thought peace could never be made without America's aid.

He said it would be a worldwide calamity if you failed to succeed yourself and he wondered whether an agitation to this effect in England would be helpful. I advised him to do nothing for the moment. It is something that needs careful thought. I have a feeling that if we could get France to raise her voice at the right time it would be better than to have it come from England.

Will you not give this some thought and let me know your conclusions. I am in such constant touch with European opinion that I could probably influence this question as you desire.

Buxton said it was thought in England that your proposal merely rested upon your individual word and that if you were defeated, or even if you were re-elected, the plan might fall through because of opposition in Congress. I reassured him in this direction by pointing out that when you made your proposal it was merely an individual matter, but since then it had been written into the Democratic Platform which meant that it had been endorsed by our party and if the party was successful in November, the proposal would have been ratified by the people.

He considered this of enormous importance and he will undertake to help bring that point out in England. It is fortunate you placed it in the platform for it gives an invaluable leverage.

In my letters to Bryce, Gardiner and others I shall call their attention to this feature.

Affectionately yours,   E. M. House

TLS (WP, DLC).

E N C L O S U R E   I

James Viscount Bryce to Edward Mandell House

Forrest Row, Sussex.

Dear Colonel House: England. June 12, 1916.

Your letter which reaches me today has crossed one which I wrote you last week about the President's recent speech, for a full copy of which I have now to thank you.

As I mentioned, one sentence was misunderstood by the undiscerning section of the English press and the expression regarding "freedom of the seas" caused some doubt, as it is thought doubtful in what sense the term "inviolate security of the seas" was used. We of course have never interfered with that security in peace time. The term "freedom of the seas" has for the last year or more been used in several different senses.

To me the speech seemed, and seems on re-reading, to be a pronouncement in favor of American cooperation for preventing future wars throughout the world of great and permanent value.

As I told our Government, it is an event of high moment, having regard to the previous course of the United States policy; and I believe that in what he said as to American cooperation, the President expressed the best sense of the American people.

It marks, as you say, a long step forward, and I am most anxious to hear what impression it has made in America. Of course all men of knowledge and judgement here feel that without American help any scheme for creating machinery to preserve peace in future will have little prospect of success.

We continue to believe that though the victory of the Allies is coming slowly, it is coming surely, and hope that within a few months Germany will realize that she must abate her pretentions.

I am,   Sincerely yours,   James Bryce.

ENCLOSURE II

Alfred George Gardiner to Edward Mandell House

Dear Colonel House: London. 15th June 1916.

Thank you very much for your kind letter. I need not say with what pleasure I read the speech and how cordially I sympathize with its purpose.

It seems to me the only line of hope for the future of the world. I regret that the response has not been more enthusiastic in some of the English journals; but I am confident that as the idea is appreciated by the people there will be an overwhelming response.   Sincerely yours,   A. G. Gardiner.

TCL (WP, DLC).

From Franklin Knight Lane

My dear Mr. President: Washington June 27, 1916.

I have had a talk with Scott Ferris regarding the water power bill, which is hung up in the Senate. He tells me that he thinks it would be wise and perfectly safe to have the Myers bill pass the Senate and go to a conference committee; that he will agree that the features of the Myers bill that are objectionable will be eliminated in conference, or else the bill will not pass. He says that there is so much demand among Western Senators for some legislation upon the matter that they will accept a reasonable measure—one that properly safeguards this invaluable resource.

Let me say that Mr. Ferris of his own motion took this matter up with me last Saturday, and I told him that I would give it consideration. Before advising him I would like to have your view, which will, of course, be controlling as to what I shall say to him.

Personally I believe that this would be an entirely safe course as to both the water power bill and the leasing bill.

Faithfully yours,   Franklin K Lane

TLS (WP, DLC).

John Palmer Gavit to Joseph Patrick Tumulty

My dear Joe: [New York] June 27th, 1916.

I have just been fixing up, for publication in the Evening Post tomorrow, excerpts from a sermon delivered last Sunday evening by Dr. Washington Gladden at Columbus, Ohio, in the course of which he advanced an idea which will not get out of my head. That was that we should send to Mexico a commission consisting of such men as Doctor Eliot, Mr. Taft, Justice Brandeis, and some others—the particular names are of no consequence—to convince the Mexicans of our good will and desire to help them work out their problem. The precise details do not matter, but the more I think of it, the more it seems to me that there is a great big idea here well worth bringing to the attention of the President at the earliest possible moment.

If I understand Woodrow Wilson at all, nothing would give him the satisfaction—whether or not it contributed to his political success—that he would get out of an escape from the necessity of using violence against Mexico. Hitherto he has communicated with Mexico largely through soldiers and in terms which, in the last analysis, rested upon physical force. It strikes me (without having deeply thought about it) that a proposal on his part now to send to Mexico City a commission composed of men of the largest moral and mental calibre at his command, to work out face to face the desperately important problems now threatening war under the most disgraceful conditions, would be a step so sensationally dramatic and so absolutely in line with his profession, as to command the admiration even of the Mexicans, and startle the attention of the world.

The President has exercised such admirable patience hitherto that it would be infinitely more than a pity to have the whole business spoiled and wasted, and end after all in a welter of blood and hatred.

If I had time and he would see me, I would go to Washington with this suggestion myself. In lieu of that, won't you take this letter in to him right now and make him read it? It is the suggestion of a friend, who has absolutely no axe of any kind to grind, and who would like to take off his hat in the years to come to the man who had had the courage to do this big thing. Tell the President I have a hat that I would like to use for that purpose right now.   Cordially yours,   John P. Gavit

TLS (WP, DLC).

To Joseph Patrick Tumulty

Dear Tumulty: [The White House, c. June 27, 1916]

This is a most interesting letter and I thank you for having called my attention to it. You may assure Mr. Gavit that it will receive my most serious consideration, if the opportunity should arise to do what he suggests.   The President

TL (WP, DLC).

Frederick Funston to Henry Pinckney McCain

Fort Sam Houston, Texas. Received at the
War Department June 27, 1916, 7:20 P.M.

Number 1809. Replying your telegrams 1581 and 1584 have communicated with General Pershing and learn that his troops are at present concentrated in vicinity El Valle and Dublan with such detachments as seem necessary along his line of communications. It is believed that this is a good strategic position for him to hold for the present. Arrangements have been made with General Pershing that as soon as there is an open break with Mexico his force is to move to the east and strike Mexican Central in vicinity Gallego or at Ahumada. It is believed that he can do this before forces at Ahumada or Juarez are aware his coming and that he will therefore be able to cut them off and between him and General George Bell, Jr., they should be able to capture all Mexican soldiers at Ahumada or to the north. Under conditions and disposition of American and Mexican forces as they exist today it is believed that this move is practicable safe, sound, strategic and will make a good initiative. It is fully realized here and it is believed that General Pershing now realizes that it would not be wise for him to attempt any move in the direction of Chihuahua. This must of necessity follow only when larger forces shall have been assembled. The move proposed above will have effect of combining General Pershing and General Geo. Bell, Jr. forces after they have disposed of Mexican forces at Juarez and Ahumada. General Pershing's line of supply will have to be by way of Dublan until such time as Mexican Central can be opened to Ahumada. However, if railroad is seriously destroyed it will be perfectly practicable to put supplies in Ahumada by motor trucks from El Paso, Texas. General Pershing and Gen. Geo. Bell, Jr. have been informed of this plan so that their movements will be coordinated.   Funston.

T telegram (WP, DLC).

To Jane Addams

My dear Miss Addams: [The White House] June 28, 1916

I have received and have read with real feeling the telegram in which you join with Mrs. Anna Garlin Spencer, Mrs. William Kent, Mrs. Louis F. Post, Mrs. Frederick J. Taussig, Mrs. Lu[c]ia Ames Mead, and Miss Sophonisba P. Breckinridge, and beg to assure you that, so far as I have been able, I have already acted in the spirit of what you and they so earnestly urge. My heart is for peace and I wish that we were dealing with those who would not make it impossible for us.

Cordially and sincerely yours,   Woodrow Wilson

TLS (Letterpress Books, WP, DLC).

To John Hollis Bankhead

My dear Senator: [The White House] June 28, 1916

I am so deeply interested in the good roads bill that I take the liberty of writing to ask you what you think the prospects are for an early consideration and action upon the conference report. I should like to help in any way that may occur to you.

Cordially and sincerely yours,   Woodrow Wilson

TLS (Letterpress Books, WP, DLC).

From Newton Diehl Baker, with Enclosure

My dear Mr. President: Washington. June 28, 1916.

The Carrizal fight took place on the 21st of June, 1916.

On the sixth day of March, 1916, the Secretary of State received from Cobb, El Paso, a despatch saying:

"Commanding General Gavira in Juarez announced to reporters this morning that Villa was proceeding to the border and that he had asked American military authorities to be on the lookout for him."

I have not been able to find any other evidence of knowledge of Villa's whereabouts and supposed intentions on the part of any other subordinate Mexican commander.

The lady in the peace delegation which visited you this morning was Mrs. Amos Pinchot.[1]

Respectfully yours,   Newton D. Baker

TLS (WP, DLC).

[1] Mrs. Pinchot, Irving Fisher, Harry Allen Overstreet, and Alfred J. Boulton, Secretary of the Central Federated Labor Union of New York, met with Wilson

on June 28 to deliver to him H. A. Overstreet *et al.* to WW, June 27, 1916. See n. 1 to that document and the *New York Times*, June 28, 1916.

Upon her return to New York, Mrs. Pinchot reported that Wilson had told the group: "Never in my Administration shall it be said that any treaty of the United States is a scrap of paper. We have come to a crisis where acts must follow words. While we have the greatest sympathy with the problem of the Mexican people and their desire for self-government, we have come to the point where we must insist that the lives and liberty of our own people shall be safe from the depredations of Mexican bandits." New York *World*, June 30, 1916.

E N C L O S U R E

Fort Sam Houston, Texas, June 27, 1916.

Adjutant General, Washington.

No. 1820. Following received from General Pershing:

"Dublan, Mexico, June 26, 1916. Following is report Captain Morey, Tenth Cavalry:

'Colonia Dublan, Mexico, June 25, 1916.

1. Troop K, 36 men, one guide, under command of Captain Morey, after marching from Ojo Federico joined Troop C, 10th Cavalry, under command of Captain Boyd, at the Ojo de Santo Domingo ranch, eight miles southwest of Carrizal, on June 20th at five thirty P.M. Captain Boyd assumed command, and after a conference with officers and a civilian who informed us that four hundred Carranza cavalry were said to be at Carrizal. Although my original orders did not require this, and although I said it would bring on a fight, he decided to march to Ahumada via Carrizal the following day.

2. June 21st. Both troops left camp at 4:15 A.M. and reached an irrigation ditch to the west of Carrizal at 6:30. Here a message was sent in to the President of Carrizal by Captain Boyd asking permission to march through the town. The troops dismounted about 2,000 yards from the southwest corner of the town to await reply. Mexican troops began to line the trees and irrigation ditch on the west and south the town and a ditch running south from southeast edge of town. The reply came back that we could go north but not east. Our line of march lay to the northeast through the town. A conference between commanders was held between lines which lasted about an hour and a half. During this time Mexican troops were coming into position on the west and south edge of town and along the irrigation ditch to the south of town, and our troops advanced to a position about 800 yards from the line. Our troops having been finally refused permission to march through the town, Captain Boyd gave the following instructions: That a *petition* [portion] of troops "C" would march through the

south corner of the town; that Troop K then on the right of Troop C would be moved to the right and protect the right flank.

The advance began mounted. Troop C in line of foragers, the second platoon etcheloned to the left and rear; troop K some 250 yards to the right with one platoon in line of foragers, and the right platoon in column of squads echeloned to right rear.

When about 300 yards from Mexican line, all dismounted to fight on foot. Horses were sent to the rear of troop C. We then advanced in line of skirmishers and when troop C was about 200 yards to the nearest point in line the Mexicans opened fire. We replied. Troop C advanced to original main position on west end of town. The turning movement of mounted and dismounted men on the right continued and occupied troop K. The most severe fire on troop K came from the south edge of town and ditch in immediate foot. The firing began about eight A.M.

About eight five A.M. a platoon of Mexican cavalry came around troop C flank and advanced on our led horses. These went to the rear out of sight.

The turning movement on right at about eight forty-five caused troop K to be withdrawn to the northwest. In moving back the men became scattered and could not be reassembled. Members of both troops, scattered, went up the hill toward the N. W. away from the field. Captain Boyd was shot and killed early in the fight. Lieutenant Adair[1] was wounded and later in the fight was killed. Captain Morey received a slight wound early in the fight. No statement of men killed on the field can be given. The Mexican line was under cover of trees and brush for most of its length, about 600 yards, it was thinly occupied. Troop K had 26 rifles on the line. Because of divergence to troop C to the left, little was seen of that part of the line over 300 yards away.

I made my escape from the vicinity by concealment by a broken well on hillside until darkness came on. Mexicans sent out immediately after the fight to capture men fleeing toward the hills. Patrols were also sent toward the ranch Ojo de Santo Domingo.

I sent in a message by three men of troop K, reporting the engagement. I later joined four men of troop C, and with them made my way to the command of Major Howze at San Lucis, reaching there at one A.M. June 24th, 1916.

(Signed) L. S. Morey, Captain, Tenth Cavalry.'

Captain Morey stated to me that he was not present at any of the performances [conferences] had between Captain Boyd and the Mexican authorities. The following is copy of instructions telegraphed to the Commanding Officer Ojo Federico ordering a patrol sent in the direction of Ahumada:

'Major Saffarrans,[2] Ojo Aederieno.

Dublan, Mexico, June 17, 1916.

Send one troop cavalry through Sabinal to Vado de Santa Maria on the Santa Maria Valley to reconnoiter from there in the direction of Ahumada. It is reported a large force Mexican troops is assembling at Ahumada and it is desired to get information as to their numbers and movements. This is a reconnaissance and not for the purpose of bringing on a fight. It is understood General Trevino has given orders to all his troops to fire on our detachments moving out from our lines of communication. One troop 10th Cavalry leaves here tomorrow moving toward Ahumada on a similar mission. It is not known whether wagons can be taken beyond Santa Maria. The troops should take every precaution against surprise. If any large force is seen, prompt report should be made of it. Answer.   (Signed) Cabell.'[3]

These same instructions were given to Captain Boyd personally."

Funston.

T telegram (WP, DLC).
  [1] Henry R. Adair.
  [2] George C. Saffarrans.
  [3] Lt. Col. De Rosey Carroll Cabell, chief of staff of the Punitive Expedition.

From Edward Mandell House

New London,

Dear Governor: New Hampshire. June 28, 1916.

Letters come from both Page and Gerard today.

Gerard says:

"von Jagow told me that the President and you must not think because of debates in the Reich[s]tag that the President is not welcome as a mediator."

"The break in Austro-Hungarian line is reported to have been caused by wholesale desertions of Ruthenian troops to Russia."

"The editor of the National Zeitung[1] responsible for the fake interview with me[2] has been fired from the paper which has published a notice to that effect."

Page says:

"After the war we will have an interesting part to play but I see no possibility of our having any hand in ending it except, perhaps, to transmit a preliminary note from one belligerent to another as I transmit a dozen or more every day about lesser subjects."

"The Allies are going to win a real victory. That becomes more and more certain."

"A complete change has taken place in the English resolution and they wont hear the word peace. They are out for a real victory which will permanently discourage a military dictatorship. That done the task of organizing the world on a secure basis will follow; then, but not till then, will our inning come."

"Sir Edward and other men in high positions are a good deal disturbed lest the American Government continues to harp on the blockade. They will not relax it. They cannot, public opinion would not stand it an hour. As things are now an Admiral has stated in a public speech in London that it is necessary to hang Grey; they are going to win the war."

"We have planted ourselves firmly. We have stated our position on the international law involved; our record on that score stands and we have cleared the ground for claims for damages. As I see it, that is all we can do unless we are prepared to break off relations with Great Britain and get ready for war after arbitrators have failed. The greatest damage done has been done by the tone and contention of the Trade Department's instructions."

Affectionately yours,   E. M. House

I am glad Hughes has chosen Willcox[3] to manage his campaign. He is not an able man and is anything but progressive.

TLS (WP, DLC).
    [1] Unidentified.
    [2] The Berlin *National Zeitung* on June 3 published what purported to be an interview with Gerard in which the Ambassador was quoted as saying that he regarded the prospects for peace as "favorable" and that he was convinced that "only a few months separate us from peace." The alleged interview also included Wilson's recent public utterances on the subject of peace. The authenticity of the interview was immediately questioned in the summaries dispatched to London and New York newspapers. Lansing cabled Gerard on June 6 asking for information about the matter. The Ambassador replied on June 8; he declared that the interview was a "pure invention." See the *New York Times*, June 5, 10, and 11, 1916, and *FR-WWS 1916*, pp. 34-35.
    [3] William Russell Willcox, lawyer of New York; Postmaster of New York, 1905-1907; chairman of the Public Utilities Commission of New York, 1907-1913; just named as chairman of the Republican National Committee.

From Amos Richards Eno Pinchot

New York, June 28, 1916.

Suggest opportunity can be made to arbitrate under treaty of 1848. We seem clearly bound under circumstances. We have from border strong intimation of determination of army circles to see us into war. I believe we will wreck our reputation if we go into war with Mexico. Do not let any body make you believe the rank and file of people in this city will not bless your name if you keep us out of war. Peace sentiment is increasing. Scenes at departure of troops show changed atmosphere.[1] I know if we can delay matters a little the country will stand for almost anything you do toward peace.   Amos Pinchot

T telegram (WP, DLC).
[1] Wilson had called out the National Guard of Texas, New Mexico, and Arizona on May 10, just after the raid on Columbus. On June 18, confronted with the worsening Mexican situation, Wilson called out the National Guard of all the states to protect the border and free all regular army troops in the Southwest for operations in Mexico in the event of war. The Guard units of each state were to assemble at a mobilization camp within the state and then proceed to the border as rapidly as possible. Pinchot's remark about a "changed atmosphere" at "departure of troops" is difficult to understand: news reports indicate that guardsmen in New York and elsewhere were cheered by enthusiastic crowds as they marched to assembly points. See the *New York Times*, June 19-28, 1916; Link, *Confusions and Crises*, p. 301; and John Patrick Finnegan, *Against the Spector of a Dragon: The Campaign for American Military Preparedness, 1914-1917* (Westport, Conn., 1974), pp. 165-72.

From Frederic Clemson Howe

Cosmos Club
My dear Mr President: Washington, D.C. June 28 [1916]
I have seen so much of the human wreckage of Europe pass through Ellis Island during the past two years that I doubt if anyone from outside of Washington feels more blessed relief than I do tonight.[1]

I feel an abiding sense of personal gratitude for the service you have rendered America and the world
Very faithfully yours   Frederic C Howe

ALS (WP, DLC).
[1] Howe referred to the news, just received in Washington, that General Treviño had ordered the release of the American prisoners taken in the Carrizal fight. Link, *Confusions and Crises*, p. 314.

From Norman Hapgood

[New York]
Dear Mr. President: Midnight Wednesday June 28 [1916]
Raymond Robins has just left my room, after three hours talk. He will not make his decision yet, for unusual but deep and sound reasons. I believe the decision will be our way, but of course wish to leave no stone unturned. Having him not only with us but in a conspicuous position as head of our league may mean several hundred thousand votes. It may well turn Illinois, and even other States.

I gave him your invitation. He hesitated to take your time, with Mexico and so much else on your mind, but I thought it worth while. He is glad you suggested the evening, not only for the leisure but for the freedom from publicity. He can delay his return to the West long enough to call Tuesday evening or any preceding evening, if you can see him. If Mr. Tumulty will send me a wire here I will communicate with Robins at once.

And if it is arranged I will write you a type-written letter outlining ahead, as well as I can, what is on his mind.

Very sincerely Yours   Norman Hapgood

ALS (WP, DLC).

From Charles William Eliot

Dear Mr. President: Cambridge, Mass., 28 June 1916.

I venture to report to you the opinions of a great majority of the people I meet, or hear from—Republicans and Democrats—and both those who have husbands, brothers, sons, and friends departing for the border, and those who have not:—to go to war with Mexico now will be to give another example of the usual stupid and brutal jingoisms and imperialism which have so long cursed the civilized world. This example will be all the more injurious because it will be given by a great republic instead of by an empire,—big or little, ancient or upstart.

The following policies are sound, and in the long run will command the approval of most Americans:

1. Withdraw all American troops from Mexican soil.

2. Put sufficient forces on the border to really protect the American people who live near by.

3. In so doing, demonstrate the adequacy, or the inadequacy, of the state militias.

4. Prevent American munitions from entering Mexico by land, or by water.

All judicious Democrats in these parts, and many Republicans, hope that you will adhere firmly to your two original policies—no war with Mexico, and no protection by force of arms for American commercial adventurers in Mexico.

It is of course to be hoped that Carranza will be able to consolidate his government by appealing to the familiar unifying motive—let us all join to repel the invader. After the consolidation is effected, he will probably be able to take care of his border and ours.

I am, with great regard,

Sincerely yours   Charles W. Eliot

TLS (WP, DLC).

John Palmer Gavit to Joseph Patrick Tumulty

My dear Joe: [New York] June 28, 1916.

Without having the slightest idea about the way in which the suggestion embodied in my letter of yesterday may have struck you, I feel moved to amplify my thought.

By the mouth of the President personally and through sundry diplomatic documents and otherwise, we have professed great friendship for Mexico. We have recognized the difficulties under which the de facto government is trying to restore order and civilized conditions generally, but the only thing we have *done* which would make any impression upon the Mexican mind is to use violence. The fact that this was under considerable provocation and in defense of our national dignity, is neither here nor there. The Mexicans have heard our fair words; but the only thing they have *seen and felt* is OUR TEETH. We have not even attempted (so far as I am aware) on any considerable scale, to help them for example with food, clothing, blankets, seed-corn, etc. However mistaken I may be in details, I think it is true in general.

Furthermore, I find myself imagining what would have happened had the positions been reversed: a Mexican column, under General Trevino, up in Southern Colorado, its ostensible business finished, the United States Government inquiring why it did not return home; General Funston instructed to prevent its further progress, and—a couple of troops of Mexican cavalry sent out into Kansas! It would be military folly, to be sure, but what of the moral effect?

If I had the say, I think I would pull our troops out of Mexico immediately upon the release of the troopers at Chihuahua, *and let Carranza know that I was going to do so.* Then I would try again to arrange for a joint policing of the border.

The President is going to be judged more by his Mexican policy than by any other one thing. The people have now a *personal* interest in that, as they have not in the European war, or even in the Lusitania. Every man, woman and child *now* has some father, brother, sweetheart, relative or friend in the business in his *own personal skin.* Whether or not men are killed with bullets, they are going to die of the heat and of disease on the Mexican border *in midsummer.* At home, wives and children, mothers and fathers, already are suffering personally inconvenience, sorrow and apprehension. To the average American individual the President's Mexican policy is *now* as real as breakfast. And the happiness and lives of Americans are in the President's own hands, to a degree that must be an almost intolerable burden of responsibility.

He is going to be accused, not of affirmative errors, but of *drifting*; of trying first this and then that and then the other thing in a more or less haphazard way, without a definite, well considered, aggressively constructive policy. I think it is not too late for him to meet that criticism, by formulating at once a program of *concrete measures* to help Mexico. If we get into an ordinary, dirty, bloody war with Mexico (and the distinction between "Mexico" and "the Mexican people" is in my judgment a foolish one) it will be the ruin of Woodrow Wilson, the idealist, the friend of man—even if he be reelected. I cannot imagine Woodrow Wilson getting any joy out of reelection on the strength or under the inertia of a war situation, or the theory that "we must not swap horses," etc.

Whether ahead of the troops or behind the troops, or better still *without* the troops, there must be a concrete program of helpfulness. Only by that means can you forestall the commercialist, the exploiter, and the annexationist, who, as surely as God lives, will ride into Mexico on the back of the present negative policy, and under escort of the army rapidly forming under the leadership of men who "know exactly what they want."

I set no special store by the suggestion I transmitted in my previous letter. I realize that Mexican pride stands in the way, and that anything we do will be received with suspicion. But I know that the way of the sword is a bad way—the *worst* way—and that it plays right into the hands of those on both sides of the border who have been scheming to bring about just the present situation. The thing to do is to forestall and defeat them, *even now*.

The problem is not easy of solution; but if it were easy *anybody* could solve it!

Make such use of this letter as you think proper. My only desire is to help.   Cordially,   John P. Gavit[1]

TLS (WP, DLC).
[1] A Hw note by Thomas M. Hendricks, one of the White House stenographers, attached to this letter, reads: "Kindly send this note of Pres to Gavit." Wilson's note is missing.

Remarks to the Associated Advertising Clubs[1]

[[June 29, 1916]]

Mr. President, gentlemen of the Associated Advertising Clubs, ladies and gentlemen: You will understand that I have not come

[1] Wilson spoke in the afternoon to an open-air mass meeting in the square behind Independence Hall in Philadelphia. The event was held under the

here to make an extended address. I do not need to explain to you the circumstances which have made it impossible that I should prepare an extended address, but I count myself very fortunate to be able to leave my duties at Washington long enough to face this interesting company of men who have the very fine conception that it is their duty to lift the standards and ideals of their profession.

I understand, gentlemen, that you have associated yourselves together in order to promote candor and truth in the advertisement of your business. I wish very much, gentlemen, that candor and truth might always be the standard of politics, as well as the standard of business. I want to challenge your attention for a moment to this aspect of your activities. I do not see how a man can devote himself to candor and truth in the promotion of a particular business without studying the life of the great nation to whom he addresses his advertising. I do not see how a man can fail, having established the horizon of his business where the great hills of truth lie, to lift his eyes to the great multitude of laboring men and striving women who constitute a great nation like ours, and, in the very act of addressing them, get in his own consciousness some part of the impulse of their life. You cannot commend your business to people that you do not understand, and you cannot understand the people of the United States without wishing to serve them.

So I come to you with this thought: America is at a point, gentlemen, where it is more than ever necessary that she should understand her own ideals, not only, but be ready to put them into action at any cost. It is one thing to entertain fine principles and another thing to make them work. It is one thing to entertain them in the formulas of words, like the splendid words which were uttered and give distinction to this ancient and historic building behind me. But it is another thing to do what those same men did—make those words live in the action of their lives. And America is summoned in each new generation to renew, not only the pledges that those men made, but to renew the example which they gave to the world.

I am not interested, and I beg that you will believe me when I say that I never have been interested, in fighting for myself. But I am immensely interested in fighting for the things that I believe

auspices of the Associated Advertising Clubs of the World, then holding their annual convention in that city. The president of the organization was Herbert Sherman Houston, a vice-president of Doubleday, Page & Co. Wilson had made the decision to go to Philadelphia for the affair only that morning, following the relief of tension brought about by the Mexican release of the prisoners taken at Carrizal.

in, and, so far as they are concerned, I am a challenger to all comers. It is important, therefore, since I am in fighting mood, to let you know what are some of the things that I do believe in.

In the first place, I believe, and I summon you to show your belief in the same thing, that it is the duty of every American, in everything that he does—in his business and out of it—to think first, not of himself or of any interest which he may be called upon to sacrifice, but of the country which we serve. "America first" means nothing until you translate it into what you do. So, I believe, most profoundly, in the duty of every American to exalt the national consciousness by purifying his own motives and exhibiting his own devotion.

I believe, in the second place, that America—the country that we put first in our thoughts—should be ready in every point of policy and of action to vindicate, at whatever cost, the principles of liberty, of justice, and of humanity to which we have been devoted from the first. (Cheers.) You cheer the sentiment, but do you realize what it means? It means that you have not only got to be just to your fellow men, but that, as a nation, you have got to be just to other nations. It comes high. It is not an easy thing to do. It is easy to think first of the material interest of America, but it is not easy to think first of what America, if she loves justice, ought to do in the field of international affairs. I believe that, at whatever cost, America should be just to other peoples and treat other peoples as she demands that they should treat her. She has a right to demand that they treat her with justice and respect, and she has a right to insist that they treat her in that fashion. But she cannot, with dignity or with self-respect, insist upon that unless she is willing to act in the same fashion toward them. That I am ready to fight for at any cost to myself.

Then, in the third place, touching ourselves more intimately, my fellow citizens, this is what I believe: If I understand the life of America, the central principle of it is this—that no small body of persons, no matter how influential, shall be trusted to determine the policy and development of America. You know what you want in your business. You want a fair field and no favor. You want to be given the same opportunity that other men have, not only to make known what you have to sell, but to sell it under as favorable conditions as anybody else. And the principle of the life of America is that she draws her vitality, not from small bodies of men who may wish to assume the responsibility of guiding and controlling her, but from the great body of thinking and toiling and planning men from whom she draws her energy and vitality as a nation. I believe, and this is the reason

I am a Democrat, not merely with a big "D" but with a little "d"— I am all kinds of a democrat, so far as I can discover—but the root of the whole business is this, that I believe in the patriotism and energy and initiative of the average man. Some men say they believe in it, but when they act, they show that they do not. They show that they think the only advice that it is safe to take is their advice. (Voice in crowd: "Oh, you Teddy!")

I was not referring to any individual, but I could give you an interesting and a very short list of a group of individuals who have that opinion, namely, that it isn't safe for the United States to escape from their control. I feel perfectly safe in the hands of the average body of my fellow citizens. You are bound to feel safe in their hands. If they do not believe in you, you cannot sell anything. If they do not believe in you, you cannot conduct your business. Your vitality comes from them to you; it does not go from you to them. The theory of government which I decline to subscribe to is that the vitality of the nation comes out of closeted councils where a few men determine the policy of the country.

And so, gentlemen, I feel at home in this company, not because I advertise, but because I have got principles that I am perfectly willing to expose to the public view, and because I want, not only to express my sympathy with, but my admiration for a body of men who think it is worthwhile to get together in order to tell the truth. The only thing that ever set any men free, the only thing that ever set any nation free, is the truth. A man that is afraid of the truth is afraid of the law of life. A man who does not love the truth is in the way of decay and of failure. And I believe that, if you will just let the vitality that is in you and the enthusiasm that is in you, run beyond the confines of the businesses that you may be interested in, you will presently feel that infinite reward, as if the red blood of a whole nation came surging back into your own veins.

Can you imagine, my fellow countrymen, a more inspiring thing than to belong to a free nation and make your way among men, everyone of whom has the right and the opportunity to say what he thinks? Criticism doesn't hurt anybody. I heard an old politician once say to his son, "John, don't bother your head about lies and slanders; they will take care of themselves. But if you ever hear me denying anything, you may make up your mind that it is so." And when you see a man wincing under criticism, you may know that something hit him that was so. And, therefore, when they are saying the things that are not true, there is no credit in keeping your head and not minding it. I have such an inveterate confidence in the ultimate triumph of the truth that I feel, with old Doctor Oliver Wendell Holmes, that the truth is no invalid, and you need not mind how roughly you handle her. She has got a splendid constitution, and she will survive every trial and every lie.

I have come, therefore, as I have abundantly shown you, not to make a formal speech—if I could show you some of the things I have been obliged to do before I came here, you would know that I couldn't possibly make a speech up—but merely to show my profound interest in a body of men who are not only devoted to business but devoted to ideals. Business is all right so long as it isn't sordid, and it cannot be sordid if it is shot through with ideals. A man, no matter how humble his business, can hold his head up among the princes of the world if, as he ought to do, he will think of himself as the servant of the people and not as their master, as one who would serve and not one who would govern.

I congratulate you, my fellow citizens, upon the ideals of a profession which can lower or exalt business, as you choose, and which you have chosen to employ for its exaltation. I came away from Washington to look into your faces and get some of the enthusiasm which I always get when I come away from official-dom and touch hand to hand with great bodies of the free American people.[2]

Printed in *Address of President Wilson . . . June 29, 1916* (Washington, 1916), with a few corrections from the text in the New York *World*, June 30, 1916.
[2] There is a WWT outline of these remarks in WP, DLC.

To Franklin Knight Lane

My dear Lane: [The White House] June 29, 1916

Thank you for your letter of June twenty-seventh about your conference with Mr. Scott Ferris. I have not the least doubt that he could make good his assurances about the result of a conference on the Myers Bill, and I am perfectly willing to have the matter handled in the way he suggests. I am very anxious indeed to have this legislation passed at this session provided it does not keep the houses here all summer.

Always   Faithfully yours,   Woodrow Wilson

TLS (Letterpress Books, WP, DLC).

From Norman Hapgood

Dear Mr. President: New York. June 29th, 1916.

This letter is an explanation of the short one I wrote you at midnight last night. Before I explain, however, just what is in

Robins' mind let me state that Bainbridge Colby[1] requests me to tell you that he is coming out energetically for you in about two or three weeks, but that for strategic reasons his speech tomorrow night will be merely support by implication.

Robins will not commit himself publicly to a final decision until after Mr. Hughes has published his formal letter of acceptance. I think that Robins' mind is almost, but not quite, made up. He thinks he owes it to his many followers, however, to listen to the prevailing arguments of his party up to the time I have mentioned. It was in deference to the wishes of his followers and associates that he had a long talk with Mr. Hughes and will have another one today, both of them being carefully kept private. It is Robins' opinion that if he comes out for you after weeks of full consideration to the arguments of his party friends he will bring many more of them with him than if he jumped now without consideration for their wishes.

Robins is a very religious man. It is the deepest note in his composition. In the leadership which he has, that part about which he is most solemn pertains to the young men in the colleges, whom he is constantly addressing. He thinks that these earnest young adherents of his are prevailingly Republican. That is one of his difficulties, and I may add that his difficulties concern himself as an individual almost not at all, and himself in his responsibilities of leadership almost altogether.

The difficulties he feels about the South and the Catholic elements in the North I have already mentioned to you, and he was much impressed when I repeated your answer.

He put four questions to Mr. Hughes. The answer on Woman Suffrage Robins described as superb in its frankness about his former way of thinking and in the ability with which he described the reasons fpr [for] his change.

The answer about conservation was very able and very satisfactory. This was asked not so much to satisfy Robins himself as because of the interest of Gifford Pinchot and others who wish to make an issue on some parts of the Democratic record regarding conservation.

What Robins cares agout [about] most of all things in the world is the life of the laboring class. Here is where Mr. Hughes fell very short. He was vague and stumbling, and in such matters as the boycott he was old-fashioned. Robins tried to get him to state clearly his feeling about the relative importance of labor and capital, along the lines of Lincoln's famous statement, but got small satisfaction. He asked his views on the Clayton Act and the Seaman's Act and was not satisfied with the answers. It is those

Acts and the appointment of Brandies [Brandeis] that make Robins feel so strongly that I feel sure he will ultimately be with us.

I shall be at Windsor, Vermont from July 1st to July 4th, inclusive and then back here again.

Very sincerely yours,   Norman Hapgood

He found Mr. Hughes without imaginative and warm interest in the way the masses live, feel, and think.

TLS (WP, DLC).
  1 Lawyer of New York and a founder of the Progressive party.

From John Hollis Bankhead

My dear Mr. President: [Washington] June 29, 1916.

Replying to your esteemed letter of the 28th instant with reference to "The Good Roads Bill," I beg to advise that the conference report was agreed to by the House yesterday, and the only thing remaining is your signature, the report having been previously agreed to by the Senate.[1]

I have only one request to make and that is—that you give me the pen with which you sign the bill.[2]

Sincerely yours,   J. H. Bankhead

TLS (WP, DLC).
  1 This was H.R. 7617, a bill "to provide that the United States shall aid the States in the construction of rural post roads," first introduced in the House of Representatives by Dorsey William Shackleford, Democrat of Missouri, on January 6, 1916. Bankhead managed the bill in the Senate. As agreed to by the conference committee, the bill provided for the distribution, under the supervision of the Secretary of Agriculture, of federal funds to state highway departments to assist in the construction of roads in rural areas. The funds to be distributed ranged from a maximum of $5,000,000 in the first year of the program to $25,000,000 in the fifth year. In addition, $1,000,000 a year for ten years was to be provided for the construction of roads in or adjacent to national forests. The state highway departments were required to submit plans and specifications of all roads to be federally funded to the Secretary of Agriculture for his approval. 39 *Statutes at Large* 355.
  2 Wilson signed the bill in a brief ceremony at the White House on July 11.

From Cleveland Hoadley Dodge

My dear President   New York. June 29th, 1916

It is needless to say that I have thought of little else lately but the awful burden of new troubles which you have had to bear. I have been on the point, several times of writing to let you know how profoundly I have admired your course from day to day. All the way along I have been optimistic & I firmly believe that you can find a way out of the apparently hopeless deadlock which the stupidity & impotence of Carranza have brought about. The American people are with you almost to a man & no one wants war except a few crazy people or traitors.

The effect on your own future, I know doesn't worry you, but nevertheless I feel sure that what you are doing will make your election sure. Your friends are getting things in good shape for the campaign and I think that the dear old reactionary Republicans, after spending three or four millions to defeat you will look pretty sick next November.

I am awfully sorry that I can't be at the dinner tomorrow[1] & fear I will not see you this trip, but sincerely hope that when you get to the summer capital we can have you on Corona for a day or two & give you a few hours of real rest, (if such is possible)

We are busy getting ready for Elizabeth's wedding the end of next month, & with seeing the last of Cleveland who is in squadron A. What is the use of children when they all go away.

Wasn't it splendid that the St. Louis convention went off so harmoniously? How long ago it seems

God bless you, dear old friend & give you new strength day by day, like what-do-you-call him who rose refreshed every time he struck the ground. Grace joins me in warm regards to Mrs Wilson & you all,   Ever affectionately   C H Dodge

ALS (WP, DLC).
   [1] The annual dinner of the New York Press Club, at which Wilson was to speak.

John Temple Graves[1] to Joseph Patrick Tumulty

My dear Mr. Tumulty: Washington, D. C., June 29, 1916

The President is so much absorbed at this time that I do not care to worry him with a personal letter, even in his own interest.

But I cannot forbear to say to you that I think the President's superb diplomacy in Mexico has brought him to the psychological and critical moment in our relations with that republic. The attitude of Carranza, if it means anything at this time, distinctly means "anything but a fight." There could be no more fortunate frame of mind in which to find him for the prosecution of the President's plans. Any wise diplomat of the administration—say Mr Fletcher—after talking with the President, ought to be able to persuade both Carranza and Obregon that their mutual interest, if not their mutual preservation, depends now absolutely upon real and active cooperation with the American Government in Mexico. If Carranza and Obregon can be made to see this, a fact which is so plainly evident to common-sense people in both countries, they will give over the insincere and hypocritical pretense of cooperation which they have heretofore given and will bring their forces in full and actual accord with the American troops now in Mexico until order is established throughout the northern provinces at least. With real and genuine cooperation, this can unquestionably be done within the present summer. It is the only way in which it can be done without tremendous expense and tremendous loss.

I think the psychological hour has come when the President can intervene without intervention, when he can establish order in Mexico without war or blood except that of the bandits who are sporadically destroyed in the establishment of law. To do this will crown all the past diplomacies of the President's administration and make him absolutely invincible in the coming campaign. I believe it to be entirely possible to be done, because it is so eminently the common-sense thing to do. I wish you would urge upon the President to prosecute this idea with all possible vigor and dispatch.

With very sincere regards, and with all good wishes for the campaign, I am

Very truly yours,   John Temple Graves

TLS (WP, DLC).
[1] At this time, a feature writer for the Hearst newspapers.

Remarks to the New York Press Club[1]

June 30, 1916

Mr. Toastmaster, Mr. Mayor, gentlemen of the Press Club, ladies and gentlemen: I realize that I have done a very imprudent thing: I have come to address this thoughtful company of men without any preparation whatever. If I could have written as witty a speech as Mr. Pulitzer, I would have written it. If I could have written as clear a definition of the fundamental ideals of American patriotism as the Mayor, I should have attempted it. If I could have been as appealing a person and of as feeling a heart as Mr. Cobb, I would have felt safe. If I could have been as generous and interesting and genuine as Mr. Colby, I should have felt that I could let myself go without any preparation. But, gentlemen, as a matter of fact, I have been absorbed by the responsibilities which have been so frequently referred to here

[1] At the organization's annual dinner at the Waldorf-Astoria Hotel. The toastmaster was Edward Percy Howard, president of the New York Press Club and news editor of the *New York Press*. The other speakers were Mayor John Purroy Mitchel, Ralph Pulitzer, Bainbridge Colby, and Irvin Shrewsbury Cobb, journalist and humorist, at this time associated with *The Saturday Evening Post*.

tonight, and that preoccupation has made it impossible for me to forecast even what you would like to hear me talk about.

There is something very oddly contradictory about the effect you men have on me. You are sometimes, particularly in your photographic enterprises, very brutal to me, and you sometimes invade my privacy even to the extent of forming my judgments before they are formed. And yet I am tempted, when I stand face to face with you, to take off all guard and merely expose myself to you as the fallible human being that I am.

Mr. Colby said something that was among the few things I had forecast to say myself. He said that there are certain things which, really, it is useless to debate, because they go as a matter of course. Of course it is our duty to prepare this nation to take care of its honor and of its institutions. Why debate any part of that, except the detail, except the plan itself, which is always debatable? Of course it is the duty of the government, which it will never overlook, to defend the territory and people of this country. It goes without saying that it is the duty of the administration to have constantly in mind, with the utmost sensitiveness, every point of national honor. But, gentlemen, after you have said and accepted these obvious things, your program of action is still to be formed. When will you act, and how will you act?

The easiest thing is to strike. The brutal thing is the impulsive thing. No man has to think before he takes aggressive action. But before a man really conserves the honor by realizing the ideals of the nation, he has to think exactly what he will do and how he will do it. Do you think the glory of America would be enhanced by a war of conquest in Mexico?[2] Do you think that any act of violence by a powerful nation like this against a weak and distracted neighbor would reflect distinction upon the annals of the United States? Do you think that it is our duty to carry self-defense to the point of dictation in the affairs of another people? The ideals of America are written plain upon every page of American history.

And I want you to know how fully I realize whose servant I am. I do not own the Government of the United States, even for the time being. I have no right, in the use of it, to express my own passions. I have no right to express my own ambitions for the development of America if those ambitions are not coincident with the ambitions of the nation itself. And I have constantly to remind myself that I am not the servant of those who wish to

[2] At this point, "as one man the six or seven hundred diners shouted: "No!" New York *World*, July 1, 1916.

enhance the value of their Mexican investments, but that I am the servant of the rank and file of the people of the United States. I get a great many letters, my fellow citizens, from important and influential men in this country, but I get a great many other letters. I get letters from unknown men, from humble women, from people whose names have never been heard and will never be recorded, and there is but one prayer in all of these letters. "Mr. President, do not allow anybody to persuade you that the people of this country want war with anybody." I got off a train yesterday and, as I was bidding goodby to the engineer, he said in an undertone, "Mr. President, keep us out of Mexico." And if one man has said that to me, a thousand have said it to me as I have moved about the country. If I have opportunity to engage them further in conversation, they say, "Of course, we know that you cannot govern the circumstances of the case altogether, and it may be necessary, but for God's sake do not do it unless it is necessary."

I am for the time being the spokesman of such people, gentlemen. I have not read history without observing that the greatest forces in the world, and the only permanent forces, are moral forces. We have the evidence of a very competent witness, namely the first Napoleon, who said that, as he looked back in the last days of his life upon so much as he knew of human history, he had to record the judgment that force had never accomplished anything that was permanent.

Force will not accomplish anything that is permanent, I venture to say, in the great struggle which is now going on on the other side of the sea. The permanent things will be accomplished afterward, when the opinion of mankind is brought to bear upon the issues. And the only thing that will hold the world steady is this same silent, insistent, all-powerful opinion of mankind. Force can sometimes hold things steady until opinion has time to form, but no force that was ever exerted, except in response to that opinion, was ever a conquering and predominant force. I think the sentence in American history that I, myself, am proudest of is that in the introductory sentences of the Declaration of Independence, where the writers say that a due respect for the opinion of mankind demands that they state the reasons for what they are about to do. I venture to say that a decent respect for the opinion of mankind demanded that those who started the present European war should have stated their reasons, but they did not pay any heed to the opinion of mankind, and the reckoning will come when the settlement comes.

So, gentlemen, I am willing, no matter what my personal fortunes may be, to play for the verdict of mankind. Personally, it will be a matter of indifference to me what the verdict on the seventh of November is, provided I feel any degree of confidence that, when a later jury sits, I shall get their judgment in my favor. Not in my favor personally—what difference does that make?—but in my favor as an honest and conscientious spokesman of a great nation. There are some gentlemen who are under the delusion that the power of a nation comes from the top. It does not. It comes from the bottom. The power and virtue of the tree does not come from the blossom and the fruit down into the roots, but it comes from the roots in the obscure passages of the earth where the power is derived which displays itself in the blossom and the fruit.

And I know that among the silent, speechless masses of the American people is slowly coming up the great sap of moral purpose and love of justice and reverence for humanity which constitutes the only virtue and distinction of the American people.

Look for your rulers of the future! Can you pick out the families that are going to produce them? Can you pick out the localities that are going to produce them? You have heard what has just been said about Abraham Lincoln.[3] It is singular how touching every reference to Abraham Lincoln is. It always makes you feel that you wish you had been there to help him in some fashion to fight the battles that he was fighting, sometimes almost alone. Could you have predicted, if you had seen Abraham Lincoln's birth and boyhood, where that great ruling figure of the world was going to spring from? I have presided over a university, but I never deceived myself by supposing that, by university processes, you were producing the ruling forces of the world. I knew that all that a university could do, if it knew its business, was to interpret the moral forces of the world and let the young men who sat under its influence know the very truth of truths about where it came from, and that no man could produce it unless he felt in his blood every corpuscle spring into delighted life with the mention of the ideals which have lifted men slowly, oh, how slowly, up the arduous grades that have resisted progress since the world began.

So, gentlemen, I have not come here tonight to do anything but to remind you that you do not constitute the United States, that I do not constitute the United States, that it is something bigger and greater and finer than any of us, that it was born in an ideal.

3 By Colby.

And only by pursuing an ideal in the face of every adverse circumstance will it continue to deserve the beloved name which we love and for which we are ready to die, the name, "America."

T MS (WP, DLC), with many corrections from the text in the New York *World*, July 1, 1916.

To Amos Richards Eno Pinchot

My dear Mr. Pinchot: [The White House] June 30, 1916.

Thank you for your telegram and for the spirit and purpose which prompted it. I feel the force of every suggestion you make and you may be sure I will not yield to any influences except those which seem to indicate the necessity which comes from causes of the most serious sort concerning both our own welfare and that of Mexico.

I greatly appreciated Mrs. Pinchot's visit the other day.
Cordially and sincerely yours,   Woodrow Wilson

TLS (Letterpress Books, WP, DLC).

To Charles William Eliot

My dear Dr. Eliot: The White House June 30, 1916.

I am sure that I need not assure you that no one is more anxious to avoid war with Mexico than I am, and that I warmly appreciate the interesting suggestions contained in your important letter of June twenty-eighth, for which I thank you most sincerely.   Cordially yours,   Woodrow Wilson

TLS (C. W. Eliot Papers, MH-Ar).

To Frederic Clemson Howe

PERSONAL.

My dear Howe: [The White House] June 30, 1916.

Thank you for your note from the Cosmos Club. You may be sure it gave me deep gratification.
Faithfully yours,   Woodrow Wilson

TLS (Letterpress Books, WP, DLC).

From William Charles Adamson

Dear Mr. President: Washington, D. C. June 30, 1916.

I am sorry to say that Dr. Foster on the Rules Committee is not favorable to the kind of a rule we want on the General Dam bill.[1] I wish you would call him up and tell him to please vote with the other Democrats on the Committee. He is willing to vote for a rule to make it in order but he is not willing to limit the time for consideration and we cannot get it considered unless we can limit the time.   Yours truly,   W. C. Adamson

TLS (WP, DLC).

[1] S. 3331, otherwise known as the "Shields bill," about which see the index references in Vol. 36.

From Newton Diehl Baker

Confidential.

My dear Mr. President: Washington. July 1, 1916.

Will you consider the possibility of issuing an address at some future time, to our troops in Mexico and on the border, from you as Commander in Chief, defining the duty of an American Soldier and the spirit in which his task should be undertaken and performed? There are some modern addresses by Commanders in Chief, notably that of the German Emperor to the troops he sent to China, which I should like to see contrasted by a modern statement. He wanted his troops so to conduct themselves that whenever thereafter a Chinaman saw a German he would tremble; we want our boys so to conduct themselves that they will do their task, assuredly, but we would like them to leave an abiding recollection of honorable and fair fighting, and of generous and chivalrous regard for women, children and non-combatants, generally, and of foes who came to help rather than to hurt.

Of course no such address would be timely now, but there is a message and a lesson to mankind in it, if the opportunity should come.   Cordially yours,   Newton D. Baker

TLS (WP, DLC).

From Edward Mandell House

New London,

Dear Governor: New Hampshire. July 1, 1916.

If you continue to make such speeches as at Philadelphia and New York we will not need much of a campaign. You are stirring the hearts of the people in these simple talks.

I do not know that I could pick out any particular part that was better than any other part, but what you said about Lincoln made me feel, and will make everyone feel, that your burdens and his are not unlike and it will make the best that is in America feel that they want to help.

You have also sensed the feeling of the country concerning Mexico. The people do not want war with Mexico. They do not want war with anybody, but least of all with a country like that.

Do you not think that you could approach the problem from the economic side as I once suggested? Could not Naon help in this direction? He is the wisest, the fairest and the best of that group.

There are two things that are appealing to the plain folk of America. One in [is] keeping the country out of war and the other is the Federal Reserve Act. The working people believe that you have taken the financial control away from Wall Street, and that you have done it through that act. They feel that if this law were not in force, the prosperity we are having would be short-lived and that Wall Street by over speculation would reap the benefit and finally bring on a panic.

Affectionately yours,   E. M. House

TLS (WP, DLC).

From Francis Joseph Heney[1]

Los Angeles, Calif., July 1, 1916.

As one of the delegates who left the Republican convention in Chicago four years ago, and participated in the organization of the National Progressive Party, I desire to assure you that it is now my intention earnestly and actively to work for your re-election as President. My admiration and affection for Theodore Roosevelt, and my respect for the opinion of those Republican delegates with whom I participated in organizing the National Progressive Party, and the more than three million voters who endorsed our action at the polls, constrains me to state, with some fullness, my reasons for refusing to support Mr. Charles Hughes as the Republican candidate for President.

Like to [the] platform of the National Progressive Party, that of the Democratic Party four years ago, contained a plank declaring in favor of the direct Presidential preference primary, and in one of your first messages to Congress, you recommended its enactment, in the press, of a vast volume of important remedial

[1] Lawyer and reformer of San Francisco.

legislation. Your recommendation has not yet been carried out by Congress, and the various party platforms are silent on the subject this year.

I have full faith, however, that you will ultimately bring about the enactment of this great reform into law. The Democratic Party, of which you are the head, is not like the Republican Party, in the unfortunate position of having the balance of power in its national convention vested in delegates from a group of states which never have helped to elect its Presidential nominee and which is not expected to do so at any time in the near future. Through your personal efforts as President, most of the other important planks of the National Progressive platform of four years ago have already been enacted into law by Congress. Consequently I feel confident that you can be relied upon, if elected, further to exert your great influence to secure Federal legislation which will require a Presidential preference primary election to be held on the same day in every state in the union for every political party, under the safeguards of law.

Four years ago after the fiasco of nominating Mr. Taft, with the aid of dishonestly seated delegates and of delegates who were representatives of a mere handful of office-holders in the southern states had been perpetuated against them, a majority of the Republican delegates who had been legally elected from those states having a preponderate Republican vote, re-assembled in Chicago and organized the National Progressive Party. The primary and paramount purpose of the organization of the National Progressive Party was to place in the hands of the voters of each and every political party, through the instrumentality of a national direct Presidential preference parimary [primary] law, the power for a majority of the voters of each political party to nominate its candidate for the Presidency. All thoughtful men among the Republican delegates who organized that Progressive movement realized that the manipulation of national political conventions by corrupt methods of invisible government through political bosses constitutes an ever continuing menace to the very existence of the Republic itself. Every serious minded person must realize that a republican government in fact cannot continue to exist under such political conditions. Political freedom is a mockery under a system which permits a few unscrupulous manipulators and corruptors to defeat the will of millions of voters in any political party by substituting the will of those few for the will of the voters. To continue such a political system means to invite and promote the ultimate destruction of the republic.

By depriving Roosevelt of the Republican nomination four years ago, Senator Boise Penrose, of Pennsylvania; Murray Crane, then senator of Massachusetts, and William B. Barnes, of New York, with the aid of such men as Elihu Root, who was the permanent chairman of the convention, continued their control of their Republican National Committee and thus prolonged their power again to defeat the will of the majority of the republican voters. And they have now once more insured their control of the Republican National Committee for another four years, with the continuance of their power to again defeat the will of the republican voters in 1920 and thereafter indefinitely, so long as we are without a Presidential preference primary law. Under the circumstances, I cannot follow Theodore Roosevelt back into the Republican Party, while it is still controlled by those same men. If he had accepted the nomination of the Progressive Party at Chicago this year, I would have loyally and vigorously supported him, because he then would have represented the basic principle upon which the Progressive Party was founded, to wit, the right of the majority of voters of each political party to nominate its own candidate for President, without any few men possessing the power to prevent it.

It is reasonably certain that Mr. Hughes was not the first choice of a majority of the aggregate of Republican and Progressive voters in the United States. Hughes represents merely the consent of Penrose, Crane and Barnes, to permit the Republican Party to have as its candidate a man selected by themselves, who, therefore, if elected President would be disinclined to attempt to destroy the continuance of their control of the nominating machinery of the Republican Party, and their power thus to reward him with renomination for another term.

To my mind the nomination of Mr. Hughes represents the fruition of the political corruption which was also successfully practiced by the Republican National committee four years ago, under the guidance of the men I have named. For that reason I cannot vote for or support him. I do not question the personal integrity or character of Mr. Hughes, but I do condemn him unqualifiedly for permitting professional political tricksters to make a nation-wide canvass for his nomination while he was a member of the Supreme Court of the United States, under an appointment for life with the vast potential power which accompanies that position. Personally I shall not vote for any republican candidate for President hereafter, as long as the corrupt control of the nominating machine of the Republican Party is permitted thus to continue in existence.

Please permit me, also at this time, to offer my heartiest approval of the policy of your administration towards Mexico. It se[e]ms to me that you have consistently and amid great difficulties and discouragements, striven to treat that unfortunate neighboring nation with that patience and forbearance which one powerful and enlightened nation ought to exercise toward a much less powerful and much less generally enlightened nation, and from which it has already acquired partly through conquest and partly through purchase a magnificent empire of territory and natural resources and, in the minds of whose people, therefore, there must naturally exist apprehension as to the unselfishness of our motives and the disinterestedness of our actions. This must be apparent to any citizen of our own country who stops for a moment to consider the fact that under the dictatorship of Diaz, Americans, as well as other foreign capitalists, acquired the control and ownership of vast natural resources of fabulous value in Mexico. No patriotic citizen can fail to pray that we shall be delivered from the necessity of entering into a war with the distracted people who inhabit Mexico.

But finally, if no other course shall lie open to us, I shall realize that you in the full performance of your duty have done everything within your power to prevent such an issue.

Your temperate restrained but lofty exercise of the powerful weapons of diplomacy have kept this country safely out of the terrible struggle in Europe, without any sacrifice of American honor or prestige, and you have wrung the most important concessions from belligerent foreign rulers while steadfastly maintaining the dignity, peace and safety of the United States. Arguments that we should replace experience with inexperience in this vital field will be without avail.

The legislative accomplishments of your administration constitute a record little short of marvelous. In three short years your administration has wrested the financial control from Wall Street and lodged it with the people, thus rendering future trust-creating panics and manipulation practically impossible. You have provided an Income tax for the raising of revenue, thus placing the burdens of government where they belong and where they can best be borne; you are providing a non-partisan tariff commission as advocated in the National Progressive platform of 1912, that will take the tariff out of partisan politics where it has long been an agency for evil. I might also speak of other important enactments, such as the Trade Commission law, the Clayton anti-trust law, the Agricultural Expansion [Extension] Act, the Industrial Employees Arbitration Act, the extension of the Parcels Post system, the driving of the notorious lobby out of Washington, the consummation of the Constitutional amendment providing for election of United States senators by the people, and scores of other pieces of important legislation, for which the country is largely indebted to you and your administration.

I trust that you will feel free to call upon me to aid in any way that I can in your reelection to the Presidency next November.

Sincerely,   Francis J. Heney.

T telegram (WP, DLC).

From Warren Worth Bailey

My Dear Mr. President: Washington, D. C. July 1, 1916.

Permit me to congratulate you on the fine spirit of your addresses in Philadelphia and New York and to express the hope that the obvious way out of the delicate Mexican situation may be taken with the least possible delay.

Our troops on Mexican soil are a continuing menace to good understanding, a certain invitation to a recurrence of incidents similar to that which took place at Carrizal. Their mission has been fulfilled. They have already dispersed the bandits after whom they were sent. It seems that if patrol duty alone is required, this can be better done at the border and within our own territory than two or three hundred miles below the international boundary. At all events troop movements should be northward rather than in any direction which may tend to excite the apprehensions of the people of Mexico.

Nothing can be more certain than that the continued operation of American armed forces upon Mexican soil will eventuate in a breach of our friendly relations with the distracted republic which we should be helping toward the solution of its difficult and perplexing problems rather than adding to them. We can lose nothing in dignity or in honor by doing a just thing in the removal of a disturbing factor which is under our control.

I am emboldened to address this letter to you by your own lofty words and by the sentiments they imply. I believe with you that "America should be ready in every point of policy and of action to vindicate at whatever cost the principles of liberty, of justice and of humanity to which we have been devoted from the first * * * * It comes high. It is not an easy thing to do. It is easy to think first of the material interests of America, but it is not easy to think first of what America, if she loves justice, ought to do in the field of international affairs. I believe that at whatever cost America should be just to other peoples and treat other peoples as she demands that they should treat her." Brave words voicing high thoughts! Their appeal can not fail to reach the heart of the great masses of our countrymen who have no sordid interest to subserve by the bringing on of war with our distracted and unhappy neighbor.

It seems to me that you must have the sympathy and the cordial and enthusiastic support of the great plain people in this magnanimous and entirely just position. I am certain that the vast majority of Americans do not want war. They have loved you because you have stood for peace, because you have stood between the country and those who for selfish and sordid reasons would have dragged it into the vortex of that horrible maelstrom of blood in which Europe is being engulfed. They will love you with even a more consuming passion if you shall bring your great powers to bear in averting the breach with Mexico which has been so threatening ever since American troops began their operations on the soil of that unhappy and hapless land.

This is but a feeble and halting expression of what I feel and hope, but may I not trust that you will receive it in the spirit which animates me in writing? I am anxious as a public servant, anxious as a citizen, that we shall not sully the flag by having it stained with the blood of a people who, as a people, have done us no hurt and have dreamed of none.

Yours sincerely,   Warren Worth Bailey

TLS (WP, DLC).

From Manuel Castro Quesada[1]

Washington, D. C.,
My dear Mr. President: July the first of 1916

It is so unusual, so difficult, to find among the leaders of peoples one who says what he thinks and who does what he says—particularly in this epoch of bankruptcy in the principles controlling world conduct—that I find myself unable to resist the impulse to say to you, in offering my warmest congratulations, that in you if the coming November should find this country submerged beneath the horrors of war, your triumph at the Presidential polls may be counted upon as an accomplished fact.

Nevertheless, so complete and perfect is your devotion to principles that, for you, not even a political triumph is sufficiently weighty or enslaving incentive to induce you to turn aside from the path which your conscience counsels you to follow.

As a fellow of humanity, as a citizen of the world, and laying aside for the moment the diplomatic character with which I am invested, I beg that you will honor me by accepting my respectful expressions of admiration for your present course.

Very sincerely yours   Manuel Castro Quesada

ALS (WP, DLC).
[1] Costa Rican Minister to the United States.

From James Alphonsus Hamill

Washington, D. C., July 1, 1916.

I take the liberty to solicit you who are a lover and champion of justice to use all the power of your great office that you can properly exert to intercede in behalf of Sir Roger Casement, recently condemned to be executed, and confidently assure you that this petition represents the heartfelt desire of a great portion of the American people who will gratefully appreciate your noble and generous action.   James A. Hamill

T telegram (WP, DLC).

From William Bauchop Wilson

My dear Mr. President: Washington July 1st, 1916.

I am enclosing you herewith copies of telegrams recently exchanged between General Carranza, First Chief, Constitutionalist Government of Mexico, and President Gompers of the American Federation of Labor, which I know you will be very much interested in.[1]   Faithfully yours,   W B Wilson

TLS (WP, DLC).
[1] S. Gompers to V. Carranza, June 28, 1916; V. Carranza to S. Gompers, June 29, 1916; and S. Gompers to V. Carranza, June 30, 1916, all TC telegrams (WP, DLC). Gompers appealed to Carranza on June 28 to release the American soldiers captured at Carrizal in order to avoid war; Carranza replied on the 29th that he had ordered their release, whereupon Gompers expressed his appreciation.

From John Clinton Parker[1]

Philadelphia, Pa., July 1, 1916.

Your New York speech tempts me to support you. Will you meet a committee of progressive engineers face to face and satisfy them regarding your course in Mexico? How can we attain the fine ideals you express so well if we fail to protect the fellow citizens along our border? Will we not rot away in peace if we fail to protect our extremities? Has Carranza the right to protect highwaymen? Have you the right to sacrifice the people along our border and block the scientific engineering development of Mexico merely to check exploitation and profit for those who do the work.   John Clinton Parker.

T telegram (WP, DLC).
[1] Engineer and president of the Pardel Corp. of Philadelphia, which produced steam boilers designed by himself; editor of *Lefax*, a monthly magazine of business comment, and of *Lefax Technical Data Sheets*.

To Edward Mandell House

My dearest Friend,   The White House. 2 July, 1916.

Your recent letters throw a great deal of light upon the stupidity of English opinion, the brave struggle a few men and a few journals are making to set it right and throw a little real intelligence into the discussion of the things that lie at the very foundation of the peace and right administration of the world.

Buxton has tried, and is still trying, to see me, but I have not thought it wise to meet any member of Parliament or to deal directly in any way with representatives of particular views over there. Do you not think I am right in that judgment?

Undoubtedly you are right about What Page oought [ought] to accomplish and might accomplish if he were to follow the same course that Penfield follows and that even Gerard would follow if he recognized the occasion. I wish that I could bring Page back, as Secretary of Agriculture, for example, in the place of Houston when Houston is promoted to some one or other of the many posts in which he is needed.

As to the expediency of having the press of *any* foreign country urge the international importance of my re-election, I am clearly of the opinion that it would do much more harm than good. Suppose, for instance, that the press of one of the Allies should press that point, would not a chance be created for this situation to be made to appear to exist: that in Hughes we had a candidate of Germany's choosing and in me a candidate of the Allies' choosing? That would never do. I hope they can be persuaded to let our politics alone.

The fact that my views expressed in the address to the League to Enforce Peace have been embodied in the platform ought, I should think, to give them immensely increased importance. That ought to soak in on the other side, with all parties to the war.

As to the Governorship of the Federal Reserve Board, I think I shall reappoint Hamlin *for one year*, and give the matter of the future selection of Governors time to be worked out. Hamlin is the only man on the Board who *is* fit to be Governor. The others entertain the opinion of him which they have expressed to you because he has so often differed with them in judgment.

It is a difficult matter, which I think it would be unwise for me to decide amidst so many other pressing things of greater consequence. Hence my determination to give myself a year's time.

I wonder what you think of the general situation as to party politics and my re-election? The selection of Willcox is of a piece with everything else Hughes has so far done. It means nothing; or, rather, if it means anything, it means that Hughes is compromising with the influences which I expect ultimately to pull him down.

My experience at the New York Press Club dinner on Friday was intensely interesting. I never before attended a dinner in New York at which the atmosphere seemed to me so thoughtfully serious or the sentiment so genuine, or so friendly to me and what I have attempted to represent and accomplish.

What is the line of the fighting going to be? It is already quite evident that they can get nowhere on the line of attacking our foreign policy. The average man is satisfied with its results.

All join in affectionate messages.

Affectionately Yours,   Woodrow Wilson

WWTLS (E. M. House Papers, CtY).

To William Bauchop Wilson

My dear Mr. Secretary: [The White House] July 3, 1916

Thank you for letting me see the telegrams exchanged between Mr. Gompers and General Carranza. They are certainly most interesting and throw an unexpected sidelight on the man.

With warm regard,

Sincerely yours,   Woodrow Wilson

TLS (Letterpress Books, WP, DLC).

To Warren Worth Bailey

My dear Mr. Bailey: The White House July 3, 1916

Thank you warmly for your candid and interesting letter of July first, to the spirit and purpose of which, I need not tell you, I heartily subscribe. There are many matters of judgment which must puzzle all of us in handling this delicate Mexican situation, and I warmly appreciate such contributions to the formation of a judgment as letters like yours supply me with.

Cordially and sincerely yours,   Woodrow Wilson

TLS (W. W. Bailey Papers, NjP).

To Cleveland Hoadley Dodge

My dear Cleve: The White House July 3, 1916

I do not know when I have been more touched or encouraged than by your letter of June twenty-ninth. Thank you for it, my dear fellow, from the bottom of my heart.

I cannot tell you how often I think of you or how happy it makes me to think of your generous support and friendship. These are hard days, but such friendship makes them easy to bear.   Affectionately yours,   Woodrow Wilson

TLS (WC, NjP).

To John Clinton Parker

My dear Sir: The White House July 3, 1916.

Your letter of July first interests me very much. I have never at any time questioned our duty to protect our fellow-citizens along the border or to shut out and punish highwaymen, and I have sought in every way to protect the legitimate interests of citizens of the United States in Mexico. But the process is not as simple as it looks, and the point of my New York speech was that there is a difference between self-protection and aggressive warfare.

I am sincerely obliged to you for your message.

Very truly yours,   Woodrow Wilson

TLS (received from Jessica Lobel).

To Martin David Foster

My dear Doctor Foster: [The White House] July 3, 1916

I think you will know how interested I am in what is known as the General Dam Bill, and I hope that you will not think I am taking too great a liberty in asking you if you would not be kind enough to favor a rule which would limit debate upon the measure and give it a chance for passage this session. It seems to me of very great consequence to the industry of the country. I beg that you will pardon me if I ask too much.

Cordially and sincerely yours,   Woodrow Wilson

TLS (Letterpress Books, WP, DLC).

To Amos Richards Eno Pinchot
and Gertrude Minturn Pinchot

My dear Friends: [The White House] July 3, 1916

That was an exceedingly generous telegram you were gracious enough to send me on the first,[1] and I thank you for it with all my heart. I am ambitious to deserve such confidence as you repose in me.

Cordially and sincerely yours,   Woodrow Wilson

TLS (Letterpress Books, WP, DLC).
[1] It is missing in both WP, DLC, and the A. Pinchot Papers, DLC.

From Robert Lansing

My dear Mr. President,   Washington July 3, 1916.

In view of your request this morning for a memorandum on the policy to be adopted in regard to Mexico I will endeavor to present an idea which is not new but which in the present circumstances I think may be worked out in a new way.

The idea is simply the naming of a joint American-Mexican Commission of four or six members to study the various questions relating to the boundary troubles and the necessary means to prevent them in the future.

If the Carrizal incident was a clear case of Mexican aggression I doubt if I would be favorable to this policy, but it appears to me that Captain Boyd was possibly to blame. At least there is sufficient contradiction in the statements of those present to put us on inquiry as to the facts before taking drastic action.

In regard to the creation and work of a joint commission I would offer the following suggestions:

1st. The proposal should be made by the *de facto* Government in answering our note of June 25th as evidence of its friendly intentions. (I feel convinced that this can be accomplished through Arredondo and through the financial agent of Carranza, Dr. Rendon.[1] In fact I know the latter is already making representations to his chief in favor of a commission of some sort).

2nd. The Commission should be composed of an equal number of Americans and Mexicans, and should sit in Washington as soon as possible.

3rd. The members should be diplomatic commissioners clothed with formal powers to negotiate a protocol or protocols *ad referendum* and to make joint or several reports.

4th The subjects to be considered by the Commission should embrace—

(a) The Carrizal incident.

(b) The raids which have taken place across the border.

(c) The general state of lawlessness and brigandage which has prevailed in Mexican territory contiguous to the international boundary.

(d) The treatment of Mexican citizens on the American side of the boundary.

(e) Efficient means of suppressing the lawless elements and restoring peace and safety by cooperation of the military and civil authorities of the two countries.

(f) The right to pursue marauders within a fixed or flexible zone without regard to territorial sovereignty, the pursuers to be properly restricted in dealing with the civil and military authorities of the other country.

(g) The use of the railroads in exercising the right of pursuit.

(h) A cooperative scheme of border protection which will insure safety to life and property.

(i) Any other pertinent subject which will aid in the accomplishment of the ends desired.

Subjects *a, b, c* and *d* should be covered by a report or reports. The other subjects, included in a protocol or protocols

5th. Until the Commission has met and completed its labors and the Governments have acted upon their reports and protocols, the *status quo* as to American troops in Mexico should continue, and in case of raids into American territory American military authorities should be permitted to cross the boundary in "hot pursuit" of the raiders.

This in crude form is the general scheme which I have in mind as offering a possible amicable solution of the present difficulty.

At the same time I would not abate for one hour the military preparation which we are making for this effort at peaceable settlement may in the end fail. If it does, we ought to be fully prepared—and I think that we will be by the time the Commission completes its work. We certainly would be better off than we are now if force is necessary. I believe too that our increasing show of strength would have a saluatory [salutary] effect on the negotiations. It is what the Mexicans appreciate better than anything else.   Faithfully yours   Robert Lansing

ALS (WP, DLC).

¹ Dr. Victor A. Rendon, attorney for the Comision Reguladora del Mercado de Henequen (Regulatory Commission for the Henequen [sisal] Market), at this time in New York.

From Robert Lansing, with Enclosure

PERSONAL AND CONFIDENTIAL:

My dear Mr. President: Washington July 3, 1916.

I enclose for your consideration a confidential memorandum which Mr. Phillips left with me and which I intended to give you at the last Cabinet Meeting, but overlooked it.

Faithfully yours,   Robert Lansing

TLS (WP, DLC).

E N C L O S U R E

A Memorandum by William Phillips

CONFIDENTIAL MEMO.   June 29, 1916.

Mr. Barclay showed me this afternoon copies of telegrams from Mr. Hohler to the British Ambassador, dated June 28th, in substance to the effect that:

1. If there is to be a real war with genuine hostilities and effective measures, the British interests on the coast will not be seriously endangered; but that if a peaceful blockade is contemplated local spirit will be stirred up, more especially in ports where American ships would be visible. Mr. Hohler adds that in case of the above peaceful blockade he sees little hope of saving oil fields;

2. Mr. Hohler is of the opinion that it would be desirable not to have a U. S. ship go to Tuxpam unless the U. S. Government has in contemplation serious and broad action, in which case rapidity is the essential point to protect the wells. He adds that a warship of any nationality would have the same effect;

3. Being in doubt as to the attitude of General Tejada at Tuxpam,¹ Mr. Hohler made inquiry of the Mexican Foreign Office and was given a definite statement that oil wells would be protected up to the last by every means in their power, but that they will destroy them rather than have them fall into the hands of the Americans.   W Phillips.

TS MS (WP, DLC).
[1] Col. Adalberto Tejeda, *Carrancista* military commander in the State of Veracruz.

From Edward Mandell House, with Enclosure

Dear Governor:

New London,
New Hampshire. July 3, 1916.

I am enclosing you a copy of a letter just received from Lord Loreburn.

Loreburn has assured me that he will cooperate with you in any way you desire when the times comes and that we could count upon him to make a strong speech in the House of Lords.

I am enclosing a copy of a letter from Jacob Shiff.[1] He is very anxious for Mr. Robinson's appointment. Robinson is a Jew who has had charge of a society for lending funds to needy farmers and is familiar with the duties required. I think, however, there is danger of overdoing the recognition of the Jews.

Affectionately yours,   E. M. House

TLS (WP, DLC).
[1] J. H. Schiff to EMH, June 30, 1916, TCL (WP, DLC). Schiff reiterated his desire that Leonard George Robinson, general manager of the Jewish Agricultural and Industrial Aid Society, be given a position in one of the land banks to be set up under the Federal Farm Loan Act of 1916.

E N C L O S U R E

Robert Threshie Reid, Earl Loreburn,
to Edward Mandell House

My dear Colonel House:

Deal. June 13, 1916.

I am very much obliged for the copy of President Wilson's speech which I had not seen.

It is a very powerful speech and I need not say how much I agree in the thought of conference and arbitration instead of war, which underlies it all. I do not see my way to "common force," not because it is in itself objectionable but because the carrying of it out must depend upon fidelity to treaty engagements, and the proved infidelity of so many nations in the past leaves little hope of their adherence to such engagements in the future.

And I feel that the honorable nations might be called on to interfere in arms possibly against their own friends, while the dishonorable nations would snap their fingers when called on to carry out their promises. But I will not pursue that theme.

But possibly the President has some ideas of his own and I shall be deeply interested when he unfolds them. He will I hope render priceless services to the cause of common sense when the nations meet in council to consider the future of mankind.

My idea is that the *people* will take things more into their own hands on the Continent of Europe when peace comes.

With kind wishes from,

Your very sincere,   Loreburn.

I enclose a print of a letter I have just published in the Economist[1] which may interest you.   L.

TCL (WP, DLC).
[1] House did not send this enclosure to Wilson. However, it was Loreburn to the Editor, June 7, 1916, printed in *The Economist*, LXXXII (June 10, 1916), 1109-10.

From Herbert Bayard Swope[1]

My dear Mr. President: New York July 3, 1916.

In behalf of the members and the Board of Trustees of the Press Club, as Chairman of the Dinner Committee, I beg to thank you warmly for your attendance at the dinner and for the speech you made there. It was singularly human in its appeal and so frank and manly in its sentiments that it made a profound impression. I say this not as a matter of opinion, but as a result of observation among some of our Republican and likewarm [lukewarm] Democratic guests. And, if I may be pardoned the liberty, let me add that David Belasco[2] himself could not have staged a dramatic climax better or more sincerely than you did when you shook hands with Bainbridge Colby after his speech, which was unusually interesting.

All of us were delighted that Mrs. Wilson was able also to be our guest.

Personally, I thought the pleasant compliments you paid each of the other speakers were well deserved, for I cannot recall offhand any public dinner that I have ever attended at which the speaking was of such a distinctive order.

I am sure that a few more talks, such as you made to us, will remove any doubts as to your re-election, and with the hope that this thought may be translated into truth on November 7th, I beg to remain,   In sincerity,   Herbert Bayard Swope

TLS (WP, DLC).
[1] City editor of the New York *World*.
[2] The well-known theatrical dramatist, director, and producer.

Joseph Patrick Tumulty to Rudolph Forster

Asbury Park, N. J., July 3, 1916.

In case Congressmen or other prominent men write or telegraph asking President to intercede in case of Sir Roger Casement please send following form reply: "The President wishes me to acknowledge receipt your telegram in the case of Sir Roger Casement and requests me to say that he will seek the earliest opportunity to discuss this matter with the Secretary of State. Of course he will give the suggestion you make the consideration which its great importance merits."   Joseph P. Tumulty

T telegram (WP, DLC).

Walter Hines Page to Robert Lansing

London. July 3, 1916.

4521. CONFIDENTIAL. Your 3483, July first.[1]

I fear that a request made to the British Government in this matter will produce very disagreeable impression. Not only does Casement, a British subject, stand convicted of treason but I am privately informed that much information about him of an unspeakably filthy character was withheld from publicity. If the Government will permit me to deliver his sister's telegram they will permit Doyle. I respectfully suggest that she can send it to Doyle. Thus the same result will be accomplished and our Government will not become the channel of communication. If all the facts about Casement ever become public it will be well that our Government had nothing to do with him or his case even indirectly.   Page.

T telegram (WP, DLC).
    [1] "Please transmit following message to Foreign Office for communication to Sir Roger Casement, with approval of British authorities: Quote. Keep up dear heart, my dearest brother. Am doing everything possible. Love. End quote." RL to WHP, T telegram (SDR, RG 59, 841.00/17a, DNA).

An Address at the Dedication of the American Federation of Labor Building[1]

[July 4, 1916]

Mr. Secretary, Mr. Gompers, and my fellow citizens: Mr. Gompers is generally very happy in his choice of words, but he used

    [1] Delivered on an open air platform at the Federation's new headquarters building at Ninth Street and Massachusetts Avenue, N.W., in Washington, before an audience estimated at 10,000 persons. William B. Wilson and Samuel Gompers also spoke. *Washington Post*, July 5, 1916.

one word just now from which I wish to demur. I am not here to adorn the occasion, but I am here to express my very deep interest in it and to show how near it lies to my own heart that the legitimate objects of the great labor movement should be achieved.

It seems to me that it is a happy conjunction of time and occasion, because we should never make any new move or establish any new instrumentality which will affect the national life without thinking of the national life and how it will be affected and how we can serve it. It is very proper that this great building should in this wise be dedicated on the birthday of the nation. You know, my fellow citizens, that the mind needs air to breathe, just as the body does. You cannot rise to the tasks of the day with any kind of zest and interest unless you know their significance; and they have a very narrow significance if you merely look upon them as a means of keeping body and soul together. It seems to me, therefore, that the most heartening thing that a man can do is to think, as often as he can, of the relation which his work bears to the place he lives in, to the state he lives in, and to the country he lives in. You know that every man, who is a man, takes some pride in doing his work well, but why should he take pride in it? Merely to glorify and distinguish himself from the common run of workers? That will only make a prig of him. A man who works in order that he may be distinguished is sooner or later going to do some selfish thing that will disgrace him, because his object is himself and not the ideals which he serves. And, therefore, it seems to me that every one of us should remind himself every day that he is working for something besides wages; that he is working for some persons whom he loves, for some community that he wishes to assist, for some nation that he is ready to serve and defend. That is the reason why it seems to me that this is a happy conjunction of day and occasion. Because, my fellow citizens, you will realize that in a position, such as I occupy for the time being, I am not at liberty to think of any one class of our fellow citizens to the exclusion of any other class. And since I have been asked to make the dedicatory address of this building, I am going to take the liberty of dedicating it to common counsel and a common understanding. I am going to take the liberty of dedicating it to the thing that I believe in most —the accommodation of the interests of various classes in the community by means of enabling those classes to understand one another and cooperate with one another.

The way we generally strive for rights is by getting our fighting blood up, and I venture to say that that is the long way and not the short way. If you come at me with your fists doubled, I think I can promise you that mine will double as fast as yours. But if you come at me and say, "Let us sit down and take counsel together and, if we differ with one another, understand why it is that we differ with one another, just what the points at issue are," we will presently find that we are not so far apart after all—that the points in which we differ are few and the points in which we agree are many, and that if we only have the patience and the candor and the desire to get together, we will get together.

The trouble in a great many of the labor contests we have had, my fellow citizens, as you will bear me out in saying, is that one side or the other side did not wish to sit down and talk it over, and that the great difficulty in the settlement of a great many labor disputes has been the difficulty of getting candid and dispassionate conference with regard to the points at issue. The great difficulty about the relationship between capital and labor is this: Labor is in immediate contact with the task itself—with the work, with the conditions of the work, with the tools with which it is done, and the circumstances under which they are used; whereas, capital, in too many instances, is at a great remove. It is owned and controlled by many who have not taken the pains to go and see the workers at their work and know just what the circumstances are. And the thing most to be desired is that capital should be humanized by being brought into a comprehending contact with the conditions of labor. You have seen what has happened in some instances. You have seen men, who had sat in their offices in some great city and directed the use of capital, presently realize that they did not know how it was being used and themselves go to the factory which their capital operated or the mines which were worked by the use of their capital; themselves don overalls and go into the bowels of the earth or through, it may be, the greasy processes of the factory, and come out with an entirely different range of comprehension as to what it was all about and a signally increased capacity to understand the point of view of the man who was actually doing the work. That is the kind of thing which I like to see done, and that is the kind of thing that we ought to talk about on the Fourth of July.

The Fourth of July was a day when a great union was formed, but it was not a union of any one class or body of persons in that little nation of three millions that formed it. It was a union of all the people for common objects. And no man is a true American who does not realize that all the objects of our national life are common objects, and not separate objects. But it is easy to say, my fellow citizens, and it is very hard to put it into practice. A great many men come to see me and tell me a great many things, some of which I believe. But if I were to listen with greater comprehension than I have to everything that they tell me, I would realize, when the day's work was over, that I could not hold in my single comprehension the infinitely varied, complex life of this great country to which we belong. It takes a multitude of minds to comprehend the United States, and that is the reason that I think a building like this should be devoted to the processes which pool our understandings. Nobody has got enough by himself to run the country. We have got to pool our understandings, and, with regard to every problem which affects labor, this great building ought to be the place to pool our understandings. Every counsel that goes forth from these offices should be a counsel of confidence, of mutual comprehension, if possible of mutual accommodation; because every one of us has some part in the infinitely difficult task of driving this nation as a team, not as a body of contesting elements. We ought to be all comprehended in one spiritual organization from which no individual or group of individuals will allow himself or itself to be torn away.

You know we used to hear very ornate orations on the Fourth of July. All the highly colored words of the very varied vocabulary of our great language were called into commission on that day to glorify the Stars and Stripes, and I remember that, when I was younger and had been immersed in fewer difficulties than recently, I used to thrill to those words and think they meant something. But I know now that rhetoric does not get to the heart of it. Flag after flag went by in that procession just now. Every one of those flags ought to have suggested to every one of us that we have not yet fulfilled the full conscientious duty of America in understanding each other and, through comprehension of each other, understanding and serving the world. America did not come into existence to make one more great nation in the family of nations—to show its strength and to exercise mastery. America opened her doors to everybody who wanted to be free and to have the same opportunity that everybody else had to make the most of his faculties and his opportunities, and America will retain its greatness only so long as it retains and seeks to realize those ideals. No man ought to suffer injustice in America. No man ought in America to fail to see the deep dictates of humanity.

Mr. Gompers was referring just now to the sixth section of the Clayton Anti-trust law, the section in which the obvious is stated, namely, that a man's labor is not a commodity but a part of his life, and that, therefore, the courts must not treat it as if it were a commodity, but must treat it as if it were a part of his life. I am sorry that there were any judges in the United States who had to be told that. It is so obvious that it seems to me that that section of the Clayton Act were a return to the primer of human liberty. But if judges have to have the primer opened before them, I am willing to open it. If any part of the United States, through habit, through ancient prejudice, through long addiction to technical ideas, insists upon living in an age, which everybody else with his eyes open knows has gone by, why, then, we have got to sound some great note that will wake them up. But wake them up always to the same thing, with which we should thrill as well as others—that it is take as well as give; that the other man has as much right as we have; that we are not to seek for an advantage but for an equality; that, though we have been put upon, we do not desire to see any other man put upon, or any other class, but that we should all have as our highest ideal merely to bask in that only nourishing sun that has ever shone upon the human heart—the sun of justice and of truth and of humanity.

Mr. Gompers spoke just now, and I dare say truthfully, as if it were somewhat a matter of surprise that the President of the United States should recognize the great labor movement by his presence on an occasion like this. I am sorry for any President of the United States who does not recognize every great movement in the nation. The minute he stops recognizing it, he has become a back number. And how anybody could overlook this movement, I cannot imagine—a movement so fraught with all sorts of things that appeal to the reason and to the heart. You cannot go deep into any argument with a workingman interested in the rights of other workingmen, as well as his own, without finding that a deep emotion underlies the argument. And, my fellow citizens, I want to remind you that we are governed by our emotions very much more than we are governed by our reason. It is a very dangerous fact, but a very profoundly interesting one, that a man follows his heart more often than he follows his head, and, when he follows his heart, it is of primary importance that his heart should be right and not wrong. Somebody said to me once that this was the day in which mind was monarch, and I replied that, if that was true, I ventured to say that mind was one of those modern monarchs that reigned but did not govern; that, as a matter of fact, we were governed by a great popular assembly made up of the passions, and that the most we could effect was that the handsome passions should be in a working majority. It is the business, therefore, of every organization like the American Federation of Labor to see to it that the handsome passions have a working majority and to summon everybody with whom they deal to put their best representative handsome passions into the conference, so that heart may meet with heart, as well as mind with mind, and one great emotion shall at once sway and unite us —the emotion of a mutual affection and a mutual comprehension.

T MS (WP, DLC).

To Francis Joseph Heney

[The White House] July 4, 1916.

Your telegram of July second I need hardly say gives me sincere satisfaction, not only because of the support it so generously promises, but also because of the added emphasis it contributes to the real issues of the campaign and the objects which all true friends of popular government should keep most prominently in mind. I am glad you have given such prominence in your kind message to the question of the Presidential Primary. I have, of course, never lost sight of it, even when many other matters of constructive legislation were pressing for early action. The delay in effecting legislation has been due to the many practical difficulties which have disclosed themselves in the attempt to frame adequate and workable laws. I shall welcome your advice and assistance in surmounting those difficulties. Meantime the voters of the country are not likely to lose sight of the immediate necessity of seeing to it that those who have tried personally to conduct and control our choices of Presidents and of policies should not again get command of either the executive or the legislative branches of the Government. With much appreciation of your characteristic candor and independence,

Woodrow Wilson.

T telegram (Letterpress Books, WP, DLC).

To Manuel Castro Quesada

My dear Mr. Minister: [The White House] July 4, 1916

Your letter of July first has given me the deepest gratification and I want to thank you for it most warmly and sincerely. It does me more than justice in its great generosity, but I think I can say that it does not misinterpret my principles and my earnest desires in this time of stress and temptation.

With warm regard and appreciation,

Cordially and sincerely yours,   Woodrow Wilson

TLS (Letterpress Books, WP, DLC).

To Newton Diehl Baker

My dear Baker: [The White House] July 4, 1916

Thank you for the suggestion about a possible address to the troops on the border. If a proper occasion should offer, I think it an admirable suggestion and shall certainly keep it in mind.

Cordially and faithfully yours, Woodrow Wilson

TLS (Letterpress Books, WP, DLC).

From Martin David Foster

My dear Mr. President: Washington, D. C. July 4, 1916.

I am in receipt of your kind letter of July 3d, and in reply beg to say, I shall be pleased to cooperate in securing the passage of the General Dam Bill. A rule limiting general debate to two hours and then consideration of the bill under the five minute rule has already been reported by the Committee on Rules. I do not think there will be any difficulty in passing the bill in a very short time. There is no reason why it should not be speedily passed under this arrangement.

If a disposition is shown on the part of Members of the House to delay the passage of this bill, I shall be pleased to vote for a rule to pass it without further delay.

Beg to assure you again, I shall gladly cooperate in bringing this matter to an early conclusion.[1]

Yours very truly, M. D. Foster.

TLS (WP, DLC).

[1] On March 21, 1916, the House Committee on Interstate and Foreign Commerce had reported on the Shields bill (S. 3331). The committee struck out all but the enacting clause of S. 3331 and substituted for it an entirely new bill which protected the public interest in water-power development much more adequately than did the original measure. For the committee report and the full text of the substitute bill, see 64th Cong., 1st sess., House Report No. 404. It was this new bill on which the House began debate on July 5 under the rule mentioned by Foster in the above letter. The House passed the revised bill on July 14. The Senate refused to accept the substitute bill and asked for a conference committee on July 15. On February 13, 1917, in the second session of the Sixty-fourth Congress, the conference committee declared itself deadlocked over the House and Senate versions of the bill. The two houses then appointed a second conference committee but it, too, was unable to reach any agreement before the end of the Sixty-fourth Congress on March 4, 1917. See *Cong. Record*, 64th Cong., 1st sess., pp. 10446-70, 10833-44, 10971-76, 11058, 11123, 11401; *ibid.*, 2d sess., 3187-89, 3213-15, 3423, 3692-97.

From John Adams Wilson

My dear Woodrow, Franklin, Pa. July 4th, '16

A letter from my friend (and your friend also) G. W. Megeath[1] this morning has the following—

"A box will be received at The White House from Omaha, in the near future, consigned to the President from Mr. John A. Wilson. It will contain twelve good sized bottles of good old *Scotch* and I hope it will enable the President to survive the coming campaign in first class shape."

When this box reaches you it is to our friend and not to me that you may send a line. With love from all to all

Affectionately yours   Jno. A. Wilson.

ALS (WP, DLC).

[1] George W. Megeath, president of the Sheridan Coal Co. of Omaha, Neb.

From Robert Lansing, with Enclosure

PERSONAL AND CONFIDENTIAL:

My dear Mr. President: Washington July 5, 1916.

Here is a translation of the Mexican answer to our notes of June 20th and 25th.

I believe from the tone of this note that the suggestion in my letter of the 3rd instant may possibly be worked out. Just how we should approach the Mexican Government on the subject I am not quite sure. Would you think it advisable for me to talk the matter over with Mr. Arredondo informally?

Faithfully yours,   Robert Lansing

TLS (WP, DLC).

E N C L O S U R E

Eliseo Arredondo to Robert Lansing

Mr. Secretary: Washington, D. C. July 4, 1916.

I have the honor to transcribe herein below the text of a note I have just received from my Government with instructions to deliver it to Your Excellency:

"Mr. Secretary:

With reference to the notes dated the twentieth and twenty-fifth of the month of June just passed, I have the honor to say to your Excellency that the immediate release of the Carrizal prisoners was additional evidence of the sincerity of this Government's desire to arrive at a peaceful and satisfactory adjustment of the present difficulties. This Government is anxious to solve the present conflict and any erroneous interpretation put upon its attitude would be unfair.

"It was also the Mexican Government [which] studiously suggested during the Ciudad Juarez and El Paso Conferences a plan for cantonments along the boundary line. This Government is now, as it has always been, disposed to seek an immediate solution of the two points which constitute the true causes of the conflict between the two countries, viz: the American Government thinks and rightfully so that the insecurity of its border is the source of difficulties and for its part, the Mexican Government regards the stay of the American troops in Mexican territory as being, besides an invasion of the sovereignty of Mexico, the immediate cause of the conflicts. The withdrawal of the American troops on the one hand and the protection of the border on the other being therefore the two essential problems their solution should constitute the direct object of the two Governments' efforts.

"The Government of Mexico is disposed to give quick as well as practical consideration in a spirit of concord to the remedies that may be applied to the existing condition.

"Several Latin-American countries have tendered to it to that end their friendly mediation which it has accepted in principle. The Mexican Government, then, merely wants to know whether that of the United States would be disposed to accept the said mediation to the above stated effect or still believes it possible to achieve the same result by means of direct negotiations between the two Governments.

"This Government in the meanwhile proposes to use every effort it may put forth on its part to avoid the occurrence of new incidents that might complicate and aggravate the situation. At the same time it hopes that the American Government on its side will take every pains to prevent also new acts of its military and civil authorities giving rise to fresh complications.

"I avail myself of this opportunity to renew to Your Excellency the assurances of my very distinguished consideration.
                    "(Signed)   C. Aguilar."

Having thus carried out the superior instructions of my Government, I take pleasure in renewing to Your Excellency the Assurances of my highest consideration.   E Arredondo.

CCL (WP, DLC).

From Robert Lansing

PERSONAL AND CONFIDENTIAL:

My dear Mr. President: Washington July 5, 1916.
Ambassador Naón called to see me yesterday afternoon by appointment to discuss a plan which he has to visit Mexico and ex-

plain personally to General Carranza his views as to the friendly and unselfish attitude of this Government toward Mexico. He thinks that he can remove the suspicions of our motives, which he considers the stumbling block to a full and frank understanding being reached between the two Governments.

He would go to Mexico entirely on his own motion, carefully avoiding any intimation that he had consulted me before leaving. He will be careful to explain that he is in no sense acting as a mediator or intermediary (the fact is he does not approve mediation), and has only made the journey because of his sincere friendship for Mexico and his feeling that the spirit and purposes of the United States are misunderstood.

I told the Ambassador that I would talk the matter over with you and give him a definite answer later, but that I could not see any objection to his visiting Mexico as long as he did so without the sanction of this Government.

The Ambassador came from New York on purpose to lay this matter before me and returned yesterday afternoon. I shall be in New York on my way to Henderson Harbor for several hours Friday evening and could arrange to see him then and give him a definite answer.

In case we decide to adopt the plan of seeking the appointment of a Joint Commission what would you think of the idea of explaining it to Naón and having him, if opportunity offers, urge the acceptance of the plan by Carranza in case he goes to Mexico?   Faithfully yours,   Robert Lansing.

TLS (WP, DLC).

From Norman Hapgood[1]

Dear Mr. President: New York, N. Y. July Fifth, 1916.

In the course of our very interesting conversation on Monday, there was one point I did not mention; partly because it was not relevant to our main purpose, and partly because I thought it might not be necessary to mention it at all. Information that has reached me, however, makes me feel it is well to put it before you.

I have rather prompt and full information about Mr. Hughes' ideas, as I am in touch with so many people who are closely in touch with him. He intends, later in the summer, to make a large point out of administrative efficiency, and to take up the record of the present administration in detail. It is this fact which leads me to say one or two things about the situation in the Federal Trade Commission.

There has been introduced into Congress a bill taking foreign trade out of the operation of the Sherman Act. This bill was introduced by Mr. Webb. It was drawn by George Rublee and revised by Louis Brandeis. For six years Mr. Brandeis has been using Mr. Rubely [Rublee] in cases where he thought a high degree of expert efficiency was necessary, combined with a deep knowledge of the Law. I have, of course, no information whatever about whether you contemplate re-appointing Rublee. He failed of confirmation on the second vote by only a tie, and I imagine that the howl that went up around the country will have impressed some of the Senators. I know that Mr. Gallinger is anxious to get out of it on a suggested deal which is characteristically improper. Of course, Senatorial courtesy, as interpreted in this case, works grossly against administrative efficiency.

Mr. Rublee has not felt comfortable remaining on the Commission. He thought it would be easier for you if he retired at once, but Hurley, Harris, Senator Hollis, Mr. McAdoo and myself thought differently. Mr. Rublee does not feel, however, that without subjecting himself to the general suspicion of holding on to an office, he could stay more than a couple of weeks longer. I suppose there cannot be much doubt that if the Federal Trade Commission is to do the very big work it was originally intended to do (as recognized by Judge Hand's disposal of the Corn Products Case)[2] it must have really first class efficiency on it. Whether it is possible to get in the United States another man as well equipped as Rublee, is not for me to say. Hurley and Harris do not think it is, nor, I fancy, does Brandeis.

I confess political considerations intrude themselves on my mind also just now when we are all playing for what we can get of the Bull Moose vote and, as Mr. Rublee is a member of that party,[*] a re-appointment of him would, naturally, make our work easier.

Another thing has come along, by the way, helping to indicate that we shall get a fair share of them. Mr. Wicker,[3] who is State Chairman of New Hampshire for the Bull Moose party, sends me word that he wishes to organize, in your behalf, the elements in that State which cannot work with the regular Democratic machine, and we shall turn him loose at once.

Sincerely,   Norman Hapgood

* Hence Senator Gallinger's opposition to him

TLS (WP, DLC).

[1] He was writing from the headquarters of the Woodrow Wilson Independent League at 280 Madison Avenue.

[2] 234 Fed. 964. Judge Learned Hand, on June 24 in the federal district court, southern district of New York, ordered the dissolution of the Corn Products

Refining Co. on the ground that it was a monopoly in violation of the Sherman Antitrust Act. For the first time in such a case, the Federal Trade Commission, acting as master in chancery under Section 7 of the Federal Trade Commission Act, was to present a plan for the dissolution of the company. For an extensive summary of the case and its significance, see the *New York Times*, June 25, 1916.

[3] George Ray Wicker, Professor of Economics at Dartmouth College, chairman of the Progressive state committee in New Hampshire, 1913-1915.

From Edward Mandell House

New London,

Dear Governor: New Hampshire. July 5, 1916.

I agree with you that it would be best not to see Buxton or anyone like him from the belligerent countries. I explained this to Buxton and he seemed to accept it as being wise, although he indicated his intention of trying to see you.

It is now that you need someone in England, rather than later, who would bend his every effort towards bringing public opinion there to a realization of what you are striving for. Brand Whitlock could do this I think if you could only find a suitable lighting place for Page on this side. Every day this work is neglected is a day lost.

I was sure you would agree with me that it would be unwise to have the English press do what Buxton suggested.

If I were you, I would feel like paying no attention to the Federal Reserve Board controversy, but prudence dictates a different course. You have no idea how strongly they feel upon the subject and how critical that situation is. I believe that after a commission has been once appointed, the less they are directed by the Executive, the better. It means trouble in almost every instance. The Only fear I have is that something disagreeable may be precipitated between now and November.

As to the general political situation, I think it is too early to prophesy. If the election were held today, I have no doubt you would win. Conditions and issues are so different from the usual that it is idle to speculate as to the final result.

This is my reason for urging a complete organization in certain vital states. If we once get this organization we will know where we stand and the opposition will probably not know. If we do not get it, everything must necessarily be guesswork up to the last moment.

It looked at one time as if the "hyphenate" issue would be the paramount one and the one upon which you could easily win. However, if Germany pursues her present course one can imagine a radical change of feeling here. Even now, I notice a lack of interest in that question. If the Allies continue their blockade rigorously and if they push the Germans back to their boundaries, a feeling of something akin to sympathy may arise in this country. Germany's complete change of attitude, both here and abroad, has done much towards lessening the war spirit in America.

I believe that certain lines of attack should be agreed upon in the campaign and the fight forced in these directions. If we center our fire, it will inevitably put the opposition upon the defensive and that is what we want. Fortunately, we have all the arguments on our side, but they have the money.

It is the plain people that will determine the result, and we must get the issues properly before them. The keeping the country out of war and the great measures you have enacted into law, should be our battle cry. It will be the aim of the opposition to bring into line against you every dissatisfied element. It is their only chance for success.

I am wondering what you have decided about the Supreme Court vacancy. That seems to me an important problem. If you cannot find a proper man in New York or in the Middle West, and do not think it wise to go to Connecticut for Wheeler, my judgment is that it would be best to appoint Davis.

Would John Bassett Moore do? Is he enough of a democrat and does he know more than international law? The fact that the next President will probably have the appointing of four or five Justices, may make the appointment of this one, an important issue of the campaign.

I am getting in great shape here and by the first of September I shall be ready for the fray.

My heart foes [goes] out to you every day in admiration, in gratitude and in devotion.

Affectionately yours,   E. M. House

TLS (WP, DLC).

From Samuel Gompers

Sir: Washington, D. C., July 5, 1916.

In response to an invitation, a copy of which I sent you, from the American labor movement to the organized workers of Mexico to participate in a joint conference of the workers of both countries, representatives from the Mexican workers have held conferences with the Executive Council of the American Federation of Labor during its recent session, which began June 26th.

These conferences were devoted to discussions and explanations necessary to bring about mutual understanding and to the consideration of a practical plan for dealing with present problems.

A declaration was signed by all of those participating in the joint conference, and in accord with the instruction contained therein, a copy of it is hereby transmitted to you.[1]

Sincerely yours,   Saml. Gompers.

TLS (WP, DLC).

[1] TC MS dated July 3, 1916 (WP, DLC). It urged a peaceful solution to the dispute between Mexico and the United States and stressed the fundamental role of the laboring classes of both countries in bringing about such a solution. It further declared that a "general conference" of workers of both nations to discuss "plans for maintaining permanent relations" was highly desirable but admitted that such a meeting was "untimely" in view of the present tense relations between the two countries. It did, however, urge the appointment of a joint commission of "high-minded citizens" of both countries "to consider differences that have brought our nations to the verge of war and to make such recommendations for adjustment as shall fitly express the highest ideals of the great rank and file of the citizenship of our two countries."

John Worth Kern to William Gibbs McAdoo

PERSONAL

Dear Mr. McAdoo: Washington July 5, 1916.

I am obliged to go to my family in Virginia to-night, to remain until Sunday, and I deem it important that you and the President should know that our Democratic conference to-night was far from satisfactory. The question was whether we would declare for the passage of the Ship Purchase Bill at this session. While a majority would have doubtless voted aye, yet those opposed and indifferent jockeyed about until at 11 o'clock the caucus adjourned until Friday night without action. As I can't be here that night, I want to advise you and the President of the following discouraging facts:

1. Although the call for the conference was urgent, at least 24 Democratic Senators remained away.

2. Of those present, a few Senators supposed to be close to the Administration manifested indifference, and one, presumed to be particularly close, *expressed* indifference.

3. Some Senators expressed a willingness and desire to agree to Gallinger's proposition to allow the Bill to go over until December.

I think it important that you have a conference at once with Senators Stone, Simmons and Fletcher, and see if something cannot be done to insure a full attendance of the friends of the Administration at the conference on Friday night. It would be well for the President to insist that Senator Hughes give his *active* support and that Senator James (who was absent to-night) attend. The situation demands immediate attention. It is the most urgent matter that calls me away.

Yours,   John W. Kern.

TCL (WP, DLC).

From Robert Lansing

PERSONAL AND PRIVATE:

My dear Mr. President: Washington July 6, 1916.

I send you herewith a note which I purpose to send to Mr. Arredondo, acknowledging the receipt of his communication of the 4th and indicating to the *de facto* Government that we are ready to consider any suggestions which it may make as to composing our differences.

You will see in certain parts of the note that I have followed the translation of Mr. Aguilar's note, which I cannot say is in exceptional English.

Will you kindly indicate any changes you would desire; and I would be very much pleased if you could send this note to my house tonight, or else have it at the Department very early in the morning.

I have just had a long and satisfactory talk with Mr. Arredondo in which the matter of a Joint Commission was discussed in general terms, and which he considers a very satisfactory arrangement. He asked me if I intended to reply to their note and if I would make any suggestions in it. I told him that I proposed to reply and that I intended to invite suggestions. This seemed to please him very much.

Faithfully yours,   Robert Lansing.

TLS (SDR, RG 59, 812.00/17715½, DNA).

To Robert Lansing, with Enclosure

My dear Mr. Secretary,   The White House. 6 July, 1916.

I herewith return the reply to the last note from Mexico, with a few verbal alterations which I think clarify the expression a little.

Perhaps it would be well to bring the note with you to Cabinet to-morrow morning for an interchange of views.

Faithfully Yours,   W.W.

WWTLI (SDR, RG 59, 812.00/17716½, DNA).

E N C L O S U R E[1]

Sir: Washington July 6, 1916.

I have the honor to acknowledge the receipt of your communication of July 4, 1916, in which you transcribe a note addressed to me by the Secretary of Foreign Relations of your Government, and to request that you will transmit to him the following reply:

Mr. Secretary:

I have the honor to acknowledge the receipt of your courteous note transmitted to me by Señor Arredondo on the 4th instant in which you refer to my notes of June 20th and June 25th, and to assure you of the sincere gratification of my Government at the frank statement of the difficulties which have unfortunately arisen in our relations along the international boundary, and the unreserved expression of the desire of your Government to reach an adjustment of these difficulties on a broad and amicable basis. ⟨It is⟩ The same spirit of friendship and of solicitude for the continuance of cordial relations between our two countries ⟨, which⟩ inspires my Government ⟨to a similar desire for⟩, *which equally desires* an immediate solution of the matters of difference which have long vexed both Governments.

It is especially pleasing to my Government that the *de facto* Government of Mexico is disposed to give quick as well as practical consideration in a spirit of concord to the remedies which may be applied to the existing condition. Reciprocating the same desire, the Government of the United States is prepared to ⟨enter⟩ *take* immediately ⟨upon the⟩ *under* consideration ⟨of⟩ any plan which your Government may deem ⟨proper to make⟩ *it desirable to adopt* looking toward remedial measures, and earnestly invites suggestions and discussion of practical means to remove finally and prevent a recurrence of the difficulties which have been the source of controversy.

Accept, Mr. Secretary, the renewed assurances of my highest consideration.   Robert Lansing.

I am, Sir,   Yours very sincerely,

T MS (SDR, RG 59, 812.00/17716½, DNA).

[1] Words in angle brackets deleted by Wilson; words in italics (except *de facto*) added by him. This letter was sent to Arredondo on July 7 and is printed in *FR 1916*, p. 600.

To Samuel Gompers

My dear Mr. Gompers: The White House July 6, 1916

May I not acknowledge in this more formal way the receipt of the paper you handed me yesterday concerning the conference of American and Mexican workers?

I am sincerely glad that the workers of the two countries should be drawn together in this vital way by which they can comprehend each other's interests, but I entirely agree with the judgment of the paper you handed me that it would not be wise to hold a general conference at this time.

Cordially and sincerely yours,   Woodrow Wilson

TLS (photostat in RSB Coll., DLC).

To John Franklin Shafroth

My dear Senator: [The White House] July 6, 1916

Thank you sincerely for your letter of July third.[1] I am heartily glad the Porto Rican Bill is on the ways and hope that it may soon be launched as a seaworthy ship.

Cordially and sincerely yours,   Woodrow Wilson

TLS (Letterpress Books, WP, DLC).
  [1] It is missing.

To Herbert Bayard Swope

My dear Swope: The White House July 6, 1916

Thank you with all my heart for your generous letter of July third. The dinner seemed to me also a very unusual one in its whole tone and atmosphere, and you may be sure that I felt the inspiration and encouragement of it. I agree with you that the speeches to which I paid my compliments were of a quite unusual character and quality, and altogether I think that the Club is to be congratulated on what was a very enjoyable and memorable occasion. I felt it an honor to be there, and I am heartily glad that you thought my own speech was worth while.

Cordially and sincerely yours,   Woodrow Wilson

TLS (received from Bruce Gimelson).

To John Adams Wilson

My dear John: [The White House] July 6, 1916

The whiskey came but I do not know Mr. Megeath's address. I wish very much you would send it to me so that I can thank him. It was certainly fine of him to think of me so generously.

In haste   Faithfully yours,   Woodrow Wilson

TLS (Letterpress Books, WP, DLC).

From Franklin Knight Lane, with Enclosure

My dear Mr. President: Washington July 6, 1916.

I had a talk yesterday with a Member of Parliament named Buxton, who to-day left me this note and memorandum that may interest you.   Cordially yours,   Franklin K Lane

TLS (WP, DLC).

E   N   C   L   O   S   U   R   E

Noel Buxton to Franklin Knight Lane

Dear Mr Lane   Washington July 5 [1916]

May I enclose a note on the point which arose in our conversation. I do not speak in any official capacity but as a Liberal politician. I look forward to seeing you at the Cosmos Club at 1 tomorrow.   Yours sincerely   Noel Buxton

ALS (WP, DLC).

A Memorandum by Noel Buxton

Confidential   [July 5, 1916]

1. TERMS OF SETTLEMENT ARE NOT IMPOSSIBLE.

The most influential English views accord with American (as to national rights, etc.) and Germany might concur if the Allies agree to mediation on American lines.

2. BUT RESPONSE TO THE PRESIDENT'S SPEECH (TO THE TAFT LEAGUE) IS HAMPERED.

Because,

(a) Fear of insecurity in the future makes us rely only on strategic gains. It is felt that we are "fighting for the nursery" and cannot be secure unless Germany is weak.

(b) We are pre-occupied with the business of war.

(c) The fear of discouraging the army and navy, silences even reasoning men.

(d) We are confident of "victory."

These points apply not only to the public but to the official world also.

3. THE GREAT SOLVENT OF THE ABOVE IS THE IDEA OF THE LEAGUE OF PEACE.

Those who believe that America will adhere to the proposal tend to support negotiation but the proposal itself is not understood or familiar in England. Ministers cannot preach it without risk of blame. Mr. Asquith and Sir. E. Grey have experienced this in some degree when they put forward the idea.

4. THE PRESIDENT HAS TAKEN THE FIRST STEP AND HAS MET WITH A GOOD RESPONSE.

The significance of this has been missed in America.

(a) The chief liberal papers in England had to fact [face] the charge of breaking the party truce, yet they were most cordial.

The hostility of the "yellow" Press, especially the Harmsworth papers, is natural. It means no more than the hostility of partisan Republican papers to the President's policy.

(b) The public opinion of England is equally shown by the half-million trade unionists affiliated to the movement for urging negotiation; by the large number of meetings held to discuss terms of settlement; and by the new group in the House of Commons on terms of peace. The fact that a public man Like Lord Brassey[1] should have begun to advocate negotiation is a sign of the times.

A reasoning attitude is widespread, though it waits for a policy before expressing itself.

5. IF THE PRESIDENT'S POLICY IS UNDERSTOOD GREAT BODIES OF OPINION WHICH HAVE HITHERTO BEEN SILENT WOULD COME OUT INTO THE OPEN.

For instance, the Parliamentary Group, known as the Liberal Foreign Affairs Group, which numbered seventy members before the war, has been silent since the war began. A great public following exists potentially if the President shows that he means to push the League of Peace.

6. THERE ARE TWO STEPS WHICH WOULD PRODUCE WIDESPREAD SUPPORT IN ENGLAND.

1. Organization of the League of Peace.

If agreement in principle, even without the draft treaty being known, were secured (even from England alone), it would be seen that terms of settlement thereby become possible, because the safety for which we are fighting is secured. The issue of a despatch to the Great Powers on the subject would of itself have a similar effect.

11. Education of opinion in Europe by speeches.

The President's prestige as a statesman and speaker is immense. The May 28th speech appeared to be a first installment only. It seemed to foreshadow further utterances.

Objections may be raised in America that,

(a) The absence of response from England and France shows disapproval.

In our view official response at this point from England was difficult.

Grey and Asquith have already expressed approval of the League idea in a marked degree.

(b) That there is not much more to say.

Englishmen need to be shown that America adheres to certain principles, which are also held by the Allies.

Nationality and right of self-government which were stated on May 28th admit of further treatment.

It needs also to be shown that a Peace League is the answer to the main reasons which compel us (and also our enemies) to fight to the last.

(c) That a movement in England has no value unless it leads to Governmental action, and that the movement would be small amd [and] only such as to provoke a reaction.

I think that the demand for negotiation hitherto has been of this kind, but the movement I contemplate would be quite different.

It would be in support of a safe and "unsentimental" policy.

It would not be injurious to National unity, but would be in line with the utterances of our Ministers.

T MS (WP, DLC).
    1 Thomas Brassey, 1st Earl Brassey (1836-1918); M.P., 1868-1885; Governor of Victoria, Australia, 1895-1900; expert on naval affairs.

From Norman Hapgood, with Enclosure

Dear Mr. President: New York, N. Y. July Sixth 1916.

I spent last evening with Mr. Brandeis and I think perhaps you may be interested in having before you his views on the Supreme Court vacancy.

He thinks, as I do, that the political effect of locality in such an appointment is so much over-estimated as to amount to a superstition; that selecting a man from a particular state would influence about six votes in that State. On the other hand, he believes, as I do also, that it is of the greatest immediate political importance—as well as of the greatest ultimate importance—to select a man who will be recognized as eminently fit and eminently progressive. We both believe that to select the type of a man now being urged from New York City, Brooklyn and Buffalo would be a wet blanket and would have a noticeable effect in chilling enthusiasm.

Of course, nobody could question the fitness of Senator Walsh, but I presume it will be decided that the situation in the Senate does not warrant his being taken away from that body.

Mr. Brandeis elaborated what he has often expressed to me before—his belief that the Attorney General is a good lawyer and that it is extremely difficult to get a sufficiently good lawyer who is as genuine a progressive as he is. After all, it is the progressive spirit that we have to consider at the moment, as well as from the more permanent point of view.

As my letter of to-day to Raymond Robins touches one of the points we discussed on Monday, I am enclosing you a copy.

> Sincerely yours,   Norman Hapgood

TLS (WP, DLC).

E N C L O S U R E

Norman Hapgood to Raymond Robins

My dear Raymond: [New York] July Sixth, 1916.

I have just had a talk with Vance McCormick, which pleased me a good deal, especially his talk about the Keystone party[1] and how they were able to put the old time Democratic crooks out of business, through the President's help. He believes you can do the same thing, with President Wilson's help, in Illinois, if you decide to come with us in this election.

Mr. McCormick would like very much indeed a chance to tell you about his Pennsylvania experiences and sends you an invitation, through me, to dine with him in his rooms alone, at the Biltmore Hotel, if you are coming East.

I am going up to Windsor, Vermont, on the fourteenth and, if I am not prevented by political developments, I shall stay there until the twenty-third, inclusive. Colonel House is not far away and Rublee and other friends of yours are very near my house.

Is there any chance that you can visit me during that time? Of course, I should especially like it if Mrs. Robins could come along also.

I see the Hughes' statement has been postponed.

With very charming recollections of Monday,

Sincerely yours,   Norman Hapgood

TCL (WP, DLC).
    [1] See V. C. McCormick to WW, Feb. 6, 1911, n. 2, Vol. 22, and F. F. Kane to WW, July 25, 1911, n. 7, Vol. 23.

From Edward Mandell House

New London,
Dear Governor: New Hampshire. July 6, 1916.

I am enclosing you a preliminary statement of the National Research Council as organized at your request by the National Academy of Sciences.[1]

This in connection with the work done by men like Godfrey, Crampton, Coffin and others will be a complete surprise to the American people when the full facts are known and will reflect credit upon your Administration.

Such work has never been done in America and, until recently, has never been done anywhere except in Germany.

As soon as it is better under way, I shall suggest to our Publicity Department to give it wide circulation.

Affectionately yours,   E. M. House

TLS (WP, DLC).
    [1] G. E. Hale to W. H. Welch, July 3, 1916, TCL, together with TC of enclosed preliminary statement, both in WP, DLC. The letter and statement discussed the purpose, membership, and work to be done by the proposed National Research Council. The purpose of the council, according to the statement, was "to bring into co-operation existing Governmental, educational, industrial, and other research organizations with the object of encouraging the investigation of natural phenomena, the increased use of scientific research in the development of American industries, the employment of scientific methods in strengthening the national defense, and such other applications of science as will promote the national security and welfare."

To Norman Hapgood

My dear Hapgood: [The White House] July 7, 1916

I have your letter of July fifth.

My scruple about Rublee is this: While his rejection by the Senate was by a very narrow margin, he was twice, as a matter of fact, rejected, and while I could give him successive recess appointments, it would put him in a doubtful light not only, but it would clearly, I fear, be in contravention of the spirit of the Constitution. I think his rejection was one of the worst pieces of business the Senate has engaged in in our time, but my present feeling is that I ought to find somebody else and I would be mighty obliged for suggestions. Have you any in mind?

I do not see what Mr. Hughes is going to make out of an efficiency campaign. I think we can very successfully challenge comparison in respect of efficiency with any preceding administration.

Thank you warmly for your letter.

In haste

Cordially and faithfully yours,   Woodrow Wilson

TLS (Letterpress Books, WP, DLC).

To Franklin Knight Lane

My dear Lane: [The White House] July 7, 1916

Thank you sincerely for the memorandum from Mr. Buxton. I would have been glad to see Mr. Buxton myself if I had not thought it unwise at this time to see any Member of Parliament not officially accredited to me in some way, formal or informal.

Cordially and faithfully yours,   Woodrow Wilson

TLS (Letterpress Books, WP, DLC).

From Joseph Patrick Tumulty

Memorandum for the President: The White House. July 7, 1916.

Senator Simmons has just telephoned that the Commerce Committee is having a great many difficulties in connection with the Shipping Bill, and that he and Senators Reed, Fletcher, and Shields feel that they ought to talk with the President before three o'clock, if possible, or at least some time this afternoon.

Can the President see them?[1]

T MS (WP, DLC).

[1] Wilson saw the senators at 2 P.M. on July 7.

From Sara Bard Field

My dear Mr. Wilson: San Francisco July 7, 1916.

Your kind answer of June 16, to my telegram of June 12, sent from St. Louis has only just reached me due to my Arab wanderings about the country.

You say that you sincerely hope that the outcome of the platform declaration for woman suffrage has been acceptable to me.

In reply I am sorry to have to tell you that not only is the platform declaration not acceptable to me and to hundreds of thousands of voting women of the West, but that we also greatly depricate [deprecate] the interpretation you gave of this plank to Mrs. D. E. Hooker of Richmond.[1] It is my sincere hope as a democratic woman that you will not allow any menance [menace] to the democratic party in the fall election through your unwillingness to face the desire of the West for speedy action upon the Susan B. Anthony Amendment.

Sincerely yours,   Sara Bard Field

TLS (WP, DLC).
[1] Della E. (Mrs. J. W.) Hooker, of Richmond, Va., called on Wilson at the White House on June 21 on behalf of the Congressional Union for Woman Suffrage and the Virginia State Federation of Labor, and asked him for an interpretation of the suffrage plank in the Democratic platform. She told reporters afterward that Wilson had said that the plank meant that the question should be decided by the states and that he still held to his refusal to urge the passage of a suffrage amendment to the Constitution. She also quoted him as saying that he was a friend of the suffrage movement and sympathized with it, but that suffrage forced upon a state would not be well received and would do more harm than good. New York *Evening Post*, June 21, 1916.

From David Franklin Houston

Dear Mr. President: [Washington] July 7th, 1916.

May I say a word about the income tax feature of the new revenue measure? I notice that the exemption remains as heretofore at $4,000. for married people and $3,000. for unmarried people. The rate of taxation, I believe, is doubled. From the beginning it has seemed to me to be a question whether the exemption was not too high. I am very definitely of the opinion that the exemption is too high with the increased rates on the amounts above the exempted amounts. I should be inclined to lower the exemption to $2,500. to married people, and to $1,800. to unmarried people.

I believe the students of taxation almost unanimously favor this lowering of the exemptions, and I have the impression that thoughtful independent men generally over the nation will think it unjust to leave the exemptions so high, especially in view of the increases in the rates.

I recognize that the burden of taxation heretofore has been heavier on the lower middle classes, but I do not think there would be included in these classes those with incomes over $3,000. or $4,000. I think I know the thought in the minds of the members of Congress who framed the bill, and I think it is largely a political thought. They probably feared the effect on the greater numbers that would be involved if the exemption were lowered. They think the lowering of the exemption would be bad politics.

I think they are mistaken. They certainly are if the thing is wrong economically, as I think it is. Furthermore, since this particular measure is an emergency measure in part, and is caused by the unusual circumstances, I believe the people with the smaller incomes would respond very patriotically. In any event, those who are looking at the matter simply from the political point of view should recognize that the tax would not become operative for a considerable time.

I have discussed the matter this morning with McAdoo. In his annual report he recommended a lowering of the exemption. He agreed with me this morning that it was a mistake not to make the reduction, and suggested that I write to you. I feel quite strongly about it, and wonder if it would not be worth your while to speak to the House leaders, or, if it is too late to speak to them, to speak to the Senate leaders. I have a sort of feeling that the reduction will be made before the measure goes through Congress, and, if it is to be made the initiative ought to come from the Democrats.[1]

Please do not trouble to reply to this. I am with Mr. Crane for the afternoon. He joins me in cordial greetings.

Faithfully yours,   D. F. Houston

CCLS (D. F. Houston Papers, MH).

[1] The exemptions remained at $3,000 for a single person and $4,000 for a married person or head of a household. 39 *Statutes at Large* 756.

From Edward Percy Howard

Dear Mr. President: [New York] July 7, 1916.

Great pressure upon my time has prevented me from writing to you before now to express to you my deep personal appreciation, as well as the deep appreciation of the New York Press Club, of your presence as our guest of honor at our annual banquet. I am sure it was one of the most brilliant nights in the history of the club, and the importance of the occasion has been most emphatically impressed upon us by the attitude of the entire press of the country and the attitude of the press abroad in connection with the event. I have even heard it expressed that that night marked the passing of the Mexican crisis, and if this be so even in part, then surely we have all reason to be happy over being present on such an occasion. Your truly wonderful address made the deepest impression on everyone who heard it, and I am sure on all who read it.

And now Mr. President I am going to press upon your kindness by asking if you will not bee [be] good enough to write your name for us on the few menus forwarded under another cover, so that the members of our Board of Trustees may have a real souvenir of the occasion, and also on Macauley's cartoon so that we may have it framed to hang in our club rooms.

Trusting you and Mrs. Wilson reached your home without discomfort, hoping at some future time to have the great pleasure of meeting with you again, and conveying once more to you an expression of my deep appreciation and respect, permit me to remain, Mr. President,

Yours sincerely,   Edward Percy Howard

TLS (WP, DLC).

Joseph Patrick Tumulty to Vance Criswell McCormick

Dear Mr. McCormick: [The White House] July 7, 1916.

I am writing at the request of the President to lay before you the following facts:

I understand that Mr. Woolley has announced that he proposes to discontinue at once all publicity efforts in Washington. One moment's discussion with you would convince you that this change will be fraught with the gravest consequences.

The scheme and scope of The Bulletin which is issued weekly in Washington is the concrete development of what Tom Pence thought was the best way to interpret and represent the administration to newspapers and public men. He gave a great deal of thought and attention to this sheet, tried many experiments, patiently watched the results in many newspapers before making up his mind as to the best way to quickly and acceptably present administration ideas. His main idea was not so much to get actual stuff in the newspapers, but to educate, instruct and inform editorial and news minds so that they could be relied upon to give us favorable and sympathetic consideration and attention on special matters from day to day. (Not merely print part of what we sent). His constant effort was to create a newspaper atmosphere which would be favorable to a sympathetic understanding of the administration, its acts and policies. A careful and general reading of the newspapers is necessary even to attempt this. Also a close connection with what is going on here and a constant inspiration and guidance is required if the right thing is to be done quickly and if the results are what we want.

There is one thing more. Much of our publicity is work among the newspaper correspondents. This to be effective must be tactful and unobtrusive. *Most of the men who write national political news for the country are here and will be here until Congress adjourns and you leave. General and special work among these is very important.*

I think we should keep Steckman[1] here to continue The Bulletin and to work in various ways among correspondents until Congress adjourns and you leave. It is proposed to place him in charge of work in New York under Woolley and to do it somewhat differently. Interest in the campaign there will not develop for a month or six weeks. We would be out of close touch. The Democratic campaign is yourself and the Democratic Administration. That is here, and certain phases of the publicity efforts which have been so carefully developed here, should not be abandoned until Congress adjourns. New York has plenty to do in getting ready for a general campaign of publicity.

There isn't a newspaper man in Washington of the most mediocre ability who would agree that this change is wise. If you will consult Secretaries Burleson, Lane and McAdoo, I think they will agree that my judgment is entitled to some little consideration in this matter.

With best wishes,   Sincerely yours,   J. P. Tumulty

TCL (WP, DLC).
[1] Frederick W. Steckman, formerly Washington correspondent of various newspapers, successor to Thomas Jones Pence as editor of the *Democratic Bulletin*.

A Memorandum by Franz Hugo Krebs[1]

Washington July 7th, 1916.

I had a talk to-day with President Wilson regarding Sir Roger Casement. Some days before the time fixed for Sir Roger's trial, I went to Boston in order to get letters that, as I thought, might obtain me an audience with the President. Finally, after consultation with a man who has known President Wilson very well, for years past, I decided to chuck all my letters of introduction away and come on to Washington relying entirely on the "human interest" side of the case. I first called to see Joseph P. Tumulty, Secretary of the President. I found him a most sympathetic listener and he gave me a letter of introduction to Mr Polk, who is now acting Secretary of State. Mr Polk is thoroughly posted on every phase of the Casement matter and showed by his questions that he had read everything that has appeared in our papers regarding Sir Roger, from the time that he first arrived in Germany. It was rather interesting to have Mr Polk quote to me from signed statements that Sir Roger had given me for the American press, on the different occasions that I have interviewed him in 1915 and 1916. Finally I was informed that President Wilson would be willing to have me see him in order for me to tell him regarding the physical and mental condition of Sir Roger at the time he left Berlin, on the evening of April 11th, to go to Ireland. I told the President that the first time I saw Sir Roger this year was on Feb 12th and that he was merely a shadow of what he was when I last saw him in April 1915. I also told President Wilson that for some months Sir Roger had been in a rest cure and that he was suffering from a severe nervous break down, that he left the rest cure about the middle of March to come to Berlin and that for weeks before April 11th he suffered severely from insomnia and had to take opiates in order to sleep.

President Wilson gave me a most sympathetic hearing and when I spoke to him about the great work Sir Roger had done in collecting the evidence on which the British Parliament acted and did away with King Leopold's rule on the Congo, further when I mentioned Sir Roger's work in connection with stopping the Putumayo outrages,[2] President Wilson signified that he was fully informed regarding Sir Roger's activities in the past.

Sir Roger is legally a British subject and there are many difficulties of custom and precedent against direct interference by the President along the lines of requesting commutation of the sentence already imposed. There is no question however that indirectly and unofficially it is already understood in Great Britain that there is great interest in the United States, in the final disposition of this case, and the general feeling in Washington is that the death penalty will be commuted.

Franz Hugo Krebs.

HwS memorandum (WP, DLC).
    [1] Lawyer, businessman, and journalist of New York. He had recently published a series of articles on Germany in the Sunday magazine section of the *New York Times*, based upon two recent trips to Germany. He had interviewed such political leaders as Theobald von Bethmann Hollweg, Gottlieb von Jagow, and Karl Helfferich, Imperial Secretary of the Treasury.
    [2] About these investigations, see B. L. Reid, *The Lives of Roger Casement* (New Haven, Conn., 1976), pp. 35-71, 93-130 *passim.*

From Newton Diehl Baker

My dear Mr. President: Washington. July 8, 1916.

The Senate Committee has reported the Army appropriation bill with an amendment striking out the entire provision for the

Council of Executive Information and substituting therefor a provision for a "Council of National Defense." I have examined the new provision carefully, and it is in effect the draft drawn up by Professor Dennis,[1] who spoke with you on this subject. In my judgment the provision substituted by the Senate is less desirable, for the following reasons:

1. It leaves off of the Council the Secretary of Labor, the Secretary of Commerce, the Secretary of the Interior, and the Secretary of Agriculture. All of these Departments have facilities and deal with subjects intimately associated with the general proposition of a coordination of the national resources.

2. The Senate proposal puts upon the Council the Chief of Staff of the Army and an officer of the Navy, thus placing subordinates of the War and Navy Departments on the Council with their superior officers, which I think will serve no useful purpose and is a wrong principle in organization.

3. The civilian members provided by the Senate amendment are six in number and are associated directly with the Secretary of War, the Secretary of the Navy, the Chief of the General Staff of the Army, and a naval officer to be designated by the Secretary of the Navy, thus associating persons with official responsibility and persons acting in a voluntary, unofficial way. I am persuaded it is better to have those under official responsibility in one group, and the citizen members as an advisory body.

4. The Senate provision strikes out authority to employ experts.

5. The Senate provision substitutes an appropriation of $10,000 for the original proposal of $200,000, and limits the expenditure to traveling expenses and subsistence of the citizen members of the Council. This, of course, would destroy the efficiency of the whole plan, by making it impossible to employ the necessary clerks to carry on the work.

I have taken the matter up with Senator Chamberlain and Mr. Hay, and I am assured that the original provision will be restored and the Senate substitute taken out. I send you this information, however, so that if any member of either the Senate or the House should speak to you on the subject, it will not be necessary for you to analyze the two provisions before you are equipped with full information to deal with any argument which may be presented.

Cordially yours,   Newton D. Baker

TLS (WP, DLC).
[1] Alfred Lewis Pinneo Dennis, Professor of History at the University of Wisconsin.

From William Joel Stone

Mr. President: [Washington] July 8 1916.

At a meeting of the Committee on Foreign Relations held this morning I was directed to request that you would, if not incompatible with the public interests, transmit to the Committee, in confidence, such information as you may have at this time respecting the treaty said recently to have been made between Japan and Russia relating to China, and also to keep the Committee advised as to any new developments relating to the subject that may arise in future.

I have the honor to be,

Very sincerely, etc.,   Wm J Stone

TLS (SDR, RG 59, 761.94/103, DNA).

From Margaret Woodrow Wilson

Darling Father,   Waterford Conn. July 9th, 1916.

It seems perfect ages since I last saw you! I am having a wonderful time here, but I am happy in the thought that I shall see you and Edith and Helen next week. I shall probably get to Washington on the seventeenth, that is if Nell can have me over Sunday. I wrote to her a few days ago asking if I might go to her after my concert on Saturday in Ocean Grove and stay over Sunday. If, however, she has not room for me I shall go to Washington on Sunday.

I have never before studied under such ideal conditions as these here. The place is beautiful, unusually so, it is very secluded, and I have no responsibility of any importance aside from my studies. So you see I am having a wonderful holiday. My voice is in fine condition and improves constantly. I am full of hope that I shall be able to give of my very best to that fine audience that they promise me for Saturday.

Aunt Annie and little Annie seem to be improving already in this delicious air. They have a room in one of the hotel cottages, you know. Did you hear Annie sing when she was in Washington? Her voice is really getting very beautiful. If mine were half as flexible I should be further ahead in my profession than I am now, much. My voice is stubborn, but I will get the best of it in time, and then it will be my servant as long as it lives, probably a better servant than if I had not had to learn how to master it. I cannot help feeling that what comes as a result of struggle is finer than that which comes of itself, easily—and that in spite of my belief in the Montessori method for little children!

Thank you dear Father so much for making it possible for me to work at the thing I love the best in this ideal spot. You are so generous to me!

I hope you are well, dear Father and not warn [worn] out by the complications of problems that you are having to settle just now.

Your speeches—Oh Father they are so wonderful and at the time of a crisis they are most wonderful! They never cease to thrill me and move me.

Well I shall see you next week. Give my dear love to sweet Edith and Helen if she is back.

I love you so much darling Father.

Your devoted,   Margaret.

TLS (WC, NjP).

An Address in Detroit to Businessmen[1]

[[July 10, 1916]]

Mr. Chairman, ladies, and gentlemen: It is with a great deal of gratification that I find myself facing so interesting and important a company as this. You will readily understand that I have not come here to make an elaborate address, but I have come here to express my interest in the objects of this great association, and to congratulate you on the opportunities which are immediately ahead of you in handling the business of this country.

These are days of incalculable change, my fellow citizens. It is impossible for anybody to predict anything that is certain, in detail, with regard to the future, either of this country or of the world, in the large movements of business. But one thing is perfectly clear, and that is that the United States will play a new part, and that it will be a part of unprecedented opportunity and of greatly increased responsibility.

The United States has had a very singular history in respect of its business relationships with the rest of the world. I have always believed, and I think you have always believed, that there is more business genius in the United States than anywhere else in the world. And yet America has, apparently, been afraid of touching too intimately the great processes of international exchange. America, of all countries in the world, has been timid

[1] Wilson spoke before the World's Salesmanship Congress in Arcadia Hall. The general chairman of this organization, D. Milton Barrett, introduced Wilson. For a report of this and the other events of the day, see the *Detroit Free Press*, July 11, 1916.

and has not, until recently, has not, until within the last two or three years, provided itself with the fundamental instrumentalities for playing a large part in the trade of the world. America, which ought to have had the broadest vision of any nation, has raised up an extraordinary number of provincial thinkers—men who thought provincially about business, men who thought that the United States was not ready to take her competitive part in the struggle for the peaceful conquest of the world. For anybody who reflects philosophically upon the history of this country, that is the most amazing fact about it.

But the time for provincial thinkers has gone by. We must play a great part in the world, whether we choose it or not. Do you know the significance of this single fact—that, within the last year or two we have, speaking in large terms, ceased to be a debtor nation and become a creditor nation, that we have more of the surplus gold of the world than we ever had before, and that our business hereafter is to be to lend and to help and to promote the great peaceful enterprises of the world. We have got to finance the world in some important degree, and those who finance the world must understand it and rule it with their spirits and with their minds. We cannot cabin and confine ourselves any longer. So that, as I said, I came here to congratulate you upon the great role that lies ahead of you to play. This is a salesmanship congress, and hereafter salesmanship will have to be closely related in its outlook and scope to statesmanship, to international statesmanship. It will have to be touched with an intimate comprehension of the conditions of business and enterprise throughout the round globe, because America will have to place her goods by running her intelligence ahead of her goods. No amount of mere push, no amount of mere hustling, or, to speak in the western language, no amount of mere rustling, no amount of mere active enterprise, will suffice.

There have been two ways of doing business in the world outside of the lands in which the great manufactures have been made. One has been try to force the tastes of the manufacturing country on the country in which the markets were being sought. And the other way has been to study the tastes and needs of the countries where the markets were being sought and suit your goods to those tastes and needs. And the latter method has beaten the former method. If you are going to sell carpets, for example, in India, you have got to have as good taste as the Indians in the patterns of the carpets, and that is going some. If you are going to sell things in tropical countries, they must, rather obviously, be different from those which you sell in cold and Arctic countries. You cannot assume that the rest of the world is going to wear or use or manufacture what you wear and use and manufacture. Your raw materials must be the raw materials that they need, not the raw materials that you need. Your manufactured goods must be the manufactured goods which they desire, not those which other markets have desired. And so your business will keep pace with your knowledge, not of yourself and of your manufacturing processes, but of them and of their commercial needs. That is statesmanship, because that is relating your international activities to the conditions which exist in other countries.

If we can once get what some gentlemen are so loath to give us—a merchant marine! The trouble with some men is that they are slow in their minds. They don't see. They don't know the need. And they will not allow you to point it out to them. But if we can once get in a position to deliver our own goods, then the goods that we have to deliver will be adjusted to the desires of those to whom we deliver them, and all the world will welcome America in the great field of commerce and manufacture.

There is a great deal of cant talk, my fellow citizens, about service. I wish the word had not been surrounded with so much sickly sentimentality, because it is a good, robust, red-blooded word, and it is the key to everything that concerns the peace and prosperity of the world. You cannot force yourself upon anybody who is not obliged to take you. The only way in which you can be sure of being accepted is by being sure that you have got something to offer that is worth taking. And the only way you can be sure of that is by being sure that you wish to adapt it to the use and the service of the people to whom you are trying to sell.

I was trying to expound, in another place the other day, the long way and the short way to get together. The long way is to fight. I have heard some gentlemen say that they want to help Mexico, and the way they propose to help her is to overwhelm her with force. That is the long way to help Mexico, as well as the wrong way. Because after the fighting you have a nation full of justified suspicions and animated by well-founded hostility and hatred. And then will you help them? Then will you establish cordial business relationships with them? Then will you go in as neighbors and enjoy their confidence? On the contrary, you will have shut every door as if it were of steel against you. What makes Mexico suspicious of us is that she does not believe as yet that we want to serve her. She believes that we want to possess her. And she has justification for the belief in the way in which some of our fellow citizens have tried to exploit her privileges and possessions. For my part, I will not serve the ambitions of these gentlemen, but I will try to serve all America, so far as intercourse with Mexico is concerned, by trying to serve Mexico herself. There are some things that are not debatable. Of course, we have got to defend our border. That goes without saying. Of course, we must make good our own sovereignty. But we must respect the sovereignty of Mexico. I am one of those—I have sometimes suspected that there were not many of them—who believe, absolutely believe, in the Virginia Bill of Rights, which was the model of the old bills of rights, which says that a people have the right to do anything they please with their own country and their own government. I am old-fashioned enough to believe that, and I am going to stand by that belief. That is for the benefit of those gentlemen who wish to butt in.

Now, I use that as an illustration, my fellow citizens. What do we all most desire when the present tragical confusion of the world's affairs is over? We desire permanent peace, do we not? Permanent peace can grow in only one soil. That is the soil of actual good will, and good will cannot exist without mutual comprehension. Charles Lamb, the English writer, made a very delightful remark that I have long treasured in my memory. He stuttered a little bit, and he said of someone who was not present, "I h-h-hate that m-man." And someone said, "Why, Charles, I didn't know you knew him." "Oh," he said, "I-I-I don't; I-I can't h-hate a m-man I know." That is a profound human remark. You can't hate a man you know. I know some rascals whom I have tried to hate. I have tried to head them off as rascals, but I have been unable to hate them. I have liked them. And so, not to compare like with unlike, in the relationship of nations with each other, many of our antagonisms are based upon misunderstandings, and, as long as you do not understand a country you cannot trade with it. As long as you cannot take its point of view, you cannot commend your goods to its purchase. As long as you go to it with a supercilious air, for example, and patronize it, and, then, as we have tried to do in some less developed countries, tell them that that is what they ought to want, whether they want it or not, you can't do business with them. You have got to approach them just as you really ought to approach all matters of human relationship.

These people who give their money to philanthropy, for example, but cannot for the life of them see from the point of view of those for whose benefit they are giving the money, are not philanthropists. They endow and promote philanthropy, but you cannot be a philanthropist unless you love all sorts and conditions of men. The great barrier in this world, I have sometimes thought, is not the barrier of principle, but the barrier of taste. Certain classes of society find certain other classes of society distasteful to them. They don't like the way they dress. They don't like the infrequency with which they bathe. They don't like to consort with them under the conditions in which they live, and, therefore, they stand at a distance from them. And it is impossible for them to serve them, because they do not understand them and do not feel that common pulse of humanity and that common school of experience which is the only thing which binds us together and educates us in the same fashion.

This, then, my friends, is the simple message that I bring to you. Lift your eyes to the horizon of business. Do not look too close at the little processes with which you are concerned, but let your thoughts and your imaginations run abroad throughout the whole world. And, with the inspiration of the thought that you are Americans and are meant to carry liberty and justice and the principles of humanity wherever you go, go out and sell goods that will make the world more comfortable and more happy, and convert them to the principles of America.

Printed in *Addresses of President Wilson at Detroit, Mich.* . . . (Washington, 1916), with corrections from a printed transcript in WP, DLC., and from the text in the *Detroit Free Press*, July 11, 1916.

A Luncheon Address in Detroit[1]

[[July 10, 1916]]

Mr. Chairman, Judge Murphy, ladies and gentlemen: I am glad to find myself as popular as Judge Murphy, and I must say, in his behalf, that you know him better than you know me. I am glad to find myself in Detroit and face to face with the men who have played the principal part in giving it distinction throughout the country and throughout the world. Looking about among you, I see that it is true in this matter, as in others, that the only men fit for such a job are young men and men who never grow old. There is the liveliness of youth in the eyes even of those of you who have shared with me the painful parting with the hirsute appendage.

And I have been interested in some things that Mr. Denby[2] has said to me today. He has shamefacedly admitted that he has

[1] Delivered before the luncheon meeting of the World's Salesmanship Congress in the gymnasium of the Detroit Athletic Club. Alfred J. Murphy, judge of the third judicial circuit of Michigan, presided and introduced Wilson. "Mr. Chairman" was D. Milton Barrett.

[2] Edwin Denby, at this time a lawyer in Detroit; Republican congressman from Michigan, 1905-1911; Secretary of the Navy, 1921-1924.

found himself enjoying the companionship of Democrats. Now, I have long enjoyed the friendship and companionship of Republicans, because I am by instinct a teacher, and I would like to teach them something. We have been trying, some of us, for a good many years to teach, in politics as well as elsewhere, this lesson—that we are all in the same boat. We have common interests, and it is our business to understand and serve those common interests. The great difficulty that has confronted us, gentlemen, has often been that we have deliberately looked at these common interests from self-chosen angles, which made them look as if some of us were separated from others; and as if some of us wanted to depress business, for example, and others of us wanted to exalt business. I dare say that you have noticed that the same necessity to make a living is imposed upon Democrats as Republicans, and I dare say you are ready to believe that Democrats are just as willing to make a good living as Republicans. And therefore, it seems to me logically to follow, though I have been quoted as having no regard for logic, that Democrats are naturally as much interested in the business prosperity of the United States as anybody else. So that if you believe that they are not as fitted to guide it as other persons, you cannot be doubting their interest; you are only impugning their intelligence.

And some Democrats had noticed that the inclination to suppose that only some persons understood the business of America had a tendency to run into the assumption that the number of persons who understood that business was very small, and that there were only certain groups and associations of gentlemen who were entitled to be trustees of that business for the rest of us. I have never subscribed, in any walk of life, to the trustee theory. I have always been inclined to believe that the business of the world was best understood by those men who were in the struggle for maintenance, not only, but for success. The man who knows the strength of the tide is the man who is swimming against it, not the man who is floating with it. The man who is immersed in the beginnings of business, who is trying to get his foothold, who is trying to get other men to believe in him and lend him money and trust him to make profitable use of that money, is the man who knows what the business conditions in the United States are. And I would rather take his counsel as to what ought to be done for business than the counsel of any established captain of industry. Because the captain of industry is looking backward, and the other man is looking forward. The conditions of business change with every generation; change with every decade; are now changing at an almost breathless pace. And the men who have made good are not feeling the tides as the other men are feeling them. The men who have got into the position of captaincy, unless they are of unusual fiber, unless they are of unusually catholic sympathy, unless they have continued to touch shoulder with the ranks, unless they have continued to keep close communion with the men they are employing and the young men they are bringing up as their assistants, do not belong to the struggle in which we should see that every unreasonable obstacle is removed and every reasonable help afforded that public policy can afford.

So I invite your thoughts, in what I sincerely believe to be an entirely nonpartisan spirit, to the democracy of business. An act was recently passed in Congress that some of the most intelligent businessmen of this country earnestly opposed—men whom I knew, men whose character I trusted, men whose integrity I absolutely believed in. I refer to the Federal Reserve Act, by which we intended to take, and succeeded in taking, credit out of the control of a small number of men and making it available to everybody who had real commercial assets. And the very men who opposed that act, and opposed it conscientiously, now admit that it saved the country from a ruinous panic when the stress of war came on, and that it is the salvation of every average businessman who is in the midst of the tides that I have been trying to describe. What does that mean, gentlemen? It means that you can get a settled point of view and can conscientiously oppose progress if you do not need progress yourself. That is what it means. I am not impugning the intelligence even of the men who opposed these things, because the same thing happens to every man if he is not of extraordinary makeup, if he cannot see the necessity for a thing that he does not himself need. When you have abundant credit and control of credit, you, of course, do not need that the area of credit should be broadened.

So I say that the suspicion is beginning to dawn in many quarters that the average man knows the business necessities of the country just as well as the extraordinary man does. I believe in the ordinary man. If I didn't believe in the ordinary man, I would move out of a democracy, and, if I could find a decent monarchy, I would live in it. The very conception of America is based upon the validity of the judgments of the average man, and I call you to witness that there have not been many catastrophes in American history. I call you to witness that the average judgments of the voters of the United States have been sound judgments. I call you to witness that this great impulse of the common opinion has been a lifting impulse, and not a depressing impulse. What is the object of associations like that which is gathered here today, this salesmanship congress? The moral of it is that a few men cannot determine the interests of a large body of men, and that the only way to determine them and advance them is to have a representative assembly chosen by themselves get together and take common counsel regarding them. And do you not notice that, in every great occupation in the United States, there is beginning to be more and more of this common counsel? And have you not noticed that the more common counsel you have, the higher the standards are that are insisted upon?

I attended the other day the congress of the advertising men, and their motto is "Truth and fair dealing in what you represent your business to be and your goods to be." I have no doubt that, in every association like this, the prevailing sentiment is that only by the highest standards—I mean the highest moral standards—can you achieve the most permanent and satisfactory business results. Was that the prevalent conception before these associations were drawn together? Haven't you found the moral judgment of the average man steadying the whole process and clarifying it? Do you not know more after every conference with your fellows than you did before? I never went into a committee of any kind upon any important public matter, or private matter, so far as that is concerned, that I didn't come out with an altered judgment and knowing much more about the matter than when I went in; and, not only knowing much more, but knowing that the common judgment arrived at was better than I could have suggested when I went in. That is the universal experience of conferences. And if it were not so, there would be no object in congresses, like this. And, yet, whenever we attempt legislation, we find ourselves in this case: We are not in the presence of the many who can counsel wisely, but we are in the presence of the few who counsel too narrowly. And the thing that we have been trying to break away from is not that these gentlemen, who constituted the narrow circles of advice, should be excluded from the advice, but that they should be associated with hundreds of thousands of their fellow citizens.

I have heard some say that I was not accessible to them, and, when I inquired into it, I found they meant that I did not personally invite them. They did not know how to come without being invited, and they did not care to come if they came upon the same terms with everybody else, knowing that everybody else was welcome whom I had the time to confer with.

Am I telling you things unobserved by you? Do you not know that these things are true? And do you not believe with me that the affairs of the nation can be better conducted upon the basis of general counsel than upon the basis of special counsel? Men are colored and governed by their occupations and their surroundings and their habits. If I wanted to change the law radically, I would not consult a lawyer. If I wanted to change business methods radically, I would not consult a man who had made a conspicuous success by using the present methods that I wanted to change. Not because I would distrust these men, but because I would know that they would not change their thinking overnight, that they would have to go through a long process of reacquaintance with the circumstances of the time—the new circumstances of the time—before they could be converted to my point of view. You get a good deal more light on the street than you do in the closet. You get a good deal more light by keeping your ears open among the rank and file of your fellow citizens than you do in any private conference whatever. I would rather hear what the men are talking about on the trains and in the shops and by the firesides than hear anything else, because I want guidance, and I know I could get it there. And what I am constantly asking is that men should bring me that counsel, because I am not privileged to determine things independently of this counsel. I am your servant, not your ruler.

One thing that we are now trying to convert the small circles to, that the big circles are already converted to, is that this country needs a merchant marine and ought to get one. I have found that I had a great deal more resistance when I tried to help business than when I tried to interfere with it. I have had a great deal more resistance of counsel, of special counsel, when I tried to alter the things that are established than when I tried to do anything else. We call ourselves a liberal nation, whereas, as a matter of fact, we are one of the most conservative nations in the world. If you want to make enemies, try to change something. You know why it is. To do things today exactly the way you did them yesterday saves thinking. It does not cost you anything. You have acquired the habit; you know the routine; you do not have to plan anything. And it frightens you with a hint of exertion to learn that you will have to do it a different way tomorrow. Until I became a college teacher, I used to think that the young men were radical, but college boys are the greatest conservatives I ever tackled in my life, largely because they have associated too much with their fathers. And what you have to do with them is to take them up upon some visionary height and show them the map of the world as it is. Do not let them see their father's factory. Do not let them see their father's countinghouse. Let them see the great valleys teeming with laboring people. Let them see the great struggle of men in realms they never dreamed of. Let them see the great emotional power that is in the world—the great ambitions, the great hopes, the great fears. Give them some picture of mankind, and then their father's business and every other man's business will begin to fall into place. They will see that it is an item and not the whole thing. And they will sometimes see that the item is not properly related to the whole, and what they will get interested in will be to relate the item to the whole, so that it will form part of the force, and not part of the impediment.

Because this country, above every country in the world, gentlemen, is meant to lift; it is meant to add to the forces that improve. It is meant to add to everything that betters the world, that gives it better thinking, more honest endeavor, a closer grapple of man with man, so that we will all be pulling together like one irresistible team in a single harness. That is the reason why it seemed wise to substitute for the harsh processes of the law, which merely lays its hand on your shoulder after you have sinned and threatens you with punishment, some of the milder and more helpful processes of counsel. That is the reason the Federal Trade Commission was established—so that men would have some place where they could take counsel as to what the law was and what the law permitted; and also take counsel as to whether the law itself was right and advice had not better be taken as to its alteration. Because the processes of counsel are the only processes of accommodation, not the processes of punishment. Punishment retards but it doesn't lift up. Punishment impedes, but it does not improve. And so we ought to substitute for the harsh processes of the law, wherever we can, the milder and gentler and more helpful processes of counsel.

It has been a very great grief to some of us, year after year, year after year, to see a fundamental thing like the fiscal policy of the government with regard to duties on imports made a football of politics. Why, gentlemen, party politics ought to have nothing to do with the question of what is for the benefit of the business of the United States, and that is the reason we ought to have a tariff commission. And, I may add, are going to have a tariff commission. But, then, gentlemen, the trouble will be with me. The provision, as it stands, makes it obligatory upon me not to choose more than half the commission from any one political party. The bill doesn't undertake to say how many political parties there are. That, just now, is a delicate question. But I am forbidden to take more than two of the same variety, and yet the trouble about that is I would like to find men for that commission who were of no one of the varieties. I would like to find men who would find out the circumstances of American business, particularly as it changes and is going to change with perplexing rapidity in the years immediately ahead of us, without any regard whatever to the interest of any party whatever, so that we should be able to legislate upon the facts and upon the large economic aspects of those facts without stopping to think which party it was going to hurt and which party it was going to benefit. That is the idea. But almost everybody in this county wears a label of some kind, and under the law I suppose I will have to turn them around and see how they are labeled, how they are branded. And that is going to be a very great blow to my spirit and a very great test of my judgment. I hope, after the results are achieved, you will judge me leniently, because my desire would be not to have a bipartisan, but an absolutely nonpartisan, commission of men who really applied the tests of scientific analysis of the facts, and no other tests whatever, to the conclusions that they arrived at.

Did you ever think how absolutely supreme and sovereign facts are? You can make laws all the year through contrary to the facts, and the facts will overrun the laws. Do not let a fact catch you napping, because you will get the worst of it if you do. And the object of the tariff commission is that we should see the facts coming first, so that they could not get us. I remember a cynical politician saying to me once, when I was thanking him for having voted the way I hoped he would vote, knowing that that had not been his initial inclination, "Well, Governor, they never get me if I see them coming first." He had heard from home, and he saw them coming. Now, I have that attitude towards facts. I never let them get me if I see them first, and it is because I want to see them that I want commissions of this sort and the spirit of this sort that I have tried to describe in the commission as it is constituted.

Because, as I was saying this morning, there is a task ahead of us of most collossal difficulty. We haven't been accustomed to the large world of international business, and we have got to get accustomed to it right away. All provincials have got to take a back seat. All men who are afraid of competition have got to take a back seat. All men who depend upon anything except their intelligence and their efficiency have got to take a back seat. It will be interesting to see the sifting process go on. I have some men in mind to nominate for back seats, and I will not draw all of them from the same party. It won't need an act of Congress for that purpose. And some gentlemen are going to be surprised at the keenness of the air into which they are thrust out. They are going to be thrust out, and we are either going to make conquest—peaceful conquest—of the markets of the world, or we are going to be prevented forevermore of boasting of the business ability of America. I have never been afraid of trusting an American businessman out in the air, but some men have. They have said, "Give us a wall to crouch behind for fear these fellows should get us." And when it has come to finding out who were crouching behind the wall, it was found that all sorts were crouching behind the wall—the capable and the incapable—and that the main object of the wall was to shelter the incapable.

As an American, I am too proud to submit to anything like that. I believe that Americans can manufacture goods better than anybody else; that they can sell goods as honestly as anybody else; that they can find out the conditions and meet the conditions of foreign business better than anybody else. And I want to see them given a chance right away, and they will be whether I want them to be or not. And we have been trying to get ready for it. The national banks of the United States, until the recent currency act, were held back by the very terms of the law under which they operated from some of the most important international transactions. To my mind, that is one of the most amazing facts of our commercial history. The Congress of the United States wasn't willing that the national banks should have a latchkey and go away from home. They were afraid they would not know how to get back under cover. And banks from other countries had to establish branches where American bankers were doing business, to take care of some of the most important processes of international exchange. That is nothing less than amazing, but it isn't necessary any longer. It never was necessary; it was only thought to be necessary by some eminently provincial statesmen. We are done with provincialism in the statesmanship of the United States, and we have got to have a view now and a horizon as wide as the world itself. And, when I look around upon an alert company like this, it seems to me in my imagination they are almost straining at the leash. They are waiting to be let loose upon this great race that is now going to challenge our abilities. For my part, I shall look forward to the result with absolute and serene confidence, because the spirit of the United States is an international spirit, if we conceive it right. This is not the home of any particular race of men. This is not the home of any particular set of political traditions. This is a home, the doors of which have been opened from the first to mankind—to everybody who loved liberty, to everybody whose ideal was equality of opportunity, to everybody whose heart was moved by the fundamental instincts and sympathies of humanity. That is America, and now it is as if the nations of the world, assembled and united here, were, in their new union and new common understanding, turning about to serve the world with all the honest processes of business and of enterprise. I am happy that I should be witnessing the dawn of the day when America is indeed to come into her own.

Printed in *Addresses of President Wilson at Detroit, Mich.* . . . (Washington, 1916); with corrections from a reading of the CLSsh notes (C. L. Swem Coll., NjP) and from a nearly complete text in the *Detroit News*, July 11, 1916.

Remarks to Employees of the Ford Motor Company[1]

July 10, 1916.

My friends: I am not a living megaphone, and, therefore, I can't hope that my voice will reach more than a few of you, but I did want to give myself the pleasure of congratulating you upon being associated with a concern, not to say with a man, who knows the human relationships of men to each other, and who knows that the real foundation of business is efficiency and the interest of those who work in the things that they are doing. I wish that I could reach all of you, so as to convey to you these personal congratulations and good wishes.

It is out of the question that I should make a speech in these circumstances, but I can, and do, wish you the best fortunes in the world, and assure you of my own deep personal interest.

T MS (WP, DLC).
[1] Delivered from the back of an open car before all the employees of the Ford Motor Company. Henry Ford had personally designed a banner of greeting with the caption: "We take our hats off to the man who kept us out of war." *Detroit Free Press*, July 11, 1916.

Remarks at Union Station in Toledo, Ohio

[July 10, 1916]

My fellow citizens: This is an entirely pleasant surprise to me. I did not know that I was going to have the pleasure of stopping long enough to address any number of you, but I am very glad, indeed, to give you my very cordial greetings and to express my very great interest in this interesting city.

General Sherwood[1] said that there were many things we agreed about, but there is one thing we disagree about. General Sherwood has been opposing preparedness, and I have been advocating it, and I am very sorry to have found him on the other side. Because, I think, you will bear me witness, fellow citizens, that, in advocating preparedness, I have not been advocating hostility.

You will bear me witness that I have been a persistent friend of peace, and that nothing but unmistakable necessity will drive me from that position. I think it is a matter of sincere congratulation to us that our neighboring republic to the south shows evidences of at last believing in our friendly intentions; that, while we must protect our border and see to it that our sovereignty is not impugned, we are ready to respect their sovereignty, also, and to be their friends, and not their enemies.

Because the real uses of intelligence, my fellow citizens, are the uses of peace. Any body of men can get up a row, but only an intelligent body of men can get together and cooperate. So that peace is not only a test of a nation's patience; it is also a test of whether the nation knows how to conduct its relations or not. It takes time to do intelligent things, and it doesn't take any time to do unintelligent things. I can lose my temper in a minute, but it takes me a long time to keep it, and I think that, if you were to subject my Scotch-Irish blood to the proper kind of analysis, you would find that it was fighting blood, and that it is pretty hard for a man born that way to keep quiet and do things in the way in which his intelligence tells him he ought to do them. I know, just as well as that I am standing here, that I represent and am the servant of a nation that loves peace, and that loves it upon the proper basis; loves it, not because it is afraid of anybody; loves it, not because it doesn't understand and mean to maintain its rights, but because it knows that humanity is something in which we are all linked together, and that it behooves the United States, just as long as it is possible, to hold off from becoming involved in a strife which makes it all the more necessary that some part of the world should keep cool while all the rest of it is hot. Here, in America, for the time being, are the spaces, the cool spaces, of thoughtfulness. And so long as we are allowed to do so, we will serve and not contend with the rest of our fellow men. We are the more inclined to do this because the very principles upon which our government is based are principles of common counsel and not of contest.

And so, my fellow citizens, I congratulate myself upon this opportunity, brief as it is, to give you my greetings and to convey to you my congratulations that the signs that surround us are all signs of peace.

JRT transcript (WC, NjP) of CLSsh (C. L. Swem Coll., NjP).
1 Isaac Ruth Sherwood, Union officer in the Civil War, Democratic congressman from Toledo.

From William Joel Stone

Dear Mr. President: [Washington] July 10 1916.

I am sending you herewith a Document, printed by order of the Senate, which I think is of great importance to the country.[1] I would be very glad indeed if you would apply your discriminating and enlightening thought to the subjects covered by this Document. Does it not seem plain that we are about to face a serious consideration? Representing the party in power we must ourselves develop a public policy; we must not wait upon others.

I am leaving for St. Louis to attend a meeting of our State Committee, at which numerous leading Democrats are expected to be present. I wish you would talk over the matters covered by the enclosed Document with Mr. McAdoo and other gentlemen upon whose wise judgment you place reliance—and among them I hope you will include Senator Simmons, Mr. Kitchen, and other members of the two Committees that must deal with these subjects—and after I return, the last of the week, I suggest that a conference of our friends be held to debate these subjects. Whether you should be present, I leave you to determine.

I have the honor to be, Mr. President,

Very sincerely yours,   Wm J Stone.

TLS (WP, DLC).

[1] 64th Cong., 1st sess., Senate Document No. 491, *Trade Agreements Abroad: Articles Relating to the Resolution (S. 220) "Requesting the President to Ascertain Certain Information Relating to a Recent Commercial Conference Held in Paris, France, by Certain European Nations," Together with the Remarks of Senator William J. Stone and Senator Henry Cabot Lodge Delivered in the United States Senate Thereon and the Message of the President in Response Thereto* (Washington, 1916), copy in WP, DLC. The remarks of Stone and Lodge, delivered in the Senate on July 10, dealt with the dangers which the postwar economic policies of the Allies might pose for the United States. Wilson's message to the Senate, dated July 10, 1916, was a brief note covering a report from Lansing setting forth what was known of the Allied Economic Conference held in Paris, June 14-17, 1916. The "articles" were various newspaper and magazine commentaries on possible postwar economic policies of both the Allies and the Central Powers.

From Newton Diehl Baker

My dear Mr. President: Washington. July 10, 1916.

This morning I had a long talk with Judge Clarke of Cleveland.[1] I have known him so intimately that the talk was natural and, to my mind, most satisfactory.

He tells me that since he has been a Federal Judge he has not been called upon to pass upon any question affecting the interpretation of the anti-Trust Laws, but that while he was still a practicing lawyer he declined several requests from clients to act for them in building business aggregations which would monopolize certain fields of industry. We then talked general[ly] about this subject, and I feel entirely free to commend his views to you without reservation or doubt on my part.

The Attorney General and I have discussed this matter since I saw Judge Clarke, and I have told him that my conversation of this morning with the Judge removed any hesitancy I had on the subject.   Cordially yours,   Newton D. Baker

TLS (WP, DLC).
  ¹ John Hessin Clarke, United States district judge for the northern district of Ohio.

From Edward William Pou

Dear Mr. President: Smithfield, N. C. July 10th, 1916.

I am very deeply touched that I should be remembered by your kind telegram and the box of flowers when so many things of nation wide importance are pressing for attention.

Since I have come to know you better I begin to understand how political success comes to you almost as a matter of course. You do not forget the seemingly little things which draw men close to-gether.

I have been pretty sick with nervous indigestion; and I can truthfully say, that my greatest cause of annoyance and chagrin has been the fact that I am kept away from Washington, and therefore, deprived of the pleasure and pride of helping put through the last parts of the administration program. I have gone over the things we have done and I say, Mr. President, that nothing but sheer madness on the part of the people can encompass your defeat. I think it significant that the nomination of Justice Hughes has caused so little enthusiasm—practically none at all.

I am glad to say I am very much improved and hope to be in my seat by the last of the week.

Again thanking you for your thoughtfulness, I remain,
                    Sincerely your friend,   Edwd W. Pou.

TLS (WP, DLC).

Henry Prather Fletcher to Edward Mandell House, With Enclosure

My dear Colonel House,   Washington July 10th, 1916

I enclose to you a translation of a note I received last week from Ambassador Naon, in which he says that he has asked his

Gov't for instructions to sign, but fears that as long as the Mexican situation remains so threatening he will not be authorized to sign etc. etc. After the receipt of this note I went to New York to see Mr Naon, and told him that the President was particularly anxious in view of the Mexican complications to show by signing the treaty the unselfishness of the U. S. A. &c. He said he appreciated that as much as anyone but could not escape the thought that his Gov't would believe the present moment inopportune. He agreed however to let me know as soon as he was authorized to proceed.

Meanwhile I have added—with Secretary Lansings approval—a clause fixing the life of the treaty at ten years—automatically renewing itself for another ten years, unless denounced a year before the expiration of this term.

I am having these articles prepared in English and Spanish for submission to the other countries who have accepted the idea, but until the Argentine answer is received I do not believe it expedient to take it up with the smaller countries.

Mr Lansing has asked me to remain on duty here in the Dep't during his absence, helping Mr Polk on Latin American and Mexican affairs and since his departure I have been so engaged.

It begins to look as if I may be able to start for Mexico sooner than I expected, but the situation, while greatly improved, is far from clear. Something constructive must be done, but I fear the Mexican Gov't will not or can not do more than patchwork at present. However the atmosphere is a great deal better and I still have hope.

With my kind regards,

Sincerely yours   Henry P. Fletcher

ALS (E. M. House Papers, CtY).

E N C L O S U R E

Rómulo Sebastian Náon to Henry Prather Fletcher

My dear Mr. Ambassador: New York, N. Y., June 27, 1916.

I have had the pleasure of receiving your kind note of last Saturday, with the copy of the draft of the Pan-American Treaty, and I note an omission therein which it would be convenient to correct, and of which I forgot to speak to you in our last conversation. I refer to an article establishing that the Treaty should last for ten years and should be renewed for another ten years automatically, unless some of the parties should decide to the contrary within one year of the expiration of the term.

It is not possible to answer you immediately with respect to the signing of the Treaty without previously consulting my Government. I fear that the present conditions of the Mexican conflict may make it necessary to consider convenient the suspension of the signature until said conflict disappears. It is difficult to sign treaties which tend to impose concord and union on the continent while threats of war are passing between two of the most important nations of America, as is the case at present. I fear, therefore, and have my motives for so doing, that in Buenos Aires it may be considered that the signature of the Treaty is incompatible with this situation. You understand how decided is the friendship of our country and how intense is its admiration for this great country of yours—you understand also that Pan-Americanism is one of the political principles of our Government, and my most profound personal conviction in the field of international American politics. It will be understood on the same grounds that only a very sincere scruple would prevent me giving you my definite answer immediately with respect to this.

Today I have telegraphed to Buenos Aires asking instructions, and I shall transmit to you the answer as soon as received. I shall send you also at an early date the Spanish translation as requested.

With my most distinguished consideration and personal regard, I repeat I am your very obedient servant and friend,

Rómulo S. Náon.

TCL (E. M. House Papers, CtY).

From Frank Lyon Polk

My dear Mr. President: Washington July 11, 1916.

I have heard from several sources in Mexico City and here, that the Mexican de facto government was on the point of suggesting a joint commission to discuss Mexican affairs in general.

Mr. Arredondo called yesterday and said he was not prepared for any discussion, but that Mr. Carranza would undoubtedly make the suggestion for a joint commission and he wished to discuss with me the question of having representatives of the Government as members. He apparently had the impression that Mr. Lansing felt that the commissioners should be men outside of the Government. I think this was a misunderstanding and that what Mr. Lansing meant was that they should be civil and not military men. I told him that I felt it would be unfortunate if some member of their Government were not on the commission. The understanding is that they wish to appoint Cabrera.

He said that General Carranza favored two commissioners. I told him that while I could not voice your opinion on the subject, I personally felt that three from each government would be an advantage, my reason being that in that way this Government could have the different elements represented.

Mr. Arredondo's attitude was apparently frank and he showed every wish to be helpful. I think he realizes that if these negotiations work out successfully, it will strengthen him in his own country

I expect to hear again from Mr. Arredondo, today or tomorrow.

Yours faithfully,   Frank L Polk

TLS (WP, DLC).

From Frank Lyon Polk, with Enclosure

My dear Mr. President: Washington July 11, 1916.

I attach a copy of a telegram from Mr. Page, which you have probably already seen. I know the Secretary felt that it would be most desirable to have Mr. Page come home, and this telegram seems to open the way.

Recently the Secretary received a letter from Mr. Page which showed extraordinary ignorance of our point of view, and it was quite querulous in its tone in regard to the many complaints which we were sending him to present to the British Government. He seemed to feel that we were imposing on the good nature of the British Government.

I think we all feel here that it would be very helpful all around, if he should come home for a short vacation.

Yours faithfully,   Frank L. Polk

TLS (WP, DLC).

E N C L O S U R E

London, July 7, 1916.

4538. There are a number of proposals which I should like to present for your consideration. If approved by you they will, I am confident, result in greatly increased efficiency of this Embassy. These proposals are difficult to present in writing but should be the subject of full personal discussion. Some of them you will doubtless wish to discuss with other departments. I should very much like to go to Washington myself but quite realize the objections to leaving my post. As a satisfactory alternative I venture to suggest that the Department summon to Washington Shoecraft[1] who has been acting as my private secretary for over a year. He is fully informed and could, I am sure, present these matters satisfactorily. I should like to have them considered by you as soon as possible. If you approve Shoecraft can be ready to sail by the first steamer on Wednesday next.   Page.

T telegram (WP, DLC).
   [1] Eugene Claire Shoecraft, Second Secretary of the embassy in London.

From Edward Mandell House

Dear Governor: New London, N. H. July 11, 1916.

Frank Walsh of Kansas City talked with me yesterday over the telephone concerning the commission which he thought Carranza would ask you to appoint.

If this commission is named he thinks it would be wise to appoint only such men as thoroughly agree with your Mexican policy. He also thought that an influential Catholic should be on it so when the report came back, it would satisfy that sect.

The man he suggested as best fitted for this was a Col. P. H. Callahan of Louisville, Ky.[1] If a labor man is appointed he suggested John Fitzpatrick of Chicago, President of the Federation of Labor.[2] Of course, if Callahan was appointed, Fitzpatrick could not be because there would be two Irish Catholics. Charles R. Crane was also suggested by him.

I am giving you this because I promised to do so.

Of your Press Club Speech Amos Pinchot says: "It was the most important utterance in recent years."

Noel Buxton said: that he felt that the journey here was well worth while just to have heard it for it struck a new high note that it would be very difficult to think of an English state[s]man taking.   Affectionately yours,   E. M. House

TLS (WP, DLC).
   [1] Patrick Henry Callahan, president of the Louisville Varnish Co.
   [2] That is, the Chicago Federation of Labor.

From Samuel Gompers

Sir: Washington, D. C., July 11, 1916.

There is a general report that you have under consideration at the present time the proposition to appoint a commission to in-

quire into conditions which have existed and now exist along
the border line of the United States and Mexico which are subversive to the best interests of both countries and are dangerous
to international peace.

In the document which I had the honor of handing you a few
days ago, when I had the pleasure of presenting to you the representatives of the British Trade Union Congress at the dedication
of the A.F. of L. office building, was the declaration of the representatives of the organized labor movement of Mexico and the
United States. That document concludes with the request that a
commission be appointed such as is reported you now have under
consideration.

I am sure I need only to call your attention to the relations
that have existed between the workingmen of the two countries
and the part that the workers have had in bringing about greater
freedom and greater opportunities in Mexico to convince you
that a representative of organized labor ought to be named on
that commission.

Out of the revolution in Mexico there has come one fundamental result—the organization of the workers. It is being more
generally recognized that the labor movement everywhere represents distinctively the cause of humanity and human rights.
There is no phase of any problem which such a commission
would have to investigate that would not affect the lives and the
work of many of both countries.

The agencies that have been most active in trying to excite a
national opinion favorable to war and which have done so much
to bring about the injustice of which the workers of both countries complain are concerned in conditions that have so nearly
precipitated both countries into what would have been a deplorable war.

These are matters of which wage-earners have information
and in which they are vitally concerned. They should be considered by any commission that is to make any recommendation
that will look for the removal of the causes of friction and of war.

I urge, therefore, for your earnest consideration that should
such a commission be appointed you appoint a representative of
organized labor upon the commission, whose work and whose
findings will have so great a potentiality in the future development of both countries.

Very sincerely yours,   Saml. Gompers.

TLS (WP, DLC).

From Charles Pope Caldwell[1]

My dear Mr. President: Washington, D. C. July 11, 1916.

Enclosed herewith is a resolution introduced by me in the House on July 10th.[2] From conversations with various members of the House, I believe that the resolution will meet with approval if it will not interfere with your plans.

I am not in a position to know what negotiations are in progress in connection woth [with] the Mexican situation; but I feel that because of the loss of American lives and property that sooner or later compensation must be demanded and this action at this time would eliminate these questions and lead to a permanent peace.

I would like to have your opinion on this resolution and would appreciate an interview for this purpose.

Very respectfully,   Chas Pope Caldwell.

TLS (WP, DLC).
    [1] Democratic congressman from New York.
    [2] 64th Cong., 1st sess., *H.J. Res.* 258, printed resolution (WP, DLC). It authorized the President to appoint a commission of five members to negotiate for the purchase by the United States from Mexico "of such portion of northern Mexico, including Lower California, as may be obtained." It also invited Mexico to appoint a similar commission.

An Address from the Polish Central Relief Committee

[Washington?] July 12th, 1916.

In the hour of the greatest calamity confronting a nation, we, the chosen representatives of organizations united in the Polish Central Relief Committee, embracing nearly all of the four million residents and citizens of the United States of Polish birth or extraction, present to you, Mr. President, our appeal, that you as President of the United States, raise your voice in protest against what appears to be a deliberate sentence of death passed upon the inhabitants of the kingdom of Poland. Galicia or Austrian Poland from the very beginning of the war suffered almost complete devastation by repeated movements of armies over her territory. Russian Poland, although visited by the hardships of war, was not in danger of starvation. A year ago the Russian armies, which were in possession, began to evacuate and a hurried retreat over Polish territory took place, followed by the invasion of German and Austrian forces.

Tremendous stores of food and provisions were destroyed and thousands of villages and towns leveled with the ground by the retreating Russian armies as "an inevitable necessity of war." In a comparatively brief period of time nearly the whole of the kingdom of Poland was occupied by the armies of the Central powers. Then reports came that requisitions by the occupying armies stripped the entire country of the rest of its native stocks and stores. The situation became more acute from day to day, until in the months of November and December 1915, it became so appalling that representatives of the American Red Cross Society, the Rockefeller Foundation and the Commission for the Relief in Belgium, took notice and endeavored to inaugurate relief work. In the month of January, 1916, the United Polish Organizations of America, actuated by humanitarian motives, and mindful of their blood relationship, organized a relief movement for the sending of food and provisions to the stricken districts in Poland. Efforts were made to secure from Great Britain a modification of the blockade which would permit landing of ships at Danzig. The American organizations mentioned above promised generous assistance. Great Britain was appealed to, Germany, Russia and Austria were approached through their embassies at Washington. Our State Department rendered assistance. Mr. Herbert C. Hoover, Chairman of the Commission for Relief in Belgium, made heroic efforts to bring about an understanding between Great Britain and Germany. American Ambassadors undertook mediation. Exchanges of telegrams and communications continued for months. In the meantime, the Polish people starved. At last there was hope of success. Great Britain agreed to permit shipment from America under conditions to be observed by the Central powers. These conditions, however, were rejected.

Now word comes from the other side: "Abandon all hope for Polish Relief." This sounds like a death sentence. There can be no illusion about it. The treatment of, and the attitude of the neighboring powers towards, the Polish people during this war clearly demonstrates their design to obtain control and hold possession of Polish territory unincumbered by its hereditary owners. Germany declines to give the guaranty demand[ed] by the Allies, that food sent to Poland from America and such supply of food as may still exist there, be not requisitioned by the occupying armies, but be taken as a whole and preserved for the civil population. Russia does not reply to a telegram sent two months ago by the United Polish Organizations of America relative to her position on the food situation in Poland.

Outraged civilization which has for two years witnessed the most startling disregard for human life and the unprecedented destruction of property created by human industry and ingenuity during centuries of time, is now further to be outraged by the deliberate murder of an ancient, civilized and noble nation.

Those who are about to die make this last appeal through their brethern here to the chief of the greatest republic on earth. You, Mr. President, have raised your voice in protest against the sinking of the Lusitania and the Sussex; you protested against the massacres of Armenians; you have repeatedly proclaimed that you stand for justice and humanity; to you, then, Mr. President, this appeal is made on behalf of these millions of human beings.

We are unwilling to abandon hope and we bring our protest to the only tribunal of humanity and justice, the United States of America. We most respectfully submit, the justice of our claim, that the President of the United States has the right to demand that America and American citizens who are willing to share in the work of salvation, be given the opportunity of sending to Poland necessaries of life which will save its remaining population from a lingering death.

Let the world be told by the President of the United States that humanity cannot acquiesce in the murder of millions of innocent people. Military considerations affecting nations at war, and their mutual distrust and hatred should not be permitted to further delay and frustrate these humanitarian efforts.

We most respectfully pray that request be made upon Great Britain by the State Department at Washington, that ships carrying provisions for the civilian population in Poland be permitted to pass the blockade, and upon Germany for a guaranty that neither such shipments will be molested, nor the still existing native stocks of food be requisitioned for the use of occupying armies.

We make this appeal in all sincerity and with due respect. Our feelings cannot be expressed in words, but we are conscious of our duty, which we hereby perform, not alone for the sake of our loved ones abroad, but in the broadest sense of universal justice.

Into your hands, Mr. President, do we entrust what we believe to be a question of life and death of millions of Polish people

Most respectfully,
Polish Central Relief Committee
John F. Smulski[1]

TLS (WP, DLC).

[1] This address was signed by John Franklin Smulski, lawyer, banker, and Republican politician of Chicago, and thirty-seven other representatives of the Polish National Council, the Polish National Alliance, the Polish Roman Catholic Union, the Polish Falcons' Alliance, the Polish Women's Alliance, the Polish Association of America, the Polish Alma Mater, the Association of the Polish Clergy, the Polish Union of America, the Polish St. Joseph's Union, and the Polish Uniformed Societies. Senator Gilbert M. Hitchcock presented a delegation representing the Polish-American societies to Wilson at the White House on July 12. Their spokesman was Smulski.

A Dialogue with John Franklin Smulski

[July 12, 1916]

[Wilson] Mr. Smulski, fellow citizens: This is a matter which has engaged my thoughts constantly, I might say without exaggeration, and I don't think that there is any matter to which the State Department has devoted a more constant effort, and repeated effort, than this matter of trying to get relief into Poland.

I know the terrible conditions, the tragical conditions that exist there, and nobody could know them without feeling his heart torn with the knowledge. Just the other day, Mr. Smulski, we issued a special appeal to the governments concerned to make concessions and allow this humane thing to be done.

Now, I am simply up against a stone wall in the matter. If they don't yield, obviously there is nothing I can do. I cannot force food in there without complicating the situation still further, and, I should conjecture, of doing a greater disservice to Poland than service, because her only friends are apparently at a disadvantage. But I can assure you that every kind of pressure that can be brought, will be brought, and is being brought in the accomplishment of this object.

I desire, as well as all those associated with me desire, to help. But, as a reminder it was most unnecessary that you should come. I mean, I was not forgetful of Poland and was not likely to be forgetful of her, but that makes your visit none the less impressive and none the less welcome, and you may be sure I will continue to do everything that is possible.

I don't quite understand what Mr. Smulski had in mind when he suggested a personal appeal on my part. Certainly you didn't mean a public paper of any sort, because I can assure you, gentlemen, that I will renew my efforts, and I will consider the ways of sending, perhaps, a personal appeal.

[Smulski] Would it be objectionable for you, as President of the United States, to address a personal letter to the Kaiser of Germany, the King of Great Britain, the Czar of Russia, representing that, in the United States, there were many hundreds of thousands of Poles and other relatives desiring to succor them and urge in some way—

[Wilson] It is quite possible that might be done.

[Smulski] We ask you, Mr. President, on behalf of humanity, to appeal to the press, Mr. President, to save Poland from extermination, and we ask you personally to appeal to the rest of the nations of Europe not to continue the starvation of Poland.

JRT transcript (WC, NjP) of CLSsh (C. L. Swem Coll., NjP), with corrections from the incomplete text in the New York Times, July 13, 1916.

To William Joel Stone

My dear Senator: [The White House] July 12, 1916

I have your letter of July eighth conveying the request of the Committee on Foreign Relations for information about the treaty recently made between Japan and Russia with regard to China. I am going to take the liberty of referring your letter at once to the Secretary of State to see if we have any information regarding it other than that which all the public has.

Cordially and sincerely yours,   Woodrow Wilson

TLS (Letterpress Books, WP, DLC).

To Robert Lansing

My dear Mr. Secretary: The White House July 12, 1916

Here is a letter from Senator Stone.[1] I am writing to ask if there is any information, other than that which all the public has upon this matter, which we could send the Committee in response to this very reasonable request.

Cordially and sincerely yours,   Woodrow Wilson

TLS (SDR, RG 59, 761.94/103, DNA).
[1] That is, W. J. Stone to WW, July 8, 1916.

To Vance Criswell McCormick

My dear McCormick: The White House July 12, 1916

The enclosed scenario by Mr. Edward Lyall Fox[1] seems to me to have a great many things to commend it. I wish that you might find time to look it over and help me assess its value to us as an instrument of the campaign; and if you are not overwhelmed with callers, I wish you would have a talk sometime with Mr. Fox himself, who, I think, writes from the Beta Theta Pi Club, No. 1 Gramercy Park.

Cordially and faithfully yours,   Woodrow Wilson

TLS (V. C. McCormick Papers, CtY).
[1] T motion picture scenario (V. C. McCormick Papers, CtY), a series of suggested scenarios contrasting the Wilson administration with its Republican predecessors in their respective treatments of such problems as big business, labor relations, banking and currency, and preparedness. Fox was a journalist of New York.

To Azel Washburn Hazen

My dear Doctor Hazen: The White House July 12, 1916

Your letters always give me the keenest pleasure, and I am certainly your debtor for the generous letter of July tenth.[1]

It interests me very much that you are about to give up your active pastorate, and it causes me a pang to hear it, because I know how much you have meant to the church and to the community in your active work as a pastor. It must be a source of the deepest gratification to you to realize the place you have established in their affection and confidence, and to think of the wide circle of friends who trust and admire you as I do.

Always   Affectionately yours,   Woodrow Wilson

TLS (received from Frances Hazen Bulkeley).
 [1] It is missing.

To Herbert Adams

[The White House] July 12, 1916

Will be very glad to see you tomorrow evening at eight if you can get here by that time; if not please let me know upon your arrival and I will find an hour.   Woodrow Wilson.

T telegram (Letterpress Books, WP, DLC).

To George W. Megeath

Personal.

My dear Mr. Megeath: [The White House] July 12, 1916

The fine whiskey came as if from John Wilson, but I know it was from you and I wanted to let you know how warmly and sincerely I appreciate your generous thought of me. You are indeed thoughtful and gracious.

Cordially and sincerely yours,   Woodrow Wilson

TLS (Letterpress Books, WP, DLC).

From Frank Lyon Polk, with Enclosure

My dear Mr. President: Washington July 12, 1916.

I enclose a translation of a communication which Mr. Arredondo handed me this morning. I have only read it very hurriedly but it seems to me that the questions to be considered by the Commission are rather too limited and there does not seem to be any provision in this communication for an investigation along the broad lines you and the Secretary have in mind.

I told Mr. Arredondo that we would probably wish to discuss the matter informally tomorrow, and possibly you would like to talk with me before I see him.

I do not suppose that it will be well for us to make a counter proposal, broadening the scope of the inquiry; but if they are sympathetic, we might suggest to them informally to amend the proposal to broaden the powers of the Commission.

Yours faithfully,   Frank L. Polk

TLS (WP, DLC).

ENCLOSURE

Eliseo Arredondo to Frank Lyon Polk

Mr. Secretary: Washington, D. C. July 12, 1916.

I have received instructions from my Government to transmit to Your Excellency the following note:

"Mr. Secretary: I have the honor to refer to Your Excellency's note dated the 7th instant, which was transmitted to me by our Confidential Agent in Washington, Lic. Eliseo Arredondo; and in doing so, inform you that I have received instructions from the Citizen First Chief of the Constitutionalist Army, Charged with the Executive Power of the Union, to propose through you to His Excellency President Wilson, that each of our Governments name three commissioners, who shall hold conferences at some place to be mutually agreed upon, and decide forthwith the question relating to the evacuation of the American forces now in Mexico, and to draw up and conclude a protocol or agreement regarding the reciprocal crossing of the frontier by the forces of both countries, also to determine the origin of the incursions to date, in order to fix the responsibility therefor and definitely to settle the difficulties now pending or those which may arise between the two countries on account of the same or a similar reason; all of which shall be subject to the approval of both Governments.

The Mexican Government proposes that these conferences shall proceed in a spirit of the most frank cordiality and with the earnest purpose of reaching an arrangement satisfactory and honorable to both countries, in the belief that if the Government of the United States should accept the proposal contained in this note, the foregoing should be the principal recommendation given to the representatives which it may name.

The Government of Mexico considers that this is the most efficacious means of arriving at the desired result, and hopes that the Government of the United States will be kind enough to state whether it accepts this proposal, in order to carry it into effect forthwith, and in order that the Government of Mexico may communicate immediately the names of the persons which it may designate as its representatives.

Accept, Excellency, the assurances of my distinguished consideration.   Aguilar."

In complying with the superior instructions of my Government, I take pleasure to renew to Your Excellency the assurances of my high consideration.   E. Arredondo.

TCL (WP, DLC).

From Edward Mandell House, with Enclosure

Dear Governor: New London, N. H. July 12, 1916.

I am enclosing you a copy of an autograph letter from Sir Edward Grey.

He makes it clear I think why the English cannot take the initiative for peace. It is true that Germany has been trying to make a separate peace with both Russia and France.

What he says about a change in conditions after this offensive has been tried out is interesting and important. They should know by September 1st whether it is to be a success or failure. Then would be the time to press some proposal on them.

Arthur Bullard is just back from Europe. He tells me that while he was in London, Sir Horace Plunkett said he had seen a cable from Spring-Rice to the Foreign Office saying that in no event would this country go to war with Germany. This was at the most acute stage of our last crisis with Germany.

What a lot of unfortunate circumstances and people we have to contend with. Spring-Rice goes only with your enemies like Roosevelt, Morgan and Senators Lodge and Root and gets their point of view and conveys it to his government.

Have you any suggestions to make in my reply to Sir Edward['s] letter? He gives us a good chance to say whatever you may think advisable.   Affectionately yours,   E. M. House

TLS (WP, DLC).

ENCLOSURE

Sir Edward Grey to Edward Mandell House

Private.

Dear Colonel House: London, S. W. June 28, 1916.

Your letter of June 1st reached me on the 26th. I am very glad you had a talk with Jusserand and got the French view at first hand.

Germany has made it known, sometimes to France, sometimes to Russia, that she is ready to make an easy peace with either of them but not with us, and the French have with perfect good humor and loyalty said so sometimes to us in conversation.

But the result of this German action is that we must at all times leave our Allies in no doubt as to our readiness to support them as long as they wish to continue and as long as they can both say truly that they are fighting to clear the enemy out of their country and I would add in the case of France to get back Alsace and Lorraine.

That each wants more than this is true, but they cannot be said, with the military map as it is and Bethmann-Hollweg's speeches as they are, to be so far prolonging the war for more than this. While this is so, German overtures to them and her concentrated hostility to us, have limited our influence with our Allies and have placed the decision as regards peace entirely in their hands, especially in those of France on whom the brunt and fury of the fight has fallen for these last months.

No Englishman would at this moment say to France after Poincare's and Briand's speeches made in face of the Verdun struggle "Hasn't the time come to make peace?" It is also true I think that if France said "I am exhausted" no Englishman would in face of the French sacrifices at Verdun say in reply "You must go on."

I ought in fairness to add that I think independent English opinion feels just as strongly as France that the time for durable peace is not yet. At any rate the British Army has to make its effort and its sacrifices if need be to help France before we can be the first to call a halt.

I want you to understand the limitations imposed upon our influence with the Allies, partly by the action of Germany and partly by circumstances and why therefore I was so desirous that the President or you should not approach France through us, but direct.

As to the President's speech of May 27th and its reception by the Allied Press, which I think is what you refer to in the fifth paragraph of your letter, I read the speech in the light of my talks with you and welcomed it. But the phrase about not being concerned with the objects and causes of the war was sure to chill the Allies. And the mention of the security of the highway of the seas as the first object of the universal cooperation of nations without any definition of what is meant made our Press suspicious.

Our Press will have it that Germany means by freedom of the seas reduction of the British Navy to a size at which it must be impotent, and when impotent to interfere with enemy trade, also impotent to protect us from invasion, and they will continue to shy at the phrase in the absence of any definition of what is meant. And there are other points e.g. is blockade in any form to be allowed or is it to be completely abolished?

All this however is by way of explanation and not a discussion of merits. I remain of opinion that we ought to agree to rules of war for land and sea approved by nations, who will bind themselves to support us and each other in a dispute in which we or they are prepared to adopt some other method of settlement than war and the opponent is not.

We are now in a very intense moment of the war—everybody in the next few weeks is going to make their maximum effort; if the result is a distinct sweep to one side or the other the situation will be changed; even if the result is deadlock, the situation will not be the same as before the effort was made and must be reviewed afresh. For the moment that is about all I can say as to future prospects.   Yours sincerely,   E. Grey.

As you say Kitchener's death is a great loss. He had not got some of the qualities that the Press universally attributed to him; but he had the quality of personality which is more valuable and uncommon and his courage was magnificent and he was a great asset to his country.

TCL (WP, DLC).

To Charles Pope Caldwell

My dear Mr. Caldwell: [The White House] July 13, 1916

I am sincerely obliged to you for having sent me a copy of House Resolution 258, and having sought my advice about it. I beg that you will not at this time press the resolution. It would constitute a very serious embarrassment and probably make a new complication in our Mexican affairs. I make this very frank response to your inquiry because I know it is only frankness that you desire.

　　　　　Cordially and sincerely yours,　Woodrow Wilson

TLS (Letterpress Books, WP, DLC).

To Frank Lyon Polk

My dear Mr. Secretary:　　　　　The White House July 13, 1916

　Here is a very earnest appeal made to me yesterday by representatives of our fellow-citizens of Polish blood. The whole thing appeals to me, as I know it does to you, and I would like your very candid advice as to whether it would be wise or in any way efficacious, so far as we can judge, for me to address personal letters to the King of England, the Emperor of Germany, the Emperor of Austria, the Czar of Russia, and the President of France, appealing to them to cooperate with us in making arrangements which will enable the Polish citizens of the United States to send food to their suffering friends and kinsmen in Poland. That is the only thing I can think of that we have not yet done.

　　　　　Cordially and sincerely yours,　Woodrow Wilson

TLS (WP, DLC).

William Phillips to Frank Lyon Polk

Dear Mr. Polk,　　·　　　　　[Washington] July 13 [1916]

　I think that this is a splendid suggestion and will follow well after *our* recent appeal.

　It seems to me that the sooner the President can address his letters the better,—we might then inform our Embassies that the letters are in fact on their way.　　　　　　W. P.

ALS (WP, DLC).

An Address on the American Spirit[1]

　　　　　　　　　　　　　　　[[July 13, 1916]]

　Mr. Chairman, ladies and gentlemen: I have come here for the simple purpose of expressing my very deep interest in what these conferences are intended to attain. It is not fair to the great multi-

---

　[1] Delivered before the Citizenship Convention, held under the auspices of the Bureau of Naturalization, at the Wilson Normal School in Washington. Richard Kenna Campbell, Commissioner of Naturalization, introduced Wilson.

tudes of hopeful men and women, who press into this country from other countries, that we should leave them without that friendly and intimate instruction which will enable them, very soon after they come, to find out what America is like at heart and what America is intended for among the nations of the world.

I believe that the chief school that these people must attend after they get here is the school which all of us attend, which is furnished by the life of the communities in which we live and the nation to which we belong. It has been a very touching thought to me, sometimes, to think of the hopes which have drawn these people to America. I have no doubt that many a simple soul has been thrilled by that great statue standing in the harbor of New York and seeming to lift the light of liberty for the guidance of the feet of men. And I can imagine that they have expected here something ideal in the treatment that they will receive—something ideal in the laws which they would have to live under—and it has caused me, many a time, to turn upon myself the eye of examination to see whether there burned in me the true light of the American spirit which they expected to find here. It is easy, my fellow citizens, to communicate physical lessons, but it is very difficult to communicate spiritual lessons. America was intended to be a spirit among the nations of the world, and it is the purpose of conferences like this to find out the best way to introduce the newcomers to this spirit, and by that very interest in them to enhance and purify in ourselves the thing that ought to make America great and, not only ought to make her great, but ought to make her exhibit a spirit unlike any other nation in the world.

I have never been among those who felt comfortable in boasting of the superiority of America over other countries. The way to cure yourself of that is to travel in other countries and find out how much of nobility and character and fine enterprise there is everywhere in the world. The most that America can hope to do is to show, it may be, the finest example, not the only example, of the things that ought to benefit and promote the progress of the world.

So my interest in this movement is as much an interest in ourselves as in those whom we are trying to Americanize, because, if we are genuine Americans, they cannot avoid the infection, whereas, if we are not genuine Americans, there will be nothing to infect them with. And no amount of teaching, no amount of exposition of the Constitution—which I find very few persons understand—no amount of dwelling upon the idea of liberty and of justice will accomplish the object we have in view, unless we, ourselves, illustrate the idea of justice and of liberty. My interest in this movement is, therefore, a two-fold interest. I believe it will assist us to become self-conscious in respect of the fundamental ideas of American life. When you ask a man to be loyal to a government, if he comes from some foreign country, his idea is that he is expected to be loyal to a certain set of persons, like a ruler or a body set in authority over him. But that is not the American idea. Our idea is that he is to be loyal to certain objects in life, and that the only reason he has a President and a Congress and a governor and a state legislature and courts is that the community shall have instrumentalities by which to promote those objects. It is a cooperative organization expressing itself in this Constitution, expressing itself in those laws, intending to express itself in the exposition of those laws by the courts.

And the idea of America is not so much that men are to be restrained and punished by the law as instructed and guided by the law. That is the reason so many hopeful reforms come to grief. A law cannot work until it expresses the spirit of the community for which it is enacted. And, if you try to enact into law what expresses only the spirit of a small coterie or of a small minority, you know, or at any rate you ought to know beforehand, that it is not going to work. The object of the law is that there, written upon these pages, the citizen should read the record of the experience of this state and nation—what they have concluded it is necessary for them to do because of the life they have lived and the things that they have discovered to be elements in that life. So that we ought to be careful to maintain a government at which the immigrant can look with the closest scrutiny and to which he should be at liberty to address this question: "You declare this to be a land of liberty and of equality and of justice. Have you made it so by your laws?" We ought to be able, in our schools, in our night schools, and in every other method of instructing these people, to show them that that has been our endeavor. We cannot conceal from them long the fact that we are just as human as any other nation, that we are just as selfish, that there are just as many mean people amongst us as anywhere else, that there are just as many people here who want to take advantage of other people as you can find in other countries, just as many cruel people, just as many people heartless, when it comes to maintaining and promoting their own interest. But you can show that our object is to get these people in harness and see to it that they do not do any damage and are not allowed to indulge the passions which would bring injustice and calamity at last upon a nation whose object is spiritual and not material. America has bulit up a great body of wealth. America has become, from the physical point of view, one of the most powerful nations in the world—a nation which, if it took the pains to do so, could build that power up into one of the most formidable instruments in the world, one of the most formidable instruments of force, but which has no other idea than to use its force for ideal objects and not for self-aggrandizement.

We have been disturbed recently, my fellow citizens, by certain symptoms which have showed themselves in our body politic. Certain men—I have never believed a great number—born in other lands, have in recent months thought more of those lands than they have of the honor and interest of the government under which they are now living. They have even gone so far as to draw apart in spirit and in organization from the rest of us to accomplish some special object of their own. I am not here going to utter any criticism of these people, but I want to say this—that such a thing as that is absolutely incompatible with the fundamental idea of loyalty, and that loyalty is not a self-pleasing virtue. I am not bound to be loyal to the United States to please myself. I am bound to be loyal to the United States because I live under its laws and am its citizen, and, whether it hurts me or whether it benefits me, I am obliged to be loyal. Loyalty means nothing unless it has at its heart the absolute principle of self-sacrifice. Loyalty means that you ought to be ready to sacrifice every interest that you have, and your life itself, if your country calls upon you to do so. And that is the sort of loyalty which ought to be inculcated into these newcomers—that they are not to be loyal only so long as they are pleased, but that, having once entered into this sacred relationship, they are bound to be loyal whether they are pleased or not; and that loyalty which is merely self-pleasing is only self-indulgence and selfishness. No man has ever risen to the real stature of spiritual manhood until he has found that it is finer to serve somebody else than it is to serve himself.

These are the conceptions which we ought to teach the newcomers in our midst. And we ought to realize that the life of every one of us is part of the schooling, and that we cannot preach loyalty unless we set the example, that we cannot profess things with any influence upon others unless we practice them also. This process of Americanization is going to be a process of self-examination, a process of purification, a process of rededication to the things which America represents and is proud to represent. And it takes a great deal more courage and steadfastness, my fellow citizens, to represent ideal things than to represent anything else. It is easy to lose your temper, and hard to keep it. It is easy to strike and sometimes very difficult to refrain from striking. And I think you will agree with me that we are most justified in being proud of doing the things that are hard to do and not the things that are easy. You do not settle things quickly by taking what seems to be the quickest way to settle them. You make the complication just that much the more profound and inextricable. And, therefore, what I believe America should exalt above everything else is the sovereignty of thoughtfulness and sympathy and vision as against the grosser impulses of mankind. No nation can live without vision, and no vision will exalt a nation except the vision of real liberty and real justice and purity of conduct.

Printed in *Address of President Wilson to the Citizenship Convention* . . . (Washington, 1916).

From Frank Lyon Polk

Dear Mr. President: Washington July 13, 1916.

I have the honor to acknowledge the receipt of your letter of July 12, 1916, enclosing a letter to you from Senator Stone requesting you to transmit to the Committee on Foreign Relations, for its confidential information and if not incompatible with the public interest, such information as you may have relative to the new Russo-Japanese treaty. You ask if the Department has any information other than that which has already been published on this subject.

The American Ambassador at Tokyo telegraphed the Department on July 7 that the Foreign Office at Tokyo had announced the "following statement of the settlement of the Russo-Japanese Convention" which was signed at Petrograd on July 3:

"Article I. Japan will not become a party to any political arrangement or combination directed against Russia. Russia will not become a party to any political arrangement or combination directed against Japan.

"Article II. In case either the territorial rights or the special interests in the Far East of one of the contracting parties, recognized by the other contracting party, should come to be menaced, Japan and Russia will confer in regard to the measure to be taken with a view to mutual support or cooperation for the safeguarding and defense of these rights and interests."

The Department was informed also by the American Ambassador at Petrograd on July 7 that the treaty had been signed. The two articles above mentioned were quoted.

The Foreign Office at Tokyo on July 7 gave to a representative of a news bureau a statement substantially as follows:

The new Russo-Japanese Agreement is designed to take a conspicuous part in the series of international compacts intended to make certain the lasting peace and stability of Eastern Asia. The wording is brief but the reasons to which it owes its origin are of far reaching moment. This agreement is a testimony to the strong determination of both powers to preserve between them the relations of perfect accord and mutual confidence and to harmonize their efforts in protection of their legitimate rights and interests in the Far East. In nature it is strictly conservative and does not prejudice, in any degree, the position of any other power equally committed to peaceful aims, and it is fully in harmony with and adds strength to the Anglo-Japanese alliance, of which it is a corollary.

The Department telegraphed Ambassador Guthrie at Tokyo on July 7, directing him to forward by mail a detailed report and to give his interpretation of the treaty. He was instructed also to telegraph to the Department any further statements the Foreign Office may issue defining the purpose, scope and intent of the treaty.

Certain newspaper articles having intimated that possibly other matters are embraced in the treaty in addition to the two paragraphs herein quoted, the Embassy at Tokyo has been directed also to telegraph whether it has any reason to believe that there are other provisions in the treaty which have not been made public, whether the Embassy has received any assurance that the full text will be published and, further, to keep the Department informed by telegraph of any important developments and whether, in the Embassy's opinion, any American rights are jeopardized.

Ambassador Francis at Petrograd telegraphed the Department on July 12 that he had arranged an interview at the Foreign Office for today to make inquiry regarding the treaty. This Department will keep you informed of any developments of importance.

Very sincerely yours,   Frank L Polk

TLS (WP, DLC).

From Edward Mandell House

Dear Governor:

New London,
New Hampshire. July 13, 1916.

Would Lane be an impossibility for the Hughes vacancy?

Houston could be moved up to Interior and Page could be moved into Agriculture.

Mezes, who is here, tells me that when Lane was on the Interstate Commerce Commission he wrote all but one of the important cases that went to the Supreme Court and was never reversed. As City Attorney of San Francisco he wrote several hundred opinions and was reversed but once by the Supreme Court.

He therefore knows Interstate Commerce law, land law and municipal law. McKenna[1] is very old and a vacancy in the course of nature must soon come there.

Affectionately yours,   E. M. House

TLS (WP, DLC).

[1] Associate Justice Joseph McKenna, then seventy-two years old. He retired from the court on January 25, 1925.

William Luke Marbury to Albert Sidney Burleson

My dear General: Baltimore July 13th, 1916.

Referring to my talk with you in Washington a day or two ago I feel impelled to write for the purpose of expressing the earnest hope that you will urge upon the President the importance of appointing a southern man to the vacancy in the Supreme Court of the United States.

What we commonly call the race problem in this country has not been finally settled.

Quite a number of those who have given most serious study to the subject are disposed to fear that we have only reached the threshold of the question.

The Supreme Court is not unlikely to be called upon from time to time to pass upon legal questions affecting the status of the negro in the south, and the relations between the races, of the most delicate character. Upon the correct decisions of these cases may depend in no small degree the peace and happiness of our people.

It is certainly of a great importance to southern people that there should be on that bench a fair number of judges who can see these questions from their standpoint. It is impossible for anybody not born and bred in the south, and in constant contact with the facts of the situation, to have the actual knowledge and understanding of these facts without which it is impossible to act with sanity and with justice in cases of the kind in question.

Frankly I feel that the President owes this much absolutely to our people.

Knowing your own partiality for myself in this connection I feel justified in repeating what I have already said, and that is that my name is absolutely not to be considered in connection with the appointment as I could not accept it if it were offered me for the reasons which I stated to you. For that reason, however, I feel more free to speak.

Sincerely yours, W. L. Marbury

TLS (WP, DLC).

From John Cardinal Farley and Others

Sir: [New York, c. July 14, 1916]

Your petitioners learn, with deep regret, that satisfactory arrangements, have not yet been secured with the European powers, whereby the people of America may render, out of their abundance, adequate assistance to the suffering peoples in Poland.

We express our grateful recognition of the most generous appeal which you made in behalf of our brothers and sisters in this devastated region, as well as your earnest efforts to open the doors for the fullest relief for these innocent sufferers.

While the appalling need of these people is so great, we believe that the relief as yet offered by the American people has been sadly incommensurate, in part because of the difficulty in conveying food supplies into Poland.

While it is possible now for the American people to transmit money, we believe that gifts would be incomparably increased by this means as well as by others, if the opportunity for rendering all kinds of assistance were made possible.

The American people honor the memory of Kosciuszko, Pulaski, and other names which are dear to our hearts, and all that we can do is but the paying of a debt which we owe rather than an expression of philanthropy. We, therefore, desire the fullest opportunity for rendering this just recompense to a people whose history is one of noble deeds and brave suffering.

We believe that we express the feelings and utter the voice of the great bodies of American people with which we are connected, and of all the people, in respectfully asking that in every legitimate way, you seek to resume and continue your good offices with the governments of Europe, in the effort to obtain access for the help which we believe our people may yet be persuaded to render.

> John Cardinal Farley
> (Archbishop of New York)
> Shailer Mathews
> President, Federal Council of
> the Churches of Christ in America
> Charles S. Macfarland
> General Secretary, Federal Council
> of the Churches of Christ in America
> Joseph Silverman
> Rabbi, Temple Emanu-El.

TLS (WP, DLC).

From Edward Mandell House, with Enclosure

New London,
Dear Governor: New Hampshire. July 14, 1916.

I am enclosing you a copy of a letter to Sir Edward.

There is no special proposal in it, otherwise I should have submitted it to you. It will not go, however, until some time next week and if there is anything in it to which you object please telegraph me.

It seems to me that the less you say and do in regard to European affairs at this time the better. Everything is in the making and I believe it is wise to wait developments. I have given Spring-Rice a slight thrust which Sir Edward may or may not recognize.

In forming your Mexican commission, if indeed, one is formed, I hope if a Catholic is put on you will be certain of his loyalty to you. If the Church comes first and you second I can see great possibilities for trouble. The Chief Justice for this reason does not appeal to me.   Affectionately yours,   E. M. House

TLS (WP, DLC).

E N C L O S U R E

Edward Mandell House to Sir Edward Grey

New London,
Dear Sir Edward: New Hampshire. July 15th, 1916.

I am very glad to get your letter of June 28th. I know the circumstances under which you work, and I know how difficult it is for England to discuss peace.

It was certain that Germany would attempt a separate peace with both France and Russia. On the other hand, it is natural that we should turn to you in our endeavors to bring about not peace alone but a better and more permanent state of affairs, for where save here do the fires of liberty and democracy burn so brightly as in England.

The world must not live, when this war is over, under the old cloud of suspicion and uncertainty. Surely our statesmanship is not so feeble, our civilization not so thin that we cannot meet the requirements that are demanded of us. But if England and America cannot come to an understanding of the needs of the hour and of the methods by which they should be compassed, how indeed, can a beginning be made?

The President and you are almost the only responsible statesmen that I know that see clearly beyond the immediate problems in which this war has enmeshed the world. If you can bring England to see what is required of her in the final adjustment in order that she may justify her potential place in the world of today, the President I feel sure will be able to bring America to see and do her part.

In his address before the League to Enforce Peace the President was speaking more or less his individual opinion. However, at the Saint Louis Convention the Democratic Party placed in their platform the substance of this speech. Therefore if the President is re-elected the people will have endorsed his position upon this question and the country will stand committed to it. This is a matter of great importance.

Now that Germany has ceased her illegal submarine practices and has completely discontinued her irritating propaganda, the feeling against her here has largely subsided. It has also caused a recession of what war feeling there was. If there is one thing clearer than another it is the general commendation of the President's foreign policy. His successful duel with Germany has given the people so large a measure of confidence in him that they would, I think, follow wherever he might think it wise to go.

I am constantly amazed at the lack of accurate information which the people of both England and France have of America. This information comes from our eastern seaboard and represents the country but a little way back. In fact, it does not represent the seaboard itself for under the surface the heart of the East beats in unison with the rest of America.

As an instance of what I mean France, and perhaps England also, was told that Mr. Roosevelt or Mr. Root would surely be the republican nominee, and those alienated Americans that constantly sow misinformation concerning their country wherever they chance to be, advised the French to express openly their sympathy for the Roosevelt candidacy. This advice was to a limited extent followed. The surprise which came with the Chicago Convention must have been great. Roosevelt received sixty-five votes out of a thousand and Root but few more, and this, bear in mind, in a republican convention.

I am not sure that there is anything further that the President can do for the moment, for he gets but little support or encouragement outside of America. Like the war itself it is all a huge gamble and the stakes are the future welfare and liberty of humanity. We are standing it seems at the roads of destiny, waiting to see which way to turn. In the meanwhile forces are at work which may soon make a choice impossible and we may all be driven down that road which it has been the life work of some of us to try to make forever impossible. We need not look as far as Germany to find such forces at work. They are in England and here, and this war has given them courage to try again to win what they had come to think a losing cause.

Though you cannot see it clearly at your distance, yet the forces against which we have to contend are nearly as great as those against which you are battling. Here it is centered upon the President and the lies, hate and vituperation that are sown broadcast are beyond belief.

But he stands unshaken and undismayed. No people ever had a wiser leader—no cause was ever lifted on a higher plane and no country has ever had to bear its burdens, a braver, loftier soul.

Sincerely yours,   [E. M. House]

CCL (WP, DLC).

From Edward Mandell House, with Enclosure

New London,
Dear Governor: New Hampshire. July 15, 1916.

I am enclosing you a copy of a letter from Bernstorff which came this morning and which explains itself.

I am fearful that the situation he speaks of in Germany may come about and the Chancellor be overthrown. It is clearly to our interest to have him remain in power.

Have you any suggestions to make to Bernstorff through me?

I have a letter from Ellery Sedgwick of the Atlantic Monthly in which he says:

"Can nothing be done to let the people of the United States

have a clear idea of the Administration's Mexican policy? It seems to me very likely that the election will be lost on this issue, for the prevailing public impression unquestionably is that the Mexican policy has been a combination of meddling and muddling without any definite cohesive plan from beginning to end. The President has done very little in his speeches to give the public any definite idea of how painstaking and consecutive his policy has been. I am satisfied that it simply has to be done before the Autumn."

I think myself if you would outline in one of your speeches just what you had in mind from the beginning, and how consistently you have adhered to it, it would have a wholesome effect. You could start with your entire Pan-American policy and point out how closely it related to Mexico.

Affectionately yours,   E. M. House

TLS (WP, DLC).

E N C L O S U R E

Count Johann Heinrich von Bernstorff
to Edward Mandell House

My dear Colonel House: New York, July 14, 1916.

I received your letter of June 17th with best thanks.

Since then, I am happy to say, the improvement in all American and German relations has continued. The acquittal of Tauscher[1] and the reception of the "Deutschland"[2] gave evidence of such improvement.

Nevertheless, however, as you will have seen yourself by the newspapers, my Government is having a hard time and has been strongly attacked for having given up the U-boat war at the request of the United States. You know the situation in Berlin so well that I need not discuss it at any length. I will only mention that there seems to be danger of the Chancellor being forced to retire on account of these attacks. That would, of course, mean the resumption of the U-boat war and the renewal of all our troubles.

The chief argument which is being brought to bear against the Chancellor is that he gave in to the United States Government although he knew that this Government was not neutral and was bringing pressure on Germany only, whilst it willingly permitted violations of International Law by England. There is certainly some truth in these attacks, as the British violations of International Law are increasing daily—eg, for instance the latest Order in Council which abolished the Declaration of London.

I do not know what can be done. You said in your last letter that there is no question of a suggestion of peace at the present moment. Furthermore you and I have always agreed, that there is no hope of England giving up her violations of International Law out of deference to the United States as we gave up our reprisals for that reason. It might, however, relieve the situation, if at least a new protest were made, even if nothing came of it. That would help our Government a great deal without doing any harm here.

The German political opponents of our Chancellor would not be able to repeat continually that the United States Government does not object to violations of International Law, when they are perpetrated by England, and submits to them quietly, although Mr. Lansing in his note publicly called the British blockade "illegal, indefensible and ineffective."

If you wish to talk matters over with me and think that any good may come of such a confidential conversation, I am, as you know, always ready to pay you a visit from Dublin as I suggested to you before you left New York.

My present address is Hotel Ritz-Carlton.

Yours very sincerely,   J. Bernstorff.

TCL (WP, DLC).

[1] Hans Tauscher, captain in the German army reserve, representative of the Krupp industries in New York, and husband of the famed Wagnerian soprano, Johanna Gadski, was arrested in New York on March 30 on the charge of having conspired on American territory in August 1914 to destroy the Welland Canal connecting Lake Erie and Lake Ontario. Tauscher was acquitted on June 30, after a well-publicized trial in the federal district court in New York. *New York Times*, March 31-July 1, 1916, *passim*.

[2] A large, commercial submarine, *Deutschland*, docked in Baltimore on July 10. It had sailed from Bremerhaven on June 23 with a cargo of 750 tons, approximately 280 tons of which were dyestuffs, reputedly worth $750,000. After careful inspection of the vessel, officials of the State, Navy, and Treasury departments decided that *Deutschland* was a *bona fide* merchantman and entitled to all the rights and privileges usually accorded to belligerent commercial vessels in a neutral port. *Deutschland* and her voyage captured the imagination of the American public. The press hailed the vessel as a triumph of German technical skill and her captain and crew as heroes. *Deutschland* sailed for Germany on August 2 and returned to her home port on August 23. See David W. Hirst, "German Propaganda in the United States, 1914-1917" (unpublished Ph.D. dissertation, Northwestern University, 1962), pp. 184-96, and Paul König, *Voyage of the Deutschland: The First Merchant Submarine* (New York, 1916).

From Wilhelmina Caroline Ginger Van Winkle[1]

Dear sir: Newark, New Jersey July sixteenth [1916].

Mrs. Harriot Stanton Blatch[2] has just returned from a tour of the twelve states where women vote.

Her report will not only interest you but it will prove a direct campaign contribution. I am therefore writing to secure an appointment with you at an early date for Mrs. Henry O. Havemeyer,[3] Mrs. Borden Harriman, Mrs. Harriot Stanton Blatch and two or three others including myself.

Will you kindly instruct your secretary to telegraph at my expense, the date, hour and place of appointment. I will forward the word to the members of the suffrage Committee.[4]

Respectfully,   (Mrs. A.) Mina C. Van Winkle.

ALS (WP, DLC).

[1] Mrs. Abraham Van Winkle, widow of a chemical manufacturer of Newark, president of the Women's Political Union of New Jersey.

[2] Harriot Eaton Stanton (Mrs. William Henry) Blatch, active in the Congressional Union for Woman Suffrage. She was a daughter of Elizabeth Cady Stanton (1815-1902), one of the great pioneers in the fight for woman suffrage.

[3] Louisine Waldron Elder (Mrs. Henry Osborne) Havemeyer, widow of the former head of the American Sugar Refining Co., noted art collector, and a founder of the Congressional Union for Woman Suffrage.

[4] Wilson saw the delegation on July 24. Those who actually came to the White House were Mrs. Van Winkle; Mrs. Blatch; Anna Isabel Vaill (Mrs. George Mason) La Monte, wife of the New Jersey Commissioner of Banking and Insurance; and Helen Todd, formerly of California but now working for the suffrage movement in New York. For accounts of the meeting, see the *New York Herald* and the *Washington Post*, July 25, 1916, and Harriot Stanton Blatch and Alma Lutz, *Challenging Years: The Memoirs of Harriot Stanton Blatch* (New York, 1940), pp. 267-69.

Remarks Upon Signing the Rural Credits Bill[1]

July 17, 1916.

Gentlemen: On occasions of this sort, there are so many things to say that one would despair of saying them briefly and adequately, but I cannot go through the simple ceremony of signing this bill without expressing the feeling that I have in signing it. It is a feeling of profound satisfaction not only, but of real gratitude, that we have completed this piece of legislation, which I hope will be immensely beneficial to the farmers of the country.

The farmers, it seems to me, have occupied hitherto a singular position of disadvantage. They have not had the same freedom to get credit on their real assets that others have had who were in manufacturing and commercial enterprises, and, while they sustained our life, they did not, in the same degree with some others, share in the benefits of that life. Therefore, this bill, along with the very liberal provisions of the Federal Reserve Act, puts them upon an equality with all others who have genuine assets and makes the great credit of the country available to them. One cannot but feel that this is delayed justice to them, and cannot but feel that it is a very gratifying thing to play any part in doing this act of justice. I look forward to the benefits of this bill, not

with extravagant expectations, but with confident expectations
that it will be of very wide-reaching benefit; and, incidentally, it
will be of advantage to the investing community, for I can
imagine no more satisfactory and solid investments than this
system will afford those who have money to use.

I sign the bill, therefore, with real emotion, and am very glad
indeed to be honored by your presence, and supported by your
feeling, I have no doubt, in what I have said regarding it.

T MS (WP, DLC).
    [1] Wilson signed the bill at the White House in the presence of several sena-
tors and congressmen and representatives of various farm organizations.

To James McMahon Cox

My dear Governor Cox: [The White House] July 17, 1916
    Accept my hearty thanks for your generous telegram of the
fourteenth of July.[1] It was a pleasure to be able to raise Judge
Clarke to the Supreme Bench,[2] and I am gratified to learn that
you think so well of the appointment.
                    Cordially and sincerely yours,   Woodrow Wilson

TLS (Letterpress Books, WP, DLC).
    [1] It is missing.
    [2] Wilson had appointed Clarke to the Supreme Court on July 14. He was
confirmed by the Senate on July 24.

To Charles Pope Caldwell

My dear Mr. Caldwell: [The White House] July 17, 1916
    I am warmly obliged to you for your generous letter of July
twelfth[1] and for the public spirit which it displays.
                    Cordially and sincerely yours,   Woodrow Wilson

TLS (Letterpress Books, WP, DLC).
    [1] It is missing.

From Josephus Daniels

My dear Mr. President: Washington. July 17, 1916.
    I desire to call your attention to a speech made by Senator
Gallinger which will be found in the Congressional Record of
Friday, July 14th, on pages 12719 and 12720, and particularly to
this statement: "The minority, and I speak advisedly, are anxious
that the child-labor bill, the immigration bill, and the workmen's
compensation bill shall be considered at this session of Congress,
but the burden for that legislation rests upon the majority and

not upon the minority, as the minority is powerless to force any measure for consideration that the majority opposes, they having the votes and the power to dictate what shall be considered and what shall not be considered." And at the end of his speech he adds: "I will repeat, Mr. President, that the minority are warmly in favor of the child-labor bill;" etc.

I understand that this statement of Senator Gallinger was made for the purpose of representing to the country that the Republicans warmly favored the child-labor bill but that the Democrats were opposing it. In view of the closeness of the vote in many of the states, and that women will vote in a large number of states, I feel that it would be a grave mistake if the Senate does not pass the child-labor bill as well as the workmen's compensation bill before it adjourns. I know that many Southern Senators oppose it but I believe that the failure to pass that bill will lose us more votes in the close states than our Southern Senators appreciate. Besides, I strongly feel that it is essential to protect child labor and that such protection is the very basis of the social legislation which gave the Progressives hold on the conscience of that portion of their party that cannot be controlled by Perkins.[1]   Faithfully yours,   Josephus Daniels

TLS (WP, DLC).
[1] That is, George Walbridge Perkins.

From Alexander Jeffrey McKelway

Dear Mr. President: Washington, D. C. July 17, 1916.

I enclose a memorandum which may be of some use to you.[1] I was surprised myself to find how closely Democratic achievement matched Progressive promise.

I fear greatly, however, that the failure to pass the child labor bill at this session will give your opponents an issue which will be costly enough before the campaign is over. After the Democratic Steering Committee had put this on the programme and after the Republicans, according to Senator Gallinger's statement in the Record of Friday last, had announced their willingness to facilitate the passage of the child labor bill, the workmen's compensation bill, etc., the Democratic Caucus, under the influence of Senator Hardwick, Senator Overman, Senator Smith, of S. C., Senator Vardaman, Senator Bryan and Senator Shields, left the child labor bill off of the programme to be passed at this session. Some of these Senators have promised their constituents not to filibuster against the bill.

I understand that Mr. Hughes is to hold a conference next

week with social workers and has already agreed to swallow the social justice programme whole. In spite of the progressive record of the Democratic Party, I fear that the action on the child labor bill will be regarded as a test of genuine interest in humane measures opposed by commercial interests.

I wish that you could see your way clear to use your influence in furtherance of this important measure.

Cordially yours,   A. J. McKelway.

TLS. (WP, DLC).

1 "The Progressive Record of the Democratic Party," T MS (WP, DLC). This nine-page document quoted many passages from the Progressive platform of 1912 and showed in each instance that the desired reform had been entirely or largely achieved during the Wilson administration, either by executive action or by legislation already, or soon to be, enacted.

From Samuel Gompers

Sir: Washington, D. C., July 17, 1916

Recently I have written you several communications in regard to matters affecting this country and Mexico in order to present the human side of the matters and the human interests concerned therein. Among other things I urged that a commission be authorized to inquire into conditions and causes that brought about friction and misunderstanding along the border between the United States and Mexico and also that a representative of Labor be appointed upon the commission.

The welfare of the workers of both countries is indissolubly bound up with the industrial and social conditions existing within the separate countries as well as the international aspects of these conditions. The workers of every country represent the heart of the nation and their well-being is fundamental for national life and progress. The labor movement is the organization through which they express their needs, purposes and ideals. It is a force that is part of their very lives. It is close to the plain, rugged red-blooded people who labor and who are the bones and sinews of the nation.

For these reasons I urge that a representative of organized labor ought to be appointed on the proposed commission. In thinking over names for submission there came to me what seems an inspiration—if I may use the expression as a plain statement without egotistical suggestion—and I wish to suggest the name of the Secretary of Labor, Honorable William B. Wilson, who in addition to his splendid qualities of heart and mind, has knowledge of the forces and their methods used in creating border hostilities and in prostituting governmental agencies for personal gain.

Secretary Wilson is wholly unaware that I am making this suggestion to you or that I am writing upon this subject. In all honor, I say that he and I or others have never directly or indirectly associated his name with the personnel of the commission under consideration.

Permit me to urge this suggestion for your earnest consideration with the hope that it will commend itself for your favorable action. Respectfully yours, Saml. Gompers.

TLS (SDR, RG 59, 812.00/18823, DNA).

To Josephus Daniels

My dear Daniels: The White House July 18, 1916

Thank you sincerely for your memorandum of June seventeenth about Gallinger's speech. I am going to try to see some of the Senators at once and see if we cannot assist to get them out of the hole that the old fox has put them in.[1]

Cordially and faithfully yours, Woodrow Wilson

TLS (J. Daniels Papers, DLC).
[1] At noon on July 18, Wilson, accompanied only by two Secret Service men, made an unannounced visit to the President's Room in the Capitol. There he conferred with Senator Kern, the Democratic majority leader; Senators Martin, Williams, James, and Owen, of the Democratic steering committee; and Senators Simmons and Hughes. Wilson said that the Senate, during the current session, should approve the Keating-Owen child labor bill and the Kern-McGillicuddy bill for workmen's compensation for federal employees. Wilson based his argument on the merits of the measures and reminded the senators of their duty to honor their party's platform pledges. The senators, in reply, promised Wilson that the Kern-McGillicuddy bill would be passed before adjournment and also agreed to put the child labor bill on the calendar. On July 25, the Democratic senatorial caucus voted to pass the child labor bill before the end of the session. See the *New York Times*, July 19 and 26, 1916, and Arthur S. Link, *Wilson: Campaigns for Progressivism and Peace, 1916-1917* (Princeton, N. J., 1965), p. 59.

To John Hessin Clarke

My dear Judge Clarke: [The White House] July 18, 1916

May I not thank you sincerely for your letter of July sixteenth?[1]

You may be sure that it gave me genuine pleasure to appoint you to the Supreme Court, and I shall look forward with the greatest confidence to your winning real distinction as a member of that great tribunal, upon which the country is so dependent for the liberal and enlightened interpretation of its laws.

I shall look forward with real pleasure to being associated with you here in Washington.

Cordially and sincerely yours, Woodrow Wilson

TLS (Letterpress Books, WP, DLC).
[1] It is missing.

To William Kent

My dear Mr. Kent: The White House July 18, 1916.

It gratifies me very much that you should have been selected as the Chairman of the Woodrow Wilson Independent League and that you should be willing to serve in that capacity. The support of independent men whose convictions I share and whose purposes are my purposes also gives me the greatest encouragement not only, but makes me feel that the political processes of the country are clearing for a new and more effective combination in the work of advancing all reasonable reform to early consummation.

Cordially and sincerely yours,   Woodrow Wilson

TLS (W. Kent Papers, CtY).

To Ole Hanson[1]

My dear Mr. Hanson: [The White House] July 18, 1916

My attention has been called to the very generous and interesting "Appeal to the Progressives of the State of Washington"[2] which you and other leading Progressives of Washington were generous enough to issue, and I cannot deny myself the pleasure of saying to you how deeply I appreciate it, not merely as an expression of personal confidence, but also as a step towards the kind of cooperation among progressive men the country over which our beloved country so much needs and which, if it can be secured, will be such a stimulating reinforcement of everything that is worth while in our politics.

I hope that you will be kind enough to express to those associated with you in the signature of the paper my deep and cordial appreciation.

With much regard,

Sincerely yours,   Woodrow Wilson

TLS (Letterpress Books, WP, DLC).
    [1] Real estate dealer of Seattle, unsuccessful Progressive candidate for United States senator in 1914.
    [2] The Editors have been unable to find a copy of this statement.

From Frank Lyon Polk, with Enclosure

My dear Mr. President: Washington July 18, 1916.

I enclose a draft of a letter to the various rulers of the warring countries, on the matter of Polish relief, prepared by Mr. Phillips after consulting Mr. Jerome Green, of the Carnegie Foundation.[1] We think it would be better not to be specific in the letter as to details of the relief, as it might give the foreign governments an opportunity to make arguments on particular points.

I also attach a memorandum which could be handed to the various governments by our Ambassadors. This memorandum contains the details, and the discussion could be on the memorandum and not on your general letter of appeal.

If you prefer to be definite in the letter, you could incorporate such suggestions contained in the memorandum as meet with your approval.   Yours faithfully,   Frank L Polk

TLS (WP, DLC).
   [1] He meant Jerome Davis Greene, secretary of the Rockefeller Foundation. Wilson's redraft of the letter to various monarchs is printed at July 20, 1916.

E N C L O S U R E

William Phillips to Frank Lyon Polk

Dear Mr. Polk: [Washington] July 18, 1916.

There have been numberless proposals and counter proposals by the contending powers regarding relief for Poland. If it is permitted for the United States to conduct new negotiations, we might do so on the following general lines:

1. That the present executive organization of the Commission for Relief in Belgium be utilized for the purchase, transportation, importation and distribution of food supplies in Poland, such organization to operate under the name of the Commission for Relief in Poland.

2. That food imported by the Commission will be used exclusively for the actual non-combatants of Poland.

3. That food imported for the inhabitants of Poland shall be used to supplement, not in place of, other available supplies; in other words, that it shall be used to give food to those who would otherwise go without.

4. That the Commission shall be in a position to guarantee that the food reaches the prescribed destination and no other, and that the terms and conditions under which importation and distribution are agreed to shall be faithfully observed. To this end a sufficient number of neutral inspectors shall be given every necessary facility.

5. That the funds for the purchase and transportation of food supplies shall be

    a. Not less than 15,000,000 marks (per month) gold to be furnished by the German and Austrian Governments, in accordance with the plan heretofore proposed.

    b. Funds furnished by popular subscription in America and elsewhere.

A further appeal could be made to treat the plan as an experiment and, if, after reasonable and actual trial, there existed definite obstacles, the whole undertaking could be abandoned without the risk of any significant injury having been done to the military interests of any belligerent during the short period of the experiment.   Sincerely,   W Phillips

TLS (WP, DLC).

From Joseph Patrick Tumulty, with Enclosure

Dear Governor: The White House. July 18th [1916].

I am in receipt of a letter from one of our newspaper friends, and beg to send you herewith an excerpt from it.

                Respectfully,   J P Tumulty

TLS (WP, DLC).

E N C L O S U R E

I recommend your careful attention to the situation which is coming to a head in railroad circles. The Brotherhoods of Locomotive Engineers, Firemen and Trainmen are voting as to whether or not to strike. A strike at this time would be a calamity. It would throw out of work not only the 300,000 men who threaten a strike but 150,000 men who are engaged in other branches of railroad service and who do not wish to strike but who can't work if the trains aren't running.

It would be a terrible thing too for the country. If milk shipments, food shipments of other kinds (particularly into the big cities) and mail and express shipments were stopped, all traffic jammed, etc., it would be one of the worst things that could happen to this country. I am informed that many railroad men who are tired of annual and semi-annual strikes are willing to let this thing go to a show-down to try to convince the people of the country that the organized trainmen are pulling off a "hold-up" game. Others want arbitration. I am told the trainmen don't want arbitration.

It looks now as if the President would certainly be called into the thing. He has just signed the Newlands bill AT LABOR'S REQUEST, which provides for arbitration of such difficulties. If he could step in and prevent a strike at this time by demanding that arbitration be agreed upon, or by getting both sides to let the Interstate Commerce Commission decide the merits of the case, it would avert what now seems to be an inevitable clash. It would be a great stroke, I believe. At any rate I'd suggest you keep him watching sharp at developments because a crisis in the darned thing is at hand.

T MS (WP, DLC).

Samuel Huston Thompson, Jr., to Cary Travers Grayson

Dear Dr. Grayson: Denver, Colorado, July 18, 1916.

I arrived here in Denver four days ago, and have been looking the situation over very carefully from a political point of view. I find that in the clubs and the business world there is very strong sentiment against us. But over against this, I find that there is a fine attitude among the middle class voters. In order to ascertain this, I employed three men whom I have known intimately, to go among the people, sounding them as to their views. One was a Swede who through his position as teller in a bank, comes in contact with the Swedish element. The second one is a seller of teas to all the small retail stores in this community. The third sells fire insurance in the poor districts of the city. The report I get from them and in fact from every other source is that the women are very strongly in favor of the President on his war policies, and they don't want him to go into Mexico. I have interviewed Mr. Costigan,[1] twice nominated for governor of this state on the Progressive ticket, and a number of the Progressives, and they tell me we will get over 50 per cent of the Progressive vote. I have also interviewed the editorial writer on a Republican paper, but an independent admirer of the President, and I have interviewed the editor of the leading Republican paper of Pueblo, both of whom being friends have confided to me confidentially that they thought the state was for the President. Everyone thinks, however, that he should make a trip out here in order to solidify the vote. His visit would be very impressive with the Progressive vote. I found on the train coming here, after talking to the conductor, engineer, and fireman, all of whom reside in western Nebraska, that the newspaper called the "Menace"[2] has done us some damage in western Nebraska and Kansas. To my surprise I found these men were all Hughes men and when I inquired why, that [they] explained that the "Menace" had done it.

I am going up into Wyoming the latter part of this week, and after I have sounded out that state, I will drop you a line. You can use your judgment as to whether you should show this letter to the President. I think, however, that he may be interested. I can sum up my general impression by saying, that with a visit by the President out here, this state would be safely within the Democratic column. You may say to the President that the appointment of Brandeis has had a greater effect upon the Progressives here than anything else.

With kind regards,

Very truly yours,   Huston Thompson

TLS (WP, DLC).
   1 Edward Prentiss Costigan, lawyer of Denver.
   2 A virulently anti-Catholic weekly, published in Aurora, Mo.

To Samuel Gompers

My dear Mr. Gompers: The White House July 19, 1916

I am afraid that the commission to discuss Mexican affairs will be too small to be really made representative, but you may be sure that I have very much in mind the interests and considerations which you urge in your interesting letter of the seventeenth, and that it will be my earnest desire to have those interests influential in the discussion of this whole difficult matter.

Cordially and sincerely yours,   Woodrow Wilson

TLS (S. Gompers Corr., AFL-CIO Ar).

To Alexander Jeffrey McKelway

My dear Doctor McKelway: The White House July 19, 1916

Thank you sincerely for your letter of July seventeenth with its accompanying memorandum, which is indeed a noteworthy calendar.

I went up to the Senate yesterday to urge the immediate passage of the Child Labor Bill and am encouraged to believe that the situation has changed considerably.

In haste

Cordially and sincerely yours,   Woodrow Wilson

TLS (A. J. McKelway Papers, DLC).

From Frank Lyon Polk, with Enclosures

My dear Mr. President: Washington July 19, 1916.

I have had two talks with Mr. Arredondo today. At the afternoon conference he brought a new clause to be added to the original Note, which new clause I enclose. I told him his suggestion would not do at all and went at length into the reasons. I then suggested that their original Note might be changed by the addition of "as quickly as possible," in connection with the settlement of the border difficulties, and by adding a general clause.

I enclose a draft of their Note with the changes suggested by us added, and I have underlined this new matter. Mr. Arredondo is consulting his Government and is coming in tomorrow morning and I will be very much obliged if you will give me your views.[1]   Yours faithfully,   Frank L Polk

TLS (SDR, RG 59, 812.00/18790½A, DNA).
  [1] Attached to these documents is the following WWhw note: "Returned & approved   W.W." Polk's underlined text is printed in italics.

E N C L O S U R E   I

Mr. Secretary:

I have the honor to refer to Your Excellency's note dated the 7th instant, which was transmitted to me by our Confidential Agent in Washington, Lic. Eliseo Arredondo; and in doing so, inform you that I have received instructions from the Citizen First Chief of the Constitutionalist Army, Charged with the Executive Power of the Union, to propose through you to His Excellency President Wilson, that each of our Governments name three commissioners, who shall hold conferences at some place to be mutually agreed upon, and decide forthwith the question relating to the evacuation of the American forces now in Mexico, and to draw up and conclude a protocol or agreement regarding the reciprocal crossing of the frontier by the forces of both countries, also to determine the origin of the incursions to date, in order to fix the responsibility therefor and definitely to settle, *as quickly as possible*, the difficulties now pending or those which may arise between the two countries on account of the same or a similar reason; *and consider such other matters as may be submitted to the Commission, the settlement of which would tend to improve the relations of the two Governments*; all of which shall be subject to the approval of both Governments.

The Mexican Government proposes that these conferences shall proceed in a spirit of the most frank cordiality and with the earnest purpose of reaching an arrangement satisfactory and honorable to both countries, in the belief that if the Government of the United States should accept the proposal contained in this note, the foregoing should be the principal recommendation given to the representatives which it may name.

The Government of Mexico considers that this is the most efficacious means of arriving at the desired result, and hopes that the Government of the United States will be kind enough to state whether it accepts this proposal, in order to carry it into effect forthwith, and in order that the Government of Mexico may communicate immediately the names of the persons which it may designate as its representatives.

Accept, etc.   Aguilar.

T MS (SDR, RG 59, 812.00/18790½A, DNA).

ENCLOSURE   II

July 19, 1916
Submitted by Mr. Arrendendo as an
·   amendment to Note of July 12 FLP

Solucionadas estas cuestiones, podrán ambos gobiernos extender sus facultades a la misma Comisión para que estudie y resuelva los demás asuntos que de común acuerdo estimaren conveniente someterle y cuyo arreglo tienda al mejoramiento de las relaciones internacionales, sujetos en todo caso los acuerdos de la Comisión, a la aprobación respectiva.

When the present difficulties may have been settled, both governments may accord their power to the same Commission, so that it may study and decide any other conflicting matters which by mutual accord of both governments may be advisable to submit to it, whose settlement would tend to improve the friendly relations between them, all decisions of the Commission being in every case subject to their approval.

T MS (SDR, RG 59, 812.00/18790½A, DNA).

From William Lea Chambers

Dear Mr. President: Washington July 19, 1916.

Relying entirely upon press statements, I observe that the representatives of the railroads are to have a conference with you either today or tomorrow in which you are to be asked to bring about an adjustment of the wage dispute between the transportation employees and the railroads of the country.[1]

It is, perhaps, not inopportune that you should be advised that neither of the parties to the controversy has as yet applied to the United States Board of Mediation and Conciliation for its services, as provided by the Act of Congress of July 15, 1913. Neither has a condition yet been reached in the controversy "in which an interruption of traffic is imminent and fraught with serious detriment to the public interest" which would authorize the Board to "proffer" its services to the respective parties to the controversy, within the contemplation of that Act. The parties, or either of them, can invoke the services of the Board at any stage of their negotiations, but the Board itself has found it the wisest policy in the past to pursue what it believes to be the intent and meaning of the Act, to wait as long as conditions seem to justify it for the parties or one of them to request its services. The vote now being taken by the employees of the railroads, if favorable to a strike, would precipitate a condition under which this Board would certainly and promptly proffer its services.

If you will pardon me, I deem it my duty to suggest that if you should be asked to intervene at this stage it would be well to refer the parties to the past efficacy of the law, enacted at the instance of both parties, providing for mediation, conciliation and arbitration in their controversies.

I hope I have not transgressed in any wise in calling your attention to this phase of the subject. You may be assured that the Board of Mediation and Conciliation is not only alert to the situation, but will use its best endeavors in the execution of the law, with the belief that we will be able to make it effective.

Very respectfully,   W. L. Chambers

TLS (WP, DLC).

[1] Actually, as WW to W. L. Chambers, July 20, 1916, TLS (Letterpress Books, WP, DLC) explains, the railroad men came to see Wilson on July 19 about another topic. Robert Scott Lovett, chairman of the executive committee of the Union Pacific System, Frank Trumbull, chairman of the board of the Chesapeake and Ohio Railway, and Alfred Pembroke Thom, general counsel of the Southern Railway, requested Wilson's assistance in securing a congressional resolution suspending for two years the operation of Section 10 of the Clayton Antitrust Act, which forbade a railroad from transacting business with any company in which any of its officials were officers or financially interested, except as the result of competitive bidding. They argued that this provision put a heavy financial burden upon the railroads and that the two-year moratorium would allow Congress to complete an investigation of the transportation needs of the country and, hence, determine whether Section 10 was really in the best interest of the nation. Wilson agreed to do what he could to secure adoption of the resolution. After the conference, the railroad officials told reporters that "no one had mentioned the subject of a railroad strike at all." *New York Herald* and *Washington Post*, July 20, 1916.

From Thomas Nelson Page

Private and Confidential.

My dear Mr. President: Paris July 19th, 1916.

I have stopped here for two or three days on my way to Rome that I may get at first hand some idea of the situation and feeling here as I did in London and as I shall have an opportunity to send a letter safely by my second Secretary, Norval Richardson, who sails from Bordeaux on Saturday for a much needed rest, I am writing you the result of my observation.

In London I met at Page's Sir Edwd. Grey and had a chance to talk with him which I was very glad to have. I found him a very natural, simple earnest man with one master motive: the desire to save England through winning the war. I do not think he knows much of America—of American feeling. He seems friendly enough to us; but hardly seems to have taken the gauge of our position regarding the war. I told him that perhaps five per cent of our people only were in favor of our intervention and that the number of those who had been originally most favorable to Engd. had appreciably diminished by the invasion, as they deemed it, of American rights by England's attitude towards us. He thought that this feeling was probably traditional; but I endeavored to correct this misapprehension. He then said that "perhaps, International law had been a little stretched at times," and added that we had done the same during our civil war. This seemed to me easy enough to set right; but I think he holds rather tenaciously to the view of similarity of the cases. I suggested that it was a pity that the correspondents of the British press in America were so critical of us and that the opinions given by them and accepted by an important section of the British press and public failed so often to reflect the situation in America. And I added that if a man like Bryce were in America and should go through the country I thought he would see what I had seen. He said he had thought at one time of that and had actually suggested it to Bryce; but the latter was averse to going. And then he added that it was a fact that the dispatches of Spring-Rice nearly always took the American side.

I have thought this of sufficient interest to send you this rather full note of our conversation for your personal eye.

I delivered your message to Page,[1] and I was glad to have an opportunity to talk informally and rather more frankly to Sir Edwd. than one can in speaking formally. The people of England according to what I heard—and so far as I can tell here the people of France also—are determined to push the war through to a conclusion. The death toll is terrible; but I see no abatement in the resolution to keep on. The new energy displayed by Engd. has had an effect here, and they are beginning to pay more attention to the British Colonies as a reservoir of force.

I find in private circles much complaint of the Belgians.

I am hoping to get a chance to run across to see the front at Verdun. And it is for this reason coupled with my desire to judge personally of conditions here that I have not hurried through France. If I get the permission I hope for I shall remain here three days longer.

I have had a good talk with Sharp over conditions in America. He thinks that Herrick will not get the nomination for the Senate.[2] He judges, of course, from letters and papers, so is not, perhaps, as well posted as if he were in America. I am enclosing clippings[3] from this morning's papers which show—assuming that "Mr. Johnson" is correct—that Mr. Hughes, Mr. Roosevelt and Mr. Herrick all agree that we should have "compulsory military service." This seems to me a very good piece of campaign ammunition and I would like the clippings sent to our friend House.

By the way, I told Sir Edwd. Grey that the "German-American alliance" boasted that they had dictated the nomination of your opponent to punish you for standing up for international law.

I hope you will pardon this long letter. I find a general impression in England and here that Germany will start in again on her submarine warfare.

As to Mexico; they are too much occupied here and in Engd. to think of it at all at present. The only thing I have heard is the expression of the view that we have got to go in there and restore order, and that now that we are in, we might as well as stay and "finish up the job." They do not appear to care anything about the matter over here—now. One interesting thing is that a newspaper man—a progressive—R. C. Mitchell[4]—who came over on the boat with us, told me that he counted that a million of the four mils. of progressives of the last campaign will vote for you—and he himself is ardently for you.

Always, my dear Mr. President,

Yours sincerely   Thos. Nelson Page

ALS (WP, DLC).

[1] T. N. Page had been in the United States on home leave. Wilson saw him at the White House on June 28, just before Page's departure.

[2] Myron T. Herrick did win the Ohio Republican senatorial nomination. He was defeated by the Democratic incumbent, Atlee Pomerene, in November.

[3] They are missing.

[4] Roscoe Conkling Mitchell, formerly a correspondent for the *New York American*.

After-Dinner Remarks to Postmasters[1]

July 20, 1916.

Mr. Toastmaster, ladies and gentlemen: I am very much interested to see the sort of crowd the Postmaster General has got me into, and, as I look about upon you, gentlemen, many of the impressions of the last three years come back upon me, because those have been three years when we have been trying to do very serious things, indeed. The thing that I have been most interested in, perhaps, has been organizing this government for the service of the country. Most of you—I am told all of you—bear commissions from the present administration. That sets me at liberty to say some things which I might not otherwise have felt free to say. If you are all Democrats, there is something I want to say to you as Democrats. There is only one way of holding the confidence of the American public, and that is by deserving it. And I know, by my intercourse with the Postmaster General, that the single object he has had in view has been to make the Post Office Department of the United States more serviceable, and more variously serviceable, to the people of the United States than it has ever been before. I know from him that he has had your hearty and loyal cooperation in that effort, and I esteem you good Democrats in proportion as you sustain him in that thing.

I tell you frankly, gentlemen, I have no interest in a political party except as an instrument of achievement. I cannot imagine how a man can be interested in a party that hasn't aspirations and purposes and a program which it carries out. Like a great many of the rest of you, I inherited my Democracy, but it wouldn't stay in my blood long if the red corpuscles of that blood did not have something to do. And if the Democratic party will bend all its efforts and all its intelligence to understanding the United States and, by understanding, serving it, it will be continued in power so long as it practices that devotion.

The Democratic party is cohesive. Some other parties are not. There is only one thing in this world, gentlemen, that binds men together. That is unselfishness. Selfishness separates them. Selfishness divides them into camps. Selfishness raises up men who have personal ends to serve. Selfishness leads to little coteries that have particular purposes to carry out and particular interests to advance. There is no great cohesive power except that of love and devotion. Now, as I have looked about upon you and read these quotations on one of the first pages of this program of the evening—quotations taken from the inscriptions on the post office here in Washington—I have wondered if you have pondered the significance of these lines: that you are messengers of sympathy and hope, the servants of parted friends, the consolers of the lonely; that you furnish the bond of the scattered family and the means which enlarge the common life; that you are the carrier of news and knowledge, the instrument of trade and industry, the promoter of mutual acquaintance, of peace and good will among men and nations. And have you reflected that the United States is one of the few great countries in the world in which men are free to do this thing now, in which hostility does not draw lines of separation which cannot be crossed, and that nowhere else in any great nation of the world, upon so great a scale, are the processes of peace free to move as they are in America; and that you are the instruments of the peace which comes from a mutual understanding, from a common object, from that weaving of minds together which can come only by free intercourse; and that in every community in this country the post office is the conspicuous gauge and standard of what the government is doing for the people and how it is doing it, that the administration will be judged by you, the whole machinery of government will be judged by you, the whole spirit of public service judged by you? Men judge very concretely. They do not think of things in the abstract. If they are thinking of a great organization like a government, they think of the man nearest them that they know that belongs to the organization of that government, and he is their standard by which they judge whether that government is doing its work well and doing it in the public interest or not.

So that you, gentlemen, are the custodians of the honor and distinction, not only of the great party which you represent, but of the great government which you serve. You are good Democrats only in proportion as you love that government more than you love yourselves. And that government is greater than any party, greater than any man's interest. Parties rise and fall, but that great government lives immortal. The only way parties can take immortality from it is by being true to its ideals and standards and loving the principles which it represents better even than they love the temporary success of the party itself.

It is true, therefore, gentlemen, that a great deal of the vitality of affairs is represented in this little company in this room tonight—a little company as compared with the great body of those who serve the government. Of course, it is common knowledge to you that 87 per cent of the classified service of the government is connected with the Post Office. There is more, speaking by way of its extent and its variety, of the service of the government embodied in the Post Office Department than in any other department of the government. The navy sees that nobody interferes with us; there are special subjects assigned to special departments; but the general intermediary, the general instrumentality, the general eye and ear and servant of the government, is the Post Office Department. I have sometimes wished that, as I signed your commissions, I could sit down with you and individually talk over with you the ideals of the service.

Did you ever reflect, gentlemen, upon how careful we are in using one of the most beautiful adjectives in our language? We readily call men "great," because there are many things great that are not lovable, that are not admirable—great in force, great in astuteness, great in power. We are very free with the use of the word "great." But there is one word which we hoard and reserve, and that is the word "noble." We never apply it to a man who thinks first of himself, but always to a man who has some margin of energy outside the little circle of his own self-interest to spend for the benefit of his fellow men. That ought to be the spirit of government, of government service. It ought to be touched with this rare spirit of self-forgetfulness, which is the spirit of nobility. We do not give men titles of nobility in this country, but men can win nobility by winning the love and confidence and admiration of their fellow men. And every man who covets office ought to covet it, not for its own sake, but that he may find some sphere in which he may prove that there is something that he loves better than himself. Why for any other reason a man should seek the responsibilities of office, I cannot imagine, for those responsibilities search the very heart. They not only put a burden upon the mind, but they are a constant challenge to the conscience. And how any man can sleep o'nights whose conscience is not clear with regard to the purposes for which he is using public office, I cannot see.

The simple thing I have come to say to you tonight, gentlemen, is this: Let us band ourselves together to prove to the people of the United States that we understand what they want and are readier to do it than anybody else that they can find.

T MS (WP, DLC).
¹ Wilson spoke at the banquet of the annual convention of the National Association of Presidential Postmasters at the Raleigh Hotel in Washington. The toastmaster was the president of the association, Colin M. Selph, Postmaster of St. Louis. *Washington Post*, July 21, 1916.

A Redraft of a Message to Various Heads of State[1]

MEMORANDUM.   [c. July 20, 1916]

In ⟨the face⟩ *view* of the overwhelming disasters which have befallen the millions of non-combatant inhabitants of Poland, I ⟨am impelled⟩ *feel justified* by the universal and ⟨insistent⟩ *earnest* expression of the sympathies of the American people, regardless of racial origin or political sentiments, to suggest to Your Majesty that the subject of ways and means for the saving *of these* ⟨of these millions of⟩ people *who still survive* be given the further benevolent consideration of Your Majesty's Government.

While no one can fail to appreciate the sufferings and sacrifices of the peoples primarily engaged in the existing war, nor the difficulties in the way of alleviating the hardships of those who are the incidental sufferers from the war, ⟨still⟩ the death by slow or rapid starvation of millions of innocent people is so awful a fact that such an ⟨eventuality⟩ *outcome* should be averted if it is within the compass of human effort *to avert it*. In ⟨such an effort⟩ *the effort to avert it* I confidently pledge the cooperation of the people of the United States, if only the way can be found to make their cooperation effective.

May I therefore be permitted to suggest that an entirely fresh consideration be given to the possibility, and method, of relief for Poland, and to tender the friendly offices of this Government in negotiations to this end; it being understood that any plan proposed shall be of such a character as to be adapted ⟨for⟩ *to* the accomplishment of no other result than that of the relief of the distressed inhabitants of Poland?

In conclusion I can only add that it is my sincere hope⟨,⟩ that Your Majesty will see in this note no intention to interfere with the rights and policies of Your Majesty's Government but merely the attempt to express to Your Majesty the sympathy and compassion towards the starving inhabitants of Poland felt by the citizens of the United States—a sympathy and compassion which they do not desire shall be evidenced merely by idle words, but which they hope they may be permitted to express by assisting in the actual work of furnishing food to the starving inhabitants of Poland.[2]

T MS (WP, DLC).

[1] Words in angle brackets in the following document deleted by Wilson; those in italics added by him.

[2] This letter was sent, *mutatis mutandi*, on July 20, 1916, to George V, William II, Francis Joseph, Nicholas II, and Raymond Poincaré. *FR-WWS 1916*, pp. 903-904. Wilson addressed the sovereigns as "Your Majesty" and the President of France as "Your Excellency," instead of using the traditional salutation, "Great and Good Friend." When Page, among other ambassadors, questioned this form

of address, the State Department replied on July 24: "Letter is purely personal in character, sealed with President's personal seal. Formal and more usual superscription 'Great and Good Friend' purposely omitted." *Ibid.*, p. 903, n. 2. Perhaps there were other reasons for Wilson's unusual salutation.

To Norman Hapgood

My dear Hapgood: [The White House] July 20, 1916

I ought long ago to have acknowledged your interesting letter of July sixth, but things have rather run away with me and I have neglected everything that I could neglect without stopping the public business.

I hope and believe that progressives of all sorts will have reason to approve of my nomination of Mr. Clarke of Ohio to the Supreme Bench, but I agree, you may be sure with the general views which you quoted in your letter from Mr. Brandeis.

In haste

Cordially and sincerely yours,   Woodrow Wilson

TLS (Letterpress Books, WP, DLC).

From Joseph Patrick Tumulty, with Enclosure

For the President—   [The White House] July 20th [1916].

The Secretary would like the President to read the attached letter, and wishes to know his feeling in the matter.

It would be inexcusable for me to touch this. It w'd involve serious international embarrassment   W.W.

TL (WP, DLC).

E N C L O S U R E

Michael Francis Doyle to Joseph Patrick Tumulty

Dear Mr Tumulty: London. July 6, 1916.

I am about to cable you asking if the President will not be good enough to write a letter to Sir Edw. Grey or Mr Asquith asking the British Government to spare the life of Roger Casement. Of course I know he can do nothing officially, but a personal request from the President *will save his life*. An appeal has been lodged and will be heard July 17. It will be decided immediately, but if dismissed, execution of the sentence takes place within a few days. It is possible a further appeal may be allowed to the House of Lords, but this is doubtful. The Criminal appeal act only recently enacted, provides that the fiat of the Atty. Gen'l. is required. There is absolutely no doubt that Casement never intended to assist Germany. *His sole object was to defend Ireland, and in furtherance of the Volunteer movement.* He was unable to call a single witness or produce any document because all were in Germany. Thus he could call the 52 men who joined the Brigade, and others in Germany, but it was impossible on account of the war. The Government declined to permit me to go to Germany or send any one there for the documentary proof necessary for his defense. Owing to the fact that I did not desire to involve our country in any controversy I submitted to the order of the Home Office.

The prejudice is strongly against him, but he has many powerful friends interested in him, such as Lord Haldane, Hon John Simon,[1] Bernard Shaw, Conan Doyle, Mr Massinger (Editor the Nation)[2] the Congo Societies and of course all of Ireland is behind him.

John Redmond and Lord Northcliffe both told me the Presidents word would save him. His great services to the world in exposing the Congo outrages and in So. America surely would justify the President, (to say nothing of the Irish question). Attempts have been made lately to discredit his character by spreading vile stories concerning him. It is done by his enemies, and his counsel at this time have not been able to verify them. They may have reached your ears by this time, but they should not affect the President. The charge against him is treason, and that only. It is an awful thing to listen to stories spread broadcast against him which are never substantiated.

I expect to return on the Finland, (July 19) and will call and see you on my return. Kindly present my compliments to the President   I hope to be of great service to him during the campaign.

With every good wish, believe me,

Sincerely yours   M. F. Doyle

ALS (WP, DLC).

[1] John Allsebrook Simon, Attorney General, 1913-1915; Home Secretary, 1915-1916; resigned from office in January 1916 because of his opposition to conscription.

[2] Henry William Massingham, editor of the London *Nation*, 1907-1923.

From Alexander Jeffrey McKelway

Dear Mr. President: Washington, D. C. July 20, 1916.

This is just to express my great appreciation of your action in going to the Senate to urge the passage of the child labor bill.

The step was taken just at the right time and in just the right way. I was in New York Wednesday but the afternoon papers had a full account of it. I am very hopeful now of the early passage of the bill.

What do you think of having, among the bureaus that are projected at Democratic headquarters, a bureau of education and social service, to appeal to the teachers and social workers of the country for the support of the Democratic ticket? If the passage of the child labor bill will allow me to leave Washington, I should be glad to tender my services in helping inaugurate such a movement. I haven't yet been able to take up the matter with Mr. McCormick personally.

Cordially yours,   A. J. McKelway.

TLS (WP, DLC).

A Memorandum by David Lawrence

[c. July 20, 1916]

Recent happenings have demonstrated pretty clearly that we must take some definite steps in our foreign policy. We are at a turning point. In the sense that our course must be submitted to the voters at the polls next November, it is political. If we are fair and honest, we need have no fear of what their judgment will be. If we are not true to the trust they impose in us, we deserve to be disapproved. There is no question in my mind of what the people want, or have I any doubt as to what will be the best slogan for us in the campaign. It is, "PEACE AND PROSPERITY." But we can only have prosperity and enjoy the remarkable and unprecedented good times if we are at peace. If we should be at war, it is true that politically we may not lose but it seems to be our most imperative duty to stay out of this war if it is humanly possible to do so. The one thing that makes me fear that we will be dragged into this war is not what Germany is doing to irritate and offend us but the things which rankle in Germany's mind to make her feel that we are not neutral and that our friendship is not genuine.

Germany is perfectly well aware of what has happened in this country since the war began. She knows as all the world knows that England has pleaded "new conditions" and has changed the law to suit her own convenience. She knows that we have made feeble protests and have taken our own time about doing it. She knows by this time that we have no serious intention of pressing England to a critical point. What I feel is that since she is convinced that we *never* will do anything against

Great Britain, she will say, "America's Army and Navy cannot hurt us." "We have suspended our submarine warfare on her account; it is the only weapon by which we can make a dent in England's food supply, and retaliate." If the English blockade grows more effective, through our help, the people in Germany will themselves grow more desperate and anger toward the United States will grow to the point where public opinion will support the German Government in any course it may pursue to vindicate its position. This is taking a long look ahead but the facts and the trend of circumstances are inevitable. Now then, the thing it seems to me which we must decide first of all is: Is it necessary to the permanent interests and future of the United States that the Allies shall win this war? If it is not, our course must be one of relentless neutrality, obviously. If it is necessary that the Allies shall win, we must inquire if they can win without our help. If they can, we must then too close our eyes to sympathies and traditions and follow the law of self-preservation and by all means remove any possible cause of trouble as between us and Germany and thereby make most remote the chances of our entering the war. I think it is almost axiomatic that if the Allies cannot win without our help, we should be openly a belligerent on their side. We should have a voice in this whole matter if it thus effects us so vitally.

But I am unwilling to believe that the Allies need our help as a belligerent nor do I for a minute suppose that anything we may do as a benevolent neutral will effect the outcome of this war.

But what I am getting at is that we must have a definite policy and that policy must be based either on consideration of law and absolute fairness to all concerned or on our destiny as it is effected by the cause for which the Allies are fighting.

It seems to me that much as we love Great Britain, much as we are her kinsmen, we must take the same attitude that Washington took when he seemingly turned on our friend, France, and refused to become entangled in Europe's quarrels. We must live our own life. We must not depend on British sea power or allow the British to believe for a minute that they can dominate us.

You know and I know that Great Britain pays mighty little attention already to what we say. We are almost in a position of a vassal state. The newspapers of the East are so strongly influenced by the fact that the money of the Allies is heavily invested through loans and other things that they dare not raise an outcry. The people of the Middle West and the Far West think otherwise. Many believe we are playing Wall Street's game and we of course never will get anything in the way of political support from those gentlemen, if indeed we need to think of those things at all.

But what I want to point out is this: We took six months to write a note to Great Britain. Apparently Great Britain is taking six months to answer it. Our record is there on paper but we do not show the spirit of real neutrality. We set forth as an excuse that until we settle our matters with Germany, we cannot take things up with Great Britain. It is this very inaction that is causing us to be hated in Germany and which is causing their people slowly to sanction a break with us. What I am afraid of is that some day Germany will of her initiative break with us on the ground that we have not been neutral. This would raise a wide discussion in this country. We would not have what the people would call a just cause and the whole matter would be very much mixed up and we would not be credited with "keeping the country out of war" but dragging the country in it.

It is a fact that England pigeonholes nearly everything we send them. She has taken our mail off the high seas; she has detained our ships; she has taken passengers off of American ships on the high seas; she has discriminated against our citizens with her trading-with-the-enemy act;[1] she has undoubtedly used many of her merchantmen to attack submarines and our modus vivendi was certainly a fair proposal to which England has not even given us a formal reply. We get no satisfaction out of her at all.

It seems to me that the big thing to do is to fight this thing out, as you said in one of our notes, "without compromise and at any cost." We must press Great Britain as hard as we have Germany. We must accept the bitterness that it will stir up in Great Britain as inevitable, but we must do our duty. Nothing will be more popular with the American people than to have the President of the United States stand up before the whole world and demand that Great Britain as well as Germany must conform to international law or lose our friendship. We must even have crises with Great Britain and talk of a break in diplomatic relations. We must be ready to go through with it all. Only by such a course can we convince the whole world that we are impartial and want to live our own life. We cannot be prejudiced on either side. Think of the effect already in this country of Root's speech.[2] I have heard of German-Americans far and wide who are beginning to say that our Government has not gone as far as some of the pro-Ally Republicans would have it. We must give further

---

[1] The so-called blacklist, about which see WW to EMH, July 23, 1916, n. 1.
[2] About which, see n. 1 to a memorandum by Joseph Patrick Tumulty, Feb. 16, 1916, Vol. 36.

demonstration of our fairness. Only in that way can we get the real approval of the country—German-Americans, British-Americans, and all. The time has come to take a big and broad view of the situation and to map out a definite policy which we will adhere to without flinching. "AMERICA FIRST" must be our motto as you have well chosen it. I know that when you have given it all careful consideration, you will agree with me that we still have time to avert the catastrophe for our country. For it is clear to me that as long as Germany can cherish the slightest hope of seeing us in controversy with Great Britain, she will not care to attack us or break with us. It is the traditional policy of the United States to balance one against the other. In our early history we balanced London against Paris, later it became London against Berlin. It is still London against Berlin, and disentanglement from their quarrels that keeps us safe and secure.

T MS (WP, DLC).

Joseph Taylor Robinson to Joseph Patrick Tumulty

Dear Mr. Tumulty: [Washington] July 20, 1916.

Returning to the Senate after a prolonged absence on account of illness, I find there exists a grave controversy among Democratic Senators as to the passage of the Child Labor Bill. I reported this bill from the committee, and am anxious to secure its passage.

I wish you would inform the President that I shall be glad to render every possible assistance to that end.

With regards Very Truly   Jos. T. Robinson.

ALS (WP, DLC).

To Joshua Willis Alexander

My dear Judge: The White House July 21, 1916

Now that we are within sight of the goal we have been striving for in the matter of the shipping bill, may I not give myself the pleasure of saying how much I have valued and admired your services in this work of capital importance? Throughout my association with you, I have learned more and more to respect your motives and admire the spirit and energy and ability with which you address yourself to great matters of public business.

Cordially and sincerely yours,   Woodrow Wilson

TLS (photostat in RSB Coll., DLC).

Frank Lyon Polk to Robert Lansing

Washington, July 21, 1916.

I had a talk with Arredondo on the nineteenth. He submitted a modification for proposed agreement, which was not acceptable. I submitted a counter proposal as I telegraphed you. He said he would communicate with his Government and let me know. Yesterday he sent word through Lawrence that he had heard nothing from Mexico. This morning the Associated Press carried a despatch from Mexico City giving the terms of their original Note and stated that this Note had been presented, but no answer had been received from the United States Government. I sent for Arredondo and told him very plainly that we could not submit to such treatment, that it was discourteous and, in view of the frank way we had dealt with him, uncalled for. I said I thought some explanation was necessary. He stated that he had not heard from his Government, but that he supposed that General Carranza had been unwilling to accept any modification. He gave out this statement to show the Mexican people what was being done. This was not at all in line with our understanding and I told him so. He was rather stubborn about it and most unsatisfactory. He said as soon as he heard from his Government he would communicate with me.

Paragraph. I asked the President this morning if he had ever spoken to Senator Stone in regard to the Danish matter. He said he had not, but perhaps you had. Do not you think it would be well to have the President see Stone before the matter is finally closed, if you have not already seen him?

Paragraph. The President approved our message to Page, suggesting that he come home to discuss pressing matters. He sails tomorrow.

Woolsey returning to-morrow on Danish matter

Frank L Polk

TS telegram (SDR, RG 59, 812.00/18791½C, DNA).

From Frank Lyon Polk

My dear Mr. President: Washington July 21, 1916.

It occurred to me that possibly Mr. Arredondo may not be presenting the case to Carranza just as we see it. We have been keeping Mr. Rodgers informed, but now it might be a good time to send him a message which he could read to the Mexican Government making clear our present position. I enclose a draft of a telegram which I would like to have you read before it is sent, as it undertakes to state your views. This should go off as soon as possible, if you approve of this course.

If you decide to let it go, I could come to the White House to get it and have it sent, if you will direct some one to telephone me to that effect.   Yours faithfully,   Frank L Polk

TLS (SDR, RG 59, 812.00/18791½A, DNA).

To Frank Lyon Polk, with Enclosure

My dear Mr. Polk   [The White House, July 21, 1916]
    This has my approval. I have suggested only one or two verbal changes   W.W.

ALI (SDR, RG 59, 812.00/18791½A, DNA).

E N C L O S U R E[1]

Washington, July 21, 1916.

CONFIDENTIAL. 231. In view of the informal conferences which were being held here between Mr. Polk and Mr. Arredondo in the hope of inducing the Carranza Government to modify its note of July 11th by adding a clause which would extend the scope of the inquiry by the Commission proposed, of which you have been kept informed, the President and the Department feel very much embarrassed by the publication of the note by the Mexican Foreign Office yesterday, and feel also that the statement of the Foreign Office officials that the note had not been answered is misleading, and gives a false impression of the attitude of this Government. While it is true that the first amendment which Mr. Polk suggested to Mr. Arredondo was not accepted by the Carranza Government, the Department did not have reason to believe that that Government's rejection was final, and no later than the 19th a sugestion in another form for broadening the scope of the inquiry of the proposed Commission was made to Mr. Arredondo, who promised to telegraph it to his Government, and it should have been received by the Mexican Foreign Office before that Office gave out its statement of July 20th. These conferences were being held in a friendly and conciliatory spirit, and Department felt that the matter would be arranged to the complete satisfaction of both Governments, when final announcement would have been made. It was understood by Mr. Polk and Mr. Arredondo that until such an agreement was reached or all efforts to reach one definitely abandoned, no announcements should be made. The Department has been disposed to consider sympathetically the delicate position of the Carranza Government, and is very desirous to avoid causing embarrassment to that Government. Apparently the Foreign Office has misjudged the Department's attitude, or has deliberately attempted to limit the inquiry to the subjects mentioned in their note of July 11th. The President had intended to name as commissioners on the part of the United States gentlemen of the highest rank and standing in the country. He had hoped that as a result of the deliberations and findings of this Commission, a settlement of all the perplexing questions outstanding between the two Governments might have been arrived at. He feels that the questions arising out of the border difficulties can be settled by direct negotiations; that a commission for the settlement of these questions alone would be unnecessary.

There are, as the Carranza Government must be well aware, other and very important questions which have been raised *by* or have grown out of the disturbed conditions which have so long prevailed in Mexico. It is not the intention or desire of this Government to interfere ⟨in⟩ *in any way with* the internal administration of Mexico. But American lives have been lost and American property injured and destroyed, and the Government feels that it is its duty to spare no effort to prevent a repetition of these occurrences; and it sincerely hopes to secure this as far as possible in friendly co-operation with the de facto Government after careful and impartial inquiry by the proposed Commission. You will express to the Foreign Office the Department's ⟨astonishment⟩ *deep surprise and keen disappointment* at the abrupt turn they have given these negotiations, and endeavor to secure a satisfactory explanation. You may read this telegram to the Secretary of Foreign Relations, but do not leave with him a copy. The Department hopes that the explanation of the Mexican Foreign Office will be such that the negotiations may proceed to a satisfactory conclusion.   Polk

T telegram (SDR, RG 59, 812.00/18791½B, DNA).
    1 Words in angle brackets in the following document deleted by Wilson; those in italics added by him. This telegram was sent to Rodgers at 9 P.M. on July 21, 1916.

To Pleasant Alexander Stovall

[The White House] July 21, 1916

My dear Mr. Minister, or may I not say, My dear Stovall:

Your letter of June twenty-first about my renomination has given me the most sincere and genuine pleasure, and in return I want to send you my cordial greetings. I can say without the least affectation that I do not desire a second term as President. The first term has in this instance been enough for any man, but I could, of course, not turn away from the service of the party or of the country which had so splendidly stood by me.

And it is delightful to realize the friendship which you and others of those who are serving the nation abroad have so steadfastly maintained for the things that we believe in and are all striving for.

These are only a few lines, my dear Stovall, but they are written with a great deal of warmth of feeling.

With the best wishes,

Cordially and sincerely yours, Woodrow Wilson

TLS (Letterpress Books, WP, DLC).

From Newton Diehl Baker

My dear Mr. President: Washington. July 21, 1916.

The so-called Porto Rican Bill, which passed the House with practical unanimity and with the unanimous recommendation of the Committee on Insular Affairs, is still hanging fire in the Senate. I am going to take the matter up personally with Senator Shafroth and other Senators in the hope of securing the enactment of the Bill at the present session, and I am writing this merely to suggest that if any Senators speak to you on the subject, the main points of importance in the matter may not escape your recollection.

The Bill is chiefly important because it makes Porto Ricans American citizens. This has been urged by all of our Presidents since 1905 and included in each Porto Rican Bill which has been introduced, but failed of passage for lack of interest in insular affairs.

The particular present importance of this matter is the agitation of a man, Jose de Diego,[1] who has visited practically all of the Latin-American countries agitating for a pro-Spanish policy in Latin America and a union of the Antilles. Diego is now in Spain speaking to large audiences and urging the revival of Spanish influence in the Antilles. If the pending Bill can pass, the gift of American citizenship will destroy the independent party in Porto Rico and put an end to the Diego agitation. Should the Bill again fail of passage, however, further internal disturbance may well result from this fresh disappointment. I do not understand there is any opposition to the Bill in the Senate, but being an uncontroverted matter, it is allowed to drift without much interest even on the part of its friends to press it over.

Respectfully yours,   Newton D. Baker

TLS (WP, DLC).

1 Lawyer, poet; judge of the Supreme Court of Porto Rico, 1898-1900; member of the Executive Council of Porto Rico, 1900-1901; member of the Porto Rican House of Delegates since 1903 and Speaker of the House, 1907-1915.

From Walter Hines Page

Dear Mr. President: London 21 July 1916

The general belief here is, in and out of military circles, that the war has entered upon its last phase; that the end may be yet a long way off; but that there will be no "draw," but a decisive victory for the Allies—not a crushing defeat (responsible men do not wish to humiliate the German people) but a real defeat of their military machine and party. How true a prophecy this is, it wd. be a waste of time to conjecture. But this is now the prevailing English mood, and this mood directly affects their spirit and their actions, military and political. They fear and expect set-backs, perhaps serious set-backs, but temporary. The Western Allies now have, they think, men and guns and munitions enough to break the Germans down; and they reckon also on the continued demoralizing effect of their economic pressure.

The getting of incalculable munitions, conscription, the French tenacity at Verdun, the initial success of the French and English offensive, the onrush of the Russians, the practical certainty that the German fleet will not risk another battle, the increasing underground rumbling of discontent in Germany—these and many lesser events of similar import have moved the English spirit to its present height of endeavor: they are "awake" at last. This awakened and expectant public opinion now rules this Kingdom. The Government is its pliant tool. I have never before seen anything so swift and determined as this public opinion; and you can hardly imagine anything more obedient than the Government.

This situation has its direct interest for us. For examples: (1) Public opinion will not hear of any relaxation of the economic pressure; (2) it will not permit a single German reservist to get home even in a neutral ship; (3) it will not consent for mails to pass unexamined. Members of the Government—some of them —frankly confess to me in effect that they are no longer free agents. The public has taken the business of conducting the war in its own hands, and the public judges every measure by this one test—They ask, does it help us win the war and hasten our victory?

The following incidents and events confirm or throw some light on these general propositions: As I make it out, there was very little personal sorrow at the loss of Lord Kitchener. This was not only because his intimate friends were few: he had spent most of his life away from home—but the general feeling was that his work was done. Many people, of course, knew, too, that he was incapable of team-work and was a constant and severe trial to his Cabinet associates. Yet his death made a profound impression. He had raised the great army—or his name had; and the whole nation roused itself to keep that army in munitions and to do everything else for it. Although the Germans had nothing to do with his death, his death nevertheless acted as an extraordinary stimulus to the war-spirit of the whole English nation. You could almost see the grim determination rise in their minds as you see the hot sun raise the mercury in a thermometer.

Sir Edward Grey, who in my judgment is the greatest man in this group here, is so exceedingly considerate of the U. S., has such a profound faith in our scheme of things—is so convinced and thorough-going a democrat, practically and idealistically, and so believes in our future—this man will go the whole length that his convictions and his environment will permit to meet our wishes. He has given many proofs of this. But on the particular subjects that directly bear on the conduct of the war, be becomes more and more rigid. He has several times almost directly & openly confessed to me that the time has passed when he can always follow his own inclinations. When I find him in the right mood, I linger in his office after my particular business is done and draw him into a general conversation. Standing before his fire (we all had fires during the whole arctic June and one is burning now in the room where I write) we have gone over schemes of government, the general relations of our two countries, the future of the English-speaking peoples, Wordsworth, fishing (he wrote a book that is a sort of modern Izaak Walton)[1] —every sort of thing that is big and interesting. The other day I went to see him when I had no errand. "I surprise you," I said,

[1] *Fly Fishing* (London, 1899).

"by bringing you no trouble to-day. I calld. only to congratulate you on your elevation to the peerage."[2] He explained the drawbacks. He spoke of the wrench it gave him to leave the House of Commons after 30 years' service without a break, and he spoke with much emotion. He was put in the Lords because Kitchener's successor is a commoner and this makes an unlawful number of Cabinet Ministers in the Commons. Somebody had to become a peer, and for several reasons he is the most suitable and available man. We fell to talking at last about the whole subject of our differences. He remarked that in normal times a democracy takes too little interest in public affairs, but in times of stress it takes too dominating an interest. In normal times, it leaves the politicians too much to their own devices, in excited times it curtails too much their liberty of action. "Why, Mr. Page, if we were to open the door for German reservists to get home from North and South America—in the first place we shd. commit suicide, and in the second place—I can't say what English opinion in its present mood wd. do to the Government." There's his confession! Another remark was this: "The French Government is much more rigid than we are in construing precedents and international law. Yet their actions do not seem to stir up American resentment as ours do. Is there not in the American democracy a background of old controversies with us about shipping and no such background of any such controversies with the French?" I couldn't keep from saying, "If that be true, it shows only that the French are luckier in their past than you." Then he fell to talking about his own future, and this and that; and when I got down stairs where Tom Page was waiting for me, I found him asleep in the automobile! A few nights later Sir Edward dined with me and he gave the whole evening to talk about his eagerness that the United States shd. not pass severe judgments on the Allies during this life-and-death struggle. Tom Page and another American, just come from home, were here; and I told them to tell him quite frankly what the feeling is in the U. S., wh. he had heard from me *ad nauseam*. When they were done, he said "I know it. Now tell me what *I* can do?" He talked of little else to Mrs. Page who has come to know him quite well and to whom he talks very freely. After the people had gone, she said to me: "What's the hitch? It is impossible to believe that Sir Edward does less than he can do to meet our views and wishes. He is a simple, honest, straight-forward truthful man. Isn't he?" "Beyond question," said

2 Grey's elevation to the peerage was announced on July 6. He was at first proposed for an earldom, but, at his own request, was given the title of Viscount Grey of Fallodon in order to avoid being confused with the other Earl Grey.

I. "Well, what's the matter then—except British public opinion?" "Very little else. We've got to argue with the whole British people. They've taken the Government, foreign policies and all, in hand." I think that that is pretty nearly the whole truth.

The matter of our controversies about the mails and about shipping troubles is practically coming more and more into the hands of Lord Rob't Cecil,[3] Minister of Blockade, now of Cabinet rank. He is the ablest of the sons of the old Lord Salisbury. I think he is the only Tory to the nth. degree that I ever had a decided liking for. He was the bitterest critic of the Liberal Government, and now under the Coalition he has half his old enemies as bedfellows. I must say that he plays the game squarely. Ugly, gentle, courteous in the extreme, he told me one day that for the present there are only two articles in his working creed—"first and foremost, to win the war and save civilization on the earth, and second, to do all that I can to safeguard the rights of neutrals and especially the U. S." And some things he does see, and he has done some things of practical value. I have had a long unofficial as well as official fight about the censorship—of news to the U. S., as well as of other things. I convinced him as I convinced Sir Edward of the desirability of being open and generous to the correspondents of the American newspapers. Sir Edward agreed with me, but he brought very little to pass: it wasn't quite his job. But Lord Robert has brought much to pass: he had more time. And he has done a good deal to lessen the delay of the mails. He smooths many little paths. The broad highways are sometimes too much for him.

He is much interested in "the war after the war," *i.e.* the war of trade. That crusade was conducted here chiefly by Hughes,[4] the Labor Prime Minister of Australia. Hughes stumped the Kingdom for it. Cities gave him their Freedom in silver cases. The universities gave him degrees. The people gave him loud applause. Half the press hailed him as a Moses. I made a pretty close study of Hughes. He is not a big man. In many ways he is an ignorant man. But he is an earnest fellow and, I think, quite honest. His economic grasp is not wide—a somewhat narrow, but very earnest and surely very convincing man, a free-and-easy and ready campaigner with a colonial breeziness which "takes." He used the background and setting of Australian help and loyalty with most excellent effect. And he and Lord Rob't Cecil were among the British delegates to the Paris Economic Conference. Now some

[3] Lord Edgar Algernon Robert Gascoyne-Cecil; hereinafter referred to as Lord Robert Cecil.
[4] William Morris Hughes.

things the Allies will do in "the war after the war." Germans had used commercial and financial methods in England and in Russia in particular wh. were unmoral if not immoral—methods that might have been taken out of the books of a decade or so ago about the Standard Oil Co. They "dumped" and killed competition by starving out competitors. They conducted systems of commercial espionage &c. &c. &c. The English were slow to detect these things and sluggish to move against them. They will be neither slow to see nor sluggish to act for some time after the war. They will try, too, to prevent dependence on Germany for dyestuffs and other monopolized articles. These things and suchlike they can and probably will do. No German ships will be allowed to touch here to carry English freight and passengers. Germans will, for a time, find London a hard money-market. But the notion of a general Allied Zollverein with preferential tariffs will either never be carried into effect or it will break down so quickly that I am sure nobody need pay much present heed to it. Besides, they will find it impracticable to discriminate against neutrals in any comprehensive scheme. Trade makes its own customs and own laws—in the long run; and no nation is going to cut its own throat—very long. As the whole matter now stands, it is a warmeasure, a piece of Allied "frightfulness," like German Zeppelins; and it does seem to be annoying the Germans.

Just what effect the recent order in council which throws out even the remnants of the Declaration of London will have will depend on the way in wh. it is put into execution. The formal discarding of the whole Declaration has met popular approval: doubtless that's what it's done for. The order in council wh. buried it is popularly calld. "Grey's Elegy." I have a feeling (not a conviction exactly but a sort of intuition) that it may be executed somewhat to our relief—practically to meet some of our contentions; and I find this same feeling in the neutral section of the diplomatic corps here. I have not been able to get any very clear-cut expression about its probable effects from any official source. What they tell me falls under the popular formula—"wait and see."

The truth is, the mind of this nation now takes in only one subject. Everybody thinks about that and works towards that—in his or her own way—all the time; and that is how to win the war. Nothing else concerns them. All other things seem of so little consequence in comparison, that most other things have to wait. If you picture to yourself the feeling in Washington while the battle of Gettysburg was going on, you will have something like a parallel. That battle lasted two (?) three days. The battle in France goes on, far more fiercely, month after month. Day after day the London papers will contain less than twenty lines of despatches from the U. S. and these have some direct bearing on the war, *e.g.* the despatches about the *Deutschland*. The same is true of other neutral countries. It is a time of but one subject for this half of the world. You can not imagine the depressing monotony of this. Every American who comes here straight from home remarks after a week or less, "I didn't know it was this way. It seemed very different in the U. S."

When I went to a camp where there are 3,000 interned (civilian) Germans a few weeks ago and for nearly the whole afternoon heard the complaints of their committees, one doctor struck an original note. "Sir," said he in his most earnest address to me, "the solemn truth is we are all on the road to the mad house. We've been here—most of us—for nearly two years. We seem—or may seem to you—to have room enough; we have these grounds to walk and sit in; we do have enough air and space; but I assure you, sir, the monotony of this life is driving us to insanity. There are three men in the hospital now whose brains have gone wrong. I am a physician, and I assure you we will all be mad if we have to stay here much longer." I felt a strong impulse to applaud and to say that he wouldn't find it essentially different outside.

The English are now doing heavy fighting. My mail is loaded down with letters imploring me to inquire whether this and that "missing" man be a prisoner in Germany. It takes one man all his time to answer these letters now. My calling hours are taken up with men and women who come to make such requests orally. Sometimes they come to my house before breakfast. Yet not one of them complains or breaks down. They, too, are determined to win the war. But it's war, war, war all the time. It seems ages since July 1914 when one read and talked and heard other subjects. The people you dine with have their houses piled with parcels that they are sending soldiers or prisoners, or with bandages and other hospital supplies. Of three boys that I had in succession as servants, one is in a German prison-camp, another in a hospital in England recovering from wounds, and the third is in the trenches in France. I think I wrote you that a little while before the war began my daughter gave a party one night to which she invited the 20 young Englishmen that she knew and liked best—fine young fellows, many of them heirs to fortunes and titles; and a little while ago I happened to find a list of her guests that night. Twelve out of the twenty (perhaps more but twelve I knew) had already been killed in the war. The interned German doctor, I have no doubt, told the truth; and we are all on the road that wd. at last lead to bedlam.

Yet, strange as this paradox is, people are very cheerful. War has come to be the normal state of life: it is not only taken for granted—it gives these people activity that brings in some a sort of exaltation, in many more a form of milder excitement. But the point I had chiefly in mind is the impossibility of inducing anybody to think or to talk about anything else or to consider or to do anything that doesn't seem immediately to help to win it. We are living almost within the sound of the guns of a continuous Gettysburg. I am told that people at certain places on the East coast of England hear the guns distinctly except when the wind is against the sound; and whole trains of wounded and of prisoners are constantly arriving. There is a hospital just through the wall from where I write and another two doors from the building where our offices are. These instances are typical of most of the residential neighborhoods—A continuous Gettysburg; a tyrannical public opinion; a universal concentration on one subject; an obedient Government—to public opinion; a depressing monotony of subject and talk and work, relieved by the exaltation born of a belief in victory—this is the atmosphere we now live in. In the course of time—a long time, I hope—we'll all be on the way to the madhouse.

Since I wrote the foregoing I have spent almost a whole afternoon with Lord Robert Cecil, going over most of our controversies. He tells me just what I have written you about the Economic Conference and trade after the war—nobody yet knows what will be done; and about the New Order in Council about the blockade —it makes no necessary change but it formally discards the Declaration of London.

And the most important news of all is the Department's telegram asking if I think it advisable to go home for a personal conference. I do, decidedly—certainly for my own instruction and benefit. Three years and a half is a long time, especially when two have been war-years. Such a visit will be of infinite help to me. Nor do I think that any newspaper sensation can now be made of my going. If leave be granted me, I shall follow this letter a week later. And it will be a great pleasure, as well as a great benefit, to see you, Mr. President.

                              Sincerely Yours,   Walter H. Page

ALS (WP, DLC).

From Frederic Adrian Delano

Washington
My dear Mr. President: July twenty-first Nineteen sixteen

Referring to my visit on the nineteenth of June, with Mr. Harding, and my explanation of the desire of four members of the Federal Reserve Board that you should recognize some formal rule of rotation and succession in designating the Governor of the Board, may I venture to express the hope that it is no part of your plan to control the Board's action through the power to designate the Governor and Vice Governor?

If I may so assume, I think I may fairly ask you to say whether you will not kindly make your position clear by pointing out the importance of some such rule when, in accordance with your reported intention, you send to the Senate the name of Mr. Charles S. Hamlin as a member of the Federal Reserve Board for a ten year term.

If you do not take this action, I trust you will not feel that I would be violating the canons of propriety should I exercise the right and privilege of a freeborn American citizen in drawing the attention of the proper Committees of Congress to what appears to me a dangerous feature of the law.

Very respectfully yours,   Frederic A Delano

TLS (WP, DLC).

From Charles Samuel Jackson

Portland, Oregon, July 21, 1916.

Congratulate you on your attitide [attitude] toward child labor legislation. Those members of Congress who are in opposition deserve to be driven out of public life and into private oblivion. It is regrettable that some of them label themselves democrats. Think of child slave drivers considering themselves democrats. The virus of chattel slavery is behind this enslavement of the children of the country and popular government efficiently and economically conducted is the only remedy and you are its recognized leader and spokesman. Reactionary government so long conducted by slave drivers and those who capitalize human life and human rights has acted as a drag upon the finer senses of the justice-loving American people, but there is promised an awakening and they have you to thank for it. May you have always the strength and courage to strike for the right, so that free institutions and free men shall not perish from the earth.

C. S. Jackson.

T telegram (WP, DLC).

From Robert Lansing, with Enclosure

Henderson Harbor, N. Y.

My dear Mr. President: July 22, 1916.

I send you a letter which I have received from Ambassador Penfield which I think you will find of interest.

Faithfully yours,   Robert Lansing.

TLS (SDR, RG 59, 763.72/2832½, DNA).

E N C L O S U R E

Frederic Courtland Penfield to Robert Lansing

PRIVATE & CONFIDENTIAL

My dear Mr. Secretary: Vienna July 3, 1916

After studying conditions and circumstances recently developed by the war, I decide to take the risk of predicting, but only to you, that the chances are more than even that Roumania will this summer enter the conflict and on the side of the Entente.

From a person highly placed in Roumanian diplomacy I am assured that this is probable, and from an Austrian military expert I learn that the step is regarded by high officials of his Government as more than likely to ensue. If it comes to pass it will leave this Monarchy with an enemy on every foot of boundary with the exception of the small frontiers where Austria adjoins Switzerland and Germany. The unfortunate plight of the Monarchy of the Habsburgs with Roumania added to the list of enemies would then be more than obvious.

Roumania has always sympathized with the Entente, but the desire to enter the lists was held in check during the months when the Austro-German armies were conquering Serbia and the Austro-Hungarian forces taking possession of Montenegro.

Now, with the irres[is]tible advance of Russia into the Bukovina and the capitulation of Greece to the demands of the Entente Powers, the desire to participate in the struggle has had recrudescence, and the reports from Bucharest are that nothing short of a miracle can keep Roumania out of the war—most Roumanians believe that the psychological moment is near. The Roumanian King,[1] it is known, is doing his utmost to have his country remain neutral.

It is Roumania's ambition to restore Transylvania to its former place in the Roumanian Kingdom. A year ago the report was current that the Emperor Francis Joseph had said that he would give no part of that region to Roumania as a peace inducement, and that Roumania could never by force take a meter of soil from him.

By the sale of cereals and other essentials to Germany and Austria, at enormous profit, Roumania's finances at present are in a position of enviable solvency.

I am, my dear Mr. Secretary,

Yours very truly,   Frederic C. Penfield.

TLS (SDR, RG 59, 763.72/2832½, DNA).
  [1] Ferdinand I.

From Samuel Gompers

Sir: Washington, D. C., July 22, 1916.

Because the proposal to appoint a commission to investigate the causes of misunderstanding between the United States and Mexico is fraught with opportunities of tremendous importance in the development of two nations, I wish to urge upon you another consideration in connection with that commission.

In your recent letter to me you say the commission would probably be too small to be thoroughly representative. The scope and the nature of the work which that commission will have to perform is of such a character that it is a very serious question whether or not a commission not truly representative ought to be empowered to perform that work.

There are events and conditions extending back for years that must be examined in order that the commission may be in a position to make a report of value. There are various relations that must be inquired into and investigations that will necessitate diversity of experience and information. Commissioners not prepared to weigh all events and conditions with discernment and discrimination would not be able to put before the people of both nations conclusions and recommendations furthering the best interests of both nations.

From the standpoint of Labor alone relations with Mexico are of fundamental importance. Between the United States and Mexico there exists only an artificial boundary line which is practically no barrier to economic development and relations that must exist between people living in contiguous territories.

The retarded development, the low standards of life and work that exist among the fifteen millions of Mexicans to the south of our country is one of the most serious problems that confront the workers of the United States in promoting their economic and social welfare.

It is only necessary to refer to the fact that every borderline problem resolves itself in the last analysis into a labor problem. The labor movement of the United States has for years been fully aware of the importance of the Mexican problem. The part that organized labor has played in helping to avert the war that seemed imminent is now common information. Labor took the first step in that crisis to protect human rights.

As the labor movements of the United States and of Mexico are the only agencies that stand distinctively for human rights and have demonstrated their effectiveness in a most trying crisis, it is just and wise that the organized labor movement should be represented on this commission, empowered to investigate existing conditions and causes of misunderstanding and to report constructive measures which will have influence in molding the development of both countries for years to come.

The interests, the desires and the demands of the workers of the United States have no other agency of expression than the organized labor movement. In urging that this commission ought to be thoroughly representative and authorized to make a comprehensive investigation that would have real value, I am presenting the expressed desires of the organized workers of this country who represent the more aggressive independent workers and who have established a way to express their wishes.

Back of the organized labor movement are the millions of unorganized who, although they have not yet learned the necessity for organization, nevertheless they are in need of its protection against lower standards of life and work and the opportunities for freedom which it maintains.

From recent reports it seems that further negotiations will be necessary in order to determine all matters connected with the proposed commission. It is not inopportune, I judge, to urge for your serious consideration the enlargement of the commission to such a number as will be truly representative.

> Very sincerely yours,   Saml. Gompers.

TLS (SDR, RG 59, 812.00/18824, DNA).

To Edward Mandell House

Dearest Friend,   The White House. 23 July, 1916.

Thank you for the many useful and enlight[en]ing letters which I have not been able to acknowledge separately. They go into my thinking, and go, you may be sure, to the very heart of it, and are invaluable to me.

You will have seen by the papers that we have called Page home from London for a vacation in which it is our hope that he may get back a little way at least to the American point of view about things.

I am, I must admit, about at the end of my patience with Great Britain and the Allies. This black list business[1] is the last straw. I have told Spring Rice so, and he sees the reasons very clearly. Both he and Jousserand think it a stupid blunder. I am seriously considering asking Congress to authorize me to prohibit loans and restrict exportations to the Allies. It is becoming clear to me that there lies latent in this policy the wish to prevent our merchants getting a foothold in markets which Great Britain has hitherto controlled and all but dominated. Polk and I are compounding a very sharp note. I may feel obliged to make it as sharp and final as the one to Germany on the submarines. What is your own judgment? Can we any longer endure their intolerable course?

I dare say you were surprised by the nomination of Clarke for the Supreme Court, because I suppose you did not know him, but I am confident you will approve when you know all about him. He is a close friend of Newton Baker's and Gregory (whom I love and trust more than ever) picked him out.

I have not been very well for the past week or two,—Since I came back from Detroit. My digestion has been upset in some way. But I am slowly getting it in shape again, I believe, the undeniable truth being that a rest, a real rest, has been now a long time overdue. I wish I were in better trim for the campaign.

All join me in affectionate messages.

Faithfully and gratefully Yours,   Woodrow Wilson

WWTLS (E. H. House Papers, CtY).

[1] The British government, on July 18, issued a list of eighty-seven American and roughly 350 Latin American firms which it accused or suspected of trading with the Central Powers, and forbade its subjects from having any dealings with those companies. This caused an immediate and furious reaction among the American people and widened the growing rift in Anglo-American relations. See Link, *Campaigns for Progressivism and Peace*, pp. 65-67.

To Frederic Adrian Delano

My dear Mr. Delano: [The White House] July 24, 1916

The matter to which you and Mr. Harding called my attention, and to which you again call my attention in your letter of the twenty-first, has so many sides to it and deserves such thorough consideration that this has not seemed to me a possible time for me to give the necessary attention to it in all its aspects.

I am, as you assume, expecting to renominate Mr. Charles S.

Hamlin as a member of the Federal Reserve Board, but I shall not by that action determine my policy in the other matter, but shall try to make some arrangement which will make it possible for me to consider the whole matter thoroughly at an early date.

May I not say with the utmost cordiality that I regret that you should speak of the question as involving a "plan to control the Board's action through the power to designate the Governor and Vice Governor?" Surely, my dear Mr. Delano, you do not think that any such plan exists or could exist.

Sincerely yours,   Woodrow Wilson

TLS (Letterpress Books, WP, DLC).

To William Henry Welch[1]

My dear Doctor Welch: [The White House] July 24, 1916

I want to tell you with what gratification I have received the preliminary report of the National Research Council[2] which was formed at my request under the National Academy of Sciences. The outline of work there set forth and the evidences of remarkable progress towards the accomplishment of the object of the Council are indeed gratifying.

May I not take this occasion to say that the departments of the Government are ready to cooperate in every way that may be required, and that the heads of the departments most immediately concerned are now at my request actively engaged in considering the best methods of cooperation? Representatives of government bureaus will be appointed as members of the Research Council as the Council desires.

Cordially and sincerely yours,   Woodrow Wilson

TLS (Letterpress Books, WP, DLC).
  [1] Baxley Professor of Pathology at The Johns Hopkins University School of Medicine. As president of the National Academy of Sciences, he directed the formation of the National Research Council.
  [2] See EMH to WW, July 6, 1916.

To Edward Percy Howard

My dear Mr. Howard: [The White House] July 24, 1916

Your very generous letter of July seventh has given me the deepest pleasure, and I thank you for it with all my heart. I am taking the greatest pleasure in returning the menus with my signature.

Cordially and sincerely yours,   Woodrow Wilson

TLS (Letterpress Books, WP, DLC).

To Charles Samuel Jackson

My dear Mr. Jackson: [The White House] July 24, 1916

Thank you warmly for your telegram about the child labor legislation. I am going after it with all my heart and am hopeful of success.

In haste

Cordially and sincerely yours,   Woodrow Wilson

TLS (Letterpress Books, WP, DLC).

To Newton Diehl Baker

My dear Mr. Secretary: The White House July 24, 1916

Thank you for your letter about the Porto Rican Bill. It furnishes me with just the ammunition I want.

Cordially and faithfully yours,   Woodrow Wilson

TLS (WDR, RG94, AGO Document File, No. 2638801, DNA).

To Henry Eitel[1]

[The White House] July 24, 1916

May I not express to you my sincere sorrow at the death of James Whitcomb Riley?[2] With his departure a notable figure passes out of the nation's life, a man who imparted joyful pleasure and a thoughtful view to many things that other men would have missed. I am sure I am speaking the feeling of the whole country in expressing my own sense of loss.

Woodrow Wilson

T telegram (Letterpress Books, WP, DLC).
  [1] A banker of Indianapolis and a brother-in-law of James Whitcomb Riley.
  [2] He had died on July 22 at the age of sixty-seven.

From Frank Lyon Polk

My dear Mr. President: Washington July 24, 1916.

I enclose a draft of a telegram to be sent to the British Government in regard to the recent publication of the blacklist.[1] This is a composite effort based in the main on the views of Mr. Johnson and Mr. Phillips. We discussed the question of making some reference to a continuation of such a policy raising the presumption of unfriendliness on the part of the British Government. It would seem to us that having referred to the measure as obnoxious, the closing sentence was sufficient to impress the British Government with the seriousness of the situation.

If they refuse to yield, then a stronger note could follow this.

I must apologize for sending it over on telegram paper, but it was copied by the stenographer believing it was to be sent without further correction.   Yours faithfully,   Frank L Polk

TLS (WP, DLC).
¹ It is missing. Wilson's redraft is printed at July 26, 1916.

Frank Lyon Polk to Rudolph Forster

Dear Mr. Forster: Washington July 24, 1916.

The letters from the President to the Emperors of Austria-Hungary, Germany, and Russia, the King of Great Britain, and the President of the French Republic, in regard to the relief of the distressed non-combatant inhabitants of Poland, which you sent to me with your note of July 20, were on the 21st instant forwarded to our Ambassadors at Vienna, Berlin, Petrograd, London and Paris, respectively, for delivery; and the full text was also cabled to the Ambassadors on the 21st instant.
                        Sincerely yours,   Frank L Polk

TLS (WP, DLC).

To Samuel Gompers

My dear Mr. Gompers: The White House July 25, 1916

I have your letter of July twenty-second and know how to weigh the importance of what you say.

The present trouble is the apparent unwillingness of the *de facto* Government of Mexico to give the inquiries of the Commission any breadth of scope whatever. It is that unwillingness we are trying to remove now and that is delaying the appointment of a commission.

When the Commission is appointed, I shall try to make it up in a way that will make it certain that the many important questions you speak of are kept fully in mind. When I said that it could not be truly representative, I meant that the various elements in our life could not be separately represented in all probability.
                Cordially and sincerely yours,   Woodrow Wilson

TLS (photostat in RSB Coll., DLC).

To Alexander Jeffrey McKelway

My dear Doctor McKelway: The White House July 25, 1916

Thank you for your letter of July twentieth. I was very glad indeed to learn from Mr. Vance McCormick yesterday that he had already taken up with you favorably the matter of a bureau at headquarters upon education and social service.

Cordially and sincerely yours,   Woodrow Wilson

TLS (A. J. McKelway Papers, DLC).

From Frank Lyon Polk

My dear Mr. President: Washington July 25, 1916.

The British Ambassador called this afternoon in regard to the blacklist. It was very evident that his Government is surprised and disturbed at the irritation and excitement caused in this country. He stated that it was not the intention of his Government to interfere in any way with neutrals trading with neutrals, but that the act was directed to prevent British capital and credit being used for the support of the enemy. The point they make is that where corporations, firms, or individuals are merely dummies for German interests, that they should prevent British subjects from trading with them.

He also stated that in general there is no intention that the blacklist should affect existing contracts except in certain specified cases, which would be fully explained. He notified me that McNear and Company (a case presented by Secretary Redfield) had been acted on by his Government and existing contracts for the shipment of oil to Australia could be carried out. He said further that any mistakes made in particular cases would be gladly remedied and those firms removed from the blacklist.

I made it very clear, and he thoroughly understood, that this discussion in no way affected the principle involved and that as the matter stood, we still felt there was a great deal to be cleared up and that a protest probably would be sent. He also stated that a statement would be made in the course of the next few days, clearing up the situation.

I thought you should have this information, as you have the proposed protest before you. What the Ambassador said shows a friendly disposition, but does not materially change the question of principle involved.   Yours faithfully,   Frank L Polk

TLS (WP, DLC).

From Frederic Adrian Delano

Washington
My dear Mr. President: July twenty-fifth Nineteen sixteen.

I am very grateful to you for your cordial note of the twenty-fourth instant, and I deeply regret if the expression quoted by you conveyed a suggestion which I hasten to assure you was very far from my thoughts; for I have steadfastly refused to believe that it was your intention to control the Board's action in any way. The thought that has been clearly in my mind is that unless some rule of rotation were now adopted, a precedent would be established which might easily, at some future time, result in the law, as it now stands, being used to control the votes of one or two of the appointive members.

To make my meaning entirely clear, what I wish to point out is that if The President now adopts a policy in harmony with the rotation principle, that will in all probability determine the application of the law for all time; and without the protection of such a precedent, men of a type that would command the respect and confidence of the country would hesitate to accept service on the Board in what would then be a subordinate capacity.

Some of us, including myself, are so impressed with the importance of this matter, which we regard as fundamental, that we deem it our duty to take up the issue if it is forced upon us, regardless of the consequences to ourselves. However, I hope that, with this further explanation of our position, you will be willing to concede the merit of our contention; for may I not remind you, my dear Mr. President, that we have worked faithfully and studiously for two years to make this Act a success, and are in a position to see dangers which may not be obvious to you, absorbed as you necessarily must be, with many other problems of great moment.

I am, my dear Sir,

Respectfully yours,   Frederic A Delano

TLS (WP, DLC).

From George Ellery Hale[1]

My dear Mr. President: Madison, Connecticut, July 25, 1916.

On behalf of the Committee of the National Academy of Sciences charged with the organization of the National Research Council, I beg to express our very appreciative thanks for your telegram, containing your letter to President Welch endorsing our preliminary report and promising the full co-operation of the Government Departments.[2] With your indispensable aid, there will now be no difficulty in completing the organization and extending greatly the work already undertaken by five committees appointed to deal with urgent matters.

In the first public statement regarding the National Research Council, which I am preparing for immediate publication by the Associated Press, it will be a great advantage to be able to speak of your approval and co-operation. I trust I may have your permission to print copies of your letter to Dr. Welch for distribution to universities and other research institutions when it becomes feasible to issue a general appeal for their participation in the work of the Council.

I have seen enough of the independent project of Dr. Godfrey and Dr. Crampton to convince me of its exceptional value, and it is a pleasure to learn that you approve it so highly.

President Welch and the Council of the National Academy request me to recommend for your personal consideration that science be separately represented on the Advisory Commission of the proposed Council of National Defense. The demand for representation of other important subjects, such as medicine, industry, transportation, etc., seems certain to call for a membership exceeding the limit of six imposed by the Senate bill, and probably even that of seven, as set by the House. Under such circumstances science may be in danger of elimination or of fusion with some other subject. The latter alternative is very undesirable, since quick and intelligent action in a crisis demands complete knowledge of the situation in a given field, such as only a leading representative of that department can have.

Thus the fusion of medicine and science, which has been spoken of as a possibility, would fail of the desired object; at least, this is the opinion of Dr. Welch and also that of Dr. Simpson, Secretary of the Committee of Physicians and Surgeons,[3] who has just visited me to discuss the subject. There is no doubt of cordial co-operation between the physicians and surgeons and the men of science—this has been abundantly assured. It is merely a question of securing for each subject that able and effective representation which would be so surely needed at a time of stress. If you could see your way clear to urge upon Congress the authorization of an Advisory Commission certainly large enough to permit the separate representation of these two important subjects, and of all others actually needed, I am sure that much advantage would result.

The importance of science, as distinguished from the equally fundamental field of industry, in any adequate plan of preparedness, is too well known to you to require discussion. But you may be interested to see how the neglect of science by the British Government, at length overcome by the establishment of an Advisory Council for Scientific and Industrial Research under the chairmanship of Sir Joseph Thomson, President of the Royal Society, is reflected in the enclosed clippings from "Nature."[4] We must not prepare poisonous gases or debase science through similar misuse; but we should give our soldiers and sailors every legitimate aid and every means of protection which the fertile imagination and the painstaking research of our great body of investigators can devise.

I expect to reach Washington next Monday evening, and should appreciate an opportunity for short conferences with you and with the Secretaries of War, Navy, Interior, Agriculture and Commerce. As I have already had preliminary talks with these members of the Cabinet, and as the question of appointments, through your kindness, has recently received further consideration by them, the choice of Government representatives can doubtless be arranged with little delay.

During my visit to Washington I shall be the guest of my brother-in-law, Colonel W. W. Harts,[5] 1842 Mintwood Place.

Assuring you of my sincere appreciation of your message, I am, with much respect,   Yours faithfully,   George E. Hale

TLS (WP, DLC).

[1] Noted astronomer, director of the Solar Observatory in California of the Carnegie Institution of Washington, and chairman of the National Research Council.

[2] WW to G. E. Hale, July 24, 1916, CC telegram (WP, DLC).

[3] That is, Franklin Farrow Simpson, M.D., prominent gynecologist of Pittsburgh and secretary of the Commission of American Physicians for Medical Preparedness.

[4] What Hale actually enclosed was an advertisement listing "some of the topical articles which have appeared in NATURE since the outbreak of the war," NATURE, XCVII (June 22, 1916), cxxxiv. This list included numerous articles on the practical applications of science to industry in both war and peace and on the ways in which government might foster such applications.

[5] William Wright Harts, military aide to Wilson; also in charge of the Office of Public Buildings and Grounds in Washington.

From Edward Mandell House

New London,
Dear Governor: New Hampshire. July 25, 1916.

I am distressed to hear that you have had a recurrence of your digestive troubles. What you need, as you say, is a real rest and I wish you could get it.

I hope they will not disturb you too much about the campaign. There is no need why you should be bothered with the details.

Roper[1] was here yesterday and I feel satisfied that we will have the only efficient organization that has ever been constructed in a democratic national campaign. Roper seems to understand the job and appreciates its importance and we have agreed to keep in close touch with one another.

I suggested a coordination between the organization, public-[it]y and speakers bureaus. The center of this should be the organization and Roper will be able to tell Cummings the kind of speakers that are needed in each particular section and will tell Woolley the kind of literature to send. I have asked him to explain this to McCormick and let him bring about the coordination himself.

Hapgood thinks that Rublee would be quite willing to remain on the Trades Commission until after the election, provided you send him a note in reply to his resignation, which will go to you this week, saying that you would appreciate it if he would continue for the present.

I am glad you chose a Northern man for the Supreme Court and I am sure Judge Clark will justify his appointment. He comes from the right section.

I am also glad that you have had a chance to know Gregory as I know him. There are not many like him. In talking about himself when he was here he told me that he did not want to go on the Supreme Bench and be in a bomb-proof cellar himself while you were on the firing line.

I am sorry that a crisis has arisen with Great Britain and the Allies. Their stupidity is beyond belief. Before asking Congress for authority to prohibit loans and restrict exportations I would suggest that you let Jusserand and Spring-Rice inform their governments that you intend to do this unless they immediately change their method of procedure. I would explain to them that you did not have much leeway because of the probable early adjournment of Congress and therefore had to ask them to move with celerity.   Affectionately yours,   E. M. House

TLS (WP, DLC).
  1 Daniel Calhoun Roper, First Assistant Postmaster General. He was to resign on July 29 to become an assistant to Vance C. McCormick at the Democratic national headquarters.

From Dudley Field Malone

PERSONAL and PRIVATE.

Dear Mr. President: New York July 25, 1916.

Our friend, Father O'Callaghan of the Paulist Fathers,[1] is now the head of the Catholic Apostolic Mission House at the Catholic

University in Washington and is, as a consequence, one of the most influential men at the University.

Father O'Callaghan is going to make an effort to see you within the next few days on a matter which he has thoroughly discussed with me here in New York.[2] From many points of view it would seem to me desirable for you to attend the public meeting of the Convention in which he is interested, especially so if Archbishop Ireland is to speak.[3] As you know, however, my judgment is obedient to your personal view of the situation.

Yours faithfully,   Dudley Field Malone

P.S. Please do not acknowledge this. D.F.M.

TLS (WP, DLC).
  [1] The Rev. Peter Joseph O'Callaghan. See the news report printed at April 7, 1912, Vol. 24.
  [2] There is no record of a meeting between Wilson and O'Callaghan.
  [3] Malone probably referred to the mass meeting held in Madison Square Garden on August 20, during the convention of the American Federation of Catholic Societies, held in New York from August 18 to 24. However, neither Wilson nor the Most Rev. John Ireland, Archbishop of St. Paul, participated in the mass meeting or in any other event of the convention. *New York Times*, Aug. 18-25, 1916, *passim*.

Frank Lyon Polk to Robert Lansing

[Washington, July 25, 1916]

Have not heard from Brun or Egan.

President very anxious matter should be closed and suggests if you approve, it may be well adapted [advised] to go ahead without waiting for further information in regard to details of contract or concession that Woolsey thought should be examined.

Have not heard from the Mex. representatives for the last two days. Am told Arredondo has no instructions.

Submitted a note to the Pres. on Blacklist. Protest was made not omitting grounds that they are violating any treaty or necessarily doing anything *illegal*? but that the extension of the blacklist amounts to a boycott and unnecessary and obnoxious exercise of power. Do you wish to have it telegraphed to you in full?

Polk

Hw decode of T telegram (R. Lansing Papers, DLC).

To the British Foreign Office

English Boycott.   The White House [July 26, 1916].

The announcement that His Britannic Majesty's Government has placed the names of certain persons, firms, and corporations in the United States upon a proscriptive "blacklist" and has forbidden all financial or commercial dealings between them and citizens of Great Britain has been received with the most painful surprise by the people and Government of the United States, and seems to the Government of the United States to embody a policy of arbitrary interference with neutral trade against which it is its duty to protest in the most decided terms.

The scope and effect of the policy are extraordinary. British steamship companies will not accept cargoes from the proscribed firms or persons or transport their goods to any port, and steamship lines under neutral ownership understand that if they accept freight from them they are likely to be denied coal at British ports and excluded from other privileges which they have usually enjoyed and may themselves be put upon the blacklist. Neutral bankers refuse loans to those on the list and neutral merchants decline to contract for their goods, fearing a like proscription. It appears that British officials regard the prohibitions of the blacklist as applicable to domestic commercial transactions in foreign countries as well as in Great Br[i]tain and her dependencies, for Americans doing business in foreign countries have been put on notice that their dealings with blacklisted firms are to be regarded as subject to veto by the British Government. By the same principle Americans in the United States might be made subject to similar punitive action if they were found dealing with any of their own countrymen whose names had thus been listed.

The harsh and even disastrous effects of this policy upon the trade of the United States and upon the neutral rights upon which it will not fail to insist are obvious. Upon the list of those proscribed and in effect shut out from the general commerce of the world may be found American concerns which are engaged in large commercial operations as importers of foreign products and materials and as distributors of American products and manufacturers to foreign countries and which constitute important channels through which American trade reaches the outside world. Their foreign affiliations may have been fostered for many years, and when once broken cannot easily or promptly be reestablished. Other concerns may be put upon the list at any time and without notice. It is understood that additions to the proscription may be made "whenever on account of enemy nationality or *enemy association* of such persons or bodies of persons it appears to His Majesty expedient to do so." The possibilities of undeserved injury to American citizens from such measures, arbitrarily taken, and of serious and incalculable interruptions of American trade are without limit.

It has been stated on behalf of His Majesty's Government that these measures were aimed only at the enemies of Great Britain and would be adopted and enforced with strict regard to the rights of neutrals and with the least possible detriment to neutral trade, but it is evident that they are inevitably and essentially inconsistent with the rights of the citizens of all the nations not involved in war. The Government of the United States begs to remind the Government of His Britannic Majesty that citizens of the United States are entirely within their rights in attempting to trade with the people or the Governments of any of the nations now at war, subject only to well defined international practices and understandings which the Government of the United States deems the Government of Great Britain to have too lightly and too frequently disregarded. There are well known remedies and penalties for breaches of blockade, where the blockade is real and in fact effective, for trade in contraband, for every unneutral act by whomsoever attempted. The Government of the United States cannot consent to see these remedies and penalties altered or extended at the will of a single power or group of powers to the injury of its own citizens or in derogation of its own rights. Conspicuous among the principles which the civilized nations of the world have accepted for the safeguarding of the rights of neutrals is the just and honorable principle that neutrals may not be condemned nor their goods confiscated except upon fair adjudication and after an opportunity to be heard, in prize courts or elsewhere. Such safeguards the blacklist brushes aside. It condemns without hearing, without notice, and in advance. It is manifestly out of the question that the Government of the United States should acquiesce in such methods or applications of punishment to its citizens. Whatever may be said with regard to the legality, in the view of international obligation, of the Act of Parliament upon which the practice of the blacklist as now employed by His Majesty's Government is understood to be based, the Government of the United States is constrained to regard that practice as inconsistent with that true justice, sincere amity, and impartial fairness which should characterize the dealings of friendly governments with one another. The spirit of reciprocal trade between the United States and Great Britain, the privilege long accorded to the nationals of each to come and go with their ships and cargoes, to use each other's shipping, and be served each by the other's merchants is very seriously impaired by arbitrary and sweeping practices such as this. There is no purpose or inclination on the part of the Government of the United States to shield American citizens or business houses in any way from the legitimate consequences of unneutral acts or practimes [practices]; it is quite willing that they should suffer the appropriate penalties which international law and the usage of nations have sanctioned; but His Britannic Majesty's Government cannot expect the Government of the United States to consent to see its citizens put upon an *ex parte* blacklist without calling the attention of His Majesty's Government, in the gravest terms, to the many serious consequences to neutral right and neutral relations which such an act must necessarily involve. It hopes and believes that His Majesty's Government, in its natural apsorbtion [absorption] in a single pressing object of policy, has acted without a full realization of the many undesired and undesirable results that might ensue.[1]

WWT MS (WP, DLC).
[1] This was sent as F. L. Polk to WHP, July 26, 1916, 10 P.M., T telegram (SDR, RG 59, 763.72112/2758a, DNA). It is printed in *FR-WWS 1916*, pp. 421-22.

To Frederic Adrian Delano

My dear Mr. Delano: [The White House] July 26, 1916
Thank you warmly for your letter of July twenty-fifth. I took it for granted that the implication in your letter was not really intentional and had already put upon it the construction you do, though I must say that it is inconceivable to me that any Executive should dare, whatever his inclinations, to yield to such a temptation as you intimate.

I realize to the full the importance of the question and your own very deep feeling about it, and I can assure you that I will put myself in a position to give it very early practical consideration.   Sincerely yours,   [Woodrow Wilson]

CCL (WP, DLC).

From Frank Lyon Polk, with Enclosure

My dear Mr. President: Washington July 26, 1916.
I enclose a copy of a cable from Mr. Gerard, in regard to the Bryan peace treaty. I find that the copy of the telegram intended for you was placed on my desk and overlooked by me.

I also enclose, as requested, a copy of the message to Great Britain on the subject of the blacklist.[1]
                    Yours faithfully,   Frank L Polk

TLS (WP, DLC).
[1] Wilson sent this enclosure to Colonel House.

ENCLOSURE

Berlin (via Copenhagen) July 24, 1916.

4149. Confidential. House Code.

Think there is remote possibility that Germany might now sign Bryan arbitration treaty. Shall I pursue matter, if so, advise matter be kept secret so that if successful we may announce it suddenly. Bernstorff should not be informed as, if treaty is signed, think Chancellor wants to do everything here. Of course suggest possibility Germany signing treaty and then starting submarine war.

Please inform Colonel House.

T telegram (WP, DLC).

From Henry Lee Myers

Dear Mr. President: Washington, D. C., July 26, 1916.

I am pleased to inform you that last night the democratic senatorial caucus ordered that the public domain water power bill be taken up in the Senate and made the unfinished business immediately after the disposition of the land leasing bill, which had already been set for a day early in December.

Therefore, it will not be necessary for you to speak to Senator Kern about the matter, as you kindly agreed to do in response to my request. I cordially thank you, however, for your very kind interest in the matter.

With great respect,

Yours most cordially,   H. L. Myers.

TLS (WP, DLC).

To Edward Mandell House

Dearest Friend,   The White House. 27 July, 1916.

Here is a note we yesterday sent to Great Britain. I hope that you will approve both its substance and its method.

Polk had already intimated to Spring Rice that I would probably be obliged to go to Congress and ask for retaliatory powers, though he had not specified what powers I would ask for. Do you think it would be wise to be specific? It was evident to Polk when he last saw Spring Rice that the British Government was not a little disturbed (and surprised, poor boobs!).

Thank you for your letter of yesterday. The campaign plans

and suggestions are admirable, and I hope they will be carried out in their entirety.

I expect to act on the suggestion about Rublee, unless something turns up that it [is] not now in sight.

I am feeling much better, and am going to try hard to get a number of short rests, since I cannot have a long one. Mrs. Wilson and I will run away more frequently on the MAYFLOWER, I hope, and get Washington frequently out of our systems.

All join me in affectionate messages.

Faithfully Yours,   Woodrow Wilson

That was a lovely thing you quote Gregory as saying, bless his heart!

I attended to that matter concerning the American Academy of Sciences immediately upon the receipt of your lett[e]r,—while McCormick was still with me.   W.W.

WWTLS (E. M. House Papers, CtY).

To Claude Augustus Swanson

My dear Senator: [The White House] July 27, 1916

I have just seen the House conferees on the Naval Bill and am hopeful of very satisfactory results.[1] In the meantime, may I not express my very warm and genuine appreciation of the successful work you have done in this great matter?

Cordially and sincerely yours,   Woodrow Wilson

TLS (Letterpress Books, WP, DLC).

[1] The House of Representatives, on June 2, had passed a naval appropriations bill which greatly scaled down the shipbuilding program recommended by Secretary Daniels. The Senate, on July 21, passed a bill much more in line with Daniels's recommendations. Wilson conferred with the House members of the conference committee on July 27 and argued for the Senate bill. Wilson continued to exert heavy pressure on congressmen, with the result that the House of Representatives, on August 15, voted to accept the main features of the Senate measure. For a detailed discussion of the bills and the political maneuvering involved, see Link, *Confusions and Crises*, pp. 334-38.

To Benjamin Ryan Tillman

My dear Senator: The White House July 27, 1916

May I not send you just a line of appreciation of the fine work done on the Naval Bill? It has been a great pleasure to be associated with you in accomplishing things.

Cordially and sincerely yours,   Woodrow Wilson

TLS (B. R. Tillman Papers, ScCleU).

To Frank Lyon Polk

My dear Mr. Secretary,   The White House. 27 July, 1916.

Thank you for letting me see this letter from Penfield. He always says something that it is useful to keep in mind.

Faithfully Yours,   W.W.

WWTLI (SDR, RG 59, 763.72/2833½, DNA).

To Daisy Allen Story

My dear Mrs. Story: [The White House] July 27, 1916

I very much appreciated the call you and the ladies who accompanied you yesterday were gracious enough to make upon me,[1] and am very much interested in the object of the visit. I sincerely hope that it will be possible for the Government of the United States to become the owner of Monticello, the former home of Thomas Jefferson. I have long been interested in the consummation of such a purchase and the preservation of so interesting a memorial of one of the greatest and most influential men in our history, and shall be glad at any time to do anything I can to assist.

Cordially and sincerely yours,   Woodrow Wilson

TLS (Letterpress Books, WP, DLC).
  [1] Mrs. Story, president general of the Daughters of the American Revolution, asked Wilson to use his influence to secure the passage of Senate Joint Resolution 153, which provided for the purchase of Monticello by the federal government. As it turned out, the Senate took no action on the measure.

From Frank Lyon Polk, with Enclosure

My dear Mr. President: Washington July 27, 1916.

Mr. Arredondo called this morning and assumed all the responsibility for the publication of the Note by the Mexican Government. His story is that he never communicated to his Government the agreement not to publish the Note and that after General Carranza stated that he was unwilling to vary the terms of the Note, he did not notify General Carranza that we were still negotiating to see if we could agree on some modification which he, Mr. Arredondo, would submit to his Government.

This explanation can be very easily punctured as it does not quite agree with the statements from Rodgers and it does not agree at all with our conversations with Mr. Arredondo. However, I assumed that it would be your wish to accept this explanation. I showed no very deep interest in his story when he was confessing his fault.

The matter now stands that we have their Note before us for acceptance and he has offered that, if we will present a Note to him he will submit it to his Government informally to see if they will accept it.

There are two courses open, either to reply to their original proposal in terms satisfactory to us, without regard to what action they may take, or to submit our proposal to Carranza. If the first course appeals to you, we could submit a Note somewhat on the lines of the Note enclosed, which he could not very well refuse. At the same time, or when you appointed the Commissioners, you could give out a statement setting forth what you hoped could be accomplished.

I enclose, attached, a copy of the original Note,[1] which you may need for reference.   Yours faithfully,   Frank L Polk

TLS (WP, DLC).
[1] It is printed as an Enclosure with WW to RL, July 6, 1916.

ENCLOSURE

DRAFT OF REPLY TO MEXICAN NOTE OF JULY 12TH.

I have the honor to acknowledge receipt of Your Excellency's Note transmitted under date of July 12th by Lic. Eliseo Arredondo, your Government's confidential agent in Washington, informing me that Your Excellency has received instructions from the Citizen First Chief of the Constitutionalist Army Charged with the Executive Power of the Union to propose that each of our Governments name three commissioners, who shall hold conferences at some place to be mutually agreed upon and decide forthwith the question relating to the evacuation of the American forces now in Mexico, and to draw up and conclude a protocol or agreement regarding the reciprocal crossing of the frontier by the forces of both countries, also to determine the origin of the incursions to date, in order to fix the responsibility therefor and definitely to settle the difficulties now pending or those which may arise between the two countries on account of the same or a similar reason; all of which shall be subject to the approval of both Governments.

In reply I have to inform you that I have laid your Note before the President, and have received his instructions to state that the Government of the United States is disposed to accept this proposal of the Mexican Government in the same spirit of frank cordiality in which it was made. This Government believes, however, that the powers of the proposed Commission should be enlarged so that happily they may arrive at a solution satisfactory to both Governments, of the questions set forth in your communication, and the Commission may also consider such other pending questions, the amicable and friendly solution of which would tend to improve the relations of the two countries, it being understood that the recommendations of the Commission in this regard shall not be binding upon either Government until formally accepted by them.

Should this proposal of the President be accepted by Your Excellency's Government, I beg to state that this Government will proceed immediately to appoint its commissioners, and fix, after consultation with Your Excellency's Government, the time and place and other details of the proposed conference.[1]

T MS (SDR, RG 59, 812.00/19039, DNA).

[1] "President telephoned me at Metropolitan Club July 27, 1916 that this met with his approval, to polish it up & give it to Arredondo. He repeated these instructions at Cabinet today July 28, 1916[.] F.L.P." Hw memorandum (SDR, RG 59, 812.00/19039, DNA).

From Frank Lyon Polk, with Enclosure

My dear Mr. President: Washington July 27, 1916.

The Danish Minister telegraphed that he has already requested his Government for full powers to sign and exchange a treaty for the sale of the Danish West Indies. In view of the fact that he has already sent the message, I thought possibly you would care to see Mr. Lansing's letter to Mr. Woolsey, pointing out his objections to the treaty.[1] I also enclose a copy of the Declaration the Danish Government wishes us to make in regard to Greenland.

I understood you to say that regardless of any objections that might be presented we were to wire the Danish Minister that we accepted the text that he had mailed us and that we would make the Declaration requested. It occurred to me that as long as he has already cabled his Government, that in accepting his text we could omit any mention of the Declaration and it might be possible for Mr. Lansing and the Minister to secure modification of this Declaration when they meet to sign the treaty. This would not necessarily delay signing.

Yours faithfully,   Frank L Polk

TLS (WP, DLC).

[1] It is missing, but see RL to F. L. Polk, July 28, 1916.

ENCLOSURE

Declaration by U. S.

The Government of the United States of America will not object to the Danish Government extending their political and economic interests to the whole of Greenland.

T MS (WP, DLC).

From David Lawrence

PERSONAL AND CONFIDENTIAL   [Washington]

My dear Mr. President: Thursday July 27th 1916

Mr. Polk spoke to me today of your request that if I had anything about Mexico to communicate to you to give it to him instead. I realize that you are very busy and should not for a moment have asked to see you did I not deem it of essential interest to you. Inasmuch as it is you who is to be responsible for what happens in the Mexican situation, your directions that are to be executed, I am taking the liberty of placing before you some of the ideas that have come to me in actual contact with the situation. I regret that I cannot write as freely as I can talk but on the assumption that this letter will be seen only by you, I am going to write somewhat frankly.

It is a different point of view that I get of this situation than the official who is inside of it and wrapped up in it. I talk with Arredondo daily; he is frank and open with me, shows me his messages, expresses himself freely, much more so than he does at the State Department; I talk frequently with Mr Polk who has graciously taken me into his confidence, too. In that way, as a disinterested person I see some of the flaws in both sides and having some years of experience with the Mexican character as well as with the purposes of our own government, I take the liberty of intruding in the situation. It is no pleasant task, usually a thankless one, and I have reached the point where I believe it would be best for me to have nothing more [to] do with the situation. I am restrained by the circumstances from writing anything for my paper about Mexico, I cannot comment at all really on the situation and while that is not so essential really, for my paper understands that, I do not like to feel that my activity may be undesired by the Government.

I feel absolutely confident that if you had had the same opportunities for studying the situation from the outside as I have had, you would have had no difficulty in the present stage of the controversy. There is nothing wrong with the *purpose* of the Administration—there never has been. It is simply the *method* that is at fault. And since this is to be my last communication on the subject to you, I am going to explain just where it seems to me the trouble lies.

All of us desire an avoidance of war with Mexico or anything that resembles armed intervention. Yet if we are not cautious, we shall have another crisis just about the most dangerous time that it could happen—the midst of the campaign. Mr. Tumulty can tell you that my predictions in the Mexican situation from time to time have been usually borne out by events. And I am certain to-day that we shall have trouble with Mexico in a month or more unless we are exceedingly cautious as to our own tactics.

There always have been but two ways to deal with Mexico, one by force and the other by friendship. You have rejected time and again the idea of force but our diplomacy has not similarly and simultaneously rejected the theory of compulsion. To say to a country that "you must do thus and so because *we* want it done" is merely to intimate that we intend to use force to obtain our end. If we are resting on the assumption that friendly means are only an expedient of today and that eventually force must be used, I submit that we must make up a different record, a better case on which to appeal to the people of this country for support. And that brings me to the fundamentals of the situation today.

We are trying to settle "the Mexican problem as a whole." Mexico under the leadership of Carranza and even before he came into power (remember the Benton episode)[1] has refused to allow us to be the suzerain or the guardian. The implied privilege which the Monroe Doctrine gives us to intercede for other powers being the "nearest neighbor and friend" is something which Carranza never has and never will admit. Call it pride or nationalism in him—it is a conviction and I predict that he will never change his mind on that viewpoint. All Latin countries go through the process of rejecting America's good office and friendliness and then they come back to it. Our present good friend Argentina was not so long ago expressing serious doubts (among her statesmen) whether or not the European system was not after all the better. Is not Chile today resentful over the implications of the Monroe Doctrine and even more nationalist at times than Mexico?

Therefore, I believe that our policy toward Mexico must not be based on the theory that it is our duty and function to impose our kind of help on Mexico. Our sole interest under international

[1] See WHP to WW, Feb. 24, 1914, n. 1, Vol. 29.

law is the *protection of the lives and property of American citizens*. If Mexico wants our help, she knows we stand ready to give it. The best kind of help we can give her is not to try to impose our will but to grant such things as Mexico *asks us* to do, provided they are compatible with our own interest. Mexico will never *publicly* or even through a commission ask us to help her. It is useless to accord powers to the new commission to treat on questions of an internal character in Mexico. Carranza cannot live politically in Mexico and negotiate internal questions with a foreign government. It is out of the question to think our government can loan Mexico money or do anything except very quietly use its influence with bankers to get a loan and unless conditions are favorable (when of course government influence would not be necessary) the bankers would not listen to any proposal except that which contained a government guarantee, which of course our government is not ready to give.

From the Mexican point of view, there is no need of funds, no economic distress. What constitutes suffering from our viewpoint is almost "normal" to Mexican eyes. Mexicans subsist on very little and if conditions in the United States are taken as a standard, of course Mexico is in bad shape. But for Mexico, conditions are such that I do not wonder that Carranza denies the existence of an economic crisis. The Mexicans have a right to do as they please with their own country; if there should really be widespread starvation, we will find the Mexican government ready and willing to accept private aid. But that point has not been reached. My suggestion is that we make our record very clear of having tried to help Mexico but put the responsibility for refusing our aid exactly where it belongs; also in such fashion that Mexico will have no doubt of our willingness to aid if she will *suggest* the way. You may notice that I emphasize the necessity for all suggestions about outside help to come from Mexico. Outside help is contraband, misunderstood and distrusted if it is not asked for or sought by the Mexicans themselves.

I believe therefore that any attempt to saddle the commission with broad powers to deal with internal questions in Mexico is doomed to failure. Privately our commissioners may in their conversations with the Mexicans influence some changes or even initiate means by which private parties may help resurrect Mexican commerce and exchange but to insist on an explicit treatment of these questions by a commission is to ask what Carranza certainly will not grant or be able to without losing prestige at home.

Carranza's note suggests a commission but is limited to the

border question. Let us accept the proposal but at the same time point out that the only purpose the expedition had in entering Mexico was to remove the conditions that made the raids possible, and that in withdrawing we must feel assured that they will not be repeated; that in bringing our forces back into American territory such action shall not be misconstrued as any relaxation in the fixed purpose of the United States to obtain the fullest protection for the lives and property of foreigners; that the de facto government when recognized was recognized as responsible for *all of Mexican territory* on the understanding that it possessed the "material and moral capacity" to protect the lives and property of foreigners; that unless the de facto government can by its acts prove itself continuously capable of giving such protection, the moral support of the United States to such a government cannot be *continuous.*

I believe, in other words, that we must make our prime consideration always the lives and property of Americans resident in Mexico as well as Americans resident on our international boundary. The Republicans can get nowhere arguing about intervention as applied to economic conditions in Mexico but they can make headway if we do not continue to insist forcefully on the protection of our nationals. In the answer to the Carranza note we have the opportunity to tell the de facto government exactly what that obligation means, what the consequences may be of its violation and why it is important that we must be assured in convincing manner of their understanding of this duty for we are in the position of having ordered all our Americans out of Mexico; we cannot advise them to go back until we are sure Mexico will protect them and without them the mines cannot be reopened or industries rehabilitated, factors that are essential to Mexico's economic salvation.

My suggestion is that we make very clear our desire to help, if Mexico suggests the way; that we make the protection of Americans the paramount issue and a prerequisite to the withdrawal of the Pershing expedition, and that we do not permit ourselves to get tangled up now, before the commission meets, with the powers or scope of a commission. The less it is limited, the more effective its work.

Another thing: the people we are dealing with are radicals and like all radicals they have had little experience in responsible office. The Mexican Foreign Office is not as high class as the British Foreign Office and so if they publish a note without telling us about it (which Great Britain has done more than once, as have we in the case of Mexico,) let us not grow too belligerent about it and feel that all is lost. It is the spirit of a negotiation that counts most and unless we are ready to back up every word we say by force, we better apply the other theory of diplomatic dealing which is the method of friendly persuasion and infinite patience. A mixture of the two theories brings confusion.

If Mr Fletcher had been in Mexico we would have been further along in this negotiation. All of it is being carried on here with Arredondo, who while an honest and willing fellow, has not had sufficient diplomatic training to understand what we are trying to accomplish. He is the best the Mexicans have ever sent here but he is very timid about talking plainly to Carranza and has enemies at home who are now accusing him of being too friendly with the United States. If Mr Fletcher would start for Mexico at once and make up a record of negotiations, the American people would take his reports and feel that all that could be accomplished had been done. If Mr Fletcher after getting to know Carranza found an absolute unwillingness on the part of the de facto government to meet us half way, I for one would feel that the use of force was justified and would advocate a coercive policy that was ready for any emergency. But I have confidence that Fletcher will find Carranza reasonable and, from the Mexican point of view, consistent. It is after all Mexico's government and her country. If the people care to put up with a government that prefers unfriendliness to friendliness with the United States, it is the Mexican people who must bear the consequences of these acts for the responsibility is theirs. That is the republican theory of government and one to which you in many speeches have many times referred.

I am sorry that I cannot have the pleasure of talking with you on some other features of the situation that it is not discreet to write about but with the hope that the above may be of service to you, because it is your interest and your success that I most want to see realized.

I remain,   Very sincerely yours,   [David Lawrence]

TL (WP, DLC).

From Charles Sumner Hamlin

Dear Mr President,   Washington July 27, 1916

Permit me to express to you my deep pleasure and gratitude for the great honor you have conferred upon me in appointing me for another term upon the Federal Reserve Board. It will be my constant aim to justify the confidence you have placed in me. With again my most grateful thanks, believe me,

Sincerely yours   Charles S. Hamlin

ALS (WP, DLC).

From Samuel Gompers

Sir: Washington, D. C., July 27, 1916.

Appreciation of the nature of the obstacle which you say interferes with the consummation of the plan to have difficulties between the United States and Mexico investigated by a United States-Mexican Commission led me to send the following telegram to General Carranza:

"July 27, 1916.

"General Venustiano Carranza,
    First Chief, Constitutionalist Government,
    Mexico City, Mexico.

Permit me to urge upon you to have the United States-Mexican Commission empowered to make comprehensive investigation. The broader the scope of the Commission the more thoroughly will the people of both countries understand the machinations of those who for their own selfish interests want to provoke a conflict between Mexico and the United States.

Samuel Gompers
President, American Federation of Labor."

It is my sincere hope that the way may be cleared for the work of this Commission, which will be of tremendous importance to both countries if comprehensive and representative.

Sincerely yours,   Saml. Gompers.

TLS (SDR, RG 59, 812.00/18842, DNA).

From Joseph Patrick Tumulty

                                       The White House.
Memorandum for the President: July 27, 1916.

Mrs. Frank M. Roessing,[1] Chairman of the Congressional Committee, National Suffrage Association, asks if she and Mrs. Carrie Chapman Catt, President of the National Suffrage Association, may see the President for not to exceed ten minutes on Monday or Tuesday of next week. If it is impossible for the President to fix a time on either of these days, they ask if they may see the President any day the following week.

T MS (WP, DLC).
    [1] Jennie Bradley (Mrs. Frank Myler) Roessing, president of the Pennsylvania Woman Suffrage Association.

To Joseph Patrick Tumulty

[The White House, July 27, 1916]

Are these ladies of the "Congressional Union" variety?

W.W.

ALI (WP, DLC).

From Joseph Patrick Tumulty

[The White House,

Memorandum for the President: July 27, 1916]

The National Suffrage Association is not affiliated with the Congressional Union. Both organizations are working for the Federal Amendment, but the National Association is regarded as the conservative body and the Congressional Union as the radical body. The Congressional Union people are of the "heckling" variety and their methods are not approved by the National Association.

Mrs. Catt is to address the Democratic State Convention in West Virginia next week.

Okeh Tuesday at 2 PM.—Office   W.W.

T MS (WP, DLC).

A News Release

[July 28, 1916]

The President has given his unreserved endorsement to certain measures, not directly related to Army and Navy expansion, which are being taken in behalf of national preparedness. Preparedness does not consist merely in the enlargement of the Army and Navy, but necessitates coordination in production, transportation and industry. A provision of the Army appropriation bill for a Council of National Defense is designed to meet this requirement. This council will consist of the Secretary of State, the Secretary of War, the Secretary of the Navy, the Chief of Staff of the Army, an officer of the Navy of the rank of Captain, or of higher rank, and six persons to be appointed by the President, who shall be authorities on questions relating to public utilities, industry, or natural resources. This body will be capable of very great and material service to the Government in the vital matter of the Nation's security. Needless to say, men of the highest quality of patriotism and ability will be asked to serve upon it.

Preparedness, to be sound and complete, must be solidly based on science. In realization of this fact, the President some time ago requested the National Academy of Sciences to form the National Research Council. That body has been formed and has made a preliminary report, in regard to which the President has written the following letter to Dr. William H. Welch of Johns Hopkins University:

"My dear Doctor Welch: I want to tell you with what gratification I have received the preliminary report of the National Research Council which was formed at my request under the National Academy of Sciences. The outline of work there set forth and the evidences of remarkable progress towards the accomplishment of the object of the Council are indeed gratifying. May I not take this occasion to say that the departments of the Government are ready to cooperate in every way that may be required, and that the heads of the departments most immediately concerned are now, at my request, actively engaged in considering the best methods of cooperation? Representatives of government bureaus will be appointed as members of the Research Council as the Council desires.

"Cordially and sincerely yours,   Woodrow Wilson"

CC MS (WP, DLC).

To Samuel Miles Hastings[1]

My dear Mr. Hastings: [The White House] July 28, 1916

It was with real interest and appreciation that I received your suggestion[2] for the appointment of a commission to visit the belligerent nations for the purpose of studying the means whereby closer economic relations might be brought about between the United States and Europe. The general idea underlying your suggestion had for a long time been much in my thoughts. Whether this is the opportune moment to act upon it, however, is open to serious question.

Let me say that, when the circumstances justify it, I shall take advantage of that provision of the Rainey Bill under which the President is authorized to direct an examination or investigation by the Tariff Commission of trade relations between the United States and foreign countries, including the conditions, causes, and effects of the competition of foreign industries with those of the United States.

After all, what we are interested in is to ascertain all the facts surrounding our economic life and to disconnect a fundamental thing like the fiscal policy of the Government with regard to duties on imports from party politics. We shall strive to do this through the instrumentality of a permanent, non-partisan commission composed of able and experienced men, so that when the facts are once obtained, the handling of our tariff question may no longer be made the football of politics. It ought to be possible by such means to make the question of duties merely a question of progress and development, a question of adapting means to ends, of facilitating and helping business and employing to the utmost the resources of the country in a vast development of our business and enterprise.

Through the Federal Trade Commission, which substitutes the milder processes of helpful counsel for the harsh process of the law, we already have, for the first time, a compilation of the trust laws of the world, together with a complete analysis of the manner in which foreign governments encourage their business enterprises and associations. A committee of the House of Representatives now has under discussion a bill to permit cooperation among American manufacturers and business men exclusively for export trade, so that American enterprise may be able to meet more successfully the organized competition with which they are face to face in international markets. In addition to the information gathered and systematized by the Federal Trade Commission bearing upon foreign and domestic commerce, our consular representatives and commercial attaches abroad have kept us well supplied with information relative to the changing business conditions and the new financial processes which are proceeding with unusual rapidity; but it will be the privilege and function of the Tariff Commission to obtain and collate in an even more systematic way the information which is desired as a basis for our future action.

We have not been accustomed to the large world of international business, but it is evident that we must get acquainted with it immediately. America is already establishing new industries. Some of these, like the dyestuffs industry for example, are old and well established in Europe and have been for generations. The study of such industries, their wages, and their general organization with reference to economy and efficiency of operation, cannot fail to be helpful to the business men of the United States and to the people in general.

May I not add an expression of my sincere appreciation of the evidence you and your colleagues have given of a willingness to cooperate in all such enterprises?

Sincerely yours,   Woodrow Wilson[3]

TLS (Letterpress Books, WP, DLC).
    1 President of the Computing Scale Co. of America, president of the Illinois
Manufacturers' Association, and Republican Mayor of Highland Park, Ill.
    2 S. M. Hastings to WW, July 12, 1916, T telegram (WP, DLC).
    3 This letter was published, *inter alia*, in the *New York Times*, July 29, 1916.

To George Ellery Hale

My dear Doctor Hale: The White House July 28, 1916

Thank you sincerely for your letter of July twenty-fifth.

I am very glad to accord you permission to print copies of my letter to Doctor Welch for distribution to universities and other research institutions when it becomes feasible to issue a general appeal for their participation in the work of the Council in behalf of national preparation.

I feel the weight of your argument for a separate representation of science, and feel that it must be managed in one way or another. Whether it can be managed by an enlargement of the Council provided by Congress, certain circumstances connected with the discussion in the House and Senate lead me to doubt, but you may be sure that I am in close sympathy with the suggestion, and that the best feasible thing will be worked out.

Cordially and sincerely yours,   Woodrow Wilson

TLS (G. E. Hale Papers, CPT).

To Samuel Gompers

My dear Mr. Gompers: The White House July 28, 1916.

Allow me to thank you for your letter of July 27th, embodying a copy of your message to General Carranza.

Cordially and sincerely yours,   Woodrow Wilson

TLS (photostat in RSB Coll., DLC).

To Henry Lee Myers

My dear Senator: [The White House] July 28, 1916

Thank you for your letter of July twenty-sixth. It was thoughtful of you to apprise me of the gratifying action of the caucus.

Cordially yours,   Woodrow Wilson

TLS (Letterpress Books, WP, DLC).

Robert Lansing to Frank Lyon Polk

Watertown, New York, July 28, 1916.

I understood from what you telegraphed me that the President was disposed to waive the objections which we had raised as to the treaty, especially as you informed me that the treaty was being engrossed. As you perceive from my letter to Woolsey two of the objections I consider of especial importance. One only affects the terms of the treaty and that is the preferential treatment of Danish subjects. The other objection relates to the declaration affecting Greenland. My suggestion is that you submit these two objections to the President and if he does not think them sufficiently important to delay the signature of the treaty I am willing to waive them. I fear that the opposition in the Senate, of which we know little as yet, may assert that both of these provisions are published soon and would obtain a certain measure of support from their use.[1] I would not myself waive these two objections unless it was entirely satisfactory to the President, nor would I urge changing the text unless he felt it advisable to do so.

Sweet telephoned you, he tells me, that Brun was cabling his Government for full powers and that it would probably be two or three days before he received authority to sign the treaty. Brun will notify me as soon as he receives them and we can arrange a meeting in New York by telegraph. Possibly it would be well for you to notify Brun at once if the President is willing to accept the Danish text of the treaty without change, as well as the decision regarding Greenland.   Robert Lansing.

T telegram (SDR, RG 59, 711.5914/255, DNA).
[1] *Sic.*

Frank Lyon Polk to Robert Lansing

My dear Mr. Lansing: Washington July 28, 1916.

I enclose a copy of the Note which was sent to Great Britain in regard to blacklisting. It is to be published on Monday morning. You will have no difficulty in recognizing the style. In some ways I think it would have been better if it had a little bit more punch, but if you read it carefully, it seems to me, the punch is there.

This week has been absolutely hideous. The Danish treaty made trouble, but the blacklist has caused an awful row. The innocent and the guilty have come down here together, wildly protesting. It was an extraordinarily stupid move on the part of the British and both Jusserand and Spring Rice threw up their hands over it. I think Spring Rice is secretly pleased that the Foreign Office has made a bad break and apparently acted contrary to his advice.

I pointed out to both the French and Italians how this blacklist is going to ruin their South American business, as most of the agents down there are German firms. Spring Rice tells me that he thinks that we will have "a diplomatic victory." There were so many angles to it that they did not foresee that we really had a splendid case. I found that banks were refusing to give drafts to blacklisted firms. This even aroused the ire of that well known pacifist, John Skelton Williams. The British consuls have been sending out blacklists to a number of custom house brokers in New York.

I enclose a copy of a telegram[1] I sent you yesterday in regard to the Danish treaty. I saw the President on Wednesday and told him of your telegram and that you had also written a letter, which had not been received, pointing out your objections. He said that he felt we should go ahead at once and take a chance on the defects, whatever they might be. I told him of your objection to giving special rights to Danish subjects, and also that there was a concession the details of which we had not received. He told me that he thought we would have to take a chance on both those points and go ahead.

Thursday, yesterday morning, I called him on the telephone and told him we had received your letter addressed to Mr. Woolsey and asked if he wished to see it. I again told him what the objections were and added that there was some question in your mind as to the declaration in regard to Greenland. He again said please to notify Brun at once by telegraph that we accepted the text of the treaty.

After reading your letter, I decided to send it to him and also a copy of the declaration in regard to Greenland, which, up to that time, he had not seen. In the letter I told him that Brun had telegraphed me in the morning (this was Thursday) that he would like to have the Department telegraph a formal acceptance, but that he had already cabled for full powers to sign. I said to the President that as long as Brun had not waited to hear from the Department before cabling, I was sending over your letter so he could see what your objections were. I waited until after six and not having heard from him, I sent a message to Brun as follows:

"Your telegram July 27th. On behalf of the Government of the United States I accept the text of treaty forwarded in your letter of the 18th instant and accompanied by a memorandum of your Government dated June 28, 1916. In order to clear up the English translation, I have had to make two or three verbal changes which do not in any way affect the sense of the text. Please telegraph me what the words quote capitals allotted to the churches unquote in Article two mean. Do they mean investments made by the churches or moneys allotted to the churches out of the revenues of the Islands?"

Apparently the President called me up shortly after this, but I had gone. I called him from the Metropolitan Club a little after eight and he told me that he had read your letter and the proposed declaration in regard to Greenland and still felt that the treaty was so important that we would have to make every concession in order to get it through at once. I told him that I had already sent the message to Brun. He said that was quite right.

Arredondo stayed away and sulked for several days. Yesterday, Thursday, he came in and assumed full responsibility for everything. He said that Carranza had definitely turned down our suggestion of a modification and that he, Arredondo, had continued negotiations without informing Carranza, to see if he could not reach some settlement here. He also said that he had failed to notify Carranza of our agreement not to make any statement to the press in regard to the negotiations or the Note. I showed nothing more than a polite interest in his story, but felt compelled to accept it, with the suggestion that hereafter it will be well to see that our understanding is carried out. He put it in such a way that we had to accept it.

I then submitted to the President a suggested answer which says we are disposed to accept Carranza's proposal and that the President hopes the Commission will also take up other matters, the settlement of which would tend to improve the relations of the two Governments. I will send you this when I have it in form, some time this afternoon.

I should have written you before and kept you posted of what is going on, but I really have not had a moment as the place has been filled with Senators, Representatives, and prominent politicians bringing in victims of the blacklist. In between time, Lincoln Steffens and other gentlemen with ready reliefs for Mexico, have been on my shoulders.

It was very hot yesterday and the day before, but it is delightfully cool today, though frightfully damp.

Please give my kindest regards to Mrs. Lansing and to General and Mrs. Foster.   Yours sincerely,   Frank L Polk

TLS (R. Lansing Papers, DLC).
1 This enclosure is missing.

To Charles Sumner Hamlin

My dear Mr. Hamlin: U.S.S. MAYFLOWER, July 29, 1916

Thank you for your letter of July twenty-seventh. You may be sure that it gave me genuine pleasure to show in a very practical way my entire confidence in you and the value I attach to your public services.

Cordially and sincerely yours,   Woodrow Wilson

TLS (C. S. Hamlin Papers, DLC).

From Obadiah Gardner

Mr. President: Rockland, Maine. July 29, 1916.

On account of the large increase of the army and navy contemplated by the present Congress, which will of necessity enormously increase the expense of their maintenance, and the fact that those interests engaged in the manufacture of the instruments of war and receiving large profits by reason of the tremendous costs incurred in the construction and maintenance of large armies and powerful navies, and as the laboring people of the Country will not individually receive any considerable benefit therefrom, and in the event of war in the future as in the past, the common people will be the principle reservoir drawn upon for the defense of the country at great sacrifice of their lives and hardships to their families, while those having large incomes usually are enabled to reap financial profits because of war and are in greater need of large armies and navies from a commercial and financial standpoint, it is only just and fair that they should be required to pay in proportion to the protection they receive.

We most respectfully call your attention to those who receive large annual incomes and urge that they be made to pay a higher rate of Income Tax than at the present time. Those receiving an annual income of $1,000,000 ought to pay twenty per cent, those receiving $500,000, ten per cent and so on down to the minimum rate used, as there can be no fairer method of deriving the revenues for government maintenance than that which requires the accumulated wealth of the Country to pay the expenses of the governments rather than to impose the burdens of taxation upon that class of people whose stock in trade is their labor only and have not been able to accumulate sufficient property to provide against sickness and suffering, for the common comforts of life, when disabled or deprived of work. Very seldom has war been occasioned by the common people but always are they called upon to engage in war in defense of their country. Those people who are the direct cause of war and who are usually the beneficiaries of war should be required to pay the expenses of war. Congress should increase the rate of taxation through the income tax law upon those best able to bear it.

With great respect and admiration for yourself and the great work you have done and are doing for the people of the United States, coupled with the hope and belief that you will succeed yourself in the office you have so highly honored, and your strength and health will be preserved to the end, I am

Most sincerely yours,   O. Gardner

TLS (WP, DLC).

From John Villiers Farwell[1]

Dear Mr. President: Chicago July 29th, 1916

I have no doubt you are as much worried about the gravity of the controversy between the railroads and their employes as are the business men and thousands of employes and individuals in this country who are dependent for health and prosperity on the uninterrupted transportation of merchandise.[2]

You may have information which some of us here have not, in regard to there being no danger of a strike. If you have not such positive information, it would seem to me that the only power equal to cope with the situation is the government at Washington. City governments or governors can do nothing; business men can do nothing. It is a national question which should be settled by the powers at Washington. The railroads have made a fair proposition to submit the whole matter to the Interstate Commerce Commission, or some other competent body.

Can you not use your great influence to see that the right step is taken at the right time? It is unnecessary to enlarge on the seriousness of the calamity if this unprecedented general strike is not avoided.   Yours respectfully,   John V. Farwell

TLS (WP, DLC).
[1] President of the John V. Farwell Co., dry goods, Chicago.
[2] For the earlier stages of the developing railroad crisis, see WW to W. J. Stone, Feb. 22, 1916, n. 1, and W. C. Adamson to WW, April 4, 1916, n. 1, both in Vol. 36. Negotiations between representatives of the railroads and of the four railroad brotherhoods began in New York City on June 1. The sessions were open to the press. After two weeks of acrimonious discussion, the talks were broken off on June 15 because the railroad managers were unwilling to grant, and the unions were unwilling to recede from, the basic demand of the eight-hour day with time and a half for overtime. The union leaders immediately began the lengthy process of securing a vote of their respective memberships authorizing them to call a nationwide strike at their discretion. By late July, the voting had

been completed, and the brotherhoods announced on August 2 that the strike authorization had carried by large majorities. *New York Times*, June 2-18, July 23, Aug. 1-3, 1916.

An Unpublished Article

America's Opportunity.[1]

[July 30, 1916]

No one can doubt that the immediate future of the world will be crowded with quick changes. Every true lover of America must wish the United States to play a part in those changes which will be worthy of her ideals and her character. Almost alone among the great nations of the world, she will be unhampered in meeting a great opportunity.

In the first place, her resources are unimpaired. Not only has the war and all its attendant circumstances made no hurtful drain upon her men or her materials; it has even enhanced her skill and added to her resources, because of the very circumstances of her situation, cut off from her usual trade with many parts of the world and called upon to supply what she never supplied before, to the nations engaged in the great struggle not only, but also to her own people. She has developed industries that she had before neglected, has found new uses for her material and new materials to use. She has thus been enabled to realize what she can do more fully than ever before, and to do it better than she ever did before. No other nation will stand quite so ready as she to serve the world in every work of peace and development.

In the second place, she will probably of necessity be the chief reliance of the rest of the world in the field of finance. Probably the chief part in supplying the means necessary for the great reconstruction which will have to follow the war will fall to her. When the war began, America was, striking the large balances, a debtor nation. When the war closes, she will be a creditor of all the world. Her financiers will have it within their choice to play a part they have never played before in the economic development of other nations and of distant regions of the earth. It is to be hoped that they will have the vision to accept the opportunity with far-sighted courage and a quick adaptation to the new conditions.

In the third place, I think it is evident that the United States will understand herself better than she ever did before. The war and all its attendant circumstances have cried her wide awake to both the dangers of her life and its enormous possibilities and advantages. There have been many things to disturb us during these two years of long drawn-out tragedy. We had not realized before that there were certain elements in our citizenship which had not in their heart of hearts devoted themselves in full loyalty and allegiance to the country of their adoption. A new problem of disunion, more subtle, more difficult to meet with direct checkmate and correction than the old problem which culminated in the Civil War, has engaged and disturbed our thought, and we have realized that we must devote a new energy and ardor to binding together the forces which will produce a new union—a union of spirits triumphant over every alien force and sympathy. But this very discovery, this very anxiety, has quickened the pulse of every loyal and devoted American throughout the length and breadth of the land, whether his birthplace was on this side of the water or on the other. A new and wholesome force has arisen amongst us of thoughtful, watchful, energetic patriotism, and I venture to think that the nation is better prepared on that account to face the problems of a new day in which it will marshal all its energies and assemble all its resources to enable the country we love to play the part it should seek to play in the counsels and actions of the great world.

Fortunately, America can play her part in the days to come unselfishly and impartially, because she covets nothing that other nations have unless it be their skill and knowledge in some of the undertakings of science and industry, and these things she can obtain, not by conquest of force, but by the mere careful use of the extraordinary capacity of her people. She can produce like skill and knowledge for herself. That is one of the things these days of struggle and interrupted trade have taught her. She has nothing that she wishes to take away from the other nations of the world, and she is better prepared than she ever was before to make rich contribution to the development of other nations.

The opportunity is at hand, therefore, for which she has waited. Her principles are suited to the freedom of mankind and the peace of the world. She can now exemplify those principles in action with a new leadership, a new opportunity to exhibit them upon a great scale. She can now afford an example of energy in justice as well as in enterprise, in fair and honorable competition, in thoughtful adaptation of her resources to the needs of the world, which may help to inaugurate a new era in the intercourse and friendly interdependence of the peoples of the world.

That she will rise to this great opportunity, no man who knows her can doubt. It should be the pride and thoughtful purpose of every American so to equip himself with knowledge and so to purge his own heart that he may play a suitable part in this rebirth of American greatness.

CC MS (C. L. Swem Coll., NjP), with corrections from a reading of the CLSsh notes.

[1] Dictated aboard *Mayflower* on July 30, 1916.

From Edward Mandell House

New London,

Dear Governor: New Hampshire. July 30, 1916.

Thank you for sending me the note to Great Britain concerning the black list controversy. It is admirable. You have put it strong enough and not too strong, and I am sure, it will be well received here. There is a suspicion of a threat in it which perhaps they will heed.

I cannot but feel that if the Allied offensive on the west does not obtain better results than seems now probable that by the first of October they will be ready to discuss peace terms.

If they are not ready, I believe you should seriously consider making the proposal without their consent. There is a strong sentiment in both England and France favorable to peace and I believe a majority of the people in those two countries would demand that their governments accept your offer of mediation if they knew actual conditions.

The conservative or reactionary forces in England are getting a firm grip upon the Cabinet and Asquith is not strong enough to withstand them. They will not want the United States to be a party either to a peace conference or a settlement afterwards.

It is this force in the British Cabinet that has prevented a settlement of the Irish question. Lloyd George, acting under the advice of Asquith, made a proposal to both Nationalists and Ulsterites which was accepted, but when it was placed before the British Cabinet as a whole, the Conservatives refused to ratify it and Asquith did not have the courage to force it through.

I am afraid we will have the same difficulty in mediation. It may be necessary to arouse the latent feeling of the people in both England and France in such a way that they will compel their governments to act.   Affectionately yours,   E. M. House

TLS (WP, DLC).

From Mary Wilson Thompson[1]

North East Harbor,

My dear Mr. President,   Maine July 30, 1916.

I hear it said repeatedly that "President Wilson will come out in favor of the Federal Amendment" in his letter of acceptance.

Personally I do not believe this, as you have always maintained a firm attitude in the face of countless Suffrage audiences & I have felt that it was a matter of principle with you & of States Rights, never-the-less the Suffragists are so persevering & determined that I hear both you & Mr. Hughes may be scared into something of the kind.

A woman can be one of the most useful & ornamental creatures in her own sphere, but in Politics she is dangerous, treacherous & revengeful—therefore the sooner her political activity is curbed the better, & it is in the hands of the men, primarily the President, to curb this tendancy. The majority of the women in the United States do not want the vote, they have no taste for politics & are many of them too indifferent to even fight the Suffrage Movement. A few dissatisfied, discontented women feel that the vote will give them every thing that they lack & they start the yeast. There are some few idealists who say "the negro has a vote —why should not I have the same privilege?" The rest are merely followers of these two classes because they are friends of the leaders in the movement & want to help. As for the 4,000,000 women voters in the eleven Suffrage States, this question of voting is nothing new to them[.] They are going to vote now just like the men either to uphold your Administration or to support the Republican point of view & the "Women's Political Union" or the "Hughes Alliance" will not have the least effect on them. They are not Suffragists[,] they are Voters & cannot be controlled unless the entire population in thoses [those] States could be made Democrat or Republican.

Why should the Federal Amendment receive the slightest consideration from any sane man? The four largest Eastern States turned down Suffrage by large majorities last Fall. Iowa has just turned it down by 10,000 majority. Missouri refused to bring it before the Legislature. Delaware turned it down last winter. Why should the cause that has been defeated so constantly in the Middle West & East & only came to pass in the West through small majorities—or often indifference—be forced upon us by Federal Amendment?

There is no reason! if the men will stand fast & protect us, protect us against ourselves as a father refuses his child something he knows that child is better without. In the eyes of the world you are the Father of this great United States & you personally know that Suffrage ought not to be granted through Federal Amendment & that it never will by the States individually, that the women of this country are not fitted for the vote & that it will not come if you hold firm. Therefore I ask you to be true to your ideals of States Rights & of womanhood, & say no more for it than has already been said in the Democratic Platform. Please pardon this long letter, which has come because I have worked enough in the opposing cause to know how unfitted our women are for Public life & politics & rest assured that you will not loose [lose] any votes by opposing the Federal Amendment.

 With kind regards to Mrs. Wilson & yourself in which Harry joins I am   Sincerely yours   Mary Wilson Thompson.

ALS (WP, DLC).
 [1] Wife of Wilson's old friend, Henry Burling Thompson.

To William Bauchop Wilson, with Enclosure

My dear Mr. Secretary: The White House July 31, 1916

 I would be very much obliged if you would be kind enough to read the enclosed letter from Mr. Wheeler of Chicago and let me know what your present view of this critical matter is.

 Cordially and sincerely yours,   Woodrow Wilson

TLS (LDR, RG 174, DNA).

E N C L O S U R E

From Harry A. Wheeler[1]

Sir: Washington, D. C. July 29, 1916.

 I feel constrained to bring to your attention a matter in connection with the controversy between the Railroads and the Trainmen's Brotherhoods in the hope that you will see fit to start an inquiry on behalf of the Administration as to the near approach of an actual crisis in the matter and to verify the statement which I herewith submit.

 As Chairman of the Chamber of Commerce Committee on Railroad Situation, I met yesterday in New York with the Railway Executive Advisory Committee, Frank P. Trumbull, Chairman, and the National Conference Committee of the Railways, Elisha Lee, Chairman, to request from them a definite statement as to the position of the Roads when the Conference reconvenes to hear the result of the strike vote which was completed on July 26.

 There seems to be a prevailing opinion in Washington, and I think rather generally held throughout the country, that no interruption of freight transportation will result and that some means will be found to adjust the differences.

As a result of the meeting yesterday my conviction is deepened that an amicable settlement is remote and that while other orderly steps are yet to be taken before a final break is reached, yet such a break is inevitable unless some strong measures of intervention are speedily introduced.

On August 8 the Joint Conference will convene again, the men will announce the result of their strike vote, and the roads will reiterate their proposals which the Brotherhood chiefs have once declined.

I am assured that there will be no modification of the attitude of the Roads. Neither is it expected that the representatives of the men, with the new power of the strike vote in their hands, will recede from the position which they have heretofore taken.

The United States Board of Mediation and Conciliation may come into the matter at this point, but without effect, in my judgment, in bringing these contending factions together. Finally, arbitration may be discussed, and the break will come when the roads absolutely refuse to arbitrate *only* the demands of the men and the men refuse with equal force to admit into the arbitration the contingent proposals of the Roads.

Thus, unless there is intervention as proposed in Senate Joint Resolution 145, ratified by an almost unanimous vote of the commercial bodies affiliated with the Chamber of Commerce of the United States, or other governmental intervention on behalf of the public, nothing will be left but for the men to indefinitely defer action or exercise the authority conferred upon them by an overwhelming vote to call a strike.

In yesterday's meeting the Roads definitely expressed a determination not to recede from their present position no matter from what source an appeal is made, and while I am usually optimistic about finding a way out of difficult situations, I must confess in this situation, after talking most earnestly with both parties to the controversy, I see no ray of light nor any possibility of averting a serious catastrophe.

I beg, Mr. President, that you will regard this letter as seriously and conservatively setting forth the actual conditions as I sense them, and that you may be led to start in motion an inquiry at your earliest convenience to verify the conclusions here recited.

Very truly yours,   Harry A. Wheeler

TLS (LDR, RG 174, DNA).
    1 President of the Chamber of Commerce of the United States, 1912-1913; at this time chairman of that organization's Committee on the Railroad Situation.

From Frank Lyon Polk, with Enclosures

My dear Mr. President: Washington July 31, 1916.

I received a telegram from Mr. Brun, the Danish Minister, a copy of which I enclose for your convenience. In substance, he says his Government wishes to know if we also accepted the Declaration in regard to Greenland, and also as to when the treaty would be submitted, after signature, to the Senate.

I telegraphed him this morning, telling him that of course we would accept the Declaration as to Greenland and that the treaty would be submitted to the Senate as soon as it was signed. I urged him to do all he could to expedite the matter.

I enclose a letter from Mr. Gerard to the Secretary, which you might wish to read.   Yours faithfully,   Frank L Polk

TLS (WP, DLC).

E N C L O S U R E   I

PERSONAL AND CONFIDENTIAL.

Bar Harbor, Maine, July 29, 1916.

According to a cablegram received this morning, the Danish Government, before cabling me full powers to sign treaty, desires to receive an official statement from you to the effect that your acceptance of our proposition includes that the declaration regarding Greenland in the text agreed upon and sent you with my letter of July 18, will be given to me simultaneously with the signature of the treaty and they also desire that before signature an agreement should be reached regarding the time when the treaty should be submitted to the respective legislative bodies of the two countries. On this point I did, already ask for your intention, in my letter of July 18. These two points should already have been mentioned in my telegram to you of July 26 regarding four enclosures, but the corresponding part of the cablegram received by me had disappeared in transmission of which I could not be aware until today when the cablegram was repeated to me. I may add that the Danish Parliament is at present in session but I do not know for how long.   Brun

T telegram (WP, DLC).

E N C L O S U R E   I I

James Watson Gerard to Robert Lansing

Personal.

My dear Mr. Secretary,   Berlin. July 18th. 1916.

A committee called the National Committee for an Honorable Peace has been formed. Prince Wedel[1] is head. Most of the people are friends of the Chancellor and of the three real heads one is an editor of the "Frankfurter Zeitung" which is the Chancellor's organ. On August 1st. fifty speakers of this Committee will begin to speak, probably the opposition will come in their meetings and try to speak or break up the meetings.

The "Lokal Anzeiger"[2] also a government organ prints an editorial to the effect that Germany may take up reckless submarine war again. Great numbers of U. boats are being built and in Sept. operations will be on a big scale, though the Chancellor will try to keep them to cruiser warfare.

The prisoner question on all sides is growing acute. The Germans sent me a note today threatening stern reprisals if the alleged bad treatment of their prisoners in Russia does not stop.

We can no longer talk to prisoners alone. Von Jägow told me that after the visit of Madame Sasenoff,[3] or Samsenoff, to a Russian prisoners camp, there was almost a riot, but the real reason is that the Germans have much to conceal. The prison food now is a starvation ration.

Two Irishmen were shot recently at Limburg. How I found this out I cannot tell.

The Alliance of the Six, really organizations fostered by Big Iron Business in Westphalia, is very active for annexation.[4] They want to get the French iron mines and coal, and so control the iron business of the Continent and perhaps Europe.

The new Mexican Minister, Zuburan,[5] has been here some time and has not called on me in accordance with invariable custom.

I think if Mexican question is not settled hard, now, that later The United States will have to fight Germany, secretly through Mexico.   Yours ever   J.W.G.

TLI (SDR, RG 59, 763.72/2801½, DNA).
  [1] Count Karl von Wedel, army officer and diplomat, most recently head of the Imperial government in Alsace-Lorraine.
  [2] Of Berlin.
  [3] The *New York Times*, May 2, 1916 carried a news report, with the date line, Berlin, May 1, which stated that a "Sister Samsonava of the Russian Red Cross," in company with a "Captain von Spaeth, a Dane," had visited a prisoner-of-war camp at Havelberg, Prussia, in response to Russian complaints of conditions there. The censored report made no mention of any disturbance at the camp.

Indeed, the "Dane" praised the treatment of the prisoners after he had interviewed some of them.

⁴ Gerard here refers to the industrial, business, and agricultural organizations
which had united to present the so-called Petition of the Six Economic Organiza-
tions to the German Imperial and other entities within the German Empire on
May 20, 1915. This document, among other things, called for the annexation to
Germany of large agricultural and mining areas in both eastern and western
Europe. See Hans W. Gatzke, *Germany's Drive to the West (Drang nach Westen):
A Study of Germany's Western War Aims During the First World War* (Balti-
more, 1950), pp. 30-47.

⁵ Rafael Zubarán Capmany.

From Wilbur W. Marsh

Dear Mr. President: New York July 31, 1916.

I have the honor to acknowledge the receipt of a letter dated
July 28th from your Secretary, enclosing your check for $2500
to the Campaign Fund of the Democratic National Committee.

Your very generous contribution is gratefully accepted. It is
an inspiration to us who are working here in the interests of your
re-election to office, to know that you who must necessarily bear
the brunt of this Campaign in so many ways, are willing to assume such a large share of the incidental expenses.

With assurances of my highest esteem, I am, Mr. President,
                    Faithfully yours,   W. W. Marsh

TLS (WP, DLC).

To Edward William Bok

My dear Mr. Bok: The White House August 1, 1916

Some time ago it was kindly intimated to me that the Ladies'
Home Journal would like to publish an article from me in the
November number. At first, it seemed impossible for me to undertake anything of the kind, but I have found a little interval in
which I have written something on Mexico, which I hope you will
think worthy of publication.

With cordial regards,
                    Sincerely yours,   Woodrow Wilson

TLS (WP, DLC).

An Article on Mexico

[Aug. 1, 1916]

Large questions are difficult to state in brief compass, but they
can be intelligently comprehended only when fully stated, and

must to all candid persons seem worthy of the pains. The Mexican question has never anywhere been fully stated, so far as I know, and yet it is one which is in need of all the light that can be thrown upon it, and can be intelligently discussed only by those who clearly see all that is involved.

In the first place, it is not a question which can be treated by itself as only a matter between Mexico and the United States. It is a part, a very intimate part, of the Pan-American question. The two Americas can be knitted together only by processes of peace, friendship, helpfulness, and good will, and the nation which must of necessity take the initiative in proving the possibility of these processes is the United States.

A discussion of the Pan-American question must always begin with the Monroe Doctrine, and very little light will be thrown upon it unless we consider the Monroe Doctrine from the point of view of Latin-America rather than from the point of view of the United States. In adopting the Monroe Doctrine, the United States assumed the part of Big Brother to the rest of America. The primary purpose of the policy was to prevent the extension to the American hemisphere of European influences, which seemed likely to involve South America and eventually ourselves as well in the net of European intrigue and reaction which was in that day being spread with so wide a sweep of purpose. But it was not adopted at the request of the American republics. While it no doubt made them measurably free from the fear of European aggression or intervention in their affairs, it neither gave nor implied any guarantee on the part of the United States that we would use our power for their benefit and not for our own aggrandizement and advantage. As the power of the United States has increased, the uneasiness of the Latin-American republics has increased with regard to the use we might make of that power in dealing with them.

Unfortunately, we gave one very disquieting example of what we might do when we went to war with Mexico in Mr. Polk's time and got out of that war a great addition to our national territory. The suspicion of our southern neighbors, their uneasiness as to our growing power, their jealousy that we should assume to play Big Brother to them without their invitation to do so, has constantly stood in the way of the amicable and happy relations we wished to establish with them. Only in very recent years have they extended their hands to us with anything like cordiality, and it is not likely that we shall ever have their entire confidence until we have succeeded in giving them satisfactory and conclusive proofs of our own friendly and unselfish purpose. What is needed for the firm establishment of their faith in us is that we should give guarantees of some sort, in conduct as well as in promise, that we will as scrupulously respect their territorial integrity and their political sovereignty as we insist that European nations should respect them.

If we should intervene in Mexico, we would undoubtedly revive the gravest suspicions throughout all the states of America. By intervention I mean the use of the power of the United States to establish internal order there without the invitation of Mexico and determine the character and method of her political institutions. We have professed to believe that every nation, every people, has the right to order its own institutions as it will, and we must live up to that profession in our actions in absolute good faith.

Moreover, "order" has been purchased in Mexico at a terrible cost when it has been obtained by foreign assistance. The foreign assistance has generally come in the form of financial aid. That financial aid has almost invariably been conditioned upon "concessions" which have put the greater part of the resources of the country which have as yet been developed in the hands of foreign capitalists, and by the same token under the "protection" of foreign governments. Those who have successfully maintained stable order in Mexico by such means have, like Diaz, found that they were the servants, not of Mexico, but of foreign *concessionaires*. The economic development of Mexico has so far been accomplished by such "concessions" and by the exploitation of the fertile lands of the republic by a very small number of owners who have accumulated under one title hundreds of thousands of acres, swept within one ownership the greater part of states, and reduced the population of the country to a sort of peonage.

Mexico is one of the treasure houses of the world. It is exceedingly to be desired by those who wish to amass fortunes. Its resources are indeed serviceable to the whole world and are needed by the industries of the whole world. No enterprising capitalist can look upon her without coveting her. The foreign diplomacy with which she has become bitterly familiar is the "dollar diplomacy," which has almost invariably obliged her to give precedence to foreign interests over her own. What she needs more than anything else is financial support which will not involve the sale of her liberties and the enslavement of her people. Property owned by foreigners, enterprises conducted by foreigners will never be safe in Mexico so long as their existence and the method of their use and conduct excite the suspicion and, upon occasion, the hatred of the people of the country itself.

I would not be understood as saying that all or even the majority of the foreigners who have owned property in Mexico or who have developed her extraordinary resources have acted in a way to excite the jealousy or deserve the dislike of the people of the country. It is fortunately true that there have been a great many who acted with the same honor and public spirit there that characterized them at home, and whose wish it has never been to exploit the country to its own hurt and detriment. I am speaking of a system and not uttering an indictment. The system by which Mexico has been financially assisted has in the past generally bound her hand and foot and left her in effect without a free government. It has almost in every instance deprived her people of the part they were entitled to play in the determination of their own destiny and development.

This is what every leader in Mexico has to fear, and the history of Mexico's dealings with the United States cannot be said to be reassuring.

It goes without saying that the United States must do as she is doing: she must insist upon the safety of her borders, she must, so fast as order is worked out of chaos, use every instrumentality she can in friendship employ to protect the lives and the property of her citizens in Mexico. But she can establish permanent peace on her borders only by a resolute and consistent adoption in action of the principles which underlie her own life. She must respect the liberties and the self-government of Mexicans as she would respect her own. She has professed to be the champion of the rights of small and helpless states, and she must make that profession good in what she does. She has professed to be the friend of Mexico, and she must prove it by seeing to it that every step she takes is a step of friendship and helpfulness. Our own principles and the peace of the world are conditioned upon the exemplification of those professions in action by ourselves and by all the nations of the world, and our dealings with Mexico afford us an opportunity to show the way.

Mexico must no doubt struggle through long processes of blood and terror before she finds herself and returns to the paths of peace and order; but other nations, older in political experience than she, have staggered and struggled through these dark ways for years together to find themselves at last, to come out into the light, to know the price of liberty, to realize the compulsion of peace and the orderly processes of law. It is painful to observe how few of the suggestions as to what the United States ought to do with regard to Mexico are based upon sympathy with the Mexican people or any effort even to understand what they need and desire. I can say with knowledge that most of the suggestions of action come from those who wish to possess her, who wish to use her, who regard her people with condescension and a touch of contempt, who believe that they are fit only to serve and not fit for liberty of any sort. Such men cannot and will not determine the policy of the United States. They are not of the true American breed or motive. America will honor herself and prove the validity of her own principles by treating Mexico as she would wish Mexico to treat her.

CLST transcript with WWhw emendations (C. L. Swem Coll., NjP); printed as Woodrow Wilson, "The Mexican Question," *The Ladies' Home Journal*, XXXIII (Oct. 1916), 9.

To John Villiers Farwell

My dear Mr. Farwell: [The White House] August 1, 1916

Your letter of July twenty-ninth was very welcome. I have devoted a great deal of thought to the impending railway situation to which you refer, and am ready to do my utmost in any way that legitimately offers to prevent the impending dangers and misfortunes to the country. The situation is developing slowly, and you may be sure that I shall keep in touch with it with anxious solicitude.

Cordially and sincerely yours,   Woodrow Wilson

TLS (Letterpress Books, WP, DLC).

From George Rublee

Dear Mr. President: Windsor, Vermont August 1, 1916

When the Senate last May refused to confirm your nomination of me as Federal Trade Commissioner and then the motion to reconsider its action failed, my inclination was to resign at once, as I felt that my continuance in office might be misunderstood.

The circumstances, however, were such that it seemed to me to be my duty to go on until certain work in which my help was needed should be finished. My colleagues on the Commission also urged me strongly to keep on serving at least until my retirement would not seriously disturb the work of the Commission. So I went on.

The situation now has changed. The matters for which I was particularly wanted are either wound up, or are in such a condition that my further participation in them is not necessary. My withdrawal from the Commission would not affect its work more now than a few weeks later.

For these reasons it seems proper that I should resign, and I hereby tender to you my resignation as Federal Trade Commissioner. I hope that in accepting it you will agree with me that I am doing the right thing.

I appreciate deeply the confidence in me which you have shown both by appointing me in the first place and by continuing to support me after the appointment was opposed in the Senate.

Very respectfully yours   George Rublee

ALS (WP, DLC).

From Vance Criswell McCormick

New York August 2nd, 1916.

I would like to have your opinion upon the enclosed invitations to the Progressives whom I propose to invite to be associated with the Campaign Committee.[1] I want to make sure that this is in line with our understanding of last Monday.

Sincerely yours,   Vance C McCormick

TLS (WP, DLC).
[1] See WW to V. C. McCormick, Aug. 4, 1916.

From Dudley Field Malone

New York, August 2, 1916.

Will you see me sometime Friday so that I can tell you of New York situation. Please leave word for me with Hoover as I will come to Washington and be there Friday so you will not have to wire me. This is really important.   Dudley Field Malone.

T telegram (WP, DLC).

From John Humphrey Small

My dear Mr. President: Washington, D. C. August 2, 1916.

I am greatly gratified to read in the afternoon paper that you intend to remain firm in your past attitude regarding the proposed amendment to the Constitution for woman's suffrage.[1] Although doubting whether the best interests of women would be promoted by being clothed with right of suffrage, yet if I lived in the North, or any other state not having a large negro population, I could probably be induced to favor it as a state matter. Neither am I [a] stickler for the rights of the states in matters not fundamental. However, I am so clearly convinced that the fathers acted wisely when they declined to grant to the Federal Government the right to fix the qualifications of suffrage, that my judgment appears to be unalterable. To illustrate one evil result. It would be most unfortunate for North Carolina, because the Fifteenth Amendment would automatically apply and confer suffrage upon negro women. The same illustration would apply more acutely to South Carolina and Mississippi. Thirty-six states ought not to have the right to impose this result on Mississippi. I believe the thoughtful people of the country, regardless of their party allegiance, now regard the adoption of the Fifteenth Amendment as an error, particularly at the period of its adoption.

If the Federal Government may negatively restrain a state from regulating suffrage, it might with equal or greater propriety be granted the power by positive enactment to forbid the manufacture or sale of intoxicating liquors. I am opposed to this last amendment, and I have been gratified at your position thereon.

Unless my study of the fundamentals upon which this great Democracy is based are incorrect, its perpetuity depends upon preserving to the states the right of local self government and the full exercise of its police powers regarding all strictly local matters.

If one is to consider political expediency in considering a fundamental question of government, our Party will not lose any strength in this election by the maintenance of your position, that the states should retain the right to regulate suffrage. Mr. Hughes appears to give two reasons for his recent conversion. He says he has come to favor woman's suffrage by Constitutional amendment in order to stop the agitation, and further because the country ought to have an uniform policy on the question. I respectfully submit that his reasons are weak.

I tried to make an appointment to-day to see you, in order to make to you a similar expression, but learned that you were not making further engagements this week. This was before I read the afternoon paper.

I believe we are going to win, and in my humble way I wish to take a part in achieving the victory.

I beg pardon for this intrusion on your time.

Very sincerely, Jno. H. Small

TLS (WP, DLC).

[1] Carrie Chapman Catt, following an interview with Wilson on August 1, said that she believed that the President would be "brought over to indorsing" a woman suffrage amendment to the Constitution. The White House announced on August 2 that Wilson had not changed his mind on the question. Wilson, it was reported, "stood on the plank of the Democratic platform favoring disposal of the suffrage question by the individual states." *New York Times*, Aug. 3, 1916.

From Jane Addams

Hull's Cove Maine

My dear Mr. President   August second [1916].

May I ask you to make an appointment to see Professor Emily Balch one of the two American delegates to the Neutral Conference now sitting at Stockholm?

The Conference would be very glad to have the President of the United States understand more fully their present situation and their relation to representatives of belligerent as well as of neutral governments. Miss Balch would need very few minutes, realizing, as we all do, how especially crowded you are in these troublous times.

May I venture to express my admiration for the successful outcome of your Mexican policies and beg to remain

faithfully yours,   Jane Addams

HwLS (Jane Addams Papers, PSC-P).

From Josephus Daniels

My Dear Mr. President: Washington. Aug. 2, 1916.

This morning by accident I met Representative Keating, of Colorado, a long time advocate of woman suffrage. In talking about the latest utterance of Hughes on that subject he expressed the opinion that it would be wise for you to make no statement, further than you have made, at this time. He said even if you felt called upon to express your view later as to the constitutional method, it would have the appearance of being stampeded for you to make any declaration now. Mr. Keating feels that Mr. Hughes may have strengthened himself in Colorado, and his own earnest advocacy of the measure would incline him to wish you to take the same position. It is because of this fact I thought you would be interested in knowing his opinion. I confess it had weight with me.

He said the Congressional Union fought Senator Thomas and all the Democratic candidates for Congress last year, but controlled few votes.   Sincerely,   Josephus Daniels

Keating says it would be unfortunate for anything to be done to seem to put woman suffrage in the place of a leading issue, particularly at this time.   JD

ALS (WP, DLC).

From Thomas Riley Marshall

My dear Mr. President,   Washington. 2nd Aug. 1916.

Pardon this suggestion. Cut your speech of acceptance to 2500 words. I want the people to read and understand it. They can not or will not if it is as long as Justice Hughes' dissenting opinion.

Another suggestion. Dont worry about woman suffrage. If all the women who dont want the ballot in the equal suffrage States will vote for you, you can carry them. I know. I've campaigned there twice.   Regardfully   Thos. R. Marshall

ALS (WP, DLC).

Joseph Patrick Tumulty to Frank Lyon Polk,
with Enclosure

Dear Mr. Secretary: The White House August 2, 1916

The President directs me to send you the enclosed resolution adopted by the Senate on July 29th, and to express his desire that the request of the Senate for its transmission to the British Government be complied with promptly.

                    Sincerely yours,   J. P. Tumulty

TLS (SDR, RG 59, 841.00/20, DNA).

E N C L O S U R E

In the Senate of the United States,

                              July 29, 1916.

RESOLVED, That the Senate expresses the hope that the British Government may exercise clemency in the treatment of Irish political prisoners; and that the President be requested to transmit this resolution to that Government.[1]

Attest: James M. Baker.   Secretary.

TS MS (SDR, RG 59, 841.00/20, DNA).
 [1] Casement's execution had been set for August 3.

Frank Lyon Polk to Joseph Patrick Tumulty

My dear Mr. Tumulty   Washington August 2, 1916.

I have received your letter of today enclosing a resolution adopted by the Senate on July 29th, and have noted the Presi-

dent's desire that the request of the Senate for its transmission
to the British Government be complied with promptly.

The resolution is being sent by cable to the Embassy at London
with instructions to transmit it textually to the British Foreign
Office.[1]   Sincerely yours,   Frank L Polk

TLS (WP, DLC).

[1] Actually, as Polk and others in the State Department knew, Spring Rice
had sent this resolution to the Foreign Office on July 29, and the British government had decided to proceed with Casement's execution on August 3, notwithstanding the Senate's plea. See JPT to M. F. Doyle, Oct. 14, 1916.

To Dudley Field Malone

The White House, August 3, 1916.

Unfortunately it is literally impossible for me to discuss that
matter tomorrow. It is imperative that all such matters should be
handled through and by McCormick. You will understand.

Woodrow Wilson.

T telegram (WP, DLC).

To Thomas Riley Marshall

[The White House]
My dear Mr. Vice President: August 3, 1916

I sincerely value your letter of August second.

Your first suggestion is one I intend to act upon. I do not know
whether I can get down my speech of acceptance to quite as strait
limits as you suggest, but I am going to make it just as short and
pointed as possible. Your point about that is absolutely well taken.

And I don't mean to worry about the woman suffrage question.
I have too much confidence in the good sense and public spirit of
the women of the country to believe that they will act as unjustly
as some of their number are predicting.

Cordially and faithfully yours,   Woodrow Wilson

TLS (Letterpress Books, WP, DLC).

To George Rublee

My dear Mr. Rublee: [The White House] August 3, 1916

It is with the most genuine regret that I receive your letter of
August first, tendering your resignation as Federal Trade Commissioner, and I am going to ask if you will not be generous enough to withhold the resignation for the present, at any

rate, and continue to serve on the Commission as long is it is possible. I know how highly the Commissioners value your counsel and cooperation, and I share, as I hope you know, their high estimate of your work and service. I hope that you will not insist upon the immediate acceptance of your resignation, which I am very loath indeed to accept.

          Cordially and sincerely yours,   Woodrow Wilson

TLS (Letterpress Books, WP, DLC).

To Mary Wilson Thompson

My dear Mrs. Thompson: [The White House] August 3, 1916

Thank you sincerely for your earnest and interesting letter which I have read with the greatest interest. I want to thank you particularly for your confidence that I would not put myself in the position of merely bidding for votes by changing well formed convictions with regard to the suffrage question.

Pardon these few lines. They are not an adequate answer to your letter, but they carry the warmest friendship and appreciation both for yourself and for your husband.

          Cordially and sincerely yours,   Woodrow Wilson

TLS (Letterpress Books, WP, DLC).

To Josephus Daniels

My dear Daniels: The White House August 3, 1916

Thank you warmly for your note about your conversation with Keating. His opinion seems to me very level-headed indeed.

     In haste   Faithfully yours,   Woodrow Wilson

TLS (J. Daniels Papers, DLC).

Two Letters from Edward Mandell House

                                        New London,
Dear Governor: New Hampshire. August 3, 1916.

What would you think of answering Hughes' speeches as he goes along so that the misinformation he conveys may not become fixed in the minds of anybody.

You could call in the reporters, as you formerly did, and tell them that your duties prevent you from speaking, but at this critical juncture in the affairs of the United States and the world, you do not feel that it is right to let misinformation and unjust charges against America go unchallenged. Remind the country that what Mr. Hughes seems to have forgotten is that a criticism of your foreign policy is tantamount to a criticism of America and the weakening of her influence abroad. That to all intents and purposes we stand today in almost as delicate a position as we would were this country engaged in war.

Could you not say that Mr. Justice Hughes' seclusion on the Supreme Court has left him with but little information as to current events, otherwise, you were sure, he would not willingly make some of the statements that he has made in his speech of acceptance.

He criticizes you for upsetting our diplomatic corps in general and that of South America in particular.[1] The facts are that you retained all the ambassadors in South America excepting in Argentine where the incumbent did not desire reappointment.

Why not tell the country the truth about Herrick? He was retained for more than a year beyond his term although he wished to be relieved. Mr. Hughes evidently does not know that Mr. Sharp was appointed, confirmed and in Paris before the war began. You have letters I think from Herrick thanking you for your extreme courtesy to him.

Mr. Hughes seems not to know that the Rural Credits Bill has become a law. Someone should inform him. Would it be out of place for you to do so?

He defends Huerta. Could you not say that he was well within his rights in doing so. (Is he correct in his statement that England, France, Germany, Russia, Spain and Japan had recognized Huerta?)

He criticizes the disposition of the troops sent to Mexico. Could you not say that you were guided in this by our army officers in command and ask him would he, under similar circumstances, disregard the advice of the general staff and use his own military judgment?

He also criticizes ordering the militia to the Mexican border. Here, again, you acted under the advice of the general staff. Would he have acted upon his own initiative?

In speaking of Mexico he says, "To a stable government appropriately discharging its international duties we should give ungrudging support." Is there any citizen of the United States that would not? An anxious American public would like to know how he would suggest getting such a government.

In regard to the protection of American property on the high seas he says you have been "too content with leisurely discussion

* * * * It is entirely clear that we failed to use the resources at our command to prevent injurious action and that we suffered in consequence."

What would he do were he President? Would he have declared war or would he have negotiated as Washington, Jefferson, Lincoln and Harrison did under similar circumstances?

The platform of the progressive party four years ago contained many suggestions of value which the democratic party did not hesitate to use for the benefit of the country. Careful scrutiny of the republican platform adopted at Chicago in June fails to disclose anything of value other than the things the democrats are already writing into law.

He should be complimented I think because of his endorsement of your proposal for permanent peace made at Washington May 27th. He should be congratulated upon accepting your idea of the mobilization of our industrial resources; upon your idea of putting our transportation system upon a firmer basis. And last, but above all, upon your idea of making America first.

Did Mr. Hughes in any way indicate what his feelings were upon this subject, or did any of the republican leaders make known their feelings upon this subject prior to your speech before the D.A.R. in October?

Mr. Hughes' position upon the Supreme Court would not have deterred him from making this statement if he had felt it, because early in June he echoed in a feeble way what you had already said so many times before. Was it a coincident or was it by design that he made this declaration while the republican convention was in session and before he had been nominated.

What laws enacted under your administration is Mr. Hughes in favor of repealing or amending? Would it be the Federal Reserve Act or the Rural Credits Act? Would he be opposed to the forming of the Trades Commission or the Panama Tolls Bill or the amending of the Clayton Bill making labor no longer a commodity?

Will he not indicate what constructive legislation he will advocate should he become President? These are fateful hours and one who aspires to the Presidentcy of this great republic should offer something better than hindsight criticism.

If anyone else should say these things the papers would not carry them. You can get the entire American people for an audience and no one else can. The democratic papers will attack Hughes with intelligence and vigor, but these attacks will be read almost wholly by democrats, while what you say will be read by republicans and progressives as well.

Anyway I wanted to give you my opinion of the weak points in the speech to use or not as you think best.

Affectionately yours,   E. M. House

1 Here House begins to comment upon Hughes' acceptance speech, delivered in Carnegie Hall in New York on July 31.

New London,
Dear Governor: New Hampshire. August 3, 1916.

In your speech of acceptance I have been wondering whether or not it would not be well to speak almost wholly on foreign affairs.

There is much more involved in this election than domestic issues and much more involved in the world situation than our people realize. Democracy hangs in the balance and the result of our election may determine its fate not only here but throughout the world.

We find the reactionary forces dominant in Germany and trying for dominion in the other belligerent countries. We find, too, that the same principles are involved in the Mexican upheaval.

You could make a speech along these lines that would rally the liberals of the world and cause them to look to you as their champion.   Affectionately yours,   E. M. House

TLS (WP, DLC).

From Frank Lyon Polk

My dear Mr. President: Washington August 3, 1916.

I think you will be interested to know that the Danish Minister telegraphed me late yesterday that he had powers to sign the Treaty and I at once made arrangements for him to meet Mr. Lansing Friday morning in New York. I have just heard that that time is satisfactory to both of them. I will send all the necessary papers over by special messenger today, to meet Mr. Lansing.

I suggested to Mr. Lansing that he and the Minister settle the details as to when the Treaty should be submitted to the Senate and their Legislative Assembly. Unless you have other views. I will also suggest to Mr. Lansing that the signing be announced, as it will be very difficult to keep a matter of this kind quiet and it is better to announce it than to have it leak out.

Yours faithfully,   Frank L Polk

TLS (WP, DLC).

From Norman Hapgood

Dear Mr. President: New York, N. Y. August 3rd 1916.

I have a report to make which I make with regret, but I would rather state the incident to you myself than to have you read it first in the newspapers.

Raymond Robins is coming out for Hughes, probably on Saturday. The background of his thought you already know. His feelings in regard to the rank and file of the two parties have proved to be unshakable, and we were unhappily unable to affect the position of Dunne in Illinois;[1] so that Robins felt that he could not work in the Democratic party there without lying in the same bed with Roger Sullivan. I am extremely disappointed, but his mind has been subjected to the best possible presentations of our side, namely; those of yourself, Secretary Baker and Brandeis, as well as of labor leaders in whom he takes a particular interest. He says that you are sure to win the election as, although he thinks you will lose Illinois, you will carry New York, Indiana, Ohio and Wisconsin. He also says that he is thoroughly for you and your measures and that it is on a twenty or forty year view that he is deciding. I hope we shall have at least the small comfort of his keeping this distinction clear.

While I wanted to get this development to you in a clear shape, instead of through the newspapers, I cannot close without making the irrelevant remark that everything looks favorable, to me and to my friends. The net result of Hughes' speech is that it is the statement of an able lawyer retained for the opposition, but that it has no positive contribution and will do nothing to stir the country.   Very sincerely yours,   Norman Hapgood

TLS (WP, DLC).

[1] It was reported in various newspapers at this time that Vance C. McCormick had recently attempted to secure an arrangement whereby Raymond Robins would run for Governor of Illinois as a Progressive-Democratic fusion candidate in place of the Democratic incumbent, Edward Fitzsimons Dunne. Reportedly, Chicago Boss Roger Sullivan refused to sanction the maneuver. Dunne won renomination in the primary election in September but lost to Republican Frank Orren Lowden in the general election in November. *New York Times*, July 16, 1916, and *New York Tribune*, Aug. 7, 1916.

From Ellen Duane Davis

R. D. Newtown,

My dear Friend,   Bucks Co. Pennsylvania. 3, Aug. 1916

Perhaps you will think this letter to you is unnecessary and uncalled for, but please remember it is written, not only in the interest of what seems to me to be one of the great issues in the coming election, but because I believe the interests and needs of the whole country are involved in your being re-elected and you surely know that without good cause I would not add one feather-weight to your burden.

As a born Suffragist, having had a Mother a converted one, having been a working woman myself since I was 15 years old and fully realizing the bitter hardships women have to endure as workers without a vote—I ask you in behalf of all the women of the States where they do not vote to urge Congress at *this* session to pass the Susan B. Anthony Ammendment. If you do this great and noble deed the women of the whole country will bless you. If you do not then the votes of men and women in the 12 voting states will be solidly for Mr Hughes and the influence of the women in the rest of the States will be for him. It requires a lot of courage to change one's mind and admit it, but do this thing and I verily believe you will never regret it. E.P. feels as strongly as I do on this subject, but I told him I meant to write to you. I wish I might *speak* to you, for things written seem so very bald and different. The Child labor bill is splendid, everything you do is worth while. Now knock the supports from under all the parties, take the wind out of their sails, and prevent what is going to be the chief issue in the campaign. Through the States Suffrage will never come as all the "Interests" which are evil are against it and they have no end of money. It was proved in Penna., New Jersey, Michigan & now in Iowa that although the majority of the good people wanted it and the Suffrage Associations did all in their power to further it "the evil which men do lives after them," but the good for the women was interred in the downfall of their hopes. God bless and help you and the working women of this blessed country of ours is the earnest prayer of your

Sincere friend   Ellen Duane Davis

ALS (WP, DLC).

To Vance Criswell McCormick

My dear McCormick: [The White House] August 4, 1916

I am telegraphing you today my approval of the enclosed, which I now return. It seems to me excellent. It ought to meet with a cordial response.

I have just been reading the morning papers and am wondering what the effect of the action taken at Indianapolis[1] will be upon our plans in this matter of associating some of the Progressives with us. It certainly does not bar us, but does it bar them, do you think? I notice that Mr. Hale has accepted the chairman-ship of the committee appointed there, and that Mr. Colby is a member of the committee. I hope sincerely that this will not be deemed by them as barring their acceptance of our invitation.[2]

Cordially and faithfully yours,   Woodrow Wilson

TLS (Letterpress Books, WP, DLC).

[1] A dissident group of leaders of the Progressive party met in Indianapolis on August 3. They repudiated the vote of the Progressive National Committee at Chicago on June 26, which had committed the party to Hughes. The dissidents decided that it was too late to reassemble the party in convention to nominate a new presidential candidate and that they would, instead, put up a ticket bearing the name of John M. Parker of New Orleans, the vice-presidential candidate, in every state where a nucleus of a Progressive organization re-mained. They hoped to win enough electors to be the balance of power in the event of a close contest between Wilson and Hughes. Matthew Hale was chosen to head this campaign. He, in turn, appointed an executive committee of fifteen (including Bainbridge Colby) to assist him and also to meet after the election to formulate plans for the perpetuation of the party. *New York Times*, Aug. 4, 1916.

[2] McCormick, on August 10, announced the formation of an "Associated Cam-paign Committee of Progressives." The members were Bainbridge Colby, Mat-thew Hale, Albert D. Nortoni, Francis J. Heney, Ole Hanson, John Appleton Haven Hopkins (about whom, see N. Hapgood to WW, Aug. 14, 1916), and Henry Milton Wallace, lawyer and Progressive leader of Ann Arbor, Mich.

To John Humphrey Small

My dear Mr. Small: [The White House] August 4, 1916

Thank you sincerely for your letter of August twenty-first, which I have read with real gratification.

Cordially and sincerely yours,   Woodrow Wilson

TLS (Letterpress Books, WP, DLC).

From Newton Diehl Baker, with Enclosure

My dear Mr. President: Washington. August 4, 1916.

I inclose a letter from Walter Lippmann which gives the im-pression of a keen and honest observer of the Hughes notification meeting, and also a suggestion which may interest you. To me the significant thing about the Hughes speech is that it has no single comment of idealism or loftiness of thought in it. Everybody who heard it, and apparently most people who have read it, have felt its dead levelism.   Cordially yours,   Newton D. Baker

TLS (WP, DLC).

E N C L O S U R E

Walter Lippmann to Newton Diehl Baker

My dear Mr. Baker: [New York] August 2nd, 1916.

Thank you so much for sending me the material on mobilization.

I attended the Hughes notification meeting on Monday night, and I must say it was a dismal affair. I had never realized before how commonplace his mind is. There is something honest and likeable about him, but he is certainly bourgeois, as the Socialists would say.

I wish the President in his acceptance speech might see his way clear to laying considerable emphasis on the very serious problem of the economic war after the war outlined in the Paris conference. It seems to me that this is the biggest item in the statesmanship of the future, and Hughes ignored it. Of course it is a very delicate matter for him to touch on, but he is virtually running as a candidate for the Reconstruction Period and he has, it seems to me, a wonderful chance for leadership if he will show that he is vividly aware, first, of the international problem raised by these economic alliances, and secondly, of the fact that tariffs alone, unless coupled with something like the Australian system of wage distribution, will be quite helpless in meeting the situation after the war.

If I can clarify my own ideas on the subject in the next few days I should like to write you again about this matter.

Very sincerely yours,   [Walter Lippmann]

CCL (W. Lippmann Papers, CtY).

From William Lea Chambers

Dear Mr President,   Washington Aug 4th, 1916

The Newspaper men swarmed upon me as I left the conference with you:[1] among them the Associated Press representative. I said nothing to them, but they are insistent.

Shall I give them the substance of our interview, or will you not think it best that a statement be given out at White House office?

A telephone advice to me will of course be sufficient. I think a statement will have a quieting effect upon the excited situation

Most respectfully   W. L. Chambers

ALS (WP, DLC).
[1] Chambers conferred with Wilson at the White House at 9 A.M. on August 4. Wilson had called him in to ask him to explain the railroad strike situa-

tion in detail. They also discussed the possibility of having the Board of Mediation and Conciliation offer its services. *New York Times*, Aug. 5 and 8, 1916.

From Edward Olin Downes[1]

Dear Mr. President: Boston, Mass. Aug. 4, 1916.

I am writing this letter to you in the hope that at some good moment it may come under your personal notice. It is a letter of congratulation, in advance of the coming election. It is meant as one, no doubt, of many similar expressions which will come to you from the hearts of the people of the United States, whether the results of the 4th of November will be personally favorable or unfavorable to you.

I want very much that you should know how many people of the United States recognize and feel the deepest gratitude for the services you have done them and the world—for the essential thing accomplished. Your triumph has already taken place, and niether politicians or parties can take it from you. The great forces of which you have been the willing and intelligent instrument will reach their fulfilment as surely as the sun shines, because of what appears to me as the beginning and end of your accomplishment: the awakening of so many Americans to a sense of their duties and their destinies which they never had before.

How you have kept your faith, in the face of all that has assailed you since 1912 is beyond my ken. What has moved me most deeply has been your unfaltering trust in the right and the unbated courage and enthusiasm with which you have consistently and continually held up to the people the broadest and the highest ideals of this citizenry, and unfolded for them horizons always greater and nobler, for the coming generations.

Though I am now in my 30th year, I have voted only once—in 1912—for you. I had not used my vote before, for I had too little faith in either the men or the parties who were candidates for votes. In the candidates I felt a lack of sincerity, or efficiency, or vision, or all three. In the parties themselves I thought I saw things of incomparably greater menace to the future of the nation. American politics as a whole impressed me as the apotheosis of all that was blundering, blind, greedy and weak. America seemed a country of the grossest ignorance and provincialism, wonderfully illustrated, from time to time, in that extraordinary body of law-makers, the American Congress, and a political system of pull and preference simply beneath contempt. I grant that this betrays a person of weak faith, and puny will for the bettering of things. But so it was, and American jingoism and co [so]-

called politics seemed a mountain of a density and weight that no sensible man would waste his time in trying to lluminate or lighten.

Thanks to you, I have changed, and your presence and your power have made life and the day's work and even personal conduct finer and more hopeful issues than they have ever been before for me. I have you to thank for new convictions and all that they mean, even to the most sluggish and indifferent. If you said that it was best for every man in America to fight, I would fight, because I would believe you. I would believe in your intelligence as in your sincerity and your humanity, and in exchange for such beliefs a life would be a very cheap and insufficient payment. Next November I shall vote again, and for ampler if not better reasons than in 1912—for you. I pray that you may continue as the head of this nation for another four years. I believe that you will, for I do not think that even the unscrupulousness and the shameless attempts at misinformation which characterize our, and perhaps all political campaigns, can blind the people as a whole to what you are and what you do. But whether you are elected or not, the fundamental thing is done, and thanks to your vision and your will, the hour of gravest danger is past. Not all the self-interested politicians in the country will be able in the future to dominate the people or to hold back America from self-realization as a representative country and a representative people of the new world to come after the war. America has evolved a man we can trust in the hour of great need. He, as well as well [sic] as his fellow-citizens, can well await with confidence the hour of reward, and know that the foundations of truth and the republic have not been shaken and that truth and light will prevail.

That is why I want to send you the message that I know thousands are sending you today. We adore you, because you embody all that is best in ourselves. We believe in ourselves again, in you, and the new age.   Very gratefully   Olin Downes

TLS (WP, DLC).
  1 Music critic of the *Boston Post*, 1906-1923; and of the *New York Times*, 1924-1955; father of the music critic and historian, Edward Olin Davenport Downes.

To Jane Addams

My dear Miss Addams: The White House August 5, 1916
    Of course, I will see Miss Balch very gladly. I did not know that she was in this country.

As I write, I am off for a very much needed absence from Washington for the week-end, but just so soon as I return to Washington, on Monday morning, I will search my calendar for the earliest possible hour at which I may see Miss Balch and will let her know at the address you give.

I warmly appreciate your approval of my Mexican policy, though the plot thickens as we go.

Cordially and sincerely yours,   Woodrow Wilson

TLS (Jane Addams Coll., PSC-P).

To Norman Hapgood

My dear Hapgood: U.S.S. MAYFLOWER, August 5, 1916

Raymond Robins' action is indeed disappointing and seems to me to be based upon really unintelligible grounds in view of all the present circumstances of our politics, but it is one of those disappointments which one must bear as philosophically as possible and with as earnest an attempt as possible to understand his point of view.

I am heartily glad you think the prospects are so good. I think that your analysis of the effect of Mr. Hughes' speech is undoubtedly the correct one. I am warmly obliged to you for keeping me informed directly of the things that concern us so vitally.

In haste

Cordially and faithfully yours,   Woodrow Wilson

TLS (Letterpress Books, WP, DLC).

To Cordell Hull

My dear Mr. Hull: U.S.S. MAYFLOWER, August 5, 1916

Your forecast of what the Republicans are likely to harp on most agrees entirely with my own,[1] and I think that it is along those lines that we must tackle them. But, after all, those are the lines upon which they are most antiquated and out of touch with the world that lies about us and before us. I think we can put them in a place very satisfactory to ourselves about issues of that kind.

But, at the same time, they are complicated issues and will need to be handled with knowledge as well as skill.

I am heartily glad to know you think my position about the

woman suffrage question is wise and sound. It is clear, at any rate, that I cannot alter it for the sake of expediency.

Cordially and sincerely yours,   Woodrow Wilson

TLS (Letterpress Books, WP, DLC).
  1 Hull's letter is missing in WP, DLC, and in the Hull Papers, DLC.

To Ellen Duane Davis

My dear Friend: U.S.S. MAYFLOWER, August 5, 1916

It was not necessary for you to appeal to me on the merits in the matter of woman suffrage, but I beg you to take these things into consideration:

In the first place, my whole power and success as a leader of the party has been due to the fact that I have not had any "Wilson policies," but have insisted only upon those things to which I could get the party to subscribe in its platform. I got the most that it was feasible to get on the suffrage question from the St. Louis Convention, and must for the time rest content with that or else lose the really extraordinary confidence which the working forces of the party have reposed in me.

In the second place, if I should change my personal attitude now, I should seem to the country like nothing less than an angler for votes, because, as you know, my attitude in this matter has again and again been very frankly avowed, and I should hate to follow the example of Mr. Hughes, who has made a special pleader of himself in the misinterpretation of his party platform and is winning a great deal of ridicule and distrust as a consequence. I would a great deal rather have the respect of the women than their votes, and I am sure they would not respect me if I departed from my usual course and made such an extraordinarily humble bow to expediency.

I know that you will feel the force of these considerations and that you will not for a moment doubt the sincerity of my belief in the principle of woman suffrage.

I have all along believed, and still believe, that the thing can best and most solidly be done by the action of the individual states, and that the time it will take to get it that way will not be longer than the time it would take to get it the other way.

With warmest regards from us all,

Faithfully your friend,   Woodrow Wilson

TLS (Letterpress Books, WP, DLC).

From William Bauchop Wilson

My Dear Mr President: Allport Pa., Aug 5th, 1916.

Your letter of July 31st, inclosing letter of Mr Wheeler of Chicago relative to the railroad labor disputes, and asking my present view of the matter, has been forwarded to me.

I still believe there is a great deal of hysteria about the situation growing out of the fact that a strike vote has to be taken before the railroad companies or the Mediation Board will recognize that a labor dispute exists. It is a bad practice but it is the existing one and has to be taken into consideration in dealing with the subject. A strike vote taken under such circumstances does not reflect the attitude of the workmen towards a strike but represents their desire to press their claims to the front where the Mediation Board can be called in. Neither does the stand taken by either side at the beginning of negotiations always represent what they will be willing to accept at the end of them.

It is to be expected, then, that the vote will be almost unanimous to authorize their officials to call a strike if negotiations fail. Of course the situation is serious and ought to be carefully watched. While it is not my purpose to interfere with the work of the Mediation Board, I feel that the department should have a representative on the ground to keep us advised of developments.

In my judgement it would not be wise to provide any special machinery for the adjustment of this dispute. The passage of the Newlands resolution (SJR 145)[1] would be a serious mistake. It would upset the negotiations now pending between the men and the companies and "put everybody up in the air." No settlement could be reached until the Inter-State Commerce Commission had made its investigation and report. Our experience in the Department of Labor indicates that investigations, for purposes of publicity, and the work of mediation do not operate well together. Mediation should come first. We are in that stage now.

Within three years we have created a new Mediation Board. It has done splendid work. It has brought about adjustments where the interests involved were just as vital to the public welfare, and the determination not to yield anything just as firmly expressed by both sides, as in the present instance. There has been no indication that it is not capable of handling the situation. On the contrary, it has shown itself exceptionally competent.

Should it become necessary later on to make an investigation and give publicity to the facts, that can be done with machinery and authority already in existence in the Department of Labor or the Department of Commerce, in a much more satisfactory manner than through the Inter-State Commerce Commission, whose primary function is a restraining influence on transportation rates, from which railroad labor must ultimately recieve its compensation. My judgment, therefor[e], is that no resolutions of investigation should be passed at this time; that the course provided by existing law should be persued, and the Mediation Board be permitted to handle the situation without interference at least until it has been demonstrated that other methods should be provided.   Faithfully yours   W B Wilson

ALS (WP, DLC).

[1] Senate Joint Resolution 145 had been introduced by Senator Newlands on June 22. It directed the Interstate Commerce Commission immediately to investigate and report to Congress on "the minimum, maximum, and average wage paid, with hours of service, to each class of railroad employees in the United States, and, so far as they are comparable, the minimum, maximum, and average wage, with hours of service, paid in other industries where similar skill and risk are involved, the relation of wages to railroad revenues, the question of whether railroad revenues based on existing rates for transportation will admit of equally favorable terms to all classes of railroad employees, and any other matter in this connection that the commission may deem relevant." The resolution was referred to the Committee on Interstate Commerce, from which it never emerged. *Cong. Record*, 64th Cong., 1st sess., pp. 9746-47.

From Irving Fisher[1]

New Haven, Conn.

My dear President Wilson: August 5, 1916

As I mentioned in the interview with you a few weeks ago on peace with Mexico, I have wanted to talk with you concerning the campaign. I am putting it briefly by letter as I fear it will be impossible to see you before your speech of acceptance is completed.

As you may remember, I am not a Democrat but an Independent and supported you four years ago for the progressive program I expected you to carry out and in which I have not been disappointed—except for the postponement of the public health part.

I am expecting to support you this fall for the progressive policies I hope to see carried out in your second term. I think I am typical of many hundreds of thousands, perhaps millions, of voters most of whom followed Roosevelt four years ago but whose vote is available to you if they become convinced that their desires will better be fulfilled through you than through Mr. Hughes.

I think I know fairly well the average Progressive, as their leaders, especially Mr. Pinchot are friends of mine. I attended all three conventions and appeared before the platform committees.

So far as the two main platforms are concerned the Democratic is far and away more attractive to the average Progressive.

I have no doubt that your speech of acceptance will also be more "Progressive" than Mr. Hughes', that you will, without difficulty dispose of the accusation of non "Americanism" and emphasize that the peace which you have sought has been both "honorable" and effective—a fact and not merely a theory. I assume that you will also emphasize with warmth the whole humanitarian program past and prospective—peace, workmen's compensation, child labor, woman's suffrage, the conservation of natural resources and the conservation of human resources, or public health, as opposed to the "cold" atmosphere of your opponent.

I am writing expecially to urge two points in particular, one that you call attention to the public health plank in your platform and the absence of any in the Republican platform, saying that while our kinsmen are wasting human life abroad we should the more save it here, referring to the good work done by the United States Public Health Service recently and expressing the hope that the states and the federal government also should adopt the principle of health insurance (which was the soul of the statesmanship of Lloyd George); and the other, that instead of lagging behind Mr. Hughes on woman's suffrage you go him one better. If not I am sure you will lose the support of many Progressives, for we regard woman's suffrage as an important means of bringing about humanitarian legislation. As you know Mr. Hughes has gone beyond his platform by stating his personal approval of submitting the Susan B. Anthony amendment to the states. I earnestly hope that you will do the same but give a better reason. Mr. Hughes apparently regards woman's suffrage as a necessary evil. He would marry the suffragette to get rid of her!

By a cordial support of the proposition to submit to the states a federal amendment, I do not think you can lose much strength, while I feel sure you will gain materially. I do not think you will lose much because to the "Antis" the suffrage question is almost always a minor issue, while to the proponent it is a major issue, and, moreover, the opponent of suffrage cannot strongly object to the proposition of submission. Submission merely means letting the people have a chance to pass upon it and this includes the chance to reject, quite as truly as the chance to accept the proposed amendment.

I have been asked by Mr. Vance McCormick to publicly "come out" for you. Before doing so irrevocably, however, I would like to have all the facts. I shall probably wait until your speech of acceptance. But if you are ready to take the view of the suffrage proposition, which I hope you will, and could let me know to that effect, I should be greatly obliged and would consider your statement confidential unless you preferred to have it published now in advance of your speech of acceptance, which would be the best way to match Mr. Hughes' special announcement,—the better in a letter to someone in public life.

If, on the other hand, you are not yet willing to go so far on suffrage, I earnestly hope you will not commit yourself *against* submission but will give the matter careful consideration, with reference to possibly taking an advanced stand in your speech of acceptance.

I dislike, more than I can say, to take your valuable time either for interviews or letters and it is only because I feel so strongly what I write that I yield to the impulse to set it down.

One of the most far seeing public men I know recently said to me that there are only two great issues looming ahead, woman's suffrage and prohibition.

I should greatly regret to see you drift into the position of seeming antagonism to woman's suffrage. My suggestion would eliminate it as an issue and enable you to expose the real issue which the Republicans are trying to keep in the background and disguised,—whether the old special interests, fed on a protective tariff, are to repeat that national scandal or not.

With kindest regards and congratulations on the handling of the recent Mexican situation, I am,

Very sincerely yours,   Irving Fisher

TLS (WP, DLC).

[1] Professor of Political Economy at Yale University and a well-known crusader for many social causes.

From Dudley Field Malone

Dear Mr. President,   Washington August 5th 1916.

I asked for the appointment with you because Harris and the leaders in N. Y. asked me to see you. I hope there was nothing in my telegram that offended you. I do not now know what I said in it for I was blinded with the pain of my neuritis when I sent it. Vance McCormack is my friend. I would have told you nothing that I had not first talked over with him as he can tell you. But your wish will be faithfully observed by me. I have really always tried not to intrude on your hours of strain and great worry except in real situations for I have loved you too much to add to your burdens; but I shall not hereafter discuss N. Y. politics with you unless of course you should ask for my view and judgment. No matter what any man may tell you, I have worked and worried day and night these past two years in N. Y. politics with the *single* motive of harmonizing conditions there in order that New York might lead the column of states for your reelection *as she will*.

I do hope you are well and standing the heat of Washington.

Whether I see you often or not at all can never affect the deep affection and devotion of

Yours most faithfully   Dudley Field Malone

P.S. Please give my warmest remembrance to Mrs. Wilson, Margaret and Miss Bones.   D.F.M.

ALS (WP, DLC).

From Frederic Clemson Howe

My dear Mr. President: Ellis Island, N. Y. August 5, 1916.

I have been reading the newspaper accounts of the negotiations looking to a loan to China by American bankers, and note that the proposal has probably fallen through. Would it not be permissible for the United States to make this loan direct? There are lots of precedents for this in European countries, both England and Russia having advanced money directly to Persia at the time of her reorganization. At least, I think this is a fact. We won so much affection in China as a result of our action in connection with the Chinese loan that direct intervention by the Government itself would, it seems to me, be a very splendid international act, and at the same time might save China from the kind of financial grip which the powers expected, or at least thought possible as a result of the five power loan. Chinese integrity is above question, and the amount of the loan is relatively small.

Very sincerely yours,   Frederic C. Howe

TLS (WP, DLC).

From Edward William Bok

My dear Mr. President: Camden, Maine August 5, 1916

I appreciate more than I can say your contribution of the little article on the Mexican question to The Ladies' Home Journal, and it is with much pleasure that we will print it. It presents the question in a way that all—who will—can understand it. I thank you very much.

As you have put aside the unwritten law that the President of the United States shall not contribute to a general magazine during his encumbency of office, may I also put aside the unwritten law that you can offer no compensation to the President? I have asked my office to send you a complimentary check,[1] and if, for any reason, you feel a hesitancy to accept it, may it not go to Mrs. Wilson for one of her charities?

With every good personal regard,

Very sincerely yours   Edward Bok

ALS (WP, DLC).

[1] For $250.

From Edward Mandell House

New London,

Dear Governor: New Hampshire. August 6, 1916.

In a letter from Bernstorff which comes today he says:

"The German political situation which I mentioned in my last letter has been somewhat relieved by the black-list controversy."

I am glad you declined to come out for the Susan B. Anthony amendment. It would not surprise me if Hughes' action would cost him the election if nothing else did. In the long run your position is better for the suffrage cause.

I am communicating with Mrs. Pennybacker[1] and some of the others giving them reasons why the stand you take will in the end be of more advantage to them than the one Hughes has taken.

The more I think of it the better I like the idea of your answering all domestic and political issues through the press and before your speech of acceptance, making that document something higher and more statesmanlike than anything that has gone before. You can do it as no one else can and I hope you will.

I am to see both McCormick and Roper the end of this week. Hapgood is doing good work in the Independent as you will have noticed. Dr. Eliot is writing an article for the September issue of the Atlantic Monthly.[2]

Everyone tells me that the campaign in New York is running more smoothly and with less friction and with a better perso[n]nel than any campaign within the memory.

Affectionately yours,   E. M. House

TLS (WP, DLC).

[1] Anna J. Hardwicke (Mrs. Percy V.) Pennybacker of Austin, Tex., president of the General Federation of Women's Clubs, active in the woman suffrage movement.

[2] Charles W. Eliot, "The Achievement of the Democratic Party and Its Leader since March 4, 1913," *Atlantic Monthly*, CXVIII (Oct. 1916), 433-40.

To the Jane Jefferson Club of Colorado

My dear Friends: [The White House] August 7, 1916

I wish I could meet you face to face and tell you in person how deeply I appreciate the work your organization has done and purposes to do for the cause of Democracy and popular government.

I am told that yours was the first woman's Democratic voters organization in America, and I am sure that as such it must have been the instrument of impressing your convictions very deeply upon the politics of your state.

One of the strongest forces behind the equal suffrage sentiment of the country is the now demonstrated fact that in the suffrage states women interest themselves in public questions, study them thoroughly, form their opinions and divide as men do concerning them. It must in frankness be admitted that there are two sides to almost every important public question, and even the best informed persons are bound to differ in judgment concerning it. With such differences of judgment, it is not only natural, but right and patriotic, that the success of opposing convictions should be sought through political alignment and the measuring of their strength at the polls through political agencies. Men do this naturally, and so do women, though it has required your practical demonstration of it to convince those who doubted this. In proportion as the political development of women continues along this line, the cause of equal suffrage will be promoted.

Those who believe in equal suffrage are divided into those who believe that each state should determine for itself when and in what direction to extend the suffrage and those who believe that it should be immediately extended by the action of the National Government by means of an amendment to the Federal Constitution. Both the great political parties of the nation have in their recent platforms favored the extension of the suffrage to women through state action, and I do not see how their candidates can consistently disregard these official declarations. I shall endeavor to make the declaration of my own party in this matter effectual by every influence that I can properly and legitimately exercise.

Woman's part in the progress of the race, it goes without saying, is quite as important as man's. The old notion, too, that suffrage and service go hand in hand is a sound one, and women may well appeal to it, though it has long been invoked against them. The war in Europe has forever set at rest the notion that nations depend in times of stress wholly upon their men. The women in Europe are bearing their full share of war's awful burden in the daily activities of the struggle, and more than their share as sufferers. Their fathers and husbands and sons are fighting and dying in the trenches, but they have taken up the work on the farms, at the mill and in the workshop and counting house. They bury the dead, care for the sick and wounded, console the fatherless, and sustain the constant shock of war's appalling sacrifices. From these hideous calamities we in this favored and beloved land of ours have thus far been shielded. I shall be profoundly thankful if, consistently with the honor and integrity of the nation, we may maintain to the end our peaceful relations with the world.

Cordially and sincerely yours,   Woodrow Wilson[1]

TLS (Letterpress Books, WP, DLC).
[1] This letter was published, *inter alia*, in the *New York Times*, Aug. 13, 1916.

To Newton Diehl Baker

My dear Baker: [The White House] August 7, 1916

Thank you warmly for letting me see the enclosed suggestive letter.

You can assure Mr. Lippmann that that is one of the matters which I have, as a matter of fact, had most vividly in mind, and I hope sincerely that as his ideas clarify he will let me have the benefit of them, either directly or in an editorial expression.

In haste

Cordially and faithfully yours,   Woodrow Wilson

TLS (Letterpress Books, WP, DLC).

To Frederic Clemson Howe

My dear Howe: [The White House] August 7, 1916

I wish with all my heart that we could act upon the suggestion of your letter of August fifth about China. I am afraid that in the present need for money and the piling on of new taxes the Congress would back off from the thing, but I am going to discuss it at least with some of the men on the Hill to see if it is by any chance feasible.

Cordially and sincerely yours,   Woodrow Wilson

TLS (Letterpress Books, WP, DLC).

To Edward Olin Downes

My dear Mr. Downs: [The White House] August 7, 1916

Your letter of August fourth has touched me very deeply. It is such messages that serve to keep a man in heart; not that there are many of them, and I do not know that I have received any that breathed quite so unqualified a confidence as your letter generously breathes. I am the more indebted to you and pray God that I may never do anything to forfeit that faith and confidence.

My desire for reelection is not a personal desire, for I would like release and rest, but is a genuine desire to serve the country as best I may, whether I serve myself or not, and it is just such support as you are according me, support that comes from the heart, that I crave and value most.

Cordially and sincerely yours,   Woodrow Wilson

TLS (Letterpress Books, WP, DLC).

A Translation of a Letter from Nicholas II

[Imperial Headquarters,
Sir President, Great and Good Friend.   Aug. 7, 1916]

I have received your letter in which you propose, in the name of the people of the United States, to submit to a new examination the possibility of rendering relief to the population of Poland who are in distress.

I am profoundly grateful for the humanitarian sentiments of the American citizens and for the disinterested intervention of the Government of the United States toward alleviating the sufferings of the victims of war.

Pursuant to MY instructions MY Government, in accordance with the Governments of MY Allies, has, at many instances given its consent to propositions which have been made to this effect.

I regret that the responsible authorities of the enemy countries have consistently opposed the manifestly legitimate conditions which have been submitted by the Allies and even actually refused to accept all relief proposed for Poland.

Leaving the development of this matter to the judgment of the Government of the United States, I desire to assure you, Mr. President, that MY Government will be happy to consider any new proposition which will be made by the Washington Cabinet.

Written at the IMPERIAL Head Quarters the 7th August 1916

Your Good Friend   Nicolas[1]

T MS (WP, DLC).
[1] The TLS of this letter is in WP, DLC.

From Frank Lyon Polk

My dear Mr. President: Washington August 7, 1916.

I am sending over to you the Danish Treaty, with a formal letter of transmittal. As you will note, the Danish Government requested that the publicity of the terms be withheld until such time as the two Governments agree to announce them. In the formal letter for you to sign, sending the Treaty to the Senate, you call their attention to the necessity for secrecy. I take the liberty of suggesting that it might be well for you to write a personal letter to Senator Stone, impressing him with the necessity of carefully guarding its terms.   Yours faithfully,   Frank L Polk

TLS (WP, DLC).

From Carrie Clinton Lane Chapman Catt

My dear Mr. President: New York August 7th, 1916.

During the entire forty-eight years of its existence, the National American Woman Suffrage Association has held strictly to a non-partisan policy and sought nation-wide suffrage for the women of this country through educational methods. A vast increase of suffrage sentiment throughout our land, due to the many successful and near-successful state campaigns, makes it necessary to re-affirm that policy with such modifications as will make it conform to the new conditions. To that end, the 48th Annual Convention of our national association has been called for September 6th in Atlantic City.

We cordially invite you to address that convention. It is true that your personal views on the subject of woman suffrage are known to virtually every man and woman in this country; but, a reiteration of your belief in the right of the individual woman to share the same privileges and responsibilities of citizenship as the individual man, delivered before our convention, would be of tremendous educational value at this time.

The thousand or more women who will attend the Atlantic City convention are intelligent and representative women who are working for the ballot,—not merely because they feel it is a right,—but because they have vision enough to see the good that may be accomplished by the proper exercise of that right. We hope you will be willing to deliver a message to them personally, as you did to the thousand or more potential citizens of foreign birth in Convention Hall at Philadelphia last year.

We appreciate the number of demands that will be made upon

your time between now and November but we feel that our cause is as worthy of attention as many other issues of the campaign.

May I ask you, therefore, to honor us with an address at Atlantic City on Friday evening, September 8th?

Cordially yours,   Carrie Chapman Catt

TLS (WP, DLC).

ADDENDA

To Benjamin Franklin Hall[1]

Dear Mr. Hall,   Bryn Mawr, Pa., 30 Jany., 1886

I am glad that you have reminded me of my duty in the matter of asking for a Certificate of Dismission from the church in Wilmington. Otherwise I might have put off indefinitely connecting myself *formally* with the little church here.

I thank you most heartily and sincerely for your expressions of interest and confidence in my future. I value your good will and friendship most highly. Please give my warmest regards to Mrs. Hall[2] and to Mrs. Sprunt and her family.[3]

Very sincerely Yours,   Woodrow Wilson

ALS (First Presbyterian Church, Wilmington, N. C.).
[1] Clerk of the session of the First Presbyterian Church, Wilmington, N. C.
[2] Margaret Tannahill Sprunt Hall.
[3] Luola Murchison (Mrs. James) Sprunt.

To Theodore Dreiser[1]

My dear Sir,   Princeton, N. J. 28 June, 1909.

The pressing engagements of our Commencement season and the weeks immediately following have delayed my reply to your kind letter of the fifth of June.

I will take pleasure in preparing an article such as you suggest for the Delineator, on The Ideal University,[2] and think that I can let you have it by about the tenth of July. I am obliged this week to attend the Commencement of Harvard University; but feel confident that I can undertake the preparation of the article next week.

I am very much obliged to you for the suggestion. I know how wide an audience the Delineator commands.

Very sincerely Yours,   Woodrow Wilson

WWTLS (T. Dreiser Coll., InU).
[1] Author, at this time editor of *The Delineator.*
[2] It is printed at July 6, 1919, Vol. 19.

To Joseph Patrick Tumulty with Enclosure

Dear Tumulty,   [The White House, Nov. 3, 1915]

I want to issue this statement to help Mr. Hoover and his Commission in the splendid work they are doing, and head off mischief-makers (or, rather, one particular mischief-maker who is a little out of his mind) on this side the water.[1]

Will you not please read it to Lansing over the 'phone and, if he has no objection to offer, give it out?[2]   W.W.

WWTLI (J. P. Tumulty Papers, DLC).

[1] Lindon Bates, head of the commission's office in New York, who had charged that Hoover had violated the Logan Act which forbade private citizens to carry on diplomatic negotiations with foreign governments. See David Burner, *Herbert Hoover: A Public Life* (New York, 1978), pp. 89-90.

[2] The statement was not issued because Bates promised to make no further trouble.

E N C L O S U R E

The President and Secretary of State this morning had brief interviews with Mr. Hoover, the Chairman of the Belgian Relief Commission, and it was learned in connection with his visit that the Administration is highly pleased with the way in which the work of the Commission has been done, and with the results accomplished. It has not only kept millions of Belgians alive but has carried its work on to the entire satisfaction of all the belligerent governments concerned and with their approval and co-operation. It has not only not been the source of international complications but has, on the contrary, been a source of international good will and disinterested service and has won the confidence of everyone with whom it has had occasion to deal.

WWT MS (J. P. Tumulty Papers, DLC).

INDEX

NOTE ON THE INDEX

THE alphabetically arranged analytical table of contents at the front of the volume eliminates duplication, in both contents and index, of references to certain documents, such as letters. Letters are listed in the contents alphabetically by name, and chronologically within each name by page. The subject matter of all letters is, of course, indexed. The Editorial Notes and Wilson's writings are listed in the contents chronologically by page. In addition, the subject matter of both categories is indexed. The index covers all references to books and articles mentioned in text or notes. Footnotes are indexed. Page references to footnotes which place a comma between the page number and "n" cite both text and footnote, thus: "624,n3." On the other hand, absence of the comma indicates reference to the footnote only, thus: "55n2"—the page number denoting where the footnote appears.

The index supplies the fullest known form of names and, for the Wilson and Axson families, relationships as far down as cousins. Persons referred to by nicknames or shortened forms of names can be identified by reference to entries for these forms of the names.

All entries consisting of page numbers only and which refer to concepts, issues, and opinions (such as democracy, the tariff, the money trust, leadership, and labor problems), are references to Wilson speeches and writings. Page references that follow the symbol Δ in such entries refer to the opinions and comments of others who are identified.

Two cumulative contents-index volumes are now in print: Volume 13, which covers Volumes 1-12, and Volume 26, which covers Volumes 14-25.

INDEX

ABC powers: see Argentina; Brazil; Chile

Académie des Beaux Arts, 42n1

Achievement of the Democratic Party and Its Leader since March 4, 1913 (Eliot), 535,n2

Adair, Henry R., 318,n1

Adams, Herbert, 247,n1, 409

Adams, John, 105n4

Adamson, William Charles, 92, 96, 337

Addams, Jane, 308, 316, 515, 527-28

Addresses of President Wilson at Detroit, Mich. . . . , 387n, 395n

Address of President Wilson at Arlington National Cemetery May 30, 1916, 128n

Address of President Wilson . . . Flag Day June 14, 1916, 225n

Address of President Wilson . . . June 29, 1916, 328n

Address of President Wilson to the Citizenship Convention, 418n

Adkins, Jesse Corcoran, 176,n1

Against the Spector of a Dragon: The Campaign for American Military Preparedness 1914-1917 (Finnegan), 321n1

agriculture: and 1916 platform, 197-98; WW signs rural credits bill, 427-28

Agriculture, Department of, 198

Aguilar, Cándido, 360-61, 367, 410-11, 437-38

Ahumada, Chihuahua, Mex.: see Villa Ahumada

Alaska, 200n3

Alaska coal-leasing bill, 197

Alexander, Joshua Willis, 451

Alexander Hamilton: An Essay on American Union (Oliver), 34,n5

Alfonso XII (of Spain), 274n2

Alfonso XIII (of Spain), 19-20,n1, 274,n3

Alice's Adventures in Wonderland (Carroll), 53

Allied Economic Conference (June 1916): see Paris Economic Conference

Alsace, 179, 412

Alsace-Lorraine, 135n2, 507n1

Amador, Juan Neftali, 22,n1, 39, 254-55

American Federation of Catholic Societies, 476n3

American Federation of Labor: WW's address at dedication of new building of, 353-58; and Mexican-American labor conferences, 365-66,n1

American Group of the Six-Power Consortium, 233, 271

American Indians, 213

American Peace Movement and Social Reform, 1898-1918 (Marchand), 291n2

American Red Cross, 405

American Sugar Refining Co., 427n3

American Union Against Militarism, 75, 291n1,2

America's Traditional Isolation (Bryce), 76n1, 77n1, 290,n4

Anderson, George Weston, 152, 267

Angell, Norman, 77, 294n1

Annapolis: see United States Naval Academy

Anti-Militarism Union Works for Peace in Mexico (New York *World*), 291n1

antitrust laws, 192, 397-98

Arcadia Hall, Detroit, 383n1

Argentina, 238, 241-44, 486; see also Pan-American Pact

Arias, Desiderio, 157n1, 158

Arizona, 300, 321n1

Arlington National Cemetery, 123n1

Army (U.S.): and 1916 platform, 187, 195

army appropriations bill, 380-81, 491

army reorganization bill, 27n1, 156; and nitrate-plant resolution, 66-67, 94

Arredondo, Eliseo, 19, 130, 250, 293-94, 306n1, 348, 360-61, 368,n1, 437, 452, 453, 476, 482-83, 497; on need for U.S. troop withdrawal from Mexico, 152-53; on Carrizal incident, 292; and Joint High Commission, 367, 400-401, 409, 410-11; D. Lawrence on, 485, 489

Asquith, Herbert Henry, 5,n1, 42, 75n2, 77,n1, 89, 95, 182-83, 294n1, 371, 372, 502

Associated Advertising Clubs: WW's remarks to, 324-28

Associated Press, 75, 204n2, 452, 473, 525

Association of the Polish Clergy, 406n1

Atlantic City, N.J., 539, 540

Atlantic Monthly, 201n1, 424, 535,n2

Auchincloss, Gordon, 177-78, 238,n1, 290

Australia, 103n1

Austria-Hungary, 4-5, 19, 319; public opinion and peace moves in, 272, 273-74

Bacon, Robert, 42,n2

Bailey, Warren Worth, 342-43, 346-47

Baker, James M., 517

Baker, Newton Diehl, 9, 22, 38, 65, 74, 76, 97, 218, 467, 522, 537; WW on, 33; on Ohio politics, 84, 96; as possible vice-presidential candidate,

WOODROW WILSON

APPEARANCE

He always looks—well "natty"—well buttoned up and he has a peculiary *live* face: *live* eyes. He looks very well, though he told me that he grows very tired. His complexion is